RELIGION AND THE
MODERN EN

John Foxe's *Acts and Monuments* – popularly known as the 'Book of Martyrs' – is a milestone in the history of the English book. An essential history of the English Reformation and a seminal product of it, no English printed book before it had been as long or as lavishly illustrated. Examining the research behind the work and also its financing, printing and dissemination, Elizabeth Evenden and Thomas S. Freeman argue that, apart from Foxe's zeal and industry, the book was only made possible by extensive cooperation between its printer, John Day, and the Elizabethan government. Government patronage, rather than market forces, lay behind the book's success and ensured the triumph of a Protestant interpretation of the Reformation for centuries to come. Based on little-used manuscript sources, this book offers a unique insight not only into the 'Book of Martyrs' and the history of the English book, but into English history itself.

ELIZABETH EVENDEN is a lecturer in the Department of English at Brunel University. Her publications include *Patents, Pictures and Patronage: John Day and the Tudor Book Trade* (2008).

THOMAS S. FREEMAN is affiliated to the Faculty of Divinity at the University of Cambridge and is a Visiting Fellow at Magdalene College. His publications include *Martyrs and Martyrdom in England, c. 1400–1700* (with Thomas F. Mayer, 2007).

CAMBRIDGE STUDIES IN EARLY MODERN BRITISH HISTORY

Series editors

John Morrill, *Professor of British and Irish History, University of Cambridge, and Fellow of Selwyn College*

Ethan Shagan, *Professor of History, University of California, Berkeley*

Alexandra Walsham, *Professor of Modern History, University of Cambridge, and Fellow of Trinity College*

This is a series of monographs and studies covering many aspects of the history of the British Isles between the late fifteenth century and the early eighteenth century. It includes the work of established scholars and pioneering work by a new generation of scholars. It includes both reviews and revisions of major topics and books which open up new historical terrain or which reveal startling new perspectives on familiar subjects. All the volumes set detailed research into our broader perspectives, and the books are intended for the use of students as well as of their teachers.

For a list of titles in the series go to
www.cambridge.org/earlymodernbritishhistory

RELIGION AND THE BOOK IN EARLY MODERN ENGLAND

The Making of Foxe's 'Book of Martyrs'

ELIZABETH EVENDEN

AND

THOMAS S. FREEMAN

CAMBRIDGE
UNIVERSITY PRESS

CAMBRIDGE
UNIVERSITY PRESS

The Edinburgh Building, Cambridge CB2 8RU, UK

Published in the United States of America by Cambridge University Press, New York

Cambridge University Press is part of the University of Cambridge.

It furthers the University's mission by disseminating knowledge in the pursuit of
education, learning and research at the highest international levels of excellence.

www.cambridge.org
Information on this title: www.cambridge.org/9781107662933

First published 2011
First paperback edition 2013

A catalogue record for this publication is available from the British Library

Library of Congress Cataloguing in Publication data
Evenden, Elizabeth.
Religion and the book in early modern England : the making of Foxe's Book of martyrs / Elizabeth
Evenden and Thomas S. Freeman.
p. cm. – (Cambridge studies in early modern British history)
Includes bibliographical references.
ISBN 978-0-521-83349-3
1. Foxe, John, 1516–1587. Actes and monuments.
2. Christian martyrs – Biography. 3. Martyrologies – History and criticism.
4. Church history – Historiography. 5. Foxe, John, 1516–1587 – Influence.
6. Day, John, 1522–1584. 7. Printing – England – History – 16th century. 8. Book industries
and trade – England – History – 16th century. 9. Illustrated books – England – History – 15th
and 16th centuries. 10. Reformation – England.
I. Freeman, Thomas S., 1959– II. Title.
BR1600.F68E84 2010
272.092–dc22
2010030512

ISBN 978-0-521-83349-3 Hardback
ISBN 978-1-107-66293-3 Paperback

For Margaret Aston

Contents

Illustrations

Acknowledgements

This book is dedicated to Margaret Aston, not only for so generously sharing her remarkable knowledge of both religion and the book in Foxe's England, but also for her constant encouragement and sage advice.

One cannot write about a book as large and complicated as the *Acts and Monuments* without incurring frequent and heavy debts both to other scholars and to institutions. First among the list of scholars are Robin Myers, Giles Mandelbrote and Michael Harris, whose invitation to both of us to contribute a piece on the printing of the 'Book of Martyrs' led us to investigate topics that have culminated in this book. A second large debt, owed by Thomas Freeman, is to David Scott Kastan for a seminar he led at the Folger Shakespeare Library on historical writing in early modern England. This seminar helped him broaden his horizons to look away from the 'Book of Martyrs' itself and to the larger context in which it was created. Elizabeth Evenden would like to thank Peter Blayney, John Guy and Andrew Pettegree for encouragement in the early stages of her research and throughout this project. Both of us owe a profound debt to the British Academy John Foxe Project, which, at various stages, employed both of us; it also put us in contact with a network of scholars who have greatly advanced our work. Particular thanks are due to Mark Greengrass, the director of the Project, for his continuing advice and encouragement, and to John Wade for his expert knowledge of Latin and of Foxe's Latin style.

Important financial assistance was provided to the authors by the British Academy, the Bibliographical Society, the Folger Shakespeare Library, Newnham College, Cambridge, and the Pilgrim Trust. We could not have completed this book without access to the collections of a number of major libraries and archives. Pride of place goes to Cambridge University Library, but we also are very grateful to the Bodleian Library, the British Library, Lambeth Palace Library, Dr Williams's Library and the Bibliothèque Nationale. A number of libraries in the city of York were particularly helpful, including the Borthwick Institute, York Minster

Library and the University of York Library. We have also benefited from being able to consult the records at the Guildhall Library, London, and the National Archives (formerly the Public Record Office). We are also indebted to a number of major collections in the United States, in particular the Folger Shakespeare Library, but also the Library of Congress, the Henry E. Huntington Library and the New York Public Library. At Cambridge we were able to consult libraries at the following colleges: Corpus Christi, Emmanuel, King's, Pembroke and Trinity. We are also grateful to Magdalen College, Oxford, for allowing us to consult its holdings. The staff at all of these institutions were more than helpful and patient with our inquiries, but it would be unjust not to particularly thank the following: all the staff of the Rare Book Reading Room in Cambridge University Library; Gill Cannell at Corpus Christi College Library, Cambridge; Patricia Aske at Pembroke College; Betsy Palmer and Steve Galbraith at the Folger Shakespeare Library; and John Powell, Peter Young and Deirdre Mortimer when researching at York Minster Library and Archives.

Heartfelt thanks go to Margaret Aston, Ethan Shagan and Alexandra Walsham, who heroically read through the entire manuscript and provided valuable commentary on what they read. Readers of individual chapters, whose advice we have profited from, include: Tom Betteridge, James Carley, Patrick Collinson, Brian Cummings, Anne Dillon, Elizabeth Eisenstein, Ceri Euler, Ken Fincham, Victor Houliston, Erick Keleman, Scott Lucas, David McKitterick, Susannah Monta, John Morrill, Stephen Taylor, Brett Usher and Susan Wabuda. Generous assistance in answering particular queries was provided by Paul Arblaster, Jim Binns, John Craig, David Crankshaw, Martha Driver, Lori Ann Ferrell, Diarmid MacCulloch, John McDiarmid, Anthony Milton, Richard Serjeantson and Bill Sherman.

Personal thanks for material, intellectual and spiritual support (or any combination of the above) to: Ruth Ahnert, Stephen Alford, Ian Archer, Melanie Barber, Dorna Bewley, Janet Dickinson, Simon Ditchfield, Susan Doran, Eamon Duffy, Ken Emond, Ian Gadd, Genelle Gertz, Mark Goldie, Tess Grant, Polly Ha, Stefan Haselwimmer, Simon Healy, Megan Hickerson, Nicola Higgins, John Hinks, Ann Hutchinson, Bruce Janacek, Paulina Kewes, Peter Lake, Erica Longfellow, Barry MacKay, Tom McCoog, Peter Marshall, Natalie Mears, Marie Müller, Peter Nockles, Anne Overell, Kendra Packham, Brown and Evelyn Patterson, Ricardo Piedade, Bill Pietrucha, James Raven, Richard Rex, Alec Ryrie, Kevin Sharpe, Bill Sheils, David Smith, Andrew Taylor, the late J. B. Trapp, Nicholas Tyacke, Kristen Walton, the late Sam Walton, Vivienne Westbrook, William Wizeman and Dan Woolf.

We are grateful to Michael Watson and Elizabeth Friend-Smith, History Editors at Cambridge University Press, for their support. Our hearty thanks go to Joanna Breeze for her diligent work in producing this volume. And finally we would also like to thank past and present editors of this series (Anthony Fletcher, John Guy, John Morrill, Ethan Shagan and Alexandra Walsham) for taking this book under their wing.

Our greatest obligations are to our respective families whom we thank for their constant, if somewhat bemused, support. Both authors would like to thank each other for their support throughout what has been a long and challenging project.

ELIZABETH EVENDEN
THOMAS S. FREEMAN

Abbreviations

1563, 1570, 1576, 1583, 1596, etc. all indicate the different editions of the *Acts and Monuments*

BL	British Library
CCCC	Corpus Christi College, Cambridge
Comm.	John Foxe, *Commentarii in ecclesia gestarum rerum* (Strasbourg, 1554)
CUL	Cambridge University Library
ECL	Emmanuel College Library, Cambridge
ERO	Essex Record Office, Chelmsford
GLL	Guildhall Library, London
HOC	*The House of Commons, 1558–1603*, ed. P. W. Hasler, 3 vols. (London, 1981)
LCA	*Laonici Chalcocondylae Atheniensis, De origine et rebus gestis Turcorum* . . . (Basle, 1556)
LM	*Letters of the Martyrs*, i.e., Miles Coverdale [Henry Bull] (ed.), *Certain most godly, fruitful and comfortable letters* . . . (London, 1564), STC 5886
LPL	Lambeth Palace Library
ODNB	*Oxford Dictionary of National Biography* (Oxford, 2004 and www.oxforddnb.com)
PPP	Elizabeth Evenden, *Patents, Pictures and Patronage: John Day and the Tudor Book Trade* (Aldershot, 2008)
SCA	Stationers' Company Archives
SRO	Suffolk Record Office, Ipswich

STC   *A Short-title Catalogue of Books Printed in England, Scotland
           and Ireland and of English Books Printed Abroad, 1475–1640 ...,*
           ed. A. W. Pollard, G. R. Redgrave, P. R. Rider, K. F. Panzer,
           W. A. Jackson and F. S. Ferguson, 3 vols. (London and Oxford,
           1986–91)
TNA   The National Archives (formerly the Public Record Office)
YML   York Minster Library

Introduction

The word 'book' incorporates two related but separate concepts. The first is of the book as a text, which embodies the thoughts and attitudes of its author or authors. Thus we speak of the books of Charles Darwin, Sigmund Freud or Karl Marx, when what we really mean are the ideas and concepts presented by these authors, rather than the physical books themselves. Yet a printed book is also a material object, as well as a compendium of ideas and beliefs. Moreover, it is a material object which is only created by means of specialised labour and equipment. The production of printed books in early modern Europe was the result of a complex, cumbersome and costly industrial process. To comprehend fully the contents and influence of an early modern 'book', in the first sense of the word, it is desirable, sometimes even necessary, to understand the physical process by which it was created.

This is particularly the case with the *Acts and Monuments* (popularly known as the 'Book of Martyrs'), partly because it was a seminal book in both senses in which the word is understood. Foxe's work is an indispensable narrative source for the history of English religion from the Lollards until the accession of Elizabeth. And as scholars in several disciplines have appreciated, Foxe's text wielded a considerable influence on English religious, social and cultural life. Yet Foxe's book, in the sense of the material object itself, was also a milestone in the history of English book production. It was by far and away the largest work produced up to that time in England by a single printer. The *Acts and Monuments* was also illustrated on a scale and with a technical finesse unmatched in previous English printed books. With the 'Book of Martyrs', John Day, its printer, demonstrated to his colleagues and rivals that it was possible to print a work which rivalled that of the continental presses in size and quality and, of at least equal importance, he also demonstrated that there was a market for such a book. In this sense, Day and Foxe prepared the way for the great volumes of Holinshed, Hakluyt and Purchas; without exaggeration, the *Acts and Monuments* marked a crucial stage in the evolution of multi-volume (often illustrated) works of scholarship and reference printed in England.

Moreover, examination of the creation of the 'Book of Martyrs' sheds a great deal of light on book production in England during this period. The printing of Foxe's book was all the more remarkable an achievement for being produced in a country whose printing industry was second-rate. An indication of the inferior condition of the English printing industry, and a major impediment to its growth, was the complete lack of an indigenous paper supply.[1] Another problem, equally grave, was the lack, for reasons that will be discussed later in Chapter 1, of personnel adequately skilled in crucial aspects of early modern book production. The *Acts and Monuments* not only benefited from developments which eased these limitations, but after it had been produced, it became a catalyst for the further development of the English book industry.

Moreover, the means by which the *Acts and Monuments* was produced affected its content, just as its content affected the size and material quality of this book. Foxe's goal of producing a multi-national history of the Church from the age of the Apostles to the accession of Elizabeth placed technical demands on Day that would have been difficult for even a major European printer, operating in a major European printing centre, to meet. For a printer operating in what, in printing terms, was a provincial city, this was a formidable challenge, and meeting it was something of an adventure, marked, as adventures often are, by desperate improvisation and disappointed expectation. It was also a desperate financial adventure, with Day risking considerable sums of money on a project, which, because of its unprecedented nature, was uncertain of success.

A few years ago, Andrew Pettegree observed, 'Remarkably little attention has been paid to the technical aspects of [the] production' of the *Acts and Monuments.*[2] This situation changed somewhat with John N. King's monograph, *Foxe's Book of Martyrs and Early Modern Print Culture.*[3] Roughly half of his book is devoted to examining the production history of the *Acts and Monuments* through its first nine editions (printed from 1563 until 1684), focusing on the early modern unabridged editions of Foxe's book. However, King's approach, while pioneering, does leave room for further development in a number of areas. King's monograph essentially examines the production of the *Acts and Monuments* within the paradigm of the sociology of the text.

[1] See below, pp. 28–30.   [2] See the entry on John Day in *ODNB.*
[3] John N. King, *Foxe's Book of Martyrs and Early Modern Print Culture* (Cambridge, 2006).

Our approach, however, differs from King's in two fundamental respects. The first is that we are more concerned with investigating the making of Foxe's 'Book of Martyrs' in its fullest sense: that is, in tracing in detail the research for the work, the sources that were drawn on, and how they were acquired – in particular, we examine closely the networks of researchers that Foxe established, and the contributors such as John Bale and Henry Bull. We also examine in more depth the physical production of the work: its financing, the actual printing of the work and its role in the formation of John Day's printing empire. The second respect is that we seek to fit the work less within the study of texts in general, but rather within the specific times and context in which it was created. As a result, we, for example, pay far more attention to Foxe's Latin martyrologies and his relations with continental scholars, the relation of the *Acts and Monuments* to the investigations into the past by Matthew Parker and his circle, and also how changes in the English book trade affected both the content and the reprinting of Foxe's book.

Perhaps the differences in our approaches are best exemplified in the diverse ways in which we analyse a seminal aspect of Foxe's book: its copious – and within the context of the English book trade remarkably advanced – woodcut illustrations. King largely examines the pictures in terms of reader response. We look at their purpose within the context of Day's quest for patronage and Foxe's use of them as visual 'proof' of the veracity of his accounts. We also examine in greater detail the problems of incorporating the illustrations into the body of a highly unstable text. Perhaps as a consequence of these different approaches, we come to different conclusions about the commissioning of these woodcuts and the nature of their importance. We have studied the research behind the book, its sources, the actual process of financing it and printing it, for every unabridged early modern edition in more detail than King or any other author has done.

We hope that this study shows that Foxe's book could only have been produced by a unique confluence of individual talents, motivations and circumstances. First of all, it was made possible by Foxe's diligent researches and his remarkable ability to synthesise and organise the information he had acquired, as well as his equally remarkable commitment to this enterprise. It was also made possible by Day's own commitment to the project, his technical skills (which in England were second to none), and his resourcefulness and drive in meeting and overcoming a host of financial and technical obstacles. Perhaps most importantly, we try to demonstrate that a book of the size and complexity of the *Acts and Monuments* could probably have only been produced at this precise time when two important circumstances converged. The first was the polemical need of the Elizabethan authorities in both Church and state to indict both the policies of the preceding reign and Catholicism in general. The second was the English book trade, which at this time worked on a monopolies system. The awarding of these monopolies allowed the authorities to subsidise, indirectly but effectively, some of the production costs of the *Acts and Monuments*. Without this system, controversial as it was, it would almost certainly not have been possible – even with the Herculean efforts of John Foxe and John Day – to print an edition of a work of the size and complexity of the *Acts and Monuments*. And in fact, as we shall show, the collapse of this system adversely affected the reprinting of subsequent editions of the *Acts and Monuments*.

In conducting the research for this book we have drawn on and utilised different types of sources that have not hitherto been extensively consulted for this subject. We have closely examined the sources in both print and manuscript on which Foxe based his magnum opus. We have also gone through the correspondence not only of Foxe but of important contemporaries, such as Edmund Grindal, Kasper von Nidbruck and the Marian martyrs themselves. We have also drawn on the depositions in two major Chancery suits, which cast light on the printing practices of John Day. And we have examined cast-offs from the *Acts and Monuments*. Above all, we have closely examined the different editions of the *Acts and Monuments* themselves – in multiple copies. This has involved not only studying the text of each edition but also the raw materials used and the formatting of the different editions.

Each of the first four editions of the *Acts and Monuments* – the ones printed during the lifetimes of Day and Foxe – underwent significant changes. Sections of text were added but sections were also deleted. Material in the book was edited and emended for purposes ranging from factual correction to outright censorship. We have provided an overview of this evolving process from edition to edition. We have followed the progress of these martyrologies from Foxe's first Latin edition, printed in 1554, down to the 1583 edition, the last one printed by John Day himself. We have then not only gone on to examine the production of the subsequent early modern unabridged editions of Foxe's book, but we have also examined the afterlife of the *Acts and Monuments* in the eighteenth century.

In this study, then, we have provided a detailed account of the making of a book that is remarkable for its importance, for its role in the development in the English book trade, and for the light it casts on the English Reformation. We have also chronicled a remarkable achievement: a story of determination and ingenuity in creating a work without precedent in England and unmatched within its genre anywhere. Our study has led us to a number of conclusions about the *Acts and Monuments* itself and about its creation, but also about the history of the English book trade and the history of the book in England. Nevertheless, it should be remembered that this is a little book about a very large book and that we have not exhausted the subject, although it has at times exhausted its authors. Certainly we have not ended research on the many topics touched on in this book, but it is our hope that we have advanced it.

CHAPTER I

The text in its context: the printer's world in early modern Europe

I

In order to understand properly the accomplishments of Day and Foxe it is necessary to examine the potential and limitations of the book trade in Western Europe as a whole, and of England in particular. Like many technologies in their early stages, printing provided entrepreneurs with the opportunity to make considerable fortunes, but at considerable risk. The business fortunes of Michael Wenssler, a printer in fifteenth-century Basle, are instructive. The bulk of Wenssler's business lay in printing books in civil and canon law, which, because of the need for specialised type, were expensive to produce. For a while the strategy paid off and Wenssler flourished. He began printing in 1474 and in 1475 he paid taxes on an income of 1,400 guilders. In 1478 he paid taxes on 1,600 guilders but in 1479 this fell to 1,000 guilders. His fortunes continued to decline gradually until he fled Basle in 1491, abandoning his family, in order to escape his creditors.[1] This case may well have been atypical and the reasons for the collapse of Wenssler's business may have been personal and even idiosyncratic. However, it is worth emphasising the 'boom and bust' nature of his business, in which he, for a while, made quite considerable sums of money before ultimately going bankrupt. Part of the problem was that books were, at least in comparison to most items produced by early modern industry, relative luxuries, and as such particularly tied to the whims of the buying public, which were (and are) often hard to predict. Another problem was that the expenses for printing were entirely 'front-loaded': in other words one did not see a return on one's investment until the product was sold. A goldsmith, for example, once he had bought the necessary raw materials and the equipment with which to work them, could proceed to use only a portion of the raw materials acquired and sell the objects he made from

---

[1] V. Scholderer, 'Michael Wenssler and his Press', *The Library*, 3rd series, 3 (1912), pp. 283–321.

them, thus getting a more rapid return on his, admittedly heavy, outlay. A weaver did not have to weave all of the raw material that he had in store at once; he could make some items, sell them, and then use the money to repay or defray living or business expenses. Moreover, these and the members of most other manufacturing trades did not necessarily have to buy their raw materials in bulk. Printers, by way of contrast, had to buy all of the materials they would need for an edition in advance, and they could not sell off any of the product until all the copies of the edition were finished. This meant that a printer had to pay higher costs in advance than most other trades and had to wait longer for a return on his investment.

Worse yet, the production of a printed book was an exceptionally costly process. The first expense was for the equipment, and the most basic piece of equipment was the press itself. In Paris in 1555–60 presses were valued at about 18–20 livres tournois (l.t.); in Geneva, during a slightly later period, they were valued at *c.* 10–20 l.t., with additional equipment, such as the platen (a flat surface used to impress the type onto the paper), costing only a little less in total.[2] For an English example, Henry Bynneman's estate in 1583 included 'thre presses with there furniture valued at £13 6s. 8d'.[3] In 1563 Christopher Plantin paid 60 florins each (about the equivalent of £18) for seven presses.[4] However, it should be remembered that the value of Plantin's presses in 1565 was still equivalent to only 1.6 per cent of the total amount of money he invested in his business at that time.[5] While there is no doubt that the printing press itself was a significant expense for the early modern printer, the purchase of a single press was only the first, and not the greatest, of many expenses.

---

[2] Elizabeth Armstrong, *Robert Estienne, Royal Printer* (Cambridge, 1954), p. 47, and J.-F. Gilmont, *Jean Crespin: un éditeur réformé du XVIe siècle* (Geneva, 1981), p. 49. As a rough and ready estimate, 10 l.t. are, in this period, about equivalent to an English pound.

[3] M. Eccles, 'Bynneman's Books', *The Library*, 5th series, 12 (1957), p. 84, item 60. This 'furniture' may include type, ink balls, formes, trays and so on, all of which would be part of the additional equipment necessary to operate the press.

[4] See Léon Voet, *The Golden Compasses: A History and Evaluation of the Printing and Publishing Activities of the Officina Plantiniana at Antwerp*, 2 vols. (Amsterdam, 1969), II, p. 133, and Raymond de Roover, 'The Business Organisation of the Plantin Press in the Setting of Sixteenth Century Antwerp', in *Gedenkboek der Plantin-Dagen 1555–1955* (Antwerp, 1956), p. 244. For the exchange rate between florins and pounds in 1563 see the Database of Early Modern Prices and Wages on the website of the International Institute of Social History, Amsterdam: www.iisg.nl/hpw/, and Lawrence H. Officer, 'Comparing the Purchasing Power of Money in Great Britain from 1264 to 2002', Economic History Services, 2004: www.eh.net/hmit/ppowerbp/.

[5] Philip Gaskell, 'The Decline of the Common Press' (PhD thesis, Cambridge University, 1956), p. 43. However, it should be noted that some of Plantin's outlay was spent on the large stationery and bookselling aspects of his business as well as his printing operation.

Furthermore, the majority of printers owned more than one press. To work with any level of efficiency a printer needed at least two presses in order to avoid 'dead time': in other words, to avoid having the pressmen standing idle waiting for the compositor or vice versa. With two presses, work on either a different book or a different section of the same book could be undertaken on the second press even if the crew of the first press were delayed. When there were two presses or more in operation, the procedure would usually be for one press to print one side of a sheet and have another press print the other side *before* the sheet had dried.[6] And the more presses there were in operation simultaneously, the more efficiently the printing house operated, providing that the master printer was able to supply sufficient supporting personnel – especially correctors – and that he had the ability to organise all of these workers efficiently.

The larger continental printing houses had anywhere from four to seven presses. For example, Johann Froben had four presses when he first met Erasmus, and at the peak of his operations he had six or seven.[7] By the mid-1540s, Foxe's future employer, the Basle printer Johann Oporinus, had six presses.[8] In the early sixteenth century Anthon Koberger, the great Nuremberg printer, was said to own an astronomical twenty-four presses, while Plantin is said by some scholars to have owned twenty-two presses. These may well be exaggerations, but Plantin demonstrably had fourteen presses in two houses at the time of his death.[9] As was often the case in the world of printing, England lagged behind its neighbours. In London, in May 1583, there were twenty-two printing houses. Of these eight (over a third) had only one press, six had two presses, four had three presses, John Day and Henry Denham each had four presses, Christopher Barker and John Wolfe both had five presses. (Wolfe, however, kept two presses

[6] Ronald B. McKerrow, *An Introduction to Bibliography for Literary Students* (Oxford, 1927), pp. 20–2.

[7] Armstrong, *Robert Estienne*, p. 47.

[8] Martin Steinmann, *Johannes Oporinus: ein Basler Buchdrucker um die Mitte des 16. Jahrhunderts* (Basle, 1967), p. 38.

[9] For Koberger, see Gaskell, 'The Decline of the Common Press', p. 6. Robert Kingdon casts doubt on this claim, observing that it first appeared in a biographical sketch of Koberger written thirty-four years after his death. Robert M. Kingdon, 'The Plantin Breviaries: A Case Study of the Sixteenth-Century Business Operations of a Printing House', *Bibliothèque d'Humanisme et Renaissance*, 22 (1960), pp. 134, n. 2. It should be noted that Plantin's account books list a maximum of sixteen presses owned by the great printer in 1574. By the next year the number had declined to fifteen and this was followed by a precipitous drop on account of damage sustained during the Spanish Fury (Gaskell, 'Decline of the Common Press', p. 8). Raymond de Roover argues that Plantin never owned twenty-two presses, and has traced the fluctuating number of presses he owned in detail (Roover, 'The Business Organisation of the Plantin Press', pp. 237 and 240–1).

hidden, apparently because he was using them to print books that were unlicensed.[10]) Only four printing houses – fewer than one-fifth of the total – had over three presses, and only one printing house, that of Christopher Barker, the Queen's Printer, had (legitimately) five presses. At the height of his success, Plantin alone owned the equivalent of just under one-third of the total number of presses in London (and this was almost the total number of non-clandestine presses in England). By way of comparison, Paris, albeit six decades later, boasted no fewer than seventy-five printing houses with 181 presses between them.[11] Nevertheless, even in England the vast majority of printers owned more than one press. It must also be remembered that the costs of equipment were recurring expenses. The 'common presses' were made of wood and thus needed to be periodically repaired or refitted.[12]

The other major expenditure on equipment would be for type. This came in many different varieties, sizes and styles and often a single work would utilise numerous different types. Each set of type had to be cast by a skilled craftsman – a typefounder. It is very difficult to give reliable figures for the amount of money a printer would have to expend on type because there are so many variables involved. Gilmont has estimated that the value of type came to about two-thirds of the value of the moveable goods of a printer.[13] Type also had to be constantly replaced as it was made of soft metal, and the way it was used also resulted in a high level of wear. One of the signs of a poor establishment was the use of badly worn type, which it could not afford to replace despite the adverse effects of this on the appearance of the text. (This is why printers went to great trouble to preserve their type even in periods of crisis. John Day, for example, appears to have transferred his type to his friend, Edward Whitchurch for

---

[10] See BL, Lansdowne MS 48, fos. 189^r–193^v.

[11] Despite the disparity in the number of presses in each capital, the populations of the two cities remained roughly equivalent throughout this period. In 1591, the population of Paris was around 200,000 or less (a decline from the mid-sixteenth century due to the ravages of war), while London's population in 1600 has also been estimated at 200,000. See Mark S. R. Jenner and Paul Griffiths, 'Introduction', in *Londonopolis: Essays in the Cultural and Social History of Early Modern London* (Manchester, 2000), p. 2, and Barbara B. Diefendorf, *Beneath the Cross: Catholics and Huguenots in Sixteenth Century Paris* (New York and Oxford, 1991), p. 9. By the mid-seventeenth century, Paris had staged a spectacular recovery, with a population at 420,000, while the London population had similarly surged to about 375,000.

[12] The term 'common press' is used to describe these wooden hand presses in order to differentiate them from copperplate printer's rolling presses and, later, from the iron hand press. See Philip Gaskell, *A New Introduction to Bibliography: The Classic Manual of Bibliography* (New Castle, DE, 2002), pp. 118–24.

[13] Gilmont, *Jean Crespin*, p. 50.

safekeeping early in Mary's reign, and indeed reclaimed and reused it for years after Mary and her reign were memories.)[14]

Presses and type were the obvious items a printer had to purchase but there was a third necessity he needed to pay for as well: the space to work in. Gaskell has observed that many small printing houses struggling for existence operated in single rooms 'measuring no more than 15 by 20 feet'.[15] Such cramped quarters provided the bare minimum amount of space in which a printer could operate. However, any reasonably established printer would require far more space; he would need room for multiple presses, separate rooms to store used and unused paper, a room to store type, a room with hot water to clean type and dampen paper, and somewhere quiet for the corrector to work in peace. All of this required fairly large establishments, and here English printers in particular suffered from a disadvantage. Because the early modern English book trade was centred almost exclusively on London, printers had to buy or lease the most expensive real estate in the kingdom. Gilmont has estimated that the total cost of the basic equipment a printer required came to between 250 and 260 l.t.[16]

Yet Gaskell reminds us that early modern printers had to pay for more than equipment when establishing their business, 'for there would be considerable expenditure on paper, ink and wages before any profit could be made'.[17] The expense of obtaining paper was particularly onerous and absolutely unavoidable, as printers went through staggering amounts of it. Annie Parent has estimated that an early modern printer need 25–30 reams of paper *per day* to supply four or five presses.[18] Robert Kingdon has noted that, on the continent, the 'stock of paper for a book would sometimes cost twice as much as the money for wages for all the men engaged in composing and printing it'.[19] Gilmont has estimated that the cost of paper accounted for around 40 per cent of the price of an entire book.[20] In some cases, the cost of paper was even higher: an edition that Plantin printed of Virgil's works cost just over 197 florins to print, of which about 140 florins were

---

[14] John Wayland took over the business and stock housed at Edward Whitchurch's premises at the start of Mary's reign. Day worked for Wayland immediately upon his return to printing and so reunited himself with his stock. See *PPP*, pp. 40–5.

[15] Gaskell, 'Decline of the Common Press', p. 1.   [16] Gilmont, *Jean Crespin*, p. 50.

[17] Gaskell, 'Decline of the Common Press', p. 41.

[18] Annie Parent, *Les métiers du livre à Paris au XVIe siècle (1535–60)* (Geneva, 1974), p. 57. A ream consists of 500 sheets.

[19] Robert M. Kingdon, 'Patronage, Piety and Printing in Sixteenth-Century Europe', in *A Festschrift for Frederick B. Artz*, ed. David Henry Pinkney (Durham, NC, 1964), p. 27.

[20] Gilmont, *Jean Crespin*, p. 54.

spent on paper.[21] (These figures are for the cost of paper on the continent; as we shall see later in this chapter, the cost of paper in England was significantly higher.) And this is assuming that paper was available; thanks to war and the vicissitudes of early modern transportation, printers were continually encountering shortfalls in their paper supply. In fact, in Geneva, remoteness from the French centres for the manufacture of paper, in addition to religious and political tensions between Catholic France and its Calvinist neighbour, induced several major Genevan printers such as Robert Estienne and Jean Crespin to invest in paper mills in order to ensure a constant supply of paper.[22]

Ink, on the other hand, was relatively inexpensive. The natural resources needed for its manufacture, linseed oil (for the varnish) and resin (lamp-black from burned resin provided the colour, while resin was also used to contain the varnish and prevent it from staining the paper) were in plentiful supply throughout Europe.[23] Furthermore, ink was a commodity on which printers consistently economised; from the fifteenth century onwards there was a steady decline in the quality of ink. Good ink cost three or four times as much as bad ink, yet readers did not seem to object when inferior inks were used. Printers, probably muttering prayers of thanks to God for this small mercy, seemed to have quietly but completely shifted to utilising poorer quality inks.[24] Thus while ink was used in enormous quantities, the cost was low, even when it was bought from a specialist ink maker.

II

Wages were another substantial expense. As we shall see, the different jobs in a printing house – those of compositor, pressman and corrector – all required specialised skills, and in the case of the corrector a high degree of literacy in at least one, ideally several, languages was a prerequisite. Even pressmen, who at first glance appear to have provided little more than manual labour, had tasks that required considerable training in addition to physical stamina. The specialist status and training of all these workers were reflected in their salaries.

[21] Roover, 'Business Organisation', p. 235.

[22] Ibid., pp. 75–6, and Robert M. Kingdon, 'The Business Activities of Printers Henri and François Estienne', in *Aspects de la propagande religieuse*, ed. G. Berthoud (Geneva, 1957), pp. 262–3. Robert's son Henri further secured his supply of paper by covering a 700 florin loan to his partners in the paper mill (ibid., p. 263).

[23] Gaskell, *Bibliography*, p. 125. The colour for red ink came from grinding up red mercuric sulphide. See also C. H. Bloy, *A History of Printing Ink, Balls and Rollers 1440–1850* (London, 1967), pp. 99–126.

[24] Gaskell, *Bibliography*, pp. 125–6.

The master printer, then, was in a relatively vulnerable position as an employer. Even if religious persecution or warfare furnished silver linings to the clouds of his existence by creating pools of well-qualified but cheap immigrant labour, those skies nevertheless remained dark and overcast as printers still had to pay their workmen more than common labourers or even artisans would receive. In Italy, during the late fifteenth century, compositors in Padua were being paid between 30 and 54 ducats a year, pressmen 24–36 ducats a year, and inkers 24 ducats per year. One Venetian printer of the period set aside 5 ducats a month for the corrector.[25] An ordinary smith or mason in Florence in the same period had 'an optimum annual income of no more than 30 florins or so'.[26] A barber would receive somewhat less, whilst servants made around 6 florins a year, although of course they also received free board and lodging.[27] Plantin, a hundred years later, paid his pressmen 100 florins per annum and his compositors 150 florins per annum. One of his correctors began by receiving 4 florins a week; however, in 1566 this was changed to 100 florins per annum in addition to board and lodging for him and his daughter.[28]

A master printer's economic woes were further compounded by the fact that he not only had to pay his workers a relatively large amount of money, he also had to hire relatively large groups of them. In 1574, when Plantin was operating sixteen presses, his payroll listed fifty-six people: thirty-two press-men, twenty compositors, three correctors, and one apprentice.[29] (This lists only the people who were paid regular wages by Plantin; it does not include piece-workers such as bookbinders, engravers and typefounders. Moreover, it does not include people who were working for Plantin but were not on salaries, such as those apprentices who received only board and lodging, and also two sons-in-law, one of whom was his chief corrector, the other being the manager of the printing house.) Admittedly, Plantin's shop is anomalous because of its massive size. However, if we extrapolate these figures for a reasonably successful printing house consisting of three presses, the printer would still need to employ, at a minimum, six pressmen, three compositors and a corrector. This is a workforce of ten people, which is quite

---

[25] Martin Lowry, *The World of Aldus Manutius: Business and Scholarship in Renaissance Venice* (Oxford, 1979), p. 99. For the role of the inker, see below, p. 18.

[26] In this period, although the exchange rates fluctuated constantly, the Venetian ducat, which was worth about 6 lire in the early sixteenth century, was loosely equivalent to the Florentine florin, which was worth about 5.5 lire in 1471, and 7.5 lire in 1531.

[27] Brian Richardson, *Printing, Writers and Readers in Renaissance Italy* (Cambridge, 1999), pp. xi and 112–13.

[28] Leon Voet, 'The Personality of Plantin', in *Gedenkboek der Plantin-Dagen* (Antwerp, 1956), p. 207, n. 3.

[29] Roover, 'Business Organisation', p. 241.

considerable for an employer of the period. Furthermore, in addition to wages, the printer would also have to supply at least one meal for these workers, plus beer or wine. All in all, wages represented a considerable part of the expenses of running a printing house and, once again, these expenses had to be met in advance.

III

Nevertheless, despite the expenses and the risks, considerable fortunes could be made in the printing trade. The Augsburg printer Günther Zainer reported an income of 2,800 guilders in 1475 and he was one of the richest men in the city when he died three years later.[30] Gilmont estimates that Jean Crespin was worth 'dizanes de milliers de livres turnois' at the end of his life.[31] The great Plantin, despite years of reversals caused by the disasters that struck Antwerp in the 1570s and 1580s, still left an estate estimated at 136,000 florins.[32] In posthumous court proceedings, John Day's wealth was estimated by staff and family members as amounting to at least £5,000.[33] Even Thomas Berthelet, a smaller operator, left property after his death in 1555 worth £125 per annum.[34] These, however, were at the top end of the trade. There were numerous printers who led a much more marginal existence. For example, Thomas Hacket (or Haquet) had goods assessed at £5 in 1547, the same amount in 1550, and only £2 in 1564.[35]

Much of the difference between success and failure in this field was due to the amount of capital invested in the business at the outset. For one thing, there were all the start-up costs of equipment, paper and other necessary items, and as we have seen a greater number of presses enabled a work to be produced more efficiently, and a sufficient supply of paper allowed the operation to proceed more smoothly. If you started with money, you were also able to attract the best workers, and to produce a higher-quality product. At the same time, reserves of money could help a printer survive unforeseen downturns in his business, caused by wars, unexpected competition or simple misjudgements.

---

[30] Rudolph Hirsch, *Printing, Selling and Reading 1450–1550* (Wiesbaden, 1967), p. 44.
[31] Gilmont, *Crespin*, p. 90.
[32] F. de Nave and L. Voet, *Plantin–Moretus Museum, Antwerp* (Brussels, 1989), p. 13. Much of the estate, however, consisted of stocks of books and the equipment in his two printing houses. A considerable portion of the remainder was in real estate: Plantin, at the time of his death, owned ten houses. Voet, 'The Personality of Plantin', p. 207.
[33] TNA, C 24/180, deps. to int. 6.
[34] E. Gordon Duff, *A Century of the English Book Trade* (London, 1905), pp. 11–12.   [35] Ibid., p. 63.

Most of the great printers of early modern Europe followed one tried and true formula for success: they invested sizeable amounts of money into starting their businesses. The Genevan printer and martyrologist, Jean Crespin, invested a considerable personal fortune (mainly his wife's) into his printing enterprise, and even then he still required financial backing from affluent Genevan booksellers such as Antoine Calvin and Nicholas Barbier in order to prosper.[36] Plantin, whose first printing business foundered when officials found heretical literature in his shop, was able to restart his business when two important financiers, Charles and Corneille van Bomberghe, agreed to underwrite his new business. It was to be widely successful but it required an investment of 18,600 florins, of which 10,800 florins were invested by the van Bomberghes and their associates – Plantin himself contributed 1,800 florins of this and a further 7,800 florins were borrowed.[37]

However, for a really large printer, further advantages needed to be obtained. No matter how great the initial capitalisation was, the only way to ensure success was to receive financial support from wealthy patrons. The vicissitudes of Henri Estienne's printing business provide an instructive example of this. Although he inherited the lion's share of his father's printing business, Henri still needed further funding to meet quotidian expenses. Ulrich Fugger, a scion of the famous Augsburg banking family, subsidised Henri Estienne's printing of works of classical literature. Fugger gave Estienne an annual stipend of 300 l.t. and loaned him 1,500 l.t. outright.[38] But this state of affairs only lasted a decade; in 1568, other members of the Fugger family went to court to stop Ulrich's payments to Estienne. This was a huge blow to Estienne's business and he subsequently tried unsuccessfully to get funding from the Holy Roman Emperor and the king of France.[39]

Henri was merely following in his father's footsteps: Robert Estienne owed his prosperity to the patents he received from the king of France granting him monopolies on the printing of certain best-selling works. (In fact, according to his biographer, Estienne was a pioneer in his reliance

[36] Crespin was a lawyer from a wealthy family in Arras. Much of his family fortune was lost when he was convicted of heresy and his property was confiscated. But he was able to salvage some of it, particularly through the sale of family property outside his native Arras. Moreover, he was able to retain his wife's substantial dowry, and before he moved to Geneva his father-in-law died, and his wife inherited further money. Gilmont, *Jean Crespin*, pp. 38–41, 48–9 and 87–96. For Crespin's partnerships with Genevan booksellers see ibid., pp. 90–101.
[37] See Roover, 'Business Organisation', p. 236; De Nave and Voet, *Plantin-Moretus Museum*, p. 11; and Gaskell, 'Decline of the Common Press', p. 42.
[38] Kingdon, 'Business Activities', pp. 260–2.   [39] Ibid., pp. 260–2.

on royal privileges in the French printing industry.[40]) The cornerstone of Plantin's printing empire was the exclusive right to sell missals, breviaries and books of hours in Spanish territories.[41] Paulo Manuzio's papal press, which operated from 1561 to 1570, was supported by taxes on wine imposed by the papacy on the thirsty inhabitants of Rome.[42] And, as we shall see, Day received a range of monopolies and concessions from various Elizabethan authorities. The purpose of this patronage, from the point of view of the patrons, was to ensure the production of high-quality works which gave the patron prestige, and in some cases served political and religious purposes as well. Manuzio and the Estiennes garnered their financial support in return for producing the works of classical authors in editions of the very highest quality. Philip II not only granted Plantin extensive privileges in return for his production of the great Polyglot Bible, he also subsidised it with truly regal generosity, paying Plantin a total of 21,200 florins.[43] (Compare that with the 18,600 florins needed to initially start the business.) And John Day would reap his not inconsiderable monopolies and concessions as a reward for printing Foxe's *Acts and Monuments*, as well as other services to the English Church and state.

Modern readers think of the financial success of a book as being entirely due to its popularity and therefore its sales. In other words, profit is understood as occurring solely within the context of a free market. However, John Day operated within a different financial and economic system. Day's economic prosperity was based on monopolies over the printing of certain popular works, which were granted to him by powerful figures in the Elizabethan government who acted as his patrons. Without these monopolies Day, as we shall see, would not have been able to afford to print the *Acts and Monuments*.[44]

For great printers such as Day, patronage was the keystone of their businesses. A cycle was initiated which had to be maintained. In order to get the financial support and privileges necessary for success, these printers had to produce works that attracted the attention of patrons and demonstrated their mastery of their trade. This patronage was what overcame the natural tendencies within the early modern printing industry to produce exclusively small, inexpensive but steadily selling works, and it was what permitted the creation of some of the greatest works of the period. The

---

[40] Armstrong, *Robert Estienne*, pp. 35–45.
[41] Kingdon, 'The Plantin Breviaries', pp. 133–50, particularly pp. 134–5, 138–40 and 147–8.
[42] Hirsch, *Printing, Selling and Reading*, p. 55.   [43] Roover, 'Business Organisation', p. 239.
[44] For an overview of Day's reliance on monopolies to maintain his printing empire see *PPP*.

Polyglot Bible, for example, would not have been produced in the format that it was – eight volumes translating the Bible into five languages, completed in a breath-taking four or five years – without the largesse of the king of Spain. Similarly, the *Acts and Monuments* would not have been produced, at least in the imposing form in which we know it, unless William Cecil and other influential Elizabethans had not been willing to reward Day for his efforts.

IV

While the printed book was the end-result of a complicated process of production, it was a process that remained fundamentally unchanged throughout Day's entire lifetime. Once the printer had a text to print he or his assistant would cast off a copy, working out how much paper would be needed for the book.[45] The copy text would then be marked up indicating how much of the text should appear on each page.[46] The copy text might also indicate what size or style of type should be used, what the headings of each page should indicate, and generally dictate the format and appearance of the printed page.[47] Once it had been marked up, the copy text would be handed to the compositor, who set the type. The compositor kept his type in two cases: capitals were placed in the upper case, minuscule letters in the lower case (a practice still reflected in the present day terminology of 'upper case' and 'lower case').[48] The compositor would take the letters from these cases and arrange them in a small adjustable tray, known as a 'composing stick', which held only a few lines of type. In order to 'justify' the line, the compositor would assess it and then make the changes required: altering spelling, abbreviating words or, if necessary, adding additional but barely noticeable spaces between them in order to ensure that the left- and right-hand margins of the text remained straight. Once the composing stick was full, the compositor would then transfer the type to a

---

[45] See Gaskell, *Bibliography*, p. 41.

[46] See ibid., pp. 338–43; Paul Baender, 'The Meaning of Copy-Text', *Studies in Bibliography*, 22 (1969), pp. 311–18; G. Thomas Tanselle, 'The Meaning of Copy-Text: A Further Note', *Studies in Bibliography*, 23 (1970), pp. 191–6.

[47] For an example of this in the *Acts and Monuments*, see Elizabeth Evenden and Thomas S. Freeman, 'John Foxe, John Day and the Printing of the "Book of Martyrs"', in *Lives in Print: Biography and the Book Trade from the Middle Ages to the 21st Century*, ed. Robin Myers, Michael Harris and Giles Mandelbrote (New Castle, DE and London, 2002), pp. 38–40. For a checklist of other surviving cast-offs from the period, see J. K. Moore, *Primary Materials Relating to Copy and Print in English Books of the Sixteenth and Seventeenth Centuries* (Oxford, 1992), *passim*.

[48] See Philip Gaskell, 'The Lay of the Case', *Studies in Bibliography*, 22 (1969), pp. 125–42.

larger tray, a 'galley', which held a page of type. Once the main body of text had been completed, additional material would be added, such as folio numbers, running heads, catchwords and signature marks.[49] (Running heads and folio numbers were optional. Catchwords were necessary to ensure that the compositor began the next page with the correct word, and signature marks were absolutely necessary for working out the order in which the sheets needed to be folded before the work was even sold, let alone bound.)

In the case of a printed book (as opposed to a broadside or proclamation), the text having been set in type would be printed on sheets large enough to contain at least two printed pages (i.e., at least the contents of two galleys) on either side. Afterwards, the contents of several galleys were then transferred into an iron frame, the size of one sheet, which was called a 'chase'. This stage was called 'imposition'. Wooden blocks, known as 'furniture', were then used to fill in any empty spaces, and 'quoins' (wedges of wood) were used to lock the type and furniture in place. Once fixed into their cases they were known as 'formes'. The forme was then inked and printed onto one side of a sheet. The contents of another forme would then likewise be inked and printed onto the other side of the sheet. A single sheet run off the press was called a proof. This proof would then be compared with the original from which it was set. Either a corrector or the author would note any errors, and the compositor would use the marked proof to correct the type.

If the corrector felt a page needed to be redone, the frame was unlocked and the compositor corrected the anomalies. The frame was then relocked, re-inked and so reprinted. This, however, was costly and time-consuming. Ideally, all mistakes would be corrected in this process. However, there is a considerable body of evidence to suggest that if only a few minor mistakes were spotted they did not bother to make the corrections. (These uncorrected mistakes probably formed the bulk of the errata which appear in many early modern books and were also the subject of myriad prefaces in which authors bemoaned the carelessness of their printers.) As we shall see later on, a factual mistake was caught probably by John Foxe himself during the printing of the 1570 edition of the *Acts and Monuments*. Rather than reprint the pages, the mistake was cited and corrected in the text several formes later.[50]

Once corrected, the sheet would be reprinted as many times as was necessary to complete the number of copies required. (E.g., if the print

---

[49] See Gaskell, *Bibliography*, pp. 52–3.   [50] See below, pp. 177–8.

run for the book was to be 1,200 copies, then 1,200 sheets would be printed.) The mechanics of the press were basically the same as those of a wine press.[51] The press itself had a wooden frame with a large screw that was worked by a handle. Turning the handle forced the platen down towards the type. A moveable carriage placed both the type and the paper under the platen. The carriage would be removed in order to re-ink the type and to insert fresh paper.

Two men were needed to work the press. One fitted the paper to a hinge on the carriage, folded it down on top of the type, and then ran the carriage under the platen. This secured the paper between the type and the platen. He would then pull the handle, turning the screw down and pressing the paper onto the inked type. Meanwhile the other pressman would have inked the type while the carriage was open.[52] Because pulling the screw took immense physical effort, these roles would be reversed in order to prevent one worker becoming exhausted. To appreciate the physical strength that this job required, it should be remembered that the process would be repeated hundreds of times a day.

The paper for printing had to be prepared the day before. Multiple piles, each consisting of 250 sheets (half a ream) would be wetted and left to stand overnight. The reason for this was that the paper needed to be damp in order to allow the ink to set properly on it; the screw of the press was not powerful enough to force dry paper to absorb the ink evenly. Once printed, the sheets would be transferred to a drying room. There they would be hung up in gatherings (otherwise known as 'quires') to dry. Once dry, they were placed in proper order according to the signature marks. The final tasks in the printing house were to fold the sheets into consecutive gatherings. These folded sheets were then bundled up either to be put into storage or to be delivered to the bookshop or binder.

This was obviously a complex process. What made it truly daunting, however, was that in order for a printer to stay in business, these tasks had to be performed at considerable speed. In this period, the workers in a printing house would work an average of twelve hours a day, six days a week. (Obviously, in northern Europe, this was subject to considerable seasonal

---

[51] A major innovation in the mechanical operation of the printing press was the addition of a mobile carriage, which speeded up the output, since a sheet of paper laid on the press could now be printed on the whole of one side, although this required two pulls of the press.

[52] In Italy in the fifteenth and sixteenth centuries there seems to have been a tendency for the pressmen to specialise, with one (who was paid the higher wage) operating the handle and the other acting exclusively to ink the type. See Richardson, *Printing, Writers and Readers*, p. 19. Also see Lowry, *The World of Aldus Manutius*, p. 99.

variation, particularly because it was not only impractical but downright hazardous to work by artificial illumination.[53]) Philip Gaskell has calculated that one compositor could set 500 ems an hour.[54] A line in the 1570 edition of the *Acts and Monuments* was generally 29 ems. On Gaskell's estimate, then, a compositor could set just over seventeen lines of this edition in one hour. There are, on average, seventy-five lines to a page of the 1570 edition. In seventeen hours a compositor could set about 290 lines, or just under a sheet of this edition. In sixty-eight hours (a little less than the 'normal' working week of seventy-two hours) four sheets could be set.[55]

The pressmen could not begin their job until the compositors had completed theirs. But once they were ready, the pressmen, as long as their muscles held up, could work at an impressive rate. It has been calculated that 2,500–3,000 impressions (i.e., 1,250–1,500 pages printed on both sides) could be produced within a single twelve-hour day.[56] It has also been estimated that a single press could print 250 sheets on one side in one hour.[57] In a twelve-hour day, this would result in the printing of a maximum of 3,000 sheets printed on one side from a single press. And, as we have seen, many printers of the period had multiple presses working for them simultaneously.

v

The celerity with which books were produced was the key to profit in the highly competitive printing industry. Because the expenses in producing a book all had to be paid before it could be sold, and because a printer did not

[53] The extra hours of daylight during the summer not only allowed for a longer working day without the need for artificial light, but also made it possible for workmen to take a break during the day.

[54] Gaskell, *Bibliography*, pp. 54–5.

[55] One sheet printed on both sides with all its impressions per day seems to have been an average in sixteenth-century Europe. Throughout Italy, for example, in the sixteenth century this seems to have been regarded as the normal rate of production. Richardson, *Printing, Writers and Readers*, p. 22. Of course the speed could vary significantly, depending on the nature of the task and the particular circumstances in which the book was being printed.

[56] In 1575 the French Humanist Louis Le Roy estimated that pressmen could print between 1,250 and 1,300 sheets per day. David McKitterick, *Print, Manuscript and the Search for Order 1450–1830* (Cambridge, 2003), p. 112. Modern scholars have tended to place a slightly higher estimate on the number of impressions that could be made in a single day. Jean-François Gilmont has estimated that between 1,300 and 1,400 copies of a page printed on both sides could be produced. Gilmont, *Jean Crespin*, pp. 50–1. However, Gilmont adds a note of caution by observing that these figures could fluctuate dramatically from edition to edition.

[57] Richard W. Clement, 'A Survey of Antique, Medieval, and Renaissance Book Production', in *Art into Life: Collected Papers from the Kresge Art Museum Medieval Symposia*, ed. Carol Garrett Fisher and Kathleen L. Scott (East Lansing, MI, 1995), p. 35.

make money on the volume until it was sold, it was in the printer's economic interest to reduce the amount of time spent in producing the book as much as possible.[58] The essential importance of swift production is underscored by the fact that printing house workers' salaries were geared to their rate of production. Compositors were normally paid according to the amount of type that they set, encouraging a faster rate of production. (And they were docked for work that had to be reset. This would also inculcate a certain reluctance to reset type, even when correctors had detected errors.) It was essential that the compositor worked as quickly as possible since the next stage in a book's production could not begin until he had finished his work. 'Dead time' – a situation where the pressmen were kept waiting for the formes – needed to be avoided.[59] An idle pressman meant the printer was losing money and this often meant that the pressman was losing money as well, since he was generally paid according to the number of impressions made.[60]

In order to achieve a speed that maximised their own pay, workers in a printing house needed considerable training to develop highly specialised skills. A compositor had to be accurate as well as fast. If his work was too sloppy then it would simply have to be redone, costing both him and the printer money. In 1534 one author, observing the production of his book in the printing house of Johann Froben, described the work of the compositor in admiring terms, stating:

It is almost this man's chief usefulness and praiseworthy diligence, to compose the types themselves not only fast, but accurately as well ... Those, however, among them who perform a just task are accustomed to deliver about two formes daily; the more diligent ones, three; those who deliver four are reckoned among the most excellent; they, however, who deliver only one are deservedly branded with laziness. And indeed, if delay occurs here the work of all the other workmen suffers a hurtful delay. Accordingly printers are accustomed to look to it that the compositors in particular carry out their task diligently and complete their formes at regular intervals, by which these can once and again be placed under the press in order that thereby they may be produced and printed more carefully and perfectly.[61]

---

[58] For example, this became an acute problem for Plantin after Philip II withdrew his patronage in the aftermath of the Spanish Fury. Plantin continued operating on a large scale and continued to make large amounts of money. However, without the royal support to cover those periods when his stock was moving slowly, he needed to borrow money to make ends meet and was forced to spend much of his profit paying off the loans. Roover, 'Business Organisation', p. 244.

[59] Gilmont, *Jean Crespin*, pp. 52–3.   [60] Gaskell, *Bibliography*, pp. 140–1.

[61] Johan Gerritsen, 'Printing at Froben's: An Eyewitness Account', *Studies in Bibliography*, 44 (1991), p. 148. This is Gerritsen's translation of the original Latin, which appears on p. 162 of his article. The rates that the author of this letter describes are much faster than the more conservative estimates given by Gaskell (see above, p. 19). Apart from over-exaggeration, it is possible that workers in a sophisticated operation such as Froben's worked at a faster rate than workers in smaller establishments.

The economic imperative for swift production placed early modern print-ers on the horns of a very painful dilemma. If the works had to be printed quickly in order to make a profit, they also had to sell, and works which were sloppily printed and contained too many inaccuracies were, for obvious reasons, unattractive to the consumer. Printers, especially in the late fifteenth and early sixteenth centuries, frequently made the accuracy of their works a selling point and a justification for special privileges.[62] For example, in his celebrated *Adagia*, Erasmus derisively contrasted the boasts of accuracy made on title pages of certain printed books with the shoddy inaccuracy with which the works were actually executed.[63] The interesting point about Erasmus's caustic comments is that they indicate that printers were advertising the accuracy of their books on their title pages.

However, this punctiliousness seems to have become increasingly rare as time went on, and was confined to a handful of illustrious printers in any case.[64] As numerous authors noted with disgust, correctors were forced to work in haste because printers wanted to produce books without delay, and accuracy was increasingly regarded as a lesser priority.[65] In fact, as early as the latter part of the fifteenth century, one Italian humanist, recognising that printers and correctors had many economic incentives to work hastily and therefore carelessly, called for a chief corrector, to be appointed by papal authority, to examine the work of individual correctors.[66] In Venice in 1603, the state actually established rules for a three-stage control over compositors' work: first the work set in the forme had to be read by the master printer or another qualified person, then a sheet was to be printed and read by a corrector who had been approved by the University of Padua, and whose name would appear at the end of the volume, and finally a second proof was to be run off to ensure that all corrections had been made.[67] This law was probably a dead letter in Venice and certainly nothing similar was practised anywhere else. The fundamental problem was that the economics of the industry worked against such measures. Printers did not want to waste paper running off sheets for correction, pressmen and compositors did not want to stand around idle (and unpaid) while waiting for such corrections to

[62] See George Hoffman, 'Writing Without Leisure: Proof-reading as Work in the Renaissance', *Journal of Medieval and Renaissance Studies*, 25 (1995), p. 21, and Hirsch, *Printing, Selling and Reading*, pp. 45–6.
[63] Desiderius Erasmus, *Adagia* (Basle, 1528), sig. 2a2ʳ.
[64] See Hirsch, *Printing, Selling and Reading*, pp. 47–8.
[65] See Anthony Grafton, *Bring Out Your Dead: The Past as Revelation* (Cambridge, MA and London, 2001), pp. 147–9.
[66] Ibid., pp. 150–1. [67] Richardson, *Printing, Writers and Readers*, p. 16.

take place, and printers obviously did not want to delay the manufacture of the final product. What such proposed reforms do indicate, however, was the crucial role played by the corrector in ensuring the accuracy of the work. In effect these reforms tried to provide a safety net and another level of correctors to reinforce the harassed correctors in an individual printing house.

Ideally, a good corrector was multi-lingual and, in particular, literate in at least Latin; the ideal expressed by Joseph Moxon, was that correctors should be competent in '(beside the English tongue) ... Latin, Greek, Hebrew ... [and] to be very knowing in deviations and etymologies of words, very sagacious in pointing [i.e., punctuation], skilful in the compositors whole task and obligation and endowed with a quick eye to espi the smallest fault'.[68] Hieronymus Hornschuch, the noted physician and eminent proofreader, agreed, stating that they needed two languages (Latin and Greek) as well as extremely good eyesight.[69] Tellingly perhaps, Hornschuch also urged sobriety as a prerequisite for a corrector: 'The corrector too should shun assiduously the vice of drink, lest he should see either nothing at all, or more than is actually there.'[70]

The question was where to find such paragons. For most English, indeed European printers, the corrector of Moxon and Hornschuch was like universal peace or a sunny English April: an ideal attainable in theory but very rarely realised in practice. Men with this much education and good character tended to take up more lucrative and prestigious vocations than working in a printing house. Even Hornschuch who idealised the role of the corrector, still admitted that if they were truly well educated, most correctors 'would be off like a shot from this sweat-shop, to earn their living by their intelligence and learning, not by their hands'.[71] Henri Estienne lost the services of a corrector, despite taking him to court to stop him leaving, when the man became the minister of a congregation at Beaune.[72]

---

[68] Joseph Moxon, *Mechanick Exercises in the Whole Art of Printing*, ed. H. Davis and H. Carter, 2nd edn (London, 1962), p. 260.

[69] Hieronymus Hornschuch, *Orthotypographia 1608*, ed. and trans. Philip Gaskell and Patricia Bradford (Cambridge, 1972), p. 8. Hornschuch also stated that the corrector needed to learn the standard sequence for pages when they were set out on the forme, in order to check that the compositor had laid them out correctly. For example, he explains that if a work was printed in folio, then the corrector would need to know that for the first twelve pages printed, the first pair of formes would hold pages 1 and 12 in the first forme, the second would hold pages 2 and 11; the second pair of formes would hold pages 3 and 10 and 4 and 9 respectively; and the third pair pages 5 and 8 in its first forme and pages 6 and 7 in its second forme; ibid., pp. 9–10.

[70] Ibid., p. 9.   [71] Ibid., p. 27.   [72] Kingdon, 'Business Activities', p. 226.

VI

Apart from doing without competent correctors – a solution that might have been resorted to by small printers but was ill-advised for large ones – there were a number of expedients printers could resort to in order to work around the scarcity of competent correctors. One was for the printers themselves to correct the text. Smaller printers often had to do this as a cost-saving measure. A printer could also occasionally recruit members of his family as correctors. Richard Day, who was educated at Cambridge, worked for a time as a corrector for his father's press and Plantin's chief corrector was, as we have noted, one of his sons-in-law, François Ravelingon.[73]

It was more common for the author to be present while the work was being printed and to aid the corrector himself. The fundamental drawback with this was that it necessitated the presence of the author in the printing house for a protracted period of time and it also involved him in a long and tedious process. The great Erasmus himself corrected Greek texts which he had edited and which were being printed by Froben. He clearly regarded this work as drudgery and the fact that he had to resort to this expedient, even when his works were being produced by one of Europe's greatest printers, highlights the desperate shortage of correctors literate in Greek. In fact, a major factor forcing authors to be present during the printing of their work was a lack of correctors competent in certain classical languages or in certain specialised fields.[74] This was particularly true in England, where relatively few works were printed in the classical languages or were of a scientific or technical nature. Even John Day, one of the largest, and arguably the most technically sophisticated printer in Elizabethan England, was unable to provide a sufficiently skilled corrector to examine Henry Billingsley's translations of Euclid, and consequently, as Billingsley ruefully noted, he was forced to act as the corrector himself:

Marvaile not (gentle reader) that faultes here following, have escaped in the correction of this booke. For that the matter in it contained is straunge to our printers here in England, not having bene accustomed to print many, or rather any bookes containing such matter, which causeth them to be unfurnished of a corrector skilfull in that art; I was forced, to my great travaile and paine, to correcte the whole booke my selfe.[75]

[73] For Richard Day see below, pp. 258–9; for Ravelingon see Roover, 'Business Operation', p. 241.
[74] James Binns, 'STC Latin Books as Evidence for Printing House Practice', *The Library*, 5th series, 32 (1977), pp. 1–27, esp. pp. 5, 10 and 16–17.
[75] Euclid, *Elements of geometrie*, trans. Henry Billingsley (London, 1570), STC 10560, 'Faultes escaped', fo. 163ᵛ (sig. 3E2ᵛ). Thomas Oliver, the Cambridge mathematician, apologised in his collection of

On the continent it appears to have been fairly uncommon for the author to remain in the printing house while the work was being printed. Richardson observes that in early modern Italy 'it was unusual for an author to be involved from day to day in the correction of proofs', although he does note that there were exceptions to this, among them Ariosto, who personally corrected proofs of the 1532 edition of his magnum opus the *Furioso*.[76] Similarly, there was a marked reluctance among many French writers to spend protracted time correcting proofs, a task which many regarded as menial and beneath their dignity.[77]

In England, by contrast, it seems to have been expected that the author would be present while the proofs of his work were being corrected. James Binns has observed that in early modern England the 'author was usually present during the printing of the book, and proofs, both first and second, were read by the author and the press corrector'.[78] Apart from the lack of correctors with classical educations in England, one reason for this difference in authorial practice was the degree of centralisation, unique in European countries, of the printing industry in one city, London. Since the vast majority of English authors resided in London on a permanent or temporary basis, or in areas with reasonable access to the capital, this made it relatively easy for many English authors to spend a lengthy period of time in a particular printing house.

Moreover, dire consequences could arise if an author was not present to supervise his work through the press. John Case, who wrote a textbook of Aristotelian logic, complained that because ill health prevented his appearing at the printing house as his work was being printed, many errors occurred in his book. He provided a list of the major errors 'which wounded the meaning' ('quae sensum vulnerunt'). There were more than fifty, covering pages 5–293 of a 294-page work.[79] While John Case was prevented by illness from supervising his work, Richard Crakanthorp was similarly stricken, only this time the illness turned out to be fatal. The compositors nevertheless diligently continued working on the book while John Barkham, who would posthumously edit it, raced to the printing house. Nevertheless, as Barkham was quick to explain, he did not arrive in time to prevent numerous 'faults, even crudities in the punctuation, number and annotation' ['naevos, ex punctulis, numeris, notulis, etiam solaecismos'] of the book. Barkham continued,

---

mathematical and medical treatises, printed at Cambridge in 1604, because he had to draw and engrave the diagrams himself as he could find no one else capable of doing it. Thomas Oliver, *De sophismatum praestigiis cavendis admonitio* (Cambridge, 1604), STC 18809, sig. ¶2ᵛ.

[76] Richardson, *Printing, Writers and Readers*, p. 15.   [77] Hoffman, 'Writing without Leisure', pp. 22–3.

[78] Binns, 'STC Latin Books', pp. 1–2.

[79] John Case, *Summa veterum interpretum in universam dialecticam Aristotelis* (London, 1584), STC 4762, sig. ¶1ʳ.

'neither the author, who departed too soon, not to speak of myself, who appeared too late, are responsible for these'.[80] In the case of the *Acts and Monuments*, a work which for polemical reasons needed to appear accurate, Foxe's quotidian presence in Day's printing house would be a necessity.

The Reformation itself occasionally provided printers with very high-quality correctors. Persecution and religious wars generated waves of educated refugees, some of whom sought work in the various printing houses. Foxe himself, along with his close friends John Bale and Laurence Humphrey, worked for Johann Oporinus while in exile during Mary Tudor's reign. Coinciding with an influx of immigrants fleeing the gentle persuasions of the duke of Alva in the Low Countries, from 1566 onwards Day began to print a series of books in Dutch and French.[81] There can be little doubt that Day was suddenly able to produce works for these new markets because he was able to recruit correctors literate in Dutch and French from these recent refugees. Occasionally religious zeal could lead to a printer being supplied with additional assistance in the correcting process. As we shall see, Foxe would be able to enlist Oxford students to scrutinise the manuscript copy of his work for error.[82] On the other side of the confessional divide, thanks to the orders of Cardinal Filippo Neri, Cesare Baronio was able 'to enlist the whole [of the Roman] Oratorio in the painstaking work of checking manuscripts and correcting proof for his massive ecclesiastical history, the *Annales Ecclesiasticae*.[83]

In any case, even when allowance is made for the occasional bounties of providence to printers in the form of war, persecution and confessional hostility, correctors, because of their education and specialised skills, could command reasonably high salaries. Figures from early modern Italy indicate occasionally exorbitant rates. One scholar was hired by the Florentine printer Jacobo Giunti in the 1560s to correct Greek texts at the rate of 20 soldi a sheet. More normally, correctors in both Milan and Venice were being paid 5 ducats per month in the latter fifteenth century.[84]

---

[80] 'Quae nec Author, qui aberat nimis citus, nedum ego, qui accessi nimis serus praestando sumus.' Richard Crakanthorp, *Defensio ecclesiae Anglicanae* (London, 1625), STC 5975, sig. 4N3ᵛ.

[81] See Elizabeth Evenden, 'The Fleeing Dutchmen? The Influence of Dutch Immigrants upon the Print Shop of John Day', in *John Foxe: At Home and Abroad*, ed. David Loades (Aldershot, 2004), pp. 76–7.

[82] See below, pp. 175–6.

[83] See Eric Cochrane, *Historians and Historiography in the Italian Renaissance* (Chicago and London, 1981), p. 460.

[84] Richardson, *Printing, Writers and Readers*, pp. 14–15, and Lowry, *Aldus Manutius*, p. 99. In the same place and period, a compositor would be paid around 2.5–4.5 ducats a month, while the pressmen would be paid 2–3 ducats a month. An inker would be paid 2 ducats a month (ibid.). For other examples of extremely high rates paid to correctors during the period, see Hirsch, *Printing, Selling and Reading*, p. 46.

Unfortunately, examples of the salaries of correctors employed in England do not survive.[85] However, records from John Day's great contemporary, Christopher Plantin, indicate that correctors seem to have been paid only slightly more than compositors.[86] This is quite interesting and would seem to indicate that the quality of correctors and the salaries they could demand may have declined since the fifteenth century. A contemporary list of 760 individuals who acted as correctors in Italy in the period 1475–1500 included forty-seven priests, ten bishops, one papal overseer, one proto-notary and one archbishop.[87] (Paradoxically, the decline in the status of correctors may have been due to the need to employ them on a steady basis and their consequent professionalisation. A priest or a bishop might well have agreed to go over a manuscript on an occasional basis in his spare time; he would hardly consent to work in a printer's business on a permanent basis.) The lower status of correctors may have partially caused, and then in turn was a consequence of, the growing unwillingness of printers to pay the premium wages necessary to get highly learned correctors. Hornschuch implies as much when he says that:

> printers should realise that they need the work of correctors as well as of compositors, if they want to take proper care of printing: they should also realise that the efforts of these men should be rewarded by a fair and honourable salary, so as not to give rise to the proverb: A low price buys high [i.e., rotten] meat.[88]

Another indication of a decline in the quality of the status of correctors is the fact that, by the seventeenth century, Plantin and others were using correctors not only to scrutinise proofs but for such relatively menial tasks as collating, making indexes and compiling glossaries.[89]

VII

All of the drawbacks that afflicted printers on the continent were exacerbated by the provincial status of the English book trade. It was difficult in this relatively backward industry, which served a small and isolated market, to produce a massive work such as the *Acts and Monuments*. It was even more difficult to produce such a work if it met, as the *Acts and Monuments* did, continental standards of quality in both illustration and layout. Yet Day

---

[85] John Day would pay his son Richard a shilling a week for his work as a corrector. This seems a rather low salary, but this figure is complicated by Richard's ambivalent status within his father's business. It should also be noted that John Day did promise his son Richard free board and lodging in the house that backed onto his garden. See TNA, C 24/181, deps. to ints. 4 and 5.

[86] See Voet, 'Personality of Plantin', p. 207, n. 3.   [87] Hirsch, *Printing, Selling and Reading*, p. 47.

[88] Hornschuch, *Orthotypographia*, p. 7.   [89] See Voet, *Golden Compasses*, p. 187.

managed to surmount these obstacles, and in doing so created one of the greatest milestones in the history of English printing since Caxton.

But to understand both the extent of Day's achievement and factors that determined the nature and scope of Foxe's book it is necessary to bear in mind the limitations of the English book trade as a whole.[90] The relative isolation and lack of technical sophistication of the English book trade increased the expenses for English printers in a number of ways. One was a shortage of sufficiently skilled personnel in England, most especially type-founders. This meant that English printers had to have their type cast (or at the very least the matrices made) abroad and shipped into England, thereby substantially increasing the cost. It is worth observing that when war and persecution did create an influx of typefounders into England, Day and others snapped up their services, in many cases lodging the typefounders within their own establishment.[91]

This rapid impressment of personnel underscores a long-term deficiency in the English book trade – a chronic shortage of people trained in all aspects of printing. There were several reasons for this. One was the linguistic boundary. Because the vast majority of works printed in England were in the vernacular, employment in the English book trade was correspondingly unattractive to those for whom English was not their native tongue. Whereas French printing staff could migrate throughout the printing centres of France, western Switzerland and the Low Countries, while Germans had the Empire and Switzerland, and the Italians had the entire peninsula to seek employment in, there were few places for English printing personnel to go and, under normal circumstances, few incentives for continental workers to uproot themselves and cross the Channel. Moreover, there were laws and regulations in England restricting the hiring of foreign workers and limiting the size of the staff of printing houses, which did not exist in most continental cities. And there was little demand in the English book trade for workers skilled in the classical languages. The English labour market was, at least in terms of the printing trade, inelastic and unable to meet sudden demands for workers.

This can be seen in the reign of Edward VI when a loosening of press regulation combined with official encouragement of works of religious and political propaganda caused the industry to expand very quickly. Foreign workers were fortunately available to fill the newly created vacuum. They

[90] These limitations are analysed in Andrew Pettegree and Matthew Hall, 'The Reformation and the Book: A Reconsideration', *Historical Journal*, 47 (2004), pp. 785–808.

[91] See BL, Lansdowne 202, fo. 19ᵛ, and R. E. G. Kirk and E. F. Kirk (eds.), *Returns of Aliens . . . dwelling in London*, Huguenot Society of London x, 4 vols. (Aberdeen, 1900–8), II, p. 186, for a list of typefounders based in Day's house.

also contributed to the improved appearance, layout and design that characterised books printed in England in the reign of Henry VIII's son.[92] But,
most importantly, it was the fortuitous availability of workers from the Low
Countries, as well as political circumstances, that made this English printing
boom possible; the supply of English workers would have been inadequate
by itself to meet this demand. If Somerset's religious reforms owed something to these foreign workmen, then so did the great martyrology that
extolled Somerset; in printing Foxe's work Day would have to rely heavily
on foreign workmen and in turn Day would have to seek the help of patrons
in order to be able to employ these indispensable aliens.[93]

Perhaps an even more profound problem facing the English book trade
was the lack of an indigenous supply of paper. As we have seen, paper was an
enormous expense for printers in any case. In England this expense was
aggravated by the fact that paper for English books had to be imported, the
greatest part of it from France, particularly Normandy. Apart from the
additional expense that transporting vast quantities of paper from abroad
entailed, this situation created at least two other obstacles for printers in
England. The first was that the supply of paper was vulnerable because of
war or international turmoil. The second was that English printers, particularly when printing a large book, had to plan their work and the amount of
paper they would require very carefully, as any miscalculation would be
difficult and time-consuming to rectify. This planning needed to be even
more precise for a large work, as any error in calculating the paper needed
would be correspondingly more difficult to correct.

It is worth considering why the English did not build a mill capable of
producing paper suitable for the English book trade until the Restoration.[94]
It was not that there was a lack of demand for such a mill. In 1585 the printer
Richard Tottle wrote to William Cecil complaining that for twelve years the
Stationers of London had been petitioning unsuccessfully for a mill on
English soil.[95] Tottle was motivated by more than disinterested concern for

---

[92] See Pettegree, 'Printing and the Reformation: The English Exception', in *The Beginnings of English Protestantism*, ed. Peter Marshall and Alex Ryrie (Cambridge, 2002), pp. 157–79, at pp. 162–5 and 174.

[93] See below, p. 163.

[94] There were two paper mills in Kent prior to the Restoration but both were small-scale and only produced writing paper. Finally, in 1670, George Gill established a mill near Maidstone, which produced paper for the printing trade. See Richard L. Hill, *Papermaking in Britain 1488–1988, A Short History* (London, 1988), p. 50. For an overview of the importation of paper into England, John Bidwell, 'French Paper in English Book', in *The Cambridge History of the Book*, vol. IV: *1557–1695*, ed. John Barnard and D. F. McKenzie (Cambridge, 2002), pp. 583–601.

[95] Edward Arber, *Transcripts of the Registers of the Company of Stationers of London . . . 1554–1640 A.D.*, 5 vols. (Birmingham, 1875–94), I, p. 242.

his fellow Stationers: he sought a monopoly on the right to manufacture paper in the kingdom. Tottle claimed that this was necessary because the French had sabotaged every English effort to establish a domestic printing industry and that only government support would enable him to triumph over this foreign competition.[96]

Why then was the English government unresponsive to these urgings? Writing in the twenty-first century, John Bidwell has concluded with Tottle, writing in the sixteenth century, that French competition was simply too powerful to overcome.[97] It is difficult to see why this should be the case and how the French could have stopped the English from building paper mills in England. It was not a question of natural resources. Essentially all you needed to produce paper were linen rags and running water, and England did not lack either. (Tottle urged the Privy Council to ban the export of linen rags to France, thus cutting off the French supply and at the same time ensuring that they remained in England.) The government failure to back this scheme, and more importantly their failure to sponsor a paper mill at all, may well have stemmed not from a fear that an English paper mill was not practical but from a fear that it would be.

As Pettegree and Hall have observed, the need to import paper through well-regulated English ports made the operation of a clandestine press quite difficult.[98] John Day's career as a printer of heretical works during Mary Tudor's reign came to an end when he was apprehended receiving a shipment of paper in Norfolk.[99] Certainly the failure to establish successful underground presses in England on anything approaching a permanent basis is striking. For example, there were three Catholic presses at work in London between 1578 and 1582 – William Carter's press on Tower Hill, Steven Brinkley's press at Greenstreet House (in East Ham), and Richard Rowlands' press in Smithfield. Together these three presses printed only about ten books before they were all discovered and dismantled, with Carter being executed, Brinkley imprisoned, and Rowlands forced to flee into exile, where he published under his alias of Richard Verstegan. Furthermore, Brinkley's press had to move three times during its three years of operation.[100] A major reason for the risk and impermanence of these operations was the difficulty in supplying them covertly with large

---

[96] Bidwell, 'French Paper', pp. 584–5.   [97] Ibid., p. 585.
[98] Pettegree and Hall, 'Reformation and the Book', p. 795.   [99] See below, pp. 67–8.
[100] Nancy Pollard Brown, 'Robert Southwell: The Mission of the Written Word', in *The Reckoned Expense: Edmund Campion and the Early English Jesuits*, ed. Thomas M. McCoog (Woodbridge, 1996), p. 194.

quantities of paper.[101] A press producing small works, such as the Marprelate tracts, could escape detection because it used limited quantities of paper, but any attempt to print *books* in early modern England foundered on reams of paper – or rather the lack of them.[102] In fact most of the printing of illicit, illegal and seditious English books was not done by clandestine presses in England; instead they were printed abroad and smuggled in. It was easier to smuggle the finished product into England in varying amounts of varying sizes than it was to smuggle the raw material necessary for creating the product. In one illuminating case the Catholic priest Thomas Alfield, who was hanged at Tyburn on 6 July 1585, had smuggled hundreds of copies of William Allen's *True, Sincere and Modest Defence* into England. He was only detected when a clandestine press was discovered and his involvement in it was traced.[103] It is quite possible that the English government wished to discourage domestic paper mills simply because the importation of paper facilitated their control of illicit printing.

The need to import both trained personnel and paper impeded the printing of large works in England. There were few of these – editions of Chaucer, Hall's *Chronicle*, Rastell's *Works of More* – before the *Acts and Monuments*. Many of these were only printed because of patronage, and some of them, such as Hall's *Chronicle*, had to be printed by several printers working together, as the task was too large for any single one of them.[104] The case of English Bibles, for which there was an imperative demand for religious, ideological and political reasons, is particularly illustrative. In the first decades of the English Reformation, these books were printed abroad, despite the considerable expense and risk involved. (The Great Bible was initially printed in the printing house of François Regnault, but the French authorities arrested the printer and confiscated both the type and the sheets already printed.) Not until Becke's Bible in 1549 would a complete Bible be printed entirely in England. (It is worth remembering, in this context, that

---

[101] Of course printers such as John Wolfe could print large quantities of illicit books under the cover of running legitimate printing houses. This gave them a plausible explanation for buying quantities of paper. The difficulty for those printing illicit books for political or religious, as opposed to commercial, motivations was the difficulty in finding an explanation for their purchases of paper. In fact, Persons was afraid that attention had been drawn to the clandestine press at Greenstreet House by the purchase of quantities of paper. Brown, 'Robert Southwell', p. 195.

[102] Clandestine presses in England, because of the need for concealment, were often so small as to border on the inadequate. Stephen Brinkley's press 'was so small that only half sheets could be printed; there was no Greek fount, and some types were in such short supply that substitutes from mis-matched founts had to be used; completed formes had to be printed off before the next pages could be set.' Brown, 'Robert Southwell', p. 195.

[103] A.C. Southern, *Elizabethan Recusant Prose, 1559–1582* (London: Sands, 1950), pp. 35–6 and 279.

[104] See STC under Halle, Edward for a discussion of the complicated printing history of this work.

Foxe's book is over six times the length of the entire Bible.) Richard Montagu, at the time bishop of Chichester, was apparently reminded of the realities of the printing business and, apparently reluctantly, he decided to produce his *De originibus ecclesiasticis* in two parts, 'bearing in mind the tedium of its reader, the purse of its buyer and the profits of its printer'.[105] As late as 1662, Thomas Fuller had to distribute the manuscript of his *Worthies of England* among different printers because no single one would undertake to print the entire work.[106] Because of the expense of producing large volumes, an expense compounded by a shortage of skilled workmen and the expense of obtaining paper, English printers had tended to avoid printing large volumes and had never attempted anything remotely approaching the size of Foxe's book.

As it was, the printing of the *Acts and Monuments* strained the capabilities of early modern book production. Its sheer size would have made it expensive and time-consuming to produce in any printing centre.[107] The technical skill lavished on it – particularly on its illustrations – would have further increased its cost and the time needed to produce it. And because it was a work both of fact and of bitterly contested facts, it had to be closely proofread and checked. This not only required correctors but the close supervision of the author as well. Both Foxe and the correctors were further challenged by the fact that additional data came in while the work was being printed, which had to be either ignored or inserted into the text. This in turn created serious difficulties in organising and cross-referencing the material in the text, which were never completely overcome. In other words, because the means of book production were so slow and cumbersome in early modern Europe, the different editions of the *Acts and Monuments* became layers of labyrinths, which have remained largely unexplored to this day.

The challenge of bringing this colossus to life was even greater when it was being done in a country where the production of a printed book of such size and complexity was unprecedented. Simply recruiting a sufficient number of skilled personnel was a considerable labour, made more

---

[105] 'ut Lectoris taedio, Emptoris compendio, Typographi lucello consuleretur'. Richard Montagu, *De originibus ecclesiasticis* (London, 1636), STC 18034, sig. 3H4ᵛ. A second part of this work was eventually issued – by a different printer – in 1638 (STC 18036).

[106] Thomas Fuller, *The History of the Worthies of England*, ed. P. Austin Nuttall, 3 vols. (London, 1840), I, p. 7.

[107] It is true that a major establishment such as Plantin's would have been able to produce the work more quickly, simply because it would have been able to devote more presses to the job; on the other hand, the logistical difficulties in producing a single work on more than four presses over what would still have been a protracted period of time might have created further difficulties of its own.

demanding by English laws regulating the employment of aliens. However, the heel of this Talos was made of paper. Because the *Acts and Monuments* necessitated astronomical quantities of paper, all of which had to be imported, the cost of the volume spiralled dangerously high. Moreover, the need to calculate accurately the amount of paper required became correspondingly more urgent.

Over the centuries we have grown accustomed to the vast size of the 'Book of Martyrs' and have ceased to marvel that mid-sixteenth-century England witnessed the printing of a work of over two million words. We are no longer surprised that four editions of this work, three of them considerably re-written, were produced in only twenty years. Yet when we consider the state of the printing industry in early modern Europe, and especially its backward condition in England, we can appreciate that producing the *Acts and Monuments* stretched the sinews of the possible. Foxe's book was only printed, in spite of all the limitations of early modern printing in general and of English printing in particular, because of the determination of a small group of people to see it printed. These included John Bale and Edmund Grindal, who first envisioned such a work, Matthew Parker and, *primus inter pares*, William Cecil, who provided the indispensable patronage. But, above all, it was a product of the zeal, willpower, resolution and self-sacrifice of two men – John Foxe, the author of the book, and John Day, its printer.

CHAPTER 2

Ancient fragments and 'noythy bokes': the early careers of John Foxe and John Day

I

John Foxe, the martyrologist, was born in Boston, Lincolnshire, around the year 1517.[1] His father, who may have been related to Henry Foxe, an affluent merchant who became mayor of the town in 1551, died while John was very young. His mother subsequently married Richard Melton, a prosperous yeoman of the nearby village of Coningsby.[2] John Hawarden, a fellow of Brasenose College, became rector of Coningsby, and around the year 1534 John Foxe entered Brasenose College.[3] The natural assumption that Hawarden paved the way for Foxe to enter Brasenose is confirmed by the fact that three decades later Foxe thanked Hawarden, by this time principal of Brasenose, for making his university career possible. In fact, Foxe seems to indicate that it was Hawarden who persuaded an apparently reluctant Richard Melton to send him to university.[4] While attending Brasenose Foxe's roommate was Alexander Nowell, the future dean of St Paul's, who would be closely associated with Foxe in later years.[5]

However, it is not clear how long Foxe remained at Brasenose; he probably studied for a time at Magdalen College school, and he certainly

---

[1] The precise date is unknown. Foxe's son, Simeon, declared that his father was born in 1517 (*1641*, II, sig. A4ᵛ). Foxe's funeral monument, erected in the parish church of St Giles Cripplegate, London (destroyed during World War II), also declared that Foxe, who died on 18 April 1587, was seventy years old when he died.

[2] Richard Melton appears in the 1523 subsidy roll, described as a yeoman. In the 1551 subsidy roll he was valued at £60 and was the wealthiest individual in the village. John Mozley, *John Foxe and his Book* (London, 1904), p. 15.

[3] On John Hawarden, the rector of Coningsby, being the same person as the former fellow of Brasenose see ibid., pp. 13–14.

[4] In 1563 Foxe dedicated his *Syllogisticon* to Hawarden. John Foxe, *Syllogisticon hoc est argumenta* (London, 1563) STC 11249. In the dedication he called Hawarden his 'Maecenas', which may indicate that he received some financial help from the rector of Coningsby. He went on to attribute his attendance at university to 'divine providence' and to Hawarden having put 'pressure' on his step-father ('Divina per te providentia, tuoque apud Socerum impulsu primum attractus sum') (sig. A4ᵛ).

[5] *1641*, II, sig. A4ᵛ.

became a probationer fellow at Magdalen College in July 1538.[6] (The probable reason for these peregrinations is that there may have been a dearth of places at Brasenose for students from Lincolnshire; the majority of its places were for students from Cheshire and Lancashire. Foxe may have attended Magdalen College school as a means of securing admission to Magdalen College which did not have the same geographical restrictions.) He was elected a full fellow in 1539 and he would hold that fellowship for about seven years. On 11 July 1543 he proceeded Master of Arts.[7]

Up to this point Foxe's career had been the easy one of a youth blessed with talent, a relatively privileged background and a modicum of good fortune. In an earlier time Foxe would have remained a fellow for some years and ultimately passed on to serve as a minister in one or more livings. He might have done some writing and attained a respectable reputation as a scholar. But the advent of the English Reformation, together with the fact that Foxe, apparently by happenstance, attended one of the handful of Oxford colleges with a significant and active evangelical minority, diverted Foxe's life into different courses.[8] For it was during his time at Magdalen that Foxe became a committed evangelical. Valuable evidence of his religious beliefs and of the confessional divisions within the college survives in a letter that Foxe wrote to Owen Oglethorpe, the president of Magdalen College, around September 1544. Writing to defend himself from unnamed accusers who charged him with not attending Mass, Foxe claimed that his actions were being monitored by some of the masters who suspected him of belonging to a 'certain new religion' ('novae cuisusdam religionis') because of his intense study of Scripture and theology. Foxe stated that such accusations had been made against him for five years, which suggests that he first gave outward indications of evangelical sympathies in 1539. In the letter Foxe also states that two other fellows of the college had been similarly accused: Robert Crowley, who would later be one of Foxe's closest friends, and Thomas Cooper, who would rise to become bishop of Winchester and one of the chief targets of the Marprelate tracts.[9] Though Foxe may have exaggerated the animus against him for rhetorical effect, it is clear that he belonged to an evangelical minority at Magdalen and one that was coming

[6] See Mozley, *John Foxe and his Book*, pp. 16–17.   [7] Ibid., pp. 17–18.
[8] For evangelicalism at Magdalen in the 1540s, see C. M. Dent, *Protestant Reformers in Elizabethan Oxford* (Oxford, 1983), pp. 4–6 and 11; Brett Usher, 'Backing Protestantism: The London Godly, the Exchequer and the Foxe Circle', in *John Foxe: An Historical Perspective*, ed. David Loades (Aldershot, 1999), pp. 116–17.
[9] BL, Lansdowne MS 388, fos. 53ʳ–58ʳ. Owen Oglethorpe, who was later promoted to the bishopric of Carlisle by Mary Tudor, was removed as president of Magdalen College in 1552 at the petition of the evangelical members of the college (Dent, *Protestant Reformers*, pp. 11–13).

under increasing pressure from conservatives at the college. This pressure certainly took its toll on Foxe – in a letter of 1545 he referred to Magdalen as a 'treadmill' ('ergastula') – and contributed to his decision to resign from the college.[10]

The specific reason for this decision, however, was a college statute requiring every fellow to take priest's orders within one year of completing an obligatory regency.[11] In Foxe's case, this meant that he had to enter holy orders by Michaelmas 1545. He was unwilling to commit to a life of celibacy; in a letter to one friend he explained that he could not remain at Magdalen 'unless I wish to castrate myself and leap into the priestly band'.[12] He was only slightly less blunt in writing to another friend: 'Michaelmas is approaching and you know the ruling of our statute; and I will not allow myself to be circumcised this year.'[13] Foxe resigned his fellowship in 1545.

Although this was a disappointing end to a promising career, Foxe's years at Magdalen were not fruitless. His religious convictions may not have pleased the Magdalen authorities but they placed him firmly within a network of evangelicals. Many of Foxe's closest friends in later years – Robert Crowley, Thomas Bentham, Henry Bull and Laurence Humphrey in particular – were part of this same evangelical circle at Magdalen. Of more immediate importance, Foxe had also made valuable contacts with prominent evangelicals outside Oxford. Now suddenly without a livelihood, Foxe turned to his evangelical friends for help. He sowed a plentiful crop of pleading letters but initially reaped a meagre harvest, receiving a great deal of advice but little practical assistance. One friend sent him a crown (five shillings) but added that he could not do anything more to help him.[14] Foxe also garnered an invitation from the great evangelical preacher, Hugh Latimer, to come and stay with him for a few months.[15] Initially Foxe tried to secure a post as a schoolmaster; he even asked Sir John Cheke to intercede on his behalf.[16] However, ultimately he set his sights lower and accepted a job as a tutor to Thomas Lucy, the son of William Lucy of Charlecote, Warwickshire, a friend of Hugh Latimer's. (This is the same Thomas Lucy whose deer were allegedly poached by the young William Shakespeare decades later.)

---

[10] BL, Lansdowne MS 388, fo. 117[r].

[11] The regency was a one-year period of public lecturing normally carried out upon attaining an MA degree.

[12] 'nisi in sacerdotale genus memet castrari ac praecipitare velim'. BL, Lansdowne 388, fo. 80[v].

[13] 'Michaelis iam festum appetit, et nosti statutis nostri decretum, neque libet hoc anno circumcidi'. Ibid., fo. 117[r].

[14] Ibid., fo. 82[r].   [15] Ibid., fo. 119[v].

[16] See ibid., fos. 83[v], 111[r] and 119[r–v]. The letter to Cheke is on fo. 118[r].

While at Charlecote, Foxe met a woman from Coventry named Agnes Randall and married her on 3 February 1547.[17] Shortly afterwards, for reasons that remain unclear, he left the Lucy household. The next period of Foxe's life is obscure and illuminated only erratically by the brief, occasionally confusing and sometimes inaccurate memoir of him written by his son, Simeon Foxe.[18] According to Simeon, John Foxe first stayed with his wife's family in Coventry and then returned home to live with his mother and stepfather in Coningsby. Simeon Foxe claimed that his father's relations with Richard Melton were strained and that, as a result, Foxe moved to London. All of this is possible, but the only part that is verifiable is that Foxe arrived in the capital some time in the summer or autumn of 1547.

Simeon also relates a dramatic and often uncritically repeated story of his father sitting destitute in St Paul's when a mysterious stranger came up to him, gave him some money and assured him that he would be employed within a few days.[19] Within (according to Simeon) three days an offer came from the duchess of Richmond, inviting Foxe to be the tutor to the children of her brother, the earl of Surrey, who had been executed in January 1547. Comforting as it is for all of us to believe in the idea of a benign providence that looks after impoverished scholars, the few available facts tend to discredit Simeon's tale. Some time in 1547 Foxe's translation of a sermon by Martin Luther was printed; in the dedication of this work Foxe stated that he lived in Stepney.[20] This must have been before he became tutor to Surrey's children and indicates that he lived in London for some time before he was employed by the duchess. In fact in 1547–8 three translations by Foxe were printed by the evangelical printer Hugh Singleton.[21] These works were

---

[17] Mozley, *John Foxe and his Book*, p. 27.

[18] The memoir was originally written in Latin and was first printed at the beginning of the second volume of the 1641 edition of the *Acts and Monuments*, along with an English translation. (All future citations from this memoir will be from the English translation.) For the history of this memoir, its authorship and a discussion of its accuracy and biases see Mozley, *John Foxe and his Book*, pp. 1–11; Thomas S. Freeman, 'Through a Venice Glass Darkly: John Foxe's Most Famous Miracle', in *Signs, Wonders, Miracles: Representations of Divine Power in the Life of the Church*, ed. Kate and Jeremy Gregory (Woodbridge, 2005), pp. 314–15, and the entry on John Foxe in *ODNB*.

[19] *1641*, II, sig. A6ʳ. Devorah Greenberg claims that Thomas Freeman 'identifies Hugh Singleton as the stranger in this case'. Devorah Greenberg, 'Community of the Texts: Producing the First and Second editions of *Acts and Monuments*', *Sixteenth Century Journal*, 36 (2005), p. 698, n. 14. Freeman, in the article Greenberg cites, merely *suggests* that Singleton may have recommended Foxe to future patrons. He does not indicate anywhere that Singleton was this providential stranger.

[20] Martin Luther, *A frutfull sermon of the moost euangelicall wryter M. Luther*, trans. John Foxe (London, 1548), STC 16983, sig. A2ᵛ.

[21] The first was a translation of Luther's sermon (cited in the previous note); the second was a translation of a sermon by Johann Oecolampadius, *A sarmon . . . to yong men, and maydens* (London, 1548), STC 18787; and the third was a translation of a tract by Urbanus Rhegius, *An instruccyon of christen fayth* (London, 1548?), STC 20847.

all printed cheaply and were visually unimpressive and, interestingly, they were dedicated to untitled and evidently minor people.[22] They do not appear to have been quests for patronage; in fact the dedications are hortatory and contain no hint of Foxe seeking money or employment. This would seem to indicate that his position was not desperate and that he may have received some support before he was hired by the duchess of Richmond. It would also be interesting to know how Foxe came to be associated with Hugh Singleton, who would print the first four works that Foxe translated, although it is quite likely that Foxe's evangelical connections brought the two men together. Certainly someone influential must have introduced Foxe to the duchess, who was a noted patron of evangelicals. During these early years Foxe seems to have received much more assistance from a network of evangelical contacts than from enigmatic strangers.

II

Foxe was entrusted with educating the three eldest children of the earl of Surrey: Thomas Howard, later the fourth duke of Norfolk; Jane Howard, afterwards countess of Westmorland; and Henry Howard, afterwards earl of Northampton. Subsequently, Charles Howard, the future commander of the English fleet against the Spanish Armada, would also be one of Foxe's charges. At first Foxe dwelt in the duchess's London residence; later, he and his pupils resided at her manor at Reigate in Surrey. The post of tutor not only provided Foxe with the first financial security he had known since leaving Charlecote, it also led to his forging a strong bond with Thomas Howard, which was later invaluable to the martyrologist. During his stay in Reigate Foxe rounded out his evangelical credentials by suppressing the cult surrounding a shrine to the Virgin Mary at Ouldsworth, Surrey. Apparently this involved the destruction of a statue of the Virgin Mary at the shrine, which was credited with healing powers.[23]

Moreover, the duchess's patronage further facilitated Foxe's entry into the ranks of England's evangelical elite. He was ordained deacon by Nicholas Ridley, the bishop of London, on 24 June 1550, and stayed at the duchess of Suffolk's house before the ceremony.[24] In 1548 Foxe also

---

[22] Two of these, a Henry Kuoche and a Mr Segrave, are untraceable. (The first of these names might be Dutch, which is suggestive in light of Foxe's ties to members of the Strangers' Church.) The third work was dedicated to Richard Melton.

[23] John Foxe, *Christ Jesus Triumphant*, trans. Richard Day (London, 1607), STC 11232, sig. A4r.

[24] Mozley, *John Foxe and his Book*, p. 30.

moved from translating the works of Protestant reformers into the authorship of works relating to theology and Church discipline. He got into a
heated controversy with the evangelical author George Joye when he
maintained that the death penalty should not be imposed on adulterers.[25]
This controversy led, by a circuitous route, to another work by Foxe, *De
censura*, which, among other things, called for a new code of canon law.[26] At
the same time Foxe turned his attention to education with his plan to issue a
book consisting of tables of Latin grammar, a project which drew important
support.[27]

Foxe forged another friendship that would also shape the contours of his
life in the summer of 1548 at the duchess of Suffolk's London residence.[28]
Here he met John Bale, the polemicist and antiquarian. Although Bale's
importance as a pioneering dramatist, a collector of manuscripts, a biblio-
phile, a biblical commentator and a historian have often been acknowledged, it is difficult for many scholars to appreciate fully these different
aspects of Bale's activities.[29] This is particularly true because Bale combined
these intellectual pursuits with a brass-knuckled polemical style, which was
egregious, even in an area of no-holds-barred confessional brawling. Patrick
Collinson once remarked to one of the authors of this book that if John Bale
were alive today he would be the editor of the *Sun* newspaper. There is truth
in this observation, but it can also be observed that if Bale were alive today

---

[25] John Foxe, *De non plectendis morte adulteris consultatio* (London, 1548), STC 11235; George Joye, *A contrarye (to a certayne manis) consultacion* (London, 1549?), STC 14822. It is an indication of how unpopular Foxe's stand on this issue was that the dedicatee of *De non plectendis*, one Thomas Picton, apparently objected to having the work dedicated to him. A reissue of the work, *De lapsis in ecclesiam recipiendis* came out the following year with the dedication to Picton removed. John Foxe, *De lapsis in ecclesiam recipiendis consultatio cum pastoribus* (London, 1549), STC 11235.5.

[26] John Foxe, *De censura sive excommunicatione ecclesiastica rectoque eius usu* (London, 1551), STC 11233. For a detailed discussion and analysis of this work see C. Davies and J. Facey, 'A Reformation Dilemma: John Foxe and the Problem of Discipline', *Journal of Ecclesiastical History*, 39 (1988), pp. 37–65. For Foxe's continuing interest in the reform of canon law see below, pp. 236–7.

[27] We will discuss this further, see below, pp. 54 and 88–9.

[28] *1570*, p. 830. In his *Catalogus*, written in 1557, Bale stated that he had known Foxe for almost ten years. John Bale, *Scriptorum Illustrium maioris Brytanniae . . . catalogus* (Basle, 1557), p. 763. This declaration by Bale would suggest that the two did not meet before 1548.

[29] For Bale as a dramatist see Peter Happé, *John Bale* (New York, 1996), and Thora B. Blatt, *The Plays of John Bale: A Study of Ideas, Technique and Style* (Copenhagen, 1968). As a collector of manuscripts, see Mary McKisack, *Medieval History in the Tudor Age* (Oxford, 1971), and Timothy Graham and Andrew G. Watson, *The Recovery of the Past in Elizabethan England: Documents by John Bale and John Joscelyn from the Circle of Matthew Parker* (Cambridge, 1998). For Bale's exegesis of Revelation see Katherine R. Firth, *The Apocalyptic Tradition in Reformation Britain, 1530–1645* (Oxford, 1979), pp. 38–68 and 78–80. For Bale's controversial writings see Jessie W. Harris, *John Bale* (Urbana, IL, 1940), Honor C. McCusker, *John Bale: Dramatist and Antiquary* (Bryn Mawr, PA, 1942) and Leslie P. Fairfield, *John Bale: Mythmaker for the English Reformation* (West Lafayette, IN, 1976), which is especially strong on Bale's polemical and historical writings, as well as on his influence on Foxe.

he would also have been the head of the *Oxford Dictionary of National Biography* (a work which, in all seriousness, still owes a considerable debt to Bale, not only in its general concept but in its specific contents).

Bale's influence on Foxe was like a torch touched to dry kindling. In fact the word 'influence' does not do enough justice to a relationship that was to form the predominant preoccupations and to inspire the undertakings that would occupy the rest of Foxe's life. Born in Suffolk in 1495, Bale entered the Carmelite Priory in Norwich in 1506, over a decade before Foxe was born. During the 1520s Bale travelled throughout East Anglia, northern France, Italy and the Low Countries, visiting Carmelite libraries and copying the texts there. Some of this work seems to have been inspired by the English antiquary John Leland.[30] During the early 1530s Bale increasingly leaned toward the evangelical cause. By 1536 he had renounced his clerical vows and had married. Now he devoted his literary energies and his antiquarian researches to furthering the Reformation, and in particular to setting forth the 'true' history of the English Church. At the time he met Foxe, Bale was building on Leland's researches to compile the first of his biographical dictionaries of English authors.[31] In 1549 he would print his *The laboryouse iourney [and] serche of Iohan Leylande*, in which Bale appealed for royal support in rescuing and printing the manuscript sources of medieval English history.[32] This activity in turn was bracketed within the two volumes, printed in 1546 and 1551, of Bale's *Actes of the Englysh Votaryes*, a history (or perhaps more accurately a *chronique scandaleuse*) of the medieval English clergy.[33]

III

The most important early dividend of the relationship with Bale was Foxe's first martyrology, the *Commentarii in ecclesia gestarum rerum*.[34] It is worth looking at the *Commentarii* in some detail, as it establishes three important points: how Foxe became interested in martyrologies and Church history, the beginnings of his unique approach to the writing of martyrologies, and the genesis of his relationship with John Bale, who would be the dominant intellectual influence on Foxe in the early part of his life.

---

[30] For Bale's travels in 1526 and 1527 see Richard Copsey, *Carmel in Britain: Studies on the Early History of the Carmelite Order*, vol. III (Faversham, Kent, and Rome, 2004), pp. 283–326. For Bale's years with the Carmelites see Fairfield, *John Bale*, pp. 1–30.
[31] This was described by Foxe himself. See *1570*, p. 830.
[32] John Bale, *The laboryouse iourney and serche . . . for Englandes antiquities* (London, 1549), STC 15445.
[33] John Bale, *The actes of Englysh votaryes . . .* (Antwerp, 1546), STC 1270, reprinted in London in 1551, STC 1273.5.
[34] John Foxe, *Commentarii in ecclesia gestarum rerum* (Strasbourg, 1554) (henceforth *Comm.*).

Foxe's sources for the *Commentarii* clearly demonstrate Bale's influence. About three-quarters of the *Commentarii* (an octavo of just over 400 pages) is compiled almost entirely from two sources. By far and away the most important of these is the manuscript (now Bodley MS e Musaeo 86), which is generally known as the *Fasciculi Zizaniorum*. This is a collection of documents dealing with the early history of the Lollards, which had been compiled by the Carmelites in the first half of the fifteenth century. Bale almost certainly obtained it from the Carmelite house in Norwich before he defected from the order in 1536.[35] Foxe would later identify Bale as the person from whom he obtained the *Fasciculi Zizaniorum*. After printing Richard Lavenham's articles, which were alleged against the Lollard John Purvey, Foxe went on to declare 'And thus much out of a certeine old written boke in parchment borowed once of J.B. which boke conteinyng divers auncient recordes of the universitie, semed to have belong sometimes, to the librarie of the sayd universitie: bearing the yeare of the compiling therof, 1396'.[36]

Most scholars have agreed that the unique manuscript copy of the *Fasciculi Zizaniorum* was lost with almost all of Bale's library when he fled from Ireland in the autumn of 1553.[37] There are two basic reasons for this assumption. The first is that Bale included the *Fasciculi Zizaniorum* in the list of manuscripts that he left behind when he hastily fled to the continent.[38] The second, less compelling, reason is that the manuscript eventually came into the possession of Archbishop James Ussher of Armagh. Neither of these objections is insuperable. First of all, Bale's list needs to be taken with a grain of salt; there is some evidence that he exaggerated the extent of his losses, perhaps for the same reason that some people exaggerate their losses in insurance claims today: in order to receive a greater amount of compensation.[39] And as for Ussher's ownership, the archbishop acquired a number of books and manuscripts from England; there is no evidence that he found the *Fasciculi Zizaniorum* in Ireland.

[35] See Anne Hudson, 'John Purvey: A Reconsideration of the Evidence for his Life and Writings', in *Lollards and their Books* (London, 1985), p. 96, n. 50. On the composition and dating of the *Fasciculi Zizaniorum*, see James Crompton, '*Fasciculi Zizaniorum*', *Journal of Ecclesiastical History*, 12 (1961), pp. 35–45 and 155–6.

[36] *1570*, p. 653. For a valuable discussion of this material see Hudson, 'John Purvey: A Reconsideration', pp. 100–1.

[37] Crompton, '*Fasciculi Zizaniorum*', pp. 39 and 43, and Hudson, 'John Purvey', p. 101. This assumption is apparently reinforced by the fact that the *Fasciculi Zizaniorum* later came into the possession of Archbishop James Ussher of Armagh. For Bale's disastrous sojourn in Ireland, see Happé, *John Bale*, pp. 16–20.

[38] Crompton, '*Fasciculi Zizaniorum*', p. 43.

[39] See W. O'Sullivan, 'The Irish "Remnaunt" of John Bale's Manuscripts', in *New Science out of Old Books: Studies in Manuscripts and Early Printed Books in Honour of A. I. Doyle*, ed. R. Beadle and A. J. Piper (Aldershot, 1995), pp. 374–87, and Graham and Watson, *Recovery of the Past*, p. 2, n. 3.

This problem casts light on the composition of the *Commentarii*, since Bale departed from his living at Bishopstoke, Hampshire, for Ireland, with his library, in December 1552.[40] If Bale took the *Fasciculi Zizaniorum* with him, then Foxe, who drew on it (and on Bale's notes in it) throughout the *Commentarii*, must presumably have ceased writing the work by the end of 1552. If so, why was it not printed until August 1554? Moreover, Foxe not only quoted from the *Fasciculi Zizaniorum* extensively, he quoted it throughout the *Commentarii*, from the beginning until the end of the book.[41] This would indicate either that the *Fasciculi Zizaniorum* was with him throughout the period when he composed the *Commentarii* or that his notes from it were so extensive as to form virtually another copy of the work.

It might be argued that Foxe made his own notebook of the contents of the *Commentarii* or copied out extracts from it before Bale left for Ireland. There is some evidence to support this hypothesis. Foxe, in 1570, said that the book was 'borowed once of J.B.', which would seem to imply that Foxe no longer possessed it, although this is not conclusive. More importantly, an extract from the *Fasciculi Zizaniorum* does survive in Foxe's handwriting, and it is, in fact, the copy of John Purvey's heretical articles that Foxe had printed in 1570.[42] However, this extract actually works against the theory that Foxe compiled a notebook from the *Fasciculi Zizaniorum*, as the extract is on several loose sheets. The most likely explanation for the existence of this separate copy of the articles against Purvey is that it was written by Foxe as the 1570 edition was being printed, in order to provide a copy text for the compositors, who otherwise might not have been able to read the original manuscript.

We would suggest that Bale left the *Fasciculi Zizaniorum* with Foxe when he departed for Ireland. Foxe would have taken it with him when he went into exile, eventually returning it to Bale when they shared a residence in Basle. Bale in turn would have been able to consult the *Fasciculi Zizaniorum* when he was preparing his own encyclopaedia of British authors, the *Catalogus*. At this point, possession of the manuscript becomes unclear. It may very well have remained in Bale's hands. If so, Bale was less than candid when he was compiling his list of books lost in Ireland. There is, however, strong evidence that Foxe had access to the *Fasciculi Zizaniorum* on various occasions between 1559 and 1570. This can be demonstrated in Foxe's account

---

[40] Happé, *John Bale*, p. 18.
[41] Apart from a brief apostrophe to the University of Oxford, which concludes the *Commentarii*, this work essentially ends on fo. 205[r]. Fos. 172[v]–99[r] reprint material from the *Fasciculi Zizaniorum*. (Cf. *FZ*, fos. 118[v]–27[r].)
[42] BL, Lansdowne 388, fos. 165[r]–73[r].

of the Lollard John Purvey. Initially in the *Commentarii* Foxe simply gave a brief account of Purvey's life, drawn from one of Bale's notes written in the *Fasciculi Zizaniorum*, together with a summary of opinions extracted from Purvey's writings.[43] In his next martyrology, the *Rerum in ecclesia gestarum*, Foxe repeated this material without change.[44] However, in the first edition of the *Acts and Monuments*, Foxe added a list of the articles that Purvey recanted in 1401, and this material came from the *Fasciculi Zizaniorum*.[45] In the second edition of the *Acts and Monuments* Foxe reprinted all of the material on Purvey from 1563, and also printed in full the commentary on Purvey's articles and his recantations of them.[46] In the 1570 edition Foxe also added another document from the *Fasciculi Zizaniorum*: a list of clerics who, in 1389, condemned articles alleged to have been held by Wiclif.[47] It seems hard to avoid the conclusion that the *Fasciculi Zizaniorum* was back in England in the 1560s and that Foxe had at least some access to it during this period.[48]

Although the *Fasciculi Zizaniorum* is an invaluable collection of sources about Wiclif and the Lollards, there is another facet of it, which, for our purposes, is of at least equal value. Bale wrote extensive notes in various blank spaces in the manuscript, containing biographical entries on the Lollards and their leading opponents, as well as episodes of Lollard history, and a copy of William Thorpe's account of his examinations. In effect what Bale did was to transform this work into both a priceless anthology and a personal notebook.[49] In the *Commentarii*, Foxe

---

[43] Cf. *Comm.*, fo. 43^{r-v} with *FZ*, fos. 91^v and 62^r. We will be discussing Bale's notes written in empty spaces in this medieval manuscript very shortly.

[44] John Foxe, *Rerum in ecclesia gestarum* (Basle, 1559), p. 20.

[45] Cf. *1563*, pp. 140–1 with *FZ*, fos. 91^v–5^r. (Foxe only printed the articles and not the recantations to each article.) It is possible that Foxe drew on the account of Purvey's trial in Archbishop Arundel's Register (LPL, Arundel Register II, fo. 184^r). However, there are a number of objections to this. One is that there is no other evidence that Foxe consulted the Arundel Register in the period before the 1563 edition was printed, and if he did it is odd that he just consulted it for Purvey's trial and ignored material on other Lollard martyrs that would have been of considerable interest to him. Second, Foxe did not print biographical material on Purvey, which would have been available from Arundel's Register, had he seen it.

[46] Cf. *1570*, pp. 649–53 with *FZ*, fos. 91^v–6^v. This is where he first stated that he drew these documents from an old book borrowed from 'J.B.', which indicates that he was still drawing this material from the *Fasciculi Zizaniorum* and not Arundel's Register.

[47] Cf. *1570*, p. 534 with *FZ*, fos. 72^r–3^r.

[48] It might be objected that the *FZ* contains no annotations by Foxe. But this may well be because Foxe had borrowed the work and was unwilling to mark up a manuscript that belonged to a close friend, to whom he was expecting to return it.

[49] For Bale's annotations see *FZ*, fos. 61^v–3^v, 105^v–10^v, 161^v, 293^{r-v}. An examination of Bale's annotations in this manuscript very strongly suggests that he used it when compiling the two editions of his great biographical dictionary of British authors, the *Illustrium maioris Britanniae Scriptorum ... Summarium* (Wesel, 1548), STC 1295, and the *Scriptorum Illustrium maioris Brytanniae ... Catalogus*, 2 vols. (Basle, 1557–9) (hereafter, we will refer to this work as the *Catalogus*).

quarried extensively from both the *Fasciculi Zizaniorum* itself and Bale's annotations.[50]

Throughout the *Commentarii* there are occasional small sections that are almost certainly based on material Bale gave to Foxe but which are not contained in the manuscript of the *Fasciculi Zizaniorum*. It is likely that Bale gave Foxe other notebooks that he had compiled, which no longer survive. The largest of these sections is a list of medieval writers and preachers who either identified the papacy with the Antichrist or, at the least, had supposedly claimed that the Antichrist appeared in the Middle Ages (which would allow the papacy to be identified with the Antichrist). All of the examples listed in the *Commentarii* also appear in Bale's *Catalogus*.[51]

At first sight it would appear that Bale simply drew them from Foxe. But several considerations militate against this. The first is that, with only one

---

[50] The documents from the *FZ* printed by Foxe were: the commentary Wiclif presented to parliament (cf. *Comm.*, fos. 17^r–26^r with *FZ*, fos. 64^v–6^v), William Burton's edict banning Wiclif and his followers from Oxford University and Wiclif's confession of faith (cf. 1, fos. 26^v–7^v with *FZ*, fos. 36^r–9^v), the story of the earthquake synod of 1382 (cf. *Comm.*, fos. 26^r–8^r with *FZ*, fos. 70^{r-v}), articles by Wiclif, which were condemned as heretical in the 1382 synod (cf. *Comm.*, fos. 28^r–9^v with *FZ*, fos. 71^{r-v}), a list of ways in which the proctors at Oxford were supposed to have favoured the Lollards (cf. *Comm.*, fos. 29^v–31^v with *FZ*, fos. 76^r–7^v), Henry Cromp's complaint against Robert Rigg (cf. *Comm.*, fos. 31^v–2^r with *FZ*, fos. 77^v–8^v), the trial of William White in 1428 (cf. *Comm.*, fos. 82^v–3^r with *FZ*, fos. 98^r–101^r), Wiclif's letter to Urban VI (cf. *Comm.*, fos. 33^r–4^v with *FZ*, fos. 83^{r-v}), Wiclif's answers to Richard II and his Privy Council (cf. *Comm.*, fos. 34^v–7^r with *FZ*, fos. 66^v–8^v), Philip Reppingdon's sermon at Oxford (cf. *Comm.*, fos. 40^v–2^r with *FZ*, fos. 75^r–7^v), the careers of Philip Reppingdon and Philip Hereford (cf. *Comm.*, fos. 42^{r-v} with *FZ*, fo. 79^r), the confession of John Aston (cf. *Comm.*, fos. 42^v–3^r with *FZ*, fos. 80^v–1^r), the process against Sir John Oldcastle (cf. *Comm.*, fos. 90^v–107^v with *FZ*, fos. 101^r–5^v), the 'twelve conclusions' of 1395 (cf. *Comm.*, fos. 108^r–15^v with *FZ*, fos. 87^r–9^v), and articles by Wiclif condemned at the Council of Constance (cf. *Comm.*, fos. 177^v–99^r with *FZ*, fos. 118^v–27^r). Material drawn from Bale's annotations consists of: the account of William Swinderby (cf. *Comm.*, fo. 43^r with *FZ*, fo. 62^r), a list of followers of Wiclif (cf. *Comm.*, fo. 44^{r-v} with *FZ*, fos. 61^v–3^v), a list of pre-Wiclifite martyrs (cf. *Comm.*, fos. 58^v–9^r with *FZ*, fos. 161^v and 166^v), the account of an unnamed friar who had to flee Scotland to avoid execution for heresy (cf. *Comm.*, fo. 62^v with *FZ*, fo. 161^v), an account of William Taylor (cf. *Comm.*, fos. 81^v–2^r with *FZ*, fos. 97^{r-v}), an account of William White and his wife Joan (cf. *Comm.*, fos. 90^v–107^v with *FZ*, fos. 101^r–5^v), an account of Joan White (cf. *Comm.*, fos. 82^v–3^r with *FZ*, fo. 63^r), an account of Richard Hoveden (cf. *Comm.*, fo. 83^r with *FZ*, fo. 623^r), an account of Thomas Bagley (cf. *Comm.*, fo. 83^{r-v} with *FZ*, fo. 63^r), an account of Paul Craw (cf. *Comm.*, fo. 83^v with *FZ*, fo. 63^{r-v}), an account of the martyrdom of Thomas of Rennes (cf. *Comm.*, fos. 83^v–9^v with *FZ*, fo. 293^{r-v}), an account of William Sawtrey (cf. *Comm.*, fo. 115^v with *FZ*, fo. 115^v) (except the fact that Sawtrey was condemned for seven heretical articles comes from the articles themselves, which are listed in *FZ*, fos. 96^v–7^r), a brief account of two Franciscans executed in 1354 (cf. *Comm.*, fo. 174^r with *FZ*, fo. 161^v), an account of 'the mother of Lady Yong' (i.e., Joan Boughton), burned for heresy in 1494 (Joan was the mother of a daughter, also named Joan, who married Sir John Yonge) (cf. *Comm.*, fos. 174^v–5^r with *FZ*, fo. 63^v), an account of John Ball (cf. *Comm.*, fo. 175^{r-v} with *FZ*, fo. 61^v), an account of Phillip Norris (cf. *Comm.*, fo. 176^{r-v} with *FZ*, fo. 63^v), and an account of Roger Acton (cf. *Comm.*, fos. 176^v–7^r with *FZ*, fo. 62^v). The *Commentarii* also contains an abridged version of the copy of William Thorpe's account of his examinations that Bale made in the manuscript of the *FZ* (cf. *Comm.*, fos. 118^r–56^v with *FZ*, fos. 105^r–10^v).

[51] Cf. *Comm.*, fos. 55^r–7^v with Bale, *Catalogus*, pp. 232–3, 168, 161, 169, 191, 628, 428, 536, 358–9, and 342.

exception, Bale's recounting of these examples is more detailed than Foxe's and he frequently lists more sources.[52] If Bale did draw on Foxe for this material then he subsequently not only looked it up but also did more extensive research on it. Moreover, in at least two cases, the direction the borrowing took becomes very clear. Foxe relates an incident drawn from Roger Howden's *Chronica*, in which Joachim of Fiore told Richard I that the Antichrist would arise in the Holy See. Bale, however, had already related this story in his *Actes of the Englysh Votaryes*, citing Howden as his source.[53] Foxe also claimed that Peter John Olivi, the Spiritual Franciscan, had prophesied that a law of liberty would appear in the end times; Foxe cited 'Guidoni Perpinianensi' as his source for this, but, in his *Brefe chronicle*, Bale had already listed the prophecies of Joachim of Fiore, the first of which began with the words 'in the latter dayes shall apere a law of lyberte'. Bale declared that these prophecies were taken 'ex compendiario Guido Perpiniani, de heresibus'.[54] Clearly these prophecies were uncovered by Bale's research and borrowed by Foxe, not, as chronology would seem to indicate, the other way round.[55] There were also isolated examples where Foxe definitely drew from Bale but the exact source from which Bale took it does not survive. For example, Foxe must have taken his erroneous claim that 'Roger Onely' and Eleanor Cobham were Lollards, punished for their religious opinions, from Bale.[56] Foxe himself acknowledged (the only time he did this in the *Commentarii*) that his narrative of Savonarola came 'ex I. Balaeo'.[57]

---

[52] The exception regards prophecies allegedly made by Savonarola. Here Foxe relates these in more detail than Bale does. (Cf. *Comm.*, fo. 56[r] with Bale, *Catalogus*, p. 628.)

[53] See *Comm.*, fo. 55[r–v] and John Bale, *The first two partes of the Actes of the Englysh Votaryes* (London, 1551), STC 1273.5, fos. 108[v]–9[r].

[54] See *Comm.*, fo. 57[r] and John Bale, *A brefe chronicle concerning the examinacyon and death of syr J. Oldecastell* (Antwerp, 1544), STC 1276, fo. 5[v].

[55] There is another example which is also suggestive. Foxe mentions a prophecy of the Antichrist 'in lib. de conversatione seruoru[m] Dei Geraldus Larodicen. episc' (*Comm.*, fo. 55[v]). The reference is to *De conversatione servorum Dei*, a now lost work by Gerard of Nazareth, a twelfth-century suffragan bishop of Laodicea. It is highly unlikely that Foxe had encountered this obscure work but Bale knew of it by 1533 at the latest from references in the Carmelite histories he researched. Andrew Jotischky, 'Gerard of Nazareth, John Bale and the Origins of the Carmelite Order', *Journal of Ecclesiastical History*, 46 (1995), pp. 214–36. Bale gives a fairly precise reference to this prophecy – Book 1, chapter 1 of *De conversatione servorum Dei* – in *Catalogus*, p. 191.

[56] Cf. *Comm.*, fo. 177[r] with Bale, *Summarium*, fo. 201[r–v]. 'Roger Onely' is Roger Bolingbroke, who was executed in 1441 for his involvement with Eleanor Cobham, the duchess of Gloucester, in a plot to kill Henry VI by means of sorcery. The mistaken identification of these two as Lollards was Bale's error, which Foxe repeated in the first edition of the *Acts and Monuments*, until Nicholas Harpsfield, Foxe's bitter critic, pounced on the mistake.

[57] *Comm.*, fo. 177[r–v].

IV

However, while Foxe's debt to Bale, both for the loan of the *Fasciculi Zizaniorum* and for Bale's notes, was immense, the *Commentarii* also owes something to Foxe's own researches as well.[58] Much of the remainder of the *Commentarii* was drawn from what is now College of Arms Arundel MS 7, which is one of the versions of Thomas Walsingham's *Chronica maiora*, which covered the years 1376–1422.[59] Foxe used Walsingham's chronicle to supply a historical framework for the documents drawn from the *Fasciculi Zizaniorum* and drew from it details of Wiclif's life and his supporters (most particularly John of Gaunt), and information about the reigns of Edward III, Richard II and Henry IV.[60] While there is no doubt that Foxe obtained the *Fasciculi Zizaniorum* from Bale, the provenance of the Arundel manuscript, before it came into Foxe's hands, remains obscure.

[58] This is a point that has been hitherto neglected, most recently in Thomas Freeman's account of Foxe in the *ODNB*.

[59] For the composition of Walsingham's *Chronica* see *The Chronica Maiora of Thomas Walsingham 1376–1422*, trans. David Preest and ed. James G. Clark (Woodbridge, 2005), pp. 10–13, and *The St Albans Chronicle: The Chronica Maiora of Thomas Walsingham*, ed. and trans. John Taylor, Wendy R. Childs and Leslie Watkiss (Oxford, 2003), pp. xxvii–lxx. This manuscript was printed as the *Historia Anglicana*, ed. H. T. Riley, 2 vols. (Rolls Series 28, London, 1863–4). The material in the Arundel manuscript for the years 1272 to 1392 is a copy of CCCC MS 195 made in the fifteenth century. From 1392 to 1422 it copies another, imperfect, version of Walsingham's history, with an independent continuation covering the years 1419 to 1422, found in CCCC MS 7 (3). See *St Albans Chronicle*, ed. Taylor, Childs and Watkiss, pp. xxxix, xlvi–xlvii and lxviii. Admittedly, Foxe also owned another version of Walsingham's *Chronica*, BL Harley MS 3634 (see below, p. 149, n. 58). However, it can be demonstrated that Foxe used Arundel MS 7 and not this manuscript as a source for the *Commentarii*. In the *Commentarii* Foxe prints an account of an old priest being burned at Smithfield in 1401 and states that he drew this out of 'vetustae historiae' (*Comm.*, fo. 60ʳ). This story is in Arundel MS 7 (p. 510) but it is not in Harley MS 3634. Foxe speculated incorrectly that this unnamed figure was actually the Lollard William Swinderby (it was actually the Lollard martyr William Sawtry; *Comm.* fos. 60ᵛ–1ʳ). In the margin of Arundel MS 7 Foxe wrote 'Guilel. Swinderby'. Foxe also took his account of the Lollard martyr John Claydon from a version of Walsingham. (Walsingham mistakenly gives 'William' as Claydon's first name, a mistake which Foxe repeats. *Comm.*, fo. 62ᵛ.) Furthermore, in Arundel MS 7 Foxe wrote in the margin, next to Walsingham's account of Claydon 'W. Claydon combustus martyr' (p. 559).

[60] Material from College of Arms, Arundel MS 7, printed in the *Commentarii* consists of: Gregory XI urging the clergy to attack Wiclif (cf. *Comm.*, fo. 10ʳ with Arundel MS 7, p. 199), Gregory XI's letter to Richard II (cf. *Comm.* fos. 10ᵛ–12ʳ with Arundel MS 7, p. 220), Lewis Clifford and Londoners intervene on Wiclif's behalf (cf. *Comm.*, fos. 15ʳ–16ʳ with Arundel MS 7, p. 222), the preamble to Wiclif's commentary on articles attributed to him (cf. *Comm.*, fo. 16ʳ⁻ᵛ with Arundel MS 7, p. 222), the death of Gregory XI, the execution of Simon Sudbury and William Courtenay becoming archbishop (cf. *Comm.*, fo. 26ʳ⁻ᵛ with Arundel MS 7, pp. 226, 230, 300 and 354), the persecution of Philip Repingdon and other followers of Wiclif at Oxford University (cf. *Comm.*, fos. 29ᵛ–31ᵛ with Arundel MS 7, pp. 362–3), gentry and nobles who support Wiclif (cf. *Comm.*, fos. 37ᵛ–8ᵛ with Arundel MS 7, pp. 366–7, 487 and 508), a priest burned in Smithfield in 1401 (cf. *Comm.*, fos. 60ᵛ–1ʳ with Arundel MS 7, p. 510), and the burning of 'William' [*sic*] Claydon (cf. *Comm.*, fo. 62ᵛ with Arundel MS 7, p. 559).

Bale's knowledge of Walsingham's chronicle seems to have been rather sketchy. Strikingly, Walsingham is not mentioned in Bale's first dictionary of British authors. In one of his notebooks Bale indicates that he knew of Walsingham's *Chronica maiora* and that it was in the library of John Leland. Bale appears to have known also of Walsingham's *Ypodigma Neustriae*.[61] But there is no direct evidence that Bale ever owned a copy of Walsingham's *Chronica*.[62] If Bale had owned Arundel MS 7, this absence of references to it in his various writings would be inexplicable, as would his failure to mention Walsingham at all in his letter of 30 July 1560 to Matthew Parker, listing works on British history and other topics that the archbishop should consult.[63] It is therefore very probable that Bale did not supply Foxe with Arundel MS 7 and that Foxe procured it on his own.

Foxe also acquired documents relating to the late fifteenth-century theologian Reginald Pecock, whom both Foxe and Bale regarded as a proto-Protestant martyr. In the wake of Pecock's conviction for heresy and the public burning of his books, a vigorous effort was made to destroy all of his works; nevertheless, Foxe obtained a letter from Thomas Bourchier, the archbishop of Canterbury who condemned Pecock, forbidding discussion of the case while it was *sub judice*.[64] The other document is a version of a recantation that Pecock made publicly at Paul's Cross on 4 December 1457. With one important exception – to be discussed a little later – Foxe's version of this recantation conforms with the other known versions of the text.[65] From whom did Foxe obtain these unrelated but authentic documents? It is very unlikely that either of these documents came from Bale. Nowhere in any of his writings does Bale give any indication of having known of their existence before Foxe printed them. Bale's information, at least according to his citations in his account of Reginald Pecock, came from what John

---

[61] John Bale, *Index Britanniae Scriptorum*, ed. R. L. Poole and Mary Bateson (Oxford, 1990), p. 459. (This is a printing of Bodleian Library, MS Selden Supra 64, which is a notebook Bale compiled, listing British authors and the locations of manuscript copies of their works.)

[62] In his list of the books that he had owned and lost in Ireland, Bale does mention owning 'continuationes' of the *Polychronicon* made 'per Thomam Vualsingham'. John Bale, *Scriptorum Illustrium maioris Brytanniae posterior pars* (Basle, 1559), p. 160. However, this reference is very vague and we cannot be sure which of Walsingham's historical writings Bale is referring to.

[63] Graham and Watson, *Recovery of the Past*, pp. 17–30, esp. pp. 24–5 where histories and chronicles are listed.

[64] *Comm.*, fos. 169ʳ–71ʳ. There is no other surviving copy of this letter.

[65] Cf. *Comm.*, fos. 141ʳ–72ʳ with Devon Public Record Office, Register of George Neville, fos. 38ʳ⁻ᵛ; 'John Benet's Chronicle for the Years 1400–1462', ed. G. L. and M. A. Harriss, Camden Society, 4th series, 9 (1972), pp. 212–13; *Registrum Abbatiae Johannes Whethamsted, abbatis monasterii Sancti Albani*, ed. H. T. Riley, 2 vols. (Rolls Series, London, 1872), 1, pp. 285–7; *An English Chronicle*, ed. J. S. Davies, Camden Society, original series, 64 (1856), pp. 75–6; Trinity College Dublin MS 516, fo. 183ʳ⁻ᵛ and Bodleian Library, Ashmole MS 789, fos. 303ᵛ–4ʳ.

Leland and Thomas Gascoigne had written about the disgraced bishop. The account of Pecock in the *Commentarii* contained items of considerable interest to Bale, and he repeated them in the *Catalogus*, but when he did so, he cited Foxe as his source.[66]

Over fifty pages further on in the *Commentarii* Foxe printed a 'Collectanea quaedam ex Reginaldi Pecocki Episcopi opusculis exustis conservata, ex antiquo psegmate transcripta'.[67] This was in effect a series of articles or bullet points, which, judging from Foxe's description of them, appear to have been copied out of an 'ancient' manuscript fragment.[68] The first of the articles was identified by Foxe as coming from a now lost work of Pecock's, *The Book of Signs*.[69] The remaining eleven articles are all drawn from Reginald Pecock's *Book of Faith*; although they are abridgements, they are fairly accurate reflections of what Pecock does say in portions of his text.[70] Once again, we do not know where Foxe got this document or even if it came from the same person or place from which he acquired his other documents on Pecock. However, it was clearly not from Bale. Admittedly, in the *Catalogus* Bale includes 'De fide' among the works of Pecock and it is the only work of Pecock's for which he supplies an incipit, indicating that he had some knowledge of the *Book of Faith*.[71] Less than ten years earlier, however, Bale did not even know this work existed: in the *Summarium* it is not included in the list of Pecock's writings.[72] If anything, it would appear that Bale learned about this work from Foxe.

---

[66] Bale, *Catalogus*, p. 595.   [67] *Comm.*, fos. 199[r]–203[v].

[68] This was probably drawn up by a contemporary of Pecock's, possibly for use in the proceedings against him or as notes for a sermon denouncing him.

[69] *Comm.*, fos. 199[v]–200[v].

[70] The only surviving copy of the *Book of Faith* is Trinity College, Cambridge, MS B.14.45. It has been printed by J. L. Morrison as *Reginald Pecock's Book of Faith* (Glasgow, 1909). (Readers who wish to consult the original should be advised that, while Morrison does indicate the manuscript folio numbers, unfortunately they have been renumbered since his work was published.) Cf. *Comm.*, fos. 200[r]–3[v] with Trinity College, Cambridge, MS B.14.45, fos. 100[v]–3[v], 115[r]–17[v], 125[v]–6[v], 113[r]–15[r], 3[r]–4[r], 71[r]–6[r], 79[v]–80[v], 33[r–v], 24[r]–6[r].

[71] Bale quoted the incipit as 'Filii mei perditi quoniam invalvit' (*Catalogus*, p. 594). This is in fact a slightly garbled version of the book's opening words: 'Facti sunt filii mei perditi, quia invalvit inimicus'. This leads to several interesting but perhaps irresolvable questions. Had Bale actually seen a copy of 'De fide'? Unfortunately, there are no annotations by either Foxe or Bale on Trinity College, Cambridge, MS B.14.45, although annotations by the antiquary John Stow are on it. However, this is not conclusive, since Foxe did not always annotate manuscripts he consulted or even owned. It is also possible that Foxe had other extracts from Pecock's works, including the opening of 'De fide', which he did not print, or even that he owned another copy of the manuscript that is now lost. In any case, it seems likely that Bale acquired these details about Pecock from Foxe, rather than the other way round.

[72] Bale, *Summarium*, fos. 204[v]–5[r].

The conclusion is inescapable. Some of the sources for the *Commentarii* were acquired by Foxe and were hitherto unknown by Bale. This may help explain how Foxe came to write the work. Nevertheless, it is on some levels rather surprising. By any standard, the work was based largely, although not entirely, on Bale's research, and it was a remarkable indication of confidence in Foxe that Bale loaned him the *Fasciculi Zizaniorum*, a manuscript that must have been invaluable to Bale, not only because of the documents it contained, but because of the extensive notes that Bale had made within it. Moreover, the *Commentarii* has to be seen as the first step in the culmination of a long-cherished, although unrealised ambition of John Bale's. A decade before the *Commentarii* was printed, Bale had written 'I wolde wyshe some lerned Englyshe manne, as there are now most excellent fresh wyttes, to set forth the Englyshe chronicles in theyr ryght shappe, as certen other landes hath done afore them, all affeccyons set a part.'[73] This passage is the faint stirring of a breeze that acts as a harbinger to an impending storm, in this case a torrential rain that would cut across the landscape of the English Reformation, transforming it forever. It is the birth announcement of the *Acts and Monuments*. Why did Bale leave it to Foxe to realise his dream? Why did the sorcerer need an apprentice?

v

The major reason was that Foxe possessed one important talent that Bale lacked: Foxe was an elegant Latin stylist, who had mastered the devices of classical rhetoric. Bale's Latin prose, by contrast, was straightforward and unadorned; while modern readers (including the authors of this book) appreciate the relative lucidity and simplicity of Bale's Latin writing, nevertheless among the educated elites of the sixteenth century this was a liability.[74] It is useful to remember that Bale's call for a learned *Englishman* to write a history of the English was written just after he had denounced Polydore Vergil, the author of the admired and influential *Anglica Historia*, for his 'Romyshe lyes and other Italyshe beggerye'.[75] Both Bale and his mentor John Leland, the great Tudor antiquary, were

---

[73] Bale, *A brefe chronicle*, fo. 5ᵛ.

[74] Bale's *Anglorum Heliades*, a history of the Carmelite order (written in 1536 but subsequently revised), is a partial exception to this, probably because Bale wished to impress John Leland (to whom the work was dedicated). In the event, the *Anglorum Heliades* was written in a florid but rather stilted style, which is atypical of Bale. The work was never printed and is now part of BL, Harley MS 3838.

[75] Bale, *A brefe chronicle*, fo. 5ʳ. For Polydore Vergil's career and writings see Denys Hay, *Polydore Vergil: Renaissance Historian and Man of Letters* (Oxford, 1952), and the article on him in the *ODNB*.

hostile to Vergil. Bale regarded Vergil (who had initially come to England as a collector of papal taxes and stayed on to forge a career in the English Church) as an unscrupulous hireling, whose history slandered the true martyrs of God and championed the interests of the papal Antichrist.[76] Leland and Bale also viewed Vergil as a foreigner who was ignorant of authentic English chronicles and who unjustly disparaged the heroic 'British' past.[77]

Yet Bale and Leland both admired and envied Vergil's classical learning and the elegant Latin style of his work.[78] Leland acerbically commented that 'Polydore has firmly persuaded himself that the soul of eloquent Cicero has migrated directly into his own breast after so many centuries. With its help he has so thoroughly mastered the golden river of flowing eloquence that, relying on it alone, he can easily turn flies into elephants and elephants back into flies.'[79] After vehemently attacking Vergil's accuracy and honesty, Bale (who was not inclined to wax lyrical on the virtues of his opponents) likewise went on to pay the Italian humanist a very uncharacteristic compliment: 'This do I not wryte in dyspraise of his lernynge, which I know to be verye excellent, but for the abuse therof beyng a most syngular gyft of God.'[80] Four years later Bale, while denouncing Vergil as a defender of Roman 'superstitionem' who was ignorant of the true history of the English, went on to praise the eloquence of his history, lauding him as the possessor of 'outstanding erudition in all good literature'.[81] Yet to Bale and Leland,

---

[76] In addition to *A brefe chronicle*, fo. 5[r], see also Bale's attack on Polydore Vergil, in his play *King Johan*, for slandering John 'At the suggestyon of the malicyouse clergy'. John Bale, *King Johan*, ed. J. H. P. Pafford (Oxford, 1931), pp. 108–9.

[77] For outraged reactions by Leland and other British antiquaries towards Vergil's scepticism regarding the historicity of King Arthur and the accuracy of Geoffrey of Monmouth's narrative, see James P. Carley, 'Polydore Vergil and John Leland on King Arthur: The Battle of the Books', in *King Arthur: Casebook*, ed. Edward Donald Kennedy (New York and London, 1996), pp. 185–204, and Hay, *Polydore Vergil*, pp. 157–61. These works will also have to be supplemented with James Carley's forthcoming edition of John Leland's *De uiris illustribus*, which will be published in the Oxford Medieval Texts series.

[78] On Vergil's classicism and polished Latin style see *The Anglica Historia of Polydore Vergil A.D. 1485–1537*, ed. and trans. Denys Hay, Camden Society, new series, 74 (1950), pp. xvi and xxiii, and Thomas S. Freeman, 'From Cataline to Richard III: The Influence of Classical Histories on Polydore Vergil's *Anglica historia*', in *Reconsidering the Renaissance*, ed. Mario Di Cesare (Binghamton, NY, 1992), pp. 191–214.

[79] This is James Carley's translation from chapter CLXI of his forthcoming edition of Leland's *De viris illustribus*. This passage does not appear in Anthony Hall's abridged edition of this work, *Commentarii de scriptoribus Britannicis: auctore Joanne Lelando Londinate. Ex autographo Lelandino nunc primus edidit Antonius Hall* . . . (Oxford, 1709). We are grateful to James Carley for allowing us to quote from his edition before publication. John Leland, *De viris illustribus: On Famous Men*, ed. and trans. James P. Carley with Caroline Brett (Oxford, 2010).

[80] Bale, *A brefe chronicle*, fo. 5[v].

[81] 'insignem omnium bonarum literarum eruditionem', Bale, *Summarium*, fos. 223[r–v].

Vergil's eloquence simply made his 'lies' more convincing and his work all the more dangerous. It was a golden chalice which contained poison, a mellifluous voice which softly whispered falsehoods, and it would take a writer of equal elegance to counter it.

Thus there were distinct advantages in having Bale's researches displayed within the bejewelled reliquaries of ornate Latin writing. Having found an associate who possessed the necessary Ciceronian style, and who shared his commitments and interests (perhaps even to the extent of the younger man acquiring Bale's own medieval manuscripts), it was natural, if rather selfless, for Bale to delegate Foxe to counteract the eloquence of Polydore Vergil and other 'popish' authors. In some ways the *Commentarii* is not an ideal piece of classically inspired humanist historical writing; it lacks a number of the devices that characterised such works (for example, elaborate speeches put into the mouths of the historical characters in the work). It also suffered from what, according to the paradigm of classical historiography, was a stylistic blemish: it reprinted documents.[82] Nevertheless, there are clearly purple passages in the work where Foxe declaimed on various topics in as sophisticated and ornate a Latin style as he could muster.[83] It is noteworthy that Bale cites the *Commentarii* three times in his 1557 dictionary of British writers. On one occasion this was on a 'factual' point that Foxe had uncovered himself: that Reginald Pecock denied transubstantiation.[84] But on the other two occasions Bale was simply drawing the reader's attention to stylistic passages in Foxe's martyrology that he felt were particularly admirable.[85]

Moreover, the *Commentarii* is edited carefully and skilfully, if somewhat tendentiously, by Foxe. The most striking example of this tendentiousness is

[82] A seminal analysis of the differences between classical and ecclesiastical historical writing, describing the inclusion of documents as a particular feature of the latter, is Arnaldo Momigliano, 'Pagan and Christian Historiography in the Fourth Century A.D.', in *Essays in Ancient and Modern Historiography* (Middletown, CT, 1977), pp. 107–26, esp. pp. 113–14. For the persistence of this distinction see Cochrane, *Historians and Historiography*, pp. 470–1. It may even be that the decision to place the two largest collections of documents – the articles alleged against Wiclif at the Council of Constance and the collection of writings attributed to Reginald Pecock – at the end of the book may have been Foxe's effort to minimise this rebarbative feature of the *Commentarii*.
[83] Examples include a diatribe on the superstition and corruption of the Church in Wiclif's era (*Comm.*, fos. 2ᵛ–6ʳ), a denunciation of the execution of people for their religious beliefs (*Comm.*, fos. 12ʳ–15ʳ), another denunciation of execution for heresy, claiming that the practice was unknown in the early Church (*Comm.*, fos. 44ᵛ–55ʳ), an encomium of Sir John Oldcastle (*Comm.*, fos. 90ᵛ–2ʳ), a comparison of Oldcastle to Elijah (*Comm.*, fo. 107ʳ⁻ᵛ), and an excursus on the tyranny of the Roman Church and the godly remnant who did not bow their knee to Baal (*Comm.*, fo. 157ʳ⁻ᵛ).
[84] Bale, *Catalogus*, p. 595.
[85] Ibid., pp. 469 and 557. The first of these references is to Foxe's flamboyant description of the spiritual darkness that enveloped England in the time of Wiclif; the second is to Foxe's comparison of Oldcastle to Elijah.

Foxe's claim that Pecock had stated that 'quod non est necessarium, ponere corpus materialiter in sacramento'.[86] This surprising utterance appears in none of the other surviving versions of Pecock's recantation; instead, they say that Pecock had stated that it was not necessary for salvation to believe in the Holy Spirit. It is hard to avoid the conclusion that Foxe arbitrarily altered this passage in order to avoid having a figure whom he regarded as a proto-Protestant denying the Trinity, and also in order to add another link to the chain of pre-Reformation theologians who denied the Real Presence. Similar considerations led Foxe to omit one article from a list of heresies attributed to Wiclif: the allegation that Wiclif believed that God owed obedience to the Devil.[87] And Foxe, reprinting a list of Wiclif's responses to questions put to him by Richard II and his council, omitted a large section of these replies because in them Wiclif declared his belief in Purgatory.[88]

Sometimes Foxe's editing simply consisted of seamlessly merging two separate texts together to achieve the desired effect. For example, there is an account of Wiclif's defence at Lambeth in 1377 in both Walsingham's *Chronica* and, in an abbreviated form, the *Fasciculi Zizaniorum*. Foxe printed the preamble to the defence, in which Wiclif protested his ortho-doxy and proclaimed his willingness to defend his opinions to the death, from the full account in Walsingham.[89] However, he then gave the abridged version of the defence itself from the *Fasciculi Zizaniorum*.[90] In this way, Foxe was able to present Wiclif's passionate defence in his preamble in full and then merely give a summarised version of what was a very long docu-ment. Similarly, Foxe took an account of Robert Rigg, the chancellor of Oxford, defying Archbishop Courtenay's orders to suppress Lollardy in the university from the *Fasciculi Zizaniorum*, but he added the claim that Rigg was a secret Lollard sympathiser from Walsingham.[91]

The *Commentarii*, then, is not simply a compilation of documents interwoven with occasional passages of polished rhetoric. It was, as all of Foxe's martyrologies were, carefully and cleverly edited to attain a desired polemical effect. When did Foxe write the work? It is impossible to answer this question precisely, but there are some clues. It must have been started after Bale had written the *Summarium* (which was printed in 1548), as Bale

---

[86] *Comm.*, fo. 172ʳ.

[87] 'quod Deus debet obedire diabolo' (cf. *Comm.*, fo. 28ʳ⁻ᵛ with *FZ*, fo. 71ʳ⁻ᵛ). This article is undoubt-edly a distortion of what Wiclif actually believed.

[88] Cf. *Comm.*, fos. 34ᵛ⁻7ʳ with *FZ*, fos. 66ᵛ⁻8ʳ.   [89] Cf. *Comm.*, fo. 16ʳ⁻ᵛ with Arundel MS 7, p. 222.

[90] Cf. *Comm.*, fos. 17ʳ⁻26ʳ with *FZ*, fos. 64ᵛ⁻6ᵛ. In fairness, it should also be observed that Foxe stated that he was presenting an abbreviated version of Wiclif's defence.

[91] Cf. *Comm.*, fos. 40ᵛ⁻1ʳ with *FZ*, fo. 75ʳ and Arundel MS 7, pp. 360⁻2.

had clearly used his notes in the *Fasciculi Zizaniorum* for this work. The *Commentarii* was very probably completed just prior to the end of Edward VI's reign at the beginning of July 1553. A dedication, which was never printed, survives for the *Commentarii*. Unfortunately the 'amico et patrono', who was the intended recipient of the original dedication, is unnamed.[92] But the fact that the dedication was changed would seem to indicate that the intended patron was suddenly either unwilling or unable to help Foxe. By far and away the most likely explanation of this is that the intended dedicatee was rendered suddenly powerless by the accession of Mary Tudor to the throne in the summer of 1553. The dedication would not have been written until the work was complete, so therefore it seems a reasonable inference that Foxe had finished the work just in time for the sudden dynastic changes to render it unprintable in England.

On the other hand, it is unlikely that it took Foxe five years to write a 400-page work. There are, moreover, indications in the *Commentarii* that the work was written when Foxe was in relative isolation and certainly away from London. In the *Commentarii* Foxe repeatedly cites the chronicle of Robert Fabian. However, these citations are, in every instance, repeated verbatim from Bale's notes in the *Fasciculi Zizaniorum*.[93] When writing his second Latin martyrology, the *Rerum*, during his exile in Basle, Foxe incorporated the *Commentarii* into it with very few changes. However, among these changes were the additions of crucial passages from Fabian's chronicle regarding Sir John Oldcastle and other fifteenth-century Lollard martyrs.[94] Clearly Foxe knew of Fabian's chronicle when he was writing the *Commentarii* and, equally clearly, he did not have access to it. It is difficult to believe that Foxe would not have had access to such a popular work had he been in London. Since the work was completed before the end of Edward's reign, and hence before Foxe's exile, this means that it was almost certainly written in the final years of Edward's reign, while Foxe was tutoring the Howard children at the duchess of Richmond's manor at Reigate.

VI

Mary Tudor was proclaimed queen in London on 3 August 1553. Her accession to the throne blasted the careers of many Edwardian

---

[92] BL, Lansdowne MS 335, fo. 2ᵛ. See below, p. 54, for a discussion of who the dedicatee might have been.

[93] Cf. *Comm.*, fos. 83ʳ⁻ᵛ and 115ʳ with *FZ*, fos. 62ʳ⁻3ʳ.

[94] Foxe, *Rerum*, pp. 98–107 and 107–9 are unmistakably drawn from Robert Fabian, *The newe Cronycles of Englande and of Fraunce* (London, 1516), STC 10659, fos. cliiiiᵛ, clxxvᵛ and clxxixᵛ. The passages are not in the equivalent sections of the *Commentarii* (fos. 90ᵛ–107ᵛ and 62ᵛ).

Protestants, among them Foxe himself. The third duke of Norfolk was released from the Tower and on 27 August, by order of the Privy Council, his grandchildren, Foxe's pupils, were placed in his custody. The old duke, a religious conservative, would have had no desire to retain Foxe as the tutor of his heir. Instead, he placed his two grandsons in the households of two of the most important bishops in the new regime. Thomas Howard, the eldest of the grandchildren, now a youth of seventeen, was lodged with Stephen Gardiner, the bishop of Winchester. His younger brother, Henry, was sent to John White, the bishop of Lincoln.[95]

However, what exactly happened to Foxe in this period is rather obscure. Apparently he returned to London and remained in contact with Thomas Howard. Simeon Foxe goes further and states that his father was sheltered by Thomas, and that it was only at the young nobleman's urging that John Foxe did not flee immediately into exile.[96] Much of Simeon's account of these events, which took place fifteen years before he was born, is unreliable. Yet there is a certain amount of corroboration of it in an inscription written in a copy of the *Acts and Monuments* now housed in the British Library.[97] This inscription, dated 3 December 1578, states that the owner of the book travelled on an errand with John Foxe from Whitehall to Southwark. It goes on to relate that Foxe told him that this trip reminded him of a journey he had taken at the beginning of Mary's reign across the river to visit Thomas Howard in Stephen Gardiner's palace in Southwark. The note goes on to declare that this visit was reported to Gardiner and nearly led to Foxe's apprehension. Simeon recounts a more elaborate and less convincing story in which Foxe inadvertently met Stephen Gardiner while the latter was visiting his young charge. According to Simeon, both Foxe and Howard took fright at this encounter and Foxe resolved to head into exile.[98] Another brief account of John Foxe's life, written by John Day's son Richard before Simeon's memoir appeared and independently of the aforementioned inscription, agrees that Gardiner sought Foxe out and that Howard sent him away for his safety into Germany.[99]

How much truth is there in these narrations? All of them very probably originate from John Foxe himself. How greatly Foxe dramatised the details of an admittedly tumultuous period of his life can only be guessed at, but it seems likely that he did stay in London in the early part of Mary's reign with some sort of assistance from the young Thomas Howard. It is possible that Foxe came to the attention of Stephen Gardiner; it is also possible that he

---

[95] Mozley, *John Foxe and his Book*, p. 37. [96] *1641*, II, sigs. A6ᵛ–A7ʳ. [97] BL, C.37.h.2.
[98] *1641*, II, sig. A7ʳ. [99] Foxe, *Christ Jesus Triumphant*, sig. A4ʳ.

merely feared that he had done so. In any case, it does seem as if Foxe's decision to flee abroad was both sudden and reluctant. On 31 January 1554, Foxe wrote a letter to a friend, Pieter Deleen, a leader of the Dutch Stranger Church in London, about the impending flight into exile of the foreign congregation. Yet although Foxe was pessimistic about the future, he seems to have had no plans to leave England. Interestingly, in the letter Foxe sounds as if he wishes to go into exile but is unable to do so, exclaiming 'would that the situation were such that I might share not only in your labours but also in your dangers'.[100] Yet sometime in the late winter or early spring of 1554 Foxe set sail from Ipswich, accompanied by his pregnant wife.

Whatever the cause, it must have been a wrenching decision for Foxe to leave England. In the years since he had first come to London, he had managed to penetrate the circles of the evangelical and social elites of Edwardian England. He was friends with the noted evangelicals John Rogers and William Turner, he remained in touch with Hugh Latimer, and appears to have known Bishop Ridley of London.[101] The most tantalising indications of how well connected Foxe may have been revolve around the question of to whom he originally dedicated the *Commentarii*. When it was eventually printed, the *Commentarii* was dedicated to Duke Christoph of Württemberg. However, the original manuscript survives and it contains a different dedication made to 'domino charo amico et patrono'.[102] Who was the patron to whom Foxe originally dedicated the work? Theoretically, there are six likely candidates: the young Thomas Howard, William Cecil, John Bale, the duchess of Richmond, Hugh Latimer or Nicholas Ridley. The last three can be eliminated fairly readily. The case endings indicate that the dedicatee was male. The address also does not suggest that the dedicatee was a cleric, much less a bishop; terms referring to the dedicatee as 'reverend' or 'pious' are not present. Furthermore, while Foxe was indebted to Bale, it is unlikely that he would have referred to him as a patron, and even less likely that he would have addressed him as 'domino'. The young Thomas Howard is a much stronger candidate. He certainly was of sufficient rank to be addressed as 'lord'. But would a tutor have addressed a recent pupil (who was still an adolescent) as an 'amico'?

[100] 'Utinam ita res ferret, ut non solum laborum sed et periculorum tuorum queam esse particeps'. J. H. Hessels, *Ecclesiae Londino–Bataviae Archivum*, 3 vols. in 4 (Cambridge, 1889–97), II, pp. 38–9; the quotation is on p. 38.
[101] For Foxe's friendship with Rogers see *Rerum*, p. 202, and for Turner's friendship with Foxe see BL, Harley MS 416, fo. 132r. Foxe claimed that he had discussed his treatise on ecclesiastical discipline and canon law with Ridley, and that Ridley had directed him to write the work. Foxe also claimed that Latimer had not only encouraged him to write the work but 'authoromento etiam quodam sui nominis in hoc negotio communivit' (Foxe, *De censura*, sig. B7v).
[102] The dedication is BL, Lansdowne MS 335, fos. 2v–9r.

At first glance, William Cecil seems an unlikely possibility. However, there is some evidence of Foxe's association with him, even by this early date. In May 1551, Foxe wrote to Cecil, who had recently been made a Privy Councillor, seeking Cecil's support for a book he had written, presenting the fundamentals of Latin grammar in tables.[103] Significantly, Foxe apparently obtained the support of the Privy Council. According to Anthony Wood, when Foxe's tables of grammar were printed in 1552 they were 'subscribed in print by eight lords of the Privy Council'.[104] This certainly is the first hint of the future close patron–client relationship between Cecil and Foxe. It is possible, although sadly it cannot be proved, that the dedication of his first martyrology was to Cecil and that this marked a further milestone in their association.

As we have seen, the *Commentarii* was essentially completed when Foxe fled England. The work, however, was printed soon after his arrival on the continent. Foxe migrated to Strasbourg, where the work was printed, in September of 1554. The original work probably concluded on fo. 205^v, which simply quotes Revelation 7:14–15 from the Vulgate. However, this is followed by an apostrophe to Oxford University, which helps to clarify the printing history of this book.[105] In the apostrophe Foxe reproaches the Oxford colleges for accepting transubstantiation and contrasts this acquiescence with twenty-six scholars who left Cambridge rather than subscribe to this doctrine. The Cambridge men (there were actually twenty-five, including their leader, Thomas Lever) had left Cambridge on 28 September 1553 and arrived in Strasbourg on 24 February 1554. Foxe is also referring to the visitation of Oxford colleges on 16 April 1554, when the fellows of the colleges were all forced to subscribe to Catholic orthodoxy. Since the dedication to the *Commentarii* is dated 31 August, the work must have been printed between late April at the earliest and the end of August. It was probably closer to the end of August, since the apostrophe closes with Foxe saying that he was being hurried to conclude it by the printer.[106] The reason for the haste is one that would affect the printing of all the books by Foxe that were printed during his exile: the need to have the book ready in time to be displayed at the Frankfurt Book Fair. It would appear that the *Commentarii* was finished just in time to make this important commercial deadline.

---

[103] BL, Add. MS 34727, fo. 2^r.
[104] Anthony Wood, *Athenae Oxoniensis*, ed. Philip Bliss, 5 vols. (London, 1813–20), I, cols. 321 and 531. No copy of Foxe's Latin grammar survives today.
[105] *Comm.*, fos. 206^r–12^r.   [106] *Comm.*, fo. 212^v.

It is usual to see Foxe's martyrologies as part of the sudden torrent of Protestant martyrological writing in the 1550s and one which, like the others, poured forth in an attempt to douse the fires of persecution. Andrew Pettegree has claimed that Foxe's work 'arose out of the experience of dislocation and defeat following the death of Edward VI and the subsequent suppression of Protestantism by Queen Mary'.[107] It is, of course, certainly true that Foxe's martyrologies gained a great deal of their relevance and influence from the Marian persecution. However, it is worth remembering that the *Commentarii* was written before Mary came to the throne and was printed before the Marian burnings had actually started. This fact would have important consequences on both the reception and the content of the work, and also on the future course of Foxe's research.

To take the last point first, Foxe stated at the end of the *Commentarii* that he planned in the future to carry the work down to the time of Luther.[108] In other words, Foxe's intention, which he ultimately fulfilled, was to link the proto-Protestants of the Middle Ages with the martyrs of the Reformation in one continuous narrative. This strategy would, as we shall see in the next chapter, be somewhat at odds with the desire of Foxe's future collaborator, Edmund Grindal, whose focus was entirely on the martyrs of Mary Tudor's reign. At the same time, Foxe's martyrology would be, from its first edition, much more detailed on medieval history than any of the other contemporary Protestant martyrologies.

A comparison of Foxe's *Commentarii* with the martyrology of the Dutch minister Adriaan van Haemstede is revealing. Haemstede devotes the first sixth of his *History of the Pious Martyrs* to the Church before Luther.[109] On this basis, Andrew Pettegree has claimed that among the major Protestant martyrologists: 'Only Haemstede offers a complete view of Christian persecutions, from the first biblical martyrs, Stephen, Paul and Simon Peter, through the Early Church to the victims of the medieval papacy.'[110] While these claims are true in the most literal sense, they are misleading. For one thing, the first edition of Ludwig Rabus's contemporary martyrology,

---

[107] Andrew Pettegree, *Reformation and the Culture of Persuasion* (New York, 2005), p. 203. One problem is that Pettegree tends to blur the distinctions between each of Foxe's martyrologies by referring to them collectively as 'the English martyrology'.

[108] *Comm.*, fo. 205ʳ.

[109] Adriaan van Haemstede, *De Geschiedenisse ende den doodt der vromer Martelaren* (Emden, 1559). This work is over 450 pages long; the history of Luther commences on p. 75.

[110] Andrew Pettegree, 'Haemstede and Foxe', in *John Foxe and the English Reformation*, ed. David Loades (Aldershot, 1997), p. 282. He reaffirms this claim in *Reformation and the Culture of Persuasion*, p. 206.

printed between 1552 and 1558, went back to Abel and continued through the Old Testament, the Apostolic era and the early Church, ending with persecutions in the fifth century A D . Rabus's work then recommenced with Lollard and Hussite martyrs of the fifteenth century. So while it covered a greater range of time than Haemstede's martyrology, it did not supply a continuous narrative. Moreover, it should be pointed out that Haemstede devotes only nine pages to events and people from the Carolingian era through to the fifteenth century; therefore, praising Haemstede for providing 'a complete view of Christian persecutions' down to 'the victims of the medieval papacy' is somewhat overstated.[111]

More importantly, and of greater relevance to our argument, Haemstede is deeply indebted to Foxe's *Commentarii* for his knowledge of the medieval proto-martyrs that he does mention. Even some of Haemstede's twelfth- and thirteenth-century martyrs are lifted straight from the *Commentarii*.[112] Haemstede declares that a Dominican named 'Richard' was accused of heresy and burned in Heidelberg in 1330. He is clearly taking this from Foxe, who stated that a Dominican named 'Eckhardus' was condemned for heresy and burned in Heidelberg in 1330.[113] However, it is in connection with the Lollards that Haemstede most clearly relied on Foxe's *Commentarii*. Haemstede's account of Wiclif in particular is unmistakably drawn from Foxe, but so is his material on the Lollard martyrs John Aston, William Thorpe, William Taylor, William White, Richard Howden, Thomas Bagley (or 'Buglus' as Haemstede refers to him) and the obscure Paul Craw (who was mistakenly identified by Bale, then Foxe, as a Scottish Lollard but who was actually Paul Kravař, a Bohemian Hussite who came to Scotland and was burned there in 1433).[114] Other references to Lollard

---

[111] Pettegree, 'Haemstede and Foxe', p. 282. Also see Haemstede, *De Geschiedenisse*, pp. 35–44.

[112] Among these martyrs, Haemstede lists 'Prince van Armeryck', 'Berghardus', who was executed at Erfurt, and a 'diaken' burned at Oxford (Haemstede, *De Geschiedenisse*, p. 40). Haemstede's source for this becomes crystal clear when one consults the *Commentarii*, which lists among its martyrs 'principem Armericum suspensum', 'Erphurdiae Berghardus haereseos titulo igni traditus. anno 1218' and 'Oxoniae Diaconus.1122' (*Comm.*, fo. 58ᵛ). Interestingly, Haemstede somewhat garbled these references. He appears to have enshrined a mythical 'Berghardus' rather than a Beghard, burned at Erfurt, as a martyr and, because Foxe used the word 'principem' for 'chief' or 'leader', Haemstede described the medieval theologian, Almeric of Bone, as a 'prince'.

[113] Cf. Haemstede, *De Geschiedenisse*, pp. 43–4 with *Comm.*, fo. 59ʳ. 'Eckhardus' is Johann Eckhart (*c.* 1260–1327), the celebrated Dominican preacher and theologian. In fact, Eckhart died of natural causes and was not burned. However, two years after his death, in 1329, John XXII condemned seventeen of Eckhart's propositions as heretical and declared that another eleven were suspicious. Because of this condemnation, Foxe leapt to the conclusion that Eckhart had been burned.

[114] Cf. Haemstede, *De Geschiedenisse*, pp. 44–53 and 66–71 with *Comm.*, fos. 1ᵛ–2ᵛ, 10ʳ, 26ʳ, 27ʳ–9ᵛ, 32ʳ⁻ᵛ, 60ʳ⁻ᵛ, and 81ᵛ–3ᵛ. On Paul Kravař see Anne Hudson, *The Premature Reformation* (Oxford, 1988), pp. 126–7 and 515.

martyrs are drawn even more unambiguously from Foxe: for example, where Foxe describes an unnamed 'faber' (actually John Badby) being burned at Smithfield, Haemstede reports that this was the fate of a similarly unnamed 'ambuchtsman'.[115] And while Haemstede's account of Sir John Oldcastle is much briefer than Foxe's, he still repeats Foxe's comparison of the Lollard rebel to Elijah.[116] Furthermore, Haemstede also repeated, almost verbatim, Foxe's accounts of a number of late medieval martyrs.[117] Andrew Pettegree has strongly suggested that Foxe was influenced by Haemstede's work, in particular speculating that it was Haemstede's example that led Foxe to incorporate the pre-Wiclifite Church history into the *Acts and Monuments*.[118] In fact, the exact opposite seems to be the case. The evidence for any influence of Haemstede on Foxe remains tenuous at best, but the influence of Foxe on Haemstede's work is both significant and indisputable.[119]

The *Commentarii* is a more influential and important work than it is normally given credit for, and its contents were rapidly absorbed into contemporary Protestant martyrologies. Ludwig Rabus's use of it is instructive. In 1552 Rabus printed what would be the first volume of an eight-volume martyrology. Unfortunately for Rabus, the printing house that produced the first volume soon went out of business. He then entered into an agreement with Samuel Emmel, another printer, who printed the remaining seven volumes of his martyrology between 1554 and 1558.[120] The

---

[115] Cf. Haemstede, *De Geschiedenisse*, pp. 52–4 with *Comm.*, fos. 61ʳ–2ʳ.

[116] Cf. Haemstede, *De Geschiedenisse*, pp. 66–9 with *Comm.*, fos. 90ᵛ–107ᵛ.

[117] Among them are Thomas of Rennes (cf. Haemstede, *De Geschiedenisse*, pp. 71–2 with *Comm.*, fos. 83ᵛ–90ʳ) and 'the mother of Lady Young' (i.e., 'Mater Dominae Yonge' in Foxe; 'moder van vrouwi Jong' in Haemstede; this is really Joan Boughton, the mother of Lady Joan Young). Cf. Haemstede, *De Geschiedenisse*, p. 73 with *Comm.*, fos. 174ᵛ–5ʳ.

[118] Pettegree, 'Haemstede and Foxe', pp. 282–5.

[119] John King has observed that Foxe cites Haemstede's martyrology as a source several times in the *Acts and Monuments* (King, *Foxe's Book of Martyrs and Early Modern Print Culture*, p. 42). What King does not observe is that on each of these occasions Foxe is simply repeating the citation from another source, usually either the martyrologies of Jean Crespin or of Heinrich Pantaleon. More pertinently Guido Latré has observed striking verbal parallelisms between passages in Foxe's and Haemstede's description of the same episode, and on the basis of these parallelisms has suggested that Foxe consulted Haemstede's martyrology. Guido Latré, 'Was van Haemstede a Direct Source for Foxe? On le Blas's *Pijnbanck* and other Borrowings', in *John Foxe at Home and Abroad* ed. David Loades (Aldershot, 1997), pp. 151–5. However, the passages Latré analyses are in an account – that of the martyrdom of Bertrand le Blas – that Foxe first included in the 1570 edition. Latré has demonstrated that Foxe *might* have consulted Haemstede's work before compiling the second edition of the *Acts and Monuments*. However, this does not demonstrate that he did so before the mid-1560s or that it had any significant influence on the themes and scope of the *Acts and Monuments*.

[120] Robert Kolb, *For All the Saints: Changing Perceptions of Martyrdom and Sainthood in the Lutheran Reformation* (Macon, GA, 1987), pp. 46–7.

second volume of his work, printed in 1554, began with the martyrdoms of Hus and Jerome of Prague, then continued with early Lutheran martyrs from Johann Esch and Heinrich Voes (both executed in 1523) to Juan Diaz (murdered in 1547).[121] No English martyrs appeared in this volume, nor were there any martyrs in it from before Jan Hus. However, Rabus's third volume – printed the year after the *Commentarii* – contained accounts of a number of Lollard martyrs. These were inserted at the beginning of the volume, before Rabus continued his narrative of the Lutheran martyrs, resuming with those executed in the 1530s. The accounts of pre-Lutheran martyrs in Rabus's third volume – William Thorpe, John Oldcastle, William Taylor, William White and Thomas of Rennes – were all drawn, as Rabus acknowledged, from Foxe's *Commentarii*.[122] In other words, Rabus must have consulted the *Commentarii* very soon after its printing and almost immediately incorporated its contents into his martyrology.

Jean Crespin, the Genevan martyrologist, also incorporated material from the *Commentarii* into his own work. However, Crespin's use, and apparent awareness, of Foxe's book is more complicated. The honour of being the first martyrologist to incorporate portions of the *Commentarii* into their work belongs neither to Rabus not Crespin but to two brothers – Jean and Adam Rivery – who printed an unlicensed edition of Jean Crespin's *Collection of numerous people who have constantly endured death for the name of our lord*. While printing their pirated edition, some time around late 1554, the Rivery brothers abruptly interpolated the account of Wiclif (duly translated into French) from the *Commentarii* into their unauthorised martyrology.[123] Crespin rapidly followed with a new version

[121] Ludwig Rabus, *Der Heyligen ausserwoehlten Gottes Zeugen, Bekennern und Martyrern . . . Historien . . .* 8 vols. (Strasbourg, 1552–8), II.

[122] Cf. Rabus, *Historien*, III, fos. iʳ–xxxiiiᵛ with *Comm.*, fos. 116ʳ–57ʳ; Rabus, *Historien*, III, fos. xxxivʳ–xlviᵛ with *Comm.*, fos. 91ᵛ–107ᵛ; Rabus, *Historien*, III, fos. xlviᵛ–xlviiʳ with *Comm.*, fos. 81ᵛ–2ʳ; Rabus, *Historien*, III, fos. xlviiᵛ–xlviiiʳ with *Comm.*, fos. 82ʳ–3ʳ; Rabus, *Historien*, III, fos. xlviiiᵛ–liᵛ with *Comm.*, fos. 83ᵛ–9ᵛ.

[123] In their edition, normal pagination starts with the account of Jan Hus (on page 1); however, before this, there are thirty-two pages devoted to Wiclif and other medieval proto-Protestants. This material occupies sigs.** 1ʳ–**8ᵛ and a1ʳ–a8ᵛ. Jean Crespin, *Recueil de plusieurs personnes qui ont constamment enduré la mort pour le nom de Nostre Seigneur* (Geneva, 1555). The only possible reason for this arrangement is that the Rivery brothers came across the *Commentarii* after the printing of their edition had begun. Admittedly, the Rivery brothers nowhere cite Foxe or the *Commentarii* as their source; however, there can be no doubt of where they obtained their material. For example, they reprint Gregory XI's letter to Richard II (cf. Crespin, *Recueil*, sigs.** 2ᵛ–4ʳ with *Comm.*, fos. 10ᵛ–12ʳ) and Wiclif's letter to Pope Urban VI (cf. Crespin, *Recueil*, sigs.** 8ᵛ–a1ᵛ with *Comm.*, fos. 33ʳ–4ᵛ); unless a pair of obscure printers in Geneva had access to a manuscript copy of Walsingham's *Chronica maiora* and to the unique copy of the *FZ* that Bale had annotated, it has to be assumed that they were drawing on Foxe. The Rivery brothers' dependence on Foxe is also apparent in their

of the *Recueil*, which reprinted, word-for-word, the material the Rivery brothers had extracted from the *Commentarii*.[124] From now on, Crespin's martyrologies, which had previously commenced with Hus, now commenced with Wiclif. Through the medium of the *Commentarii* the Lollards became part of the major Protestant martyrologies of Crespin, Haemstede and Rabus.

These martyrologies in turn disseminated information in the *Commentarii* to works that had a wider readership among continental Protestants. For example, the popular Lutheran ecclesiastical calendar written by Kasper Goltwurm, the court chaplain of Count Philip of Hanau, contained accounts of Sir John Oldcastle, William Taylor, William Thorpe and William Sawtry, which were almost certainly drawn from Ludwig Rabus's martyrology and, through Rabus, the *Commentarii*.[125] Goltwurm's calendar was what Ian Green would term a 'steady seller': it went through nine editions between 1559 and 1600, in print runs of up to 3,000 copies.[126] Through this calendar generations of Lutherans would have learned some of the details Foxe provided about leading Lollard martyrs.

VIII

Thus the *Commentarii* brought the Lollard martyrs – and indeed the Lollards who followed Wiclif – to the attention of continental Protestants. (Wiclif was, of course, well known to both Hus and the Hussites and a few works attributed to him were printed by the early Lutherans. But until the printing of the *Commentarii*, knowledge of most other Lollards, particularly Lollard martyrs who had not authored books or treatises, were not widely known on the continent, even among

---

treatment of the proto-Protestants in this section, who include Almeric of Bone (once again referred to as 'Prince Almeric'), the Beghard executed in Erfurt and the deacon executed at Oxford (all of these are in Crespin, *Recueil*, sig. a6ᵛ). The Rivery brothers also mention several other Lollards clearly drawn from Foxe, including the 'faber' (or, in French, 'homme de mestier') burned at Smithfield (*Recueil*, sig. a7ʳ).

[124] Cf. Crespin, *Recueil* (1555), sigs.** 1ʳ–a8ᵛ with Jean and Adam Rivery, *Recueil de pluisiers personnes qui ont constamment enduré la mort pour le nom de Nostre Seigneur* (Geneva, 1556), pp. 1–31. For Crespin and the Rivery brothers see Gilmont, *Jean Crespin*, pp. 170–2, and Jean-François Gilmont, *Bibliographie des éditions de Jean Crespin*, 2 vols. (Verviers, 1981), I, pp. 56–9.

[125] Kaspar Goltwurm, *Kirchen Calendar* (Frankfurt, 1559), fos. 26ʳ, 31ᵛ–2ʳ and 36ʳ. Goltwurm cited 'Johannes Baleus' and 'Johannes Foxius' as his sources for these accounts (fos. 26ʳ and 36ʳ). However, it is very likely that Goltwurm derived these references, as well as these accounts, from Ludwig Rabus's martyrology, which was the major source for his calendar. On Rabus as a source for Goltwurm see Bernward Deneke, 'Kaspar Goltwurm: Ein lutherischer Kompilator zwischen Überlieferung und Glaube', in *Volkserzählung und Reformation*, ed. Wolfgang Brückner (Berlin, 1974), p. 145.

[126] Deneke, 'Kaspar Goltwurm', pp. 174–7 and Kolb, *For All the Saints*, p. 30.

Protestants.) One of the most significant aspects of Foxe's first Latin martyrology was that it focused on Protestant proto-martyrs of the Middle Ages, rather than contemporary evangelical or Protestant sufferers for the Gospel. In time, Foxe's later martyrologies would contain extensive material on the medieval Church, and would far surpass other Protestant martyrologies in the attention they paid to the history of the Church before Luther.[127] Another distinctive feature of the *Commentarii*, which would become the hallmark of the *Acts and Monuments*, was its reliance on chronicle sources. Other martyrologists, such as Crespin or Haemstede, relied heavily on documents, but these were mostly letters. Foxe's work, especially for the medieval period, would rest on the foundations laid by English chroniclers such as Matthew Paris, Thomas Walsingham and Gervase of Canterbury.

These features of the *Commentarii* show the influence of Bale upon Foxe. A particularly striking indication of this, however, is Foxe's inclusion of a brief section listing prophecies made in the Middle Ages declaring that the Antichrist was already present within the Church.[128] Not only does this listing of medieval prophecies and prophets reflect a number of Bale's preoccupations, but there is considerable evidence that Foxe drew these examples from Bale.[129] These few pages are the earliest indications of Foxe's interest in the Apocalypse, a subject in which Bale would prove to be his

---

[127] It is worth remembering that Foxe declared at the conclusion of the *Commentarii* that he intended to write another volume, carrying the history of the martyrs down to the time of Martin Luther (*Comm.*, fo. 205^r). Moreover, while many scholars repeat the common error of stating that the *Commentarii* only covers Lollard martyrs (e.g., Andrew Pettegree describes it as 'a short Latin work devoted entirely to the English Lollards' ('Haemstede and Foxe', pp. 281–2), and Katherine Firth describes it as 'more an essay on the life and doctrine of Wiclif in relation to the Reformation than the beginnings of an extensive history of martyrdom' (Firth, *Apocalyptic Tradition*, p. 77), it should also be remembered that the work deals with numerous continental figures, notably Thomas of Rennes and Savonarola as well.

[128] *Comm.*, fos. 55^r–7^v. *Pace* Katherine Firth, who declares that the *Commentarii* 'contained very few references to the Apocalyptic tradition' (Firth, *Apocalyptic Tradition*, p. 77).

[129] *Pace* Katherine Firth again who also maintains that 'Foxe's use of the Apocalypse in 1554 followed more nearly the example of Erasmus and Calvin than that of Bale' (Firth, *Apocalyptic Tradition*, p. 77). For some of the strongest examples for Bale's provenance for this material – notably prophecies by Joachim of Fiore, Peter John Olivi and Gerard of Nazareth – see notes 49 and 50 above. Foxe himself states that his material on Savonarola came from Bale (*Comm.*, fo. 177^{r-v}). Foxe does not give a source for Arnold of Villanova's prophecy – that the Antichrist would persecute the godly after 1300 – but Bale not only gives the story in more detail in his *Catalogus* (pp. 358–9), he also cites Bernard de Gui as the source for the story. A number of these prophecies – those attributed to Jean de Roquetaillade, Manfred of Vercelli and an unnamed priest of Florence – are related by Bale as well as by Foxe. (Cf. Bale, *Catalogus*, pp. 161, 169, 428, and 536 with Foxe, *Comm.*, fos. 55^v–6^v.) Both Bale and Foxe list fairly well-known authors (Sabellicus Antonius of Florence and Jean de Froissart) as the sources for these stories. It is suggestive, but hardly conclusive, that Bale's citation of Antonius is more precise than Foxe's.

mentor, and which would be the pole star for much of Foxe's later life and research. Above all, Bale has to be given credit for supporting, encouraging and possibly inspiring Foxe's research into martyrology. Admittedly, much of Foxe's work on the *Commentarii* was carried out independently of Bale and it would be Foxe who made the key editorial decisions on the volume. But nevertheless it is possible to say that, without Bale, Foxe might not have written a martyrology at all. It is certainly true that without Bale it would have been a very different martyrology.

The *Commentarii* may have earned Foxe a measure of fame and it certainly influenced other Protestant martyrologists. Nevertheless, he garnered neither money nor patronage from the book. Foxe was clearly in need; in fact he sent a letter to Duke Christoph of Württemberg, to whom the *Commentarii* had been dedicated, inquiring why he had not received any response from the duke about the work. With seeming naivety, Foxe wondered if perhaps the duke's servants were negligent and the book had not come into his hands.[130] Presumably Foxe received no response to this missive; in any case, by the autumn he had left Strasbourg and journeyed to join the English congregation at Frankfurt. There Foxe and his family lived in the same house as Anthony Gilby, later the puritan sage of Ashby-de-la-Zouche. Gilby would be Foxe's ally in a dispute over the liturgy, which tore the exiled English congregation at Frankfurt apart.[131] In this dispute Foxe was a prominent supporter of John Knox, who wanted an English translation of the Geneva liturgy to be used by the congregation. In late March 1555, Richard Cox, the leader of an opposing faction which championed the use of the 1552 Book of Common Prayer, had persuaded the Frankfurt authorities to expel Knox from the city.[132]

On 27 August 1555, Whittingham, Foxe and nearly twenty other former members of Knox's faction wrote a formal letter to the English congregation declaring their intention of departing, but asking, in a final attempt at compromise, that four arbiters, two from each side, be appointed to resolve the dispute. This request for arbitration was denied, and early in September Foxe departed for Basle, arriving in the Swiss city some time before

---

[130]   BL, Harley MS 417, fo. 122ᵛ.
[131]   On the controversy at Frankfurt see the anonymous Elizabethan narrative, *A brief discourse of the troubles at Frankfort, 1554 – 1558 A.D. ...*, ed. E. Arber (London, 1908). For the authorship and background of this work see Patrick Collinson, 'The authorship of *A Brieff Discours off the Troubles begonne at Franckford*', in *Godly People: Essays in English Protestantism and Puritanism* (London, 1983), pp. 191–212.
[132]   See Arber, *A brief discourse*, pp. 42–55.

22 September.[133] Most of Knox's followers who left Frankfurt went to Geneva; Foxe almost certainly went to Basle because Bale was already there, working for the great Swiss printer Johann Oporinus. A little earlier, Foxe had sent Oporinus a copy of the *Commentarii* and sought his patronage.[134] Quite possibly, Foxe had received some encouragement from Oporinus, and this may also have helped him decide to seek his fortune in Basle.

IX

Foxe's career and writings would be greatly shaped by his working relationships with two printers: Johann Oporinus and John Day. His relationship with Oporinus was just beginning in the autumn of 1555; meanwhile back in England the other printer, John Day, had been establishing contacts and undergoing experiences that would prepare him for his future collaboration with Foxe. While the details of Foxe's early life are relatively well known, almost nothing is known about the early life of John Day. It is commonly assumed that he was born around 1522.[135] Nothing is known of his parentage, place of birth, or indeed his childhood years.[136]

Early in 1546 Day married; by that time he had apparently already been in London for some time. He had certainly married reasonably well within the city. His wife, Alice, was the eldest child of Simon Richardson, a Merchant Taylor of the city. Her dowry of £26 13s 4d was comfortable, although not wealthy, and all the more impressive because she was one of twenty-one surviving children.[137] The likelihood then is that Day himself came from a reasonably prosperous background; the certainty is that by the end of Henry VIII's reign Day had established a foothold for himself in London. By the time of his marriage Day was already a bookseller; by the end of the year it is likely that he had begun printing works himself.[138]

Whatever printing activity Day may have been involved in prior to 1547 is surrounded by mists of obscurity; while he was actively printing by 1547, many of the works attributed to him by the Short Title Catalogue remain

---

[133] Mozley, *John Foxe and his Book*, pp. 49–50. On 22 September Foxe's daughter, Christiana, was baptised in Basle.

[134] BL, Harley 417, fo. 98[r–v].

[135] The date is based on a woodcut profile of Day, which the printer commissioned himself, dated 1562, which gives his age as forty.

[136] The traditional and often repeated belief that Day was born and raised in Dunwich, Suffolk, rests on nothing stronger than the fact that he later owned a house in the town. For a discussion of Day's origins and background see *PPP*, pp. 3–4.

[137] TNA, PROB 11/30, fos. 19[r]–20[r].   [138] See *PPP*, p. 5.

disputable.[139] Thanks to the colophon to Herman von Wied's *A Simple and Religious Consultation*, we not only know that Day was the printer of this work, we also know that he had established his printing house at the Sign of the Resurrection near Holborn Conduit by 30 October 1547.[140] Very shortly afterwards he went into partnership with William Seres, another printer in the Holborn area. (It should be noted that partnership in this period was not the formal contractual agreement that it is today. It merely meant that two printers both held the patent for a particular work. It was quite possible for one printer to be working in partnership with a number of other printers.) Both Seres and Day were just starting out as printers and it made sense for them to take advantage of their geographical proximity and to combine limited resources to maximise the speed with which individual works could be produced. Ideological proximity as well as geographical proximity very probably played a key role in cementing the partnership; together Day and Seres would produce a series of attacks on Catholic beliefs and practices. In fact half of the Day/Seres works printed during 1548 denounced Eucharistic doctrine.[141] The most notable of these jointly printed works was Luke Shepherd's *John Bon and Mast Person*, a vitriolic attack on transubstantiation, which caused great offence. Edward Underhill, an evangelical who was one of the Yeomen of the Guard, claimed that it was only his intercession that prevented Day's arrest by the Lord Mayor.[142] The following year Day and Seres turned their attentions to the most godly book of all, the Bible, collaborating on a de luxe edition of Edmund Becke's edition of Scripture.[143]

Day was clearly prospering during this period, as he opened a new bookshop at the Sign of the Resurrection in St Sepulchre's parish. (The phrase 'at the new shop' occurs in many imprints in Day's books from early 1549 onwards.) At around the same time Day moved from Holborn to Aldersgate, in the parish of St Anne and St Agnes. He established both his

[139] John N. King, 'John Day: Master Printer of the English Reformation', in *The Beginnings of English Protestantism*, ed. Peter Marshall and Alec Ryrie (Cambridge, 2002), p. 183.

[140] Herman von Wied, *A Simple and Religious Consultation by what means a Christian Reformation may Be Begun* (London, 1547), STC 13213.

[141] See Catherine Davies, *A Religion of the Word* (Manchester, 2002), pp. 19–21, 30–2, and *PPP*, pp. 9–12.

[142] J. G. Nichols (ed.), *Narrative of the Days of the Reformation*, Camden Society, original series, 77 (1859), p. 172. It is interesting that, by this account, the Lord Mayor seems to have felt that Day was primarily responsible for the book. This could be because Underhill sent his examinations in to Foxe when Day was printing the *Acts and Monuments*; in other words, he could be subtly flattering Day by ascribing the printing of Shepherd's work only to him. On the other hand, it is possible that Day was primarily responsible for the production of this work and that contemporaries were aware of this.

[143] *The Byble*, ed. Edmund Becke (London, 1549), STC 2077. The colophon is dated 17 August 1549.

household and what would remain the centre of his printing business there in buildings on the wall attached to the gate into the city. There were obvious commercial advantages to having a business on one of the major thoroughfares into the city. However, there may have been another reason behind the move. Aldersgate was one of the London parishes popular with the expanding communities of foreign refugees. Many religious refugees, particularly Protestants from France and the Low Counties, had skills and experience in the book trade and were valuable supplies of workmen for printers such as Day. In 1549 four 'Dutchmen' are listed in the lay assessments as living with Day in his new residence in Aldersgate.[144]

Day's employment of foreign workers, as well as his sincere commitment to the evangelical cause, led to his forming strong associations with the Stranger Churches in London.[145] These connections in turn may have helped him forge other links with leading Edwardian Protestants. John King has described Day as a client of the duchess of Suffolk.[146] The evidence is not clear-cut. It is true that an illustration of the duchess's coat of arms appeared in several works that Day printed at the time.[147] But it is not clear whether these illustrations advertise the duchess's support for the works or are merely bids placed by the printer on his own initiative in a quest for her patronage. *If*, however, Day received support from the duchess, then it is most likely that the connections were formed through the Stranger Churches, which they both actively supported.

From about 1550 Day had the resources, the confidence and possibly the connections to begin printing works on his own. A striking indication of his expertise and technical resources was that Day was able, in 1551, to reprint Becke's edition of the Bible by himself, without having to rely on the cooperation of Seres.[148] Becke's Bible must have cost Day a great deal of money, which suggests that he had considerable capital at his disposal, either from his own pocket or because he had obtained substantial backing from one or a number of patrons. In any case, for a young man still in his late twenties, Day had made remarkable progress in the competitive world of English printing. At the same time as Day's business was expanding, so

---

[144] R. E. G. and E. F. Kirk, *Returns of Aliens*, 1, p. 173.
[145] See Evenden, 'The Fleeing Dutchmen', pp. 65–6. [146] King, 'John Day', p. 186.
[147] William Tyndale, *An exposicion vppon the v.vi.vii. chapters of Mathew* (London, 1548), STC 24441a; Pierre Viret, *A verie familiare [and] fruiteful exposition of the .xii. articles of the christian faieth conteined in the commune crede, called the Apostles Crede* ... (London, 1548), STC 24784; Hugh Latimer, *A notable sermon of ye reuerende father Maister Hughe Latemer* ... (London, 1548), STC 15291; Thomas Some's edition of Latimer's sermons, STC 15270.5 *et seq.*
[148] STC 2087.

was his household. His first son, Richard, was born 21 December 1552, while a second son, Edward, was born the following year.[149]

One sign of Day's increasing prominence in the London book trade was that, in September 1552, the duke of Northumberland attempted to confer the patent for the works of Thomas Becon and John Ponet (including Ponet's popular *Catechism*) on Day. Admittedly, this was largely a move to strip Reyner Wolfe, Cranmer's chosen printer, of this patent, and this has to be seen in the larger context of deteriorating relations between the leading secular and clerical authorities in the second half of Edward VI's reign.[150] Nevertheless, the choice of Day to replace Wolfe is an indication of confidence in both his technical abilities and his godliness.[151] In the event, Cranmer resisted, trying to retain the patents for Wolfe, and the result was a rather awkward compromise. On 25 March 1553 Day received the rights to Ponet's *Catechism in English* and all the works of Becon and all the other work of Ponet in perpetuity. Wolfe received the patent to the less lucrative but more prestigious edition of Ponet's catechism in Latin.[152]

x

Unfortunately, Day did not have long to enjoy his triumph. Mary came to the throne that summer and Day's patents were revoked. Later, in 1560, looking back on this period, Day would describe how he was compelled to 'surcease from printing ... godly men's works'.[153] However, one thing remained to Day from the wreckage of his Edwardian career: his ties to William Cecil. Almost certainly the most important link in this chain was Day's earlier relationship with William Seres. Seres was more than a client of Cecil's; he is described several times as one of Cecil's servants.[154] Cecil apparently had great trust in Seres; when Edward VI began scheming to

[149] See the article on Richard Day in the *ODNB*. The year of Edward Day's birth is calculated from his age as given in a deposition in 1584 (TNA, C 24/180).

[150] On the struggle for power between Northumberland and Cranmer see Diarmid MacCulloch, *Thomas Cranmer: A Life* (New Haven, CT: 1998), pp. 520–38; MacCulloch's discussion of the argument over the Ponet and Becon patents is on p. 524.

[151] It is worth observing that this was more than a commercial opportunity for Day; later he would go to considerable expense to produce de luxe editions of Becon's works. See below, p. 113.

[152] TNA, 7 Ed. VI, part 3, m. 23.

[153] Roger Hutchinson, *A faithful declaration of Christes holy supper comprehended in thre sermo[n]s, preached at Eaton Colledge* (London, 1560), STC 14018, sigs. A3ᵛ–A4ʳ.

[154] Peter W. M. Blayney, 'William Cecil and the Stationers', in *The Stationers' Company and the Book Trade 1550–1990*, ed. Robin Myers and Michael Harris (Winchester and New Castle, DE, 1997), pp. 11–34, esp. pp. 26–7. Seres collected rent for Cecil and also made payments on Cecil's behalf. He also made many purchases for Cecil's household (ibid., p. 26).

place Jane Grey on the throne, the far-sighted Cecil realised that this might backfire and he made contingency plans to leave London in haste. These plans included shifting his papers, plate and money 'to one Nelsons howse in London and Seres howse yo[u]r servant'.[155] One indication of how association with Seres helped Day to forge links to William Cecil is their joint printing of sermons by Bernardino Ochino in 1551, which were translated by Anne Cooke, William Cecil's sister-in-law.[156]

Day's connection to Cecil was made manifest when, almost immediately after Mary's accession to the throne, he went up to Lincolnshire and rented land there belonging to William Cecil. Day was not retiring to the quiet life. Soon after his arrival in the village of Barholm, he printed an edition of Stephen Gardiner's *De vera obedientia*, a work that obtained new-found popularity in Mary's reign as Protestants were anxious to remind everyone that Mary's Lord Chancellor had acquiesced in the Henrician Reformation. This was the first of a series of clandestinely printed books under the pseudonym of 'Michael Wood'. These works were printed between the autumn of 1553 and the summer of 1554. They were a mixture of Protestant polemic and virulent attacks on the Church of Rome and on Stephen Gardiner in particular.[157] Foxe later declared that William Cooke, Cecil's brother-in-law, was imprisoned 'for that he suffered this oure printer [John Day] to print the boke of Wint. De vera Obed.'[158] No record of Cooke's imprisonment survives, but his involvement in Day's clandestine printing, combined with the fact that Day was living and working on Cecil's land, establishes beyond reasonable doubt that Day was sponsored and supported in this enterprise by Cecil himself.

Day's career in clandestine printing came to an abrupt end in the autumn of 1554. The contemporary diarist, Henry Machyn, wrote that, as he came out of Norfolk on 16 October 1554, he saw 'John Day the printer and hys servand, and a prest and anodur printer [under arrest], for pryntyng of noythy bokes, [being taken] to the Towre'.[159] It would seem that Day was arrested trying to collect a supply of paper from one of the Norfolk ports, most probably King's Lynn, the largest and most accessible port close to

---

[155] BL, Cotton MS, Titus B. ii, fo. 376ʳ, quoted in Blayney, 'Cecil and the Stationers', p. 27.

[156] *Fouretene sermons of Barnardine Ochyne* (London, 1551), STC 18767.

[157] Elizabeth Evenden, 'The Michael Wood Mystery: William Cecil and the Lincolnshire Printing of John Day', *Sixteenth Century Journal*, 35 (2004), pp. 383–94.

[158] *1563*, p. 1681.

[159] *The Diary of Henry Machyn, Citizen and Merchant-Taylor of London, from A.D. 1550 to A.D. 1563*, Camden Society, original series, 42 (London, 1848), p. 72. Unfortunately we have no idea who the other printer was. It was probably not Seres because he was too close to Cecil; the involvement of a member of Cecil's own household in this illegal venture would have been simply too dangerous.

him. (This explanation is conjectural but the need to replenish his paper supply is the most likely explanation for Day's journey down to Norfolk.) Day's arrest brought an end both to the Michael Wood press and to the first stages of Day's career.

As Day approached the battlements of the Tower and as, a year later, Foxe approached the spires of Basle, both men had reason to feel despondent. The fruits of early success had turned to ashes and the achievements of the first decades of their lives had been swept away on the receding tide of English evangelicalism. Both men and their families faced an uncertain future. But although neither Foxe nor Day could have realised it, it would be in this period that they laid the foundations for the success of their later great collaborative enterprise.

CHAPTER 3

Adversity and opportunity: Foxe and Day during Mary's reign

I

By 1556 John Day had been released from prison and had started to pick up the pieces of his career as a printer. He began work as an assign of John Wayland; in fact this may well have been a condition of his release.[1] If so, this form of Tudor community service indicates both the importance the Marian regime attached to printing and rather more imagination than they are usually given credit for in ensuring that skilled personnel were employed in producing officially sponsored texts. For, as Eamon Duffy has shown, the Wayland primers were a key element of the Marian regime's religious strategy.[2] Although the primers continued to come out under Wayland's name it was probably Day and Seres who took charge of their production from 1556 onwards. Both Wayland's health and his finances were poor, and the combined toll this took on him meant that he could not properly fulfil his responsibilities. (In fact, even Wayland's status as a favoured printer of the regime was not enough to keep him from being sent to prison for debt in the spring of 1558.[3]) Even before this, there are indications that Wayland was not involved in the actual printing of the primers. While both Day and Seres are listed in the Stationers' Charter of May 1557, significantly Wayland is not.[4] Moreover, the presence of Day and Seres in the charter is also an indication of their success in re-entering their profession following their disgrace and imprisonment.

Day was also City Printer from around 1556 until the end of Mary's reign. Like his co-production of the Wayland primers, this work was routine in

---

[1] William Seres, who had also been imprisoned under Mary, was another assign of John Wayland (see Seres in *ODNB*).

[2] Eamon Duffy, *The Stripping of the Altars: Traditional Religion in England, 1400–1580* (New Haven, CT, 1992), pp. 526–7 and 537–43.

[3] See Wayland in *ODNB*.

[4] Arber, *Transcripts*, I, pp. xxviii–xxii. The fact that Wayland was a member of the Scriveners' Company does not in itself account for his absence from this charter, since members of other companies were listed.

nature and neither stretched nor showcased his abilities. Most of Day's work during Mary's reign was of this character, although an exception occurred with his printing of an edition of Leonard Digges' *A Boke called Tectonicon*, a technical manual for surveyors, carpenters and masons.[5] This book was conspicuous for the quality of its technical illustrations and there is evidence that Day employed skilled foreign workmen to create these pictures.[6] If this is indeed the case, then this is another indication of the ways in which Day was quietly forging links that would be essential to his later success. Significantly, it was another printer, Thomas Gemini, who held the patent for this work (which was designed to advertise tools made by Gemini), and he commissioned Day to print this technically demanding book. This is indicative of a professional paradox Day found himself in during Mary's reign. Contemporaries recognised his skills, yet he remained in a subordinate position, dependent upon assignments from others.

All told, the last three years of Mary's reign must have been frustrating ones for John Day. He was obligated to produce texts such as the Wayland primers, which must have been deeply uncongenial. From being a printer of works subverting the Marian restoration he had gone to producing works that buttressed it. Worse yet, these works – and all of the texts that he printed during these years – were not being printed under his own name but purely as an assign to others. However, the period was not completely devoid of accomplishments for John Day. Most fundamentally, he could congratulate himself not so much on what he did during tumultuous times, but on having survived them. Day had also continued to impress others with his professional skills, and in the following reign he could bask in the glory of having suffered for the cause of the Gospel. Consequently, when Mary died in November 1558, Day was in a solid, if not commanding, position. Moreover, he had already entered into the mainstream of the book trade in London and, unlike those printers who had gone into exile or ceased trading, he was already active and in the capital when Elizabeth came to the throne.

Day spent the year following Mary's death expanding his business and he seized a few opportunities to more fully demonstrate the quality of work he was capable of. One of these came with Day's printing of Conrad Gesner's *The treasure of Euonymus*.[7] This medical treatise, by one of the

[5] Leonard Digges, *A Boke Named Tectonicon* (London, 1556), STC 6849.5.
[6] See C. L. Oastler, *John Day the Elizabethan Printer* (Oxford, 1975), p. 12.
[7] Conrad Gesner, *The treasure of Euonymus conteyninge the vvonderfull hid secretes of nature ... Translated (with great diligence, et laboure) out of Latin, by Peter Morvvying felow of Magdaline Colleadge in Oxford* (London, 1559), STC 11800.

most celebrated physicians in Europe, was a shrewdly chosen project during a time of widespread pestilence. It contained technically accomplished illustrations and was an admirably printed text. Another work that Day printed, which was even more celebrated for its illustrations, was William Cunningham's *Cosmographical glasse.*[8] By the autumn of 1559 Day was one of the rising printers in London. He was also blessed with impressive evangelical credentials to match his professional ones and, perhaps most important of all, he had ties, going back to the reign of Edward VI, with some of the leading Protestant clerics and statesmen of Elizabeth's reign. It was a combination of these factors that would lead to Day's being given the printing job that would change his life.

I I

Just as the last three years of Mary's reign were a period of trial and frustration, leavened with occasional opportunities for Day, the same could be said of Foxe's years in Basle. For one thing, Foxe had to endure financial hardship. How great this hardship was has been a matter of some dispute. On the one hand, J. F. Mozley describes Foxe as 'wretchedly poor' and claims that he suffered from illnesses 'caused by lack of good food'.[9] John King, on the other hand, is sceptical of such claims and maintains that Foxe was not 'driven to the drudgery of proofreading' by financial necessity, and further claims that Foxe and his family were 'long-term residents' at the house of Oporinus.[10] The truth lies somewhere in between. First of all, there is no evidence that Foxe, much less his family, were residents in Oporinus's household. From at least 1557 onwards, Foxe lived along with other English exiles, including John Bale and Laurence Humphrey, in the Klarakloster, an abandoned convent of the Poor Clares, which the city of Basle made available to the English exiles.[11] (We have no way of knowing whether or not Foxe and his family lived there before 1557, or indeed where they resided at all during this period.)

It is certainly an exaggeration to assume that Foxe and his family lacked food. On the other hand, it is not farfetched to assume that he undertook

---

[8] William Cunningham, *The cosmographical glasse conteinyng the pleasant principles of cosmographie, geographie, hydrographie, or nauigation* (London, 1559), STC 6119. See below, pp. 112–13.

[9] Mozley, *John Foxe and his Book*, p. 51.

[10] King, *Early Modern Print Culture*, pp. 76–7. It is true that Foxe wrote to Oporinus requesting his patronage (BL, Harley MS 417, fo. 98ʳ). However, while Foxe received employment from Oporinus, there is absolutely no indication that he was subsidised by him. It seems inconceivable that Foxe would have taken up the arduous post of corrector unless he was compelled to.

[11] Mozley, *John Foxe and his Book*, p. 51.

the tedious job of correcting because he needed to support himself and his family. While we do not know how much Foxe was paid for this labour, such jobs were generally not overly renumerative. Foxe would also supplement his salary as a proofreader with income derived from editing and translating texts for Oporinus and his fellow printer Johann Froben.[12] Even so, Foxe's letters from this period contain numerous pleas for money or grateful acknowledgements of having received small amounts of funding.[13] Foxe also appealed to his former pupil, now the duke of Norfolk, requesting an allowance. (Characteristically, in the same letter Foxe also exhorted the duke to stand firmly with the true religion and admonished him not to neglect his study of Scripture.)[14] For whatever reason, Foxe's appeal to the duke seems to have been, at this stage, unsuccessful, but he did acquire money from other supporters. In 1556, Foxe dedicated his drama, *Christus Triumphans*, to John Binks, John Escott and John Kelke, three London haberdashers, also in exile, who had supplied him, as well as other English Protestant exiles, with funds.[15]

King also maintains that Oporinus 'underwrote Foxe's ongoing research into ecclesiastical history and martyrology'.[16] If by this King means that Oporinus's *employment* of Foxe made it possible for Foxe to conduct his researches, then he is correct. However, if by this King means that Oporinus paid Foxe to undertake research, then he is mistaken. In fact, Foxe would complain to Grindal, in the autumn of 1557, that his work on the martyrology had been interrupted by the need to edit a work for Froben because 'I was then in total poverty and was reduced to my last coin.'[17] Foxe further lamented that 'two months were wasted by me in that drudgery'.[18] There were, admittedly, considerable advantages to Foxe's working with Oporinus, which will be discussed below, and occasionally Foxe received certain small benefits from the Swiss (e.g., he was allowed to matriculate at the University of Basle without fee), which were welcome to him.[19] Nevertheless, one must not overestimate Foxe's prosperity during his exile

---

[12] Ibid., pp. 50–1.   [13] E.g., BL, Harley MS 417, fos. 103ᵛ–4ʳ, 112ʳ and 113ᵛ.   [14] Ibid., fo. 115ᵛ.

[15] *Two Latin Comedies by John Foxe the Martyrologist*, ed. and trans. John Hazel Smith (Ithaca, New York and London, 1973), p. 203, n. 1, and Christina H. Garrett, *The Marian Exiles: A Study in the Origins of English Puritanism* (Cambridge, 1938), pp. 90, 151 and 202. Both of these studies should now be updated in the light of the more recent and more accurate research of Brett Usher, 'Backing Protestantism: The London Godly, the Exchequer and the Foxe Circle', in *John Foxe: An Historical Perspective*, ed. David Loades (Aldershot, 1999), pp. 131–2.

[16] King, *Early Modern Print Culture*, p. 78.

[17] 'eramque tum omnibus plane exutus pecuniis, adeoque pene ad extremum assem redactus' (BL, Harley MS 417, fo. 113ᵛ).

[18] 'in ea movenda farina perierunt mihi duo menses' (ibid.).   [19] Mozley, *John Foxe and his Book*, p. 52.

or underestimate the burdens his lack of financial security placed on him. Foxe may also have been troubled by his physical as well as his fiscal health. In a letter written to Thomas Lever in the winter of 1557–8, Foxe complained of ill health and the lack of a patron.[20]

This illness may have been aggravated, if not caused, by the overwork brought on by the need to earn a living, and other commitments. The most important and most onerous of these was a translation into Latin of Thomas Cranmer's attack on Stephen Gardiner, *An answer . . . unto a crafty cavillation*.[21] This task had been pressed upon Foxe by no less a figure than Peter Martyr and, while it was a considerable honour, it was in many ways the sort of honour one would be happier without. By the summer of 1555, Foxe was already complaining to Martyr of the difficulties involved in the task.[22] Apart from the challenges of the translation itself, Foxe was also faced with the difficulties of having it printed. By the autumn of 1557 Foxe had a draft ready, although he would still spend some time soliciting advice from friends and polishing the work.[23] Moreover, Cranmer's controversial Eucharistic theology made it nearly impossible to find a printer for it in either Germany or Switzerland.[24] Even though Christopher Froschauer, the eminent Zurich printer, finally agreed to print Foxe's translation in 1558, the work was never produced, and as late as September 1559 Foxe was, a little forlornly, writing to Bullinger to see if it might ever be printed.[25]

III

Nevertheless, despite these difficulties, Foxe pressed ahead with his martyrological labours. Moreover, the circumstances of his exile, while undoubtedly irksome, also had beneficial aspects for these endeavours. Among the greatest of these benefits were Foxe's contacts with a series of different, yet overlapping, Protestant intellectual circles on the continent. One of these was the network created by John Bale with various Protestant scholars,

---

[20] BL, Harley MS 417, fos. 103[v]–4[r].
[21] Thomas Cranmer, *An answer of . . . Thomas archebyshop of Canterburye unto a crafty cavillation by S. Gardiner* (London, 1551), STC 5991.
[22] BL, Harley MS 417, fo. 115[r–v].   [23] Ibid., fos. 119[r], 113[v] and 114[v].
[24] On the difficulties of finding a printer, see ibid., fo. 113[r].
[25] Ibid., fos. 113[v] and 114[v]–15[r] and Hastings Robinson (ed.), *The Zurich Letters*, 2 vols. (Cambridge, 1842–45), I, pp. 42–3. Mozley argues that the letter must be misdated and that the correct year must be 1557, since that was when the previous discussions on printing Foxe's translation of Cranmer had taken place. However, there is no reason to suppose that the matter might not have come up again two years later (Mozley, *John Foxe and his Book*, p. 61). Foxe's translation of Cranmer's manuscript remains among his papers as BL, Harley MS 418.

most particularly Matthias Flacius (known as Illyricus) and the Magdeburg Centuriators (i.e., the editors of the great Lutheran *Historia Ecclesiastica* known – because of its division into centuries – as the 'Magdeburg Centuries'). Bale's ties to Flacius, forged through their mutual friends, Caspar von Nidbruck and Alexander Alesius, went back to at least the early 1550s.

Flacius had announced in a letter of November 1552 that he was planning to write a catalogue of those who opposed the papacy before Luther and, interestingly, he claimed that this work would soon be ready for printing.[26] One reason why it might have been delayed was that Flacius learned about Bale's work and realised that there was a great deal of newly printed material yet to be incorporated into his catalogue. In a letter dated 28 November 1553 Flacius wrote to Nidbruck that he had read Bale's *Illustrium maioris Britanniae Scriptorum ... Summarium* and that he had found descriptions of many authors there of whom he was unaware. Flacius told Nidbruck that he had already written to Bale asking for his help.[27] Flacius probably also used Bale's close friend Alesius as a go-between; certainly, some time in 1553 Alesius wrote to Bale describing the praise he had heard of Bale's *Summarium* from Melanchthon, Bugenhagen, Joachim Camerarius and others. In particular, Alesius claimed that Flacius had marvelled at Bale's erudition and zeal in attacking superstition. He also added, somewhat inaccurately, that Flacius was planning a history of the Church, and he urged Bale to assist him. In particular, Alesius inquired about evidence of true religion in England before Gregory the Great and for references to any contemporary writings opposing the missions of Saints Augustine and Boniface.[28] Whether or not all of these letters actually reached Bale during the middle of his Irish adventures, and whether Bale found time to respond to them, is problematic, but they certainly indicate the considerable interest Flacius had taken in Bale's work.[29]

In April 1554 Nidbruck wrote to Flacius that he had found Bale in Wesel and had secured his cooperation.[30] The two authors must have made contact shortly afterwards, as Flacius wrote to Bale in a letter dated July

---

[26] Victor Bibl, 'Der Briefweschsel zwischen Flacius and Nidbruck', *Jahrbuch der Gesellschaft für die Geschichte des Protestantismus in Österreich*, 18 (1896), pp. 6–8. Flacius described the upcoming catalogue more fully in a letter to Hartmann Beyer, the Superintendent of Frankfurt, dated 7 March 1553. See Ronald E. Diener, 'The Magdeburg Centuries: A Bibliothecal and Historiographical Analysis' (ThD dissertation, Harvard University, 1979), pp. 58–9.

[27] See Bibl, 'Briefweschsel', p. 16.   [28] BL, Cotton MS Titus D.X, fo. 180ʳ.

[29] Bale certainly received a letter from Alesius, passing on the commendations from various reformers, since Bale modestly mentions it in his autobiographical *Vocacyon*. John Bale, *The vocacyon of John Bale*, ed. Peter Happé and John N. King (Binghamton, NY, 1990), p. 75.

[30] Bibl, 'Briefwechsel', pp. 205–7. Bale's presence in Wesel in 1554 has gone unnoticed among English-language scholars; very probably, Bale was there overseeing the printing of his *Vocacyon*, which was produced in Wesel that very year.

1554; in it Flacius promised Bale that he would see that the *Summarium* as well as Bale's epitome of John Leland's *De viris illustribus* were printed at Wittenberg or Leipzig if Bale would send them to him.[31] Bale later claimed to Matthew Parker that Flacius's *Catalogus testium veritatis* and the *Varia doctorum piorumque virorum*, which were printed in 1556 and 1557, were 'set fourth by me and Illyricus'.[32] Bale's claim is often dismissed as mere boasting but it needs to be taken more seriously.[33]

Bale and Foxe were both working for Oporinus when the *Catalogus testium veritatis* was printed and it is virtually certain that both corrected Flacius's text. Moreover, the possibility exists that Bale and Foxe went to Basle specifically in order to work on Flacius's book. On 23 May 1554 Nidbruck wrote to Bale, advising him on printing a new and expanded edition of the *Summarium*. In his letter he suggested to Bale that Johann Oporinus would be an ideal printer.[34] Then, in a letter to Flacius of 23 August 1554, Nidbruck similarly recommended that Flacius's projected catalogue be printed in Basle by Oporinus.[35] It raises the possibility that Nidbruck wished to have Bale working for Oporinus in order to oversee Flacius's text. In any case, it is probable that Foxe went to work for Oporinus because Bale was either working there or about to work there.

Bale's influence on the *Varia* is far more pronounced. Included in the *Varia* is a Latin poem, the *Apocalypses goliae*, which was printed by Bale – who discovered the manuscript – in 1546.[36] The *Rhithmi* was incorporated, with acknowledgement, into Flacius's *Varia*.[37] More interestingly, Flacius claimed that Walter Map was the author of the poem and cited Bale as his source for this.[38] Flacius had also printed an excerpt from the *Rhithmi* and attributed it to Walter Map in his *Catalogus testium veritatis*, which was printed a year before either the *Varia* or Bale's *Catalogus*.[39] However, in the *Summarium*, Bale had attributed the poem to either John of Salisbury or

[31] BL, Cotton MS Titus D.X, fos. 180^v–1^r.   [32] CUL, Add. MS 748, fo. 2^v.
[33] See, for example, Norman L. Jones, 'Matthew Parker, John Bale and the Magdeburg Centuriators', *Sixteenth Century Journal*, 12 (1981), p. 36.
[34] Martina Hartmann, *Humanismus und Kirchenkritik: Matthias Flacius Illyricus als Erforscher des Mittelalters* (Stuttgart, 2001), p. 69, n. 117. The choice of Oporinus as a printer may not have come entirely out of the blue; Nidbruck had already solicited his aid in finding documents, and Oporinus and Flacius had been corresponding since at least 1539. Martin Steinmann, *Johannes Oporinus*, p. 69, n. 55. However, as of 1554, when Nidbruck recommended Oporinus to Bale, the Basle printer had not produced any of Flacius's works.
[35] Bibl, 'Briefwechsel', pp. 213–20. The first work by Flacius printed by Oporinus was his *Antilogia papae*, a collection of medieval anti-clerical writings, which appeared in 1555.
[36] John Bale, *Rhithmi vetustissimi de corrupto ecclesiae statu* (Antwerp, 1546), sigs. A4^r–B4^r.
[37] Matthias Flacius, *Varia doctorum piorumque virorum, de corrupto ecclesiae statu* (Basle, 1557), pp. 133–49.
[38] Ibid., pp. 130–2.   [39] Matthias Flacius, *Catalogus testium veritatis* (Strasbourg, 1556), pp. 703–4.

Robert Grosseteste.[40] Bale's first printed reference to Map as the author came in his *Catalogus*, which was printed a year after Flacius's *Catalogus*.[41] It thus becomes fairly clear that Bale was supplying Flacius with information closely related to the contents of the *Catalogus testium veritatis* and the *Varia* as they were being printed. This assistance was probably a large part of the reason why Bale claimed virtual co-authorship of these works with Flacius. However, it should be remembered that Bale, in his turn, borrowed heavily from Flacius's *Catalogus* for his work.[42]

It was unquestionably through Bale, and through Bale's ties with Flacius, as well as his employment by Oporinus, that Foxe became aware of Flacius's *Catalogus*. Yet this work had an especially profound impact upon Foxe's *Acts and Monuments*. One area of this influence, which has already been extensively discussed, most notably by the late Frances Yates, has been Foxe's drawing on Flacius for what Yates terms the 'imperial theme'.[43] Moreover, Flacius's *Catalogus* was also the direct source for much of the material on the history of the papacy in Foxe's martyrology.[44] But, perhaps most fundamentally, Flacius's *Catalogus* was Foxe's essential source for the opponents of the papacy and for those people and groups who had, during the Middle Ages, challenged or rejected the authority of the Catholic Church. To take merely one crucially important example, Foxe's account of the Waldensians – whom he and generations of English Protestant scholars, following his lead, considered to be at the headwaters of a great continuous medieval dissenting religious movement, extending from the twelfth century to the Reformation – was drawn almost entirely from Flacius's *Catalogus*.[45] In fact, although it is too large a topic to explore here, much

---

[40] Bale, *Summarium*, fos. 91ᵛ–2ʳ.   [41] Bale, *Catalogus*, pp. 253–5.

[42] Among the places where Bale specifically cites Flacius as a source see ibid., pp. 574, 579, 580–1 and 625.

[43] See Frances A. Yates, *Astraea: The Imperial Theme in the Sixteenth Century* (Harmondsworth, 1977), pp. 42–7. Yates's claims that Foxe's work was an unqualified celebration of the 'cult of Elizabeth', and her belief that Foxe's book extolled an English imperial identity are both in need of qualification. But she is certainly correct in pointing out that Foxe saw godly emperors, kings and princes as defenders of the true Church against the papacy and she acutely observed that Foxe drew on Flacius for his account of Dante and his extracts from *De Monarchia*. In fact she could have gone even further and observed that Foxe's accounts of other great theorists of imperial authority in the Middle Ages, such as Marsilius of Padua and William of Ockham, are also drawn directly from Flacius. Cf. Flacius, *Catalogus*, pp. 488–90 and 507 with *1570*, p. 485.

[44] Thomas S. Freeman, '"St Peter Did Not Do Thus": Papal History in the *Acts and Monuments*', available online at: www.hrionline.ac.uk/johnfoxe/apparatus/freemanStPeterpart1.html.

[45] Cf. Flacius, *Catalogus*, pp. 424–47 with *1563*, pp. 42–6. The one item that Foxe did not take directly from Flacius – a letter defending 'Waldensian' beliefs on the Eucharist – was taken from a work Flacius cited and used extensively, Ortwin Gratius's *Fasciculus*. Cf. Ortwin Gratius, *Fasciculus rerum expetendarum et fugiendarum* (Cologne, 1535), fos. 87ᵛ–8ʳ and 92ʳ–3ʳ with *1563*, pp. 43–4. For the importance of the Waldensians in Foxe's interpretation of Church history see Jane Facey, 'John Foxe and the Defence of the English Church', in *Protestantism and the National Church in Sixteenth*

of Foxe's distinctive ecclesiology and interpretation of Church history is derived from Flacius's great work.[46] For example, the comparison between the Catholic Church and the Apostolic Church, which opens the second edition of Foxe's work, is a direct translation of scattered passages from Flacius's *Catalogus*.[47]

One other work edited by Flacius was to be of considerable importance to Foxe in producing the *Acts and Monuments*: Flacius's monumental edition of the works of Jan Hus and Jerome of Prague.[48] Significantly, although this work was not printed by Oporinus, Foxe was aware of it at a very early stage. He includes material from it in his second Latin martyrology, although he would draw much more material from this source in the 1570 edition of the *Acts and Monuments*. Ultimately, almost all of Foxe's account of the two Bohemian martyrs was taken from Flacius's work.[49] At a minimum, Foxe's awareness of this scholarship is yet another indication of the intellectual association, initially fostered by Bale's ties to Flacius, which Foxe had formed with the great Lutheran scholar.

It was through both Bale and Flacius that Foxe also forged links with the Magdeburg Centuriators. Although, as Ron Diener has shown, Flacius did not actually edit the Magdeburg Centuries, he initiated the project and he recruited the actual editors of the work: Johann Wigand and Matthias Judex. By 1557 Flacius had become increasingly detached from

---

Century England, ed. Peter Lake and Maria Dowling (London, 1987), pp. 165–6. Euan Cameron surveys the importance of the Waldensians in overall Protestant historical thought and also discusses the inaccuracies and ambiguities in Protestant scholars' use of this label. Euan Cameron, 'Medieval Heretics as Protestant Martyrs', in *Martyrs and Martyrologies*, ed. Diana Wood, Studies in Church History xxx (Oxford, 1993), pp. 185–207.

[46] For a useful overview of Foxe's ecclesiology and his ideas of Church history, which, however, does not mention Flacius, much less analyse the intellectual relationship between the two scholars, see Facey, 'John Foxe and the Defence of the English Church', pp. 162–92.

[47] Cf. Flacius, *Catalogus*, pp. 306–8, 32–3, 292–3, 470–1, 201–4, 68–9, 261, 270–83, 477–8 with *1570*, pp. 4–13.

[48] *Johannis Hus et Hieronymi Pragensis confessorum Christi Historia et Monumenta*, 2 vols. (Nuremberg, 1558). Although this work was edited anonymously, correspondence between Flacius and Nidbruck demonstrates that Nidbruck oversaw the collection of the writings of the two heresiarchs and that printing them had become a major preoccupation of Flacius. Oliver K. Olson, *Matthias Flacius and the Survival of Luther's Reform* (Wiesbaden, 2002), pp. 266 and 329. It was Nidbruck who recommended to Flacius that the work be edited anonymously.

[49] Foxe draws on the *Johannis Hus . . . Monumenta* in *Rerum*, pp. 24–5 and 28–52 (cf. *Johannis Hus . . . Monumenta*, I, fos. 108v–9v, 111r–21r, 124r–8r, and II, fo. 367v). Foxe's personal copy of the *Johannis Hus . . . Monumenta* is now housed in Pembroke College Library, Cambridge (shelfmark 4.II.22–3). This volume was annotated by Foxe in preparation of his account of Hus in the 1563 edition. Among other things, it contains notations of the dates of events to help him in his narration of the story (see I, fos. 7r, 14v, 23r and 25v and II, fos. 349r, 350r, 351r, 352r and 356r). Since these volumes were printed in 1558, the most likely assumption is that Foxe acquired them on the continent and brought them back home with him.

the day-to-day administration of the project and by 1562, when relations between Flacius and Wigand had degenerated into outright hostility, Flacius had ceased to have any involvement with the project whatsoever.[50] Yet during the latter 1550s, Foxe's association with both Flacius and Oporinus had blossomed into some degree of collaboration between Foxe and the Centuriators.

As ever, Bale was an intermediary here; in the dedication of the second part of his dictionary of British authors, Bale warmly praised 'Matthias Flacius Illyrius, Johann Wigand, Matthias Judex, Basil Faber, and others under whose guidance a most blessed great work of Church history has been provided'.[51] Bale therefore, apparently, was not only on good terms with both Flacius and Wigand, but he was very much aware of the evolving Magdeburg Centuries. In fact, both Bale and Foxe were consulted in the initial stages of the project. On 2 March 1559 Wigand wrote to Bale, thanking him for his encouragement of their project, and asking him that he and 'Master Foxe, a most renowned man' ('D. Foxum, clarissimum virum') supply him with lists of people 'who in this our age are or were illustrious in the Church of God' ('que hac nostra aetate illustres in ecclesia Dei sunt aut fuerunt').[52] And, of course, both Bale and Foxe were still working for Oporinus when the first volume of the Magdeburg Centuries rolled through his presses.

Yet, with the possible exception of Flacius, no one rivalled the influence of Bale himself on the *Acts and Monuments*. We have already observed Bale's crucial role in shaping Foxe's first martyrology, the *Commentarii*, and we will shortly discuss his importance as a source for Foxe's second martyrology, but Bale's influence upon Foxe far exceeded his having supplied Foxe with sources and information; he also decisively influenced Foxe's interpretation of history. Most fundamentally, Foxe appropriated Bale's concept of the relationship between biblical prophecy and human history: that the former elucidated the latter in precise detail. Bale understood Revelation in particular as a description of human history *before* the Second Coming of Christ. This concept, together with the understanding – shared by Bale and

---

[50] Diener, 'Magdeburg Centuries', pp. 19–23, 39–58, 70, 78–81, 102, 130–1, 146–60, 166, 206–17, 240, 266–70 and 356–9.

[51] 'Matthias Flacio Illyrico, Ioanne Wigando, Matthaes Iudice, Basilio Fabro, aliisque, Ecclesiae ministris, magnum Ecclesiasticae historiae opus felicissimus auspiciis adornari.' John Bale, *Scriptorum Illustrium maioris Brytanniae posterior pars* (Basle, 1559), pp. 175–6. Basil Faber worked as an assistant to Wigand and Judex, and supervised the printing of the first three volumes of the Magdeburg Centuries.

[52] BL, Cotton MS Titus D.X, fo. 179ᵛ.

Foxe – of the struggle between the true and false Churches as being the chief agents in shaping history, was the foundation of the *Acts and Monuments*.[53]

The first glimmerings of Foxe applying this scheme to history came in the *Commentarii*.[54] However, Foxe's 'apocalyptic comedy', *Christus Triumphans*, marked its dawning. This drama, printed in 1556 by Oporinus, links the history of the Church – represented allegorically by the character of Ecclesia, and her persecution by Pseudamnus (the Antichrist) and Pornopolis (the Whore of Babylon) – to the book of Revelation. Even at this stage, Foxe's interpretation of both Revelation and human history differed in some aspects from that of Bale. (For example, Foxe already parallels what he characterised as the ten persecutions of the early Church with the persecutions inflicted on the post-Reformation Church, a scheme which later appears in both the *Acts and Monuments* and Foxe's commentary on the Apocalypse, but is nowhere to be found in Bale's writings.) However, Foxe's composition and printing of *Christus Triumphans*, especially at a time when he was residing and working with Bale, indicates the impact of the older man upon his younger colleague.[55] Foxe's next martyrology, the *Rerum*, contained very little material on the Apocalypse, yet his contemporaneous drama demonstrates that Foxe had already come to interpret the history of the Church as the ongoing fulfilment of prophecies contained in Revelation.[56] As Richard Bauckham has observed, *Christus Triumphans* was 'a preliminary sketch' for Foxe's 'lifelong task of integrating a study of history and prophecy'.[57] At an even more fundamental level, the fact that Foxe continued with his work on a second martyrology, which would include the Lollard and Henrician martyrs, as well as the more recent and more topical martyrs, is another sign of Bale's continuing influence on his younger colleague.

---

[53] Firth, *The Apocalyptic Tradition*, pp. 32–110, Richard Bauckham, *Tudor Apocalypse* (Abingdon, 1978), pp. 54–90, and Paul Christianson, *Reformers and Babylon: English Apocalyptic Visions from the Reformation to the Eve of the Civil War* (Toronto, 1978), pp. 20–1 and 39–40.

[54] Here we must respectfully disagree with Katherine Firth, who observes that a list of prophecies of the Reformation given in the *Rerum* are important early indications of Foxe's apocalyptic thought (Firth, *The Apocalyptic Tradition*, p. 78). However, Firth failed to realise that these prophecies first appeared in the *Commentarii*.

[55] Bauckham, *Tudor Apocalypse*, pp. 80–2.

[56] One interesting, if slight, indication of Foxe's placing his second martyrology in an apocalyptic framework comes in its title: *Rerum in ecclesia gestarum quae postremis et periculosis his temporibus evenerunt, maximarumque per Europam persecutionum, et sanctorum Dei martyrum, caeterarumque rerum si quae insignioris exempla sint, digesti per regna et nationes commentarii.* Clearly the 'periculosis his temporibus' is a reference to 2 Timothy 3:1 and its predictions of the perils in the end times.

[57] Bauckham, *Tudor Apocalypse*, p. 76.

IV

Foxe also benefited considerably from his association with Oporinus. At the most obvious level, Oporinus printed a number of Foxe's works during this period. Some of these, such as Foxe's second martyrology, the *Rerum*, were almost certainly intended to make a profit; others, such as a Latin appeal to the English nobility to bring the persecution of Protestants to a halt, could not reasonably have been expected to sell well.[58] Oporinus clearly printed these minor writings by Foxe as a favour to his employee, and perhaps in some cases out of their shared religious sympathies. (In fact, at one point in 1557, Oporinus worried about the expense Bale's delay in producing the *Acta Romanorum Pontificum* was creating and complained that he was unable to spur Bale on. This certainly suggests a level of independence as authors, if not as employees, in the relationships between the English exiles and Oporinus.[59]) But Foxe gained much more from his association with Oporinus than the printing of his writings. Oporinus was far more than a thriving printer; he was a scholar (in fact, before he entered the printing business he had been a professor of Latin and Greek at the University of Basle) and a humanist.[60] Partly because of his leadership, and also partly because Basle was both a major printing centre and a gathering place for religious refugees from across Europe, Oporinus was at the centre of a network of Protestant scholars.

Working for Oporinus, Foxe had access to a wide range of scholarship, including Flacius's *Catalogus*, which he would draw upon for the *Acts and Monuments*. In one case, Foxe openly acknowledged this borrowing, stating that his source for a particular anecdote was the autobiography of Francisco de Enzinas, 'whose [manuscript] book written in Latin, I my self have sene and read remaining in the hands of John Oporine at Basill'.[61] A particularly striking example of how Foxe took advantage of the scholarship Oporinus made available to him came with the account, in the *Acts and Monuments*, of the Ottoman Empire. Most of the historical information in Foxe's account came from five books. Two of these were Sebastian Münster's *Cosmographia*, a standard reference work, and Carion's *Chronicle*, a universal history written by Caspar Peucer, Philip Melanchthon's

---

[58] John Foxe, *Ad inclytos ac praepotentes Angliae proceres* (Basle, 1557).
[59] Steinmann, *Johannes Oporinus*, p. 96.   [60] For Oporinus's academic career see ibid., pp. 9–17.
[61] *1570*, p. 1022. For Foxe's use of Enzinas's autobiography see A. Gordon Kinder, 'Spanish Protestants and Foxe's Book: Sources', *Bibliothèque d'Humanisme et Renaissance*, 60 (1998), pp. 107–16. On Oporinus's friendship with Francisco de Enzinas and his printing of several of his books, see Steinmann, *Johannes Oporinus*, pp. 82–5.

son-in-law.[62] Three of these books dealt exclusively with the Islamic world and its history. One of them was Johann Cuspinian's *De Turcorum origine*.[63]

Foxe was probably guided to Cuspinian's work by the inclusion of excerpts from it in *De origine et rebus gestis Turcorum*.[64] This was a compilation of extracts on the history of the Turks from the works of twenty-five authors, beginning with an extract from *De origine et rebus gestis Turcorum* by the Byzantine historian Laonikos Chalkokondylas. (Because this work was the first in the collection, its name appears on the title page, yet Chalkokondylas had nothing to do with the compilation of Oporinus's collection. The work was edited anonymously, and translated by Conrad Clauser, a Swiss scholar of Greek.)[65] Whoever edited the collection, it was a major source of historical data for Foxe's account of the Ottoman Empire. This one work, for which Foxe was very probably one of the correctors, was Foxe's paramount source for Ottoman history from the accession of Mehmed II to the death of Suleiman the Magnificent (Foxe cites twenty-one authors as his sources for the history of the Turks; for seventeen of these Foxe drew on the *LCA*.[66])

Foxe's other major source, which he drew on particularly for the history of both Islam and the early Turks, was Theodor Bibliander's translation of the Qu'ran.[67] Oporinus's printing of this work in 1543 brought him into conflict with the municipal authorities of Basle. Luther wrote to the Basle authorities urging that it be printed, on the grounds that Christians needed to know the nature of their 'diabolical' adversary, and they reluctantly acquiesced.[68] Although Foxe did not arrive in Basle until well after this work had appeared, the notoriety surrounding its printing would have

---

[62] Cf. Sebastian Münster, *Cosmographia* (Basle, 1559), pp. 947, 957 and 967–9 with *1570*, pp. 872–3, 874, 884, and 886–7, and Caspar Peucer, *Chronicon Carionis* (Wittenberg, 1580), pp. 583–9, 642–55 and 657–8 with *1570*, pp. 873–4, 874–6, 876–7, 878–9, 881, 882–4 and 885–6.

[63] Cf. Johann Cuspinian, *De Turcorum origine* (Antwerp, 1541), fos. 14ᵛ–16ᵛ and 22ᵛ–5ᵛ with *1570*, pp. 876 and 877–8.

[64] *Laonici Chalcocondylae Atheniensis, De origine et rebus gestis Turcorum . . .* (Basle, 1556). Hereafter this work will be referred to as *LCA*.

[65] Clauser wrote a dedicatory preface that appears in some, but not all, copies of the work, and which is dated 19 February 1556. The colophon, in every copy, states that it was printed in March 1556. In some copies of the work, the Clauser dedication is replaced with a dedication written by one Johann Herold and dated April 1556. Because of this it is impossible to tell whether Harold or Clauser edited the work or whether it was someone else.

[66] *1570*, p. 897.

[67] Cf. Theodor Bibliander, *Machumetis Saracenorum principis . . . Alcoran* (Basle, 1550), pt. I, pp. 218–22, pt. II, p. 9 and pt. III, pp. 132, 166–71, 177–9, and 192–236 with *1570*, pp. 872, 873, 884, 897, 871 [recte 899]–900, and 913–14.

[68] Steinmann, *Johann Oporinus*, pp. 20–30.

ensured that Foxe was aware of it. Foxe's very inclusion of the Turks in his history is in itself a measure of the influence that Oporinus had on his thought. Foxe included the Turks in his history because he tended to see the Ottoman Empire as the Antichrist, or at least a manifestation of it, and in doing so he departed sharply from contemporary English Protestant interpretations of Revelation.

Like most sixteenth-century Protestants, Foxe regarded the Antichrist as a spiritual force and not as an individual, as medieval tradition had portrayed him. Thus the Antichrist could be the papacy or it could be the Turks or it could even be both, as Luther, Bullinger and many other Swiss and German Protestants believed.[69] This flexibility allowed Foxe to make almost every event in human history conform to biblical prophecy. But he, at least, found it difficult to accept both the papacy and the Ottomans as the Antichrist and he wavered on the point considerably.[70] As Katherine Firth has explained, 'Foxe described as Antichrist both the Turk and the pope: but when by Antichrist he meant to indicate the second beast of the Apocalypse, or the whore of Babylon, then he meant only the Papacy.'[71] Foxe's tentative identification of the Turk as the Antichrist became problematic in England in the seventeenth century, as Laudian writers, notably Robert Shelford, Richard Montagu and John Cousins all argued, drawing on Foxe, that the Turk was the Antichrist and therefore the papacy could not be.[72] And, as he made clear in the *Acts and Monuments*, Foxe finally preferred the identification of the papacy with the Antichrist.

In *Christus Triumphans* Foxe explicitly rejects the suggestion that the Turks were the Antichrist.[73] But clearly works that Foxe had studied while employed by Oporinus, in particular *LCA* and Bibliander's edition of the Qu'ran (which included excerpts from a number of scholars, ranging from Luther to Paolo Giovio, identifying the Turks as the Antichrist), influenced him into accepting the Turks as either the Antichrist or, at a minimum, significant actors in the Apocalypse. Before Foxe, the Turks were not central to English Protestant Apocalyptic thought; in fact, they are barely mentioned, even by John Bale. After Foxe, most English Protestant commentators on the Apocalypse, including such major figures as Thomas Brightman

---

[69] Bauckham, *Tudor Apocalypse*, pp. 94–6.   [70] *1570*, pp. 904–10.
[71] Firth, *Apocalyptic Tradition*, p. 99.
[72] Christopher Hill, *Antichrist in Seventeenth Century England* (Oxford, 1971), pp. 34–40. Although these writers and Foxe himself tended to assume that the pope and the Turks could not *both* be the Antichrist, some other English writers were not troubled by this. The notorious separatist Robert Browne, for example, believed that 'the Turks' and 'Saracens' were 'fellow Antichrists' to the 'chief Antichrist', the pope. See Christianson, *Reformers and Babylon*, p. 64.
[73] See Foxe, *Two Latin Comedies*, p. 353.

and Joseph Mede, accorded the Turks a crucial role in the unfolding of the end times.[74] The *Acts and Monuments* brought these views, hitherto not widely disseminated in England, into the mainstream of English Apocalyptic thought. It also contributed powerfully to creating a demonic conception among the English of the Ottoman Turks.[75] In these, as in numerous other ways, the intellectual currents that Foxe navigated during his exile contributed significantly to his interpretation of history.

However, Foxe's fellow countrymen, especially Edmund Grindal, also had a profound influence on Foxe's historical writing during his exile. Sometime during his exile, Grindal, who had previously been Nicholas Ridley's right-hand man in the diocese of London, started to organise materials for what he termed a 'history of the martyrs'.[76] Although the origins of this project are not clear, it was probably conceived independently of Foxe's work. In a letter to Foxe dated 18 June 1557, Grindal gave the clearest depiction of his original intentions: a history of the Marian martyrs, written in English and based on materials gathered by a team working loosely under his supervision, to be paralleled by a history of the martyrs in Latin, based on the same material and written by Foxe.[77]

It is probable that Foxe was chosen as the author of the Latin martyrology when Grindal learned of the *Commentarii*. Grindal apparently planned that the parallel martyrologies would cover only Mary's reign, and he initially conceived of Foxe including material on earlier martyrs in a second edition of the *Commentarii*. Grindal had hoped to have both editions on the Marian martyrs ready for the press by the autumn of 1556, but this proved to be over-optimistic.[78] Foxe continued to flounder in the quicksands of the Cranmer translation, while Grindal's team was distracted by personal concerns and competing priorities. In the event, like so many committee projects, the English-language martyrology was never completed, while Foxe pressed ahead with the Latin edition. However, the work of Grindal's team was not fruitless; they had amassed a considerable collection of documents, which were passed on to Foxe and were printed in his second martyrology. Grindal was also able to provide Foxe with advice, encouragement and a modest amount of financial support while Foxe was preparing the *Rerum*.

Grindal was based in Strasbourg and, while he contemplated joining Foxe in Basle, in the end he remained in Strasbourg.[79] As Collinson has

[74] Christianson, *Reformers and Babylon*, pp. 104–5 and 126.
[75] See Matthew Dimmock, *New Turkes: Dramatizing Islam and the Ottomans in Early Modern England* (Aldershot, 2005), pp. 76–81, 135–61 and 198–207.
[76] 'Historium Martyrum'. BL, Harley MS 417, fo. 102ʳ. [77] Ibid. [78] Ibid. [79] Ibid.

observed, by remaining in Strasbourg, he was in a strategic location to receive news and materials from England and from a network of Protestant exiles scattered across Germany and Switzerland.[80] Thus by the time that he was working on his second martyrology, Foxe already had an advantage, which separated him from most contemporary Protestant martyrologists: he was able to benefit from the work of a team of researchers. In his subsequent martyrologies, management of an expanding network of collaborators and associates would become a characteristic and distinctive strength of Foxe's work. Can we identify those beyond Grindal who aided Foxe in gathering the material for his second martyrology?

Unfortunately, it is hard to be precise and accurate here. Grindal did mention Thomas Sampson in a reference, which makes it clear that Sampson was playing an important editorial role in the project.[81] Beyond this, there is a considerable amount of mythology and not much substantive evidence. Patrick Collinson, in the mistaken belief – dispelled by Susan Wabuda – that Miles Coverdale edited the volume known as *The Letters of the Martyrs* (which will be discussed in the next chapter), misidentified Coverdale as a 'manager' of the project.[82] John Aylmer is frequently and carelessly mentioned as aiding Foxe in the *Rerum*. It is true that Foxe wrote to Aylmer requesting information on Lady Jane Grey; however, it is also true that Aylmer wrote back saying that he had none.[83] The late seventeenth-century ecclesiastical historian, John Strype, in a biography of Aylmer, dedicated to one of Aylmer's descendants, claimed that Aylmer played an important role in the making of the *Rerum* and this declaration, despite Strype's obvious bias and the lack of evidence he produced to support it, has been difficult to exorcise from scholarship.[84] Further identification of Grindal's team remains shrouded in the mists of time.[85] The

---

[80] Patrick Collinson, *Archbishop Grindal 1519–1583: The Struggle for a Reformed Church* (Berkeley and Los Angeles, 1979), p. 80.

[81] BL, Harley MS 417, fo. 102ᵛ.

[82] Collinson, *Grindal*, p. 80. John King has recently repeated this, now claiming that Coverdale was to be one of the editors of Grindal's projected English martyrology (King, *Early Modern Print Culture*, p. 25). In fact, Coverdale was in Denmark while Foxe was working on the *Rerum* and there is no evidence that Coverdale contributed to it. For Coverdale's very limited involvement with the *Letters of the Martyrs* see below, p. 131.

[83] BL, Harley MS 417, fos. 122ʳ–3ᵛ.

[84] John Strype, *Historical Collections of the Life and Acts of . . . John Aylmer* (Oxford, 1821), pp. 8–10. The dedication is sig. A1ʳ⁻ᵛ.

[85] Devorah Greenberg's list of those involved in Grindal's project, although extensive, does not distinguish between the different roles they might have had or their level of involvement. There was probably a wide network of individuals who supplied or transmitted information but a rather small circle of people redacting the documents or deciding general editorial strategy (Greenberg, 'Community of the Texts', pp. 700–1).

important point, however, is that Foxe had moved, between his first and second martyrologies, from writing as a solitary author to drawing on material assembled by a network of others.

v

This shift is reflected in the contents of the *Rerum*, Foxe's second martyrology. This was at once his promised continuation of the *Commentarii* and also the Latin 'Book of Martyrs', which Grindal had assigned to him. In terms of the sources upon which the contents are based, the *Rerum* can be divided into three sections. The first section was a reprinting of the *Commentarii* with relatively minor changes.[86] These additions were based on sources that Foxe acquired while on the continent, such as Ortwin Gratius's *Fasciculus rerum expetendarum et fugiendarum* and Flacius's edition of Hus's works.

The second section of the *Rerum*, dealing with the history of the True Church in England and Scotland from the end of the fifteenth century until the death of Edward VI, is stylistically a continuation of the *Commentarii* but it is based on different sources.[87] The most important of these was Hall's *Chronicle*, which Foxe must have had with him during his exile.[88] It supplies all of the factual material in the accounts of the Richard Hunne case; the posthumous excommunication of William Tracy; the martyrdom of Andrew Hewet; Wolsey's reception of Cardinal Campeggio in 1518 and 1529; the execution of John Forrest; the martyrdom of Robert Barnes, William Jerome and Thomas Garrett; the articles against Sir John Borthwicke; the Act of the Six Articles; the execution of Richard Mekins; the account of four martyrs executed at Windsor in 1542; and the story of a virtuous matron.[89] Out of ninety-five pages in this section, thirty pages are taken directly from Hall's

---

[86] This section corresponds to pp. 1–118 of the *Rerum*. The changes are: the addition of two stories about Wiclif's opponents (cf. *Comm.*, fo. 28ʳ with Foxe, *Rerum*, p. 13); details of the Council of Constance and of Jan Hus (cf. *Comm.*, fo. 44ᵛ with Foxe, *Rerum*, pp. 21–52); and additional material on Sir John Oldcastle and his followers (cf. *Comm.*, fo. 107ᵛ with Foxe, *Rerum*, pp. 100–9).

[87] For reasons that will be discussed more fully below, in contrast to the *Commentarii*, the *Rerum* deliberately deals only with events in the two kingdoms and not with anything that happened on the continent.

[88] Edward Hall, *The vnion of the two noble and illustre families of Lancastre and York* (London, 1550), STC 12723a (hereafter referred to as Hall's *Chronicle*). There had been three previous editions of the work prior to this edition; it is uncertain which edition Foxe used.

[89] Cf. Hall's *Chronicle*, Hunne: fos. 50ʳ–5ᵛ; Tracy: fo. 211ʳ⁻ᵛ; Hewet: fo. 235ᵛ; Wolsey: fo. 84ʳ⁻ᵛ; Forrest: fos. 232ᵛ–3ʳ; Barnes, Jerome and Garrett: fos. 242ʳ–3ʳ; Borthwicke: fos. 245ᵛ–7ʳ; Act of the Six Articles: fo. 134ʳ⁻ᵛ; Mekins: fo. 244ʳ; Windsor four: fo. 256ʳ⁻ᵛ; and the virtuous matron: fos. 256ᵛ–7ʳ with *Rerum*, Hunne: pp. 119–21; Tracy: pp. 125–6; Hewet: pp. 135–6; Wolsey: pp. 136–7; Forrest: p. 146; Barnes, Jerome and Garrett: pp. 165–6; Borthwicke: pp. 166–79; Act of the Six Articles: pp. 179–80; Mekins: p. 181; Windsor four: pp. 182–3; and the virtuous matron: pp. 183–4.

Chronicle, often in a word-for-word translation. Moreover, that is hardly the extent of Foxe's dependence on Hall for this portion of the *Rerum*: his account of John Frith's arrest, trial and execution comes from Hall, as does almost all of his material on Tyndale, except for the story of Tyndale and a magician. Foxe also based his account of the arrest and trial of Anne Boleyn, as well as the details about Robert Packington's assassination, on Hall.[90]

In two other cases in this section, Foxe reprinted either large extracts from a work or an entire work. This is particularly noteworthy because the incorporation of smaller works would become a characteristic feature of the *Acts and Monuments*, but this was the first time Foxe employed this technique. He reproduced, in translation, Alexander Alesius's account of a dispute that he had with Bishop Stokesley of London in 1537 on the number of the sacraments.[91] Foxe also translated one of Bale's editions of the examinations of Anne Askew in its entirety.[92]

Apart from these two examples, and apart from Hall's *Chronicle*, Foxe relied on unprinted information from individual informants. The most important of these was John Bale. (It seems probable that another printed work consulted by Foxe during his exile was Bale's *Epistle exhortatorye*, which contains a list of English martyrs and details about their executions that are repeated in the *Rerum* but were not available in any other source.[93] On the other hand, in at least one case, that of the account of the Scottish martyr Patrick Hamilton, Foxe's source was unquestionably Bale's *Catalogus*.[94]) It is clear that Foxe's accounts of a number of Henrician martyrs came from Bale, notably the accounts of James Bainham and the martyrs executed along with Anne Askew.[95] In certain cases, Foxe clearly followed Bale closely but added additional information that he had gleaned. For example, in the *Epistle*

---

[90] Cf. Hall's *Chronicle*, Frith: fo. 285^{r-v}; Tyndale: fos. 186^{r-v} and 227^{r-v}; Boleyn: fos. 286^{v}–7^{r}; and Packington: fos. 231^{v}–2^{r} with Foxe, *Rerum*, Frith: pp. 129 and 135; Tyndale: pp. 138–9; Boleyn: pp. 144–5; and Packington: p. 146.

[91] Cf. Alexander Alesius, *Of the auctoritie of the word of God* (Strasbourg, 1548?), STC 292, sigs. A5^{r}–B7^{v} with Foxe, *Rerum*, pp. 159–64.

[92] Cf. Anne Askew, *The exawinacion* [sic] *of A. Askew* (London? 1550?), STC 852.5, with Foxe, *Rerum*, pp. 186–99. For identification of this edition as the one Foxe translated in the *Rerum*, see Thomas S. Freeman and Sarah Elizabeth Wall, 'Racking the Body, Shaping the Text: The Account of Anne Askew in Foxe's "Book of Martyrs"', *Renaissance Quarterly*, 54 (2001), pp. 1171–6.

[93] Cf. John Bale, *The Epistle exhortatorye of an Engliyshe Chrystyane* (Antwerp, 1554), STC 1291, fos. 13^{r-v} and 14^{v}–15^{r} with Foxe, *Rerum*, pp. 126–7 and 181–2.

[94] The wording of the two accounts is remarkably similar. Cf. *Catalogus . . . posterior pars* (Basle, 1559), p. 222 with Foxe, *Rerum*, pp. 121–3.

[95] In the *Rerum*, Foxe misidentified James Bainham as George Bainham (*Rerum*, p. 126). Bale had invariably but erroneously identified this martyr as George Bainham in various works. Bale, *Epistle exhortatorye*, fo. 13^{v} and *Select Works of John Bale*, ed. Henry Christmas (Parker Society, Cambridge,

exhortatorye, Bale stated that three people were burned at St Giles's Field in Southwark at five o'clock in the morning. He identified one of these as a man named Giles, who was a joiner, one as one of the king's servants, and one as a painter. In the *Catalogus*, Bale described the same incident and dated it to around 1538. He dropped the information that the burning took place at five in the morning but added that the name of the painter was John.[96] Foxe combined elements of these two accounts in the *Rerum* but he also added material that was in neither: i.e., that Giles's last name was 'Germaine' and that the king's servant was named 'Launcelot'. He also added that Launcelot, at the trial of Giles and John, had displayed such sympathy for the defendants that he was examined and condemned along with them.[97] Clearly Foxe had supplemented the material he got from Bale with material obtained from an informant, who was probably present at the trial.

Similarly, in both the *Epistle exhortatorye* and the *Catalogus*, Bale declared that three young men from Suffolk, Robert King, John Debenham and Nicholas Marsh, were executed for destroying the rood in the church at Dovercourt, Essex.[98] Foxe repeated this in the *Rerum*, but added a detail that is not in Bale: that there was a fourth participant, a 'Robertus Gayrnerus' who fled and survived.[99] In the first edition of the *Acts and Monuments*, Foxe has a version of the episode but he also added that he had consulted a letter that Robert Gardner had written to someone named Chapman, describing the incident.[100] It seems fairly clear that Foxe either saw the letter when writing the *Rerum* or else that he heard about it from another informant. In either case, Foxe obtained information while in exile, which extended that supplied by Bale, and which he was able to develop further in the 1563 edition of the *Acts and Monuments*.

1849), pp. 394 and 586. Which one of these works Foxe consulted is unknown, but clearly it was ultimately Bale who was the source for this. Similarly, in the *Rerum* Foxe identifies the martyrs burned with Askew as John Lascelles, John 'Adams' and 'Nicholas Belenian' (*Rerum*, p. 199). Only Bale's *Catalogus* (p. 670) gives these names for these martyrs.

[96] Cf. Bale, *Epistle exhortatorye*, fos. 14ᵛ–15ʳ with *Catalogus*, p. 665. This episode is well established by independent sources. Charles Wriothesley wrote that on 3 May 1540, 'were three persons brent without Sainct Georges Barre in Southwark in the high waie almost at Newington for heresies against the Sacrament of the aulter, one was a groome to the Queene named Maundevild, a French man borne, another an painter, an Italian, and an Englishman'. Charles Wriothesley, *A Chronicle of England During the Reigns of the Tudors*, ed. William D. Hamilton, vol. 1, Camden Society new series (1875), p. 118.

[97] Foxe, *Rerum*, p. 181.   [98] Bale, *Epistle exhortatorye*, fo. 13ᵛ.

[99] Foxe, *Rerum*, p. 126.   [100] *1563*, p. 496.

As can be seen from these examples, Foxe was able to draw on information from informants that was not available in print for the Henrician section of the *Rerum*. Foxe declared his indebtedness to such informants in a preface to the *Rerum*, when he declared that, although he was hampered by not writing in England where the events he was describing took place, certain English people supplied him with information.[101] Among these were friends and family members. Foxe probably obtained at least two accounts in the *Rerum* either from his wife or from members of her family. One was the narrative of the 'murder' of John Randall, an evangelical who was a relation by marriage of John Foxe.[102] The other was an account of the execution of Joan Smith and six other Lollards executed in Coventry in 1520. This account is brief but it contains certain circumstantial details that were almost certainly based on the testimony of an eyewitness.[103] It seems probable that this material was transmitted to Foxe by his wife, whose family came from Coventry. It should also be noted that Foxe drew on his own memory for certain incidents described in the *Rerum*: the trial and execution of William Cowbridge at Oxford in 1538 and the panic that ensued at the public recantation of a heretic in the church of St Mary's, Oxford, in December 1536, because of the false alarm of a fire. Foxe stated specifically that he was an eyewitness to both events.[104]

Foxe also drew extensively on friends and earlier contacts he had made in England for information about Henrician martyrs. Foxe's account of the martyrdom of John Lambert, a sacramentarian executed in 1538 after a spectacular show trial by Henry VIII, was based on an eyewitness account from Anthony Gilby, with whom Foxe shared a house in Frankfurt.[105] Another instance of Foxe drawing on an old acquaintance, this one made during Edward VI's reign, occurs when Foxe relates a story of the humanist Leonard Coxe coming to the aid of the evangelical John Frith.[106] In a letter

[101] Foxe, *Rerum*, p. 1.

[102] Randall was a student at Trinity College, Cambridge, who was found hanged in his room. In the *Rerum* and in the first edition of the *Acts and Monuments*, Foxe declared that he was murdered by Catholics (*Rerum*, p. 121 and *1563*, p. 490). Nicholas Harpsfield wrote a scathing attack on the credibility of this account, and Foxe quietly withdrew all mention of Randall from subsequent editions of the *Acts and Monuments*. Nicholas Harpsfield, *Dialogi sex contra summi pontificatus, monasticae vitae, sanctorum, sacrarum imaginum oppugnatores et pseudomartyres* (Antwerp, 1566), pp. 747–8.

[103] Foxe, *Rerum*, p. 116.

[104] Ibid., pp. 139–44. Foxe declares that he was an eyewitness to both events on p. 139.

[105] Ibid., pp. 146–54. Foxe did not identify the source for this narrative until the 1570 edition, when he identified it as coming from his friend, 'A.G.' (*1570*, p. 1284). However, since the story first appeared in 1559, Foxe must have learned of it before then, and Gilby, the only Marian exile whose initials are A.G. – who is known to have been a friend of Foxe – is most likely to have been the source for this dramatic episode. For Foxe residing in Gilby's house see BL, Harley MS 417, fo. 113[r].

[106] Foxe, *Rerum*, p. 128.

to William Cecil, written in 1551, Foxe mentions that he had sent his work on Latin grammar 'to other most learned men, especially to Leonard Coxe, who has the most discerning judgement in these matters'.[107]

However, Foxe did not only quarry information from friends and relations; he also mined in unfamiliar territory; either with the assistance of mutual friends or by his own diligent inquiries, he was able to obtain information from people he did not know personally. A remarkable example of this came with Foxe's account of the 'martyrdom' of William Gardiner, an English merchant who was executed in Lisbon in 1552 for desecrating the host in the Portuguese royal chapel. Foxe's account, full of vivid and corroborative detail, was obtained from one 'Pendigrace', an Englishman from Bristol, who had shared a house with Gardiner in Lisbon.[108] What is particularly striking is that this eyewitness account is verified in its details by the records of the Portuguese Inquisition.[109] Somehow, and we do not know by what means, Foxe was able to obtain this accurate and dramatic account from a Bristol merchant with whom, as far as we know, he never came in contact. On occasion Foxe was even able to get documents of the Henrician era from contacts in England. For example, we know that he was able to consult documents concerning the execution of four martyrs in Windsor in 1543.[110]

Foxe used basically the same types of sources, but in different proportions, for the section of the *Rerum* dealing with Mary's reign. For the Marian period, he was not able to rely on a single source in the way that he had relied on Hall's *Chronicle*. By way of compensation, he incorporated a number of printed works into his narrative of recent events. In fact, Foxe's account of Mary's reign in the *Rerum* is much less a narrative than his account of Henry's reign had been. Rather, it is a collection of writings strung together by bits of narrative. One reason for this may be that, for this section, Foxe was very dependent on material obtained from Edmund

---

[107] 'aliis doctissimus quibusdam, tum principe Leonardo Coxo exquitissimae in iis rebus sententiae'. BL, Add. MS 34727, fo. 2ʳ.

[108] Foxe, *Rerum*, p. 206.

[109] These records are printed in Thomas S. Freeman and Marcello J. Borges, '"A grave and heinous incident against our holy Catholic Faith"': Two Accounts of William Gardiner's Desecration of the Portuguese Royal Chapel in 1552', *Historical Research*, 69 (1996), pp. 1–17. This article compares the account of these records with Foxe's narrative and also attempts to identify Pendigrace.

[110] Later, in 1570, while explaining an error he had made, which had been spotted by Harpsfield, Foxe claimed that he had been misled in his first account by the wording of the writ authorising their execution (*1570*, p. 1399). Furthermore, although Foxe based much of his account of these martyrs on Hall's *Chronicle* (fo. 256ʳ⁻ᵛ), he had some information that was not in Hall – e.g., the charges against one of them, named Bennet – that were almost certainly obtained from trial documents (Foxe, *Rerum*, pp. 182–3).

Grindal, and Grindal's interest seems to have been in a collection of writings by the Marian martyrs, rather than a narrative about them. Another reason may simply have been that this latter part of the *Rerum* was written, for reasons we shall discuss shortly, in considerable haste.

First of all, Foxe drew on printed works that were available to him; in some instances, these were reprintings of works that he had authored. The first of these was Foxe's appeal to the English nobility to end the persecution, *Ad inclytos*, which had been printed in March 1557.[111] The other was a translation of Philpot's examinations into Latin, which Foxe had made and which was apparently printed in 1557.[112] Foxe also reprinted Valérand Poullain's Latin translation of Philpot's account of the disputes in the 1553 Convocation about the Sacrament.[113] Finally, Foxe also translated an English pamphlet on the tribulations of James Hales, which, ironically, had been printed by John Day as one of the works from the Michael Wood press.[114] Although this is a relatively small number of works, they amount to 139 pages of the 527 pages of the *Rerum* devoted to Mary's reign.

By far and away the most important source of material that Foxe drew on for the Marian portion of the *Rerum* was the writings of the martyrs, which, up until then, had remained in manuscript. Although it is possible to overstate the amount of organisation involved, clearly Foxe was able to draw on the desultory but impressive efforts of contacts to acquire this material from England. Thanks to the correspondence that survives between Foxe and Grindal, we know that Grindal procured a number of these items, including a narrative of Thomas Cranmer's death, which Foxe reprinted, Cranmer's and Ridley's disputations at Oxford, an account of Bradford, together with some of his letters, as well as a number of Hooper's writings.[115] Grindal and his associates were very probably responsible for other items that are not mentioned in the correspondence, especially

[111] This is reprinted on pp. 239–61 of the *Rerum*.

[112] No copy of this work survives. However, John Strype declared that such a work was printed, entitled *Mira ac elegans cum primus Historia vel Tragoedia potius, de tota ratione examinationis et condemnationis. J. Philpotti Archidiaconi Wincestriae, nuper in Anglia exusti. Ab autore primum lingua sua congesta; nunc in Latinum versa, Interprete J.F.A.* See John Strype, *Memorials of . . . Cranmer*, 4 vols. (Oxford, 1840), vol. 1, pp. 515–16. This was reprinted on pp. 215–32 of the *Rerum*. In a letter to Foxe, Bullinger noted that Foxe was considering printing the Philpot examinations as a separate work (BL, Harley MS 417, fo. 112[r]).

[113] Cf. Anon., *Vera expositio disputationis . . . in Synodo Ecclesiastica, Londini in Comitiis regni ad 18 Octob. Anno 1553* (Rome [i.e., Cologne], 1554), fos. 4[r]–29[v] with Foxe, *Rerum*, pp. 215–32. Foxe states on p. 215 that he was following this Latin translation. However, it should be noted that he omitted the beginning and added his own conclusion.

[114] Cf. *The communication betweene my lord chancelor and judge Hales . . .* (Stamford, 1553), STC 11583 with Foxe, *Rerum*, pp. 262–3.

[115] BL, Harley MS 417, fo. 113[r–v]. Also see *LM*, STC 5886, pp. 50–1 and ECL, MS 260, fo. 114*[r]. Grindal did not specify which of Hooper's writings he had acquired but it is almost certain he was largely

Hooper's examinations and his letters, as well as the disputations of Latimer at Oxford.[116]

It is, of course, entirely possible, even likely, that Foxe obtained other writings of the martyrs through the good offices of Grindal and his team. However, it is unlikely that he obtained all of the manuscripts that he printed from them. In some cases there are indications that Foxe had cultivated other sources. For example, Foxe states that the Marian martyr, Lawrence Saunders, wrote numerous letters to friends on the outside who sustained him during his imprisonment and that, in particular, Saunders had written a number of letters to a certain 'nobilis foemina'.[117] Foxe prints the examinations of John Rogers, who was an old friend of his; Foxe would later describe how these documents were retrieved from Newgate by Rogers' son, Daniel, and it is certainly likely that Foxe ultimately obtained them from the family.[118] Moreover, as we shall see shortly, Foxe obtained information about the martyrs themselves from various informants, and it seems likely that at least some of these passed along writings of the martyrs as well. Whatever Foxe's sources were for these manuscript writings, they formed a substantial portion of his section on Mary's reign: 168 out of 527 pages. However, it would be a mistake to assume that the entire English exile community acted as sources for Foxe. For example, Jean Crespin the martyrologist was able to print letters of the martyrs that were unavailable to Foxe because they had been sent to Geneva; Foxe apparently had few contacts there.[119]

As with the Henrician section of the *Rerum*, Foxe relied on oral sources for Mary's reign. As before, he was able to draw on friends for information. For

referring to Hooper's treatise on the Lord's Supper, which Foxe reprinted in the *Rerum*, along with his own commentary. Foxe, *Rerum*, pp. 298–396. Foxe's commentary is on pp. 396–403. Grindal informed Foxe of concerns by Bullinger and Peter Martyr about printing, without revision, the writings of Hooper that Grindal was sending to Foxe. At the same time, we know that Hooper had sent Bullinger his treatise on the Lord's Supper in December 1554. *Original Letters Relative to the English Reformation*, ed. Hastings Robinson, 2 vols. (Parker Society, Cambridge, 1846–47), I, pp. 105–6.

[116] Peter Martyr and Heinrich Bullinger, at a minimum, took an interest in the printing of Hooper's writings, and almost certainly played a role in gathering them and transmitting them to Grindal. As we have seen, Cranmer's and Ridley's disputations were certainly acquired by Grindal, who may also have obtained those of Latimer.

[117] Foxe, *Rerum*, p. 412. Depending on whether 'nobilis' is a description of class or character, this most likely refers to either Lady Fitzwilliam or Lucy Harrington, both of whom were correspondents and sustainers of Saunders. The point here, however, is that while Foxe did not print any of these letters, he clearly knew about them, which would suggest that he had his own contacts for Saunders' life and writings.

[118] Foxe, *Rerum*, pp. 266–79. For the account of Daniel Rogers retrieving these documents see *1570*, p. 1663.

[119] David Watson, 'Jean Crespin and the First English Martyrology of the Reformation', in *John Foxe and the Reformation*, ed. Loades, pp. 196–8.

example, he relates in detail the escape of Alexander Wimshurst (formerly a chaplain of Magdalen College and described by Foxe as 'veteri amico meo') from Bonner's custody.[120] Foxe also has detailed accounts of the execution of Robert Samuel in Ipswich in 1555.[121] These were clearly furnished by an informant from Ipswich. The identity of this informant is probably revealed when Foxe later describes Andrew Ingforby, a merchant, and his family fleeing Ipswich; in this tale, Foxe mentions that Ingforby was a friend of Samuel.[122] The link to Foxe becomes apparent when one realises that Foxe's close friend, Laurence Humphrey, married Andrew's daughter, Joan.[123]

In a surprising number of cases, Foxe was able to obtain eyewitness accounts of the deaths of Marian martyrs: for example, the very circumstantial description of Hooper's journey from London to Gloucester and his execution there, the graphic account of the execution of John Cardmaker and John Warne, and the vivid account of the capture and gory execution of George Eagles.[124] Foxe may have obtained these narratives through Grindal's network or he may have acquired them through his own contacts. One very interesting example of the scope of what Foxe learned from his informants is his knowledge of the tribulations of Robert Ferrar, bishop of St David's. Ferrar had been at the epicentre of bitter controversy, which extended back to his appointment, and which resulted in his trial back in the reign in Edward VI. Foxe relates quite a few of the details of these controversies and he was also able to supply circumstantial details of Ferrar's execution at Carmarthen in Mary's reign.[125] Clearly Foxe was able in this case to rely not merely on an eyewitness to an execution but to a partisan who was very familiar with the martyr's career.[126]

The authorship of the *Rerum* marked an important milestone in Foxe's growth as an historian. In the *Commentarii*, Foxe had derived all of his information from a limited pool of sources. In order to compose the *Rerum*, he had to gather his own information. Whereas in the *Commentarii* he was relying to a considerable extent on what he had obtained from Bale, in the *Rerum* he not only obtained his own information, but he worked closely with a research team to acquire it. He also drew on a diverse range of sources: different types of manuscripts and printed sources, with

---

[120] Foxe, *Rerum*, pp. 637–8.   [121] Ibid., pp. 523–5.   [122] Ibid., p. 636.
[123] See the entry on Laurence Humphrey in *ODNB*.
[124] Foxe, *Rerum*, pp. 290–6, 441–3 and 726–8 respectively.   [125] Ibid., pp. 423–5.
[126] In later editions, Foxe would present an incredibly detailed account of the welter of charges and counter-charges that swirled around Ferrar. These stemmed from a massive collection of documents relating to the Ferrar case, which still survive in Foxe's papers (BL, Harley MS 420, fos. 80ʳ–178ʳ). These documents are copies of the originals – which do not survive – and they were clearly sent to Foxe by a supporter of Ferrar, very probably one with whom Foxe was in contact during his exile.

information from informants also. In this respect, the *Rerum* was quite similar to the contemporary martyrologies of Crespin, Haemstede and Rabus. But the *Rerum* differed from these works in one important respect: it was the first Protestant martyrology to provide *continuous* coverage of the late medieval as well as the Reformation periods. Already, particularly through his determination – despite Grindal's reservations – to include the pre-Marian history in the *Rerum*, Foxe was taking the first steps towards writing an ecclesiastical history, rather than a simple martyrology.

VI

Although Foxe was slow to abandon hope that his translation of Cranmer's work on the Eucharist would be printed, and although he continued to author a number of works throughout his exile, from the spring of 1557 onwards he seems to have been largely preoccupied with work on the *Rerum*. He was faced with the challenge of assembling his material and integrating it into a narrative at a very rapid rate. There were two reasons for this haste. The first was the death of Mary I on 17 November 1558, which animated Foxe with the desire to return home to England. At the same time, Oporinus was clearly anxious that the book be finished in time for the Frankfurt Book Fair.[127] Thus both printer and author wished to complete the *Rerum* as swiftly as possible. Certainly there are signs of haste throughout the volume, most notably that no details are given for any of the martyrs executed after Thomas Cranmer was burned on 20 March 1556; instead, these martyrs are merely listed.[128] In any event, the book was barely finished in time for the September fair. The colophon states that the work was printed in August 1559. In the dedication, which is dated 1 September 1559, Foxe declared that the printers gave him only one day to write it.[129]

The most important consequence of this haste, however, was that it caused Foxe and Oporinus to drop any plans for including continental material in the *Rerum*. Instead, this volume concentrated – apart from some discussion of Jerome of Prague and Jan Hus – solely on martyrs in England and Scotland. However, this decision was apparently made only on the eve

---

[127] Foxe repeatedly referred to the haste with which the *Rerum* was completed and printed in his preliminaries to the book (*Rerum*, sig. A3ʳ and p. 1).

[128] The list appears in Foxe, *Rerum*, pp. 729–32.

[129] Ibid., sig. A3ʳ. In order to hasten the printing of the work, it was divided between Oporinus and Nicholas Brylinger, another Basle printer. The imprints gave joint credit to the two men but, more unusually, different copies also manifested different devices, that is to say that some copies bear the device of Brylinger, whereas others bear that of Oporinus.

of its printing. On 13 May 1559, Foxe wrote to Heinrich Bullinger asking him to try to obtain from Bernardo Ochino and other Italians in Zurich accounts of the persecution of Protestants in Italy. He also asked Bullinger to send him an account of events in Zurich: 'For although I am more immediately concerned with British history, yet I shall not pass over the sacred history of other nations, should it come in my way.'[130] In a subsequent letter to Bullinger, just over a month later, Foxe pressed him for material on Zwingli and promised that anything he sent would be printed in England, if it was not printed in Germany.[131] By this point in time, Foxe (and Oporinus) had already decided that there would be a second part to the *Rerum*, covering continental history, which would be completed by Foxe after he returned to England.[132] Writing to Bullinger as late as 2 August 1559, Foxe again repeated the request for information on Zwingli and assured Bullinger that he would be printing an account of Zwingli in England.[133] In these letters we can see Foxe, and presumably Oporinus, gradually coming to the decision to abandon, temporarily, the non-British martyrs, presumably in order to get the book finished by September.

Nevertheless, Foxe had not forgotten about the Protestants on the continent, and in fact he was very concerned that his new martyrology be widely disseminated in Europe. Apparently he planned to have a French translation of the work printed in Geneva; at least this is what he maintained in an introduction to the *Rerum*, where Foxe declared that 'he hoped that two editions [of his martyrology] would be printed, one in Latin in Basle, the other in French at Geneva'.[134] It would appear that this ambitious plan came close to fruition. On 16 October 1559, Nicholas Barbier asked the Genevan consistory for 'privilege pour quatre ans d'imprimer Historia ecclesiastica Iohannis Foxi'. On the same day, Jean Crespin petitioned the consistory 'de luy permettre imprimer et augmenter le Livre des martirs, y adjoustant les Martirs d'Angleterre et autres pays, avec bon privilege'.[135]

---

[130] Robinson, *Zurich Letters*, 1, p. 26.   [131] Ibid., p. 36.

[132] When the decision was made for Foxe to work on a second part in England is unknown, but by the time the work had gone to press the decision had been made to divide the work into two parts, one covering Britain, the other the German territories. In the *Rerum*, Foxe praised Martin Luther 'auspicatissimae vir memoriae' but regretted that an account of his life 'longa hic texenda mihi esset narratio: nisi institutam historiae seriem sequutus de Anglis in praesentia et Scotis: post vero de Germanis hominibus, atque inter hos de Luthero, suo ordine referre decrivissem' ('is too long to weave into my narrative unless it follows in the next instalment of this history, [which is] presently on the English and the Scots. Truly afterwards I will focus on the German people, Luther among them, in their turn'). *Rerum*, p. 121.

[133] Robinson, *Zurich Letters*, 1, p. 42.

[134] 'duo pariter Typographi, alter Basiliensis, qui latine imprimeret, alter Genevensis, qui Gallicam etiam huius historiae editionem efflagitabat' (Foxe, *Rerum*, p. 1).

[135] Gilmont, *Bibliographie*, 1, p. 140.

This wording seems to indicate that Barbier sought permission to print a French translation of the *Rerum*, while Crespin sought permission to print a new edition of his own work, incorporating new material – probably derived from a reading of the *Rerum* – on the English martyrs. (In the light of Foxe's subsequent utilisation of Crespin's work – and vice versa – it is interesting to note that it would seem that Foxe had negotiated with Barbier, not Crespin, for a translation of the *Rerum*.) The Geneva council gave permission to both parties to print a French translation of the English 'collection of the martyrs'.[136] In the event, neither printer ever produced a translation of the *Rerum*.

However, a great deal of the *Rerum* was incorporated into Crespin's next martyrology the *Actiones et monumenta martyrum*, printed in Geneva in 1560.[137] In fact, apart from the long theological discussions (e.g., Philpot's account of the debate in the 1553 Convocation or Hooper's treatise on the Eucharist), Crespin incorporated all of the *Rerum* into his new martyrology.[138] Crespin's borrowing from the *Rerum* continued; Gilmont estimates that 85 per cent of Crespin's subsequent martyrology, the *Quatrième partie*, was a translation into French of material from the *Rerum*.[139] In the long term, it was the incorporation of the material from the *Rerum* into the martyrologies of Crespin, Pantaleon and Adriaan van Haemstede that provides the most enduring influence of the *Rerum*. However, the *Rerum* was disseminated rapidly across Protestant Europe. In 1560, Mihály Sztárai, a Hungarian humanist who was also a Protestant archdeacon in Ottoman-occupied Hungary, was inspired by the *Rerum* to write a narrative poem – in Hungarian – celebrating the life and martyrdom of Cranmer.[140] In a letter dated 4 May 1574, Simon Budnaeus, a Lutheran preacher in Lithuania, wrote to Foxe praising the work and declaring that he studied it regularly.[141] The tribute that probably mattered the most to Foxe was a letter from the great Heinrich Bullinger congratulating him on the

---

[135] Gilmont, *Bibliographie*, I, p. 140.

[136] 'ung recueuel des martirs' (ibid.).

[137] As always, the borrowing between Foxe and Crespin was mutual. Almost certainly Foxe took the title, *Acts and Monuments*, from Crespin's martyrology.

[138] The one exception to this, which demonstrates the rule, is that Crespin omitted Foxe's account of the persecution and suicide of Judge Hales. The reason for this was that Foxe praised Hales's suicide as a form of martyrdom. Crespin was doubtless wary of the theological implications of this.

[139] Gilmont, *Bibliographie*, I, p. 140.

[140] Mihály Sztárai, *Historia Cranmerus T. Erseknek* (Debrecen, 1582). We are grateful to Diarmid MacCulloch for providing us with this reference.

[141] Bodleian Library, Add. MS 14995, fo. 97ʳ.

book.[142] Now, for the first time, while in his early forties, Foxe had attained an international reputation as a writer.

The surest indication of the success of the *Rerum*, however, was that Oporinus was determined to print the second part of it, dealing with the history of the Reformation on the continent. Eventually this second part would appear but it would be written by Heinrich Pantaleon rather than Foxe. Pantaleon proclaimed in the subtitle of his martyrology, the *Martyrum historia*, that it was 'Pars Secunda quum autem in prima parte Martyres saltem Angliae et Scotiae, a D. Johanne Foxe Anglo, superioribus annis sint annotate'.[143] In the dedication of the *Martyrum historia*, Pantaleon also declared that Foxe had intended for a subsequent part of the *Rerum* to be printed separately, which would cover the 'res Martyrum' for areas outside England and Scotland.[144] Pantaleon went on to declare that he was only taking over the composition of the second part 'since truly we have waited, in vain, for several years' for Foxe to complete it.[145] But Oporinus apparently was reluctant to abandon hope that Foxe would, at least, collaborate with Pantaleon in the second part; as late as September 1562, Oporinus wrote to Foxe asking him if he had any intentions of contributing to this work.[146] Foxe's response must have been rapid and negative, as the work would be printed seven months later, with Heinrich Pantaleon credited as the sole author.[147]

Pantaleon was a close friend of Foxe and Bale.[148] He was also a remarkable polymath. He was a theologian, but also a highly successful physician, as well as Professor of Medicine at the University of Basle. At the same time he was also an accomplished translator, rendering, amongst other works, Sleidan's *Commentaries* into German. (Although this translation was strongly opposed by Sleidan it was a considerable

---

[142] BL, Harley MS 417, fo. 124ʳ.

[143] Heinrich Pantaleon, *Martyrum historia* (Basle, 1563), fo. 3ᵛ.   [144] Ibid.

[145] 'quum vero per aliquot annos frustra' (ibid.).

[146] BL, Harley MS 417, fo. 108ᵛ. This letter is particularly interesting because it shows that Oporinus was significantly involved in the preparation of the *Martyrum historia*, even though the work would eventually be printed by his close associate, Nicholas Brylinger.

[147] See n. 23, p. 110 below.

[148] Pantaleon was part of the circles in which Foxe and Bale moved in Basle. He contributed a Latin poem to Bale's *Catalogus*, which praised 'learned Bale' for glorifying Britain and degrading the papacy (Bale, *Catalogus*, sig. β2ʳ). Pantaleon would also declare in his dedication to the *Martyrum historia* that Bale had encouraged him to write historical works (*Martyrum Historia*, fo. 3ᵛ). In the text of the *Martyrum historia*, describing the English exiles, Pantaleon refers to Bale and Foxe as 'amici mei integerrimi' (ibid., p. 336.)

success.) Like Foxe, he wrote a neo-Latin comedy, entitled *Philargyrus*. He had also established himself as a historical writer with his *Chronographia Christianae Ecclesiae* (Basle, 1550), a work that presented Church history in parallel tables showing the dates of emperors, kings, popes, great theologians, and Church councils. Pantaleon's most famous work, however, was his *Prosopographia herorum atque illustrium virorum totius Germaniae*, which, in addition to coining the name of a historical methodology, was also a greatly admired biographical dictionary of great Germans.[149]

Scholars have paid little attention to Pantaleon's martyrology. German scholars have focused almost all of their discussion on Pantaleon's *Prosopographia* to the neglect of his other works.[150] Scholars from other language groups have also ignored Pantaleon's *Martyrum historia*, partly because of an obsession with vernacular martyrologies and also because of a linked obsession with tying martyrologies to national confessions. Yet Pantaleon's *Martyrum historia* is one of the most important martyrologies of the Reformation. In the dedication, Pantaleon put his finger on its greatest strength: while other Protestant martyrologies had focused on particular nations and regions, his work covered martyrs in Germany, Switzerland, the Low Countries, France and Italy. Pantaleon even envisioned a third part to the martyrology that Foxe had started and he had continued, dealing with martyrs in Spain, Sicily, the Balkans, Greece, Hungary, Poland, Denmark and other Christian countries.[151]

Because of its international scope, because it drew on the martyrologies of Foxe, Crespin and Rabus, and because it was written in Latin rather than a vernacular language, Pantaleon's work allowed other European martyrologists to access material originally contained in books that they could not read. For example, Foxe was able to draw on Ludwig Rabus's German martyrology through Pantaleon's

---

[149] The account of Pantaleon in *Allgemeine deutsche Bibliographie*, 56 vols. (Leipzig, 1875–1912), XXV, pp. 128–31, still remains the standard source for his biographical information. On Pantaleon's translation of Sleidan's *Commentaries*, see Alexandra Kess, *Johann Sleidan and the Protestant Vision of History* (Aldershot, 2008), pp. 21–2.

[150] Hans Buscher's *Heinrich Pantaleon und sein Heldenbuch* (Basle, 1946) focuses almost exclusively on the *Prosopographia*, its contents and its printing history. Matthias Pohlig provides nuanced discussion of the *Prosopographia* and its relationship to Reformation historical writing but it says little about the martyrology or indeed Pantaleon's career and most of his writings. Matthias Pohlig, *Zwischen Gelehrsamkeit und konfessioneller Identitätsstiftung* (Tübingen, 2007), pp. 259–69.

[151] Pantaleon, *Martyrum historia*, fos. 3ᵛ–4ʳ.

work.[152] The drawback to Pantaleon's approach was that he was heavily dependent on what earlier martyrologists had written and he did little original research of his own. Pantaleon also made a conscious decision to eliminate lengthy documentation from his work, including the writings of the martyrs. He stated that he did this because he could not otherwise include the range of people and countries that he did without making the work too long to print.[153] Pantaleon and his work deserve much more study than they have received, partly because his *Martyrum historia* not only continued Foxe's *Rerum* but it became, in turn, an important source for the *Acts and Monuments*. Friendship and association with Pantaleon was yet one more way in which Foxe's exile linked the *Acts and Monuments* to continental historical scholarship.

Of course it was Mary Tudor who was ultimately responsible for Foxe's not undertaking the second part of his projected martyrology with Oporinus. Her death caused the English exiles to return from Switzerland to England with alacrity. Foxe himself was anxious to take wing and join the flock but, in the event, he had to wait and finish the *Rerum*. However, from at least the beginning of 1557, Foxe was casting an eye towards his eventual return. In January 1559 Oporinus printed a short Latin oration by Foxe, the *Germaniae ad Angliam de Restituta Evangelii Luce Gratulatio*, which took the form of an address by Germany to England in which Germany offered a great deal of advice on how the English state and Church should be run.[154] Almost the moment it came off the press, Foxe dispatched three copies of the work. The first, in a gesture that epitomises Foxe's enduring ties to the Swiss Reformers, was sent to Heinrich Bullinger; the other two, with an eye

---

[152] For examples of Foxe drawing on Rabus via Pantaleon, cf. Rabus, *Der Heyligen ausserwoehlten Gottes Zeugen, Bekennern und Martyrern ... Historien ...*, III, fos. 186ʳ–205ᵛ with Pantaleon, *Martyrum historia*, pp. 200–6 and 263–5 and *1570*, pp. 1066–70. Robert Kolb has mistakenly claimed, regarding Rabus's martyrology, that 'Foxe and Crespin probably could not read his German, and there is no indication that they used his volume as a source for their works.' Robert Kolb, *For All the Saints*, p. 82. However, Kolb cites Rabus as a source for Pantaleon's martyrology, apparently unaware of the extent to which Foxe drew on Pantaleon (ibid., p. 83, n. 57).

[153] Pantaleon, *Martyrum historia*, fo. 4ʳ. The fact that Pantaleon, working with established printers in one of the great European printing centres, felt that a work of under 400 pages was in danger of becoming too lengthy is another reminder of Day's determination and resourcefulness in printing the different editions of the *Acts and Monuments*, all of which approached or exceeded 2,000 pages.

[154] *Pace* John King, the *Gratulatio* is a work by Foxe, not 'a congratulatory address composed by partisans in Germany' (King, *Print Culture*, p. 78). For a discussion and translation of this work see John Wade, 'Thanksgiving from Germany in 1559: An Analysis of the Content, Sources and Style of John Foxe's *Germaniae ad Angliam Gratulatio*', in *John Foxe at Home and Abroad*, ed. David Loades (Aldershot, 1997), pp. 157–222.

to Foxe's future prospects, were sent to Elizabeth and to the duke of Norfolk.[155]

A major theme of the *Gratulatio* was that both Elizabeth and Norfolk had been preserved by providence during Mary's reign and were duty-bound to serve God now that they were in power. Foxe, being Foxe, was full of suggestions on exactly how this could be done.[156] But his gift of the book also served more practical purposes. Although he did not directly ask Norfolk for financial assistance, he clearly wanted not only to instruct the duke but to remind him that his worthy old tutor was out there. This time, Norfolk took the hint. In a letter dated 5 March the duke warmly greeted his former tutor and thanked him profusely for the *Gratulatio*.[157] Foxe's joy at receiving this encouraging epistle may have been somewhat tempered by the duke's confession that this was the first Latin letter that he had written in five years. But otherwise it was all that the martyrologist could have wished for. However, although Norfolk expressed the hope that he would see Foxe within a few days, it was actually over six months before the two were reunited. Although most of the English exiles were streaming back home, Foxe needed to stay in Basle to finish the *Rerum*. Sometime after the work was finished, in early September, Foxe and his family started on the long journey home.

Foxe almost certainly returned to England without much wealth to show for the years he had spent abroad, but nevertheless he returned with several important, if less tangible, prizes. The first was an international reputation, established by the two Latin martyrologies, as a scholar and an accomplished writer. The second consisted of connections, begun in Edward VI's reign and continued through his exile, with some of the leaders of the Elizabethan Church and state. The third was a mission, a goal that was to dominate his life completely for the next eleven years and one which he would never completely achieve. Foxe aspired to write a martyrology covering the late Middle Ages and the Reformation on both the continent and in Britain.

VII

Foxe must have arrived sometime in October, since the duke of Norfolk wrote to him, in a letter dated 30 October, from his house in Kenninghall, telling his former tutor that he would meet him shortly in London.[158] In the

---

[155] Foxe's dispatch of these copies is described in a letter to Heinrich Bullinger, which is now Zurich Zentralbibliothek MS F 62, fo. 411[r]. The letter is printed and translated in Wade, 'Thanksgiving', pp. 221–2.

[156] For a discussion of this see ibid., pp. 160–9.   [157] BL, Harley MS 417, fo. 102[r].

[158] Two copies of this letter survive: BL, Harley MS 417, fo. 115[v] and 118[r].

following month, John Day printed an octavo entitled *A frendly farewel.*[159] This work, edited by John Foxe, was one of the letters that Nicholas Ridley had written during his imprisonment in Mary's reign. However, what is of greatest interest about this work is a statement Foxe made in a letter to the reader, which deserves to be quoted in full:

> Amongest manye other worthy and sundrie histories and notable acts which we have in hande, and intende (by the grace of Christe oure Lorde), shortly to set abrode, of such as of late daies have ben persecuted, murthered and martyred for the trewe Gospell of Chrst, in Quene Maries raigne, Firste to begin with this litell treatis of Doct. Nicholas Ridley, late Byshoppe of London, thys shalbe to desire thee (gentle Reader) to accept it, and studiouslye to peruse it in the meane tyme, whyle the other Volumes be addressing, which we ar about, touching the full Historie, processe and examinations of all our blessed brethren, lately persecuted for rightousnes sake. Whiche histories whan they shal come to light, (I suppose) thou shalt see as horrible a slaughter of the Sainctes joyned with as much crueltie of some English hartes, as ever in any one realme before Christe, or after was sene. In the meane time because all thynge can not be done at once, and the Volumes be long, accept well in worth this litle (but pithie) worke of this forsaid Bishoppe, in expectation of greater thynges, which shall (perchaunce) more largely satisfie thy desire.[160]

This is one of the earliest examples of Day employing a tactic that he would use repeatedly to promote sales for the *Acts and Monuments* and other books: that of advertising forthcoming works in books on related topics. What was being promised in these comments was the first edition of Foxe's magnum opus, the *Acts and Monuments.*

The question is, how did Foxe and Day come to form a collaboration for such a mammoth project within a few weeks of Foxe's return to England? (It is worth observing that the phrase 'which we are about' would seem to indicate that the new work was already in progress.) It is, of course, quite likely that Foxe, immediately upon his return, began looking for someone who would print a new martyrological work. If this is the case, then it is another indication of Foxe's determination that the hastily finished first section of the *Rerum* would simply be a milestone on the path to further martyrological labours. But, even accepting that Foxe was endeavouring to find a printer, how did he decide upon Day as the person to execute this project?

---

[159] Nicholas Ridley, *A frendly farewel, which Master Doctor Ridley . . . did write*, ed. John Foxe (London, 1559), STC 21051. The title page is dated 10 November 1559.

[160] Ridley, *A frendly farewel*, unpaginated preface.

There is no direct evidence that Foxe and Day knew each other before 1559, but they certainly moved in the same circles and had mutual contacts. Foxe's patron, the duchess of Richmond, is known to have employed Day by 1550, and there are tantalising hints that Day might have been associated with Bale about this time.[161] Moreover, both Foxe and Day, as we have seen, had another common patron during Edward's reign: William Cecil. It is likely that, upon returning to England, Foxe communicated his plans to Cecil, and that Cecil put him in touch with Day. From Foxe's comment in the introduction to the *Frendly farewel*, it is clear that some decisions about the forthcoming martyrology had already been made. It was not to be the second part, dealing with continental martyrs, of Oporinus's planned two-volume martyrology; rather it was to focus on England. It was, however, intended from the outset to be a massive work. To what degree these decisions, including the choice of printing the work in English, reflected Foxe's original intentions and to what degree they were modifications made after consulting with Day, and probably Cecil, will never be known. It is very probable that Day would not have undertaken such a massive work without promises of financial support from Cecil. Yet even though Foxe and Day had, with remarkable speed and self-assurance, made plans to produce a major martyrology, they could not have realised just how long, arduous and costly (in more than the financial sense) this project would prove to be.

[161] See *PPP*, p. 24.

CHAPTER 4

The making of the first edition of the Acts and Monuments

I

When Foxe and Day promised 'Volumes ... touching the full Historie, processe, and examinations, of all our blessed brethren, lately persecuted for righteousnes sake' they did not specify what language these volumes would be written in.[1] At some point, we do not know when, the decision was made to produce the new work in English. This decision had important consequences for both the development and the reception of the work. Obviously this made the work potentially accessible to all those who could not read Latin and thus ensured that the intended audience for the work would be largely English. The decision, which today seems perfectly natural, indeed almost inevitable, did not seem so to Foxe. He was apparently concerned that his reputation as a writer would suffer. When he presented a copy of the first edition to Magdalen, his old college, his long inscription repeatedly apologises for presenting a work written in English rather than Latin, and he justifies this by saying that he was driven to do so in response to the needs of ordinary people.[2] Nor were these anxieties without foundation. Foxe would be remembered in the seventeenth century, most unjustly, as a writer illiterate in Latin.[3] It can be safely assumed that the decision to write the work in the vernacular was less than satisfactory to Foxe.

On the other hand, this probably fitted in with Day's plans rather well. A work printed in English could be expected to sell better, thereby increasing potential profits. At the same time, Reyner Wolfe held the monopoly on works printed in Latin; this was not an insurmountable obstacle but it was one that it was preferable to avoid. Most probably, however, the driving force behind the decision to print the work in the vernacular was William

[1] Ridley, *Frendly farewel*, unpaginated preface.   [2] Mozley, *John Foxe and his Book*, p. 136.
[3] Thomas Fuller, *The Church History of Britain*, ed. J. S. Brewer, 6 vols. (Oxford, 1845), IV, p. 391.

Cecil. Foxe's declaration to the fellows of Magdalen College that he was compelled to write the work in English in order to make it more accessible, if it is taken at face value, would indicate that it was the needs of propaganda, rather than of profit, that dictated this decision.

Cecil's role as the facilitator and sponsor of this edition was acknowledged by a woodcut capital 'C', which appeared at the beginning of Foxe's dedication of the work to Elizabeth (see Figure 1). The image shows an enthroned Elizabeth with three men in attendance. The three figures are readily identifiable as, from front to back, William Cecil, John Foxe and

Figure 1 Initial 'C' from John Foxe's *Acts and Monuments* (1570), sig. *1^r. By kind permission of the Dean and Chapter of York Minster.

John Day.[4] This remarkable visual acknowledgement of his role as patron
leaves no doubt of Cecil's paramount importance as facilitator and patron of
this book. No one would have been in a better position to insist that the
book be written in English.

The printing of the work in the vernacular served to make a distinct break
with Foxe's previous martyrologies. A resolution was also made that the new
English martyrology would not merely be a continuation of the old, but
would be based on new types of sources, requiring further extensive research
on the part of Foxe. It was the decision to extend the factual foundations of
the work and the research required to do this that meant that, although the
new martyrology had been announced in November 1559, it would not be
printed until March 1563.

II

During this time Foxe held no living within the English Church, although
he had been ordained as a priest on 25 January 1560, soon after his return to
England.[5] Foxe's biographer, and a number of writers following him, have
attributed Foxe's lack of preferment to his scruples about vestments and an
unwillingness to conform.[6] This explanation really does not hold water. For
one thing, vestments were hardly an issue in the first years of Elizabeth's
reign. Later anti-vestiarian leaders, such as Laurence Humphrey and
Thomas Sampson, gained rapid preferment in the Elizabethan Church.
Moreover, Foxe appears to have been offered the deanship of Christ
Church, Oxford; certainly he was congratulated on this new position in a
letter Laurence Humphrey wrote to him on 13 August 1560.[7] Humphrey,
who was Lady Margaret reader at the time and soon to be made president of
Magdalen, is unlikely to have been misinformed about this. The only
reasonable conclusion is that Foxe was offered it and turned it down. If
this is true, it is another indication of Foxe's determination to concentrate
on preparing the first edition of what would become the *Acts and
Monuments*.

Foxe had the luxury of being able to turn down this post, despite the fact
that he had a wife and children to support, because of the patronage of his
former pupil, Thomas Howard, now the fourth duke of Norfolk. For about

---

[4] For the evidence supporting these identifications see Evenden and Freeman, 'John Foxe, John Day
and the Printing of the "Book of Martyrs"', pp. 27–9, 31 and 33.
[5] Mozley, *John Foxe and his Book*, p. 63.   [6] Ibid.   [7] BL, Harley MS 417, fo. 133ʳ.

a year after his return from exile Foxe lived at Norfolk's London house, just inside Aldgate. Foxe also resided there from August 1562 until he moved to his own house in St Giles Cripplegate at the end of the decade. Meanwhile, in the autumn of 1560, Foxe went to Norwich, where he and his family lived with his friend John Parkhurst, now bishop of the diocese.[8] This trip was not made lightly. Agnes Foxe was in an advanced stage of pregnancy at the time of the journey and Foxe's eldest son, Samuel, would be born in the episcopal palace on 31 December 1560. Undoubtedly Foxe assisted Parkhurst by spreading the Gospel in the diocese. One reason for the trip was that Foxe could act as a reliable preacher in a diocese where there was a shortage of trained clergy who were doctrinally sound. A number of letters written to Foxe during this period mention his preaching activity.[9] However, the major purpose of the trip was probably to conduct research for the *Acts and Monuments* in this part of the realm. Certainly in the 1563 edition Foxe would make use of archival sources, particularly the episcopal records for the diocese. Foxe also took advantage of his preaching tours to conduct interviews with victims of past persecutions and their families.

Meanwhile, printing of the first edition had started in the autumn of 1561.[10] We do not know if Foxe was in Day's printing house when the printing began, although this seems very probable; in fact, it was probably Foxe's absence, while doing research in Norwich, that delayed the printing of the volume. Foxe had certainly returned to Day's business premises by 24 August 1562, when a letter was sent to him there.[11] In the meantime Foxe had left his family in the care of Parkhurst and they remained until after the first edition had been printed.

Foxe's research in the diocese of Norwich provides insight into the sources he would cultivate for his first edition – sources which made the new edition unlike his Latin martyrologies and at the same time also unlike other continental martyrologies. One major difference was in Foxe's increasing reliance on information derived from local informants. Most of

---

[8] William Winthrop, a godly London clothworker, wrote to Foxe in Norwich on 18 November 1560. Winthrop begged for Foxe's assistance in obtaining preferment for some worthy ministers in Essex: an interesting indication that Foxe was presumed to have some influence with Edmund Grindal, who was now bishop of London (BL, Harley MS 416, fo. 106ʳ). Since Parkhurst was only consecrated bishop in September of that year it is unlikely that Foxe journeyed up to his palace prior to the autumn.

[9] Ibid., fos. 106ʳ and 170ʳ.

[10] This is based on a statement Foxe made in a preface to the work, 'Ad Doctum Lectorem', that the work took eighteen months to print (*1563*, sig. B3ᵛ). This statement will be discussed in more detail further on.

[11] We know this from a letter addressed to Foxe on that date, 'inaedibus Johannis Daii typographi' (BL, Harley MS 416, fo. 173ʳ⁻ᵛ).

the major Protestant martyrologists (Haemstede is the major exception to this) lived and worked in places that were fairly distant from the events and people they described. They tended to rely very heavily on accounts written by the martyrs themselves or their sympathisers. While preparing the 1563 edition, Foxe had the advantage of actually being in places where the persecution had taken place and being able to interview the friends and families of the victims. This enabled him to derive information from groups of people generally not available to other martyrologists: to take one obvious example, people who were illiterate and who would not be able to send accounts of events.

A particularly instructive example of the painstaking effort Foxe put into obtaining information from such people occurs in the case of his handling of a Protestant named John Cooper who was executed for sedition in Mary's reign. Foxe heard the story of Cooper from two youths – one of whom was almost certainly a member of Cooper's family. Apparently Foxe heard about the youths and their story from two other Suffolk ministers, John Kelke and John Walker, and he was with Thomas Sutton, a Suffolk minister, and William Punt, a former Marian exile and another denizen of Suffolk, when he interviewed them.[12] Foxe included this story in the 1563 edition; almost immediately after it was printed, aspects of the story were challenged. Foxe sent Punt back to verify the story with Kelke, Walker and Sutton. In addition, Punt and Sutton 'with another honest man' went to the two youths who had first related the story and they swore to its accuracy. However, just to make sure, Punt also brought Cooper's wife and children to Ipswich to make a statement before William Cavendish, a JP from the area, and he promised to send that statement to Foxe in London 'with spede'.[13] This was hardly the end of the controversy surrounding Cooper's death, but for our purposes what is instructive about this episode is the light that it casts on Foxe's careful gleaning of sheaves of information for his magnum opus. There were few, if any, precedents in English historical writing for this meticulous assembling and utilisation of first-hand testimony; such sources would contribute greatly to the apparent verisimilitude of Foxe's narrative.

While working in Norwich, Foxe also made extensive use of archival sources. Once again, Foxe had not used such material in his Latin martyrologies, and once again his reliance on it distinguished his martyrology from

---

[12] For all of this see Thomas S. Freeman, 'Fate, Faction, and Fiction in Foxe's *Book of Martyrs*', *Historical Journal*, 43 (2000), pp. 601–7.

[13] Ibid., pp. 605–7.

that of his Protestant counterparts on the continent. Admittedly, unlike Haemstede, who was a fugitive, or Crespin, who was in exile, Foxe had the opportunity to visit the archives and could rely on the cooperation of their keepers and, more importantly, those in high office. For example, a letter survives, which is unfortunately undated but which must have preceded the 1563 edition, in which Foxe requests the assistance of both Matthew Parker and Edmund Grindal in obtaining an official copy of the disputations Ridley, Cranmer and Latimer held at Oxford in 1554.[14] (This is the first surviving sign of what would become a close working relationship between Day and Parker and a close, if sometimes fraught, relationship between Foxe and the archbishop.) Foxe was keenly aware of the probative value of these archival materials. In an introduction to the 1563 edition, written 'Ad Doctum Lectorem', Foxe asserted that one sign that his history was more accurate than traditional hagiographies was that its 'whole cloth was drawn and woven together from the archives and registers of the bishops themselves'.[15] Foxe certainly took advantage of his trip to Norfolk to gather diocesan records; probably the most important of these is a court book for heresy trials in the diocese between 1428 and 1431.[16] Foxe's printing of this material, much of which no longer survives, was the first official record of a pre-Reformation heresy trial printed in English. But Foxe also made considerable use of court books and diocesan records for later heresy trials in the area.[17]

Undoubtedly with the active cooperation of Edmund Grindal, Foxe began systematic research into the London episcopal archives. Interestingly, Foxe began with the Marian period and worked backwards, being forced by lack of time to conclude his researches in the early English Reformation.[18] In the next edition he would work backwards in the London registers to the episcopate of William Courtenay in the late fourteenth century. The abrupt termination of

---

[14] BL, Additional MS 19400, fo. 97^r.

[15] 'tota textura ex ipsis Episcoporum Archivis atque Registris . . . hausta et conflata' (*1563*, sig. B3^v).

[16] What remains of this court book is now Westminster Diocesan Archives, MS B.2, pp. 205–362. Foxe printed material from this court book in the 1563 edition, pp. 348–58. Although we are not certain how Foxe acquired this manuscript, the date when he used it, together with the fact that it was from Norwich, point to his having obtained it on this trip. What survives of this court book has been printed as *Heresy Trials in the Diocese of Norwich, 1428–31*, ed. Norman P. Tanner, Camden 4th series, 20 (1977).

[17] BL, Harley MS 421, fos. 140^r–217^v consists entirely of transcriptions made from no longer extant court books covering heresy prosecutions in the diocese of Norwich during Mary's reign. These copies are for the most part not in Foxe's handwriting. It is possible that he had someone transcribe these records for him after he uncovered them; it is also possible that the transcriptions were made, for purposes of legibility, from Foxe's notes, when the volume was printed. In either case, however, the notes were made before the 1563 edition was printed and it is virtually certain that they were among the fruits of Foxe's stay while he was in the diocese.

[18] In the 1563 edition virtually the first thing printed from the London registers (and remember, because Foxe is working in reverse order, this would have marked the end of his researches) was a list of people

Foxe's work on the London registers, when he reached the period around 1527, demonstrates not only that he was working deliberately backwards in time, but also that his researches in these records were ongoing as the 1563 edition was being printed. It seems safe to assume that Foxe began work on these records after he returned from his sojourn in Norwich. This raises the question: did Foxe get the idea of including archival material after examining the episcopal records in Norwich? It is perhaps noteworthy that of the three sets of episcopal archives that Foxe seems to have used in the 1563 edition – i.e., records from the dioceses of Norwich, London, and Coventry and Lichfield – the latter two came into Foxe's hands at a very late stage.

In fact, only a small amount of material came to Foxe from Coventry and Lichfield and this undoubtedly reached him through his contacts in the diocese. His acquisition of this material is especially interesting as it is manifestly the product of directed investigation. In the *Rerum*, Foxe had a brief account of the wife of a former mayor of Coventry named Smith who was burned along with six other people in a ditch just outside the walls of Coventry.[19] He almost certainly acquired this information from oral sources – very probably his wife or his wife's family, as they were from the city. This provenance for the story accounts for Foxe initially dating the episode to 1490 – three decades out. In the text of the 1563 edition Foxe included a revised and expanded account of this incident. He named the mayor and the sheriffs at the beginning of his account and this, along with his more correct dating of the incident to 1520, suggests that he consulted a mayoral list or city annal, although the detail in his account strongly suggests that he obtained further information from local informants as well.[20]

Later, in an appendix to the 1563 edition, Foxe included a transcription, translated into English, of Lollard abjurations from the years 1486–8. This material was taken from the register of Bishop John Hales. It is virtually

who had abjured in a sweeping prosecution of heresy in the diocese of London, which began in 1527 (*1563*, pp. 418–20). In the next edition, however, Foxe not only listed these individuals, he also printed the charges against them, as well as background information – for example, age, vocation, place of residence, etc. – which the records provided (*1570*, p. 1184). At the same time, the list in the 1570 edition contained a number of names that Foxe apparently overlooked in his haste. The 1563 list included the names of people who were prosecuted and abjured much later, in 1541, and these names were placed in the proper chronological order in the second edition (*1570*, pp. 1378–80). Similarly, Foxe first printed documents from Bishop Tunstall's records pertaining to Humphrey Monmouth, a London alderman, who was arrested for heresy in 1528, in the appendix to the 1563 edition, while in the next edition these documents were incorporated into the main text (*1563*, pp. 1737–8 and *1570*, pp. 1133–4).

[19] Foxe, *Rerum*, pp. 116–17.

[20] *1563*, p. 420. In the 1570 edition Foxe cited a 'Mother Halle' as his source; she may well have been his source back in 1563 (*1570*, p. 1107).

inconceivable that Foxe actually visited Coventry to consult the register (for one thing, he would not have left Day's printing house on the eve of the book's completion). It is much more likely that transcripts of sections of the register were sent to Foxe from the city. (It is worth noting that Thomas Bentham, the bishop of the diocese, and Thomas Lever, the archdeacon of Coventry, were close personal friends of Foxe.) It would seem, therefore, that Foxe alerted them to the existence of trials of Lollards in the diocese in the past and asked them to uncover the relevant records. The fact that the material was not printed until the end of the book indicates that Foxe did not obtain it until the printing of the edition was well underway. Foxe's account, in his first edition, of the Coventry Lollards thus provides an excellent example of how he conducted his research for this first edition. It is noteworthy that the only episcopal records that Foxe consulted for the first edition were either from places where he resided – i.e., London and Norwich – or, in the case of Coventry, where he was able to rely on close friends. In future editions Foxe's use of archival materials, aided significantly by a larger network of friends and associates, would increase tremendously.

III

There was another respect in which the first edition of the *Acts and Monuments* differed from its predecessors: it drew on continental Protestant martyrologies. It is interesting that Foxe's martyrologies – English and Latin – expanded in two different directions: both chronologically, in covering an increasingly larger scope of time, but also geographically, in increasingly covering the True Church beyond the British Isles. One particular reason for this growing engagement with these continental martyrologies stemmed from Foxe's original commitment to undertake a second volume of the *Rerum*. Given that he embarked on the *Acts and Monuments* almost immediately upon his return to England, any assurances that he would have given to Oporinus about completing the second volume were either wildly optimistic or less than completely sincere. Oporinus, however, was in earnest about finishing this project. On 1 December 1562 he wrote to Foxe, asking him if he had any intention of actually writing the second volume.[21]

---

[21] Pantaleon, *Martyrum historia*, fo. 3ᵛ. In the preface to the second volume, Pantaleon, who would actually produce it, wrote that he only agreed to do so because 'multique pii et docti viri una cum Bibliopolis partum secundam efflagitarent' (A copy of Pantaleon's letter is BL, Harley MS 417, fo. 108ᵛ).

As we have seen, Oporinus then delegated the task to Heinrich Pantaleon. This, however, appears to have been done with Foxe's full knowledge and consent. First of all, Pantaleon insisted that he was writing his martyrology with the blessing of 'my singular good friend, Master Foxe'.[22] More decisively, although Pantaleon's martyrology, the *Martyrum historia*, was printed shortly after the first edition of the *Acts and Monuments*, Foxe unmistakably borrows accounts from Pantaleon's work.[23] This obviously would not have been possible had Pantaleon not sent a copy of his work to Foxe in advance.

Foxe also drew on a number of works by the Genevan martyrologist Jean Crespin. The most accessible of these, at least to Foxe, was Crespin's first Latin martyrology, the *Actiones et monumenta martyrum* (very obviously the title of Foxe's first English martyrology seems to have been taken from Crespin).[24] Among the accounts of early modern martyrs that Foxe undeniably took from this edition are those of Jean Castellane, Peter Spengler and Leonard Keyser.[25] More interesting was Foxe's reprinting part of Jean Crespin's account of the massacres of Waldensians in Provence.[26] For reasons that will be discussed further on, only part of this work (87 out of 135 pages) was printed in the first edition of the *Acts and Monuments*. Nevertheless, Foxe's interest in including this work in his martyrology is striking, particularly since it was printed in French, a language that Foxe did not read. This means that arrangements had to be made for someone to translate this work. Foxe would draw much more extensively on the martyrologies of both Crespin and Pantaleon in future editions, but in the 1563 edition he had already started to utilise these sources.

Foxe also consulted previously printed works for use in this edition. In some cases these were works that Foxe had already known of but was unable to obtain during his exile, such as William Thorpe's account of his

---

[22] 'D. Foxii amici mei singularis' (Pantaleon, *Martyrum historia*, fo. 3ᵛ).
[23] The colophon of the first edition has a date of 20 March 1563. The dedicatory epistle to Pantaleon's *Martyrum historia* is dated 13 April 1563. Some of Foxe's account of Savonarola in the 1563 edition – from his preaching in Florence in 1496 through to his execution on 23 May 1497 – follows Pantaleon's account quite closely. Cf. Pantaleon, *Martyrum historia*, pp. 33–5 with *1563*, pp. 371–3. Two accounts, originally from Oecolampadius, of the martyrdom of Lutheran ministers, are reprinted word-for-word from Pantaleon. Cf. *Martyrum historia*, pp. 46–8 and 51–4 with *1563*, pp. 432–5. Similarly, Foxe's account of Simon Grynaeus's near arrest in Speyer in 1529 is taken virtually word-for-word from Pantaleon. Cf. *Martyrum historia*, pp. 71–2 with *1563*, pp. 441–2.
[24] Jean Crespin, *Actiones et monumenta martyrum* (Geneva, 1560).
[25] Cf. ibid., fos. 44ʳ–6ʳ, 47ᵛ–9ᵛ, 55ʳ⁻ᵛ with *1563*, pp. 428–32 and 437–8.
[26] Jean Crespin, *Histoire memorable de la persecution et saccagement du peuple de Merindol et Cabrieres et autre circonvoisins, appelez Vaudois* (Geneva, 1555).

examinations.[27] A particularly interesting example of this is Bale's account of Sir John Oldcastle's examinations. Foxe clearly knew of this work while he was in exile; the *Rerum* includes a picture of Oldcastle, which is clearly based on the title page of Bale's treatise.[28] However, Foxe did not have the treatise to hand, as his account of Oldcastle is once again a reprinting of Bale's notes and extracts from Fabian's chronicle.[29] In at least one case Foxe was apparently able to draw on John Day's stock. There is only one new account of a Scottish martyr in the first edition: it describes the martyrdom of George Wishart. It was the complete reprinting of a relation of Wisehart's trial and burning that had been appended to the only edition of Sir David Lindsay's *The tragical death of David Beaton*.[30] John Day had printed this work and it is reasonable to assume that Foxe, who had not even mentioned Wishart in his Latin editions, obtained this work from Day.

While Foxe was researching the *Acts and Monuments*, he and Day together managed to produce one or two works (aside from Ridley's *Frendly farewel*) generally related to the first edition. One of these was a work printed anonymously in September 1560: *A Solemne Contestation of Divers Popes*.[31] This is a first-person narration putatively delivered by the papal Antichrist, describing the extent of his power and the nefarious means by which he obtained it. The purposes behind the work are not easy to ascertain. One possibility is that Foxe initially planned to begin the 1563 edition with Wyclif and that this was his nod to the early eras of Church history. If this was the case, he subsequently revised his plans for the scope of the *Acts and Monuments*, as we shall see. Some time during the years 1560–4, Foxe and Day also printed the *Syllogisticon* – a series of tables outlining arguments over the Eucharist.[32] It is quite likely that this was an outgrowth of the work Foxe was doing on the *Acts and Monuments* itself.

---

[27] In the *Commentarii* and the *Rerum* all that Foxe was able to print from these was a summary, which John Bale had made in the *FZ*. Cf. *FZ* fos. 105ᵛ–10ᵛ with *Comm.*, fos. 118ʳ–56ᵛ and *Rerum*, pp. 80–96. In the 1563 edition for the first time Foxe reprinted the entire work. Cf. *The examinacion of Master William Thorpe*, ed. William Tyndale [?] or George Constantine [?] (Antwerp, 1530), STC 24045, sigs. A6ᵛ–H2ʳ with *1563*, pp. 144–71.

[28] Foxe, *Rerum*, p. 97.

[29] Cf. Foxe, *Rerum*, pp. 98–107 with *FZ*, fos. 101ᵛ–5ᵛ and Robert Fabian, *The Chronicle of Fabian* (London, 1559), STC 10664, pp. 390 and 389 [recte 397].

[30] Cf. *1563*, pp. 648–54 with David Lindsay, *The tragical death of David Beaton* . . . (London, 1548?), STC 15683, sigs. C7ᵛ–F6ʳ.

[31] *A Solemne Contestation of Divers Popes* (London, 1560), STC 20114. For the arguments that this work was actually written by John Foxe see Thomas S. Freeman, 'A Solemne Contestation of Divers Popes: A Work by John Foxe?', *English Language Notes*, 31 (1994), pp. 35–42.

[32] John Foxe, *Syllogisticon hoc est argumenta, seu probationes & resolutiones* (London, 1563), STC 11249. The work is undated and the only indication of when it was printed is a dedication to John Harding, the principal of Brasenose. Harding was principal until January 1565.

IV

Apart from producing the minor works that Foxe authored, John Day spent the period between Elizabeth's accession and the autumn of 1561, when he probably started printing the *Acts and Monuments*, securing the patents that would be the financial pillar for printing Foxe's magnum opus. Unfortunately the letters patent granting Day a monopoly over the metrical psalms in English and the English primer have not survived. However, they were renewed in 1567 and patents normally ran for seven or ten years. Since it is extremely unlikely that he received these patents under Mary, it is very probable that he received his patent in 1560, as the preparations for printing the 'Book of Martyrs' were well underway. Day could only have secured these lucrative patents through the intervention of a powerful patron. Almost certainly this was Cecil.

However, at no time could he rest on his laurels. His receipt of patronage, which was the keystone of his printing empire, depended on his continually demonstrating his technical mastery. Day seized the opportunity to do this with the production of William Cunningham's *Cosmographical glasse*. This was protected by Day's first known Elizabethan patent.[33] This patent was interestingly open-ended, in that it covered not only Cunningham's work but also all new works printed at Day's expense. Day seized the opportunity to produce a visual masterpiece. It contained numerous impressive pictures and it also marked the first appearance in England of a double-pica italic type by the renowned typographer François Guyot.[34] In printing, as in so much else in life, it costs money to attain quality and Day's outlay for this was so generous that even Cunningham was grateful for the 'charges the printer hath sustained ... that shalbe evident conferring [comparing] his beautiful Pictures & letters, with suche workes, as herto hath bene pub-lished'.[35] Day was not recompensed through sales of the book and it is quite possible that he never expected to be.

Significantly, the book was dedicated to William Cecil and it is quite possible that the printing of this book was designed to serve two related purposes: the first was to demonstrate to Cecil, and to anyone else, Day's virtually unrivalled – in England – technical mastery. This in turn might have provided sufficient assurance to Cecil that Day was indeed the man to carry out important printing assignments and thus resulted in Day's obtain-ing the crucial patents for the primers and the metrical psalms afterwards.[36]

---

[33] TNA, 1 Eliz., part 1, m.24.   [34] *PPP*, p. 59.
[35] Cunningham, *Cosmographical glasse*, sig. A6ᵛ.   [36] See *PPP*, pp. 59–61.

Still concerned to impress the powers that be, Day celebrated his patent by printing a good-quality edition of the metrical psalms. (In later years, when he had less to prove, Day would save money and effort by letting these standards slip in the printing of these steady sellers.[37]) During the period between his obtaining the patents and the start of printing the 'Book of Martyrs', Day continued to churn out these reliable pillars of his prosperity. Afterwards, when his presses were fully occupied in printing Foxe's mammoth work, he would have surely farmed the work out in order to secure an income and to ensure a steady supply of available copies of these works; after all, demand for primers and metrical psalms was not going to cease during the lengthy period when Foxe's book was being printed.

It is doubtful that Day fully anticipated how long Foxe would take in researching his martyrology. In 1560 Day would feel confident that he would have time to print Thomas Becon's *Reliques of Rome* (a book of around 260 octavo pages), and to print the first volume of his monumental folio collection of Becon's writings.[38] (The entire production of Becon's works provides another dramatic example of Day printing a work so lavish that it simply could not have made a profit. This may have stemmed partly from a desire to impress the great and the good but it also owed something to Day's friendship with Thomas Becon.[39]) The following year Day still felt he had enough time to print Becon's *Sick Man's Salve* (which ran to in excess of 500 pages in octavo).

However, Day was also turning down work in the years 1560–1. He was also putting major projects on hold; the Becon collection was stalled following the printing of volume 1 and Day ceased work on another book, the *Certaine notes set in foure and three parts*, which would, in the event, not be printed until 1565. During the first half of the 1560s, Day lost quite a bit of business, especially in musical works, because of his commitment to printing the *Acts and Monuments*.[40] All of this meant that he would have been naturally anxious to begin work on Foxe's martyrology, as the incomplete work was a sword of Damocles hanging over his head. The printer was losing money by having to delay or turn down other projects while he was waiting to cast copy. At the same time, he had to endure a massive logistical headache in trying to

---

[37] See Oastler, *John Day*, pp. 23–5.
[38] The conclusion to volume 1 was complicated by a late insertion, which may have been done at a later date. See *PPP*, pp. 71–2 for details.
[39] Significantly, Day guaranteed Thomas Becon's payment of first fruits in 1563, the only case where Day did this for any clergy. Brett Usher, 'Backing Protestantism'.
[40] See *PPP*, pp. 72–3.

assemble the necessary supplies and staff for all his projects and the lengthy period of uncertainty was only aggravating it.

Day may also have been under pressure from Cecil to produce the first edition of the *Acts and Monuments*. Certainly Foxe came to feel the pressure and complained about it in a preface to the 1563 edition:

But indeed even now I hear that there is also muttering by some who say that they are seized by long expectation until this [book] – our *Golden Legend* as they call it – is set forth . . . In this matter we have indeed worked to the best of our ability, we have, I hope, done our duty, if not swiftly enough in regards to time . . . we certainly acted more prematurely than was fitting for a book of such size and importance.[41]

It is interesting to observe that it was apparently not only the Catholics that were referring to this work as a counterpart to the *Golden Legend* (*Legenda Aurea*, by Jacobus de Voragine). But what is more important is that this comment shows that there were people who were anxiously awaiting Foxe's work and who were putting pressure on the martyrologist, and presumably the printer, to get the job done. Foxe was clearly unhappy and, as we shall see, not without cause, about this rush to press, whatever its source.

V

The combination of delay and then frenetic speed in producing the first edition of the *Acts and Monuments* destabilised the format of the work and created additional problems in printing it. For one thing, Day had decided, in an apparent moment of caution, not to commission any of the pictures until the printing of the work was just about to begin. This can be seen, first of all, in the fact that two of the pictures must have been created in 1562. One of these pictures, a woodcut portrait of Day, which would be included at the end of the *Acts and Monuments* (see Figure 2), is dated 1562. Another, a picture of Latimer preaching before Edward VI, was almost certainly intended for the *Acts and Monuments*, where it would appear, but in the meantime Day also used it in a 1562 edition of Latimer's sermons.[42]

[41] 'Quin et iam nunc mussitari etiam anonnullis audio, qui longa sese tenere dicant expectatione, quad haec tandem (Legenda nostra ut appellant Aurea) evulganda sit . . . Egimus in hac quidem re pro viril nostra, egimus spero et pro officio, si non satis pro temporis modo expedite . . . certe maturatius egimus, quam tanti momenti et magnitudinis negotio conveniebat'. *1563*, sig. B3ʳ⁻ᵛ.

[42] Hugh Latimer, *27 sermons preached by the rught Reverende father in God and constant martir . . . Hugh Latimer* (London, 1562), STC 15276. This image appears as a tip-in, usually at the front of the volume. It needed to be folded at least twice to fit within the book. The picture was reprinted in the 1563 edition of the 'Book of Martyrs' on p. 1353.

Figure 2 Portrait of John Day from John Foxe's *Acts and Monuments* (1570), sig. 4U4ᵛ. By kind permission of the Dean and Chapter of York Minster.

The result of this was that the opening portions of the *Acts and Monuments* were sparsely illustrated because there was simply not enough time to prepare so many woodcuts for portions of the book that were being printed imminently. It also meant that the work, being done in haste, was being produced somewhat sloppily. The first two illustrations (both for Book 1 of the 1563 edition) were paste-ins, in itself an ad hoc arrangement, and moreover the woodcuts were larger than the space allotted for them. The final illustration in Book 1, depicting the poisoning of King John, was a tip-in. Admittedly, this may well be due to the chaos involved in a reprinting of the last portion of Book 1, which will be discussed shortly. But in either case, whenever the picture of King John's murder was actually made, tipping it in was clearly a strategy to buy time. The next illustration, appearing towards the beginning of Book 2, showing Wyclif's bones being posthumously burned and scattered, was initially imposed incorrectly.[43] The illustration that follows this, over 170 pages into the book, of the burning of William Sawtre, is a small woodcut, which nevertheless is larger than the single column width allotted to it. After this the situation appears to stabilise and fewer mistakes are in evidence. Nevertheless, Day's apparent prudence in not committing himself to the expense of woodcuts, together with the haste in printing the volume, marred the presentational value of these early illustrations. This was one of a number of problems (many of them caused by haste) that both Foxe and Day would seek to correct in a subsequent edition.

Whether it was due to pressure from Cecil or Day or both, Foxe ended up having to abandon his research so that the printing of the volume could commence. Foxe states that 'scarcely eighteen full months were given to us for preparing material, for collecting and compiling, for comparing copies, for reading manuscripts, for rewriting transcripts, for correcting type, for arranging the history in a balanced manner and order etc.'[44] From this description, it would appear that Foxe is referring to the process of casting off as well as to the actual printing of the volume. Since the printing of the first edition was completed in March 1563, it would appear that the initial casting off of the volume began in the autumn of 1561. It is hard to say when the printing itself started, partly because we do not know how many presses Day had or the size of the print run for this edition, but, most particularly, because the compilation and translation were ongoing, even after the printing process had begun.

The confusion, and the haste that caused it, are perfectly preserved in Foxe's account in this edition of the persecution of the Waldensians in Provence, which culminated in the notorious massacres at Mérindol and Cabrières. Work began on printing an accurate translation of Crespin's *Histoire memorable*. However, about two-thirds of the way through, this

---

[43] The details of this are described in our full discussion of the illustrations in Chapter 6.

[44] 'cum a nobis vix integros datos esse menses octodecim praeparandae materiae, comportandis componendisque rebus, conferendis examplaribus, lectitandis codicibus, rescribendis his quae scripto mandata errant, castigandis formularis, concinnandae historiae et in ordinem redigendae etc.' (*1563*, sig. B3ᵛ).

translation was abandoned and the account of the massacres was completed with a much briefer narrative of these events, taken from an English translation of Johann Sleidan's *Commentaries*, which had been printed by Day in the previous year.[45] In the next edition of the *Acts and Monuments* Foxe would entirely omit the Sleidan translation and instead base his account on translations of the *Histoire memorable* and Pantaleon's martyrology.[46] The only conceivable reason for not completing the translation from Crespin in the first edition was that it was taking too long and the printing had reached the stage where the text concerning the massacres needed to be completed. At this point it was quicker and easier to print Sleidan's already translated text than to wait for the Crespin translation to be finished and run the risk of dead time in the printing house. Like an onrushing avalanche, the printing swept ongoing work, such as the Crespin translation and the transcription of the London registers, before it.

The fact that the printing process was taking place while information from different types of sources was continuing to arrive greatly intensified the complexity of Day's task. Throughout the edition Day had to employ a number of ad hoc tactics to keep the volume in some form of coherent order. Most of the problems that arose during printing stemmed from one of two causes. The first entailed simple errors in casting off. These could be rectified in a number of different ways. It is possible that, on occasion, the compositor shifted to a smaller typeface to increase the amount of text on a page.[47] However, caution is called for on this point, as there are a number of different reasons why compositors would change typeface. Another expedient was simply to widen the columns on a page in order to fit in more words. A particular egregious example of this occurs on page 1500 (see Figure 3).[48]

---

[45] Cf. *1563*, pp. 628–46 with Crespin, *Histoire memorable*, sigs. 3ᵛ–4ᵛ and pp. 1–41 and 66–87, and *1563*, pp. 646–8 with Johann Sleidan, *A famouse cronicle of our time, called Sleidanes Comantaires*, trans. John Daus (London, 1560), STC 19848, fos. 219ʳ–20ᵛ.

[46] Cf. *1570*, pp. 1075–86 with Crespin, *Histoire memorable*, pp. 1–121 and Pantaleon's *Martyrum historia*, pp. 111–13 and 142–5.

[47] See, for example, the letter by John Careless in *LM*, pp. 560–4 (cf. cast-off markings on ECL, MS 262, fos. 58ᵛ–9ᵛ and 53ʳ⁻ᵛ).

[48] King argues – although in an apparent typographical error he describes the excessively wide columns on p. 1500 (sig. 3Rr6ᵛ) as being 'excessively narrow' – that this expedient was utilised to allow Foxe 'to substitute a lengthier version of Thomas Cranmer's rescinding of his recantation' (King, *Print Culture*, p. 97). However, a closer examination of this material undermines this assertion, since Cranmer's oration runs on to the next page (p. 1501), which casts doubt on the idea that these changes occurred as a result of late acquisition of the document. Rather, it appears that the compositors were slightly off in their calculations for the end of the gathering (or the person calculating the casting off had made a mathematical error) and they had to make adjustments as best they could.

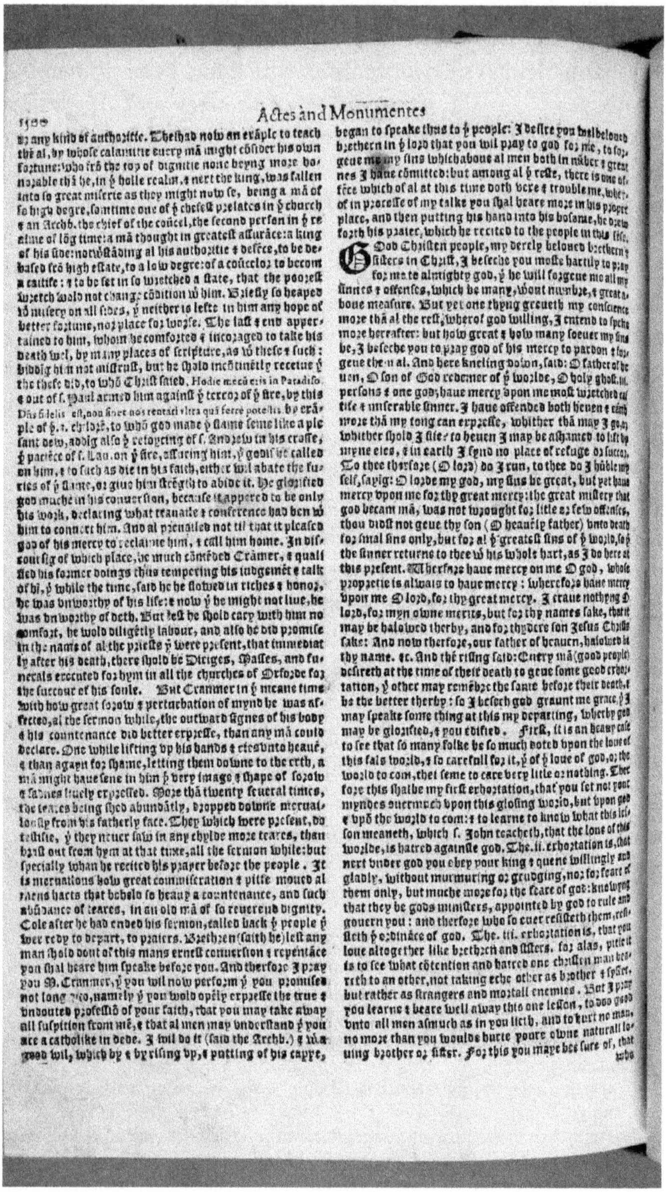

Figure 3 John Foxe, *Acts and Monuments* (1563), p. 1500. Courtesy of Lambeth Palace Library. Note the lack of indentation to fit more words onto the page. These columns are about 9 cm in width; normally columns in the 1563 edition are 7 cm.

An even greater challenge was created by Foxe's continual acquisition of material during the printing process. In such cases, Day essentially had four options. The first was to ignore the new material, and in fact, although this may indeed have happened on occasion, in general this option ran counter to Foxe's editorial principles. Two other options were to put the new material into an appendix or to include it in the work out of chronological order and to rely on cross-referencing to guide the reader. Increasingly in later editions Day would rely on both of these devices. However, in the first edition he seems to have preferred, when possible, to rely on a fourth option. This was to interpolate the late material into the text through the insertion of extra sheets or gatherings. The obvious challenge here was to avoid as much as possible disrupting the pagination of the book. The additional sheets would usually be marked with letters and/or additional symbols (most often an asterisk), to indicate to both the compositor, and later the binder, where the additional sheets were to be included. At the same time, the reader was usually alerted to the changes by symbols, such as parentheses, to indicate the revised pagination.

A good example of this occurs in the first edition in correspondence between Edward VI and his Privy Council, on the one hand, and the King's sister Mary, on the other, concerning her lack of conformity to recent changes in religion. As King has observed, 'this material has the appearance of a cache of recently discovered documents that the compiler felt concerned to include out of chronological order'.[49] Most of this correspondence was printed on an inserted gathering, which was placed between sigs. 2Kk6ᵛ (p. 888) and 2Llrʳ (p. 889), at the end of the fourth section. (The additional pages were numbered: 877–88, with each number encased in parentheses.) Clearly the renumbered gathering was, in this case, a solution for dealing with the problem of incorporating material after the relevant section had already been printed.[50]

However, the delayed acquisition of material was not the only reason for such interpolations. For example, there is another major interpolation of documents, which were inserted between sigs. 3Vv6ᵛ (p. 1536) and 3Xx1ʳ (p. 1537). Unlike the correspondence between Mary and her brother, the

---

[49] Ibid., p. 97.

[50] We agree with King that the insertion of material was caused by the untimely acquisition of these documents. Where we would disagree is over his insistence that a change in typeface from that on the 2Kk gathering – and that in the inserted material, beginning on sig. *2Kkl ʳ – was caused by a need to save space in order to incorporate the documents, and at the same time end the section at the close of a gathering. The change in typeface probably stemmed from the new gathering being printed by a different printer from those who had printed the bulk of the text, rather than from any calculations, in this case, to save space. King, *Print Culture*, p. 98.

interpolated material is a heterogeneous collection including letters of the Marian martyrs John Philpot and John Careless, as well as accounts of a number of martyrs who died in the summer and autumn of 1556. The desultory nature of this material is in itself a major reason for doubting that this interpolation was caused by their tardy acquisition. It would be a coincidence that beggars belief that a series of accounts of martyrdoms ranging from July to September 1556 all arrived at Day's printing house after this section had been printed. The unlikelihood of this is even further increased by the wide range of locales in which these martyrdoms took place, ranging from Guernsey and Sussex up to Derby. At the same time, among the inserted material is a large woodcut depicting the burning of three women and a baby at Guernsey in July 1556.

If a woodcut was commissioned to illustrate this horrific episode then it follows inescapably that Day knew about this material and that it could not have been a late acquisition. Rather, it appears that an entire tranche of material relating to these particular months was somehow mislaid in the printing house and only rediscovered after the relative section had been printed. Clearly unwilling to discard a woodcut, to say nothing of the accounts of some prominent martyrs, Day chose to interpolate this material in its proper chronological place. Such a blunder provides a vivid reminder of the time pressure under which the 1563 edition was being produced.

The same haste is undoubtedly responsible for the slap-dash conclusion to the first edition. The book ends with an appendix, which is a collection of anecdotes that reached Foxe too late to be included in the text of the book. The penultimate anecdote is of Gertrude Crokhay, a Protestant confessor who died towards the end of Mary's reign. In an ideal world this probably would have been the final account in the book, as the anecdotes in the appendix proceeded in chronological order. However, inconveniently, the account of Crokhay ended with about 60 per cent of the final page left blank. With more time, there were a number of expedients that could have been employed to fill in the empty space and disguise this defect. But with Time's wingèd chariot at his heels Day simply looked for any material still available at hand to fill in this space. Interestingly, what he came up with was a short account from Francisco de Enzinas's autobiography of a Spanish sculptor who was burned for heresy because he defaced a religious image he had carved in a dispute with its buyer.[51] This story was, if not pointless, then

[51] For Foxe's use of Enzinas see above, p. 80. It was Gordon Kinder who first suggested that this story was used to fill out the last page of the edition. A. Gordon Kinder, 'Spanish Protestants', p. 111.

rather anti-climactic, and it almost certainly would not have been included in Foxe's book at all if it were not for the speed and concomitant carelessness of the process.

VI

The most spectacular example of the ad hoc improvisation that character-ised the making of the 1563 edition, however, came in the first book. The pagination of this book is chaotic, even by Day's less than rigorous stand-ards. In fact – and this at least is very unusual – the collation is also haphazard. The first forty-nine pages of this book are orderly enough.[52] However, immediately afterwards, in the account of Thomas Becket, the pagination suddenly switches to foliation for the next two dozen pages.[53] The next five pages, finishing the account of Becket and dealing with the remainder of Henry II's reign, return to pagination.[54] Then the material reverts back to foliation for the remainder of the reigns of Henry II and Richard I and the beginning of John's reign.[55] Up to this point, the signatures follow an expected sequence. Now it reverts to '*I' signatures for a gathering of six. At this point the pagination becomes completely idiosyncratic: the equivalent pages are identified as pages (62)–(67), fol-lowed by folios (68^r)–(71^v). These new pages cover the reign of King John, his death, the fourth Lateran Council, the rise of the mendicant orders, and denunciations of clerical abuses by Saint Hildegard of Bingen and others. This in turn is followed by a new gathering of two, which are signatures *I*1*^{r}–*I2*^{v} and pages)70(–)73(. Finally, there is a single sheet, **I1*$^{r-v}$, which contains pages 73( )–( )74. These last two gatherings take the story into the reigns of Henry III and the Holy Roman Emperor Frederick II, with the emphasis on papal financial exactions and usurpation of secular authority. Book 2 begins with the K gathering, where a normal sequence is restored. This gathering commences with page 85.

What could explain this apparent abandonment of the normal collation? The most likely explanation is that Book 1 was initially printed and ran up to page 84. At some point after the first book was printed Foxe obtained new material and felt it was important enough to insert into the volume, thus replacing the original end to Book 1. So what was this additional material? The only way to answer this is to examine what the sources are for those sections of the first book where the pagination becomes irregular. On page 47,

---

[52] These first forty-nine pages are sigs. C1^r–F6^r.   [53] Sigs. G1^r–H6^v.
[54] Sigs. I1^r–I3^v.   [55] Fos. 68^r–72^v, which are sigs. I4^r–I6^v.

just before the irregularity begins, Foxe begins basing his account of Becket on the edition of the *Quadrilogus* printed in Paris in 1495.[56] In this account of Becket, which was so clearly a late insertion, Foxe also drew in Roger of Howden's chronicle.[57] Finally, Foxe also quoted contemporary denunciations of Becket from the chronicler William of Newburgh and John Bale's *Catalogus*.[58] He continued drawing on Howden as his primary source for the reigns of Henry II and Richard I.[59] For John's reign he drew on a wide range of sources, most notably Matthew Paris's *Chronica maiora*.[60] The remainder of Book 1 is drawn chiefly from Matthius Flacius's *Catalogus*, Walter of Guisborough's chronicle and, more especially, Matthew Paris's *Chronica maiora*.[61]

One thing should be clear from this: Foxe did more research into medieval chronicles in preparation for the 1563 edition than has been previously acknowledged. However, the question remains how much of the material that was added to the first edition was directly the product of Foxe's own researches. It is, of course, possible that he began delving into some of the major English medieval historical works as the 1563 edition was being printed, and, if so, he must be given credit as the scholar who 'discovered' Matthew Paris's *Chronica maiora*, just as the *Acts and Monuments* is indisputably the first early modern English book to be based on Paris's magnum opus.

---

[56] Henry of Croyland, *Vita processus sancti Thomae Cantuariensis martyris super libertate ecclesiastica* (Paris, 1495). Cf. *Vita processus*, sigs. a5ʳ–a6ᵛ, a7ᵛ–a8ʳ, b4ᵛ–c4ᵛ, c8ᵛ, d1ᵛ–2ʳ, d3ᵛ–4ʳ, e1ʳ–ᵛ, e6ᵛ–8ᵛ, g5ᵛ–6ᵛ, g7ʳ–ᵛ, g8ʳ–h1ʳ, h3ᵛ–h4ʳ, h5ᵛ–6ʳ, h7ʳ–k2ʳ, k3ᵛ–4ʳ and k8ᵛ–l1ʳ with *1563*, p. 47–fo. 49ᵛ, fos. 50ʳ–52ᵛ, fo. 53ʳ, fos. 53ᵛ–64ᵛ and fo. 64ᵛ–p. 63. The *Quadrilogus* is a collection of four contemporary hagiographies of Becket. See Anne Duggan, *Thomas Becket: A Textual History of his Letters* (Oxford, 1980), pp. 205–23.

[57] Cf. Roger of Howden, *Chronica magistri Rogeri de Hovedene*, ed. W. Stubbs, 4 vols. (Rolls Series 51, London, 1868–71), I, pp. 222–4, 226, 228–30; II, pp. 15–17 and 28–9 with *1563*, fos. 49ᵛ–50ʳ, 51ᵛ and 52ᵛ–3ʳ and p. 63.

[58] Cf. *Chronicles of the Reigns of Stephen, Henry II and Richard I*, ed. Richard Howlett, 5 vols. (Rolls Series 82, London, 1884–89), I, pp. 140, 142–3 and 160–1 and Bale, *Catalogus*, p. 210 with *1563*, pp. 63–5. Foxe also declares that he took material on a threatened interdict of England, following Becket's murder, from 'libro annotationum historicarum manuscripto' owned by one 'J. Skenii'. We are unable to identify this source.

[59] Cf. Howden, *Chronica*, II, pp. 33–6, 77, 85–8, 92–3, 102–4, 120, 141–3, 148–9, 174–5, 177–8, 182–3, 185–8, 260, 264, 269, and 366–7; III, pp. 13–16, 28, 31–2, 75–9, 145–7, 195–6, and 202–3; IV, pp. 82–3 and 76–7 with *1563*, pp. 65 and 68 [recte 66]–fo. 71ʳ.

[60] This is discussed in detail in Thomas S. Freeman, 'John Bale's Book of Martyrs?: The Account of King John in *Acts and Monuments*', *Reformation*, 3 (1998), pp. 175–223.

[61] Cf. Flacius, *Catalogus*, pp. 391–3 and 403–4, *The Chronicle of Walter of Guisborough*, ed. Harry Rothwell, Camden Society, 3rd series, 89 (1957), pp. 150–1 and pp. 156–7, and Matthew Paris, *Chronica maiora*, ed. H. R. Luard, 7 vols. (Rolls Series, 1872–83), III, pp. 78–9, 151–3, 208–9, 381–3, 404, 413, 416–17, 419–41, and 473; IV, pp. 6–7, 9–10, 31–2, 35, 37–8, 526–9 and 558 with *1563*, fos. (70)ʳ–( )74.

However, there is another explanation. It has been argued that the account of King John, at least – which draws extensively on Paris's work – was written by John Bale.[62] Of course some of the other sources used in the revised sections of Book 1, such as the *Quadrilogus*, could plausibly have been obtained by either Foxe or Bale. Similarly, it is difficult to be definitive about Howden's chronicle, not least because many other medieval writers incorporated large sections of it into their own work. However, it is worth observing that Bale was very familiar with Howden's work and there is no source used in the revised section of Book 1 that was not demonstrably known to Bale. Three pieces of evidence in particular, however, point to Bale as the source for this material. The first is the extensive use of Paris's *Chronica maiora*, which is more likely to have been Bale's discovery than Foxe's.[63] The second is that the available evidence points to Bale rather than Foxe as the author of a large part of these revised sections – that dealing with King John.[64] Yet another feature of the revised sections – a catalogue of the mendicant orders – has deep affinities with Bale's earlier work. This list is very close to the roll call of mendicant orders enumerated by 'Clergy' in Bale's *King Johan*.[65]

However, even if this material came from Bale, this does not in itself explain how Foxe would have acquired it suddenly as the 1563 edition was being printed. By 1551 Bale had completed the first two parts of his *Actes of the Englysh Votaryes*, a salacious account of the English clergy. The second part concluded with the end of the reign of Richard I. At the end of this second part, Bale promised that he would continue with a third part, which would run from the reign of John until the end of Richard II's reign, and that he would conclude it with a fourth part running from the reign of Henry IV to the Reformation.[66] We would suggest that the accounts of the reigns of John and Henry III in the first book of the 1563 edition are based

---

[62] Freeman, 'John Bale's Book', pp. 175–223.   [63] See ibid., pp. 190–2.   [64] See ibid., pp. 185–202.

[65] Cf. *The Complete Plays of John Bale*, ed. Peter Happé, 2 vols. (Woodbridge, 1985–6), 1, pp. 40–1 with *1563*, fo. (70)[v]. Thora Blatt observes that the list in *King Johan* is itself based on earlier lists drawn up by John Bale around 1525, in what is now Bodleian Library, Bodley MS 73. She further observes that Bale drew some of the names in the *King Johan* list from François Lambert's *In regulam Minoritarum* (Wittenberg, 1523) and a poem, *The Image of Ipocracy*, falsely attributed to John Skelton. Blatt, *The Plays of John Bale*, p. 38. Some of the names in the 1563 list are not found in *King Johan* or any of these other works. We cannot determine the sources for all of these additional groups but 'Saynct Helens brethren' and the order of 'Vallis umbrose' come from Polydore Vergil, *De rerum inventoribus* (Basle, 1536), pp. 497–9. The listing in 1563 of the 'Ammonites' and 'Moabits' and the 'Sicarii' and 'Zelotes order' suggests that whoever the compiler of this list was, he saw Old Testament pagans and ancient Jewish religious sects as being fundamentally linked to mendicant orders.

[66] Bale, *The actes of Englysh votaryes*, fo. 116[r–v].

on an unfinished continuation of the *Votaryes* that Bale never completed. Realising, perhaps, that he would never live to finish this work – Bale died on 15 November 1563 – he may have given his notes, as well as some of his key sources such as Howden and Paris, to Foxe, who then proceeded to incorporate them into the *Acts and Monuments* with alacrity.

In any case, three important observations can be made about this material and its probable authorship. The first is that it provides an obvious and dramatic example of the fundamental instability of the text of the *Acts and Monuments*, as Foxe's acquisition of sources considerably outpaced the printing process itself. Second, the fact that Foxe – whether with or without Bale's intervention – was making extensive use of Matthew Paris's great chronicle suggests that a revision of Parker's relationship to both Matthew Paris and John Foxe is in order. It would appear that one of Parker's greatest achievements – the acquisition of the different manuscript versions of the *Chronica maiora*, along with its printing – was inspired by Foxe's work.

Finally, it is a fitting note on which to end Foxe's relationship with Bale. As has already been observed repeatedly in this book, Foxe's intellectual debt to Bale was enormous; indeed, in writing the *Acts and Monuments* Foxe was carrying out a project that not only epitomised many of Bale's views but which Bale had envisioned much earlier. Nevertheless, Foxe was as necessary a part of this achievement as Bale was. The latter lacked the ability to work as part of a team, the ability to synthesise the work of others, and perhaps above all the patience of his protégé. In many ways Bale was rather like Moses: he was able to see the Promised Land from a distance, although his temperament prevented him from reaching it himself. Nevertheless, he was able to appoint his successor and he lived just long enough to see the goal attained.

VII

As we have discussed, a major reason for the haste with which the first edition was printed was a fervent desire on the part of the great and the good in Elizabethan England for the book to appear. Foxe's friend, Bishop John Parkhurst, who in his own quiet way had contributed significantly to the making of the book, informed Bullinger in a letter dated 26 April 1563 that Foxe's martyrology had just been printed and crowed that it would make the papists universally unpopular.[67] The most interesting and somewhat problematic response to Foxe's book came from a letter written to the

[67] Robinson, *Zurich Letters*, 1, p. 128.

martyrologist, dated 26 November 1563, by the eminent evangelical William Turner. He began by noting that throughout his journeys people had been praising Foxe's new book, but he also noted a persistent complaint: that the volume was too expensive and was thus unobtainable for a large proportion of the population. Turner was clear that the fault lay with John Day:

almost every printer would prefer large books, for the sake of large profits, rather than have them useful to, and easily procured, by the poor and wretched flock of Christ. Would that you had a rich living to support you, so that you were not compelled to serve mean, avaricious, vainglorious, and ignorant booksellers. I hear that you are badly treated by your master, to call him nothing worse.[68]

Turner had put his finger on a major and enduring problem with the *Acts and Monuments*: its incredible size meant that the book was expensive, which limited its dissemination. However, Turner's strictures about printers in general, and Day in particular, are misguided to the point of being unjust. At least in England, printers had shied away from producing large books because there was no assurance that the sales would be sufficient for the printer to recoup his investment. There is absolutely no indication that Day was pressuring Foxe to increase the size of the book. The features that Turner specifically objected to in increasing the size and cost of the volume – the inclusion of Latin documents, the coverage of subjects apart from the martyrs, and the discussion of Catholics and Catholic writers – were all features that Foxe regarded as essential to establishing the veracity of his work. (In fact, apart from the deletion of documents in their Latin versions, Foxe disregarded Turner's specific suggestions on decreasing the size of the book, although, as we shall see, a determined purge of materials took place in the second edition.) And perhaps most crucially, Turner made the same mistake that many other scholars since then have made: that of assuming that Day's motivations in printing the book were entirely profit-orientated and that patronage played no role in its production.

Turner's letter also raises the question of the relationship between Foxe and Day. It is quite difficult to believe that it was anywhere near as adversarial as Turner describes, since the two of them would go on to collaborate on a number of different books, including a further three editions of the *Acts and Monuments*. Yet while Foxe has to be credited

---

[68] 'Typographus fere quisque mavult libros suus esse magnos ob magnum suum quaestum, quam misello et parvo gregi Christi utiles et facile parabiles. Utinam tum lautus tibi victus supperet, ut non cogares miseris, avaris, gloriosis et amusis libariis servire! Audio enim te maligne a tuo domino, ne quid durius dicam, tractatum esse.' For Turner's letter see BL, MS. Harley 416, fo. 132r. This letter is printed in *The Works of Nicholas Ridley*, ed. Henry Christmas (Parker Society, Cambridge, 1841), pp. 487–95; these passages are on p. 488.

with most of the major editorial decisions regarding the scope and contents of the book, the question remains: did Day play any role in these decisions? Or was he simply the gifted technician and entrepreneur who turned Foxe's ideas into reality? There are at least two important aspects of the first edition of the *Acts and Monuments* where it can be established that Day played a major creative role.

The first of these was also the most controversial: a calendar in imitation of traditional liturgical calendars, which listed various martyrs and confessors, the vast majority of whom were mentioned in the first edition. This calendar and the bitter controversies that surrounded it during Foxe's own lifetime and for decades afterwards have been the subject of a not inconsiderable amount of academic scrutiny.[69] Yet scholars have tended to assume that the calendar in the *Acts and Monuments* was compiled by Foxe.[70] However, it is difficult to imagine that Foxe played any role whatsoever in the composition of the calendar. For one thing, it contains Scottish martyrs not included by Foxe in his book, whom he certainly would have mentioned in the book had he known of their existence. More importantly, the calendar contains numerous errors, and lists people who Foxe believed were not recorded in the Book of Life and whom he certainly did not want recorded in his book.[71]

The person behind the calendar was very probably John Day. And if there were religious or polemical motivations behind the calendar, they were probably secondary to commercial motivations. One of Day's primary objectives was to facilitate the placing of the 'Book of Martyrs' in parish churches by giving the book a quasi-liturgical appearance. Another was to challenge Seres, who had, over the passage of years, been evolved from a collaborator into a competitor, and who held the right to print calendars

---

[69] Damian Nussbaum, 'Reviling the Saints or Reforming the Calendar? John Foxe and his "Kalendar" of Martyrs', in *Belief and Practice in Reformation England*, ed. Susan Wabuda and Caroline Litzenberger (Aldershot, 1998), pp. 113–36; King, *Print Culture*, pp. 249–67; Anne Dillon, *The Construction of Martyrdom in the English Catholic Community, 1535–1603* (Aldershot, 2002), pp. 341–55; Thomas S. Freeman, 'The Power of Polemic: Catholic Responses to the Calendar in Foxe's "Book of Martyrs"', *Journal of Ecclesiastical History*, 61 (2010), pp. 475–95; Elizabeth Evenden and Thomas S. Freeman, 'Red Letter Day: Protestant Calendars and Foxe's "Book of Martyrs"', *Archiv für Reformationsgeschichte* (forthcoming, 2012).

[70] In his important article on the calendar, Damian Nussbaum, 'Reviling the Saints', p. 114, n. 3, mentions that Foxe did not devise the calendar, yet then proceeds to assume throughout the rest of his article that the calendar was designed to serve Foxe's objectives. Nor does he suggest who else, apart from Foxe, might have devised the calendar or at least been responsible for it. John King, on the other hand, observes that Foxe completely disclaimed responsibility for it. See King, *Print Culture*, p. 257.

[71] For a detailed discussion of these points see Evenden and Freeman, 'Red Letter Day'.

bound with metrical psalms.[72] In the event, the calendar did not succeed in accomplishing these objectives. Instead, it stirred up a hornets' nest of critics. For our purposes, however, it is merely important to note that Foxe explicitly denied his authorship of the calendar and appears to have been anxious to disassociate himself from it. (It was perhaps the martyrologist's objections, as well as those of outraged Catholics, that caused the calendar to be withdrawn in the next edition.) However, the fact that the calendar was printed at all seems to provide an example of where Day overrode the objections of his author to influence the contents of the work.

Day almost certainly was responsible for a fundamental aspect of the first edition: its copious, well-executed illustrations. The purposes behind these and the relative roles of Foxe and Day in determining their content will be discussed further on in this book; for now it is important to note this as perhaps the chief sphere of Day's creative involvement with the book. It also undermines Turner's claim that Day was solely motivated by a desire for profit. Had this been the case, Day could have saved a great deal of money by simply not producing the illustrations or producing ones of inferior quality. It would appear that one of Day's reasons for lavishing such care on these commissioned illustrations was the same as had underlain his display of expertise in producing the *Cosmographical glasse*: the desire to impress patrons and potential patrons with his technical mastery.

And in fact the labours of Foxe and Day seem to have been appreciated by those on high. Shortly after the first edition was printed, Foxe received his first ecclesiastical preferment: the prebend of Shipton at Salisbury Cathedral. Valued at just under £40 a year, it combined the two prerequisites that Foxe seems to have required: a decent income joined with a lack of administrative responsibility. This appointment was the only benefice that Foxe held for any significant period, but it allowed him, and almost certainly was intended to allow him, to pursue his career as an author and a preacher. The timing of the appointment is suggestive. Peter Vannes, the previous incumbent, died some time between 28 March and 30 April 1563. Foxe was presented to the living on 22 May. It would appear that Foxe was granted the first suitable and suitably remunerative benefice that became available after the *Acts and Monuments* was printed. Foxe's son Simeon would later declare that William Cecil procured this living for his father.[73]

In the long term, Day had clearly impressed Cecil, Parker and others with his skill and drive, and Day established himself beyond question in the top rank of English printers. This was given quasi-official recognition by his

---

[72] For detailed analysis of this see ibid.   [73] See the life of Foxe in *ODNB*.

peers when he was elected a warden of the Stationers' Company in 1564. During the course of his life, Day would hold this post on four separate occasions but he first attained it at the first available opportunity following the appearance of the first edition of the *Acts and Monuments*.[74] Day appears to have also taken the opportunity provided by the appearance of the first edition to elevate his standing among his customers. The first edition of the *Acts and Monuments* advertised, for the first time (although this would become a regular feature in Day's most expensive volumes), that it was only to be purchased at Day's Aldersgate shop. In doing this, Day was establishing his Aldersgate shop (where he lived and worked and which was closely associated with him), in contrast to his other shops, as the place where London's elite could buy deluxe books.

Nevertheless, while the first edition seems to have been a success for both printer and author, neither was completely satisfied with it. Paradoxically, the feeling that there was room for improvement may well have facilitated the decision to print a second edition of the work. The decision was certainly made quickly. The *Letters of the Martyrs*, a work that will be discussed in more detail shortly, which was printed in 1564, contains a note referring the reader to 'the next edition of the booke of martyrs'.[75] This means that within a year or so of its appearance, Day and Foxe had already decided to reprint the edition. Furthermore, they must have obtained the backing of Cecil and perhaps other important figures for this endeavour, as it is very unlikely that Day would have committed himself to such a mammoth undertaking without continued assurance of the continuation of the patents, which were so necessary to sustain his business during the printing of the *Acts and Monuments*.

It must have been clear from the outset that this was to be a mammoth undertaking. First of all, Foxe's first edition was larger than any other book hitherto printed in England. But the reasons why Foxe and Day were dissatisfied would have inevitably entailed an increase in the complexity of the task of the new edition if it were to increase its size further. In the next edition Foxe would take the opportunity, afforded by the fact that he had more time, to edit the documents in the work with incredible precision. Not with a concern to making them more accurate – in certain fundamental areas, such as chronology, Foxe made only the most minimal effort. Where he devoted a great deal of attention was to the excision of material that he felt might undermine the messages that he wanted to advance in his book.

[74] See *PPP*, pp. 78–9.　[75] *LM*, p. 46.

One particularly sore subject was that the translation of Latin documents in the first edition had been done by other people. In the second edition Foxe would go over these translations very carefully to remove compromising passages that the translators had understandably but unguardedly included in their work. At the same time, sometimes embarrassing howlers were made by the translators. For example, the happily anonymous individual who translated *The Twelve Conclusions of the Lollards* (which had been printed in the *Commentarii* and the *Rerum*) rendered the passage 'potestate angelus altiori' as 'a higher power unto England'.[76] In the second edition, this was corrected to 'a power higher than aungels'.[77] Judging from the woodcut illustrations in the second edition, Day, concerned about the appearance of the new edition, was anxious to see that this time the new small pictures included in the volume were the width of one column of text.

But, most fundamentally, Foxe was determined to complete and round out his archival research. The two most important aspects of this were finishing his work in the diocesan archives of London, and beginning to make use of the rich archives of the diocese of Canterbury. Moreover, two books appeared in 1564 that provided Foxe with abundant new material to quarry. One of these, which may have been a surprising but welcome development to Foxe, was Jean Crespin's new martyrology. In the next edition, Foxe and Day would go to great pains to incorporate material from this work in the *Acts and Monuments*.[78] The other book, which Foxe had not only been aware of for some time, but which indeed was intertwined with his own work on several levels, was the collection of the letters of the Marian martyrs edited by Foxe's friend and colleague Henry Bull and printed by John Day.

VIII

Henry Bull and John Foxe had been moving in the same circles for some time. They had both been fellows at Magdalen College in the 1540s.[79] Early in Mary's reign, Bull gave subtle indications of his religious sympathies when, along with Foxe's friend Thomas Bentham, he snatched the censer from the hand of a priest celebrating Mass. Bull was subsequently expelled

---

[76] Cf. Foxe, *Rerum*, p. 76 with *1563*, p. 137.   [77] *1570*, p. 606.

[78] Tom Freeman is continuing to work on this project.

[79] Much of what follows regarding Henry Bull is based on Susan Wabuda's pioneering research. See her seminal article, 'Henry Bull, Miles Coverdale and the Making of Foxe's *Book of Martyrs*', in *Martyrs and Martyrologies*, ed. Diana Wood, Studies in Church History xxx (Oxford, 1993), pp. 245–58. See also her *ODNB* article on Henry Bull.

because of this incident and appears to have gone underground in England. William Winthrop, in his letter to Foxe of November 1560, described Bull as one of those who 'have not bowed theyr knees to baall', which would suggest that Bull had been a member of one of the clandestine Protestant congregations during Mary's reign.[80] This background would be of enormous benefit in tracking down the letters to and from the Marian martyrs, and at the same time it established his credentials not only with Foxe but with some of the people who were supporting him.

It is unknown when Bull decided to start collecting these letters, but in 1562 he broadcast his intentions to the reading public with much the same tactic that Foxe had employed in printing Nicholas Ridley's *Frendly Farewel*. Instead of Nicholas Ridley's work, Bull chose to memorialise Ridley's sometime adversary, the equally formidable John Hooper.[81] Even if he did not know of Bull's project before this, Foxe certainly would have known of it from this point onwards. (In fact Foxe would print all four of the letters in his 1563 edition.[82]) Interestingly, Edmund Grindal himself personally approved this work for the press.[83] In itself, this is not an indication that Grindal supported the project, but it would be surprising if he did not. In effect, it was Bull rather than Foxe who was actually continuing Grindal's long-standing plans for a collection of the writings of the major English martyrs.[84]

Foxe's surviving correspondence clearly shows that he and Bull were good friends throughout this period, and ultimately each, as we shall see, would incorporate portions of the other's work.[85] Moreover, ultimately Day would print Bull's collection. Nevertheless, there are two significant features

[80] BL, Harley MS 416, fo. 106ʳ. It is of course possible that Bull went into exile, but it is unlikely, as there is no evidence of this. Winthrop was almost certainly a member of the main underground congregation in London; significantly in Elizabeth's reign he stood first fruits for Robert Cole, one of the congregation's leaders. On the congregation, see Brett Usher, 'In a Time of Persecution: New Light on the Secret Protestant Congregation in Marian London', in *John Foxe and the English Reformation*, ed. Loades, pp. 233–51. For Winthrop's role in this congregation, see p. 248. It seems reasonable to suppose that Winthrop was referring to Bull's participation in this congregation.

[81] The work is *An apologye made by the reverende father and constante Martyr of Christe John Hooper . . .* (London, 1562), STC 13742. In addition to the letter described in the title, this work contains a letter informing Hooper of the arrest of a Protestant congregation at St Mary le Bow on New Year's Day 1555, Hooper's reply to that letter, and a letter to the members of that congregation who were imprisoned in the Bread Street Counter.

[82] *1563*, pp. 1020–2 and 1057.

[83] The manuscript for the book is ECL, MS 261, fos. 1ʳ–14ʳ. On the final recto the notation appears: 'aprobator Edm. London'.

[84] Another indication of Grindal's support for this project is the fact that Bull would print for the first time a letter from Grindal to his mentor Ridley as well as Ridley's reply (*LM*, pp. 49–51 and 51–6).

[85] See BL, Harley MS 416, fos. 113ʳ⁻ᵛ and 118ʳ⁻ᵛ as well as BL, Harley MS 417, fo. 108ʳ⁻ᵛ.

about the work. One is the poor quality of production of this edition. The major problem was that the work was printed in (probably early) 1564 and Day clearly had expended most of his supply of good-quality paper on the *Acts and Monuments*. As a result, the *Letters of the Martyrs* is printed on inferior paper. Moreover, even this poor-quality, rough paper was apparently in short supply, as Day tried to squeeze as much text onto a single page as was possible, in order to minimise the amount of paper used but thereby reducing even further any aesthetic qualities that the book might have had. Interestingly, the *Letters of the Martyrs* was edited anonymously.

In fact, Bull's identity as the compiler was only revealed by Susan Wabuda in the late twentieth century. This may have been due to modesty on Bull's part but it is possible that there was a marketing reason behind this and that Day was trying to make as much money as he could from the book. The work opened with a preface by Miles Coverdale, and since then, although there is actually no evidence that Coverdale had anything to do with the making of the book, it has generally been attributed to him. Coverdale, a former Edwardian bishop, who had only narrowly escaped burning in Mary's reign and who then went into exile, was a venerable and almost venerated figure in the early Elizabethan Church, and one closely associated with the major Marian martyrs. Having him write a preface for the work was a shrewd stroke of public relations, which may well have sprung from the fertile brain of John Day.

Yet despite the fact that the two projects eventually converged, they appear to have begun independently of each other. The timing of Bull's printing of Hooper's apology while Foxe's tome was making its slow progression through the press is suggestive. Moreover, a look at the contents of the two works reveals that, initially at least, they were pursuing different lines of research. There are 219 letters in the *Letters of the Martyrs*; 173 of these were printed by Bull for the first time and are presumably the fruits of his investigations. Although we have no certain knowledge of how Bull obtained many of these letters, it is quite possible to trace some of his sources. A very important figure who contributed letters to Bull and who had very possibly known him during Mary's reign was Augustine Bernher, another of the leaders of the London underground congregation.[86] Bernher, who had also been Latimer's close friend and amanuensis, almost assuredly put Bull in touch with Mary Glover, Latimer's niece, as Bull printed a letter

---

[86] Bull would print six letters sent to Augustine Bernher: three from Ridley (*LM*, pp. 70–2, 72–3, 73–4), two from Bradford (*LM*, pp. 468–9 and 469–70) and one from John Careless (*LM*, pp. 607–11).

from Philpot and two letters from Lawrence Saunders, each sent to Mary's husband, the martyr Robert Glover.[87]

This list goes on, as Bull clearly solicited the aid of a roll call of surviving friends and family of the leading Marian martyrs. In many cases, a survivor not only contributed letters that he or she had received, but passed on letters that friends had also received. For example, Thomas Upcher, a correspondent of John Careless, gave Bull four letters that Careless had written to him. However, he also gave Bull six letters that Careless had written to Margery Cooke; we know this because the letters contain inscriptions instructing that they be returned to Upcher.[88] Often these survivors gave Bull letters that were surprisingly personal, even intimate, although in a few cases it is interesting to note that they held back letters that were especially cherished.[89] In any case, what is clear from this pattern is that Bull and Foxe had initially established different sources of information for their respective works. It was only in the second edition that Foxe renewed contact with some of the sources that Bull had originally cultivated.

Bull was not only pursuing different lines of research, he was also pursuing them after the first edition of the *Acts and Monuments* had been printed. It is clear on two occasions in the *Letters of the Martyrs* that last-minute material was inserted into the volume. Day inserted it out of order at the end of book, but the apparent ending of the book kept being moved further and further back, as new material seems to have kept on dribbling in.[90]

[87] *LM*, pp. 206–7, 207–8, and 241–2.

[88] ECL, MS 260, 132[r–v], 236[r], 238[r], 240[r] and BL, Add. MS 19400, 66[r] and 71[r].

[89] For example, Elizabeth Fane gave Bull five letters she had received from Bradford but a series of letters sent to her by the martyr John Philpot were only obtained by John Foxe after her death and were first printed in the 1570 edition of the *Acts and Monuments*. These letters from Philpot are both intimate and passionate – the two clearly had formed a close relationship – and it is very probable that Elizabeth Fane refused to part with these letters and the memories they contained while she was alive. To appreciate their intimate nature, the letters need to be seen in their originals and not in their expurgated versions provided by Foxe: see ECL, MS 260, fos. 160[r]–1[v], 184[r]–5[r] and BL, Add. MS 19400, fo. 50[r–v]. Similarly, the Marian martyr John Careless acted as a sort of matchmaker between Augustine Bernher and Elizabeth, the woman he married (see BL, Add. MS 19400, fo. 64[v]). Careless wrote a letter to each of them individually on the duties and joys of marriage. Again, although Bull received quite a few letters from the Bernhers, these letters were not printed until after the recipients had both died. See ECL 260, 237[r–v], printed *1570*, pp. 2116–17. The letter to Augustine Bernher does not survive in manuscript but the printed version is *1570*, pp. 2115–16.

[90] The first insertion consists of one letter each from the martyrs Rowland Taylor, John Philpot, John Bradford and Bartlett Greene, as well as two letters from the martyr Thomas Whittle (*LM*, pp. 640–56). Unfortunately this material took them past the end of the gathering of eight (Vv) and onto the first page of what would become the Xx gathering (again, a gathering of eight). This gathering was then filled out with letters that Foxe had already printed in his first edition of the 'Book of Martyrs'. The text tapers to a close on the final leaf of this gathering and is followed by an ornamental fleuron, suggesting an intended close to the book. But this was not to be. A subsequent gathering of six (Yy) is

In his second edition, Foxe would appropriate much of Bull's work. He reprinted about half of the letters (eighty-three of them) that had first appeared in the *Letters of the Martyrs*. Foxe seems to have had several criteria for selection. Some of these were pragmatic. As we shall see, saving paper became an acute issue as the 1570 edition was being printed, and some of these letters were clearly dropped simply because of a lack of space. Thus if a particular person wrote several letters to the same correspondent, Foxe would print only one or two of them.[91] Foxe also had polemical motives behind his selectivity. Some letters that Bull had printed referred to the disputes among Marian Protestants over the question of free will. Writing in 1564, revealing the existence of such disputes did not trouble Bull; in fact, these letters provided him with an opportunity to associate the Marian martyrs with predestination.[92]

In 1566 the Catholic controversialist, Nicholas Harpsfield, made the theological divisions among Protestants a major part of his scathing and effective criticism of Foxe's work. In response to this, Foxe deleted almost all references to any religious divisions among the Marian Protestants, and this included many of the letters that Bull had printed.[93] However, it is still accurate to describe Foxe as appropriating Bull's work. Almost invariably, when Foxe reprinted Bull's letters he preserved the editorial changes that Bull had already made in them. He also (and this was unusual for Foxe)

then included, which, curiously, contains further material that had already been previously printed in Foxe's book. Again, the gathering draws to a close with tapered text and another fleuron. However, at this point, a previously unknown letter from Nicholas Ridley to Sir John Cheke must have come to hand and it was inserted on pp. 683–5, which carry the signatures ☙ Yr[r]–2[r]. On sig. Y2[v] commences a description by Cuthbert Symson of his racking, which had already been printed by Foxe (sigs. ☙ Y2[v]–Y[r]; note the irregularity in the signatures). This is then followed by an inscription written by Bradford in a New Testament, which had not previously been printed. This is only a short piece of text, which tapers to a close on sig. ☙ Y[r], which is followed by yet another fleuron at the foot of the page. Once again, however, another letter appears to have come to hand – one from Thomas Leaver to John Bradford (no signature, p. 688). This is then followed by a blank page, a list of errata and the index.

[91] Simply by way of example, Foxe printed one out of the three letters that Bradford wrote to Joan Wilkinson (cf. *LM*, pp. 342–3, 343–4 and 423–5 with *1570*, p. 1825), and he printed three out of five that Bradford wrote to Elizabeth Fane (cf. *LM*, pp. 334–5, 335–6, 336–8, 403–8 and 467–8 with *1570*, pp. 1824 and 1829–31). Bull had printed four letters that Careless wrote to Thomas Upcher; Foxe printed two of these (cf. *LM*, pp. 580–2, 582–5, 618–20, and 620–4 with *1570*, pp. 2109 and 2112). Lawrence Saunders wrote two letters to the brothers Robert and John Glover; Foxe only printed one of them (cf. *LM*, pp. 206–7 and 207–8 with *1570*, p. 1674).

[92] The most prominent Marian martyrs, and indeed the ones that were the subject of his book, were outspoken champions of predestinarianism. On this see Thomas S. Freeman, 'Dissenters from a Dissenting Church: The Challenge of the Freewillers, 1550–1558', in *The Beginnings of English Protestantism*, ed. Marshall and Ryrie, pp. 152–3. As Susan Wabuda has observed, Bull's animus towards the Freewillers 'is clear from a comment he wrote on one manuscript, and printed in a marginal gloss, that their spirit was "arronyous, forward, & unquiet"'. Wabuda, 'Henry Bull', p. 256.

[93] Freeman, 'Dissenters', pp. 154–5.

tended to reprint Bull's marginal comments rather than add his own. Foxe also profited from Bull's research on other levels. Ultimately, many of the letters of the martyrs that Bull had gathered came into Foxe's hands after they had been used in Day's printing house. It is a sign of the value that Foxe and later generations would attach to these letters that they remained in Foxe's hands throughout his lifetime and that they were then preserved in Emmanuel College Cambridge.[94] Furthermore, as we have seen, Foxe was able in the 1570 edition to follow up on Bull's original research and to glean more letters from fields that Bull had initially harvested.

In fact, between them Foxe and Bull all but stripped these fields bare. Apart from the fortuitous discovery of a treatise of Ridley's and two letters of John Careless, which were printed independently of Foxe (and Day) in 1566, the two martyrologists between them had obtained every surviving copy of the voluminous correspondence of the Marian prisoners for the Gospel.[95] It was this massive incorporation of the writings of the martyrs that helped to ensure that Foxe's work had no rival. Indeed, the only potential rival to his undertaking was Bull's collection, and much of that, as we have seen, was assimilated by Foxe. In the end, Foxe's text completely overshadowed that of Bull. The *Letters of the Martyrs* would not be reprinted until the nineteenth century. This relative lack of success, at least in printing terms, may have been partly due to Bull's inclusion of controversial material, such as that on disputes about free will, which Foxe had prudently excised from his own work. But much of this lack of success was also due to Foxe's persistent, albeit selective, appropriation of the material in Bull's collection. Although Foxe was less than satisfied with his first edition, and although he was soon to endure bitter criticism of it, Foxe at least had the satisfaction of knowing, after his first edition had been printed, that he completely dominated this genre of literature in England.

---

[94] On the history of these letters see Wabuda, 'Henry Bull', p. 258.

[95] These letters were printed as *A pituous lamentation of the miserable estate of the church of Christ in Englande, in the time of the late revolt from the gospel. Never before imprynted. Whereunto are also annexed letters of J Careless* (London, 1566), STC 21052.

CHAPTER 5

Sources and resources: preparing the 1570 edition

I

In the *Letters of the Martyrs* a marginal note appeared promising forth-coming material that 'you shall read in the next edition of the boke of martyrs'.[1] Preparations for the new edition began within two years at the latest. At the beginning of 1566, Ralph Morice, Thomas Cranmer's former secretary, wrote a letter to John Day – in response to Day's requests for information for the new edition – relating anecdotes about the archbishop and offering to provide material.[2] Internal evidence shows that Foxe was already writing his account of the history of the Ottoman Empire in the same year.[3] By the beginning of 1567, arrangements were being made to have manuscript drafts of Foxe's text copy-edited.[4]

These instances not only show the early date at which work on the new edition commenced, they also demonstrate that almost from the first it was designed to be of different and far greater scope than the first edition. Apart from brief excerpts from Hall's *Chronicle*, dealing with the sieges of Rhodes and Vienna, Foxe had said nothing in his first edition about the Ottoman Empire, yet by 1566 he had already decided to include its history in the new edition of his work.[5]

---

[1] *LM*, p. 46.   [2] BL, Harley MS. 416, fos. 183[r]–4[r].
[3] In the 1570 edition Foxe states that as he was writing his section on the Turks he received 'a certaine writyng out of Germany' relating (prematurely, as it turned out) the news of a victory over the Ottoman armies at the fort of Gyula in Hungary (*1570*, p. 896). Foxe was referring to a pamphlet, *Newes from Vienna the 5 day of August 1566* (London, 1566), STC 24716. According to the title page, this pamphlet was printed on 21 September 1566. On the next page, Foxe wrote that he was unsure if the Ottoman sultan Suleiman was still alive; in fact, Suleiman had died on 6 September 1566. A little later in the same edition, Foxe relates that he had heard news that Gyula had indeed fallen to the Turks (*1570*, p. 904). The fort had in fact fallen on 1 September 1566. From these references, it seems clear that Foxe was writing this section of the *Acts and Monuments* some time in late September or early October 1566.
[4] BL, Harley MS 416, fo. 185[r].   [5] *1563*, pp. 442–3.

The reasons for Foxe's readiness to embark on a new edition are both clear and self-evident. We have already seen that he was unhappy about the haste with which the first edition had been produced – haste so great that he had been prevented from fully utilising the sources already at his disposal. The opportunity to create a 'perfect' edition would have been very attractive to Foxe. The advantages of this for Day, however, were less obvious. The production of two editions of a work of this physical magnitude by the same printer, one edition following on the heels of the other, was unprecedented in the history of the English book. The first edition could not have sold out by the time the decision was made to print the second, although Day may well have waited until a sufficient stock of the first edition had been sold before he proceeded with the actual printing of the second edition. In fact, the available evidence seems to indicate that the sales of the first edition were disappointing. In a Latin poem prefacing the second edition, the scholar, mathematician and poet, Robert Record, praised the new edition: 'Certainly the work is worthy, however large the volume, to be approved by the pious multitude and judged worthy by posterity.'[6] Record goes on to predict that future generations will indeed find the work worthy and will admire Foxe's genius, but he admits that contemporaries have been less insightful:

> Nevertheless, the insanity of a demented populace does not permit [this],
> Alas, neither, does it endure or suffer learned men.
> The actor, the jester, the wit, the parasite, the hypocrite, the mime
> [And] the wastrel are more attractive; the pimp [and] the papist please.
> You do not know how to flatter, Foxe, or to be silent about the truth,
> And you wonder that your writings have not found favour?[7]

So why would Day reprint a work that did not sell well? The only reason can be that Day received assurances from someone in power, very probably William Cecil, the great patron of Foxe's book, that measures would be taken to protect the printer's investment. Nevertheless, Day's anxiety about the possible monetary loss he would incur from this new edition haunted him throughout its printing.

Another poem, this one anonymous, prefacing the 1570 edition, read:

> Although many have sold frivolous nonsense and
> Unadulterated foolishness for a high price

---

[6] *1570*, sigs. C3^v – C4^r. 'Dignum certe opus est, quamvis sit grande volumen, / Quod pia turba legat, posteritasque probet'.

[7] *1570*, sig. C4^r. 'Non tamen insani sinit haec dementia vulgi / Hei mihi nec doctos fert partitur ve viros. / Histrio, scurra, dicax, parasitus, hypocrita, mimis, / Vappa mage arrident, leno, Papista placent. / Nescis adularia, nec verum (Foxe) silere / Scriptaque mirais non placuisse tua?'

Do not doubt that you will recoup the great profit you wish,
Day, even if the Monuments is costing you dear.[8]

Clearly, despite the assistance he would receive from his patrons, Day was
anxious about the sales of the new edition of the *Acts and Monuments*. (This
in itself is another indication that the sales of the first edition were not
encouraging.) The decision to launch another edition is a clear indication
that market forces did not necessarily dictate when – or even if – subsequent
editions of the *Acts and Monuments* would be produced. Nevertheless, Day's
concern about sales also indicates that these were not of negligible importance. Rather, there was a complicated relationship between patronage, sales
and the printing of a given edition of the *Acts and Monuments*.

II

One thing that needs to be remembered (and which will be examined in
detail further on) is that the evidence suggests that Day believed that this
second edition would be about the same size as the first. One cause of the
unforeseen size of the new edition was the wave of Catholic attacks on the
first one. While Robert Persons' *A Treatise of Three Conversions*, printed in
1604, was the first work devoted exclusively to rebutting the *Acts and
Monuments*, almost every English Catholic polemical work of the 1560s
contained at least one or two desultory attacks on Foxe's book. In 1565
Thomas Harding coined what would become a Catholic trope by sneering
at 'that huge dungehill of your stinking martyrs which you have intituled
the Actes and Monumentes'.[9] In 1567 Harding returned to the fray with a
more substantial attack on the veracity of Foxe's account of the martyrdom
of three women in Guernsey.[10] Thomas Stapleton printed an edition of
Bede's *History of the Church of England*, as well as a separate companion
work, *A Fortress of the Faith*; both were designed to provide a 'true' alternative account of the Anglo-Saxon Church to that presented by Foxe.[11] In
another work published a few years later Stapleton vehemently challenged

[8] *1570*, sig. C4ʳ. 'Frivola quum multi deliramenta, meramque; / Stultitiam magno vendiderint pretio, /
Ne dubita optato referes vel singula lucro / (Daie) licet magno stent Monumenta tibi.'
[9] Thomas Harding, *A Confutation of a Book Intituled An Apology of the Church of England* (Antwerp,
1565), STC 12762, fos. 13ᵛ–14ʳ.
[10] Thomas Harding, *A Reioinder to Mr Jewels Replie Against the sacrifice of the Masse* (Louvain, 1567),
STC 12761, fos. 184ʳ–5ᵛ.
[11] *The History of the Church of England, Compiled by Venerable Bede, Englishman*, trans. Thomas
Stapleton (Antwerp 1565), STC 1778, and Thomas Stapleton, *A Fortresse of the Faith* (Antwerp
1565), STC 23232.

the accuracy of a number of narratives in Foxe's book.[12] Foxe's text was like a caribou attacked by a pack of wolves: no single animal in the pack was large enough to take on the beast by itself, but by darting in and out, striking and retreating, they could hope to weaken, and ultimately slay it. The leader of this pack was Nicholas Harpsfield, whose *Dialogi sex* contained a 250-page attack on the first edition of Foxe's work.[13]

Foxe was very sensitive to these attacks. In a letter prefacing the 1570 edition the martyrologist complained of the 'stingyng waspes' that his first edition had stirred up. He went on to say, with injured disingenuity, that while he had no objections to those who pointed out 'true faultes' in his work, nevertheless:

to carpe where no causes, to spye in others straws and to leap over their own blockes: to swallow camels, and to strayne gnattes: to oppress truth with lyes, and to set up lyes for truth, to blaspheme deare martyrs of Christ and to canonise for saintes [those] whom Scripture would scarce allow for good subjects, that is intolerable.[14]

In the dedication to Queen Elizabeth, rewritten for this edition, Foxe was even more caustic about these criticisms of his first edition:

A man would have thought Christ to have bene new borne agayn, and that Herode with al the Citie of Jerusalem had bene in an uprore. Such blustryng and styrring was then against that poore booke through all quarters of England even to the gates of Louvaine: so that no English Papist almost in all the Realm thought himself a perfect catholicke, unlesse he had cast out some word or other, to give that book a blow.[15]

In fact what is ostensibly a dedication to the queen is largely taken up with Foxe's expressions of outrage at the volume and vehemence of the Catholic attacks on his first edition. Moreover, a sense of personal resentment against his Catholic critics burns slowly throughout the *Acts and Monuments*, occasionally igniting bursts of invective, such as this one, directed against the Catholic critic Thomas Dorman, in which Foxe reminded his readers that one of the Buckinghamshire Lollards persecuted by Bishop Longland was a Thomas Dorman and that:

this Thomas Dorman (as I am credibly informed of certeine about Amersham) was then uncle to this our Dorman . . . which nowe so uncharitably abuseth his penne

[12] Thomas Stapleton, *A counterblast to M. Hornes Vayne blast against M. Fekenham* (Louvain, 1567), STC 23231, fos. 60ʳ–1ᵛ, 306ᵛ–10ᵛ, 312ʳ–14ᵛ and 317ᵛ–19ᵛ.
[13] Nicholas Harpsfield, *Dialogi sex*, pp. 638 [recte 738]–1002.   [14] Sig. ☞ 2r.   [15] *1570*, sig. *1ʳ.

in writing agaynste the contrary doctrine, and rayleth so fiercely agaynst the bloud of Christes slayne servaunts, miscalling them to be a dong hill of stinking martyrs.[16]

III

However, while Foxe took these attacks personally, he also took them seriously. One indication of this is shown by two introductions that Foxe added to the 1570 edition. One of these was straightforwardly addressed 'To all the professed frendes and folowers of the Popes procedynges' and adhering to the dictum that the best defence is attack, it attacks the Catholic Church as persecutors of God's word. This introduction also denounces the supposed Catholic reliance on works and ceremonies to achieve salvation and identified the papacy with the Beast in Revelation.[17] The other introduction, a very important statement of Foxe's concept of history, is also directed, albeit more subtly, against his Catholic opponents. A major Catholic argument lodged not only against Foxe but against Protestants in general was: where was your Church before Luther?[18] To answer this question Foxe had to engage with the history of the Church continuously from its beginnings until the Reformation. A long prefatory letter to the 1570 edition addressed 'To the True and Faithful congregation of Christ's universal church' contains Foxe's response, and in effect it sketches the existence of a faithful remnant preserving apostolic doctrines and practices and existing in every era, linked solely by the Holy Spirit.[19] More importantly, one of the most notable features of the second edition is the increased chronological scope of the work, which now ran continuously from the Apostolic era to the end of Mary Tudor's reign. Demonstrating the existence of 'Protestantism' before Luther not only demanded that the chronological range of the book be increased but that its documentary base be expanded as well. In fact, on occasion, Foxe explicitly cited documents asserting that this material proved the existence of the true Protestant Church before Luther. For example, after printing long extracts from

---

[16] *1570*, p. 964.   [17] *1570*, sig. *4ʳ, C1ʳ.

[18] The importance of this issue is demonstrated by the way that Protestants tried to turn it on its head, as when John Jewel famously challenged the Catholics to prove their doctrines and practices had existed in the first six centuries of the Church. *The Works of John Jewel*, ed. J. Ayre, 4 vols. (Parker Society, Cambridge, 1845 – 50), I, pp. 20–I.

[19] *1570*, Sigs. ☞ 1ʳ–4ʳ. For a discussion of Foxe's concept of this faithful remnant see Facey, 'John Foxe', in *Protestantism and the National Church in Sixteenth Century England*, ed. Lake and Dowling, pp. 162–92.

Bishop John Langland's court books describing the persecution of Lollards in the years 1520 and 1521, Foxe threw down the gauntlet:

And this was before the name of Luther was heard of in these countreys amongest the people. Wherfore they are much beguiled and misse informed, which comdemne this kinde of doctrine now receaved of noveltie askynge where was this Church and Religion . . . before Luthers tyme? To whom it may be aunswered that this Religion and forme of Doctrine first planted by the Apostles and taught by true bishops, afterward decayed, and nowe reformed agayne, although it was not receaved nor admitted of the Pope's clergie before Luther's tyme, neither yet it was receaved of other, in whose heartes it pleased the Lorde secretly to worke, and that of a great number which both professed and suffered for the same, as in the former times of this hystorie may appeare. And if they thinke this doctrine to be so newe that it was not heard of before Luther's tyme, how then came such great persecutions before Luther's time here in England?[20]

Moreover, rebutting the specific charges made by Foxe's Catholic adversaries often necessitated archival research and the printing of documents. For example, when Thomas Harding criticised Foxe's account of an atrocity (the burning of an infant child along with its mother) in Guernsey in 1556, Foxe responded by soliciting records and oral testimony from Guernsey to confirm and corroborate his account.[21] When Nicholas Harpsfield challenged Foxe's claims that the Lollard rebels Sir Roger Acton and Lord Cobham had been guilty of treason and sedition, Foxe responded with research into previously unused chronicle and archival sources (e.g., Roger Wall's *De Gesti Henrici Quinti*, the Parliament Rolls, the Patent Rolls, and registers of the diocese of Canterbury) in an attempt to make his case. All of this saw a substantial growth in the amount of space Foxe devoted to a subject. In 1563 it had taken twenty-two pages to deal with Acton and Oldcastle; in the 1570 edition it took fifty-seven.[22]

Any attempt to depict, even at a cursory level, the history of the Church during the Middle Ages and the Reformation demanded the use of continental sources. Ideally, it would have entailed the use of continental archives but this was not done by Foxe. Instead, he relied on a vast range of books printed on the continent for his history. There was nothing new about this; we have previously noted Foxe's dependence upon Matthias Flacius's *Catalogus testium veritatis* and Ortwin Gratius's

[20] *1570*, p. 945.
[21] Harding, *Reioinder*, fos. 184[r]–5[v]; *1570*, pp. 2130–4. Also see D. M. Ogier, *Reformation and Society in Guernsey* (Woodbridge, 1997), pp. 57–9, 62–3, 69–70.
[22] Cf. *1563*, pp. 173–5 and 261–81 with *1570*, pp. 644–700 and 761–3. Also see Harpsfield, *Dialogi sex*, pp. 832–6 and 953–4.

Fasciculi, but his use of continental works now expanded even further. These earlier sources remained important. In fact, Flacius's *Catalogus*, along with Bale's *Catalogus*, remained essential works for Foxe's interpretation of the Middle Ages. Foxe also expanded his use of some works that had been previously used in a limited way. For example, in the 1563 edition Foxe had drawn on Johannes Cochlaeus's history of the Hussite wars simply for a brief account of Hus's excommunication.[23] In the new edition of 1570, Foxe drew on Cochlaeus for a range of documents, especially those detailing measures taken to repress Hus and the Hussites.[24] At the same time Foxe also used, for the first time, a number of works on more specific topics. For example, Foxe took Pierre de Cugnières's oration to the 1329 Parlement denouncing abuses in the French Church from a fifteenth-century incunabulum attacking Pierre de Cugnières.[25] And Nicholas Cisner's oration on Frederick II was the basis for almost all of Foxe's account of the great Hohenstaufen emperor.[26] Strikingly, almost all of Foxe's extensive history of the Ottoman Empire was drawn from two works, both of which Foxe almost certainly acquired during his exile, and both of which had been printed by Foxe's employer, Oporinus. The first of these was Theodore Bibliander's controversial edition of the Qur'an (which included a number of historical and ethnographic works on the Turks). The second work – which, very probably, Foxe had corrected himself – was Laonikos Chalkokondyles's collection of sources of Turkish history.[27] And of course the entire section on the first 400 years of the Church that was added to the new edition was based on the *Magdeburg Centuries*. In other cases Foxe appears to have followed up references and then acquired the necessary works from abroad. For example, John Jewel and Thomas Harding had debated the veracity of a story about Pope Clement V putatively humiliating the Venetian doge, Francesco Dandalo, and each had cited the Venetian historian Sabellico as his source. By 1570 Foxe drew a fairly detailed account

[23] Cf. *1563*, pp. 190–1 with Johannes Cochlaeus, *Historiae Hussitarum* (Mainz, 1549), pp. 19–24.

[24] Cf. *1570*, pp. 659, 701–5, 741 and 763–4 with Cochlaeus, *Historiae Hussitarum*, pp. 19–25, 29–33, 38–55, 165–8, and 175.

[25] Cf. *1570*, pp. 443–57 with Petrus Bertrandus, *Libellus de iurisdictione ecclesiastica contra Petrum de Cugnieres* (Paris, 1495).

[26] Cf. *1570*, pp. 373–4 and 377–95 with Nicholas Cisner, *De Fredericus II Imp. Oratio* (Strasbourg, 1608), pp. 97–102, 104, 107–10, 123–30, 133–6, 139–43, 153–6, 159–69, 176–9, 183–97, 199–201 and 204–9.

[27] An edition of this work, *Laonicii Chalcondylae Atheniensis, De origine et rebus gestis Turcorum* ... (Basle, 1566) was printed by Oporinus while Foxe was working as a proofreader in his printing house. Foxe cites the work as a source on *1570*, pp. 897 and 898. For an example of Foxe's use of Chalkokondyles, cf. *1570*, p. 898 with *De origine*, pp. 179–80. For a complete documentation of Foxe's use of this work see the online edition of the *Acts and Monuments* at: www.hrionline. sheffield.c.uk/foxe/editions/html.

of the incident from Sabellico's *Enneads*, which he had clearly consulted to verify Jewel's account.[28] For the Reformation itself Foxe drew on a great number of continental sources – too many to discuss here. Of special importance though was his extensive use of Jean Crespin's 1564 martyrology and his increasing reliance on Heinrich Pantaleon's martyrology.[29]

Foxe not only widened his use of printed sources, he extended his use of manuscript sources also. As we have seen, the dominant archival sources of the 1563 edition were the London diocesan records and, as we have also seen, Foxe had not completed his work on these. Working backwards from Mary's reign, he had only reached the register of Bishop Cuthbert Tunstall (1522–30). In the 1570 edition Foxe resumed working backwards on the London records, taking material from a now lost court book or books, which covered (at least) heresy trials held under Richard Fitzjames and Cuthbert Tunstall.[30] Foxe also made use for the first time of the registers of Richard Fitzjames (1506–22).[31] Also during the period between the first and second editions, Foxe began systematically quarrying the archiepiscopal registers at Lambeth Palace. Interestingly, the procedure seems to have been the exact opposite of that Foxe used for the London episcopal records; instead of beginning at the present and working backwards in time, he began with the registers of William Courtenay (1381–96)

---

[28] Jewel, *Works*, III, p. 23, and IV, pp. 692–7. Cf. *1570*, p. 460 with *M. Antonii Cocci Sabellici Opera Omnia*, 2 vols. (Basle, 1566), II, col. 791–2.

[29] Many of Foxe's accounts of Protestant martyrs in the Low Countries and almost all of his accounts of Protestant martyrs in France were reprinted from Jean Crespin's *Actiones et monumenta martyrum*, which was printed in Geneva in 1560. But in the 1570 edition Foxe also drew accounts of individual martyrs from the 1564 edition of Crespin's martyrology. Cf., for example, the group of French martyrs described in *1570*, pp. 1047–59 with Jean Crespin, *Actes des martyrs* (Geneva, 1564), pp. 792–7, 828–37, 839–44, 847–53, 855–7, 871–902 and 906–7. Strikingly, Foxe's account of the auto-da-fé at Valladolid on 21 May 1559 is also taken from Crespin's 1564 edition (cf. *1570*, pp. 1063–5 with Crespin, *Actes des martyrs*, pp. 903–6). Pantaleon's martyrology was used extensively by Foxe for his accounts of Protestant martyrs outside England. Merely as an example of this, it is worth observing that all the accounts of Italian Reformation martyrs in Foxe – except for the story of Francisco de Enzinas's imprisonment and escape in Rome in 1545 – were drawn from Pantaleon's martyrology (cf. *1570*, pp. 1066–73 with *Martyrum Historia*, pp. 101, 177–8, 200–9, 263–5 and 296–9).

[30] Foxe is apparently drawing on this book or books in *1570*, pp. 928–30 and 1184–92. There is some evidence for the provenance of these books. In the seventeenth century Archbishop Ussher took notes from these records, which he states had been kept at Lambeth Palace. Some of his notes duplicate material that Foxe had used (cf. Trinity College, Dublin, MS 775, fos. 122ʳ–5ʳ with *1570*, pp. 928–30).

[31] Cf., for example, GLL, MS N531/9, fos. 25ʳ–6ᵛ with *1570*, pp. 927–8. In a rare acknowledgement of the help a copyist had given him, in the text of the *Acts and Monuments* Foxe mentioned that one R. Carket, citizen of London, had copied records from the registers of Bishop Fitzjames of London (*1570*, p. 927). Foxe also mentioned that John Medwel, servant to a 'Master Carket, scrivener' was imprisoned for owning heretical books under Bishop Stokesley (*1570*, p. 1189). It appears that Foxe received this report of Medwel's ordeals from Carket. It is also an indication that Carket was aiding Foxe out of his religious zeal and was probably a volunteer.

and worked forwards.[32] In addition, documents were also copied for Foxe from the registers of Durham, Bath and Wells, Rochester, Lincoln and Hereford.[33]

The 1563 edition had opened the floodgates for torrents of personal testimony. Participants in the events described in the book, or their friends and families, often sent material to Foxe or to Day, presenting their versions of what had happened. These individual informants ranged across the social spectrum, from the lowly Isobel Malt of Horn Alley in London, who provided a far-fetched story of a plot to have her son declared Mary Tudor's child, to Bishop Grindal of London who contributed his reminiscences of Nicholas Ridley and other Cambridge evangelists.[34] Such testimony was accompanied by rivers of documents praising people, vilifying people, justifying individual conduct or condemning it, all flowing into Day's printing house.

This material was often of the highest value and placed biographical flesh on the dry bones supplied by the official records. In some cases testimony from individual informants resurrected Protestant heroes from almost total oblivion. In the 1563 edition Foxe had the merest mention, totalling only twenty-five words, of the burning of Rawlins White, a Cardiff fisherman. In 1570 this was replaced by an extremely detailed and vivid account of the life and death of this self-taught gospeller and martyr.[35] Similarly Foxe has no mention before the 1570 edition of Thomas Dusgate (or Benet), who was burned for heresy in Exeter in 1532. In the second edition, however, Foxe

---

[32] Cf. LPL, Courtenay Register, fos. 26^v–34^r and 69^r with *1570*, pp. 535–44. The inference that Foxe worked forward can be gleaned from the fact that the documents he drew from the register of William Warham (1503–22) were printed out of chronological order. Thus the first document reproduced from the register, a decree banning heretical books, is only printed in the section detailing events after 1546 (cf. LPL, Warham Register, fos. 182^r–6^v with *1570*, pp. 1429–38). Foxe also printed, even later in the book, material on heresy trials conducted by Warham back in 1511 (cf. LPL, Warham Register, fos. 169^r–74^r with *1570*, pp. 1453–6).

[33] For Foxe's use of Durham records see below, p. 148. Foxe's account of the trial of Richard Lush (*1570*, p. 2196) was copied from the registers of Gilbert Bourne, bishop of Bath and Wells. The transcript of this extract survives among Foxe's papers (BL, Harley MS 421, fos. 113^r–14^r). For Foxe drawing material from the registers of Maurice Griffith, bishop of Rochester, see *1570*, pp. 1859–60 and 1869. For Foxe drawing from Hereford material on the Lollard martyrs, William Swinderby and Walter Brute, cf. *Registrum Johannis Trefnant, Episcopi Herefordiensis, AD MCCCLXXXIX–MCCCCIV*, ed. William W. Capes, Canterbury and York Society XX (London, 1916), pp. 231–396 and 401–11 with *1570*, pp. 553–660. Foxe also drew on now lost court book(s) of Bishop John Longland of Lincoln for his persecution of Lollards in 1521: see *1570*, pp. 117 [recte 917]–18 and 946–64. Ussher also copied a small extract from this court book or books, which are currently in Trinity College, Dublin, MS 775, fos. 128^v–9^r.

[34] *1570*, pp. 1772, 1152 and 1566.   [35] Cf. *1563*, p. 1101 with *1570*, pp. 1726–9.

reprinted a detailed narrative, which covered four pages, of Dusgate's eventful life and even more eventful death, which he had received from the distinguished Exeter antiquary John Hooker (alias Vowell).[36] These accounts from informants vastly swelled Foxe's original material. For example, thanks to testimony from William Hunter's brother, the account of Hunter's martyrdom more than doubled in length in the 1570 edition.[37]

Yet denunciation went hand-in-hand with acclamation and this denunciation in turn stimulated justification and self-exculpation, all of which increasingly swelled the size of Foxe's text. For example, most of Foxe's material on the martyrs of the early Scottish Reformation was supplied to him by John Winram, superintendent of Fife, in an adroit attempt to forestall criticism of his pre-Reformation past.[38] The account of the martyr Julins Palmer in the 1563 edition motivated two Protestant ministers, Thomas Perry and John Moyer, to collect materials on Palmer's life. Among the details of this material was the claim that one Thomas Thackham had betrayed Palmer. This provoked Thackham into sending an elaborate defence of his character and conduct to Foxe. This in turn elicited an even longer and more detailed denunciation from Perry and Moyer. This welter of denunciation, defence and renewed denunciation survives in hundreds of pages of manuscript material in Foxe's papers. Foxe himself was also tossed to and fro by these countervailing blasts: in the 1583 edition he printed a qualified retraction of the charges against Thackham, only to later – having apparently been further persuaded by Thackham's adversaries of his guilt – print a renewed attack on this controversial figure.[39]

---

[36] *1570*, pp. 1280–4. Coincidentally, Foxe also received an account of Dusgate from Ralph Morice, which the martyrologist did not utilise, although he may have consulted it (BL, Harley 419, fo. 125[r–v]). Dusgate's martyrdom underscores the value of the information communicated to Foxe in personal testimonies. Not only had Dusgate's death previously eluded Foxe entirely, it had also escaped the notice of John Bale, Edward Hall and every other contemporary historian or martyrological source.

[37] Cf. *1563*, pp. 1109–10 with *1570*, pp. 1712–16.

[38] Thomas S. Freeman, '"The reik of Maister Patrik Hammylton": John Foxe, John Winram and the Martyrs of the Scottish Reformation', *Sixteenth Century Journal*, 27 (1996), pp. 43–60.

[39] Thackham's self-defence is BL, Harley MS 425, fos. 18[r]–32[v]. Foxe sent Thackham's account to Perry who wrote back to Foxe declaring that Thackham was a liar and vowing that 'no diligence shall be spared' in refuting him (BL, Harley MS 416, fo. 100[r]). Perry was as good as his word: a portion – only a portion – of the detailed denunciation of Thackham survives as BL, Harley MS 425, fos. 33[r]–64[r]. Foxe's retraction of the charges against Thackham is in *1583*, p. 1937, but later in the same edition he printed a letter from Moyer to Perry, summarising Thackham's alleged misdeeds (*1583*, p. 2141).

Another example of the swirling riptides of condemnation and justification which battered Foxe throughout successive editions of the *Acts and
Monuments* was the conflicting accounts of the role one Robert King, a
'deviser of Enterludes', played in the execution of the Marian martyr
Rowland Taylor. In the 1563 edition King was described as one of those
who 'studiously' piled faggots around the martyr at the stake. In the second
edition, the negative implications of this description became overt. King,
now denounced as a 'common rayler', was castigated for 'diligently' piling
faggots around Taylor. However, in the third edition Foxe said that King
placed gunpowder around the martyr and did it moreover 'onely for quick-
ness and for love of him [i.e., Taylor] and his cause as he himselfe [King]
testifieth'. But by the time the fourth edition was printed, Foxe metaphorically threw up his hands, stating that King did place gunpowder around
Taylor but 'what he meant and did therein (he himself sayeth he did it for
the best, and for quick dispatch), the Lord knoweth which shall judge al,
more of this I have not to say'.[40] The hothouse climate created by the
passions of recent persecution stimulated a luxuriant growth of innuendo,
rumour, accusation and denial, which provided an abundance of material
for Foxe's martyrology but one whose extent was clearly not foreseen by
Day and probably not by Foxe himself.

The chronological scope, moreover, of these individual informants was
surprisingly wide-ranging. For an account of the execution, which first
appeared in the 1570 edition, of two Lollards burned at the stake in 1506,
'William Tylsley' and a miller named Roberts, Foxe cited as his sources two
eyewitnesses to the execution: one William Page, 'an aged father and
yet alyve' and one Agnes Wetherley, 'wydowe, being about the age of an
hundreth yeares, yet lyving and witness hereof'.[41] Foxe's only source for his
account of Lawrence Ghest, burned in Salisbury, 'for matter of the sacrament in the dayes of King Henry VII' was the 'credible reporte' of William
Russell, 'an aged man dwelling late in Colmanstreate' who was not only
present but was branded on the cheek at Ghest's execution. Russell's
reminiscences were reported to Foxe by Russell's daughter and confirmed
by Richard Webbe who lived in Russell's house and had heard him relate

[40] *1563*, p. 1079, *1570*, p. 1703, *1576*, p. 1453, *1583*, p. 1527. Next to this brief account of King, a marginal
note appeared in the 1570 edition of the *Acts and Monuments*. This note related that King was also one
of the armed guards who escorted Protestant martyrs to be burned at the stake in Bury St Edmunds.
This note was retained in all subsequent editions of the book, although this is probably due as much
to the neglect of the critical apparatus in these later editions as to anything else.
[41] *1570*, p. 117 [recte 917]. Wetherley, who is Foxe's source for 'Tylsley's' execution, seems, despite her
age, to have been fundamentally accurate: the writ from Chancery authorising the execution of
William Tilsworth for heresy in 1506 survives (TNA, C 85/115/10).

the incident.[42] Webbe in turn was also the source for information about the young Hugh Latimer and, in a classic demonstration of the dangers of oral testimony, for the fictitious story of the death of Dr Thomas Wodyngton, gored to death by a vengeful bull in Chipping Sodbury.[43]

Webbe is far from unique in being a source for several different incidents. In a number of cases people who began by contributing one anecdote to Foxe ending up supplying much more information. An example of this is Ralph Morice, who began by sending in one anecdote about Cranmer and ended up by contributing numerous anecdotes on the Henrician Reformation, as well as a substantial biography of Thomas Cranmer for Foxe's work.[44] A further interesting example of this is supplied by the brothers John and Roger Hall of Maidstone. They began by contributing a narrative of the 'cruell and unchristian handling' of their sister, Alice Benden, who was burned in Canterbury in June 1557. Apparently in answer to inquiries by Foxe for further information they also sent in accounts of other local martyrs: Edmund Allin, Thomas Read and Joan Bradbridge.[45]

In the case of the Hall brothers, and assuredly in many other cases, Foxe himself pumped informants for further information. William Maldon, explaining how he came to write an account of his being beaten during the reign of Henry VIII for the possession of heretical books, provides a vivid description of Foxe's relentless quest for information:

jentyll reader, understand that I do not take in hande to ryte this lytyll tratys as followeth of myne owne provoking, but I with another chanced to goe in the company of Mr Foxe, the gatherer together of this grate boke, and he desired us to tell hym if wee knewe of any man that had suffered persecution for the gospel of Jesus Christ, to the end he myght add it unto the boke of marters. Then said I that I knew one that was whipped in king Henryes time for it, of his father. Then he enquired of me his name then I bewrayed and said it was I myself, and told him a

---

[42] *1570*, pp. 918–19.

[43] Ibid., p. 919 (Foxe calls the bull's victim 'Whittington'). On this story see Mozley, *John Foxe and his Book*, p. 164, and Thomas S. Freeman, 'Fate, Faction and Fiction in Foxe's "Book of Martyrs"', *Historical Journal*, 43 (2000), pp. 613–14.

[44] BL, Harley MS 416, fos. 183ʳ–4ʳ. Stories contributed by Morice are in *1570*, pp. 1355–6, 1359–60 and 2043–5; Foxe also cited him explicitly as his source for an improbable story that Henry VIII promised the French Ambassador in 1546 that he would completely abolish the Mass in England (*1570*, p. 1426). Magnus Williamson persuasively argues that Morice is also the source for the famous story of Thomas Cromwell obtaining papal indulgences for Boston, which is first related in *1570*, pp. 1346–7. 'Evangelicalism at Boston, Oxford and Windsor under Henry VIII: John Foxe's Narratives Recontextualised', in *John Foxe: At Home and Abroad*, ed. Loades, pp. 38–9. Morrice's biographical sketch of Archbishop Cranmer is CCCC MS 128, pp. 405–40; to see how extensively Foxe drew on this narrative for his life of Cranmer, cf. *1570*, pp. 2032–43.

[45] Thomas S. Freeman, 'Notes on a Source for John Foxe's Account of the Marian Persecution in Kent and Sussex', *Historical Research*, 67 (1994), pp. 203–11.

pece of it. Then was he desirous to have the whole surcomstance of it. Then I promised him to wryght it.[46]

On occasion, Foxe apparently rounded up oral testimony in order to support an important, but contested, point. Thus when Nicholas Harpsfield stated, citing Thomas More as his authority, that the prominent evangelical Thomas Bilney had recanted at the stake, Foxe mustered a list of witnesses, including William Turner, the dean of Wells; a citizen of Norwich (where Bilney had been burned); a brother-in-law of Matthew Parker; and the Archbishop himself, all denying that Bilney had retracted his beliefs.[47] In a striking indication of the importance Foxe attached to oral reports, he actually had John Field, the future co-author of the controversial *Admonition to Parliament*, working for him as an informal (and certainly unpaid) research assistant, gathering and verifying them.[48] It was inevitable that the publication of a book covering events that were recent and extremely controversial should have induced people to send their historical gleanings to Foxe's vast granary. But it was not inevitable that Foxe was not only prepared to include so much of this material in his martyrology, but that he personally hunted for even more of it with a zeal that bordered on insatiability, and which placed an enormous logistical burden on Day's shoulders.

Another consequence of the increased scope of the book was the reliance on chronicles and histories – many of them unpublished at this time – covering the history of medieval England. Foxe himself was a not inconsiderable collector of medieval manuscripts, some of which he seems to have inherited from John Bale.[49] But these were not enough to sustain the

---

[46] BL, Harley MS 590, fo. 77ʳ; printed in Nichols, *Narratives*, pp. 348–9. Maldon, like so many of Foxe's informants, went on to contribute other anecdotes to Foxe about himself and others. See *1570*, pp. 2278, 2302–3.

[47] *1570*, p. 1150; cf. Harpsfield, *Dialogi sex*, p. 822. (This is another example of Harpsfield stimulating Foxe's research.) On the controversies surrounding Bilney's various trials and his execution, see John F. Davis, 'The Trials of Thomas Bilney and the English Reformation', *Historical Journal*, 24 (1981), pp. 775–90, and Greg Walker, 'Saint or Sinner? The 1527 Heresy Trial of Thomas Bilney Reconsidered', *Journal of Ecclesiastical History*, 40 (1989), pp. 219–38.

[48] BL, Harley MS 416, fo. 188ʳ.

[49] Among these are twelve manuscripts currently in the library of Magdalen College, Oxford, which belonged to the martyrologist and were given by his son Samuel to the college in 1614. On these manuscripts see N. R. Ker and A. J. Piper, *Medieval Manuscripts in British Libraries*, 4 vols. (Oxford, 1983–92), III, pp. 644–5. Also see Ralph Hanna, 'An Oxford Library Interlude: The Manuscripts of John Foxe the Martyrologist', *Bodleian Library Record*, 17 (2002), pp. 314–26, although this article must be used with caution and overestimates the number of manuscripts that came from the Foxe family to the college. For the purposes of this book it is simply worth noting that three of these manuscripts were once owned by John Bale and contain his annotations. These are Magdalen College Library, Latin MSS 53, 36 and 172.

necessary research into the medieval past. Foxe's essential problem was that he needed to demonstrate the existence of proto-Protestants in England before the Reformation and at least the remnants of pure doctrine within the English Church during the centuries preceding Luther. For these purposes the standard post-medieval history of England, Polydore Vergil's *Anglica historia* was of no use to Foxe.[50] He had to blaze his own trail through the distant past, which at that time was virtually untouched, and to create his own historical narrative. This entailed thorough, if far from impartial, reading and analysis of medieval English historical works. And given the lack of institutional research centres at this time, this meant that Foxe had to have the cooperation of individual manuscript collectors and bibliophiles. Previously Foxe had relied largely on the collections and research of one of the greatest of these, John Bale, but now, especially since he was confronted with hostile and erudite critics, he required much more assistance.

This came from numerous people. For example, Foxe stated that he consulted an old chronicle borrowed of 'one Permynger'.[51] Foxe also reprinted a bull of Pope Martin V, which he copied from a manuscript belonging to Richard Hakluyt, the cousin and guardian of the future author of *The Principal Navigations*.[52] Foxe's old friend, James Pilkington, had described in a work printed in 1563 a letter from Richard II to Boniface IX, in which the king cited historical precedents to demonstrate that secular authorities had supremacy over clerical authorities.[53] This letter was subsequently printed by Foxe in the second edition of the 'Book of Martyrs', where Foxe declared that the letter came 'ex fragmento libri cuisdam Dunelm'.[54] Similarly Thomas Blundeville, the noted Elizabethan writer, showed him a document which Foxe used to demonstrate that priests had been married in medieval England.[55] Medieval documents gathered by John le Hunte (John Day's brother-in-law) from the records of Little Bradley,

---

[50] For Foxe specifically denouncing Vergil's 'slaunderous penne' and putative inaccuracy in denouncing such Protestant heroes as John Wiclif and Sir John Oldcastle, see *1570*, pp. 526 and 686–8. Also see *1570*, p. 832, for Foxe rejecting Vergil as an authority because of his alleged pro-Catholic bias.

[51] Ibid., p. 830.

[52] The bull is *1570*, pp. 768–73; the citation of Hakluyt as the owner is on p. 773.

[53] See *The Works of James Pilkington*, ed. James Scholefield (Parker Society, Cambridge, 1842), p. 640.

[54] *1570*, pp. 608–11. That this was the same letter that Pilkington had previously mentioned is demonstrated by the fact that he cites the same historical precedents that appear in the letter Foxe prints.

[55] *1570*, p. 1335. Interestingly Foxe recorded the date that he saw this document – 24 November 1567 – which indicates that he was collecting this material well in advance of the printing of the second edition.

Suffolk, and by John Ford (a member of the Inner Temple) were also used by Foxe as part of his argument against clerical celibacy.[56]

IV

But by far and away the most important of the collectors who aided Foxe was Matthew Parker, archbishop of Canterbury.[57] It was from Parker that Foxe obtained many of his most important sources for post-Conquest medieval English history: most especially Matthew Paris's *Chronica maiora*, Gervase of Canterbury's chronicle, and the version of Thomas of Walsingham's *Chronica maiora*, now known as the 'Chronicon Angliae'.[58] On at least one occasion, Foxe explicitly acknowledged that his source was a manuscript – from the library of Worcester Cathedral – loaned to him by Parker.[59] A number of manuscripts once belonging to the prelate and surviving with the bulk of his collection in Corpus Christi College, Cambridge, were either owned by Foxe or at the very least consulted by him, as they contain his marginal notes.[60] Researches conducted

[56] Ibid., pp. 1337–8.

[57] For an overview of Matthew Parker as a collector and editor of historical manuscripts and especially for the religious motivations that lay behind these activities, see Benedict Scott Robinson, '"Darke speech": Matthew Parker and the Reforming of History', *Sixteenth Century Journal*, 29 (1998), pp. 1061–83, and McKisack, *Medieval History in the Tudor Age*, pp. 26–49.

[58] Foxe cites Matthew Parker as having given him 'a chronicon monasteri Albani' (i.e., one version of Walsingham's great chronicle history). *1570*, pp. 525–6. Two copies of this manuscript belonged to Parker: Cotton MS Otho, Cii and BL, Harley MS 3634. One of Walsingham's nineteenth-century editors believes that Foxe used Cotton MS Otho Cii (*Chronicon Angliae*, ed. E. M. Thompson (Rolls Society, London, 1874), pp. xiii–xiv and xviii). This is incorrect; Foxe demonstrably used Harley MS 3634. For Parker's ownership of one of the extremely rare copies of Gervase of Canterbury, see *The Historical Works of Gervase of Canterbury*, ed. William Stubbs, 2 vols. (Rolls Series, London, 1879–80), I, pp. li–lii. For an example of Foxe's use of Gervase of Canterbury see *1570*, pp. 309–11; drawn from *Gervase of Canterbury*, I, pp. 364–9 and 383–8. Note also Foxe's explicit, repeated citation of Gervase's chronicle as a source in *1570*, pp. 302–7 and 311–12. Matthew Paris's *Chronica maiora* was Foxe's paramount source for English and even some European history for the first six decades of the thirteenth century. Foxe particularly relied on this work because Paris's consistently anti-papal interpretation of events was quite congenial to the martyrologist. This chronicle was Foxe's most important source for the crucial pontificates of Innocent III, Honorius III, Gregory IX, Innocent IV and Alexander IV. Cf. *1570*, pp. 328–33, 337, 344–8, 354–9, 363–70, 377–9, 405–7, 409–11, 437–8, 503 with Paris, *Chronica maiora*, II, pp. 517–20, 529, 536, 539–44, 569–71, 647–8, 650–3; III, pp. 102–3, 113–14, 145, 151–3, 169–72, 184–9, 207–8, 219, 303–8, 313–17, 397, 414, 448–60, 469–71, 480, 493, 499, 567, 610–11; IV, pp. 6–7, 9–11, 14–15, 31–2, 35–8, 55, 73, 101–2, 137, 161, 224, 259, 284–5, 314–15, 321–4, 368, 374–6, 391, 401–2, 412–17, 419–23, 431–2, 441–55, 478–9, 504, 506–10, 526–9, 536–7, 550, 552, 554–7, 558, 560–1, 564–6, 580; V, pp. 38–40, 97–8, 109–10, 177–8, 355, 389–93, 429–30, 497–8; VI, pp. 229–31. At the time Foxe was writing the *Acts and Monuments*, Matthew Parker had collected all the surviving manuscripts for Paris's *Chronica maiora*. See May McKisack, *Medieval History*, p. 34.

[59] *1570*, p. 605.

[60] These include the chronicle of John of Brompton (CCCC, MS 96), Nicholas Trivet's *Annals* (CCCC, MS 1152), a transcribed excerpt from *Life and Death of Edward II* (CCCC, MS 281, fos.

under Parker's auspices into the Anglo-Saxon Church also produced a harvest in which Foxe shared, most notably in the martyrologist's reprinting of sections of William Lambarde's *Archaionomia*, and of a sermon by the tenth-century English abbot, Aelfric, which had previously been printed as part of the Parker-sponsored collection of writings, *A Testimony of Antiquity*.[61] The reproduction of the *Testimony of Antiquity* reveals Parker's active involvement in the reprinting of this material. Although Foxe largely repeated Aelfric's translation in the *Testimony* on a word-for-word basis, he did make some significant changes. He omitted two sacramental miracles, demonstrating the corporeal presence of Christ in the Eucharist, which Parker had dismissed as 'monkish' interpolations but had nevertheless retained in his text. Foxe also arbitrarily changed the word 'Mass' to the more anodyne word 'supper'. These changes were almost certainly editorial decisions made by Foxe himself. However, in other places mistranslations of the Old English in the *Testimony* were corrected.[62] Foxe did not have the linguistic expertise to make these corrections himself; one of Parker's associates must have reread and corrected the text before it was printed.[63] (This, by the way, is another indication of the concern with accuracy manifested throughout the editing of the second edition.)

An egregious example of the way in which Matthew Parker replaced John Bale as the primary conduit of antiquarian materials to Foxe comes from the letters of the so-called 'Volusianus'. These were actually letters defending clerical marriage that had been composed in the eleventh century as part of the opposition to the Gregorian reform movement. One of these letters was well known in Europe: it had been tendentiously attributed to Ulric, the bishop of Augsburg (c. 890–973), a venerated figure who had been

---

48^v–49^r) (which was mistakenly attributed to Thomas De la Moore), a copy of the letters of Archbishop Anselm (CCCC, MS 135), and a thirteenth-century chronicle attributed to Walter of Coventry (CCCC, MS 175). According to a note by John Joscelyn, Foxe actually owned this last manuscript. See M. R. James, *A Descriptive Catalogue of the Manuscripts in the Library of Corpus Christi College Cambridge*, 2 vols. (Cambridge, 1912), 1, p. xix. Fascinatingly, this manuscript had previously belonged to Sir John Cheke; Foxe may well have obtained it through the good offices of Cheke's close friend William Cecil.

[61] Cf. William Lambarde, *Archaionomia, sive de priscis anglorum legibus libri, sermone Anglico, vestustate antiquissimo, aliquot abhinc seculis conscripti, . . .* STC 15142, with *1570*, pp. 146–7. The extracts from Anglo-Saxon law codes, which appear later in the volume, are also translated from the *Archaionomia*. Cf. *Archaionomia*, fos. 1^r–2^r, 19^r, 29^r–31^r, 41^r, 52^r–8^r, 60^r, 72^r–4^r, 77^r–8^r, 82^r, 84^r and 98^r–104^r with *1570*, sigs. 2M2$^{r–v}$.

[62] See Theodore H. Leinbaugh, 'Aelfric's *Sermo de Sacrificio in Die Pascae*: Anglican Polemic in the Sixteenth and Seventeenth Centuries', in *Anglo-Saxon Scholarship: The First Three Centuries*, ed. Carl T. Berkhout and Milton McGatch (Boston, 1982), pp. 56–8.

[63] On Foxe's ignorance of Old English, see note 108 below.

canonised in 993. The letter was supposed to have been sent by bishop Ulric to Pope Nicholas I.[64]

Later Protestants, including Matthias Flacius and at first John Bale, followed this attribution in good faith.[65] However, in a letter to Matthew Parker written in 1560, Bale rejected the idea that St Ulric of Augsburg was the author of this letter.[66] Then in 1563 Bale discovered a manuscript that had belonged to the monastery of St Augustine, Canterbury.[67] This contained, inter alia, a copy of two letters, both supporting clerical marriage and both attributed to a bishop of Carthage named Volusianus. (There was a bishop of Carthage named Volusianus in the fifth century; he was fairly well known to medieval Christians because he had corresponded with his fellow North African bishop, St Augustine. But there was no bishop of Carthage in the ninth century, much less one named Volusianus. Both Bale and Parker did not explicitly identify the supposed author of these letters with Augustine's correspondent, nor did they make any attempt to identify this enigmatic figure at all.) The first of these letters was the same one that had been previously attributed to St Ulric. Bale gave the manuscript to Matthew Parker.[68] Years later, in 1569, Matthew Parker had these letters printed.[69]

Foxe was initially unaware of these developments when he was penning his second edition of the *Acts and Monuments*. Towards the beginning of

---

[64] See *Libelli de lite imperatorum et pontificum saeculis XI et XII*, ed. Ernst Dümmler et al., in *Monumenta Germaniae Historica*, 3 vols. (Hanover, 1896), I, pp. 254–60, and E. Frauenknecht, *Die Verteidigung der Priesterehe in der Reformzeit* (Hanover, 1997), pp. 176–80.

[65] Flacius, *Catalogus*, pp. 101–9, Bale, *Catalogus*, p. 118, and John Bale, *Acta Romanorum Pontificum* (Basle, 1558), pp. 116–17.

[66] See Graham and Watson, *The Recovery of the Past in Early Elizabethan England*, pp. 28 and 48, n. 156. Both Bale and Parker were troubled by the intractable chronological discrepancy between the pontificate of Nicholas I (d. 867) and the tenure of Ulric in the see of Augsburg (924–73); see Catherine Hall, 'The One-Way Trail: Some Observations on CCC MS. 101 and G&CC MS. 427', *Transactions of the Cambridge Bibliographical Society*, 11 (1998), pp. 278–9. Although neither Graham, Watson nor Hall mentions this, Bale's doubts had almost certainly been inspired by the Catholic polemicist Fredericus Staphylus who had recently pointed out discrepancies in the putative provenance and dating of the pseudo-Ulric letter. Fredericus Staphylus, *Defensio pro trimembri theologia* (Augsburg, 1559), sigs. B4ʳ–C1ʳ. At first Bale came up with his own ingenious and spurious 'solution' to the problem of the authorship of this manuscript – he claimed that the author was (another non-existent) bishop, one Huldericus or Guldericus of Utrecht (see Hall, 'One-Way Trail', p. 279).

[67] This is now Gonville and Caius College Library MS 427. This manuscript is discussed in Hall,' One-Way Trail', pp. 274–5.

[68] *1570*, p. 1320; cf. Hall, 'One-Way Trail', pp. 279–80.

[69] *Epistolae duae D. Volusiani Episcopi Carthaginensis … de celibatu cleri* (London, 1569), STC 24872. Parker's sudden decision to print these letters is almost certainly due to Nicholas Harpsfield having repeated Staphylus's criticisms of the attribution to Ulric (*Dialogi sex*, pp. 146–52). Once again we see Nicholas Harpsfield's attacks influencing the content of Foxe's work.

this edition, Foxe printed an English translation of Flacius's version of the Ulric/Volusianus letter, and repeated Flacius's claim that the letter had been written by St Ulric.[70] Yet over a thousand pages later, Foxe printed the two 'Volusianus' letters together. Moreover, Foxe made it clear that he had examined the actual manuscript containing these letters, and furthermore that Matthew Parker had loaned it to him:

> As touching the antiquitie of thys epistle above prefixed, it appeareth by the copie, which I have seene, and received of the right reverend ... Matthewe Archbyshop of Canterbury, to be of an old and auncient writing, bothe by the forme of the characters and by the wearing of the Parchment almost consumed by length of years and tyme.[71]

Foxe went on to admit that St Ulric was not the author of this letter, as he had previously stated, and now identified Volusianus as its author.[72] (Foxe did not look a gift horse in the mouth, by trying to determine whether or not there had actually been a bishop of Carthage named Volusianus who could have written this letter.)

v

But Parker was more than a collector; he maintained a circle of scholars in his household who annotated, cross-referenced and compared the texts of the different manuscripts that the archbishop consulted, commandeered, begged, borrowed and perhaps even stole.[73] And the work of these scholars seems, at least on occasion, to have been placed at Foxe's disposal. For example, in the 1563 edition Foxe had asserted that King John was poisoned by a monk from Swineshead Abbey. This claim was pounced on by Foxe's Catholic critics who were anxious to disassociate a Catholic cleric from an act of regicide. In 1565 Thomas Harding listed sources that stated that King John had not been poisoned but had died of natural causes instead.[74] Two years later, Harding's colleague, Thomas Stapleton, issued a detailed and incisive criticism of the poisoning story.[75] In rebuttal Foxe cited no fewer than thirteen chronicles in the 1570 edition, affirming that the king was

---

[70] *1570*, pp. 182–4.   [71] Ibid., p. 1321.

[72] As we shall see, it is typical of the third and fourth editions of the *Acts and Monuments* that they did nothing to clarify a potentially confusing situation created in the 1570 edition. Both versions of the first 'Volusianus' letter, one attributed to St Ulric and the other to the fictitious prelate of Carthage, were reprinted in the 1576 and 1583 editions with Ulric and Volusianus both credited as authors, yet without any further explanation of this inconsistency (*1576*, pp. 138–40 and 1129–33; *1583*, pp. 137–9 and 1154–62).

[73] For information on Parker's circle, apart from Graham and Watson, *Recovery of the Past*, see Robinson, '"Darke speech"', pp. 1061–8 and 1072–6; also see McKisack, *Medieval History*, pp. 26–49.

[74] Harding, *Confutation*, fo. 184[r–v].   [75] Stapleton, *Counterblast*, fos. 312[v]–14[r].

indeed poisoned.[76] The evidence suggests that the references to these thirteen sources were gathered by Matthew Parker himself from manuscripts in the archbishop's possession, some of which were not used by Foxe anywhere else in his text.[77] Apparently Parker, or his associates, combed through the archbishop's manuscript collection to find evidence supporting Foxe on a point where the martyrologist was vulnerable.

Sometime before the publication of the 1570 edition, Parker also supplied Foxe with eyewitness testimony about the contested circumstances surrounding the execution of his mentor, Thomas Bilney.[78] Moreover, John Joscelyn, the archbishop's secretary and chief researcher in antiquarian matters, also supplied Foxe with his own personal testimony about Edmund Bonner having struck his father Sir Thomas Joscelyn, during that choleric prelate's visitation of Essex in 1554.[79] Joscelyn's assistance points us to the area where Parker made perhaps his greatest contribution to the *Acts and Monuments*: he enabled Foxe to reap the benefits of an elaborate network of antiquarians, collectors and scholars that he had carefully constructed. Foxe's debt to these people for his medieval English history cannot be overestimated.[80]

For example, Foxe frequently borrowed material from William Carye, the London clothworker and manuscript collector.[81] Carye had earlier loaned a number of important manuscripts to John Bale and Bale drew Archbishop Parker's attention to Carye's collection.[82] Foxe frequently acknowledged borrowing a number of manuscripts from Carye, 'a citizen of London, a worthye treasurer of most worthy manuscripts of antiquitie'.[83] Among them was a 'certayne auncient written history', which Foxe

---

[76] *1570*, sig. NN3ʳ (for reasons that will be discussed in the next chapter, this section is not paginated).

[77] See Freeman, 'John Bale's Book of Martyrs?', pp. 208–10.   [78] *1570*, p. 1150.

[79] See ibid., pp. 1645–6. One of the sources Foxe listed for the story was 'Rich.K.', very probably Richard Kitchin, who was in Essex in 1554 and tied to Parker and Joscelyn. See J. and J. A. Venn, *Alumni Cantabrigienses*, 10 vols. (Cambridge, 1922–58), I, p. 37.

[80] Devorah Greenberg ('Community of the Texts') lists members of the 'scholarly and technical community, as named by various researchers' who assisted Foxe. Some of these names, such as Coverdale, Nowell (Alexander or Laurence? – Greenberg does not specify), Sampson, Becon (who died in 1567) and Bullinger are distinctly problematic. However, Greenberg supplies no evidence on exactly how these figures assisted Foxe.

[81] For what biographical information there is on William Carye and a description of his collection see Andrew G. Watson, 'Christopher and William Carye, Collectors of Monastic Manuscripts, and "John Carye"', in *Medieval Manuscripts in Post-Medieval England*, ed. Andrew G. Watson (Aldershot, 2004), section V, pp. 135–42.

[82] John Bale, *Index Britanniae Scriptorum: John Bale's Index of British and Other Writers*, ed. Reginald Lane Poole and Mary Bateson, rev. Caroline Brett and James P. Carley (Woodbridge, 1990), pp. xxi, 62, 366, 427, 438–9, 477–8, 486, 490 and 492. Also see H. R. Luard, 'A Letter from Bishop Bale to Archbishop Parker', *Cambridge Antiquarian Society Communications*, 3 (1864–79), p. 166.

[83] *1570*, p. 198.

christened 'by the name of whom I borrowed this boke, with many other likewise without name, Historia Cariana'.[84] Nor did Foxe only borrow histories and chronicles from Carye; at one point he also acknowledged consulting 'certeine olde papers and recordes of William Carye', which described the execution of an old man in Smithfield for heresy in 1500.[85]

Particularly interesting is the cooperation between John Foxe and John Stow. The relationship between the two greatest Elizabethan historical writers is a subject that needs to be explored much more thoroughly. On a preliminary level it is certain that Foxe and Stow both consulted the sole manuscript of the so-called 'Great Chronicle' of London.[86] It is also clear that Foxe and Stow both used the sole copy of the Greyfriars chronicle. The manuscript was annotated by John Stow, but the chronicle was Foxe's source for his tale of John Street (or Streate), a London joiner arrested in 1554 for assaulting a priest during the Corpus Christi procession.[87] Given the almost polar opposition between the religious and social views of the two men, it is reasonable to assume that Parker, who was an indispensable patron to Stow, was the intermediary between these two scholars.[88] The use of a manuscript version of Walsingham's chronicle (now BL Harley MS 3634) would seem to demonstrate this. The manuscript is paginated and annotated by Parker but also annotated by Foxe and by John Stow.[89] This manuscript almost certainly came from William Carye, and Foxe states that he obtained it from Matthew Parker.[90] It ended up in the hands of John Stow from whence it eventually entered the collection of Robert Harley. Thus, in this case, we have a manuscript which Parker apparently obtained from Carye, and subsequently loaned to Foxe, who must have returned it to

---

[84] Ibid., p. 153. This is probably the same work also cited in *1570*, p. 326. For other citations by Foxe of Carye manuscripts see *1570*, pp. 185, 298–9, 463 and 494. One 'historia manuscripta, cui initium "Rex pictorum" ex bibliotheca Cariensi mutuata' (*1570*, p. 299), which Foxe cited, had previously been consulted by Bale (*Index Britanniae Scriptorum*, p. 477).

[85] *1570*, p. 117 [recte 917].

[86] *The Great Chronicle of London*, ed. A. H. Thomas and I. D. Thornley (London, 1938), pp. xvi–xvii.

[87] See *Chronicle of the Grey Friars of London*, pp. viii and 89. Foxe's version of the story first appears in *1563*, p. 1005.

[88] On the ties between Parker and Stow see Oliver Harris, 'Stow and the Contemporary Antiquarian Network', in *John Stow (1525–1605) and the Making of the English Past*, ed. Ian Gadd and Alexandra Gillespie (London, 2004), p. 29. On Stow's religious views and general outlook, see Patrick Collinson, 'John Stow and Nostalgic Antiquarianism', in *Imagining Early Modern London: Perceptions and Portrayals of the City from Stow to Strype 1598–1720*, ed. J. F. Merritt (Cambridge, 2001), pp. 27–51, and Ian W. Archer, 'John Stow: Citizen and Historian', in Gadd and Gillespie, *John Stow*, pp. 20–1.

[89] For Foxe's annotations see fos. 131^r, 152^v–3^v, 154^v, 173^v, 184^v, 186^r and 191^v; these annotations are devoted almost exclusively either to John Wiclif or to episodes of medieval religious history.

[90] See Watson, 'Christopher and William Carye', p. 140.

Parker, who then loaned the manuscript to Stow. This is probably only the tip of an iceberg but it goes some way towards indicating the fecund cross-pollination of various historical works, with the same manuscripts shared among a circle of historians and antiquarians which had Matthew Parker at its centre. Ian Archer has recently suggested that Stow's claims that Parker inspired his work were self-serving and so they may have been; nevertheless, the codicological commerce between Foxe, Parker and Stow should not be minimised.[91]

In contrast to Stow, the great antiquarian and fellow Parker protégé William Lambarde was a friend of Foxe and also shared his religious outlook.[92] In fact Foxe sent a copy of Lambarde's *Archaionomia* to a friend of his, William Bradbridge, dean of Salisbury, with a letter that not only praised that 'vir multis et egregiis dotibus ornatissimus Gulielmus Lambardus' but also recommended that Lambarde be admitted to Bradbridge's friendship as well as his library.[93] But Lambarde's friendship not only warmed Foxe's heart, it also benefited the *Acts and Monuments*. Lambarde was another important collector of manuscripts. The peregrinations of one particular manuscript provide an interesting example of the way in which manuscripts passed between the different members of Parker's circle. As part of a long argument against clerical celibacy, Foxe reprinted an extract from Florence of Worcester's *Chronicon ex chronicis*, transcribed, according to Foxe's handwritten note, from a 'codex Wigorniensis'.[94] The manuscript of the *Chronicon ex chronicis* passed through the hands of John Joscelyn and John Stow (who used it in compiling his contribution to Holinshed's *Chronicles*), ending up in William Lambarde's possession.[95]

Two very important sources for Foxe's history – the manuscript histories by Robert of Avesbury and Thomas Walsingham – similarly migrated within the Parker circle.[96] In the 1570 edition Foxe frequently confused these two

---

[91] Archer, 'John Stow', p. 22.
[92] On Parker's patronage of Lambarde, see below, p. 160. It should be remembered, however, that Lambarde and Stow were also friends – another indication of the interlinking ties between this circle of scholars. See Harris, 'Stow and the Contemporary Antiquarian Network', p. 32.
[93] The letter is found on a fly-leaf of a copy of the *Archaionomia* in the Henry E. Huntington Library in San Marino, California (shelfmark RB 62136). The authors would like to thank Professor Lori A. Ferrell for providing a copy of this letter.
[94] *1570*, pp. 1331 and 1334; BL, Harley MS 419, fos. 1ʳ–2ᵛ (this MS is the extract from Florence of Worcester).
[95] *The Chronicle of John of Worcester 1118–1170*, ed. J. R. H. Weaver (Oxford, 1908), pp. 5–7.
[96] Robert of Avesbury's *De Gestis Mirabilibus Regis Edwardi Tertii* was Foxe's major source for the events of this king's reign. Cf. Robert of Avesbury, *De Gestis Mirabilibus Regis Edwardi Tertii*, ed. E. M. Thompson (Rolls Series, London, 1889), pp. 312–20, 323–7, 330–9, 353, 355, 362–3, 367–9, 376–81, 383–4, 390–1, 395–6, 406–14 with *1570*, pp. 473–84.

sources. He corrected these mistakes in the 1576 edition. (In itself this is very
revealing. Foxe made very few changes of any kind to this edition and he
clearly felt that these corrections were of particular importance.) One of the
mistaken references and its correction reveals the provenance of these manuscripts. In the second edition Foxe stated that a particular letter from Edward
III was 'to be found in the story of Robertus Avesbury remaining in the library
of J. Stevenson, citizen of London'. This letter is actually to be found in
Thomas of Walsingham's *Historia Anglicana*, and Foxe noted this in the next
edition, adding that Walsingham's history was also in Stevenson's library.[97]
One of the manuscript copies of Robert of Avesbury's chronicle is now in the
Bodleian Library and has the name of 'John Stephynson' written in a
sixteenth-century hand at the beginning of the volume.[98] This copy, clearly
the one used by Foxe, belonged to Matthew Parker and subsequently to
William Lambarde.[99] It is very likely that Foxe confused Avesbury and
Walsingham because he obtained both manuscripts from Stevenson and
was using them both at the same time. Once again, a manuscript used by
Foxe then proceeded to circulate within Matthew Parker's network.

There is one further antiquary to whom both Foxe and Parker were
immensely indebted, but whose connections with both remain obscure:
William Bowyer, the keeper of the Tower records. On one occasion
Foxe cited Bowyer as a source, declaring that a royal document that Foxe
printed was an 'extract out of an old written volume remayning in
the handes of Maister William Bowyer'.[100] (Significantly, a copy of this
document is in a manuscript in the Parker Library, with passages underlined in the archbishop's trademark red crayon.) A copy of Ranulph of
Higdon's *Polychronicon* consulted by John Foxe apparently once belonged
to William Bowyer; Foxe states that he 'borrowed of one maister Bowyer'
another anonymous chronicle.[101] And Bowyer was the owner of numerous

[97] *1570*, p. 472 and *1576*, p. 376. The letter is in Thomas of Walsingham, *Historia Anglicana 1272–1422*, 2
vols., ed. H. T. Riley (Rolls Series, London, 1863–4), I, pp. 201–8. In the 1570 edition Foxe also cited
Robert of Avesbury's chronicle as the source for two stories – one of a fraudulent miracle denounced
by Edward I, the other of a miracle that allegedly led to the conversion of a Mongol prince to
Christianity – which actually came from Thomas of Walsingham's *Historia Anglicana* (cf. *1570*,
p. 440 with Walsingham, *Historia Anglicana*, pp. 21, 82 and 113). This error went uncorrected in later
editions (*1576*, p. 335 and *1583*, p. 351).
[98] Bodley Douce MS. 128.   [99] Robert of Avesbury, *De Gestis*, p. xxv.
[100] *1570*, p. 837. This document is found in Bodley MS Tanner 165, fos. 81ʳ–82ᵛ, which did in fact belong
to William Bowyer.
[101] This is now College of Arms, Arundel MS 4. Bowyer's name appears on fo. 1ʳ. Foxe stated that he
obtained a reference to an anonymous martyr, burned in Smithfield in 1500, from 'an old written
Chronicle borowed of one in the tower, intituled Polychron' (*1570*, p. 117 [recte 917]). For the
anonymous chronicle see *1570*, p. 700.

manuscripts that eventually came into the possession of Archbishop Parker.[102] On several occasions Foxe introduced material into the second edition that came from the Parliament Rolls and that must have been obtained with Bowyer's cooperation.[103]

VI

The interaction between Foxe, Matthew Parker and the archbishop's network of antiquarians marks an important milestone in the history of manuscript scholarship. Those manuscripts that survived the dissolution of the monasteries had, by the eighteenth and nineteenth centuries, largely been gathered in either the libraries of the universities and their colleges or, ultimately, in the British Library. Previously, in the sixteenth century, these manuscripts were often owned by private collectors – some such as Carye and Stevenson, of relatively modest status – whose libraries varied in size. As we have already seen, Foxe in his Latin martyrologies and in the first edition of the *Acts and Monuments* was very much the heir to the researches of John Leland and John Bale. Now, thanks largely to Archbishop Parker and the network of manuscript collectors he had assiduously created, Foxe was able to benefit from these small private collections at a time when access to their contents must have been difficult. Historians primarily concerned with Foxe's value as a historical source, still tend to underestimate the importance of the medieval sections of Foxe's book, but to Foxe's contemporaries – both Catholic and Protestant – this aspect of his work had enormous value. For generations the *Acts and Monuments* would be the narrative history of medieval England which was most thoroughly grounded in manuscript sources.

Previous English Protestant writers – William Tyndale, John Bale, William Turner and John Jewell among them – had, with varying degrees of success, sought to demonstrate that the English Church was indeed Protestant before

---

[102] Graham and Watson, *Recovery of the Past*, pp. 10, 58, 68, 74, 100 and 102–3.

[103] Cf. *1570*, pp. 519–22, 611–12 and 662 with *Rotuli Parliamentorum vt et Petitiones et Placita in Parliamento*, 6 vols. (London, 1761–83), II, pp. 143–5, 153–4, 162–3, 228, 283–5, 289–90, 337–9, 363, 367, 370 and 377; III, pp. 18–20, 46–8, 95–6, 214, 246–7, 264, 270, 304, 341, 419, 594–5 and 614–16. Bowyer had his own ulterior motives for cooperating with Foxe. Since 1564 he had been in a bitter battle with the Master of the Rolls over who had jurisdiction of the Chancery Rolls, the Parliament Rolls and the Patent Rolls. By June 1567, Bowyer had largely won this argument, with the intervention of Cecil and the queen, and he had succeeded in securing at least the Parliament Rolls and the Chancery Rolls. *Calendar of State Papers Domestic, 1547–1625*, 12 vols. (London 1856–72), I, pp. 234, 290, 292 and 293. A few months later, on 29 August 1567, Bowyer wrote to Cecil informing him that he had collected historical material from his official records showing 'how happy it is for England to have nothing to do with the Pope' (ibid., p. 298). From this it is pretty clear that Bowyer's assistance to Foxe was part of the price that he paid for increasing the authority of his office.

Luther, but none had done so with the detail and the documentation that Foxe was able to muster. This detail gave the English Protestants an enormous polemic edge over their English Catholic opponents. To undermine Foxe's interpretation of the history of the English Church, Catholics had to be able to refute his massive documentation in detail. Merely reprinting chronicle sources, such as Stapleton's edition of Bede, or citing them, as Harpsfield had done, was no longer sufficient. Protestants countercharged that these chroniclers were Catholic and therefore inherently biased, and so sought to conceal the 'truth' revealed by the documents that Foxe, Parker and scholars supported by Parker had printed.[104] The Catholics had the scholarship but they did not have the access to the manuscripts necessary to refute Foxe and these antiquarian works. Standing on a mountain of manuscripts, Foxe could plausibly claim that he could see more clearly into the hidden vales of the English past than his opponents could. The dominance that this elevated position gave to Foxe's work can be seen in the fact that Catholic antiquarians, such as William Blundell, were forced to rely on the *Acts and Monuments* for their own researches into medieval English history.[105]

An appreciation of this ascendancy, along with a determination to maintain it, were qualities that Parker shared with Bale and Foxe. The intensity and force of this motivation has proved to be a blessing to modern scholars in that it led to the preservation and publication of crucial sources for English history. It has also proved to be something of a curse in that it impelled Parker to edit, indeed rewrite, sections of these priceless documents in a way that one scholar has recently characterised as 'a chamber of codicological horrors'.[106] This powerful desire to lay a secure historiographical foundation for the

[104] Foxe emphasised the need to go back beyond the chronicles to the original sources (*1570*, pp. 686 and 830–2). For Foxe on the bias of medieval chronicles and their unreliability, see *1570*, pp. 687–9. For an example of the triumphant emphasis placed on the rediscovery of authentic documents relating to the medieval English Church, see the preface to Aelfric, *A Testimonie of Antiquities Shewing the Auncient Faith in the Church of England* (London, 1566?), STC 159, pp. 1ʳ–18ᵛ. The obverse side to this positivist insistence on the primacy of original documents was an almost unbounded paranoia about the success of the Catholic Church in either eradicating or tampering with writings that demonstrated the 'truth' about the English past. Foxe, for example, claimed that Lanfranc and other Norman bishops destroyed books which 'proved' that the pre-Conquest English clergy did not believe in transubstantiation (*1570*, p. 1304). He even went so far as to claim that the Catholic humanist historian Polydore Vergil actually burned, at the pope's behest, old English books which 'proved' that transubstantiation and other Catholic doctrines were only introduced into the English Church at the time of the Norman Conquest (ibid.).
[105] Daniel Woolf, *The Social Circulation of the Past: English Historical Culture 1500–1730* (Oxford, 2003), pp. 248, 252–3.
[106] Ibid., pp. 170–1. Of course, scholars need to beware of judging the work of sixteenth-century editors by modern-day standards. The editorial premise that 'the textual editor relates the authorial time to the present' must be remembered *in its historical context* when considering sixteenth-century editing

English Protestant Church also led Parker to accept without comment – perhaps even to tolerate – features of the *Acts and Monuments* that were distinctly uncongenial to him, notably its insistent attacks on the wearing of ecclesiastical vestments and its less subtle and even vehement impatience with the torpid pace of Elizabethan ecclesiastical reformation.[107] Eventually there would be a rupture between Foxe and Parker, and the archbishop would publicly humiliate his troublesome collaborator, but for now the uneasy alliance between Lambeth and Aldersgate continued and even thrived. Parker also cashed in on the success of the *Acts and Monuments* by having Foxe write a preface to an edition of the *Anglo-Saxon Gospels*, a work which the archbishop sponsored and which, once again, was printed using Anglo-Saxon characters.[108] In this preface Foxe did pay some of his debt to Parker by praising 'the reverend and learned father in God Matthew, Archbishop of Cant. . . . by whose industrious diligence & learned labours this booke, with others moe, hath been collected & searched out of the *Saxon* Monume[n]tes'. Foxe went on to elucidate the reason for all these 'learned labours': they showed 'how the Church at thys present, is no new reformation of the thinges lately begonne, which were not before, but rather a reduction of the Church to the Pristine state of olde conformitie'.[109]

VII

Another consequence of Parker's intense desire to publish the appropriate and polemically useful sources for English history was the close working

of earlier works. See Claire Badaracco, 'The Editor and the Question of Value: Proposal', *TEXT*, 1 (1984), p. 42, cited in the introduction to Ian Small and Marcus Walsh (eds.), *The Theory and Practice of Text-Editing: Essays in Honour of James T. Boulton* (Cambridge, 1991), p. 6.

[107] On Foxe's critiques on the Elizabethan ecclesiastical policy see Tom Betteridge, 'From Prophetic to Apocalyptic: John Foxe and the Writing of History', in *John Foxe and the English Reformation*, ed. Loades, pp. 230–1; Thomas S. Freeman, '"The Reformation of the Church in this Parliament": Thomas Norton, John Foxe and the Parliament of 1571', *Parliamentary History*, 16 (1997), pp. 135–6; Thomas S. Freeman and Sarah Elizabeth Wall, 'Racking the Body, Shaping the Text: The Account of Anne Askew in Foxe's "Book of Martyrs"', *Renaissance Quarterly*, 54 (2001), pp. 1186–9, and Thomas S. Freeman, 'Providence and Prescription: The Account of Elizabeth in Foxe's "Book of Martyrs"', in *The Myth of Elizabeth*, ed. Susan Doran and Thomas S. Freeman (Basingstoke, 2003), pp. 27–55.

[108] *The Gospels of the fower Evangelistes* . . ., ed. John Foxe (London, 1571), STC 2961. For Foxe's very limited editorial role in this work see p. 239, n. 35 below.

[109] *The Gospels of the fower Evangelistes*, sig. ¶ 2ʳ.

relationship he forged with John Day. It has traditionally been assumed that Parker was in fact Day's most important patron, a myth that has been demolished by Oastler.[110] It was not until 1566 (and remember that by this time Foxe had already begun preparing the second edition) that Parker gave Day the first and perhaps most important commission he would bestow upon him: an order for Day to have cast new special sorts for the Anglo-Saxon characters.[111] This was a technically demanding job for which Day's connections with foreign (most likely Dutch) typefounders were invaluable.[112] It was also an expensive job, costing the archbishop in the region of £200.[113] Having received the essential type, Day used it in printing the *Testimony of Antiquity*, the first of a number of works commissioned by Parker and printed by Day that would utilise Anglo-Saxon characters.[114]

The next work that Day printed with Anglo-Saxon sorts was one of the major antiquarian works published in the sixteenth century, William Lambarde's *Archaionomia* – a parallel Old English/Latin translation of the laws of various Anglo-Saxon kings, which, like *A Testimonie*, contained a key to understanding the Anglo-Saxon characters used, as well as a glossary of Anglo-Saxon legal terms.[115] The work also included a map showing the Anglo-Saxon Heptarchy which would later be reutilised in the third and fourth editions of the *Acts and Monuments*. In fact sections of Lambarde's text were reprinted in the second edition of Foxe's book.[116] The following year, 1569, the connection between Day and Parker was further reinforced when Day printed *A christall glasse of Christian reformation*, a devotional work by Stephen Bateman, one of the archbishop's chaplains. Bateman had

---

[110] Like many other myths concerning Foxe and his associates this appears to have originated with John Strype. See John Strype, *The Life and Acts of Matthew Parker*, 3 vols. (London, 1821), II, pp. 113–14. Oastler points out that there 'is no evidence at Lambeth Palace or amongst Archbishop Parker's papers at Corpus Christi College, Cambridge, to support the picture of him as Day's 'patron' (Oastler, *John Day*, p. 19). See also *PPP*, pp. 128 and 151–6. In fact John Strype's exaggeration of the working relationship between John Day and Matthew Parker has tended to obscure the importance of the patronage of other influential figures such as William Cecil and Robert Dudley on Day's business (see *PPP*, *passim*).

[111] See Peter J. Lucas, 'Parker, Lambarde and the Provision of Special Sorts for Printing Anglo-Saxon in the Sixteenth Century', *Journal of the Printing Historical Society*, 28 (1999), pp. 41–70. Recently, Devorah Greenberg has maintained that Parker's close working engagement with Day began in 1560 with the metrical translation of the psalms (Greenberg, 'Community of the Texts', pp. 705–6). While Parker put his name to this work, there is no other evidence of his close involvement with its production or its printer at that stage.

[112] For Day's intimate connections with foreign workmen, see Evenden, 'The Fleeing Dutchmen?', pp. 63–77.

[113] See Lucas, 'Parker, Lambarde and the Provision of Special Sorts', pp. 44–5.

[114] STC 159. See also *The Gospels of the fower Evangelistes* (1571) and John Asser's *Aelfredi Regis res gestae* (London, 1574), STC 863.

[115] STC 15142.   [116] Cf. Lambarde, *Archaionomia*, fo. 13[r–v] with *1570*, pp. 146–7.

become a zealous procurer of books and manuscripts for Parker and was probably introduced to Day while the printer was engaged in the archbishop's projects.[117]

The connection between Parker and Day was of enormous value to both men. It enabled Parker to print works such as *De antiquitate*, his history of the archbishops of Canterbury, which, if the matter had been left to popular demand alone, would never have seen the light of day.[118] (Parker's personal involvement with this work was so great that he had a press set up in his palace at Lambeth so that he could closely supervise the work's progress.)[119] The limited commercial appeal of such works meant that only Day's desire to gratify the archbishop made their publication possible at all. The commercial problems involved in the printing of such works are illustrated in the correspondence caused by Day's reluctance to produce Bartholomew Clerke's *Fidelis servi subdito infideli responsio* (one of many learned and indignant responses to Nicholas Sanders' seminal *De visibili monarchia ecclesiae*). On 13 December 1572 Matthew Parker wrote to Cecil – who also seems to have been concerned about the production of Clerke's response – reporting that 'I have spoken to Daie the printer to caste a newe Italian letter which he is Doinge, and it will cost him xl marke[s]'.[120] While Day agreed to have the new type made for the book, he made his reservations about the task clear to Parker. The archbishop informed Cecil that 'Loth he [and] other printers be to printe any lattin booke, bicause they will not heare bee uttered, and for that Bookes printed in Englande be in suspition abroad'.[121]

Nevertheless, despite his concerns over the marketability of Clerke's book, Day not only printed it, he gave the printing of it precedence over

---

[117] On Bateman see Venn and Venn, *Alumni Cantabrigienses*; the important relationship between Bateman's *Christall glasse* and the second edition of the 'Book of Martyrs', already in print at this time, will be explored below.

[118] Matthew Parker, assisted by George Acworth and John Joscelyn, *De antiquitate Britannicae ecclesiae* ... (London, 1572), STC 19292.

[119] The Archbishop's son, John, wrote the following note on the fly-leaf of one of the Bodleian copies: 'liber iste et collectus et impressus est propriis in aedibus Lambethae positis'. See Oastler, *John Day*, p. 20.

[120] BL, Lansdowne MS 15, fo. 99[r].

[121] Ibid. This could possibly have been a reference to the Latin *Apologia* printed earlier by Day for sale on the continent. This book sold better in English, but Day only held the patent for the Latin edition. The English edition, provided by Lady Anne Bacon, was not available for another year or so after Day had printed the Latin edition. By that time Day was heavily involved with the printing of Foxe's *Acts and Monuments* and so the licence for the English edition was subsequently granted to Reyner Wolfe at some point between January and July of 1562. Day would not have been happy that he had not been offered the rights to the more popular English edition, especially since he had already interrupted his busy printing schedule to print the Latin edition. If this is the case, Day was pointedly reminding Parker of a *quo* for which he expected a *quid*.

John Parkhurst's *Epigrams*, a work that Day had already committed himself to producing.[122] This was not the first time that Day let Parker's projects in at the front of the queue. In 1567, for example, Day refused to print the music for a service by none other than Thomas Tallis, which would have brought prestige and a tidy profit to the printer, in order to fulfil Parker's commission of a new psalter.[123] As was so often the case, Day's repeatedly giving priority to Parker's pet projects stemmed from sound commercial motives. The paradox here, which it is essential to understand in connection with Day's business, is that by sometimes ignoring strict market forces and producing works that he knew would not sell, he was able to retain his invaluable monopoly over books that were guaranteed to sell in huge numbers.

Parker, along with Cecil and Leicester, formed an important link in the golden chain that connected Day to the lucrative patents that were the cornerstone of his prosperity. Parker was certainly in a position to do favours for Day. He enlisted the bishop of Norwich's help in the acquisition of valuable type for Day.[124] In one important matter, Day's controversial ambitions to set up a bookshop in St Paul's Churchyard, the printer not only shamelessly reminded the archbishop of services rendered, he also called in markers from the Privy Council, compelling Parker's assistance.[125] But beyond Parker's influence as a patron, the acclaim that Day garnered in executing the archbishop's prestigious but technically challenging commissions helped to seal his reputation as England's premier printer. These complicated, elaborate works were a reminder to potential patrons of John Day's readiness and ability to perform successfully the most difficult and exacting tasks.

VIII

The printing of the second edition of the *Acts and Monuments* was the most demanding job that Day had hitherto undertaken. It would require substantial financing in order to purchase the necessary supply of paper and to hire sufficient specialised staff; yet this was only the beginning of the

---

[122] See Day's letter to Parker, cited in Arber, *Transcripts*, 1, p. 454.
[123] Peter Phillips, *English Sacred Music, 1549–1649* (Oxford, 1991), p. 400. See PPP pp. 114–15.
[124] See, *PPP*, p. 130.
[125] Peter Blayney's compelling discussion of the incident suggests that the archbishop was initially reluctant to stick his hand into the jurisdictional hornet's nest of St Paul's Churchyard. Peter Blayney, 'John Day and the Bookshop that Never Was', in *Material London, ca.1600*, ed. Lena Cowen Orlin (Philadelphia, 2000), pp. 321–43.

financial burden that Day would shoulder. Once again he would have to find the means to support himself and his family and this time for the even longer period during which his presses would be occupied in printing the even larger second edition of Foxe's work. Time and considerable organisational skills, as well as money, were needed to overcome these obstacles. Day also had to arrange all his other printing assignments around Foxe's writing schedule and ultimately to decline potentially lucrative commissions in order to print the 'Book of Martyrs'. At the same time the links of patronage had to be retested, and if necessary repaired and reforged; especially the all-important patents for the primer and the metrical psalms that were due for renewal in 1567 had to be secured. Another problem which required support from the great and the good resulted from the shortage of skilled compositors and pressmen in England at the time. The current English law limited employers to hiring a maximum of four foreign workmen. However, in order to print Foxe's work, Day would need up to half a dozen compositors and another three to six pressmen. The pool of foreign labour in London offered the most promising – indeed quite possibly the only available – supply of this number of qualified workers.

Day and Foxe, keenly aware that the printer's patents were due to expire in 1567, began organising themselves to meet these challenges as early as 1566. (It is possible that the need to renew these patents may have played a role in helping them to decide on the early commencement of work on the second edition. Day may have calculated that he would be in a stronger position to have his patents renewed if he had started work on a major project that Cecil and other influential figures wished to see in print.) In July of that year, Foxe wrote a letter to William Cecil with a number of requests designed to facilitate the book's production.[126] Foxe asked Cecil to loan him manuscripts and requested that in Day's case the law limiting the number of foreign workmen be waived. In an interesting indication of the mass of material that had already been gathered for the new edition, Foxe informed Cecil that these extra workmen would be required 'since we have enough material to keep three presses continuously employed'.[127] And in a footnote that may indicate that Day was looking over the martyrologist's shoulder, Foxe reminded Cecil that Day's monopoly on the metrical psalms

---

[126] King claims that this letter is 'dated 6 July 1570' (King, *Print Culture*, p. 84). First of all, the letter is actually dated 6 July, with no year given. Second, since the letter presses for the renewal of Day's patents granting him the monopoly on the ABC, catechism and metrical psalms, were actually granted for ten years on 6 May 1567, this letter could not have been written after July 1566 (TNA, 9 Eliz., part 9, m. 19).

[127] 'quum tribus praelis materiam continue suppeditamus'. BL, Lansdowne MS 10, fo. 211ʳ.

needed to be continued because 'from this one thing his whole household is sustained'.[128] In January 1567 arrangements were made for manuscript drafts of the new edition to be read and probably corrected.[129] Clearly by 1566–7 the preparations by Foxe and Day for the second edition were well underway.

A significant pattern also emerges from Day's printing at this time. Unsurprisingly he continued ladling out generous portions of the primers, catechisms and metrical psalms, which were the bread and butter of his business, but during this time he produced very few of the specialised works that had made his reputation, and those that he did produce were demonstrably part of the preparation for the *Acts and Monuments*. The woodcuts in Stephen Bateman's *A christall glasse* of 1569 appear to have provided a small-scale rehearsal for the illustrations in the *Acts and Monuments*.[130] And, as we have seen, *A Testimony of Antiquity* and the *Archaionomia*, works using Anglo-Saxon sorts that were prepared at Archbishop Parker's behest, were not only part of the complicated mutual back-scratching between prelate and printer, they were also recycled into the second edition of Foxe's book.

IX

Nevertheless, despite all this planning and preparation, Day seriously miscalculated the amount of paper that he needed for his Herculean task. Apparently Day laid in the same amount of paper as had been used for the first edition. He must have had some idea of the increased scope of the book and the consequent additional new material. Presumably he had calculated that deletion of material from the first edition would balance the influx of new information into the second edition. After all, William Turner in his letter had called for just such a purge of material, urging in particular that the Latin documents printed in the first edition be removed from all future editions.[131] In fact this purge did take place: much of the documentation of the first edition did not make it into the second. Some of this material would have been deleted in any case because it was embarrassing to the Protestant cause.[132] Occasionally material was deleted because it

[128] 'ex hoc uno solo universa illius alitur familia'. BL, Lansdowne MS 10, fo. 211[r].
[129] BL, Harley MS 416, fo. 185[r]. This letter is dated 26 January 1567.   [130] See below, p. 195.
[131] BL, Harley MS 416, fo. 132[r]. On Turner's letter see above, p. 125.
[132] For example, Foxe eliminated a very informative list sent to Bishop Bonner by an informant of 'heretical' leaders in London (*1563*, p. 1605), and also the equally valuable list of Protestants who had been driven from their homes or otherwise harassed in Kent, Essex, Norfolk, Suffolk and Warwickshire (*1563*, pp. 1667–80). Both lists included radicals among the 'orthodox' Protestants,

offended powerful individuals. A scathing account of Francis Nunn, a Suffolk JP, hunting down Protestants in Mary's reign, which culminated with an appeal for Nunn's removal from office, was quietly dropped.[133] More often the only reason for the deletion of documents was to make room for the new material in the new edition. For example, Foxe eliminated the fifty-three pages entirely devoted to depositions alleged against Bishop Stephen Gardiner in Edward VI's reign. The ongoing relevance of these documents to Foxe can be seen in the fact that the martyrologist would continue to cross-reference back to them in the 1570 and subsequent editions: the need to save space was the sole reason for their deletion.[134] Similarly a defective writ authorising (or more accurately failing to author-ise) the execution of a Marian martyr was eliminated from the second edition and replaced by a note referring the reader back to the first.[135] Occasionally Foxe was frank about both the removal of documents and the reason for their removal; several letters of the Marian martyr Hugh Latimer were dropped 'because it woulde aske to much roume here [for them] to bee inserted' and a 'conference' held by Ridley and Latimer was also dropped because it was 'somewhat long here to be inserted and because I see thys volume swelleth already with aboundance of other matter'.[136] So great was the pressure on Foxe to save even relatively minute amounts of paper that he began to remove excess verbiage from court documents, for no other reason than to save space.[137]

Nevertheless the brutal fact remained that Day had seriously under-estimated the amount of paper the new edition would require. There were several understandable reasons for this mistake. Day did not fully perceive how much paper would be demanded by the increased chrono-logical range and wealth of material supplied by Matthew Parker and others.

giving them a legitimacy that Foxe did not wish to grant them. Another good example of a thorough suppression of embarrassing material occurred when Foxe reprinted the examinations of the Protestant martyr John Careless; admissions that Careless lied to his examiner and references to Careless's disputes with Freewillers disappeared, never to be reprinted (cf. *1563*, pp. 1529–34 with *1570*, pp. 2101–3). For a discussion of why Foxe wished to censor this material, see Thomas S. Freeman, 'Dissenters from a Dissenting Church: The Challenge of the Freewillers 1550–1558', in *The Beginnings of English Protestantism*, ed. Peter Marshall and Alec Ryrie (Cambridge, 2002), pp. 152–5.

[133] The account of Nunn's persecution is on *1563*, p. 1698. Nunn continued as a JP well into Elizabeth's reign, only dying in 1573. Diamaird MacCulloch, *Suffolk and the Tudors: Politics and Religion in an English County 1500–1600* (Oxford, 1986), pp. 190–1 and 385.

[134] *1563*, pp. 818–61; cf. *1570*, pp. 1536, 1957 and 1959.   [135] *1563*, p. 1632 and *1570*, p. 2216.

[136] Cf. *1563*, pp. 1317–20 with *1570*, p. 1912. For the earlier printing of this 'conference' cf. *1563*, pp. 1285–94 with *1570*, p. 1896.

[137] For example, such abridgements occur in the fourth and fifth articles charged against John Hallingdale (cf. *1563*, p. 1638 with *1570*, p. 2222), and the eighth article alleged against Richard Gibson (cf. *1563*, p. 1641 with *1570*, pp. 2223–4). Note that neither the charges nor the entire documents are removed; rather they are simply abridged.

Neither did he appreciate the amount of new material that had been uncovered by Foxe, Henry Bull and others assisting in the research for the volume. In fairness it would have been impossible for anyone to have predicted how much material would be included in the book. As we shall see, throughout the protracted printing process fresh material for the *Acts and Monuments* continued to arrive at Aldersgate. Day was in the unenviable position of having to base hard financial calculations on the shifting sand of a remarkably unstable text.

On this matter there may well have been some tension between Foxe and Day. Foxe seems to have perceived that the sheer size and massive documentation of the *Acts and Monuments* provided one of its best defences against further attack. Yet he was constrained both by the available paper supply and the need to have the work completed so that Day could return to his normal business. Day seems to have mollified Foxe with the promise of an appendix that would reprint many or all of the writings of the Protestant martyrs. Throughout the second edition Foxe assures the reader of his plans for this appendix. At one point he declares that 'I have differed and put over many treatises, letters and exhortations belonging to the story of the martyrs unto the later appendix in the end of this volume.'[138] A little later Foxe apologised for not including other works by Nicholas Ridley but promised 'wherof ye shall see, God willing, the effect and contents in the forepromised Appendix, which I purpose by the Lordes grace after the finishing of these storyes to adjoyne'.[139]

Still later Foxe, discussing Cranmer's works, stated:

all which writings and bookes ... our present story would require here to be inferred; but because to prosecute the whole matter at length will not bee comprehended in a small rowme, and may make to long tariaunce in our story, it shall therefore be best to put of[f] the same unto the place of the Appendix following, wherein (the Lord willyng) we intende to close up these and other diverse treatises of the learned Martyrs as to this our story shall apperteine.[140]

In the event this promised appendix would not materialise in this edition, although a modest version of it ultimately appeared at the end of the 1583 edition. An even more startling indication of the almost unlimited scope of Foxe's ambitions is the fact that he apparently planned to take this edition of

---

[138] *1570*, p. 1939. For another reference see p. 1903.   [139] Ibid., p. 1950.

[140] Ibid., p. 2045. For other passages where Foxe promises this appendix see ibid., pp. 1036 and 1903. Foxe also seems to be alluding to this appendix when he states that he would not print all of the account of Lawrence Saunders in his text because he hoped 'to prosecute the same hereafter more at large' (ibid., p. 1671).

the *Acts and Monuments*, as he advised his readers, 'to the tyme of Quene Elizabeth'.[141]

X

It is only too apparent why the desired appendix was not printed; Day ran out of paper in the course of printing the second edition. An examination of the extant copies of the 1570 edition reveals that the quality of the paper rapidly decreases from around page 1800 onwards. (It is worth remembering that the 1563 edition was around 1,800 pages long. It seems reasonable to suppose that Day assumed the second edition would be the same length and only purchased enough paper for 1,800 pages of text.) Day resorted to at least two expedients that reveal his dire need for paper. One was to use the 'cassie' (or 'cording quires') as an additional source of paper for Foxe's book. When reams of paper were shipped they were wrapped in outer sheets made up of imperfect paper. These sheets were the cassie. The purpose of this was to protect the good-quality paper in the ream from being damaged during transportation. The cassie was usually discarded upon opening the ream, but was used by Day in the later stages of this edition as an ingenious – if desperate – measure.[142]

Another expedient was to paste smaller sheets of writing paper together to form one large sheet. (This is demonstrated by the occasional appearance of the watermark in the centre of pages in the 1570 edition.)[143] These pasted-together sheets alternate with the packing sheets until around page 2050, after which the pasted-together sheets are used almost exclusively.[144] These

---

[141] Ibid., p. 1059. As we shall see in subsequent chapters, this ambition evolved into a scheme for writing a separate history of Elizabeth's reign, which was only grudgingly abandoned by Foxe and Day.

[142] A double chain line is only visible in the cassie. See Gaskell, *New Introduction*, pp. 59–60. The paper with this distinctive double chain line occurs in the last 500 pages of every copy of the 1570 edition.

[143] Watermarks were situated in the centre of a sheet. When the sheet was folded to make pages, the watermark would be less visible since it was in the gutter. With sheets comprised of two smaller sheets pasted together two watermarks would appear on one large 'sheet' and both would be visible when the sheet was folded into pages.

[144] The collation for the two volumes shows more clearly where the smaller sheets occur. It should be remembered that outside of those in the preliminaries, which were always printed last, the use of the smaller sheets in the early stages of Volume 1 suggests that cancellations of previous text were made late on in the book's production. (The use of some large paper in the preliminaries, such as in sigs. ✠⁴, suggests that some sheets may have been preserved to ensure that at least the opening pages appeared on good-quality, large paper.) The smaller sheets are indicated by underlining: volume 1: ✠⁴ *⁴ χ1, a-b⁶ c⁴ d²e-r⁶ s⁶ (-s1 + 's1'. 's2') t-y⁶, A-C⁶ D-E⁴F-H⁶ I⁶ *I*⁶K-Y⁶, Aa-Ll⁶ Mm⁶ (±Mm1) Nn-Yy⁶, AA-KK⁶ LL⁴ MM² (±MM2) NN-OO⁴; volume 11: ²χ1, Aaa-YYy⁶, AAA-ZZZ⁶ &&&⁶ ****⁶, AAAa-YYYy⁶, AAAA-YYYY⁶, AAAAa-CCCCc⁶ DDDDd⁶ (±DDDDd1) EEEEe-HHHHh⁶ IIIIi⁶ (-IIIIi1.6+IIIIi1.6) KKKKk-YYYYy⁶ ZZZZz⁶ (±ZZZZz2), AAAAA-BBBBB⁶ GGGGG⁶ HHHHH⁴ IIIII⁶.

pasted-together sheets were also used for the preliminaries to the book (which were always printed last), and also in a few gatherings that were clearly late additions of newly discovered material.[145] The use of pasted-together sheets required extra care on the part of the pressmen on account of the increased risk of tearing these fragile, hastily cobbled-together sheets. This extra care not only created additional labour for the pressmen, it probably also slowed down the overall production of the book. While it is not clear who was saddled with the task of pasting these pieces of paper together, the need to use workmen in Day's shop for this new job was a further impediment to the progress of printing the book. Beyond delaying the production of the second edition, this expedient also undermined its quality. The smaller sheets that were pasted together were thinner than the good-quality sheets. The use of thinner paper resulted in bleed-through, reducing both the book's legibility and its aesthetic appeal.

Yet even the supply of extra paper created by Day's improvisation was limited, and careful calculations had to be made to see how much of Foxe's apparently unlimited supply of material could actually be printed. A few of the original letters written by the Marian martyr John Philpot survive with markings on them made by Foxe and Day (or Day's workmen).[146] These markings are actually instructions for the compositors. Among other things they indicate a Procrustean process in which the original text of the letters was amputated in order to save paper. (The letters we are discussing are all printed in the second edition after page 1800, when the shortage of paper became acute.) These markings determine the physical layout of the page.[147] Paragraph breaks are indicated by the use of brackets or a pointing

---

[145] Roberts, 'Bibliographical Aspects of John Foxe', in *John Foxe and the English Reformation*, ed. Loades, pp. 46–7. Earlier discussions of the use of pasted-together sheets in the 1570 edition are Leslie M. Oliver, 'Single-Page Imposition in Foxe's *Acts and Monuments*, 1570', *The Library*, 5th series, 1 (1946), pp. 49–56, and Paul S. Dunkin, 'Foxe's *Acts and Monuments*, 1570 and Single-Page Imposition', *The Library*, 5th series, 2 (1947), pp. 159–70.

[146] Apart from BL, Add. MS 19400, fo. 50[r–v], which we are about to discuss, ECL MS 260, fos. 160[r]–1[v] and 184–5[r] are also original letters by John Philpot edited in Foxe's own hand with instructions to Day's staff. These markings are discussed in detail in Evenden and Freeman, 'The Printing of the "Book of Martyrs"', pp. 39–40 and King, *Print Culture*, pp. 62–4. The latter discussion, however, over-simplifies this process by assuming that all of the annotations made on these letters were by Foxe, which is clearly not the case.

[147] In contrast with the markings on epistles printed in *LM*, already discussed, the markings on Philpot's letters determined in minute detail the layout of the text and the amount of paper that would be used, demonstrating the much greater need to conserve paper, which occurred with the second edition of Foxe's book. King's analysis of these markings tends to focus on content rather than layout – even to the point of ignoring some of the markings visible in his sample – but clearly the markings were designed to deal with both of these aspects. See King, *Print Culture*, pp. 62–4.

hand.[148] Where text is being deleted, a 'hash mark' is placed in the margin of manuscript, at the point where the deletion begins and ends – often with the first words of the deleted text underlined to signal exactly where the omission is to be made.[149] In the printed text these deletions are often indicated by the use of 'etcetera' or some variant of this word. Text that was to be printed in italic type (rather than in the main font used for most of the page) was emphasised by underlining (this italic type was usually used for biblical quotations and source references). Marginal notes in Foxe's hand-writing also appear on the manuscripts; in many cases the text of these notes was reprinted without change in the *Acts and Monuments*. Foxe also wrote the headings for individual letters on these manuscripts, just as Bull had done in the *Letters of the Martyrs*.

These markings indicate a great deal about Foxe's editorial control of the 1570 edition and the ways in which he shaped both the content and the presentation of the writings of the martyrs. Because he worked so closely with Day, and tended to spend a great deal of time at Day's printing house, there are not many examples of Foxe marking up documents that were to be printed in the *Acts and Monuments*. One of the few instances of this confirms that Foxe composed the marginal notes for the *Acts and Monuments*. In the 1563 edition Foxe had misidentified the name of an individual who had been sentenced to be burned at Windsor in 1543 but was pardoned by the king. Foxe had given the man's name as Henry Filmer, but in reality Filmer was executed and it was John Marbeck who was par-doned.[150] Harpsfield pounced on this error and used it to demonstrate the general unreliability of Foxe's account.[151] Foxe responded by soliciting a detailed narrative of what happened at Windsor from John Marbeck himself. A manuscript copy text of Marbeck's narrative survives among Foxe's papers.[152] The copy text, however, is incomplete; it appears to have been begun and then abandoned. Although the main text itself is complete, only a few of the folios include any paratext whatsoever. The paratext that exists in the copy text consists entirely of marginal notes written in Foxe's handwriting (the body of the text is in another, scribal hand). These notes correspond, with only minor variations, to the marginal notes that appear in the printed version.[153] Only a few pages of the copy text contain Foxe's marginal notes; the margins in the rest of the copy text remain blank.

---

[148] Other names for this symbol are 'index', 'digit', 'fist' or 'manicula'.
[149] A hash mark looks like a continental number four with two vertical slashes and no vertical link.
[150] *1570*, pp. 1387–8. [151] Harpsfield, *Dialogi sex*, pp. 962–3.
[152] BL, Lansdowne MS 389, fos. 240ʳ–76ʳ. [153] Cf. ibid., fos. 242ᵛ–7ʳ with *1570*, pp. 1386–99.

Apparently what happened is that Foxe was, for some unknown reason, temporarily away from Day's printing house. Not wishing to delay the work, the copy text was sent or given to him to supply the missing marginal notes. Apparently his absence was shorter than anticipated and he was able to return and oversee the work in person. However, this accidental survival casts a revealing light on several aspects of the production of the second edition of the *Acts and Monuments*. It clearly indicates Foxe's responsibility for the marginal notes but it also suggests the complexity of the supervisory process. Because Foxe's book was in large part a compilation of material from a myriad number of sources, Foxe, as well as the printing house staff, had to work with numerous copy texts, all of which had to be properly coordinated and incorporated.

However, the printing house markings on the Philpot letter also demonstrate the one effective limit upon Foxe's control of the text – the practical necessities that also shaped the content of the edition, the most important of which was the need to conserve paper. In one of Philpot's letters (see Figure 4), Foxe has suggested places where the text of the letter could be deleted.[154] The small figure 20 in the top corner of the margin indicates a line estimate made by Foxe or, more likely, one of Day's staff. Calculations were being made to see how many lines of type could be fitted on one page of the book. Each block of twenty lines of type was estimated and the places where they ended indicated on the original letter. (There are four such markings on fo. 50^v.) The purpose of these unusually precise calculations was to determine how much of the contents of the letter would fit onto a given page. This in turn enabled Day and Foxe to decide how much remaining material could be printed on the very limited supply of remaining paper.

The markings on the original letter reveal the difficult decisions, and occasional vacillations, caused by the shortage of paper. One fascinating example occurs where a particular passage was scheduled for deletion but reprieved. For example, Figure 4 shows a marginal note made by Foxe that reads 'A perfect chri/stian man how/ he is knowen'. Just above this note there is an unusual shape: a hastily drawn ivy leaf marker with a circle drawn over it. Clearly the ivy leaf was meant to indicate that someone had reservations about whether this particular note and the text it accompanied should be printed; when the decision was made to include it, a circle was drawn over the mark, cancelling it out. (It is interesting that these directions

---

[154] Other letters by Philpot show similar markings by Foxe, as well as by Day or his workmen, but this letter is the most extensively annotated.

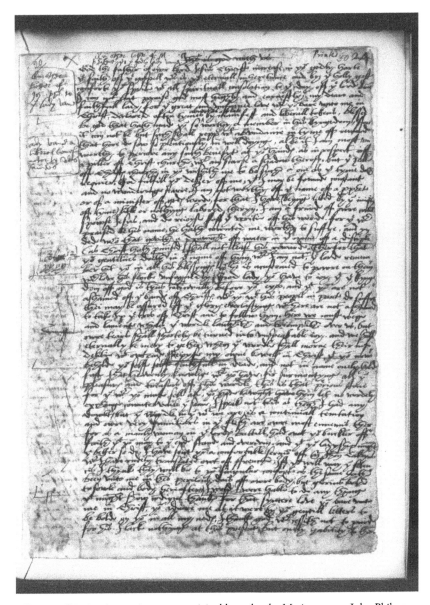

Figure 4 Printing instructions on an original letter by the Marian martyr John Philpot. British Library, Additional MS 19400, fo. 50ᵛ, courtesy of the British Library Board.

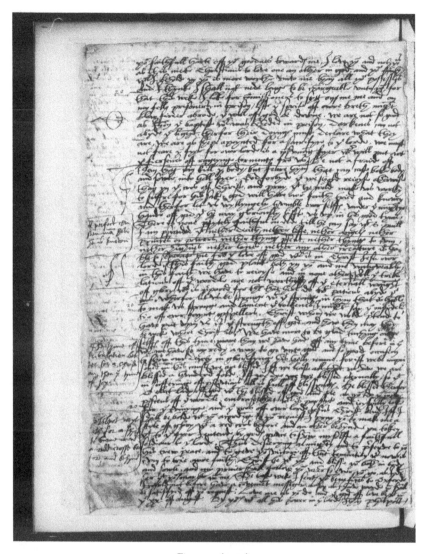

Figure 4 (cont.)

are made by means of signs and symbols, rather than being expressed in writing. This may well have been because many of Day's personnel were foreigners and could not read English.) This particular passage was probably saved when a subsequent passage was cut. In any case these markings reveal not only drastic abridgement of the letter (see Figure 4 for how extensive these deletions were) but they indicate a frantic last-minute debate over what could and should be included in the edition. The line calculations on the manuscript indicate not only that these debates were being driven by the need to conserve paper, but that the need was so acute that these decisions had to be made practically on a line-by-line basis.

Of course these were the strategies for working from manuscript sources. With sources that were already printed, these calculations of how much paper was required were easier to make, and above all the text was more legible to the compositors. The major printed source for the second and all subsequent editions of the *Acts and Monuments* printed by Day was apparently the previous printed edition. Certainly, some of Foxe's notes, which were inserted into the 1570 edition, have markings that indicate that the compositors worked from the text of the 1563 edition. Next to these notes are symbols (for example, a circle, an asterisk, a triangle and manicula) that must have corresponded with identical marks made on the printed page of the first edition being used as a copy text. The compositors would simply insert the text from Foxe's notes at the place indicated on both the copy text and the manuscript.[155]

XI

The deletion of material that had been printed in the 1563 edition was unfortunate in many respects but it did have one desirable consequence: it helped inspire one of the most impressive, albeit relatively unnoticed features of the second edition: the impressive network of cross-references. Because Foxe was anxious to cite some of the deleted material, he was careful to see that notes were added guiding readers back to the first edition. This in itself was an irritation for a number of readers who were not fortunate enough to own both editions of the work, and the problem was only exacerbated over time, as the 1563 edition became progressively harder to obtain. In fact, in 1582 Foxe would receive a letter that, among other things, complained that it was frustrating to be referred to documents in the first edition of the book when it was not to hand.[156] Another reason that these elaborate cross-references were required was a factor that has already been alluded to: the incorporation of material into the work out of

---

[155] See Thomas S. Freeman, "'As True a Subiect being Prysoner': John Foxe's Notes on the Imprisonment of Princess Elizabeth, 1554–5', *English Historical Review*, 117 (2002), pp. 104–5.
[156] BL, Harley MS 416, fo. 204[r].

chronological order. This problem had not been solved in the 1563 edition, especially for the Marian period, where the attempt to arrange the materials in chronological order ends up being perfunctory at best and virtually non-existent at worst. In the 1570 edition a real and heroic effort was made to arrange all of the material in chronological order. However, this effort was continually undermined by the arrival of new material as the work was being printed. And given the choice between leaving material out or inserting it out of its proper chronological place, Foxe unhesitatingly chose the latter. When he placed an account of the Anglo-Saxon King Edgar between Harold II and William the Conqueror (out of place by over a century), Foxe blithely remarked: 'better I judge it out of order than out of the book'.[157]

Worse yet, when material reached Foxe from different sources at different times, the result all too frequently was that portions of accounts of the same person were printed at widely separate locations within the text. For example, while an account of the martyrdom of John Newman appeared in its correct location, Foxe obtained a copy of his examinations as the second edition was being completed, so he placed it right at the end of the book.[158] In the 1563 edition Foxe printed several letters by John Hullier, a Protestant minister martyred in Cambridge on 2 April 1556. Foxe knew little about the minister and in fact in 1570, when he reprinted the letters, he prefaced them with an appeal for information about Hullier's martyrdom. Foxe asked and he received. One hundred pages later, in the middle of describing events in June 1557, Foxe inserted an eyewitness account of Hullier's execution, 'which since hath come into my hand'.[159] Similarly, Foxe printed an account of Edmund Allin's arrest, his flight, re-arrest and execution, which he obtained from two Kentish Protestant divines. Later on Foxe printed an account of Allin's escape from prison after his first arrest, which he received from Roger Hall. Foxe inserted this account around seventy pages after his earlier account of Allin's martyrdom.[160] All of these stories were linked across hundreds of pages of text by cross-references. Perhaps Foxe over-relied on this system of cross-references since these stories were never integrated in future editions. The ubiquity *and* accuracy of these cross-references is a stunning achievement, and powerful testimony to a facet of the second edition that we shall be examining shortly: the

[157] *1570*, p. 220.
[158] In *1570* the main account occurs on pp. 1865–6. The examinations occur on pp. 2135–6.
[159] See ibid., pp. 2086–9 and 2196–7: cf. *1563*, p. 1513.
[160] *1570*, pp. 2165–7 and 2197. Also see Freeman, 'Notes on a Source', pp. 203–11.

rigorous editorial oversight devoted to it. But remarkable as this intricate network of references was, it contained a potential danger. As new editions of the *Acts and Monuments* were printed, these references had to be kept up to date; in other words, new page numbers had to be supplied. No subsequent edition of the *Acts and Monuments* would receive the editorial scrutiny lavished on this edition. The cross-references were never updated and were ultimately removed. As this happened, stories whose component parts were scattered across the pages of the second edition became sources of considerable editorial confusion in later editions.[161]

But that was in the future. Meticulous – almost obsessive – attention to detail is a hallmark of the 1570 edition and testimony of Foxe's close involvement in the editing of this work. He was fiercely determined that nothing should remain in his work that would allow his Catholic adversaries the slightest opportunity to discredit any part of it. This not only meant that awkward details were airbrushed out of the volume, but that remarkable care was taken to try to avoid any mistakes whatsoever in the second edition. One ingenious step that Foxe took was designed to solve one of the great problems faced by a sixteenth-century printer: the lack of correctors educated in the learned languages. The ideal expressed by Joseph Moxon, that correctors should be available in the printing house and should be competent in 'Latin, Greek, Hebrew . . . [and] to be very knowing in deviations and etymologies of words, very sagacious in pointing, skilful in the compositor's whole task and obligation, and endowed with a quick eye to espy the smallest fault', was little more than a distant pipe dream to John Day or most early modern printers.[162] Foxe had found a shortcut to the Holy Grail of early modern printing – cheap but learned copy-editors – by sending portions of the manuscript of the second edition – before the printing had actually commenced – to Magdalen College, Oxford, where his old friend

---

[161] This will be discussed in greater detail in Chapter 8, but one example is perhaps worth adding now. At some point after the 1570 edition was printed, a manuscript copy (now extant in Foxe's papers) of a prayer of Hullier's and one of his letters were marked up in preparation for inclusion in the *Acts and Monuments*. However, there is a note in the upper left-hand corner of the first page of the manuscript: 'lok in J. Hulliers life and there this letter is prynted' (ECL, MS 262, fos. 111ʳ–13ʳ). What must have happened is that this manuscript came into the hands of someone in Day's printing house who then checked the account of Hullier's execution, did not see the letter there, and decided to insert it in the text. Someone, perhaps Foxe, caught the mistake and informed Day's staff that the letter was in fact already in the *Acts and Monuments*.

[162] Joseph Moxon, *Mechanik Exercises on the Whole Art of Printing*, ed. H. Davis and H. Carter, 2nd edn (London, 1962), p. 260. As a matter of fact, during this period Day did have at least one 'sufficient' corrector, William Gace (see TNA, C 24/181, deps. to ints. 11–13). Gace was a graduate of Clare Hall, Cambridge, and probably assisted Foxe in the task of checking the printed proofs.

Laurence Humphrey (the president of the College) and his students worked as unpaid proofreaders.[163]

It is very likely that Humphrey's team paid particular attention to material that had been translated from Latin into English in the first edition. Most of this work, which had not been done by Foxe, was unsatisfactory. Sometimes this was because it was inaccurate or misleading. For example, Foxe, translating an account of a debate between the Scottish Reformer Alexander Alesius and Bishop John Stokesley of London in 1537, which was written by Alesius himself, for inclusion in the *Rerum*, described the debate as taking place 'in consilium'.[164] In the 1563 edition this was translated as 'convocation', which misleadingly implied that the debate took place during Convocation.[165] In the 1570 edition this was altered to the accurate 'Parliament house'.[166] A slightly farcical example came in the reprinting of the 'Twelve Conclusions' – a Lollard manifesto of 1395. The second of these Conclusions spoke of the pope claiming 'potestate angelis altiori' and this was accurately reprinted in Foxe's two Latin martyrologies.[167] As stated above, in the first edition the person who translated this passage, misled by the same verbal similarity that had inspired Gregory the Great's famous pun about the English being angels, rendered this phrase as 'higher power unto England'.[168] In the second edition, however, this was silently corrected to read 'a power higher than aungels'.[169] It was almost certainly Foxe himself who spotted this small but potentially embarrassing error and this is yet another indication that he carefully read through the translations that had been made for the 1563 edition. This meticulous attention to detail is typical of the scrupulous care taken in revising the translations that had been made in the 1563 edition. Sometimes, however, the problem was that the translator was too faithful to the original text to suit Foxe's purposes.

This was a particular problem with the translation of Aeneas Silvius Piccolomini's account of the Council of Basle in the first edition. This work was of particular importance to Foxe in demonstrating that there had been resistance to claims of papal supremacy over the Church before the Reformation. But the text also presented problems to which the first edition translator was not alert: in particular the need to present the anti-papal faction at the Council as virtuous figures by sixteenth-century-Protestant standards. Thus St Augustine's famous quotation, 'Quod evangelio non

[163] BL, Harley MS 416, fo. 185ᵛ.
[164] Foxe, *Rerum*, p. 159; cf. Alexander Alesius, *Of the auctorite of the word of god agaynst the bisshop of London* (Strasbourg, 1544?), STC 292, sigs. A5ʳ–B7ᵛ.
[165] *1563*, p. 594.   [166] *1570*, p. 1351.   [167] *FZ*, fo. 61ᵛ. Cf. *Comm.*, fo. 108ʳ and *Rerum*, p. 71.
[168] *1563*, p. 137.   [169] *1570*, p. 606.

crederet, nisi autoritas ecclesiae se commoveret', a favourite passage among Counter Reformation Catholics, was quoted by the anti-papal faction at the Council. This embarrassing quotation was faithfully translated in the 1563 edition but unobtrusively deleted from the second edition.[170] Similarly a declaration by one of the pro-papal speakers at the Council that it was heresy to deny papal supremacy over the Church was included in the first edition but dropped from the second.[171] The translator was alert enough to omit Piccolomini's description of Louis d'Aleman, archbishop of Arles (the leader of the anti-papal faction), collecting relics of saints and having them brought to the Council for inspiration at a moment of crisis. In the second edition, however, Foxe added a sentence stating that d'Aleman ordered the members of the Council to pray, thus burnishing the archbishop's godly image; Foxe simply did not bother to say to whom the archbishop was actually praying.[172] All of this demonstrates the close scrutiny paid to the translations made in the previous edition.

Yet despite the careful copy-editing and the microscopic attention to detail, mistakes still made it into print. Every surviving copy of the 1570 edition also contains hand corrections that must have been made in the print room. Of course single-page impositions, slip cancels and stop press corrections inevitably occurred.[173] Far more unusual are the deletions and corrections done by hand on the actual pages of the second edition. The most striking example occurs in Foxe's accounts of a massacre of Waldensians in Provence. The massacre, which actually took place in the villages of Merindol and Cabrières, is mistakenly described as having taken place in 'the valley of Angrone' (the Angrogna river and valley are actually located in Piedmont; the mistake had occurred because someone had conflated two separate massacres of Waldensians, one of which had taken place in the Angrogne valley). The erroneous words 'in the valley of Angrone' were crossed out with a single pen stroke in every surviving copy of the 1570 edition. Foxe then refers to this hand correction *within the printed text*, referring the reader to the earlier mistake that they saw 'rased out with penne'. The original mistake occurred on page 1075. The reference to the hand correction appears only eleven pages later, on page 1086.[174] No one except Foxe is likely to have caught this

---

[170] Cf. Aeneas Silvius Piccolomini, *De Gestis Concilii Basiliensis Commentariorum*, ed. and trans. Denys Hay and W. K. Smith (Oxford, 1967), p. 90 and *1563*, p. 297 with *1570*, p. 802.

[171] Cf. Piccolomini, *Commentariorum*, p. 93 and *1563*, p. 298 with *1570*, p. 803.

[172] Cf. Piccolomini, *Commentariorum*, p. 179 and *1563*, p. 319 with *1570*, p. 815.

[173] Usually, the evidence of stop press corrections does not exist because the stop press removed all trace of the original mistake. However, the surviving evidence of hand corrections in Fox's book allows modern scholars the very rare opportunity to see where at least some of these stop presses occurred.

[174] Evenden and Freeman, 'John Foxe', p. 41.

mistake. For Foxe to have seen this error so quickly – even before the printing of this single episode had been finished – he must have been examining the pages as they came off the press.

Here again we see the consequences of the fear and anger that Foxe's Catholic critics had instilled in him; it was their onslaught that made this attention to detail necessary. Another response to Foxe's Catholic critics and another demonstration of Foxe's pervasive control were the marginal notes which proliferated in this edition, covering the empty margins like ivy on an old stone wall. By any standards the proliferation of marginal notes from the first to the second edition is staggering. There were seven marginal notes accompanying the story of William Tyndale in the 1563 edition; in the second edition there were 102.[175] Foxe's narrative of the martyrdom of John Hooper required only 12 marginal notes in the first edition. In the second edition there were 114.[176] The controversial career and martyrdom of Archbishop Thomas Cranmer had already elicited 85 marginal notes when Foxe related it in 1563. Seven years later Foxe needed 380 marginal notes.[177] (These examples, moreover, are of people already well known to Foxe and his readers in 1563. In none of these cases is the efflorescence of marginal notes a consequence of Foxe suddenly receiving vast amounts of new material on a hitherto obscure figure. There is some additional material in all of these accounts – particularly that of Thomas Cranmer – but the amount of additional annotation is vastly disproportionate to the amount of new information.)

These notes tended to be especially prominent, however, when Foxe was printing material with which he disagreed or at least had reservations. They were his way of muting an adversary's voice and refuting his arguments and of controlling the reader's response to a text which Foxe feared could be 'misread'. Thus, for example, a letter from Bishop Stephen Gardiner to Bishop Ridley is encrusted with marginal notes in the same way as the pilings of a pier are encrusted with barnacles (see Figure 5).[178] However, the most striking of the annotations added to this edition are the syllogisms inserted in the margins, replicating arguments presented in the text as logical formulae. In some cases this was done because Foxe felt that the arguments being made were of particular importance or merit. Thus the statements of Eucharistic theology made by the Marian martyr, John Bland,

---

[175] Cf. *1563*, pp. 513–22 with *1570*, pp. 1224–32.
[176] Cf. *1563*, pp. 1049–64 with *1570*, pp. 1674–84.   [177] Cf. *1563*, pp. 1470–1503 with *1570*, pp. 2031–67.
[178] For the letter see *1583*, pp. 1348–50. For other examples of this see Foxe's reprinting of a sermon Stephen Gardiner preached before Edward VI (*1570*, pp. 1952–55) or his reprinting of Nicholas Harpsfield's disputation with Archbishop Cranmer at Oxford in 1554 (*1570*, pp. 1628–30).

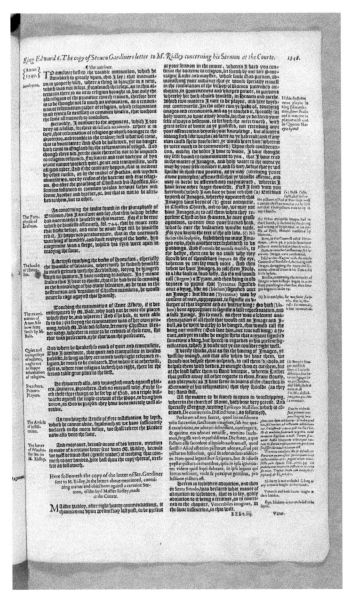

Figure 5 Letter from Stephen Gardiner to Nicholas Ridley in John Foxe's *Acts and Monuments* (1583), pp. 1348–50. Courtesy of Lambeth Palace Library.

Figure 5 (cont.)

Figure 5 (cont.)

during his examinations were converted by Foxe into a series of syllogisms
(see Figure 6).[179] Sometimes, such as when Foxe presented the arguments in
the 1554 Oxford disputations as syllogisms, they were intended to emphasise

[179] *1570*, p. 1851.

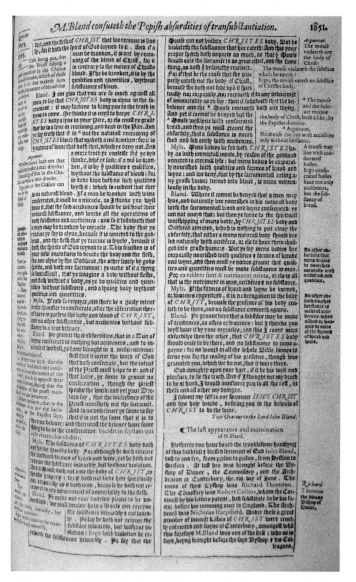

Figure 6 Syllogisms in John Foxe's *Acts and Monuments* (1570), p. 1851. By kind permission of the Dean and Chapter of York Minster.

both the truth of the Protestant arguments and the specious reasoning of the Catholics. Nevertheless, Foxe was also quite capable of taking arguments printed by fellow Protestants that he felt were limited in their theological range and converting them into syllogisms which not only made them appear irrefutable but also something that their original authors might well have regarded as rich and strange.[180]

This editorial oversight demanded a huge investment of Foxe's time and he must once again have spent a considerable amount of time in Day's printing house. In fact letters were addressed to him there in both February 1566 and January 1567.[181] Also about this time Foxe moved from the duke of Norfolk's house in Aldgate to a house he acquired in St Giles Cripplegate. There were a number of reasons for this move but one of them surely was to bring Foxe closer to Day's printing house where he would be spending much of his time.

XII

The second edition of the *Acts and Monuments* would ultimately number around 2,300 pages, divided into two volumes of unequal length. Printing a work of this size must have been a laborious and time-consuming operation. Even though Day brought at least three presses to the task, unfortunately we do not know when he commenced the actual printing of the work, and we have only a few hints as to when it was finished.[182] About 85 per cent of the way through the text Foxe made a reference to Bishop Bonner as still living; Bonner died on 5 September 1569.[183] In a section that was one of the last to be printed in the *Acts and Monuments*, Foxe referred to a visit of Muscovites to London that took place on 1 October 1569.[184] All of this, together of course with the 1570 date on the title page, points to the work having been completed in the first half of 1570. The date became important because political circumstances caused a very late addition to be made to the text. At

---

[180] An excellent example of this is Foxe's reprinting (and re-editing) of the theological tract by the Scottish martyr, Patrick Hamilton, itself edited by John Frith and later John Knox, known as *Patrick's Places*. These syllogisms and some of their arguments, particularly regarding predestination, appeared in no other edition of the work (cf. *1570*, pp. 1108–13 with STC 12731.4–12732).

[181] BL, Harley MS 416, fos. 118[r–v] and 185[r–v].

[182] These three presses are mentioned by Foxe in his letter to Cecil. See above p. 163.   [183] p. 1952.

[184] Ibid., p. 26. Although this appears early in the volume, this section was undoubtedly a very late addition, as can be seen in both the irregular pagination (with columns numbered instead of pages) and the irregular size of the gathering, where the irregular pagination occurs (sigs. c1[r]–c4[v]). It might also be worth mentioning that on p. 2305 of the second edition Foxe speaks of 'this present yeare an.1569', a reference that could extend as far as 25 March 1570.

the end of the first volume there is a section devoted to attacking papal claims to supremacy over secular rulers. It includes a reprinting of Foxe's earlier work, *A solemne contestation*.[185] It also includes a series of woodcuts, some of them newly engraved, illustrating episodes of papal 'tyranny'.[186] This section gives every evidence of having been produced in enormous haste (for one thing there is a complete absence of pagination). Even so, the inclusion of this material may have delayed the work by a few months.[187] This section was undoubtedly a response to *Regnans in excelsis*, the papal bull excommunicating and deposing Elizabeth, promulgated at the beginning of 1570.

A work of this size was unprecedented in the history of printing in England. Despite obstacles and unforeseen problems, the work was a triumph of logistics and determination on John Day's part. On Foxe's part it was a triumph of unblinking attention to detail, combined with remarkable zeal and an ability to orchestrate masses of material, shaping the individual efforts of hundreds – if not thousands – of soloists into one harmonious composition. Yet any feelings of triumph Day had as the volume was nearing completion must have been alloyed with feelings of anxiety and even fear. Day's patents protected him from loss while the work was being printed, but they did not protect his cash investment in materials and labour for the work, and of course did not recompense him for the effort and time he had personally invested in it.[188] If this work did not sell Day would suffer a significant financial reverse. Worse yet, his most basic stock in trade – his reputation as England's greatest printer – would be dented, if not damaged beyond repair.

Shrewdly, Day took some pains to protect his investment. Once again, he advertised his work to a target audience. In 1568 he printed Victor Skinner's translation of Gonsalvius Montanus's popular and influential attack on the

---

[185] See Freeman, '"A Solemne Contestation of Divers Popes": A Work by John Foxe?', pp. 41–8.

[186] These illustrations will be discussed below, pp. 215–17.

[187] There is a distinct possibility that in February 1570 the second edition was put on hold awaiting these anti-papal woodcuts, and a de luxe edition of Euclid was rushed through Day's press in the interval. This will be discussed below.

[188] How sizeable this investment was will never be definitively known. John King has estimated that Day spent about £315 on paper for the entire print run of this edition. This figure, however, rests on a number of assumptions which, while not necessarily unreasonable, are not established facts. First of all, King assumes a print of 1,250 copies, which even he acknowledges is less than absolutely certain (King, *Print Culture*, p. 90, n. 60). Second, King is assuming a consistent price for the paper, but since the paper used was of both good and inferior quality in the edition, this assumption seems open to challenge. Above all, it needs to be remembered that this estimate only covers the cost of the paper and not the cost of labour, plus the loss of income to Day, caused by having his presses tied up. It also does not factor in the cost of the illustrations.

Spanish Inquisition. Skinner declared at the end of his preface to the reader that he 'mightest use this booke as a taste in the meane space, whiles the booke of martires be finished, wherein thou shalt have a most plentiful and notable history of the like manner and argument'.[189] Moreover, as we shall see, Day seems to have been quite articulate in making those in power aware of his concerns about the marketability of this edition. Someone – quite probably Foxe himself – seems to have offered Day some assurance on this point. In a group of Latin poems that prefaced the second edition, most of which are devoted to praise of the martyrs and vilification of their persecutors and of the pope, there is a short verse that stands out in contrast to these graver themes:

> Although many have sold frivolous nonsense and
> Unadulterated foolishness for a high price
> Do not doubt that you will recoup the great profit you wish,
> Day, even if the Monuments is costing you dear.[190]

Whether Day took any comfort from this sentiment is unknown, but as the final copies of the second edition were being stitched or bound, he must have been asking himself the question that has haunted printers and publishers since Gutenberg first put type to paper: will the book sell?

---

[189] Reginaldus Gonsalvius Montanus, *A discovery and playne declaration of sundry subtill practices of the holy inquisition of Spayne*, trans. V. Skinner (London, 1568), STC 11996, sig. A4ᵛ. This statement was repeated in a new edition of Montanus printed by Day in the following year (STC 11997, sig. ¶3ʳ). In this new edition of Montanus there was also a direct reference made to Foxe's work (on sig. Dd.4ʳ).

[190] *1570*, sig.*4r (our translation).

CHAPTER 6

'*Fayre pictures and painted pageants*': the illustrations of the '*Book of Martyrs*'

I

The *Acts and Monuments* is one of the seminal texts printed in early modern England but the significance of the book goes beyond the considerable importance of its text. As we have seen, the production of this book marked a true revolution in the history of the English book. None of the physical aspects of the book are more important or more conspicuous than the scores of woodcut illustrations that accompanied the text of each edition. Certainly this aspect of the work powerfully impressed contemporaries. Robert Persons, in his three-volume attack on Foxe's text, bitterly lamented that the 'lyinge Acts and Monuments ... hath done more hurt alone to simple soules in our countrey by infectinge and poysoninge them unawares under the bayte of pleasant histories, fayre pictures and painted pageants than many other the most pestilent bookes togeather'.[1]

Persons's claim that many people scanned the book's illustrations receives indirect, but interesting, confirmation in William Cartwright's comedy, *The Ordinary* (1651), in which one character derides the lugubrious piety of another, declaring that he wishes 'to become a martyr, and be pictur'd with a long labell out o' your mouth, like those in Foxe's book: just like a jugler drawing ribband out of his throat'.[2] Here the joke depends entirely on the audience's recognition of the illustrations in the *Acts and Monuments*. The illustrations remained familiar throughout the seventeenth century. In the pope-burning procession in London in 1680, one float carried figures depicting a seated pope holding the papal keys in one hand, with his foot on the neck of a monarch lying prostrate at his feet. This is unmistakably a conflation of two woodcut pictures from the *Acts and Monuments*. One shows Pope Alexander III treading on the neck of the

[1] Robert Persons, *A treatise of three conversions of England*, 3 vols. (St Omer, 1604), STC 19416, III, p. 400 (henceforth cited as *Three conversions*).
[2] *The Plays and Poems of William Cartwright*, ed. G. Blakemore Evans (Madison, WI, 1951), p. 283.

Holy Roman Emperor Frederick Barbarossa; the other shows the pope seated on the papal throne holding the keys aloft while the monarch humbly kisses his foot.[3] In his anti-Catholic play *The Female Prelate*, written that same year, Elkanah Settle describes the duke of Saxony:

> Poisoned by a Priest, his savage Confessor,
> That cursed Slave that fed upon his Smiles,
> Fill'd the dire Bowl, and whilst the canting
> Villain was whispering Heaven into his Ear, could lift
> Damnation to his Lips.[4]

This mode of assassination is strikingly reminiscent of the death of King John as depicted in a woodcut in the 'Book of Martyrs' (see Figure 7). This parallel is underscored by a later line in the play, where the son and successor of the slain duke declares to the murderer, 'I will bequeath my dukedom to paynters and engravers to revenge me. There's not the humblest roof in all the principality of Saxony, that shall not have thy face drawn to the life in hell.'[5]

All of this, however, demonstrates merely a superficial, although widespread, familiarity with Foxe's illustrations. For some readers at least the illustrations had a more profound influence. There are several examples where the pictures in the 'Book of Martyrs' seem to have worked as powerfully on the imagination of John Bunyan as the text did. In the *Heavenly Footman*, Bunyan enumerated the tortures inflicted on the martyrs of the early Church; they had to 'endure to be *stoned*, *Sawn asunder*, to have their eyes bored out with *Augures*, their bodies broiled on *Grid irons*, their tongues cut out of their mouths, boiled in *Cauldrons*, thrown to the wild Beasts, burned at the *Stakes*, whipt at Posts and a thousand other fearful torments'.[6] Bunyan seems to have had the large illustration showing the 'X. First Persecutions of the Primitive Church' in mind, if not actually before him, when he was writing this passage.[7] This illustration not only depicts people's eyes being put out with augurs but also shows a martyr being roasted in a grid iron and others being boiled in a cauldron, whilst still others are thrown to wild animals, burned, sawn in half, stoned and whipped. In *The Pilgrim's Progress*, Faithful's execution consists of a series of tortures – 'first they scourged him, then they buffeted him, then they

---

[3] Cf. British Museum, Department of Prints and Drawings, Catalogue of Satires, no. 1085.
[4] Elkanah Settle, *The female prelate* (London, 1680) STC Wing S2684, p. 2.   [5] Ibid., p. 31.
[6] John Bunyan, *The Heavenly Foot-man* (1698), in *The Miscellaneous Works of John Bunyan*, ed. Graham Midgely, 5 vols. (Oxford, 1986), v, p. 167.
[7] See below, p. 207, for a discussion of this picture.

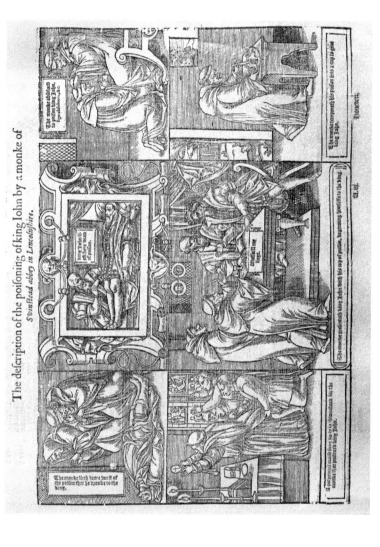

The description of the poisoning of king Iohn by a monke of *Swinsted abbey in Lincolnshire.*

The monke absolued to poison king Iohn, *byz a dobtor*, &c.

The monke tempereth his poison into a cup against king Iohn.

king Iohn ui= eth here dead of poison.

The monke presenteth king Iohn with his cup of poison, begynning, Wassheile to the king.

Theobaldus king.

The monke lieth here dead of the poison that he dranke to the king.

A perpetuall masse sung for the Munkes by the munke that poisoned king Iohn.

Figure 7 Tip-in woodcut depicting the murder of King John from John Foxe's *Acts and Monuments* (1570). By kind permission of the Dean and Chapter of York Minster. Moving clockwise from the upper right, these pictures form a narrative of John's poisoning by a monk.

lanced his flesh with knives; after that they stoned him with stones, then pricked him with their swords and last of all they burned him to ashes at the stake' – all of which were pictured in the woodcut of the 'X. Persecutions'.[8] Apparently this illustration made a deep impression on Bunyan, and he kept visualising it when he wrote about martyrdom and persecution.[9] Similarly, the East India Company reproduced a figure from one of Foxe's woodcuts, which showed persecution of the early Christians, to illustrate a 1624 pamphlet relating the massacre of Company merchants by the Dutch in Ambonya.[10]

Unsurprisingly, the illustrations in the first four editions of John Foxe's *Acts and Monuments*, which received so much attention from early modern readers, have also attracted the attention of modern scholars, most notably in the seminal work of Ruth Luborsky and Elizabeth Ingram.[11] Numerous scholars from a number of different fields, most notably students of art history and the history of the book, have also cast gimlet eyes upon the composition, content, placement and iconography of the illustrations in Foxe's book.[12]

Nevertheless, no one has examined or discussed the production of these illustrations within the context of the overall production of his book. There is a powerful tendency for modern authors and readers – as immersed in a culture of visual images as a fish is in the ocean – to take the woodcuts of Foxe's book for granted. Viewed, however, from the broad perspective of the process of producing the book, paradoxical aspects of the decision to illustrate it extensively emerge. There was a powerful tendency within Protestant book production – most particularly within Calvinist book production – to be wary of the spiritual dangers of the 'idolatrous image'.[13] Foxe himself was not only an outspoken advocate of iconoclasm;

---

[8] John Bunyan, *The Pilgrim's Progress*. ed. Roger Sharrock (Harmondsworth, 1965), p. 134.

[9] For other examples of Bunyan's writings being influenced by illustrations in the *Acts and Monuments* see Thomas S. Freeman, 'A Library in Three Volumes: Foxe's "Book of Martyrs" in the Writings of John Bunyan', *Bunyan Studies*, 5 (1994), pp. 52–3.

[10] Anthony Milton, 'Marketing and Massacre: Ambonya, the East India Company and the Public Sphere in Early Modern England', in *The Politics of the Public Sphere*, ed. Peter Lake and Stephen Pincus (Manchester, 2007), p. 175.

[11] Ruth Samson Luborsky and Elizabeth Morley Ingram, *A Guide to English Illustrated Books, 1536–1603*, 2 vols. (Tempe, AZ, 1998), 1, pp. 374–82.

[12] Among notable recent discussions are Margaret Aston and Elizabeth Ingram, 'The Iconography of the *Acts and Monuments*', in *John Foxe and the English Reformation*, ed. Loades, pp. 66–141; Deborah Burks, 'Polemical Potency: The Witness of Word and Woodcut', in *John Foxe and his World*, ed. Christopher Highley and John N. King (Aldershot, 2002), pp. 263–76, James A. Knapp, *Illustrating the Past in Early Modern England: The Representation of History in Printed Books* (Aldershot, 2003), pp. 124–61, and King, *Print Culture*, pp. 162–242.

[13] Andrew Pettegree, 'Illustrating the Book: A Protestant Dilemma', in *John Foxe and his World*, pp. 133–44; Patrick Collinson, *The Birthpangs of Protestant England* (Basingstoke, 1988), p. 117.

he had even destroyed at least one image of the Virgin Mary personally.[14] So why was the magnum opus of this iconoclast the most lavishly illustrated book hitherto produced in England?

Moreover, we have already noted (as apparently Foxe did himself) John Day's persistent fear that this book would lose money. Wariness of the dangers of iconoclasm and perhaps a similar attention to the bottom line had caused Jean Crespin to produce his massive martyrology, the nearest contemporary equivalent in size as well as purpose to the *Acts and Monuments*, without significant illustration.[15] Why then did Day commission, and more importantly pay for, these expensive woodcuts – particularly when his readers would not have expected them? There were a number of reasons, which we will explore further in this chapter, but to begin with Day's individual contribution should not be ignored. From the earliest stages of his career (e.g., his inclusion of a full picture of the burning of Anne Askew in Robert Crowley's *Confutation*) Day had been a pioneer in producing illustrations of contemporary martyrdoms. One fundamental reason why the *Acts and Monuments* was so lavishly illustrated, while Crespin's martyrology had no illustrations, may lie as much in the contrasting personalities and proclivities of Day and Crespin as in the contrasting political and religious circumstances in which they operated. In this chapter, we hope to examine not only why these illustrations were commissioned, created and printed, but also the impact that these processes had on the overall production of the work.

II

Everyone who has written about the illustrations in Foxe's book has mentioned the expense that producing the woodcuts would have entailed. Unfortunately it is impossible to be more precise about how great this expense was. Financial records simply do not survive from Day's printing house or any other contemporary English printing house to indicate the precise cost of such illustrations.[16] Nevertheless it does seem safe to say that

---

[14] See *Christ Jesus Triumphant*, trans. Richard Day, sig. A4ʳ, for a description of this episode. Foxe clearly stated his desire for a thoroughgoing purge of images in churches to be conducted by the magistrates (*1570*, p. 992).

[15] On the rarity of illustrations in any of Crespin's printed works see Gilmont, *Jean Crespin*, pp. 70–1.

[16] Greenberg estimates that 'illustrations boost[ed] the cost [of the *Acts and Monuments*] by 100 percent' (Greenberg, 'Community of the Texts', p. 708). Greenberg does not give a source for her assertion, but she is almost certainly drawing this from Tessa Watt, who maintained that the expense involved in hiring illustrators 'was reflected in the doubling of the normal prices when a book was illustrated; a practice sanctioned by a Stationers' Company ordinance of 1598'. Tessa Watt, *Cheap Print and*

the expense must have been considerable.[17] Woodcuts, especially of the quality of those used in the *Acts and Monuments*, would have been produced by highly skilled craftsmen, and their efforts would not have come cheaply. These woodcuts were prized possessions, carefully conserved and reused in subsequent editions of Foxe's book right up to 1632.[18]

However, the simple expense of commissioning these woodcuts was not the only cost involved in their production. Once created, the woodcuts had to be fitted within the book. In the 1563 edition this caused numerous

Popular Piety, 1550–1640 (Cambridge, 1991), p. 147. First of all, it should be noted that Greenberg is taking an observation made about *cheap* print and applying it to an *expensive* volume, whose economics were necessarily quite different. Watts does not make this crucial distinction either. Watts cites Francis R. Johnson's article, 'Notes on English Retail Book-prices, 1550–1640', *The Library*, 5th series, 2 (1950), pp. 84 and 90. However, Johnson is describing an ordinance of 1598 which regulated the maximum price that could be charged per sheet. This price was determined by the amount of type on a page. Simply because woodcut pictures, which obviously reduced the amount of type on a page, were not of uniform size, they could therefore not be easily regulated and so illustrated books were exempted from this ordinance. Thus Watts is in error by stating that a doubling of illustrated book prices was sanctioned by this ordinance; in actual fact, the ordinance did not affect illustrated books at all. Furthermore, Johnson actually states that 'the average illustrated book was priced *75–100 per cent* higher than other books of the same number of sheets': Johnson, 'English Retail Book-prices', p. 90 (our emphasis). Apart from the fact that 75–100 per cent is not the same as 100 per cent, the question is, what is the 'average illustrated book'? Clearly, the ordinance was aimed at cheap print and, equally clearly, the sample books mentioned in Johnson's article are predominantly cheap books. Of course an illustration would dramatically increase the price of a small, inexpensive book because the other costs involved would not be that high. Equally clearly, if the book was a large, expensive book, such as the *Acts and Monuments*, illustrations would certainly increase the price but they would not necessarily double it.

[17] King argues that 'the expense of illustration underwent dilution as pressmen reused the woodblocks in successive editions' (King, *Print Culture*, p. 168). As we will observe in more detail below, because of the specificity of their subject matter, the woodcuts from the *Acts and Monuments* were not, in fact, extensively reused.

[18] King has claimed that the woodcut used in Foxe's book to illustrate the execution of Anne Askew was a reuse of the very same woodcut first used in Robert Crowley's *The confutation of .xiii. articles, whereunto N. Shaxton, late bishop subscribed* (London, 1548), printed by Stephen Mierdman for William Seres and John Day. There is no doubt that the woodcut used in Foxe's book was identical to the woodcut first used in Crowley's *Confutation*, and King is very probably correct in maintaining that it was the exact same block; if true, this is a striking proof of the value of these woodcuts and the unwillingness of printers to discard them. (It is also another indication of Day's pioneering interest in the visual representation of historical events.) Unfortunately, King's proof that this was the exact same block falls short. King bases his claim on a 'hairline crack', which he has discerned in this woodcut. John N. King, *English Reformation Literature: The Tudor Origins of the Protestant Tradition* (Princeton, NJ, 1982), p. 439. We have been unable to spot this crack, either in the copies of Shaxton's *Confutation* or the copies of Foxe's work that we have consulted. However, the frame of the woodcut does show signs of deterioration in copies of the *Acts and Monuments*, particularly in the upper left-hand corner, but there is also further obvious deterioration in the right-hand vertical strip of the frame, where there is a small but definite break just above the background building. A similar break occurs in the left-hand vertical strip behind the group of onlookers, beginning with the first edition of the *Acts and Monuments* and continuing through to the sixth edition of 1610. (In the seventh edition the original woodcuts were replaced with copies.) Clearly the original woodcuts were used throughout the first six editions of Foxe, yet there is no absolute proof, *pace* King, that Day had retained this woodcut since 1548, although this is a reasonable hypothesis.

problems. For example, the first woodcut within the main text of the 1563 edition of the *Acts and Monuments* is a picture of the humiliation of the Emperor Henry IV at Canossa. The compositors left a space – equivalent to twenty-five lines of text – at the bottom of the second column of text for this woodcut to be inserted.[19] The space, however, turned out to be too small for the woodcut, which had to be pasted in on one side and then folded in half. Clearly an illustration had been planned for this section but was not ready when the printing of the section commenced.[20] It seems equally clear that Day was negligent here in not getting accurate measurements for the woodcut from its designer or in not passing those measurements on to his compositors. The awkward insertion of this woodcut created a number of small problems. Folding the woodcut made it more liable to damage. Pasting it in made it much more possible for it to be detached from the text and lost. The same situation occurred, with the same consequences, when a second woodcut in this edition, showing Alexander III treading on the neck of a prostrate emperor, Frederick Barbarossa, was added to Book 1.[21]

The chance survival of 'proof sheets' from the 1563 edition indicate problems that arose with the printing of a picture of Wiclif's body being posthumously burned.[22] In the first attempt to incorporate this woodcut into the text, the illustration was printed on the left-hand side of the sheet, instead of the right-hand side where it should have been printed. When the sheets were folded to make pages, this meant that the picture appeared on the wrong page. The illustration went on the side of the sheet that became sigs. $L2^{r-v}$ (pages 99 and 100) and $L5^{r-v}$ (pages 105 and 106). Thus in these early attempts, the woodcut was printed on sig. $L2^v$ (page 100), rather than on sig. $L5^r$ (page 105), where it belonged.

Beyond the simple expense of commissioning a skilled artisan to create a woodcut, their inclusion in Foxe's text, particularly given the extent to which they were used, vastly increased the complexities of producing an already technically demanding work. These challenges are a further indication of the determination of Day and perhaps Foxe to illustrate the volume despite the problems involved. In fact sometimes mistakes could not be corrected without discarding the woodcut. An example of this occurred when the names identifying several martyrs in a particular woodcut

---

[19] *1563*, p. 25.   [20] See King, *Print Culture*, p. 192.   [21] *1563*, p. 41.
[22] The sheets were identified as 'proof sheets' in the revised STC (no. 11222a). Technically, since these sheets were only printed on one side, they are not really proof sheets; they are simply pages which were wrongly imposed and therefore discarded. See Roberts, 'Bibliographical Aspects of John Foxe', pp. 45–6.

appeared backwards; rather than having the woodcut recarved, the mistake was simply repeated from edition to edition. Another woodcut, illustrating the scourging of a Lollard named John Florence, identifies his tormentor as 'Boner'. This was an incorrect assumption by someone on Day's staff, as that bishop of London was not even alive when Florence was scourged.[23]

One aspect of early modern book production that helped to justify the expensive illustrations was that they could be reused by the same printer for different works or even loaned to another printer. In fact, Day borrowed one woodcut from his colleague Richard Grafton.[24] He also quarried earlier works to supply woodcuts for various editions of the *Acts and Monuments*. Two large woodcuts that appeared in all the editions of Foxe's book were appropriated from previous works printed by or for John Day: one was the woodcut of Anne Askew and two other martyrs being burned at Smithfield, mentioned above, which first appeared in Robert Crowley's *Confutation of Nicholas Shaxton*. The second picture, of Hugh Latimer preaching before Edward VI, has an even more interesting history. It first appeared in Augustine Bernher's edition of *Certayn godly sermons vppon the lords prayer*, printed by Day in 1562.[25] This is the only time Day produced a book of sermons with an illustration. It is therefore possible that this large woodcut was actually commissioned for the *Acts and Monuments* and was finished in time to be used in Bernher's book, which was printed the previous year. Both of the woodcuts added to the 1576 edition were also used in previous books printed by Day. One of these – a map of the kingdoms of the Saxon Heptarchy – was reprinted from William Lambarde's 1568 *Archaionomia*; the other, depicting Truth weighing the 'Verbum Dei', originally appeared on the last page of Foxe's edition of *The whole workes of W. Tyndale, John Frith and Doct. Barnes*, printed by Day in 1573.

Of course the process worked in reverse as well. Day occasionally reused woodcuts from the *Acts and Monuments* in other works. The specificity of many of these woodcuts, however, made this difficult to do, and it is another example of how Day's decision to illustrate Foxe's book lavishly with pictures of particular events worked against Day's short-term economic interest. Nevertheless, he was able to recycle some of these woodcuts in a few works. Foxe's edition of the writings of Tyndale, Frith and Barnes provided an excellent opportunity for reusing the woodcuts depicting the

---

[23] See King, *Print Culture*, p. 195.
[24] The woodcut first appears on fo. 263ᵛ of Edward Hall's *The vnion of the two noble and illustre famelies of Lancastre [and] Yorke, beeyng long in continual discension for the croune of this noble realme*, printed by Richard Grafton (London, 1548), STC 12721.
[25] STC 15276.

executions of these evangelicals. Day ingeniously, if somewhat inappropriately, reused the woodcut capital 'C', which depicts him, Foxe and Cecil along with an enthroned Elizabeth, in John Dee's *Perfect arte of Navigation.*[26] A more apposite recycling of a woodcut occurred when Day took the capital 'E' showing Edward VI enthroned, which had been used in the dedication of Edmund Becke's English Bible, and placed it at the beginning of the account of Edward VI's reign in the *Acts and Monuments.*[27]

The most interesting example of the reuse of one of the woodcuts occurs not with a large woodcut but with a small one, depicting the execution of the Marian martyr Cicely Ormes, in which she appears bound to the stake, gazing straight ahead, with her hands before her in prayer. This illustration was also later used in 1592 as the title page of an anonymous pamphlet describing the execution of Anne Brewen in Smithfield on 28 June 1592 for the crime of poisoning her husband John, a London goldsmith. The Ormes woodcut, last used in the 1583 edition, was probably 'borrowed' from the stock of woodcuts when these were transferred to the Stationers' Company prior to the printing of the 1596 edition of Foxe.[28] It was apparently never returned to the stock as it never reappears in any subsequent edition of Foxe; instead, a new woodcut of Ormes appears, depicting her bound to the stake with her head looking towards the sky and her arms crossed on her breast.[29]

III

While there is no doubt that Day commissioned the woodcuts for Foxe's book, did he design them? Clearly someone must have instructed the illustrator as to which topics they were to illustrate. Moreover there are patterns and thematic unities in the woodcuts – e.g., the emphasis on martyrdom and papal tyranny – that suggest that someone assumed overall direction of their content. The only two people who could have done this

---

[26] John Dee, *General and rare memorials pertayning to the perfect arte of navigation* (London, 1577), STC 6459.

[27] Cf. Becke, *The Byble*, sig. *3ᵛ with *1563*, p. 675. This woodcut was only reused in the first edition of the *Acts and Monuments*. The royal arms of Edward VI (conveniently the initials 'E.R.' prominently displayed were equally suitable in the reign of Elizabeth) were also recycled from Becke's Bible into the *Acts and Monuments* (the arms occur on the verso of an unsigned page prior to the title page of both books).

[28] Cf. *The trueth of the most wicked murthering of J. Brewen* (London, 1592), STC 15095, with *1583*, p. 2023.

[29] *1596*, p. 1835. This new woodcut was also used to depict the Marian martyr Margery Polley (*1596*, p. 1524). It had first been used in *1570*, p. 1860.

were Day and Foxe. It can safely be asserted that Day was responsible for placing one woodcut in the book – his own portrait. Furthermore he printed numerous works, such as *The cosmographical glasse, The treasure of Euonymus* and Bateman's *A christall glasse*, that were noted for their abundance of detailed illustration.[30] More importantly, Day had also, as we have seen, commissioned woodcuts of Askew's martyrdom and of Latimer preaching for earlier works.

The production of *A christall glasse* may in fact be intertwined with that of the *Acts and Monuments*. This was one of the first works written by Stephen Bateman (or Batman), who was not only one of Parker's chaplains but one of the archbishop's chief aides in finding medieval books and manuscripts. Such activities may well have already associated him with Foxe and Day, and the care that Day devoted to producing his book may well have been another link in the chain that bound the printer to the prelate. (It is even possible that Parker may have underwritten the cost of some or all of the illustrations in his chaplain's book.)[31] What is likely is that the illustrator or illustrators of *A christall glasse* also worked on some of the illustrations for the 'Book of Martyrs'. In particular, an illustration in Foxe's book showing Thomas Bilney (an evangelical burned in 1531) being pulled from the pulpit by two friars has marked similarities to an image in Bateman's book of a godly preacher being pulled from the pulpit by 'two enemies of God's word'.[32] All of this would seem to highlight Day's role in choosing both the topics illustrated in Foxe's magnum opus and the illustrators who depicted them. As the person who would have hired and paid the illustrators, it can be assumed that Day would have had the responsibility and the privilege of determining the content of the illustrations.

Evidence of Foxe's involvement, on the other hand, is rather more mixed. Foxe's modern biographer John Mozley has claimed – and his claim has been incautiously repeated by numerous scholars as fact – that Foxe actually drew a picture of a man sentenced to carry a bag of straw as penance. The woodcut is a copy of a marginal drawing made in Archbishop Courtenay's Register (see Figures 8 and 9) and Mozley's claim rests entirely on the assumption that Foxe actually saw the register. We know that Foxe used

---

[30] William Cunningham, *The cosmographical glasse conteinyng the pleasant principles of cosmographie, geographie, hydrographie, or nauigation* (London, 1559) STC 6119; Gesner, *The treasure of Euonymus*; Stephen Bateman, *A christall glasse of Christian reformation wherein the godly maye beholde the coloured abuses vsed in this our present tyme* (London, 1569) STC 1581.

[31] As we shall see later in this chapter (pp. 225–5), Parker had a considerable interest in book illustration.

[32] Margaret Aston, *The King's Bedpost: Reformation and Iconography in a Tudor Group Portrait* (Cambridge, 1993), pp. 164–6.

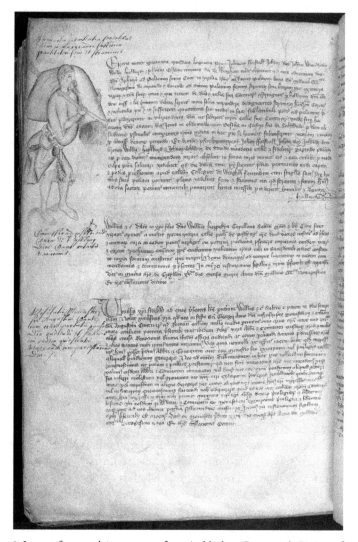

Figure 8 Image of a man doing penance from Archbishop Courtenay's Register, fo. 337^v.
Courtesy of Lambeth Palace Library.

copyists to transcribe records and it is far more likely that he consulted transcriptions of the Lambeth records rather than actually visiting the palace itself. The decision to copy the picture – both to illustrate the penance and to verify Foxe's use of the register – would have probably been made by Foxe

¶ A deſcription of the poore men doyng their pe-
naunce, with their ſtraw on theyr backe.

☐ Rroris mater ignorātia, quoſdam Hugonem Pennie. Ioh 3.

Figure 9 Woodcut of a man doing penance from John Foxe's *Acts and Monuments* (1570),
p. 661. By kind permission of the Dean and Chapter of York Minster.

(presumably the transcriber made a note that the picture was there) and an
artist would then have been sent to make a copy. It is of course possible that
Foxe saw the actual register himself and decided to make the copy, but there
is no evidence of this, and it seems to have been his usual practice to rely on
copyists – even for documents found in London and its environs.

There is, however, one case where there is some evidence that Foxe might
have had the idea for an illustration. In the 1570 edition, comparing

Protestant works banned in the reign of Mary Tudor with Catholic works promulgated at that time, Foxe wrote:

So much leave it may please the reader to graunt me, to set before hym here a payre of balaunce, wherein to waygh the bookes on the one side condemned, with the bookes on the other side allowed, to the end that we weying the one with the other, may discerne the better between them, which part weyeth best with Gods holy truth and true Catholicke church, against manifest Idolatry and palpable abomination.[33]

This verbal image seems to be a description of the woodcut of Truth weighing the Bible in a pair of scales, which first appeared in the third edition. However, apart from these few instances, and the real but unproven probability that Day would have discussed at least the major illustrations with his author, there is no evidence of Foxe's designing the woodcuts or even dictating the subjects they should illustrate.

It should also be remembered that while Day (and possibly Foxe) may have determined the subjects of the illustrations, they would not have determined their designs or even their specific details.[34] These would have been left to the craftsmen who actually designed the woodcuts. For the most part we have no idea who these people were, or any means of identifying them. There is no comprehensive list of the illustrators Day employed, nor, for the most part, did the engravers sign their work.[35] The only clues to their individual identities are idiosyncratic details in their illustrations: e.g., the manner in which they drew flames or windows. However, these anonymous craftsmen played a large part in determining the actual content of the illustrations and it was through the eyes of these craftsmen – almost certainly foreigners – that generations of English people visualised the history of 'their' Church.

---

[33] *1570*, p. 1773.

[34] It must be said that on occasion the woodcuts depict very specific details unique to Foxe's text. For examples of this with the smaller woodcuts, see below, p. 202. An interesting example of this in one of the large woodcuts occurs in the picture of Henry IV's submission at Canossa. The papal historian Platina, in his account of this story, declared that Gregory VII agreed to accept Henry IV's submission 'rogatu Mathildis et Adelai Sabvadiensis comitis et cluniacensis abbatus' ('through the pleas of Matilda and Adelaus, Count of Savoy, and the Abbot of Cluny'). Bartolomeo Platina, *Vitae pontificum* (Venice, 1479), sig. P3ᵛ. Foxe, whose account of the incident is translated directly from Platina's work, rendered this passage as 'through the intreating of Matilda, *the popes paramour* and of Adelau, earle of Sebaudia, and the abbot of Cluniake' (*1563*, p. 26, our emphasis). In the upper right-hand corner of this woodcut, looking through a window, the pope can be seen embracing his 'paramour', Matilda of Tuscany.

[35] Margaret Aston and Elizabeth Ingram have observed that the monogram 'MD' appears on both the 'ten persecutions' foldout and the illustration of the Windsor martyrs. A second set of initials, 'RB', also appears on the illustration of the Windsor martyrs. Aston and Ingram were unable to identify whose initials these were. See Aston and Ingram, 'Iconography', p. 137, n. 104.

IV

Ruth Luborsky has drawn basic but useful distinctions, based on their functions, between the three types of illustrations that occur in the book. She refers to one type as 'announcement' woodcuts because they announce a change in the major text and usually epitomise or summarise it.[36] Illustrations of this type are often allegorical and, unlike other illustrations in Foxe's work, they often express complex ideas. The purpose of these illustrations, however, is to precede and herald a major section of text and often give the reader some indication, at least thematically, of what is to follow. An example of these woodcuts is the famous title page, which shows the division between the True Church with its martyrs and its godly readers and hearers of God's word, and the False Church, with its 'superstitious' ceremonies and 'idolatrous' rituals. Other announcement woodcuts include the capital C already discussed, which opens the dedication of the work to Queen Elizabeth, and the similar image of Henry VIII trampling Clement VII underfoot. Another image of Henry VIII, this time depicted seated in majesty with his councillors, introduces Book 8. Book 9, devoted to the reign of Edward VI, opens with an image that encapsulates Foxe's conception of the godly Church and the measures taken in the young king's reign to create it. In the upper portion of the woodcut offending images are destroyed, while crosses, chalices, candlesticks and other ceremonial objects are removed from churches. Some of the obnoxious objects are shown being burned, while others are transported overseas by Catholics fleeing into exile. In the lower portion Edward VI delivers an English Bible to his bishops and a reformed Church is depicted in which only two sacraments – baptism and communion – are depicted. The communion table (ostentatiously labelled as such, rather than being described as an altar) lies in the chancel instead of against the east wall, and is aligned with its sides on an east–west axis. At the same time, a venerable minister is preaching to a congregation, some of whom are reading their Bibles, while others listen in rapt attention (see Figure 10).[37] Finally there is the allegory of Justice weighing the Word of God, which appears as the end page to the third and fourth editions of the 'Book of Martyrs'. One common theme unites all of these announcement woodcuts: unremitting hostility to the Roman Catholic Church, its sacraments, its worship and its spiritual head.

[36] Ruth Samson Luborsky, 'The Illustrations: Their Pattern and Plan', in *John Foxe: An Historical Perspective*, ed. Loades, pp. 68–9.
[37] As Margaret Aston has observed, the illustration of the king (in the bottom left of this woodcut) presenting the Bible to his bishops is an updated version of the frontispiece to Cranmer's 1548 catechism. Aston, *The King's Bedpost*, pp. 155, 158 and 161.

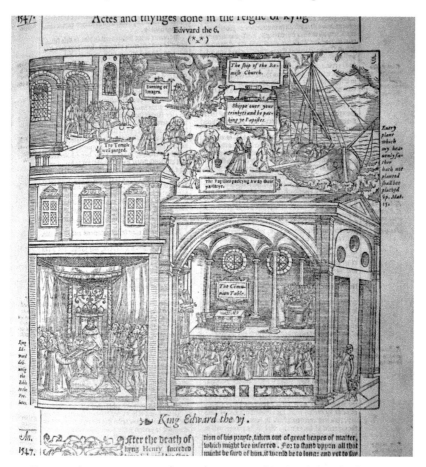

Figure 10 Announcement woodcut at the opening of Book 9 (Edward VI's reign)
in John Foxe's *Acts and Monuments* (1570), p. 923. By kind permission of
the Dean and Chapter of York Minster.

The most numerous group of illustrations in Foxe's book are what
Luborsky has called the 'narrative' woodcuts. Hitherto most illustrations,
particularly in English books, had been allegorical, and relatively few
English book illustrations had attempted to portray actual historical events
realistically.[38] Even editions of the *Legenda Aurea*, which, as we shall discuss
shortly, provided a certain precedent and perhaps even inspiration for the

[38] An important exception to this is the realistic depiction of the burning of Anne Askew which Day
printed in 1548. See above, p. 191, n. 8. John King has observed that this woodcut – particularly in its

woodcuts in Foxe's book, nevertheless tended to depict the saints and martyrs in very stylised, generic pictures, devoid of historical specificity. James Knapp has even suggested that 'the effort and expense taken to avoid the use of universal or typological illustrations indicates a desire to differentiate the book from Catholic predecessors like Jacobus De Voragine's *Legenda Aurea*'.[39] There may be some truth to this, but the historical specificity of the illustrations in Foxe's text are probably due to many other factors beyond the different confessional strategies of illustrating ecclesiastical history.

It is striking that the illustrations in the *Rerum* show a greater tendency to lean towards the symbolic than the illustrations in even the 1563 edition. There are exceptions to this. The *Rerum*, for example, does provide relatively realistic depictions of the martyrdom of John Hooper and Thomas Cranmer, although even these are, as Aston and Ingram point out, relatively stylised and much less graphic than those in the first edition of Foxe's book, published only four years later.[40] One woodcut depicting the agonising and protracted martyrdom of William Gardiner in Portugal is strikingly close in composition and design to a woodcut depicting the same incident that appeared in the first and subsequent editions of the *Acts and Monuments*.[41] Yet here too, despite the horrendous physical punishment being inflicted on Gardiner, he appears oddly serene in the *Rerum* woodcut, and the visual impact of this illustration is somehow less graphic than that in the *Acts and Monuments*. It is particularly instructive to compare the illustration of Sir John Oldcastle in the *Rerum* with that in the *Acts and Monuments*. In the *Rerum* the Lollard hero is shown – in an image modelled on the title page of John Bale's account of Oldcastle's martyrdom – as a Roman warrior, complete with trireme in the background, bearing a shield with the image of the crucified Christ. In the *Acts and Monuments* he is depicted at the moment of his martyrdom, suspended in chains over a fire, writhing in agony.[42]

depiction of Shaxton preaching and of lightning flashing during the execution – follows John Bale's famous description of this grisly event quite closely (King, *Reformation Literature*, p. 80). Many of the narrative illustrations in Foxe would draw heavily in their iconography from continental – particularly German – models. This subject has been well covered by Aston and Ingram, 'Iconography', pp. 66–141.

[39] Knapp, *Illustrating the Past*, p. 134.

[40] Foxe, *Rerum*, pp. 297 and 326, see also Aston and Ingram, 'Iconography', pp. 83–6. Aston and Ingram also point out that woodcuts in Ludwig Rabus's contemporary Lutheran martyrology are similarly restrained and 'unrealistic' (ibid., p. 87, n. 37).

[41] Cf. Foxe, *Rerum*, p. 97 with *1563*, p. 879.

[42] Cf. Foxe, *Rerum*, p. 97 with John Bale, *A brefe chronycle concernynge the examinacyon and death of the blessed martyr of Christ syr J. Oldcastell* (Antwerp, 1544), title page, *1563*, p. 277, *1570*, p. 762, *1576*, p. 620, *1583*, p. 643.

The narrative woodcuts come in various sizes: some are the size of a page or even larger, many cover at least two columns in width (we will refer to these as 'large woodcuts'). More numerous are woodcuts covering about one column in width (we will refer to these as 'small woodcuts'). These small woodcuts invariably depict the martyrdoms of various individuals. The historical specificity, which is such a novel and distinctive feature of the narrative woodcuts, is much more marked in the larger woodcuts than in the smaller ones. Many of the small woodcuts tend to be generic, and indeed are often used and reused to depict different martyrs. Yet as Luborsky has observed, these small woodcuts are not absolutely homogeneous, nor completely interchangeable. Minor differences occur between these small woodcuts, even when the designs are similar. However, many of the small woodcuts do, despite their differences, share a basic design and, most importantly, the martyrs they depict are undifferentiated to the point of being anonymous, with featureless expressions and no means of identifying them.[43] This type of woodcut was most frequently repeated and used to depict various martyrs or groups of martyrs. However, some of these small woodcuts illustrate specific episodes described in the text and were suitable for use only once. These include pictures of William Collins, executed, as Foxe recounts, along with his dog, who is shown being hurled into the fire occupied by his master; the Scottish martyr George Wishart shown being burned on a gibbet, not the customary stake, as Foxe recounted; John Lawrence whose woodcut not only shows the martyr being executed in a chair because of his physical infirmity, but also follows Foxe's text in depicting children who shouted encouragement to the elderly man as he was burned to death; George Marsh with a bucket of pitch dripping over his head, a unique feature of his execution described by Foxe; John Denley struck on the head with a bundle of faggots thrown at him at the command of Dr John Story (who is clearly labelled in the woodcut); and Hugh Laverock, a lame martyr, who, following Foxe's description, is shown waving his crutches at the stake.[44] Another small woodcut depicts the sudden death of Thomas Nightingale, rector of Crundale, Kent, struck down in his pulpit in the act of extolling the restoration of Catholicism to England.[45] This picture is unique among the small woodcuts in depicting the 'providential' punishment of a sinner rather than the heroic death of a

---

[43] Luborsky, 'Illustrations', p. 73.

[44] For William Collins see *1570*, p. 1291; for George Wishart, *1570*, p. 1448; for John Lawrence, *1570*, p. 1721; for George Marsh, *1570*, p. 1738; for John Denley, *1570*, p. 1867; for Hugh Laverock, *1570*, p. 2090.

[45] *1570*, p. 1731.

martyr. Thus small woodcuts, as well as large ones, can be used to illustrate specific historical events.

There was a third type of illustration, much less numerous than the narrative woodcuts, but nevertheless quite important. These woodcuts, for which Luborsky has coined the term 'incidental cuts', can be differentiated from the other woodcuts, not by what they depict, but by the purpose they were meant to serve. They were intended to provide visual proof and authentication of something referred to in the text. Foxe, for example, made a point of emphasising that the purpose of the woodcut copied from the Canterbury Register, reproducing the picture of a fourteenth-century penitent, was authentic. A note beside it reads that the picture was 'drawn in all proportion according to the exemplar standing in the register'. The same point is made in the text, which refers to the picture 'annexed and painted in all resemblaunce' to the drawing in Archbishop Courtenay's Register.[46] Clearly the purpose here was as much to reassure readers that Foxe had consulted the register – and that the records he was citing actually existed – as it was to depict the sufferings of medieval penitents.

Foxe demonstrated a similar desire to prove that he had consulted a printed record by including a careful woodcut copy of the front page of Clement VII's sentence declaring the invalidity of Henry VIII's divorce from Catherine of Aragon. Foxe declared that he was reproducing the very copy of the document that was sent to Catherine and that 'hath of late come to our handes'.[47] As Margaret Aston has observed of this illustration, the 'format of the papal brief is closely followed, including a woodcut of Clement's arms, but noticeably omitting the supporting figures of Saints Peter and Paul which flank these arms in the original'. The sentence imitated the form of the actual document, taking up the breadth of the page, with Foxe's text on the remainder of the page returning to a double column format.[48] A final example is a very exact copy of a medal, almost certainly struck in Bohemia in the sixteenth century, of Jan Hus, showing

---

[46] LPL, Courtenay Register, fo. 337ᵛ and *1570*, p. 661 (see Figures 8 and 9). [47] *1570*, pp. 1457–8.

[48] Aston and Ingram, 'Iconography', p. 73. The subsequent history of this woodcut is worth mentioning. Aston and Ingram have maintained that in the 1576 and 1583 editions 'there was no similar attempt made to reproduce the format [of the sentence], though in the latter (p. 1280) a new woodcut of the papal arms was introduced' (Aston and Ingram, 'Iconography', p. 73, n. 16). This is not completely accurate. It is true that in the 1576 edition the papal arms are not included and the sentence is printed continuously in columns, rather than across the page, although the headings are still faithfully reproduced (within the column width) (*1576*, p. 1243). In the 1583 edition the situation is more confusing. The sentence is printed in a column, which continues from the lower verso of one page onto the recto of the next. A papal coat of arms is reproduced but the arms are those of Julius II. What explains these changes is that the original woodcut of Clement VII's arms seems to have been lost or unavailable for Day to use. What is interesting to our argument is that in 1583 an attempt was

the Bohemian heresiarch in profile on one side and showing him being burned at the stake on the other.[49] Foxe's interest in these woodcuts, however, was not in the depiction of Hus or of his burning. These woodcuts appear twice in the *Acts and Monuments* – and this alone underscores their importance – and are used both times to illustrate passages in which Foxe recites a prophecy that Hus was supposed to have made at his death in 1415. The prophecy related that although a goose ('husa' is Czech for goose) was now being burned, in a hundred years a swan would come, which would not be burned. This was considered to be a prophecy of the advent of Martin Luther and gained great currency among Protestants.[50] The medal referred to the prophecy with a motto – clearly reproduced in Foxe's picture – circling the image of Hus at the stake, which reads 'Centum revolutis annis deo respondebitis'.[51] The purpose of this illustration was to demonstrate that there was indeed a prophecy that anticipated the coming of Martin Luther, thus 'proving' that the great reformer had been sent by God.

These then are the basic types of illustrations in Foxe's work and the purposes which they were meant to serve: to demarcate different sections of the text, to visually represent ideas and attitudes embodied in the text, to dramatise events depicted in the text, and to verify some of the sources that Foxe had consulted.[52]

v

Phrases such as 'lavishly illustrated' and 'extensively illustrated' used to describe the 'Book of Martyrs' suffer from the disadvantage of being inexact. Unfortunately, as with so many aspects of the *Acts and Monuments*, determining the number of illustrations is not as straightforward as it might appear. First of all, some illustrations were used more than once within an edition of the 'Book of Martyrs'; thus it is necessary to observe a distinction

made to reproduce the facsimile appearance of the document by restoring a papal coat of arms, albeit the wrong one. (It is only the size of the facsimile that has changed, since it is reproduced across one column, not two, in this edition.)

[49] Although the copy of the medal was accurate, Foxe somewhat confused the issue by identifying the person burning at the stake as Hus's fellow martyr, Jerome of Prague. On Foxe's use of this medal see Aston and Ingram, 'Iconography', pp. 98–9.

[50] On this prophecy see R. W. Scribner, 'Luther Myth: A Popular Historiography of the Reformer', in Scribner, *Popular Culture and Popular Movements in Reformation Germany* (London, 1987), pp. 302 and 309.

[51] *1570*, pp. 912 and 968. Foxe also printed a Latin caption under the picture of Hus at the stake, 'post centum annos vos omnes cito', emphasising the prophecy.

[52] We have not included in this analysis the woodcut picture of John Day, discussed above, which was *sui generis*.

between the number of illustrations and the number of times an illustration occurred. Second, the number of illustrations varied from edition to edition. In the first edition there are 53 illustrations with 57 occurrences; in the second edition there are 105 illustrations with 149 occurrences. In the third edition the number of woodcuts increases slightly to 107, with 150 occurrences, while the 1583 edition has the lowest number of actual illustrations, 100, but there are 153 occurrences. It is also important to remember that there is no consistent accumulation of illustrations from edition to edition. While some illustrations were added to various editions, others were quietly discarded.

Moreover, simply enumerating the number of woodcuts does not adequately convey what they represented. Although numerous, the woodcuts only treat a small number of the subjects described in Foxe's text. First of all, with few exceptions, they depict either the persecution of the martyrs or the iniquity of the papacy. Nor do they cover equally the full historical period described by Foxe; although the number of pictures devoted to the period preceding Mary Tudor's accession to the throne rose dramatically in the second edition, the number of illustrations for the three years of the Marian persecution, depending on the edition, either exceed or equal the number of illustrations for the preceding 1,500 years of Church history. Interestingly, there are some subjects that receive a great deal of attention in the text, but were barely illustrated (e.g., the providential punishment of sinners).[53] Remembering the expense and trouble it took to illustrate the 'Book of Martyrs' at all, why were particular topics and periods chosen for illustration?

The distribution of woodcuts, both topically and chronologically, changed remarkably from the first to the second edition.[54] (In the discussion below we will be considering only the large *narrative* woodcuts, for a number of reasons. First of all, because they are all non-generic and not repeated, they are much easier to be subjected to this type of analysis. Second, their smaller number makes it easier to be precise about their appearances.) In the 1563 edition there is a total of forty-five large woodcuts. Only three are for the period before the advent of John Wiclif, all of which depict the papacy humiliating or even

---

[53] For Foxe's overriding concern to relate examples of God's chastisement of the wicked, see Freeman, 'Fate, Faction and Fiction', pp. 601–23; Patrick Collinson, 'Truth, Lies and Fiction in Sixteenth Century Protestant Historiography', in *The Historical Imagination in Early Modern Britain: History, Rhetoric and Fiction, 1500–1800*, ed. Donald R. Kelley and David Harris Sacks (Cambridge, 1997), pp. 37–68. For a seminal discussion of providential thinking in sixteenth-century England see Alexandra Walsham, *Providence in Early Modern England* (Oxford, 1999).

[54] There were only two large woodcuts added to the 1576 edition; these will be discussed below. No large woodcuts were added to the 1583 edition.

murdering medieval kings.[55] Five of the large illustrations cover the period from Wiclif to Luther, and these also all depict the executions of Lollard or Hussite martyrs (as long as one includes the illustration of the exhumation and burning of Wiclif's bones).[56] The reigns of Henry VIII and Edward VI are illustrated with eight large woodcuts, seven of which depict the execution of various martyrs and one which shows the evangelical preacher, Thomas Bilney, being pulled from the pulpit as he is preaching.[57] These come to a total of sixteen large woodcuts for the entire 1563 edition prior to the execution of John Rogers, the first Marian martyr.[58] There are twenty-seven large woodcuts covering the Marian persecution. There is also a single woodcut depicting Hugh Latimer preaching before Edward VI – although depicting an event in the previous reign, this woodcut was included with the life of Latimer, which is recounted by Foxe as part of the narrative of Mary's reign – and another illustrating the execution of an English merchant, Nicholas Burton, in Spain in 1560.[59] However, these figures indicate a further chronological imbalance. Twenty-one of these illustrations depict episodes – predominantly, but not exclusively, executions – from the lives of martyrs burned between 4 February 1555 and 20 March 1556: that is, from the execution of John Rogers up to and including the execution of Thomas Cranmer. Only seven woodcuts show events of the Marian persecution from 21 March 1556 until Mary's death on 17 November 1558.

Further pictures were added to the 1570 edition; however, no new large illustrations were added to the section of the book dealing with Mary

---

[55] These pictures show the humiliation of Emperor Henry IV at Canossa (*1563*, p. 25), Pope Alexander III trampling on a prostrate Emperor Frederick Barbarossa (*1563*, p. 41), and the poisoning of King John by a monk shown acting with the blessing of the Church (*1563*, faces p. 69). Significantly, these illustrations are all tip-ins.

[56] These show Wiclif's bones being burned (*1563*, p. 105), the burning of the Lollard John Badby (*1563*, p. 172), the burning Jan Hus (*1563*, p. 240), the burning of Jerome of Prague (*1563*, p. 249), and the execution of Sir John Oldcastle (*1563*, p. 277).

[57] The picture of Bilney being pulled from the pulpit is in *1563*, p. 474; the other illustrations depict the executions of a trio of iconoclasts who burned a rood at Dovercourt (*1563*, p. 496); the double execution of John Frith and Andrew Hewet (*1563*, p. 505); the execution of William Tyndale (*1563*, p. 519); the execution of John Lambert (*1563*, p. 569); the triple execution of Robert Barnes, Thomas Garrett and William Jerome (*1563*, p. 612); the execution of Anne Askew and two others (*1563*, p. 666); and the execution of William Gardiner (*1563*, p. 879).

[58] There are no illustrations for the two years of Mary's reign preceding the onset of the Marian persecutions in February 1555.

[59] The illustration of Hugh Latimer preaching at court is in *1563*, p. 1353, and the execution of Burton is in *1563*, p. 1729. The other illustrations are on pp. 1039, 1048, 1064, 1080, 1101, 1139, 1144, 1161, 1205, 1209, 1216, 1260, 1272, 1387, 1418, 1448, 1451, 1502, 1503, 1524, 1544, 1566, 1651, 1689 and 1706. There are also two tip-in illustrations – one depicting the executions of Latimer and Ridley, which is placed between pp. 1376 and 1377, the other depicting the burning of the exhumed bodies of Bucer and Phagius at Cambridge, which is placed between pp. 1548 and 1549.

Tudor's reign. (In compensation, however, whereas there was only a single small woodcut illustrating a Marian martyrdom in the 1563 edition, the second edition saw a profusion of small woodcuts illustrating various Marian burnings.)[60] A single woodcut was added to the section before Wiclif; however, this would be the largest woodcut included in the book. In fact, this woodcut, depicting the ten persecutions of the Church before Constantine in graphic detail, had to be folded several times to fit within the covers of the book. Each copy of this illustration consisted of several sheets pasted together to form a single page. The picture itself measures 33 cm by 82 cm and it is smaller than the foldout, which has a 1.5 cm left-hand border and 9 cm between the illustration and the foot of the foldout. The foldout is larger than three folio pages (the folio page it faces measures 23 cm by 37 cm).[61]

Two new narrative woodcuts were added for the period from Wiclif to Luther. One depicted the mass hanging of the Lollard followers of Sir Roger Acton, and the other, adding an additional note to the chorus of anti-papalism in this section of the work, depicted a monstrous owl, whose ill-omened presence disrupted a medieval council.[62] The anti-papalism was further dramatically increased with the addition of ten new woodcuts to a new section of the work on 'the proud primacie of Popes paynted out in Tables', which will be discussed in further detail below. Two woodcuts were added to the reign of Henry VIII. One of these two additional woodcuts depicted the death of Richard Hunne, and the other, a depiction of the martyrdoms of Robert Testwood, Henry Filmer and Anthony Person at Windsor in 1493, was notable for its conspicuous and detailed depiction of Windsor Castle.[63] No new narrative woodcuts were added to Book 9, which was devoted to the reign of Edward VI. From all this, it is apparent that priority was given, in the second edition, to illustrating Church history before Mary's reign, and to correcting something of the imbalance that had existed in the first edition.

[60] The single small woodcut is of the joint burning of Elizabeth Cooper and Simon Miller in Norwich in July 1557 (*1563*, p. 1603). Like some of the smaller woodcuts in the first edition, it was more than one column's width; it was cropped down to one column's width in the 1570 edition.

[61] Because it covered material discussed over a wide range of Foxe's text, the illustration of the 'ten persecutions' was tipped into different copies of the book in numerous places within about the first hundred or so pages.

[62] See *1570*, pp. 699 and 706 respectively.

[63] See ibid, p. 931 and between pp. 1398 and 1399 respectively. More will be said about this illustration shortly.

There is a natural tendency to assume that the specific subjects illustrated in *Acts and Monuments* were those particularly important to Foxe. This, however, does not seem to have been the case. Martin Luther is one of the most crucial figures in the *Acts and Monuments*. Not only is his career recounted in detail, but Foxe also lists prophecies made of Luther's advent, thus further underscoring his conception of the German reformer's pivotal importance in Church history.[64] Yet there is not a single illustration of Luther or of any event in his career in the *Acts and Monuments*. Foxe devotes around twenty pages to the examinations and exploits of Richard Woodman, a prominent martyr in East Sussex, whom Foxe admired, but his death is only commemorated by a small woodcut depicting him being burned with nine other people at Lewes.[65] Similarly, Foxe's admiration for the duke of Somerset is almost unbounded. At one point he had to apologise for nearly comparing Somerset with Christ.[66] Yet although Somerset's execution is vividly related by Foxe, there is no picture of it in the book. The reason for this last exclusion is not difficult to trace: Somerset's death was a particularly sensitive issue because John Dudley, the father of the powerful Elizabethan nobleman, Robert Dudley, was widely blamed for it. This last example reminds us of the degree to which the illustrations of the *Acts and Monuments*, like all other aspects of the book, were affected by both financial, political and polemical considerations.

VI

A particularly noteworthy example of these polemical considerations is the nearly complete absence of women martyrs from the illustrations of the *Acts and Monuments*. The major exception to this, which demonstrates the rule, is the horrific woodcut of three women being burned at Guernsey in July 1556. This picture, showing one of the women giving birth to a child during her burning, is included in the *Acts and Monuments* because the incident was a graphic display of the cruelty of the Marian persecutors. It was the child, not the women, who was the real reason why this martyrdom was depicted at all.[67] The Guernsey martyrs are the only women who are

---

[64] The prophecies described are ibid, pp. 967–99, *1576*, pp. 814–16, *1583*, pp. 841–[recte 843]. Luther's career is ibid, pp. 969–94, *1576*, pp. 816–38, *1583*, pp. 841 [recte 843]–64.

[65] See *1563*, pp. 1571–602, *1570*, pp. 2171–96, *1576*, pp. 1875–95, *1583*, pp. 1984–2004. Interestingly, this woodcut only shows six people being burned and may not even have been designed with Woodman specifically in mind.

[66] See *1570*, sig. ℭ5^r.   [67] *1563*, p. 1544.

Figure 11 The burning of Anne Askew from John Foxe's *Acts and Monuments* (1563), p. 682.
Courtesy of Lambeth Palace Library.

depicted being executed in a large woodcut in the *Acts and Monuments* without being accompanied by male co-religionists (unless one counts the infant, who was a boy). Anne Askew, arguably the most famous of the female martyrs, is shown being burned along with two men, and, uniquely among the woodcuts of martyrdoms in Foxe, the image depicts a panorama of Smithfield at the time of the burning, with the martyrs at the stake just one small feature of the large topographical picture[68] (see Figure 11). Out of thirteen people burned at the holocaust in Stratford le Bow on 27 June 1556, two – Elizabeth Pepper and Agnes George – were women and they are both depicted along with their eleven male comrades in the large illustration of this event.[69] Out of the hundreds of female martyrs whose sufferings are recounted by Foxe, from the early Church to the accession of Elizabeth, the actual martyrdoms of very few are illustrated and – except for the Guernsey

[68] Ibid., p. 666. [69] Ibid., p. 1524.

martyrs – the women are conspicuously outnumbered in these large wood-cuts by their male counterparts.

There is one important exception to this rule, which seems to have arisen from a miscommunication to the illustrator. Seven martyrs were burned at Smithfield in late January 1556; of these, four were men and three were women. The illustration shows four women and three men being burned together, neatly transposing the number and, in this case, giving the female gender a fictitious majority.[70] Care was usually taken to be as accurate as possible in the large woodcuts and it has to be assumed that the erroneous gender ratio produced here was purely accidental. In any case, this certainly created considerable problems within Day's printing house. Most unusu-ally, the text blocks identifying the martyrs were left completely blank in the 1563 edition, probably because the baffled compositor was unable to sat-isfactorily match the list of the martyrs with the figures depicting them. In subsequent editions the names of six of the martyrs were supplied, but one text block (actually labelling a woman) remained blank and John Tudson's name was understandably not placed above a female martyr.[71]

Apart from this, two large woodcuts do depict female martyrs, although they do not depict their executions. The first of these is a large woodcut depicting twenty-two heretics being transported from Colchester to London; ten of these are women (the picture actually shows fifteen people – significantly only five of these are women).[72] The other woodcut – that of Rose Allin, who would eventually be executed at Colchester on 2 August 1557 – is more exceptional. It depicts the young woman carrying a jug of water to her invalid mother and having her hand burned by Edmund Tyrrel.[73] As with the Guernsey martyrs the purpose of this woodcut is to highlight the cruelty of the Catholic persecution. Here the innocence and vulnerability of the young woman become polemical assets for Foxe. By emphasising the torture of Rose Allin but not foregrounding the depiction of her martyrdom, Foxe effectively has his cake and eats it too. He is able to highlight the brutality of Catholic persecutors without raising the disturb-ing questions provoked by the martyrdom of women.

The situation is a little bit more favourable to women in the small woodcuts. Eleven female martyrs – Joan Boughton, Margery Polley, Agnes Potten, Joan Trunchfield, Katherine Hut, Joan Horne, Elizabeth Thackwell, Margaret Thurston, Agnes Bongeor, Cicely Ormes and Mrs Prest – are depicted as suffering the ultimate penalty unaccompanied by male co-religionists. However, this statement deserves closer examination.

[70] Ibid., p. 1451.   [71] *1570*, p. 2031, *1576*, p. 1751, *1583*, p. 1858.   [72] *1563*, p. 1566.   [73] Ibid., p. 1706.

All of these woodcuts were added in the 1570 edition. Furthermore, a number of them are repeated. The illustration of Joan Boughton (the one pre-Marian martyr in the group) is reused to depict Cicely Ormes.[74] The woodcut depicting Agnes Potten and Joan Trunchfield would be repeated for Margaret Thurston and Agnes Bongeor.[75] The woodcut depicting Margery Polley would not be reused in the first four editions but was used to depict Cicely Ormes in the fifth and all subsequent unabridged editions. There are also several small woodcuts depicting women martyrs being executed as part of a larger group of male martyrs. All of these woodcuts are used to depict multiple burnings, even though the numbers of people depicted in the woodcut sometimes do not correspond to the number of people actually burned.[76] Finally, there is one woodcut, first used in 1563, that depicts the Marian martyrs Simon Miller and Elizabeth Cooper being burned together at the same stake.[77] Altogether fewer than twenty women martyrs out of all the martyrs described in Foxe's book are depicted in small woodcuts, and many of these woodcuts are stylised representations used and reused to depict a number of women.

There is perhaps a practical reason for this disparity. Women were burned predominantly in the second and third years of the Marian persecution, and as we shall see there is a strong tendency within the *Acts and Monuments* to illustrate the first fourteen months of the persecution more extensively than the remaining thirty-two months. However, the more compelling reason is that women martyrs were inherently problematic. Engrained sixteenth-century gender bias held that women were less rational and less constant than men: vices that were directly antithetical to the stoicism and *apatheia* expected of a true martyr of Christ.[78] Sexual and doctrinal deviance were often linked in the sixteenth century and Catholics and Protestants frequently depicted their confessional adversaries as lustful

---

[74] *1570*, pp. 866 and 2219. [75] Ibid., pp. 2072 and 2216.

[76] A woodcut of three women in a total group of seven burned at Canterbury on 19 June 1557 (*1570*, p. 2168) is reused to depict a later burning of three men and three women at Colchester (*1570*, p. 2206). Similarly a woodcut of one woman being burned along with four men at Islington on 17 September 1557 (*1570*, p. 2215) is reused to depict the burning of three men and three women at Canterbury on 10 November 1558 (*1570*, p. 2252).

[77] *1563*, p. 1603.

[78] On *apatheia* and martyrdom see Brad Gregory, *Salvation at Stake: Christian Martyrdom in Early Modern Europe* (Cambridge, MA, 1999), pp. 50–62 and 97–138; Patrick Collinson, ''A Magazine of Religious Patterns''; An Erasmian Topic Transposed', in *Godly People: Essays on English Protestantism and Puritanism* (London, 1983), pp. 499–525; and Thomas S. Freeman, 'The Importance of Dying Earnestly: The Metamorphosis of the Account of James Bainham in Foxe's "Book of Martyrs"', in *The Church Retrospective*, ed. R. N. Swanson, Studies in Church History xxxiii (Oxford, 1997), pp. 267–88.

and debauched as well as heretical.[79] Women were also believed to be more inclined to vice – particularly carnal vice – and women martyrs on both sides of the confessional divide became targets of sexual innuendo and defamation. Consequently, the presence of women among one confession's martyrs was used by their confessional adversaries to question the very cause and doctrines for which they died.[80] Certainly Foxe and his colleague, Henry Bull, went to considerable lengths to conceal the important role played by women within Marian Protestantism; it is therefore quite likely that fears of giving the Catholics a polemical advantage led to the visual under-representation of the women who sealed their doctrine with their blood.[81]

VII

Nor were all the woodcuts simply generalised depictions of papist cruelty. Often they were used to support very specific polemical points. A striking example of this occurs in the first edition in an illustration showing the dead body of Richard Hunne hanging in his cell. Hunne was a London merchant who was under arrest for heresy, and who the authorities claimed committed suicide in 1514; his friends and supporters, on the other hand, maintained that he was murdered by the Church authorities. The woodcut shows the body of Hunne hanging on one side of the cell, while on the

---

[79] G. Wylie Sypher, "'Faisant ce qu'il leur vient à plaisir": The Image of Protestantism in French Catholic Polemic on the Eve of the Religious Wars', *Sixteenth Century Journal*, 11 (1980), pp. 59–84, is a particularly incisive discussion of Catholic attempts to view their opponents in this light. Peter Lake is similarly acute on Protestant construction of Catholics: 'Anti-Popery: The Structure of a Prejudice', in *Conflict in Early Stuart England*, ed. Richard Cust and Ann Hughes (Harlow, 1989), pp. 72–106, esp. pp. 74–5.

[80] Robert Persons devoted much of his rebuttal of Foxe in *Three conversions*, to attacks on the chastity as well as orthodoxy of Foxe's female martyrs; e.g., Persons, *Three conversions*, I, pp. 238–9, 349 and 406; II, pp. 254, 370, 495 and 510. Similarly John Harding's attack on Foxe's account of the Guernsey executions was directed against the character of the three martyred women. According to Harding, they brought their deaths upon themselves through theft, sexual immorality and heresy. Worst of all, Perotine Massy, from shame at having an illegitimate child (Harding assumes that the child was illegitimate because Foxe did not mention Massy having a husband in his 1563 account of the incident) hid her pregnancy from the officials, making her the murderer of her infant son. Harding, *Reioindre*, fos. 184ʳ–5ᵛ. On the other side of the confessional divide, Protestants circulated slanderous reports that Margaret Clitherow, the Catholic martyr, had sexual relations with fugitive priests she had sheltered in her house. See John Mush, *An abstracte of the life and martirdome of Mistres M. Clitheroe* (Newton Abbot, 1619), STC 18316.7, sigs. C2ᵛ–C3ʳ and Mush, 'A True Report of the Life and Martyrdom of Mrs Margaret Clitherow', in *The Troubles of our Catholic Forefathers*, ed. John Morris (London, 1877), pp. 420, 422 and 425.

[81] Thomas S. Freeman, "'The Good Ministrye of Godlye and Vertuouse Women": The Elizabethan Martyrologist and the Female Supporters of the Marian Martyrs', *Journal of British Studies*, 39 (2000), pp. 8–33.

Figure 12 The hanging of Richard Hunne in his cell from John Foxe's *Acts and Monuments* (1563), p. 390. Courtesy of Lambeth Palace Library.

other side one of his killers is shown blowing out a candle, placed on one of the stocks, as he leaves (see Figure 12).[82] This scene is not mere sensationalism; it illustrates one of the chief arguments (reiterated by Foxe) that Hunne was murdered. The coroner's inquest into Hunne's death (reprinted by Foxe) reported that 'an ende of a wax candel . . . we found sticking upon the stockes fayre put out, about seven or eight foote from the place where Hunne was hanged, which candle after our opinion was never put out by him'.[83]

The attacks of Nicholas Harpsfield in particular seem to have inspired a number of illustrations that were added to the second edition. For example, one of the new pictures showed the followers of the Lollard leader Sir Roger Acton being hung en masse. This was placed as part of Foxe's lengthy

[82] *1563*, p. 390. The best accounts of the Hunne affair are Susan Brigden, *London and the Reformation* (Oxford, 1989), pp. 98–103; W. R. Cooper, 'Richard Hunne', *Reformation*, 1 (1996), pp. 221–51; Peter Gwyn, *The King's Cardinal: The Rise and Fall of Thomas Wolsey* (London, 2002), pp. 34–41.

[83] *1563*, p. 391.

rebuttal of Harpsfield's (correct) claim that Acton and his followers had been rebels; here sensational illustrations were being used to undermine valid arguments.[84] Repeating More once again, Harpsfield insisted that the evangelical martyr Thomas Bilney recanted at the stake. Foxe collected testimony from informants about Bilney's final hours in order to demonstrate that he had not only died holding his evangelical convictions but that he remained calm and stoical up to the very end. One of these stories related that Bilney, in an inn on his way to his execution, stuck his finger in a burning candle to test his endurance; this was depicted in a new woodcut.[85] One reason for the inclusion of the full-page woodcut of the martyrdom of Robert Testwood, Henry Filmer and Anthony Persons in 1542 was to counter Harpsfield's embarrassing exposé of Foxe having misidentified these martyrs in his first edition.[86] And the illustration of the coin depicting Hus's martyrdom with the prophecy of Luther engraved on it, which we have already discussed, also appears to have been another illustration added in response to Harspfield.[87]

The event, however, that had the biggest impact on the illustrations of the second edition was the publication of the papal bull *Regnans in excelsis* in February 1570, which excommunicated Elizabeth and released her subjects from their allegiance to the queen. There can be little doubt that the section added at the end of the first volume of the second edition was a response to Pius V's recently articulated claims of plenary authority over the English Church. This section was probably the last of the edition to be printed. Furthermore there is every indication that it was compiled in considerable haste. The pagination for the section is not irregular – it is non-existent. Furthermore, the last page before this section is page 922, while the second

[84] *1570*, p. 699.

[85] Ibid., p. 1151. James Truman has recently posited a very different interpretation of this picture. Instead of seeing it as a visual confirmation of Foxe's disputed claims to Bilney's constancy and status as a martyr, Truman argues that this woodcut depicts Bilney in a homosexual relationship, since Bilney is depicted testing his endurance with the candle while another male looks on from a bed. According to Truman this woodcut 'exposes the interplay between the suffering of martyrdom . . . and the physical intimacy of early modern male friendship'. James C. W. Truman, 'John Foxe and the Desires of Reformation Martyrology', *English Literary History*, 70 (2003), p. 52. Truman does not explain why Foxe would have chosen to depict Bilney in this way or why no one, including generations of Foxe's Catholic critics, seemed to have understood, or commented on, the homoerotic dimensions of this picture.

[86] *1570*, between pp. 1398 and 1399; cf. *Dialogi sex*, pp. 962–3.

[87] In the *Rerum* Foxe had attributed this prophecy to Hus and had specifically described a Bohemian medal, depicting Hus's death and engraved with the prophecy. Foxe repeated this in the 1563 edition, although he also stated that the prophecy had been made by Jerome of Prague (*Rerum*, p. 67 and *1563*, pp. 249–50). Harpsfield derided the prophecy and doubted its existence (*Dialogi sex*, pp. 925–7). In the 1570 edition Foxe removed the incorrect mention of Hus making the prophecy. He also printed an illustration of the coin in question, 'proving' its existence and the existence of the prophecy.

volume commences with page 923. Therefore it can only be concluded that this section was added after the printing of the second volume was well underway. Even more striking is the irregularity of the size of the gatherings in this section: the usual practice in the second edition was for gatherings that consisted of six leaves. But sig. NN1^r, on which the section begins, is the first of only four leaves in that gathering, following the previous gathering (MM), which consisted of only two leaves; sigs. NN1–4 are then followed by a further gathering of only four leaves (sigs. OO1–4). The most plausible explanation for these anomalies would be that this section was created as an afterthought; presumably, given its subject matter, an afterthought inspired by *Regnans in excelsis*. A further indication of the late production of this section is that it is printed on the pasted-together sheets that Day used only when the supply of regular paper ran out.

In yet another indication of haste, much of the text for this section was a reprinting of an anonymous work which John Foxe had written in 1560: *A Solemne Contestation of Divers Popes*.[88] The heart of this section, however, was a series of anti-papal woodcuts illustrating the expansion of papal political power, marked especially by putative historical examples of popes humiliating European monarchs. It is very difficult to determine how many – if any – of the woodcuts were commissioned specifically for this section.[89] Some clearly were not. The woodcut of Emperor Henry IV at Canossa is recycled here (and, since it had already been used on page 292 of this edition, it appeared twice in this and all subsequent editions of Foxe's book).[90] The opening woodcut for this section – ironically captioned 'The Image of the true Catholicke Church of Christ' – depicts a king or emperor watching scenes of savage persecution (see Figure 13). This woodcut was probably designed to illustrate persecutions of the early Christians. It certainly bears a marked resemblance in style and composition to the mammoth woodcut of the ten persecutions of the early Church. Perhaps it was even a prototype for that larger woodcut, put to use in this section. Closer examination of this picture tends to support this hypothesis. The figure of the emperor or monarch seated on the throne on the far left of the picture is incongruous on several counts. For one thing, the emperor and his

---

[88] Freeman, '*A Solemne Contestation of Divers Popes*: A Work by John Foxe?', pp. 41–8.

[89] We have reservations concerning John King's confident assumption that, apart from the Canossa illustration, 'the eleven other illustrations in "The Proud Primacie of Popes" were designed and cut as a self-contained sequence'. John N. King, *Tudor Royal Iconography: Literature and Art in an Age of Religious Crisis* (Princeton, NJ, 1989), p. 139.

[90] King has plausibly suggested that the woodcut of Pope Alexander III and Frederick Barbarossa, which certainly would have been relevant to this section, was not reused here because of its smaller size (King, *Print Culture*, p. 190).

Figure 13 Image of the true Catholic Church (from the 'Proud Primacie of Popes')
in John Foxe's *Acts and Monuments* (1570). By kind permission of the Dean and
Chapter of York Minster.

courtiers are huddled into a very small space. For another, the figures are out
of proportion with the other figures in the woodcut. If the emperor in this
illustration was depicted standing, he would be about twice the size of the
torturers. Finally, the seated ruler and his courtiers, unlike the other figures
in the woodcut, bear marked similarities in style to depictions in other
woodcuts in this section of the Emperor Constantine. We would suggest
that the figure of the emperor and his courtiers were part of a larger picture
carved on a separate block, which was then joined to the original woodcut to
make a more suitable picture for this hastily improvised section.

Six of the remaining woodcuts were probably commissioned for this
section. They all depict episodes from Church history, ranging from the
fourth century to the thirteenth century, and if they had been intended to
illustrate the text of the *Acts and Monuments* themselves, they would
presumably have been placed at the appropriate places in the text, while
the volume was being printed, as were the anti-papal woodcuts of Henry IV

at Canossa and of the monstrous owl. What probably happened instead is that ten woodcuts were commissioned for this section, but only six of these were completed and duly used. Four other illustrations had to be pressed into service. This would explain why the Canossa illustration was reused and probably why the persecution woodcut was included as well. There are two remaining woodcuts: one showing the pope's horse being led on foot by the German emperor, and the other showing the pope being borne triumphantly in a litter, which have a less specific relationship to the text of this section than the other pictures do. They may well have been woodcuts intended for another work, which Day somehow obtained and used for this one. It is worth noting in this regard that these last two woodcuts are of a different size from the other woodcuts – apart from the Canossa illustration – employed in this section.

One interesting but probably unanswerable question emerges from all of this: did Day receive any official encouragement or reward from the government for producing this section? It was certainly very much in the interests of Elizabeth's government to respond quickly and as effectively as possible to the papal bull. More interestingly, John Day seems to have been the printer they turned to for producing other works responding to the bull.[91] Even if there was no direct connection between the authorities and the section on the 'proud primacie' of the popes, the inclusion of these woodcuts, with their accompanying text, in the *Acts and Monuments* would certainly have increased the desire of Cecil and other leading figures to disseminate the book. Once again, we see Day either acting at the behest of powerful figures or at the very least anticipating their desires.

Sometimes strictly practical considerations could also play a role in determining what was illustrated and what was not. We have already mentioned that of the twenty-seven large woodcuts illustrating the Marian persecution, twenty-one illustrate the execution of martyrs burned at the same time as or before the execution of Cranmer on 20 March 1556. This arrangement began in the 1563 edition and continued unchanged in

---

[91] Thomas Norton rushed into print with *A warning agaynst the dangerous practices of Papistes* (London, 1569?) STC 18685.3, which was printed by Day and devoted largely to denouncing the offending bull. John Foxe's Paul's Cross sermon on Good Friday 1570 was also a response to *Regnans in excelsis* and this work was rapidly printed by Day in both English and Latin: John Foxe, *A sermon of Christ crucified* (London, 1570) STC 11242 and Foxe, *De christo crucifixo concio* (London, 1571) STC 11247. In the meantime John Jewel had sent a copy of the offending bull to Heinrich Bullinger who obligingly printed a lengthy confutation of it, which was printed by John Day first in Latin as *Bullae papisticae ... contra reginam Elizabetham ... refutatio* (London, 1571) STC 4043, then in English as *A confutation of the popes bull against Elizabeth queene of England*, trans. Arthur Golding (London, 1572) STC 4044.

subsequent editions. Its notable imbalance – the majority of martyrs died after this date and a number of these later martyrs, such as John Careless and Richard Woodman, were figures of considerable importance – can probably be explained by the fact that the *Rerum* only covers the martyrs up to Cranmer in any detail. When decisions were made on what to picture for the Marian persecution in the first edition there was very little information available for subjects after March 1556. A few dramatic episodes became known which justified pictures: the burning of a baby at Guernsey, the exhumation of Bucer and Fagius at Cambridge, the racking of Cuthbert Symson, Edmund Tyrrel burning a young woman's hand, Bonner scourging a victim, and the mass executions of thirteen people at Stratford le Bow and twenty-two people at Colchester. But for the most part events before March 1556 were better known and hence easier to plan illustrations for, and so it was these events which tended to be depicted. As with all aspects of the *Acts and Monuments*, the planning, production and placement of the illustrations was a complicated process, which evolved from edition to edition and which was affected by current circumstances and practical needs.

VIII

No aspect of the illustrations demonstrates the complexity of their production, and at the same time the practical pressures the existing technology placed on the ambitions of both Foxe and Day, than the production of the 'labelling apparatus' for these illustrations. By labelling apparatus we mean the captions, xylographic inscriptions, scrolls, banderoles, and text blocks used to identify the people depicted and to reproduce their quotations. This was an important aspect of the pictures, although it is not a topic that has been dealt with systematically by scholars.[92] In a work that dealt with inflammatory and bitterly contentious events of the relatively recent past, the identification of individuals was a matter of pressing importance. At the same time, Foxe's book was subjected not only to intense and hostile scrutiny from his adversaries but to friendlier correction from his confessional allies.[93] The need for accuracy can be seen in the caption to the

[92] King provides an important and interesting discussion of these in *Print Culture*, pp. 193 and 196–205. However, more systematic and more detailed analysis is required.
[93] For example, Foxe was compelled to retract his erroneous declaration that Sir George Blage was a member of Henry VIII's Privy Chamber (*1570*, recto of page before pagination starts). A particularly striking example of the correction of Foxe's work by its well-wishers is a letter written around 1635 – presumably to a member of Foxe's family – correcting the martyrologist's account of the execution of

picture of Edmund Tyrrel burning Rose Allin's hand. In the 1570 edition the caption identified Tyrrel incorrectly as 'Syr Edmund Tyrrel'.[94] The mistake – Tyrrel was not a knight – was apparently caught in the late stages of production, since the offending word 'Syr' was crossed out in some – but not all – of the copies of this edition.[95] In the 1576 edition this caption was corrected.[96]

In addition to captions, essentially an external device for labelling, there were various ways of labelling a picture internally. The least complicated method was to simply engrave a name onto a figure xylographically. This had the advantage of being a fairly straightforward process but it suffered from two severe drawbacks. For one thing, on occasion it proved surprisingly difficult for Day's engravers to remember that they were producing what was in effect a mirror image. As a result, an illustration of the imprisonment of George Tankerfield, Robert Smith, Elizabeth Warne, John Newman and John Symson has each figure xylographically labelled. But the labels on all except for Elizabeth Warne appear back to front.[97] An even greater disadvantage of this method was that, once engraved, the labels were permanent and could not be corrected. (This had the additional disadvantage of preventing Day from reusing these pictures in other works as illustrations of other events.)

Increasingly, Day resorted to text blocks as a means of labelling instead. The process of producing these was complicated: a small square or rectangular section would be cut out of an existing block, into which type was inserted, spelling out the name of a person or event being identified. Smaller blank pieces of metal, which were fixed into the woodcut, held the type in place and yet remained invisible when the woodcut was printed. The great advantage of this method was that corrections and changes could be made to these labels with relative ease. One illustration demonstrates how desirable this flexibility was and how effectively this method operated. In the 1563 edition Foxe described four Protestants dying in prison of natural causes. He incorrectly gave their names as William Andrew, Thomas King, Thomas Leyes and Richard Smith. The deaths of these martyrs were commemorated in the 1563 edition with a woodcut depicting them

one Edward Horne in 1556. The author of the letter states that he wrote to correct this 'smal errour' out of 'the reverence I beare to the memory of Mr Fox . . . and the honor and love I beare to his works' (BL, Harley MS 425, fo. 121^r).

[94] *1570*, p. 1706.
[95] Among the copies where the crossing-out occurs are the ones in the Cambridge University Library, the Lambeth Palace Library, the Folger Shakespeare Library, and the copy from R. R. Mendham's collection, which is now in Canterbury Cathedral Library.
[96] *1576*, p. 1898. [97] *1563*, p. 1260.

languishing in prison. In this illustration they were labelled by means of text blocks and given the names assigned to them in the text of the 1563 edition.[98] In the 1570 edition Foxe correctly identified the four martyrs as William Andrew, George King, Thomas Leyes and John Wade. Their names were also unobtrusively corrected in the accompanying woodcut for this edition. Yet even now the labels remained imperfect, for the name 'Androws' had been inserted into the block upside down. This mistake was corrected in the next edition, when the letters were reinserted the correct way up.[99]

Another means of internal labelling was the use of scrolls and banderoles. These served both as a means of identification and as a means of reproducing quotations.[100] They also produced a particular aesthetic problem, which interestingly seems to have aroused Day's concern. While the banderoles and scrolls, following traditional iconography, all curve in the middle, it is considerably simpler to insert type on a straight line, and in the 1563 edition type was in fact placed in a straight line within the curved scrolls. However, in the 1570 edition, efforts were made to alter the position of the text so that it conformed to the undulation of the scroll.[101] This attention to detail is yet another indication of the importance Day attached to the woodcuts in Foxe's book. It is indicative of Day's approach to printing, and to the printing of the *Acts and Monuments*, that he was at least as concerned with getting the labels aesthetically correct as well as with getting them factually correct.

---

[98] It should be noted that, unusually, these text blocks were not purely rectangular, but had scroll endings.

[99] See *1563*, p. 1272, *1570*, p. 1878 and *1576*, p. 1608.

[100] Two banderoles and one scroll remained blank in the 1563 edition. The first scroll was meant to identify Sir John Shelton who presided over the execution of Rowland Taylor. This scroll remained blank in every edition (*1563*, p. 1080, *1570*, p. 1703, *1576*, p. 1454, *1583*, p. 1527). Whether this was simply an oversight or perhaps stemmed from caution about needlessly antagonising a prominent Suffolk family is unknown. Two banderoles were intended to reproduce the dying words of the martyrs William Gardiner and Lawrence Saunders. The former remained blank in all editions but the words 'Welcome life' were introduced to the latter in the 1570 and all subsequent editions. For William Gardiner see *1563*, p. 879, *1570*, p. 1544, *1576*, p. 1316, *1583*, p. 1366; for Laurence Saunders see *1563*, p. 1048, *1570*, p. 1670, *1576*, p. 1425, *1583*, p. 1499. In the 1570 edition a new woodcut was introduced, in which the scroll remained blank in that and subsequent editions. This woodcut, originally used to depict John Florence, a Lollard, was later reused; almost certainly the decision to reuse it explains why its scroll remained blank. (For example, cf. *1570*, pp. 782 and 786 with *1576*, pp. 636 and 640.)

[101] A good example of this occurs in the banderole giving Cranmer's last words at his execution. In the 1563 edition the words, essentially in a straight line, fit awkwardly into the scroll (*1563*, p. 1503); in the 1570 edition the words were obviously repositioned, forming an arch that fits neatly into the centre of the scroll (*1570*, p. 2067).

IX

Modern scholars, in discussing the illustrations, have tended to assume that their primary purpose was to make Foxe's book accessible to readers with little or no education. Warren W. Wooden, for example, states that Foxe's book 'spoke also to the non-reading public' through its illustrations, which were 'accessible to all who could look'.[102] There is a considerable amount of validity to this assumption, which Foxe's contemporaries themselves tended to make. Robert Persons maintained that Foxe's pictures 'delighteth many to gaze on, who cannot read'.[103] More importantly, the Elizabethan authorities expressly ordered that the book be displayed so that it could be consulted by the servants of the senior clergy.[104]

However, this venerable view has been recently challenged by James Knapp, who questions the ready assumption that the illustrations in the *Acts and Monuments* were intended to bring the messages of the book to the illiterate masses. In particular, Knapp observes that the illustrations increased the price of the book, placing it out of the reach of the masses, and at the same time he also observes that it cannot be assumed that the 'messages' of the illustrations were uniformly accessible and apparent.[105] Pettegree and Hall have gone even further than Knapp and questioned the use of book illustrations as a means of instructing the unlettered in general:

Much has been written about the use of visual material to bridge the gap between the literate and the unlettered. It has become a common assumption, as those of us who teach undergraduates know, that the evangelical message crossed the barrier between the literate and the illiterate with the help of visual culture. To our very visual age this seems a natural assumption and perhaps for this reason it has not been sufficiently tested.[106]

King, on the other hand, defends the more traditional view by claiming that Knapp draws too sharp a boundary between literacy and orality in early

---

[102] Warren W. Wooden, *John Foxe* (Boston, 1983), unpaginated preface.

[103] Persons, *Three conversions*, III, p. 400.

[104] *The Anglican Canons 1529–1947*, ed. Gerald Bray, Church of England Record Society VI, (Woodbridge, 1998), pp. 177–9 and 183. See also Elizabeth Evenden and Thomas S. Freeman, 'Print, Profit and Propaganda: The Elizabethan Privy Council and the 1570 Edition of Foxe's "Book of Martyrs"', *English Historical Review*, 119 (2004), pp. 1298–9.

[105] Knapp, *Illustrating the Past*, pp. 124–61, esp. pp. 124–9.

[106] Ibid., p. 806. While we think that there is a great deal of merit in this argument, it may be a little too sweeping. For example, as we have noted, the woodcuts in Foxe's book were ultimately used to instruct the illiterate, and the authorities, at least at one point, wished to take advantage of this.

modern England and neglects the role of the literate in communicating the meaning of the pictures to the illiterate.[107]

At a minimum it would seem likely that there were other motivations for going to the considerable time, trouble and expense of producing these woodcuts beyond a desire to instruct the unlettered. Elizabeth Eisenstein has helpfully observed that while the Poor Man's Bible is usually considered to have been intended almost exclusively as a tool for instructing the illiterate, it was actually used to instruct those who were instructing the illiterate. Moreover, despite its name, the Poor Man's Bible was actually a fairly expensive work, beyond the price range of the truly poor.[108] It is certainly quite possible that the pictures in Foxe's book were used by preachers in much the same way, or as a visual means of stimulating their own memories.

Moreover there is some evidence that the illustrations in Foxe's book were made as much for their aesthetic appeal to elites as for the edification of the simple. Two copies are known to have survived of the *Acts and Monuments* (both of the 1570 edition) in which all the illustrations have been painstakingly coloured. One of these copies – that in Trinity College – belonged to Archbishop Parker. His arms are stamped on the centre-piece of the cover of both volumes and on the fore-edge of the spine.[109] This copy is a twin of a coloured copy in Cambridge University Library.[110] Except for Parker's coat of arms, the bindings are clearly the product of the same workman. More importantly, the illustrations were unmistakably coloured

---

[107] King, *Print Culture*, pp. 205–6.

[108] Elizabeth Eisenstein, 'Defining the Initial Shift: Some Features of Print Culture', in *The Book History Reader*, ed. David Finkelstein and Alistair McCleery (London, 2002), pp. 160–1.

[109] The copy was given to Trinity by its first Master, Thomas Neville. Neville's initials are also stamped on the cover of the book in gold and a printed slip attached to the title page states: 'Ex dono ornatissimi viri Thomae Nevile Decani Cantuariensis & Collegi Trinitatis Praefecti'. Neville was dean of Canterbury and he may have acquired the book from the cathedral library or precincts after Parker's death. On the other hand, Thomas Neville's brother, Alexander, had been a member of Archbishop Parker's household and Thomas could have acquired the book through his brother. On Alexander Neville see McKisack, *Medieval History in the Tudor Age*, p. 48. For such high-quality centre-piece binding as a hallmark of these very expensive bindings, see David Pearson, 'English Centre-Piece Bookbinding 1560–1640', in *Eloquent Witnesses: Bookbindings and their History*, ed. Mirjam M. Foot (London and New Castle, DE, 2004), pp. 106–20.

[110] Tessa Watt, in some passages about a large foldout woodcut illustration of the ten persecutions of the primitive Church, observes that there is evidence that this woodcut was hung in private houses and then declares that 'In the Cambridge copy of 1570 the gruesome scenes of torture [in the woodcut illustration of the ten persecutions] are brightly coloured' (Watt, *Cheap Print and Popular Piety*, p. 158). This is rather misleading in that it ignores the fact that *all* of the pictures in this copy were coloured in. Furthermore, since the coloured illustrations are still in the book, they were not intended to be hung on walls. Therefore these woodcuts must have been coloured for some other reason.

by the same workmen. In almost every case they used the same colours to depict the same subjects and objects within the same pictures.[111] This demonstrates that these two copies were coloured together by the same workmen and were part of a joint project. If these copies were illustrated separately there would have been much more variation in the colours used to depict the same people and objects. (There is also considerable similarity in the ways in which certain objects in these pictures are detailed in both copies. For example, columns are given a marbled effect in both copies, which is not suggested in the black and white illustration; in the picture of Henry IV at Canossa, both illustrations have the empress wearing a lace collar which is not depicted in the original woodcut.[112]) These similarities demonstrate that the colouring of these illustrations was carried out under the same roof.

We know where that roof was: in Lambeth. Matthew Parker stated, in a letter to William Cecil, that he maintained staff skilled in book illustration and binding.[113] Another illuminated work prepared by Parker – an exquisitely hand-coloured copy of his *De antiquitate* – remains in its original binding in Cambridge University Library.[114] We know that this binding was done by the same workman who did the binding for the coloured copies of the 1570 edition of the *Acts and Monuments* held in Cambridge University Library and Trinity College Library, Cambridge.[115] Therefore it seems undeniable that the copies of both books were bound in Parker's house.

---

[111] In some illustrations, such as that of the execution of William Taylor (*1570*, p. 781), the clothing of individuals is drawn from the same stock of colours but different articles of clothing are given different colours in the two illustrations (e.g., a person who is wearing a cerise robe with yellow sleeves in the Cambridge University Library copy is wearing a cerise robe with cerise sleeves in the Trinity copy). In some pictures, such as that of the martyrdom of John Oldcastle (*1570*, p. 762), the identical colours are used throughout the picture in both copies. In the Cambridge University Library copy, however, gold leaf is often used when only yellow is used in the Trinity copy. Clearly the supply of very expensive gold leaf was limited and only used in this particular copy (e.g., in the initial 'C' depicting an enthroned Elizabeth, the queen's crown and jewellery are in gold in the Cambridge University Library copy but in yellow in the Trinity copy). Whoever the recipient of the Cambridge University Library copy was, their copy had additional time and money lavished upon it through the use of this costly gold leaf. For further discussion of the use of colour in the illustrations see *PPP*, pp. 104–17.

[112] *1570*, p. 232. The Cambridge University Library copy also has a gold necklace beneath the lace collar (the necklace is not a detail in the original cut).

[113] *Correspondence of Matthew Parker*, ed. John Bruce and T. T. Perowne (Parker Society, Cambridge, 1853), p. 426.

[114] Matthew Parker, *De antiquitate Britannicae ecclesiae* (London, 1572), STC 19292.

[115] The binding of the two copies of Foxe and the copy of *De antiquitate* are exactly the same. The artistry of the binding also matches a copy of *The Gospels of the fower Evangelistes . . .*, presented by John Foxe to Elizabeth, which is now held by the British Library. Parker told Cecil that the binding of the copy of *De antiquitate* had been 'bound by my man'. *Parker Correspondence*, p. 425.

These two copies of Foxe's book, like the copy of *De antiquitate*, would have been coloured while unbound (to avoid the risk of pages closing on top of each other, causing unwanted transferral of paint, and to allow easy access to the parts of the picture nearest the inside margins). So although it might be objected that the copies could have been coloured somewhere else and then transported to Parker's household for binding, it seems inconceivable that anyone would risk transporting these fragile illuminated pages across town.[116] These books must have been coloured and then bound under Parker's roof. As we shall discuss shortly, these copies were presented by Parker to people at the very apex of Elizabethan society – in this case, far from this colouring being the popular activity that Tessa Watt describes, it was instead a way of turning an already valuable book into a luxuriously crafted artefact exclusively for elite consumption.

Day himself appears to have presented de luxe editions of the 'Book of Martyrs' to important people in the quest for patronage. A specially prepared copy of Foxe's book valued at £10 was given by John Day to Sir Henry Killigrew as part of Day's successful efforts to re-secure his patents, up for renewal again in 1577.[117] Unfortunately the records do not specify what improvements Day made to this copy to make it worth £10 but it is certainly possible that colouring the pictures and perhaps a quality binding were part of these improvements. This in turn opens up the possibility that Day had other 'de luxe' copies of Foxe's book available to him as piquant bribes.

Yet it was the archbishop who seems to have had a real desire that books he was involved with be aesthetically pleasing. When presenting a copy of the Bishops' Bible to Elizabeth in 1568, Parker not only praised the skill and accuracy of the work's translators, he made a point of also praising the

---

[116] Although some printers began to colour editions of scientific and medical works because they enhanced their accuracy (for example, a 1506 treatise, Ulrich Pinder's *Epiphanie medicorum*, contained coloured illustrations relating the different shades of urine to specific medical conditions), such staff were not needed on a regular basis, since coloured printed books were too costly to produce frequently. Printers therefore tended to contract such work out to freelance artisans (usually referred to as 'painters'). Even a business the size of Christopher Plantin's did not have an in-house painter. We know that Plantin contracted the colouring of illustrations, such as those in Leonhardt Fuchs' *De historia stirpium commentarii insignes* (Basle, 1542), to workers not under his own employ. See Sachiko Kusukawa, 'Leonhardt Fuchs on the Importance of Pictures', *Journal of the History of Ideas*, 58 (1997), pp. 403–27. Plantin paid 13 florins and 10 stuivers for an out-of-house 'painter' for colouring the pictures in three copies of the last volume of the Polyglot Bible (see Voet, *The Golden Compasses*, II, p. 243).

[117] See TNA, C 24/182 deps. to ints. 15–18. On Killigrew see below, p. 291.

workmanship of the Queen's Printer, Richard Jugge.[118] Moreover, the presentation copy of the Bishops' Bible that Parker sent to Elizabeth is now in the Folger Library and the illustrations of Dudley and Cecil in it have been coloured.[119] As we have already mentioned, a copy of Matthew Parker's *De antiquitate*, even more exquisitely illuminated than the coloured copies of Foxe, was sent as a presentation copy to William Cecil.

These examples in turn open up several intriguing but tantalisingly unanswerable questions. Did Parker have any influence on the decision to illustrate the *Acts and Monuments*? Did he go so far as to subsidise any or all of the illustrations? While we will probably never learn the answers to these questions, it does seem safe to say that Day was pushing the restrictive boundaries of English book production and its limited tradition of book illustration. However, he was operating at an extraordinarily propitious moment, as during the primacy of Matthew Parker, the archbishop and other members of the Elizabethan elite took an exceptional interest in book illustration. Soon, as Andrew Pettegree has pointed out, the influence of Calvinist iconophobia would make itself increasingly felt within the English book trade.[120] Patrick Collinson has observed that book illustration in England regresses sharply after 1580, with realistic religious pictures being a particular casualty.[121] This opens up a fascinating counter-factual question: if Foxe's book had first been printed two decades later would it have been illustrated at all?

At some point Day may have also decided that illustrations would enhance the prestige of the 'Book of Martyrs' (and thus *his* prestige) by giving it a quasi-liturgical aura; significantly Day also introduced a calendar of martyrs into Foxe's book in a similar attempt to make it more closely resemble a service book. Certainly one precedent that must have been on Day's mind was that of the *Legenda Aurea*. First printed by Caxton in 1483, this work went through at least nine editions down to the eve of the Reformation and it was a ubiquitous presence in English churches.[122] Profusely yet crudely illustrated with images of God's saints, this book

---

[118] *Parker Correspondence*, pp. 337–8.

[119] See Peter W. M. Blayney, 'The "Bishops' Bible"', in *Elizabeth I: Then and Now*, ed. Georgianna Ziegler (Seattle, 2003), p. 43.

[120] Pettegree, 'Illustrating the Book', pp. 133–44.   [121] Collinson, *Birthpangs*, p. 117.

[122] Jacobus de Voragine, *Legenda Aurea*, trans. W. Caxton? (London, 1483), STC 24873. Subsequent editions are STC 24874–24880. On *Legenda Aurea* in churches, see Sherry L. Reames, *The Legenda Aurea: A Re-examination of its Paradoxical History* (Madison, WI, 1985). Also Fiona Kisby, 'Books in London Parish Churches before 1603: Some Preliminary Observations', in *The Church and Learning in Later Medieval Society: Essays in Honour of R. B. Dobson* (Stamford, Lincs., 2002), pp. 305–26, esp. pp. 321–3.

may have inspired Day with the hope that his new work on saints and martyrs might act as a replacement for its 'popish' predecessor. It is interesting that the *Acts and Monuments* was the first post-Reformation non-liturgical or scriptural book to be placed in numerous parish churches; in this, it fulfilled the same function as the *Legenda Aurea* and provided a Protestant equivalent to Caxton's hagiography.

Whatever Day's wider objectives in illustrating his book were, his most immediate concern was very probably to gratify aesthetically the tastes of his elite patrons, and to impress them with his technical skill. Day may also have been motivated to include illustrations in an attempt to make the work more accessible and to extend its audience. But if he did so, it was because he believed that his patrons wanted the propaganda message of the book to reach as many people as possible. What Day did not do was to include the pictures in an attempt to enhance the sales of the book among the non-literate or barely literate; after all, these were the people least likely to afford it. Tessa Watt has done invaluable work in demonstrating the influence of the woodcuts in the 'Book of Martyrs' on popular religious culture.[123] However, it is ironic that this popular influence very probably originated in a desire to impress the elites and that it was a by-product of Day's efforts to win the patronage of the great and the good.

x

The fact that the illustrations were intended to please elite readers does not in the slightest diminish their role as propaganda. As we have seen, many of the illustrations were direct responses to Catholic writers or to the events of 1569–70. The profusion of narrative woodcuts – particularly those showing recent executions – must have had a considerable emotional impact on those who looked at the *Acts and Monuments*. As Margaret Aston has observed, these images would have 'spoke[n] with a shocking directness comparable to the realistic impact of the atrocities of war on twentieth-century contemporaries who first saw photographs in *Picture Post* and, later, television imagery'.[124] These images were perhaps the most effective instruments of Protestant propaganda in early modern England and they helped to make the deaths of fewer than three hundred martyrs in the Marian period a pivotal event in English history. They would have a lasting effect on

---

[123] Watt, *Cheap Print*, pp. 158–9.
[124] Margaret Aston, 'The Illustrations: Books 10–12' in John Foxe's 'Book of Martyrs' Online Variorum Edition; see www.hrionline.ac.uk/foxe.

English religious and political life for centuries to come. If the influence of the *Acts and Monuments* was confined solely to the impact of these pictures, the work would still rank as one of the most important books printed in early modern England.

Moreover, as Kevin Sharpe has observed, early modern propaganda was most effective when it contained messages that were to some degree shared by both elite and popular audiences. This does not mean that different social, economic and educational groups understood these messages in exactly the same way but rather that they extracted certain common themes and concepts from them.[125] The illustrations in the *Acts and Monuments*, particularly the seemingly realistic portrayal of historical events and people, operated as the sort of shared propaganda that Kevin Sharpe describes. Both elite and popular 'readers' could readily perceive common themes (e.g., the cruelty of Catholic persecutors, the pride and iniquity of the papacy) in these images.

Proof of the effectiveness of these illustrations as propaganda can be found in their use by both English Catholics and English Protestants. In fact, Foxe's use of vividly realistic images – we have observed above how the graphic nature of the woodcuts in the *Acts and Monuments* contrasted even with those in the *Rerum* – may have been inspired by his Catholic adversaries. A broadsheet printed in Rome in 1555 depicted in six engraved plates the martyrdom of the Carthusians of London and York in the years 1535 and 1537. These images, although produced on the continent, were almost certainly seen by Protestants in exile in Europe, and very probably also circulated in England.[126] Paradoxically, at least in terms of Knapp's suggestion that the realism of the illustrations in the *Acts and Monuments* was an attempt to distance Foxe's work from Catholic hagiographies, it may well be that these images of the Carthusians helped to inspire the realistic, if not graphic, detail of Foxe's narrative woodcuts.

The illustrations in Foxe's book triggered a confessional war of martyrological images, which was carried on by English Catholics. In fact, Foxe's book may well have inspired Catholics to greater use of printed illustrations as propaganda. Two years after Foxe's first edition appeared, John Fowler printed a Latin oration given at the University of Louvain in 1565, which castigated Protestants as seditious and denounced the insurrections that

---

[125] See Kevin Sharpe, 'Representations and Negotiations: Texts, Images, and Authority in Early Modern England', *Historical Journal*, 42 (1999), pp. 853–81.
[126] See Anne Dillon, *The Construction of Martyrdom in the English Catholic Community, 1535–1603* (Aldershot, 2002), pp. 52–62.

Protestantism had caused.[127] The following year, in 1566, Fowler printed an English translation of this sermon and added thirty-six woodcut pictures depicting the immorality of Protestants and focusing in particular upon the violence and massacres that Protestants inflicted on Catholics.[128] This book, unquestionably a response to the illustrations in the 'Book of Martyrs', was merely the first salvo in a sustained campaign of images glorifying the English Catholic martyrs: a campaign that culminated in the magnificent murals depicting the English martyrs at the English College in Rome and in the woodcuts in Richard Verstegan's international bestseller *Theatrum crudelitatum haereticorum nostri temporis* (1592).[129]

The development in the use of historical illustrations in cross-confessional polemic is a crucial and rather neglected answer to the question of why the *Acts and Monuments* was so lavishly illustrated. Andrew Pettegree has observed that Foxe's book was produced at a particularly fortuitous time when the English printing industry had developed the skills necessary for the lavish project of illustration but before Calvinist iconophobia had made its presence felt in England.[130] Yet England was also particularly rich in the numbers of its martyrs, both Protestant and Catholic. Their deaths created enormous opportunities for the deployment of visual propaganda, and once Catholics had begun using this imagery, the English Protestants were powerfully motivated to respond in kind. In fact the 'Book of Martyrs' would itself, as we shall see, escalate the war of competing confessional images.

These illustrations were in fact particularly effective propaganda because of their seeming realism. Edmund Bonner is supposed to have marvelled at the skill with which his likeness was depicted in Foxe's book. The quote comes from Sir John Harrington, a bottomless reservoir of unreliable anecdotes, and is of course valueless for what Bonner actually said or thought.[131] However, it is fascinating evidence of the reputation for verisi-militude of the woodcuts in Foxe's book and the importance that contemporaries attached to this. Moreover, it echoes the claims of Foxe's text itself, which boasts that it is the 'true counterfeyt of Bon[n]er'. However, the picture is actually carefully stylised and, as Deborah Burks' careful analysis

---

[127] Peter Frarin, *Oratio P. Frarini . . . Quod male, reformandae religionis nomine, arma sumpserunt Sectarii nostri temporis* (Louvain, 1565).
[128] Peter Frarin, *An oration against the unlawful insurrections of the Protestants of our time, under pretence to refourme religion* (Antwerp, 1566), STC 11333.
[129] On both of these see Dillon, *Construction of Martyrdom*, pp. 170–276.
[130] Pettegree, 'Illustrating the Book', pp. 135 and 144.
[131] John Harrington, *A briefe view of the state of the Church of England as it stood in Q. Elizabeths and King James his reigne* (STC Wing H770), pp. 15–17.

reveals, it is highly effective anti-clerical propaganda, establishing Bonner (and by implication all Catholic clergy) as persecutors motivated by homosexual lust and sadomasochism.[132]

The polemical messages, overt and covert, of these woodcuts established their lasting importance in English religious and cultural life. With very few exceptions (e.g., the picture of John Day), the woodcuts are all stridently anti-Catholic. Even the capital 'C' depicting the enthroned Elizabeth has the pope chained beneath her feet, holding broken keys. The *Acts and Monuments* itself is a complicated book with numerous overlapping messages – it is at once a book of didactic advice on how to live the Christian life, a book of spiritual consolation for troubled souls, a history of the Church in its many facets, a history of England, and an exegesis of the Apocalypse unfolding through the history of the world. Like a lens the woodcut illustrations focused and intensified one aspect of the complete spectrum that was the *Acts and Monuments*: its anti-Catholicism. This intensification on the one hand simplified, perhaps even distorted, the many intertwined ideas and themes presented in Foxe's work, but it also gave the one idea that it presented a searing power. Well into the nineteenth, if not the twentieth century, Foxe's woodcuts would keep the memory of the Marian persecution green and rub salt into the wounds of sectarian hatred.[133] Foxe's rich and varied work became reduced in the late seventeenth century and onwards to a well-documented anti-Catholic screed, and the illustrations were a major part of this process. The anti-Catholicism was always there in Foxe's work but circumstances, alterations to the text (e.g., additional material on Catholic 'atrocities' such as the Gunpowder Plot and the massacres in Ireland), as well as the illustrations allowed this particular leitmotif to swell in volume, overwhelming the other strains in Foxe's magnum opus. An interesting indication of the sectarian passions ignited by these pictures is the mutilation of the images of Catholic figures in some surviving copies of Foxe's book; in one striking case, a copy of the 1632 edition, the face of the pope is eliminated on each and every

---

[132] The woodcut first appears on *1563*, p. 1689. See Burks, 'Polemical Potency', pp. 264–76.

[133] Eirwen Nicholson has questioned the extent of the impact of Foxe's iconography during the eighteenth century. Eirwen Nicholson, 'Eighteenth Century Foxe: Evidence for the Impact of the *Acts and Monuments* in the "Long" Eighteenth Century', in *John Foxe and the English Reformation*, ed. Loades, pp. 142–77. We suggest that Nicholson may be underestimating the influence of the woodcut even in the period she discusses, but even accepting that there was a diminution of the impact of Foxe's pictures during the eighteenth century, it unquestionably rebounded in the nineteenth century with the publication of four unabridged editions of Foxe's book – all including copies of the original woodcuts – as well as dozens of abridged editions, many of them illustrated.

engraving on which the pontiff appears.[134] If, as Linda Colley has argued, Protestantism was the force that unified the different British peoples, then Foxe's illustrations – much more than any direct putative statements in his text about an 'elect nation' – were part of the creation of the British nation.

The influence of the illustrations in the 'Book of Martyrs' on the history of the English book, whilst spectacular, is more ephemeral than their influence on sectarian prejudice. A number of factors converged to ensure that Day's achievement in lavishly illustrating Foxe's book was not repeated. In early modern English printed religious books Foxe is the general exception to a pervasive mediocrity in the illustrations to this type of literature. As Martha Driver has observed, 'from the point of view of illustration, execution and layout, English printed books are generally regarded as inferior to their continental counterparts until well into the seventeenth century'.[135] Scholars such as Andrew Pettegree and Patrick Collinson have seen the cause of this lack of pictorial sophistication as religious – in their view, a rising tide of Calvinist influence, which included a marked iconophobia and suspicion of the image as idolatrous. This iconophobia extended to book illustrations, and unsurprisingly most powerfully affected religious books.[136] We would suggest, however, that changes in the ways in which English book production was financed played as great a role, if not greater, in throttling the development of English book illustration. In the 1580s resentment against printing monopolies, which had been gathering steam for more than a decade, came to a head. The Stationers' Company began to lose control of the situation: book piracy proliferated and the existing monopolies became increasingly difficult to enforce. It was because of the patents he received (and possibly, although this cannot be proven, because of subsidies he might have received to defray the costs of his illustrations) that John Day was able to afford to illustrate Foxe's book on an unprecedented scale. Later printers were not as fortunate; as we shall see, the system of monopolies, which sustained Day's printing empire, effectively perished

[134] Barry McKay, 'Foxe's "Book of Martyrs": The Appleby Copy', *Bookbinder*, 18 (2004), pp. 68–9. This particular copy was part of the parish library of Appleby, Westmorland. In a more rarefied setting, the copy of the 1570 edition, which had belonged to Matthew Parker and which remained in the library of Trinity College, Cambridge, was similarly, although not as extensively, mutilated (see, for example, the removal of Bonner's face from the illustration of Bonner burning Thomas Tomkins' hand on p. 1710). The faces of popes, monks, friars and persecutors are obliterated in several other copies of the 1570 edition also, such as those in the copy in Ohio State University Library (see, for example, the removal of the pontiff's face in many of the woodcuts in the 'proud primacie' section at the back of volume 1).

[135] Martha Driver, *The Image in Print: Book Illustration in Late Medieval England and its Sources* (London, 2004), p. 33.

[136] See Pettegree, 'Illustrating the Book', pp. 133–59, and Patrick Collinson, *Birthpangs*, p. 117.

with him. To produce a large, expensive and complicated work (and an extensively illustrated volume would inevitably be all of these), printers had to form syndicates. The involvement of more people in the process had the effect of reducing the desire to take financial risks or embark on expensive technical innovations. At the same time the need to impress patrons, which spurred Day on in some of his most ambitious undertakings, was now removed. Thrift, not excellence, was the watchword of the new economic order. Illustrated books were still produced, but because their financing was increasingly complicated they became more unusual. Thus it may have been the dictates of Mammon as much as the word of God that hindered the development of English book illustration.[137]

Whatever its effect on the development of the English illustrated book, patronage made possible the wealth of technically sophisticated illustrations in the 'Book of Martyrs'. Even setting aside the possibility that these illustrations might have been subsidised or partly subsidised by Matthew Parker or some other influential figure, patronage supplied the monopolies that provided the money that Day used to finance the illustrations, among other things. There is, moreover, evidence that these woodcuts, although they played an important role in making Foxe's book more accessible, were nevertheless intended to impress and gratify elite readers as well, and to ensure continued patronage for the work's printer. The satisfaction of elite consumers as well as the edification of popular ones made the work even more effective as propaganda, thus in turn winning Day and the 'Book of Martyrs' further official support. As we shall see in the next chapter, the use of the visual images as pro-government propaganda would be referred to by the Privy Council as part of their reasons for encouraging the dissemination of the second edition of the *Acts and Monuments*.

---

[137] A major exception to this was the printing of scientific, medical and mathematical works in England, which did continue to be illustrated. Significantly these books also tended to be financed through patronage, although this took the form of direct financing from wealthy backers rather than through the granting of official monopolies.

CHAPTER 7

A parting of the ways? Foxe and Day, 1570–1576

I

With the completion of the 1570 edition, both Foxe and Day turned their attention to other projects. Apparently they had no plans to produce a subsequent edition of the *Acts and Monuments*. Some of their new enterprises, such as an edition of the works of the English evangelicals William Tyndale, John Frith and Robert Barnes, were long-standing projects, which had been announced in the 'Book of Martyrs'.[1] Others, such as the *Reformatio Legum Ecclesiasticarum* or the *Sermon of Christ crucified*, were responses to current events and unexpected opportunities. At the beginning of the 1570s, Foxe and Day were still working closely together, but by the middle of the decade their paths were beginning to diverge.

There is no exact date for the completion of the second edition. However, it seems reasonable to assume that it must have been finished in the opening months of 1570. At some time, presumably around the beginning of 1570, Bishop Grindal invited Foxe to preach the Good Friday sermon at Paul's Cross.[2] In reluctantly accepting this invitation Foxe, after pleading his own unworthiness for the job, went on to declare that he was too busy with other tasks, and although he does not say so specifically, from his description of these labours it appears clear that he was still working on the *Acts and Monuments*.[3] An invitation to preach a sermon at the most celebrated venue in England on the holiest day of the Christian year (when not only the bishop of London and the dean of St Paul's but also the mayor and all the aldermen would be present) was a signal honour. As such, it was more than a personal tribute to Foxe; it was also the first of several

---

[1] See *1570*, pp. 1226 and 1230.
[2] An undated copy of Foxe's letter accepting the invitation is BL, Harley MS 417, fo. 129ʳ. Good Friday was very early that year and fell on 24 March.
[3] 'ego iam diu literariis istis molestiis quotidie exhaurendis, pervestigandis Scriptoribus, legendis ac relegendis exemplaribus, describendis materiis, quae publico Ecclesiae usui serviant' (ibid).

quasi-official endorsements of the second edition. It was only natural that Day wanted to capitalise on this and he therefore rushed an edition of the sermon into print.[4] In doing so, however, Day was making heavy demands on his still depleted supply of paper. As a result, the work was printed on the cheap paper that had been used to complete the *Acts and Monuments*. Foxe seems to have been back working in Day's printing house on this edition, since at the end of the sermon he added a 'Postscript to the Papists', because 'here remaineth behind an emptie page of white paper'.[5]

Although the postscript would appear to have been a spur of the moment composition, it addressed one of Foxe's central concerns. Like many people who are completely convinced of the righteousness of their causes, Foxe possessed an almost naive belief that if he only presented the 'truth' to his confessional opponents they would see the error of their ways and convert to the teachings of the Gospel.[6] (This moral certitude was reinforced by Foxe's apocalyptic beliefs. He genuinely believed, as he would declare in his commentary on Revelation, that in the end times, which he believed were imminent, Catholics, Jews and Muslims would join the True Church en masse.[7]) This accounts for one of the striking features of Foxe's sermon: while anti-Catholic, it is not political, and in particular barely alludes to the papal deposition.[8] This sermon might have been expected to denounce the bull; instead, Foxe moved from attacking Catholic doctrines in the first part of the sermon to emphasising and expostulating on justification by faith and the means by which salvation is attained.

It may have been this emphasis on pastoral rather than political issues that led to the perhaps unexpected popularity of this sermon in print. The title page of the edition declared that it was 'written and dedicated to all such as labour and be heavy laden in conscience, to be read for their spirituall comfort'. The work was dedicated to this same group. In some ways this unusual dedication is at once a reversion to Foxe's past and an indication of things to come. Foxe was returning to the pattern of his first

---

[4] Jonn Foxe, *A sermon of Christ crucified* (London, 1570), STC 11242.   [5] Ibid., sig. T4^r.

[6] For examples of this, expressed in numerous works by Foxe, see the *ODNB* article on Foxe. In a particularly striking case Foxe presented the eminent recusant lawyer Edmund Plowden with a copy of his last work of anti-Catholic propaganda, a treatise on justification, printed as a response to Edmund Campion's *Decem rationes*. Glyn Parry, 'John Foxe, "Father of Lyes", and the Papists', in *John Foxe and the English Reformation*, ed. Loades, pp. 300–5.

[7] John Foxe, *Eicasmi seu meditationes in sacram Apocalypsin*, ed. Samuel Foxe (London, 1587), STC 11237, pp. 389–90.

[8] Only in a prayer at the end of the volume does Foxe mention the threat to England posed by Catholics, and he combines this with the threat posed to Christendom by the Ottoman Turks (Foxe, *Christ crucified*, sig. T2^{r-v}).

printed works of 1547–8, which were pastoral works, dedicated to friends and neighbours, rather than to the great and the good who could be expected to render him material assistance. At the same time, the concern with alleviating the pangs of afflicted consciences, anxious about their salvation, anticipated the great project of Luther translations that he would organise in a few years' time.[9]

Some time in the same year a second edition of the sermon appeared, which boasted on the title page that it had been 'newly recognised by the Author'.[10] This claim was largely a marketing ploy, as the work was barely changed at all.[11] The minimally revised version went through five editions up to 1585, with a further edition in 1609.[12] A Latin edition of the work appeared – as the title page informs us – on 1 October 1571.[13] This was clearly directed at a different and more learned audience and lacked both the pastoral dedication and the 'Postscript to the Papists'. It was also substantially larger than the English text; although it made exactly the same points, the Latin version buttressed them with abundant classical and patristic citations and historical examples. As a result, the work lost its pastoral orientation and became more of a theological treatise. This change was reflected in a new introduction, which focused on the sole sufficiency of Christ's sacrifice and the superiority of his teachings to all worldly philosophies, and urged the reader to meditate on his death and passion.[14] Perhaps unsurprisingly, this version went through only one edition, and its printing was probably a favour granted by Day to Foxe, with little expectation of profit. The relatively late printing of this volume was probably due to its being displaced by another project that occupied Foxe, and to a lesser extent Day, in the winter and spring of 1570–1.

II

The fact that the first edition of Foxe's sermon was printed on the dregs of Day's paper supply is a telling indication of how severely work on the

---

[9] Foxe quoted only one work by a contemporary theologian in the English editions of the sermon *Christ crucified* but he quoted the work twice: it was Luther's commentary on Galatians, which would be the keystone of the translations of the German reformer that Foxe sponsored (ibid., fo. 51[r–v]).

[10] John Foxe, *A sermon of Christ crucified, preached at Paules Crosse the Friday before Easter, commonly called Good fryday* (London, 1570) STC 11242.3.

[11] The beginning of the dedication was revised, eliminating passages, which emphasised Foxe's reluctance to have the sermon printed. The text of the 'newly recognised' version also contains an expanded exegesis of 2 Corinthians 5:18 (cf. STC 11242, fo. 59[v] with STC 11242.3, fos. 59[v]–60[r]).

[12] STC 11242.3–11246.   [13] Foxe, *De christo crucifixo concio* (London, 1571), STC 11247.

[14] Ibid., sigs. A1[v]–A4[v].

second edition of the *Acts and Monuments* had drained the printer's resources. (Admittedly, Day printed a major work, Henry Billingsley's translation of Euclid's *Geometrie*, prefaced by John Dee, in 1570, but this was probably because Dee had supplied Day with the necessary paper.[15]) It is certainly noteworthy that a major Parker project – the printing of Matthew Paris's *Chronica maiora* – was not printed, as one might expect, by John Day, but by his competitor, Reyner Wolfe. Instead, Day concentrated largely on picking up the threads of his business. This included a renewed emphasis on his best sellers, such as the ABC, the catechism and the metrical psalms, and it also included a determined effort by Day to ensure the profitability of the second edition of the *Acts and Monuments*. The printer lobbied certain Privy Council members in an attempt to ensure that parish churches were required to purchase copies of it, and these efforts were at least partially successful.[16]

Of course in order to obtain favours from the powerful it was necessary to render services to them in return. Day found a way to do this and also to fulfil promises that had not yet been met, by printing a number of works by Thomas Norton. Norton's relationship with Day went back to almost the beginning of Elizabeth's reign but it became particularly active in 1569–70, as Norton wrote a series of works responding to the perceived Catholic threat – fear of which grew stronger in those years of the Northern Rebellion and the papal deposition of Elizabeth. The works Day printed were largely a series of polemical tracts written by Norton as part of a propaganda campaign organised by Norton's patron, William Cecil.[17] However, a sign of an increasingly close personal relationship between Norton and the printer is revealed by the printing in 1570 of a more personal work: the revised edition of *Gorboduc*, a controversial drama co-written by Norton and Thomas Sackville. Apparently neither Norton nor Sackville intended the play, which dealt with the volatile topic of the royal succession, to be printed. However, in 1565 an opportunistic printer, William Griffith, produced an unauthorised, poorly printed edition of the play.[18] In 1570, Norton turned to Day to produce a corrected and also less contentious version.[19] Norton and Day would soon be involved with John Foxe in another politically sensitive and highly topical project.

---

[15] *PPP*, pp. 148–51. [16] See Evenden and Freeman, 'Print, Profit and Propaganda', pp. 1288–1307.
[17] See Michael Graves, *Thomas Norton: Parliament Man* (Oxford, 1994), pp. 147–96 and *PPP*, pp. 127–32.
[18] Thomas Norton and Thomas Sackville, *The tragedie of Gorboduc* (London, 1565), STC 1565.
[19] Thomas Norton and Thomas Sackville, *The tragidie of Ferrex and Porrex . . .* (London, 1570), STC 18685.

On the morning of 6 April 1571, the second full working day of the 1571 parliament, William Strickland, a zealous puritan MP, made a long speech in which he claimed that, back in the reign of Edward VI, Peter Martyr and Paul Phagius had written a confession of faith in England. Strickland then declared that this work was in the possession of his fellow MP, Thomas Norton, and asked that the House require Norton to provide it. Strickland then proceeded to a denunciation of the superstitions and errors in the Book of Common Prayer. Norton rose and corrected Strickland, declaring that he did indeed have such a work but that it was not a statement of faith but rather a collection of proposed canon laws, composed by Walter Haddon and Sir John Cheke. Norton added that Foxe had recently edited the book and that it had just been printed 'to be offered to that house'; he then produced copies of it.[20]

The work that Norton and Strickland were referring to was a code of canon law that Foxe christened the *Reformatio Legum Ecclesiasticarum*. It had been prepared in 1552 under the direction of Archbishop Cranmer in order to replace the canon law codes that had been nullified by the Henrician Reformation. Although it was submitted to parliament for approval in 1553, the duke of Northumberland's opposition doomed the code and it did not become law.[21] Sometime during the year between his delivering the *Sermon of Christ crucified* and the calling of the 1571 parliament, Foxe had edited a version of Cranmer's old law code and Day had printed it in time for parliament.

Foxe essentially based his version of the *Reformatio* on two manuscripts. One is now BL, Harley MS 426, which is an incomplete copy (probably a working draft submitted to Cranmer during the preparation of the law code), which was given to Foxe by Thomas Norton, who was Cranmer's son-in-law. The other manuscript no longer exists but was supplied by Archbishop Parker. Foxe's use of it was deduced by the great ecclesiastical historian John Strype from annotations Foxe made on Harley MS 426. Strype correctly assumed that the markings on that manuscript were cross-references made by Foxe to the Parker manuscript.[22] Foxe also consulted a

---

[20] For the events of 6 April, see *Proceedings in the Parliaments of Elizabeth I*, ed. T. E. Hartley, 3 vols. (Leicester, 1981–95), I, pp. 200–1.

[21] See *Tudor Church Reform: The Henrician Canons of 1535 and the Reformatio Legum Ecclesiasticarum*, ed. Gerald Bray, Church of England Record Society VIII (Woodbridge, 2000), pp. xli–liv and lxxiii–lxxvi.

[22] See John Strype, *The Life and Acts of Matthew Parker*, 3 vols. (Oxford, 1821), II, pp. 62–3. For Foxe's annotations referring to Parker's manuscript see BL, Harley MS 426, fos. 65ᵛ, 76ʳ, 83ʳ, 89ʳ and 150ᵛ. For further discussion of these manuscripts, see Bray, *Tudor Church Reform*, pp. liv–lxiv.

draft of a 1535 canon law code, which was a forerunner of the *Reformatio*, which he may possibly have received from William Cecil.[23]

The production of the *Reformatio* was part of a carefully organised initiative to achieve legislation mandating not only a new code of canon law but also reform of the Prayer Book. This is made clear by Foxe's explicit call, in the preface to the *Reformatio*, for reform of the Book of Common Prayer.[24] The plan (probably devised by Norton) was apparently to persuade the bishops and conservative clergy to endorse reform of the Book of Common Prayer (i.e., a purging of its 'superstitious' elements) in return for the establishment of a new code of canon law. The plan went wrong, partly because Strickland's premature intervention in the debate alarmed the bishops and partly because many MPs were reluctant to extend the authority of the clergy by establishing a new code of canon law.[25]

The fascinating thing about the production of the *Reformatio* is that it was so manifestly designed as part of an effort to lobby parliament. This effort involved the close cooperation of Norton, Foxe and Day. In addition to his ties with Day, Norton may also have formed a relationship with Foxe as part of the work on the *Acts and Monuments*. Thomas Norton's son, Robert, claimed that his father 'was the greatest helpe Mr John Foxe had in compiling his large volume of Acts and Monuments'.[26] Whenever these links between Norton and Foxe were forged, they proved enduring. In 1582, when Norton was under arrest, he entrusted his emotionally unstable wife to Foxe's care.[27] It is also possible that Cecil may well also have been a party to this parliamentary initiative. If so, as always he left no trail leading back to him.[28]

Cecil's involvement – if he was indeed involved – may have been an additional inducement for Day's involvement in this enterprise but it was hardly the only one. For one thing, Norton and Foxe were valued friends and Day would have been happy to oblige them. For another, Day shared their religious convictions and would have been willing to further the cause.

---

[23] The draft of the 1535 law code is BL, Add. MS 48040; a note stating that it had been used by John Foxe is on fo. 13ʳ. For the argument that this manuscript may have come from Cecil, see Freeman, 'The Reformation of the Church in this Parliament', pp. 137–8.

[24] *Reformatio Legum Ecclesiasticarum* (London, 1571), STC 6006, sig. B1ʳ.

[25] See Freeman, 'Reformation of the Church', pp. 139–44. Bray has a somewhat different interpretation. He feels that while Strickland's intervention was 'unsettling', it was not decisive in causing the re-establishment of the canon laws to be rejected. (Bray does not discuss the concomitant failure of reform of the Book of Common Prayer.) He instead explains the failure of the Henrician canons as being due to a desire by parliament to avoid being distracted by a controversial and divisive bill at a time of crisis. Bray, *Tudor Church Reform*, pp. xcvii–xcviii.

[26] Quoted in Graves, *Thomas Norton*, p. 44.   [27] TNA, SP 12/152, fo. 72ᵛ.

[28] For a discussion of this, see Freeman, 'Reformation of the Church', p. 145.

There is no doubt that Day was deeply involved in this project. A letter survives to Foxe passing on a message that Day was awaiting the preface to the *Reformatio* because 'the parliamente draweth nere'.[29] A letter to Foxe from Laurence Humphrey, dated 28 March 1571, is addressed to Foxe at Day's printing house.[30] Manifestly, Day and Foxe were working hand-in-glove at this time to achieve certain political and religious objectives.

In doing so, both author and printer ran the risk of offending a valued ally: Archbishop Parker. After all, Parker had loaned Foxe one of his manuscripts in preparing the *Reformatio* and it is inconceivable that Parker would have approved of its use as part of a plan for purging the Book of Common Prayer. Therefore Foxe must have concealed, or at the very least dissimulated, his true objectives from the archbishop. It is difficult to conceive how Parker could not have been affronted by this. The seventeenth-century historian, Thomas Fuller, relates a story that Foxe was summoned by Matthew Parker and ordered to subscribe to the 'canons'. According to Fuller, Foxe produced a copy of the Old Testament in Greek and said that he would subscribe to that instead.[31] At first glance, Fuller's story might not appear very credible, since he was writing almost a century after the incident would have taken place. However, Fuller was a friend of John Foxe's grandson, Thomas, who had given him access to the martyrologist's private papers.[32] The story may have gained something in the telling but it is probable that the incident took place.[33] Yet while the connection between Foxe and Parker was strained, it was too valuable to both individuals for it to be broken, at least for the moment.

In fact the intricate association between Foxe, Day and Parker is revealed in a work printed by Day later in 1571: an edition of the Gospels in Anglo-Saxon and English.[34] A striking feature of the work, and one designed to attract the attention of the reader, was a dedication written and signed by

---

[29] BL, Harley MS 416, fo. 119ʳ. For discussion of this letter see Freeman, 'Reformation of the Church', p. 134.

[30] BL, Harley MS 416, fo. 179ʳ⁻ᵛ. For a discussion of the dating of this letter see Freeman, 'Reformation of the Church', p. 134.

[31] Thomas Fuller, *The Church History of Britain*, ed. J. S. Brewer, 6 vols. (Oxford, 1845), IV, pp. 328–9.

[32] Fuller prints two letters from this collection in his Church history. Cf. *Church History*, IV, pp. 389–90 with BL, Harley MS 416, fo. 151ʳ⁻ᵛ and *Church History*, IV, pp. 391–5 with BL, Harley MS 416, fos. 152ʳ⁻3ʳ.

[33] Fuller does not date the incident. Foxe's modern biographer, Mozley, assumes that it took place in 1566 at the height of the vestiarian controversy. However, there would have been no point in having Foxe subscribe to the canons at that point in time, while there is every reason to think that Parker might have tried to get his subscription to the canons in the wake of an attempt by Foxe to reform the Book of Common Prayer (Mozley, *John Foxe and his Book*, p. 74).

[34] Foxe, *The gospels of the fower Evangelistes*.

John Foxe, presenting the work to Elizabeth. Foxe could not translate Anglo-Saxon and the dedication was clearly in part an attempt to capitalise on the celebrity of his name in order to promote sales.[35] Most of the introduction is taken up with Foxe expounding upon the need for the faithful to have the Scriptures in the vernacular and upon how, throughout history, godly rulers had ensured vernacular Bibles were made available.[36] There were probably two particular agendas behind this history lecture. One was to buttress the recent editions of the Bishops' Bible, and at the same time to remind Elizabeth very gently of her duties as a godly ruler.

Foxe was also careful to praise not Elizabeth, the dedicatee of the volume, but rather 'the reverend and learned father in God, Matthew Archbishop of Cant., a cheefe and a famous travailler in thys Church of England, by whose industrious diligence and learned labours, this book, with others moe, hath bene collected and searched out of the Saxons monuments'.[37] Foxe continued by asserting that the edition of the *Anglo-Saxon Gospels* showed that 'the religion taught and professed in this land at present, is no new reformation of thinges lately begonne, which were not before, but rather a reduction of the Church to the Pristine state of old conformitie, which once it had', and that this was to be seen in the doctrines of

transubstantiation, of Priestes restraint of marriage, of receaving under one kind, with many other pointes and articles moe of like quality thrust in, and the old abolished by the clergy of Rome: whereof part hath bene sufficiently detected already by the godly diligence of the sayd Archbyshop above mentioned, in his booke of the Saxon Sermon and other treatises; part likewise remaine to be shewed, and set forth shortly.[38]

Several agendas were fulfilled in these passages. In the first place, Day was advertising to interested readers that he would be producing more Anglo-Saxon translations in the near future. At the same time, both Parker and Foxe were signalling, particularly to Catholics, the weight of evidence they had to support their arguments that the doctrines of the Elizabethan Church were essentially those of the pre-Conquest English Church. Foxe's mention of the discussion of the doctrines of transubstantiation, clerical celibacy and receiving under one kind was a reference to the allegations against the Six Articles: a section of the *Acts and Monuments* that had been written with the active cooperation of Matthew Parker. At the

---

[35] On Foxe's inability to read Anglo-Saxon, along with a persuasive argument that his contribution to this work was limited to this dedication, see Michael Murphy, 'John Foxe, Martyrologist and "Editor" of Old English', *English Studies*, 49 (1968), pp. 516–23.
[36] Foxe, *The Gospels of the fower Evangelistes*, sigs. A2ʳ–¶2ʳ.   [37] Ibid., sig. ¶2ʳ.   [38] Ibid., sig. ¶2ʳ⁻ᵛ.

same time Foxe was also signalling that Parker had a number of other documents also testifying to the antiquity of English Protestant doctrines, which were yet to be printed. Finally, Foxe's praise of Parker and his projects, as well as his very inclusion in a volume produced under Parker's auspices, may well have been intended to alert those few, but influential, people who may have been aware of recent tension between the two men that they were back working together in harmony.

In the following year, 1572, Day continued to produce works that were designed less for commercial purposes than to suit the agenda of his two valued associates, Matthew Parker and John Foxe. For Parker he printed a book very close to the primate's heart: *De antiquitate*, a history of the archbishops of Canterbury.[39] Day also printed Foxe's *Pandectae. Locorum communium*, a much larger and more elaborate version of the *Locorum communium tituli*, the commonplace book that Foxe had printed by Oporinus in 1557.[40] This book appears to have sold as poorly as Foxe's previous commonplace book had done, although Hugh Singleton reprinted it after Day's death, in 1585.[41] Both of these texts were a reminder that more than simple market forces dictated Day's choices of project. In some cases he even printed books that were not expected to sell well at all and which were not intended to gratify friends and patrons but were instead designed to serve his own religious and ideological purposes.

IV

The next project on which Day and Foxe collaborated was their promised edition of the works of William Tyndale, John Frith and Robert Barnes.[42] Apparently this was a pet project of John Day's. When, in the *Acts and Monuments*, Foxe announced that this collection would be forthcoming, he stated that it was Day who was collecting the writings of these martyrs and that it was Day's idea to print an edition of these gathered texts. However, the parameters of what Day would be collecting and printing seemed to have changed somewhat, as Foxe also stated that it would be the works of Tyndale,

---

[39] Parker, *De antiquitate Britannicae ecclesiae*. On the production of this book see *PPP*, p. 111.

[40] John Foxe, *Pandectae locorum communium, praecipua rerum capita & titulos, iuxta ordinem elementorum complectens* . . . (London, 1572), STC 11239. Evidence for the poor sales lies in the fact Day used pages from unsold copies of the *Pandectae* in a later work. See *PPP*, pp. 166–7.

[41] STC 11239.5.

[42] John Foxe (ed.), *The whole workes of W. Tyndall, Iohn Frith, and Doct. Barnes, three worthy martyrs, and principall teachers of this Churche of England collected and compiled in one tome togither, beyng before scattered* . . . (London, 1573), STC 24436.

Frith and Barnes 'and other'.[43] Apparently the decision was made at some point to restrict the venture to just the work of Tyndale, Frith and Barnes. What is less clear is why Day was so committed to this particular project.

Whatever Day's motivations were, they almost certainly were not financial. The *Whole workes* was an expensive undertaking – a folio of over 750 pages, printed largely on fine-quality paper.[44] The cost of production was reflected in the price of the book. In the inventory of an Edinburgh bookseller, the price of an unbound copy is given as 7s 2d.[45] By way of comparison, the truly massive 1589 edition of Hakluyt's *Voyages* sold for 9s unbound.[46] Scholars have tended to assume that, despite its size and expense, Day seems to have expected to make a profit from the *Whole workes*. David Daniell asserts that the work 'must' have been commercially profitable, while John King goes even further and maintains that the 'popularity' of this work (which King describes as 'a highly saleable commodity') is an indication that revisionists have underestimated the popularity of Protestantism in Elizabethan England.[47]

There is actually no evidence that the book sold particularly well (it only went through one edition). Moreover, Day did not take measures that would have helped ensure a profit from this work. As King has explained, Day's usual strategy was to test the market for works by evangelical authors by producing single-text editions or small collections first.[48] However, in this case, significantly, he did not. Moreover, Day increased the already significant cost of the book's production by commissioning an allegorical woodcut showing the Gospel outweighing papal decretals, communion wafers and other symbols of Catholicism.[49]

---

[43] *1570*, pp. 1226 and 1230.

[44] For the change to an inferior stock of paper for the section dealing with the works of Robert Barnes, see *PPP*, pp. 145–7.

[45] Francis R. Johnson, 'Notes on English Retail Book-Prices, 1550–1640', *The Library*, 5th series, 5 (1950), p. 111.

[46] Ibid., p. 92.

[47] David Daniell, 'Tyndale and Foxe', in *John Foxe: An Historical Perspective*, ed. David Loades (Aldershot, 1999), p. 24; John N. King, '"The Light of Printing": William Tyndale, John Foxe, John Day, and Early Modern Print Culture', *Renaissance Quarterly*, 54 (2001), p. 53.

[48] King, *Print Culture*, p. 83.

[49] John King has maintained that it is 'a virtual certainty that Day commissioned this elaborate woodcut for the 1576 version of the "Book of Martyrs"' (King, *Print Culture*, p. 179). This assumes that Day was already planning to print a new edition of Foxe's book as early as 1572. As we shall see in the next chapter, the circumstances surrounding the printing of the third edition of the *Acts and Monuments* make this unlikely. Rather, it appears that the decision to print the third edition was made suddenly. Had Day planned on a third edition of the 'Book of Martyrs', this would have been the perfect place to advertise – as he had done in other works that announced the 1563 and 1570 editions – yet no such advertisement appears anywhere in the *Whole workes*.

Rather than being a work intended to make a significant profit or designed to impress 'the powers that be' (there is no indication of support for this work by Cecil, Parker or any other of Day's patrons), this appears to have been something of a labour of love for John Day. As Foxe had already announced, this collection was not only done at Day's behest but it was the printer who gathered together many, if not all, of the works in it. This project may have been developing for some time. Surviving among Foxe's papers in Emmanuel College, Cambridge, is a manuscript title page for what was presumably a copy text for a version of *Patrick's Places*.[50] The manuscript title page states at the bottom that it is 'Newly imprinted at London' in 1566. The reverse of the manuscript title page contains the beginning of John Frith's preface to the first edition of *Patrick's Places*, which appeared around 1531.[51] The remainder of the complete copy of this text occurs further on in this manuscript.[52] The text is clearly marked up in preparation for printing and also contains revisions of the text in Foxe's handwriting.[53] Obviously *Patrick's Places*, edited by Foxe, was intended for production by Day in 1566 but was presumably never printed as an individual piece. We do not know why this project was abandoned so close to fruition, but *Patrick's Places* was incorporated into the 1570 edition of the *Acts and Monuments*.[54] It would appear from this that the project of reprinting Frith's works, at least, had roots that went back to the 1560s.

By the time the *Whole workes* was printed, Day had done an impressive job of gathering together the scattered writings of the three authors. Foxe

---

[50] *Patrick's Places* is the name given by John Frith to his translation from Latin into English of Patrick Hamilton's *Loci communes*.

[51] ECL, MS 262, fo. 60[r–v]. Patrick Hamilton, *Patrick's Places*, ed. John Frith (Antwerp, 1531?), STC 12731.4.

[52] ECL, MS 262, fos. 72[r]–81[r]. William Clebsch has pointed to the existence of the text of the translation in the Emmanuel manuscript, but he appears to have been unaware of the title page, which is present in the same manuscript but separated from the body of the text. Moreover, Clebsch was not aware that the annotations on the manuscript were in Foxe's handwriting. William A. Clebsch, *England's Earliest Protestants, 1520–1535* (New Haven, CT, 1964), p. 82.

[53] For example, marginal notes are added by Foxe and their position on the (what would have been the printed) page indicated clearly, such as on fo. 73[v], where the line 'Christ bare our sinnes on his back Esa.53' is crossed out in the body of the text and moved into the margin area to indicate to the compositor where to position this text.

[54] *1570*, pp. 1109–16. The version of the text printed in the *Acts and Monuments* is not the same as the Emmanuel manuscript version and it is quite different from Frith's original edition of the work. In terms of content of the version printed in the *Acts and Monuments*, Foxe made the work more explicitly predestinarian than either Hamilton or Frith had intended. He also recast the work into syllogisms and gave it a more formal, logical structure to the theological arguments. He also added a series of interpretative comments, which were as long as the original treatise itself. These final notes discussed the distinction between the law and the Gospel in terms that anticipated the longer discussion of this in Foxe's *Sermon on Christ crucified*. See the discussion of the version of *Patrick's Places* printed in the 1570 edition of Foxe's book in Clebsch, *England's Earliest Protestants*, pp. 83–4.

and Day were quite aware that efforts to recover all of their texts had not met with complete success – a fact acknowledged in the *Whole workes*.[55] In fact all of the works of Tyndale that survive today are included in the *Whole workes*, as well as at least one item, *The Supper of the Lord*, that is now attributed to George Joye.[56] Similarly, they obtained almost all of the works of John Frith.[57] The 'whole works' of Robert Barnes, however, is something of a misnomer. Almost all of Barnes's German and Latin works, including his very influential and widely read *Vitae Romanorum Pontificum*, are not reprinted. This restricted them largely to Barnes's major work, his *Supplication*, which, however, they printed with considerable care, as well as desultory extracts from a number of his other writings.[58]

Obviously there was a long-standing personal commitment on the part of both Day and Foxe to reprinting the works of these great Henrician reformers. This personal commitment may explain another oddity about the volume: why print a collection of the writings of Tyndale, Frith and Barnes at all? All three figures had in their favour the obvious fact that they were martyrs and that they were also the three most important of the clerical martyrs of the Henrician Reformation. Nevertheless, there were significant problems with printing their writings. For one thing, the theological currents of Protestantism had moved swiftly and had left all three figures, particularly Tyndale and Barnes, aground. The central point of the theology of all three men, the doctrine of justification by faith, was, by the middle of Elizabeth's reign, almost automatically accepted by English Protestants of all persuasions. The focal point of theological disputation had shifted to other areas, leaving these three writers theologically obsolete.[59] The problem

---

[55] Foxe, *Whole workes*, sig. A3ʳ.

[56] William Tyndale, *The souper of the Lorde* (Antwerp? 1533), STC 24468. Neither did Foxe include *The examinacion of master William Thorpe* (Antwerp, 1530), STC 24045, which he attributed to William Tyndale, although there is some doubt about this attribution today.

[57] Foxe and Day did not print *A christian sentence and true judgement of the sacrament . . .* (London, 1548?), STC 5190. Modern scholars believe that this work was by Frith but it is unlikely that Foxe and Day knew this. Neither did they print Frith's translation of Martin Luther's *De Antichristo* or his translation of Patrick Hamilton's *Loci communes*.

[58] Foxe painstakingly collated both the 1531 (STC 1470) and 1534 (STC 1471) editions of Barnes's *Supplication*. (The editions varied widely, largely on account of the different political and religious circumstances in which they were written.) Foxe and an enigmatic 'T. G.' drew on whatever suited them from both editions and failed to acknowledge when they were moving between editions. For a discussion of Foxe's editing of Barnes's works see Clebsch, *England's Earliest Protestants*, pp. 58–9.

[59] See Basil Hall, 'The Early Rise and Gradual Decline of Lutheranism in England, 1520–1660', in *Reform and Reformation: England and the Continent c. 1500–c. 1750*, ed. Derek Baker, Studies in Church History: Subsidia II (Oxford, 1979), pp. 576–95; Alec Ryrie, 'The Strange Death of Lutheran England', *Journal of Ecclesiastical History*, 53 (2002), pp. 64–92; Carl Trueman, *Luther's Legacy: Salvation and English Reformers, 1525–1556* (Oxford, 1994), pp. 15–16, 72–4, 83–120, 156–98 and 200.

was exacerbated by the conservative theology of Tyndale and Barnes on the Eucharist in particular. In the *Acts and Monuments* Foxe was repeatedly embarrassed by Barnes's prominent role in persecuting sacramentarians.[60] In the *Whole workes* he repeatedly felt obliged to modify or qualify Tyndale's statements of Eucharistic theology.[61] Even Frith, who died for his relatively advanced sacramental theology, had comments that troubled Foxe.[62]

Even in the area of his greatest renown, biblical translation, Tyndale had become increasingly irrelevant by the end of the sixteenth century. In the bitter disputes surrounding the printing of the Rheims New Testament in 1582, Tyndale's name was almost unmentioned. In Patrick Collinson's words, 'Tyndale's older, paler star had been eclipsed by the newer, fiery lights of Theodore Beza, the Geneva Bible and William Whittaker.'[63] Half a century after the printing of the *Whole workes*, Thomas Goad, in a collection of works by, or attributed to, Frith, conceded that, while his writings were popular in the days of Henry VIII, 'in calmer times they seemed to have slept in oblivion'.[64]

Yet to everything there is a season and, paradoxically, the fact that the writings of the Henrician reformers were old-fashioned made them in some ways particularly relevant to the circumstances of the 1570s. (It should not, however, be forgotten that, occasionally, there were also passages, such as Tyndale's defence of the validity of the marriage of Catherine of Aragon, that could not have been more inappropriate and that Foxe had to quietly excise or modify.[65]) An important aspect of this was the fact that the writings of these three theologians were directed against Catholic doctrine

[60] *1570*, pp. 1283–4 and 1382.

[61] For example, where Tyndale declared that the term 'sacrifice' was merely used of the Eucharist because it was a memorial of Christ's sacrifice Foxe added a marginal note expanding Tyndale's meaning: 'The supper of the Lord is geven us to be a memorial of his death once offered for all' (Foxe, *Whole workes*, p. 323). Foxe also changed Tyndale's marginal note, 'the sacrament of the altere and how it must be receayved', to 'the Sacrament of the body and bloud of Christ how it must be received'. Cf. William Tyndale, *An Answere unto Sir Thomas Mores dialoge* (Antwerp, 1531), STC 24437, sig. N6ʳ with Foxe, *Whole workes*, p. 316.

[62] For example, when Frith said that the Mass represented the crucifixion, Foxe cautioned in a marginal note, 'Frith writeth of the Masse according to the common opinion that was at that time' (Foxe, *Whole workes*, p. 128). For the influence of Oecolampadius and the Swiss reformers on Frith's sacramental theology see Trueman, *Luther's Legacy*, pp. 150–5 and Clebsch, *England's Earliest Protestants*, pp. 122–7.

[63] Patrick Collinson, 'William Tyndale and the Course of the English Reformation', *Reformation*, 1 (1996), pp. 75–6.

[64] John Frith, *Vox Piscis* (London, 1627), STC 11395, p. 21.

[65] Cf. William Tyndale, *The practyse of Prelates* (Antwerp, 1530), STC 24465, sigs. H4ᵛ–K1ᵛ with Foxe, *Whole workes*, pp. 372–3. In fact, Foxe felt constrained to change the title of Tyndale's work to *The Practice of Papistical Prelates*, lest it be read as an attack on episcopacy as a whole.

on basic fundamental issues. Elizabethan theological writing might have moved away from attacks on Purgatory and the defence of justification by faith but these issues had been of primary importance to the Henrician theologians. The reprinting of the visceral, anti-Catholic writings of these authors made the collected works of Tyndale, Frith and Barnes one of the last substantial anti-Catholic works to come from Day's presses.[66] At the same time, the arguments of the three against Catholic teachings made the work a useful part of Foxe's ongoing efforts to convert those who still followed them.

In particular, Tyndale, Frith and Barnes had jousted with the greatest English Catholic polemicists of their era: John Fisher, John Rastell and Thomas More. The works of these Catholic authors were still a matter of concern to Foxe and other Elizabethan divines. In the *Acts and Monuments* Foxe lamented that More's 'bookes be not yet dead but remaine alyve to the hurt of many'.[67] Printing the controversial works of Tyndale, Frith and Barnes gave Foxe the opportunity to take two swipes at the Elizabethan Catholics. The first was through the texts of Tyndale, Frith and Barnes themselves, the second was through Foxe's marginal notes, which kept up a steady chorus of derision or praise of particular authors. For example, Frith's second response to John Rastell is enriched by such marginal notes as 'an apt and good example', 'Note here the modesty of John Frith', 'Frith the faithful servant and true martyr of Christ' and 'Note well this worthy and learned argument'.[68] In the same work Rastell is treated to a series of catcalls and jeers: 'Rastell showeth himself to be very ignorant', 'Rastell is a bitter taunter', 'Rastelles blind argument', and 'Rastel falsifieth scripture'.[69] But it is More who is the particular target of Foxe's invective. He is denounced in the following terms: 'More a lying papist', 'M. More is a lyer', 'Tyndall doth here playnly prove More an heretic', 'More blasphemeth God', 'More is maliciously blind', 'M. More is confused in the interpretation of Scriptures' and 'More purposely corrupteth the sence of the scripture'.[70]

---

[66] Day's anti-Catholic stance can be seen later still in his production of an edition of writings by Thomas Cranmer: *An aunsvvere by the Reuerend Father in God Thomas Archbyshop of Canterbury, primate of all England and metropolitane, vnto a craftie and sophisticall cauillation, deuised by Stephen Gardiner Doctour of Law, late Byshop of Winchester agaynst the true and godly doctrine of the most holy sacrament, of the body and bloud of our sauiour Iesu Christ Wherein is also, as occasion serueth, aunswered such places of the booke of Doct. Richard Smith, as may seeme any thyng worthy the aunsweryng. Here is also the true copy of the booke written, and in open court deliuered, by D. Stephen Gardiner* ... (London, 1580) STC 5992.

[67] *1570*, p. 1147.   [68] Foxe, *Whole workes*, pp. 63, 65, and 71.   [69] Ibid., pp. 65, 67, 70, and 71.

[70] Ibid. (under Tyndale), pp. 294, 309, 316, 328, 337, and (under Frith), pp. 41 and 42.

The *Regnans in excelsis* seems to have been a particular motivation behind the production of these works. Tyndale, Frith and Barnes had devoted much of their writing to attacking papal claims to primacy over Church and state; this was particularly true of Tyndale's *Practice of Prelates* and his *Obedience of a Christian Man*, and Barnes's *Supplication*. (Interestingly, at the beginning of Mary's reign, John Bale seems to have considered producing an annotated version of Tyndale's *Practice of Prelates* as part of an attack on Mary's renunciation of the Royal Supremacy.[71]) Among the marginal notes Foxe added to the text of Barnes's *Supplication* were the following, which were suddenly extremely topical in the aftermath of the papal bull: 'Popes take upon them the deposition of kings', 'we ought not to depose a king though he be wicked' and 'The Pope will dispence with the othe of obedience that subjectes make to their prince'.[72]

The importance of the papal deposition can be seen even in the selection of materials included in the *Whole workes*. As a rule, Foxe and Day confined themselves to reprinting the English-language works of these authors and did not reprint their Latin compositions. However, extracts from Barnes's *Sententiae ex doctoribus collectae* were translated and included in the *Whole workes*. Almost certainly a fundamental reason for this decision was that one of the four sections of the *Sententiae* was devoted to Barnes's attack on the validity of papal excommunication.[73] Similarly, the only one of Frith's numerous translations that was reprinted in the *Whole workes* was his translation of Melanchthon's *Passional Christi und Antichristi*, a work which contrasted the papal Antichrist with the Apostles and castigated the papacy for its worldly ambition and its pretensions to authority over secular rulers.[74]

But there was more to Foxe's interest in reprinting Tyndale, Frith and Barnes than a need to draft additional authors into the conflict against Pius V. For one thing, Foxe, as he was in the *Acts and Monuments*, was very concerned with using martyrs as models for emulation. In the preface to the *Whole workes* Foxe enjoined his readers,

---

[71] At the end of a translation of Stephen Gardiner's *De vera obedientia*, printed in 1553, the anonymous translator (who may very well have been John Bale), urged his readers to pray that England be not brought back into the papal bondage. The translator further promised: 'loke shortly to have from me the practises of prelates compyled by Willyam Tyndale the true martyr of God to the augmentacions of Joan Bale'. Stephen Gardiner, *De vera obedientia* (Wesel, 1553), STC 11587, sig. H4ʳ.

[72] Foxe, *Whole workes*, pp. 186, 187 and 188.   [73] See ibid., pp. 358–76.

[74] See ibid. (Frith section), pp. 97–106. The relevance of this work to Foxe and Day's concern to respond to the papal bull can be seen in the fact that, as Ingram and Aston have observed, Lucas Cranach's woodcut illustrations from Melanchthon's work provided an inspiration for the 'Proud Primacie of Popes' section of the *Acts and Monuments* (Ingram and Aston, 'Iconography', pp. 120–5).

Briefly, whatsoever thou art, if thou be yonge, of John Frith, if thou be in middle age of W. Tyndall, if in elder years of D. Barnes, matter is here to be founde, not onely of doctrine to enform thee, of comfort to delyte thee, of godly ensample to directe thee.[75]

It is worth observing that Foxe is rather stretching the facts in order to make the three martyrs serve as examples for three separate age groups. Frith, who was around thirty years old when he was executed, could stand as a representative for youth, but Tyndale was about forty-two when he was executed and Barnes was about forty-five when he died.

The lives of all three men were taken from the accounts of them in the *Acts and Monuments*. However, in the life of Tyndale, material was added about his daily life while in Antwerp. According to Foxe, Tyndale devoted Mondays and Saturdays of each week to wandering around Antwerp distributing alms to the poor. On Sundays he gave Scripture readings to the English merchants and the remainder of the week he devoted to study.[76] David Daniell has questioned the accuracy of this story, pointing out that Tyndale was a fugitive at the time, and would hardly have been roaming about the streets of Antwerp. (In fact Tyndale was arrested the moment that he was tricked into leaving his safe haven in the house of the Merchant Adventurers in Antwerp.)[77] Whether he invented these details or uncritically printed somone's report about Tyndale, Foxe was certainly trying to use Tyndale as a model for how clergy should live their daily lives.

Yet as Foxe had stated when recommending the *Whole workes* to the reader, among the many reasons for reading the book were not only the theological lessons and moral examples they provided, but also the pastoral comfort that the works of these three authors gave the reader. This concern had already been signposted in the *Sermon of Christ crucified* and it lay at the heart of Foxe's next big project: his series of translations of Luther's works. It was also a major part of the attraction of reprinting the works of Tyndale, Frith and Barnes. As Patrick Collinson has shrewdly suggested: 'Foxe intended his editions both of Tyndale–Frith–Barnes and of Luther to serve as a kind of prophylactic against the harmful pastoral effects of the determinism all too easily read into Calvinist soteriology'.[78]

The marginal notes Foxe included next to the texts of Tyndale, Frith and Barnes unmistakably signpost his belief that these works could be used for the benefit of afflicted consciences, including such marginal notes as 'A godly comfort agaynst desperation', 'Let no man despayre but put his hope

---

[75] Foxe, *Whole workes*, sig. A2ᵛ.   [76] Ibid., sig. B3ʳ.
[77] David Daniell, 'Tyndale and Foxe', p. 23.   [78] Collinson, 'Tyndale', p. 74.

in Christ and he shalbe safe', 'Faith is ever assailed by desperation', 'The faythfull though they slip yet they fall not', 'Mercy waiteth ever on the elect' and 'To be in God is to beleve in the mercy of God'.[79] Evidence from the title pages of the *Whole workes* indicates that the book was completed in March 1573.[80]

v

The *Whole workes* was the last collaboration between Foxe and Day for three years. There is no sign of a falling out between author and printer; relations remained apparently amicable between them. During the years 1573–6 Day appears to have gone about his usual business, returning to an assured, steady income after years of major projects undertaken at the behest of others. In a manner of speaking, Foxe also returned to what is considered his usual business – that of being a prominent London preacher and spiritual physician to those suffering from troubled consciences.[81] During the next few years Foxe channelled this pastoral commitment into a project that would be one of his most enduring contributions to English religious life: a remarkable series of translations of various writings by Martin Luther, supervised under Foxe's auspices, and edited by his friends and colleagues.

The first and most important of these was an English translation of Luther's commentary on Galatians.[82] In a short foreword to the work, dated 28 April 1575, Edwyn Sandys, the bishop of London, described the genesis of the English version of the commentary:

Which being written in the Latine tongue, certaine godly learned men have most sincerely translated into our language ... Some beganne it according to such skill as they had. Others godly affected, not suffering so good a matter, in handling to be marred, put to their helping hands for the better framing and furthering of so worthy a worke. They refuse to be named, seeking neither their owne gaine or glory, but thinking it their happiness, if by any meanes they may releve afflicted mindes, and doe good to the church of Christ, yealding all glory unto God, to whom all glory is due.[83]

Who were these translators whom Sandys refused to name? A number of scholars have maintained that Foxe was the author of a long introduction to the work, which followed Sandys' foreword, and that Foxe was responsible

<hr>

[79] Foxe, *Whole workes*, (Tyndale section) pp. 4, 91, 259, 260 and 403.
[80] Numerous surviving copies have the title page corrected to 1573 by hand.
[81] For a discussion of these activities, and of Foxe's contemporary fame as a spiritual physician, see Freeman, 'Through a Venice Glass Darkly', pp. 307–20.
[82] Martin Luther, *A Commentarie Vpon the Epistle to the Galathians* (London, 1575), STC 16965.
[83] Ibid., sig. *2ʳ.

for 'the better framing' of the translation.[84] Their arguments are very persuasive, particularly in the light of Foxe's involvement with other translations. The identity of the initial translator has remained more elusive. However, two inscriptions in copies of the first edition of the commentary on Galatians shed some light on this translator's identity. A copy in the Folger Shakespeare Library has an inscription that is somewhat difficult to decipher, since it is at the top of a title page that has been cropped. It appears to read, however, 'To Pawle Swallowe John Field ... a token of his good wyll'.[85] Fortunately the second inscription, also on the title page of the work, which appears in a copy in Cambridge University Library, is much more legible: 'To the right honourable and my very good Ladye, the Countess of Warwicke, Jo: Feilde, her most humble and faythful servaunte giveth this booke, as a token of his humble dewtye and hertie good will towards yo[ur] hono[ur]'.[86] The two inscriptions can only plausibly be explained by John Field having been one of the translators of this work. One inscription could simply mean that the book was a gift, but two inscriptions – and one of them to a valued patron – can only indicate that Field had some role in composing the work. A look at John Field's career at this point in his life supports the idea that he was the initial unnamed translator whose work had to be revised to make it acceptable to Bishop Sandys.

John Field is, of course, as notorious to historians of the period as he was to his contemporaries as the great propagandist for nascent Presbyterianism. In 1572 Field and his fellow Presbyterian, Thomas Wilcox, were imprisoned for their *Admonition to Parliament*, an incendiary attack on the bishops and on the faltering progress of the reformation of the Church in England.[87] However, Field's relationship with Foxe went back for a number of years before he walked into the limelight and then into Newgate. On 26 January 1567, John

---

[84] See William A. Clebsch, 'The Elizabethans on Luther', in *Interpreters of Luther: Essays in Honor of Wilhelm Pauck*, ed. Jaroslav Pelikan (Philadelphia, PA, 1968), pp. 111–12; G. R. Elton, 'Luther in England', in *Studies in Tudor and Stuart Politics and Government*, 4 vols. (Cambridge, 1974–92), IV, p. 236. Patrick Collinson maintains that the introduction indicates 'Foxe's prime responsibility' for this edition. Patrick Collinson, 'England and International Calvinism, 1558–1640', in *International Calvinism, 1541–1715*, ed. Menna Prestwich (Oxford, 1985), p. 215, n. 56.

[85] Shelfmark STC 16965 (copy 1). For a time, John Field had been a curate at St Giles Cripplegate and we know that in 1569–71 he lived in the parish. Collinson, 'John Field and Elizabethan Puritanism', in *Godly People*, p. 338. The parish registers for St Giles Cripplegate indicate that the son of a 'Paul Swallow, goldsmith' died in the parish in August 1584. We are grateful to Alan H. Nelson for supplying us with this latter information from his database of the St Giles Cripplegate parish records.

[86] Shelfmark SSS.22.17. We would like to acknowledge that it was Richard Duerden who pointed out the existence of these two inscriptions in a paper read at the Tyndale Society conference in Antwerp in 2002.

[87] Patrick Collinson, 'John Field and Elizabethan Puritanism', pp. 339–47.

Field wrote to Foxe from Broadgates Hall, Oxford. The letter makes it clear that Field was acting as a liaison between Foxe and Laurence Humphrey and that he was assisting in having sections of the forthcoming second edition of the *Acts and Monuments* examined by students at Magdalen.[88] By September 1569 Field was clearly assisting Foxe in gathering material for the *Acts and Monuments* and was living in St Giles Cripplegate, Foxe's parish.[89] By 1570 Field was a curate at St Giles Cripplegate and by November 1571 he was living in Grub Street, with Foxe as a near neighbour.[90] After Field's arrest, Foxe was one of his many visitors in Newgate prison.[91] Field was eventually released, thanks to the influence of two powerful patrons who had also supported Foxe: the earls of Leicester and Warwick. Between the autumn of 1573 and July 1575 Field's movements and activities remain mysterious. Patrick Collinson has suggested that he may have travelled to Heidelberg and supervised the printing of some 'manifestos of English presbyterianism'.[92] When Field next reappears in England it is in the company of John Foxe, attending the burning of two Anabaptists in July 1575.[93] Presumably Field was back in London some time before this date and working on the commentary to Galatians, which was printed around the end of April 1575.[94]

Considering this background, it seems likely that Field was the initial translator. It is hardly surprising that his translation might have contained passages, probably of an anti-espiscopalian nature, that alarmed Bishop Sandys. At this time, Sandys turned to Foxe (who had very probably obtained Sandys' tentative approval of the project in the first place) and possibly to others to revise the work and make it more acceptable. Although he would remain anonymous, Field had quite a bit to gain from his labours, apart from its strictly spiritual benefits. It was almost certainly part of a process, later continued in Field's anti-Catholic writings, of his rehabilitating himself in the eyes of his more moderate supporters, as well as of the authorities.[95] The question arises, was the commentary on Galatians Field's idea or did Foxe

---

[88] BL, Harley MS 416, fo. 185[r].   [89] Ibid., fo. 188[r-v].   [90] Collinson, 'John Field', p. 338.
[91] Inner Temple Library, Petyt MS 538/47, fo. 481[r].   [92] Collinson, 'John Field', p. 347.
[93] *The Seconde Parte of a Register*, ed. Albert Peel, 2 vols. (Cambridge, 1915), 1, p. 105.
[94] Field and Foxe apparently continued to move in the same circles after this. In 1579 Field preached at a wedding and – for reasons too complicated to cover here – Bishop John Aylmer of London took disciplinary action against him. Foxe, who was present at the wedding, sent letters to Aylmer defending Field. Dr Williams's Library, *Seconde Parte of a Register* [MS], 11, fos. 96[r]–7[r].
[95] In fact, the inscriptions in the books seem to indicate that this is exactly what Field was trying to accomplish. They are making his involvement in this highly respectable and worthy enterprise known to people whose views mattered. The value of the good opinion of the countess of Warwick goes without saying, but if the other book was dedicated to Paul Swallow, a goldsmith of St Giles Cripplegate, he may not have been just a friend but also a financial supporter in the lean years when Field was without benefice.

suggest it to him? Since it is the first of a series of translations from Luther, sponsored and directed by Foxe, it seems reasonable to suppose that the idea originated with Foxe. However, it is, of course, possible that it was Field's idea and that Foxe developed it into a larger and more ambitious project. What is safe to say is that it was Foxe who secured Sandys' support and also his imprimatur, which was extremely helpful in extinguishing the fears that many important people would have had because of Field's involvement.

What then were Foxe's goals in the project? The major reason why several scholars have been confident in attributing the anonymous introduction to Foxe, and in thus deducing his role in the commentary, has been the extent to which passages in the introduction are closely paralleled in other writings by Foxe. It is worth noting the close resemblance in two passages, the first from the second edition of the *Acts and Monuments*, the other from the introduction to the commentary on Galatians:

[Pope Leo X] sent a Jubilee with his pardons abroad through all Chrisen realms and dominions: whereby he gathered together innumerable riches and treasure. The gatherers and collectors whereof perswaded the people, that who so ever would geve x shyllynges, should at his pleasure, deliver one soule from the paynes of Purgatorie ... But if it were one less than x shyllynges, they preached that it would profit them nothing.[96]

Pope Leo the X sent a Jubiley with his pardons abroade through all Christian realms and dominions, wherby he gathered together immense riches and treasure. The collectours whereof promised to every one that would put ten shillings in the box, license to eat whitemeat and flesh in lent, and power to deliver what soule he woulde out of purgatorye, and moreover full pardon from all his sinnes were they never so heinous. But if it were one iote less then x shillings, they preached that it would profite him nothing.[97]

Again, note the similarity between the following two passages:

But hereof sufficient touchyng this division betweene the Lutherians and the Zwinglians. In which division, if there have bene any defaut in M. Luther, yet is that no cause why either the Papistes may greatly triumph or why the Protestantes should despise Luther. For neither is the doctrine of Luther touchyng the Sacrament so grosse that it maketh much with the Papistes: nor yet so discreet that he ought to be exploded.[98]

And yet in the same matter of the sacrament, not withstanding that he [Luther] altereth somewhat from Zwinglius, stick to[o] nere to the letter: yet he joyneth not so with the Papist, that he leaveth there any transubstantiation or idolatie.[99]

---

[96] *1570*, p. 970. [97] Luther, *A Commentarie Vpon the Epistle*, sig. *5ʳ. [98] *1570*, p. 993.
[99] Luther, *A Commentarie Vpon the Epistle*, sig. *5ʳ.

The resemblance even extends to works written at the very beginning of Foxe's career. In the dedication to a translation he made of a sermon of Luther's, Foxe wrote of the great reformer: 'I wyll not say this author in all poynts to stand up right and absolutely, as in the sacraments, but what humane wryter hath there ever bene but some defaute he hath left behynd hym ... In every thyng the best is to be taken.'[100]

In the introduction to the commentary on Galatians we see very similar sentiments:

And though his [Luther's] doctrine as touching a litle circumstance of the sacrament can not be thoroughly defended ... [yet] let us not be so nice, for one little wart to cast away the whole body. It were doubtlesse to be wished, that in good teachers and preachers of Christ, there were no defect or imperfection. But he that can abide nothing with his blemish, let him, if he can, name any Doctor or writer (the scripture only except) greke or latin, old or new, either beyond the Alpes or on this side [of] the Alpes, or him selfe also, what so ever he be, which hath not erred in some sentence or in some exposition of holy scripture. But if he cannot so doe, then let him selfe to beare with other, to take the best and leave the worst.[101]

If the introduction to the commentary was not written by Foxe then it was written by somebody who had closely studied Foxe's works and who held almost identical views. And since, as we shall see, there is incontrovertible evidence that Foxe had masterminded subsequent Luther translations, one has to conclude that Foxe was the anonymous author of the introduction.

The last pair of twinned quotations points to Foxe's awareness of the difficulties some of his readers might have with aspects of Luther's theology, particularly with his sacramental theology. But it also reveals why Foxe was willing, indeed eager, to overlook this: the martyrologist's profound admiration for Luther as a great spiritual physician. In the second edition of the *Acts and Monuments* Foxe criticised those who:

For a little stoupyng of Luther in the Sacrament, therefore they geve cleane over the readyng of Luther, and fall almost in utter contempt of his bookes. Wherby is declared the nicenes and curiousness of these our dayes, as the hinderance that commeth therby to the Church, is greatly to be lamented. For albeit the Church of Christ (praysed be the Lord) is not unprovided of sufficient plenty of worthie and learned writers, able to instruct in matters of doctrine, yet in the chief pointes of our consolation, where the glory of Christ, and the power of his passion and strength of faith is to be opened to our conscience, and where the soule wrastelyng for death and lyfe, standeth in need of serious consolation, the same may be sayd of

[100] Luther, *A frutfull sermon of the moost evangelicall wryter M. Luther*, sig. A2ᵛ.
[101] Luther, *A Commentarie Vpon the Epistle on Galatians*, sig. *5ʳ.

M. Luther, amongst all this other varitie of writers, that S. Cyprian was wont to say of Tertullian: *Da magistrum* geve me the master.[102]

Foxe's motive in presenting the commentary on Galatians was part of his overriding preoccupation in the last decades of his life: his ministry to afflicted consciences. In fact the introduction to the commentary was addressed 'To all afflicted consciences which grone for salvation and wrestle under the crosse for the kingdome of Christ, grace, peace and victorie in the Lorde Jesu our Saviour.'[103] (It is worth noting the resemblance of this heading to the declaration on the title page of the *Sermon of Christ crucified*: 'Written and dedicated to all such as labour, and be heavy laden in conscience, to be read for their spirituall comfort.')

The same desire to salve wounded consciences lay behind the other Luther translations supported by Foxe. In his preface to a translation by Henry Bull of Luther's commentary on the 'psalms of ascent', Foxe discerned two points of value in the translation. In the first place it should be read for 'spirituall consolation to such weake minds as in cases of conscience are distressed and wrastle in faith against the terrour of Satan, of death, of damnation, against the power of the lawe and wrath of God'. In the second place it should be read for Luther's discussion of the difference between the law and the Gospel.[104] In his foreword commending William Gace's translation of a selection of Luther's sermons to the 'Christian reader', Foxe extolled the value of the collection and rhetorically asked: 'For what more worthie matter can be then to set forth Christ in his right glorie, in his full riches and royall estate to the hears and soules of men, especially such as are heavie laden and distressed in spirit?'[105] Foxe's otherwise puzzling desire to remain anonymous in his introduction to the commentary on Galatians can probably be explained by his desire that these works become as widely read as possible. He may well have been worried, on account of his fame as the author of the *Acts and Monuments*, that he had become something of a divisive figure and that his name might alienate readers with Catholic sympathies.

---

[102] *1570*, p. 992.   [103] Luther, *A Commentarie Vpon the Epistle*, sig. *3ʳ.

[104] Martin Luther, *A commentarie upon the fiftene psalmes*, trans. Henry Bull (London, 1577) STC 16975, sigs. *2ᵛ–3ʳ. Foxe went on to observe that Luther treated these subjects in the present work just as he had done 'in his former treatise before set forth upon the Epistle to the Galathians' (sig. *3ʳ). The relationship between the law and the Gospel was, as we have seen, another preoccupation of Foxe's writings during this period, especially the *Sermon of Christ crucified* (in both its English and Latin versions) and the *Whole workes of W. Tyndale, John Frith and Doct. Barnes*. It would also be a theme in Foxe's sermon on *De oliva evangelica* in both of its versions (see below, p. 279).

[105] Martin Luther, *Special and chosen sermons*, trans. William Gace (London, 1578), STC 16993, sig. *7ʳ.

In any case, Foxe's desire for a wide readership of the commentary on Galatians was soon abundantly realised. The translation of Luther's commentary went through five editions between 1575 and 1588.[106] There were a further three editions up to 1635,[107] and another in 1644.[108] The work became a puritan classic. John Bunyan declared 'I do prefer this Book of Mr Luther upon the Galathians, (excepting the Holy Bible) before all the Books that I have ever seen, as most fit for a wounded conscience.'[109]

Apart from the ever-popular translation of the commentary on Galatians, there were definitely two other works, and possibly a third, that can be attributed to Foxe's programme of Luther translations. In an undated draft of a letter to an unnamed bishop (almost certainly Sandys), Foxe wrote that Henry Bull had just written an English translation of Luther's commentary on the fifteen psalms, work that Foxe recommended as being of great use to the Church. He also urged the bishop's approval of its production.[110] Bull died some time during the first half of 1577 and it was very probably Foxe who shepherded the work through the press. He certainly added an address to the reader, assuring them that their labour in reading it 'shall be recompensed with no less spiritual consolation to thy soules health than the godly translator thereof M. Bull did receave in translating of the same'.[111]

The other translation of Luther's writings that can be tied to Foxe is William Gace's translation of a selection of Luther's sermons. William Gace had been the corrector of the second edition of the *Acts and Monuments*.[112] In the dedication to the collection, Gace described how he was 'first procured' to translating the sermons 'by a learned Father of this lande, whose wordes and judgement I make no small account of'.[113] Since Foxe was not only an associate of William Gace's, but the work contains an admonition to the reader by the martyrologist, it can safely be assumed that Foxe was the 'learned Father' Gace described.[114] In his address to the reader Foxe implicitly linked this work to the other recent translations by contentedly observing that a great many of Luther's works had already been 'set abroad'.[115] Gace was also the translator of another collection of Luther's

[106] STC 16965–9. [107] STC 16970, 156973 and 16974. [108] STC Wing L 3510B.

[109] John Bunyan, *Grace Abounding with Other Spiritual Autobiographies*, ed. John Stachniewski with Anita Pacheco (Oxford, 1998), p. 38.

[110] BL, Harley MS 417, fo. 130ᵛ. [111] Luther, *Commentarie on the fiftene psalms*, sig. *3ᵛ.

[112] TNA, C 24/180, dep. 2. [113] Luther, *Special and chosen sermons*, trans. sig. *4ᵛ.

[114] Foxe's address to the reader is on sigs. *7ʳ–8ʳ. It is also worth observing that Gace's work was dedicated to a major patron of Foxe, in the martyrologist's later years, Sir Thomas Heneage. On Heneage and Foxe see below, p. 297.

[115] *1570*, sig.*7ʳ.

writings.[116] This work bears no overt sign of Foxe's involvement; however, like the other works, it was printed by Thomas Vautrollier, and like the others it was concerned with pastoral care for afflicted consciences. If it was not directly supervised by Foxe, it was certainly inspired by the other Luther translations.

All of these translations seem to have met a real need. Whatever reservations Elizabethan readers may have had regarding Luther's theology, his writings as a spiritual physician enjoyed real popularity. None of the other Luther translations sponsored by Foxe enjoyed the enduring popularity of the commentary on Galatians. However, they all achieved a certain success. Henry Bull's translation of the psalms went through two editions in 1577, a third in 1615 and a fourth in 1637.[117] The *Treatise containing fourteene pointes* went through three editions in 1578, 1579 and 1580, while Gace's translation of Luther's sermons went through two editions in 1579 and 1581.[118] All of the Luther translations initiated by Foxe were printed by Thomas Vautrollier. This may point to Cecil's at least tacit cooperation in these translations, since Vautrollier was another printer favoured by Cecil. But this raises the question, why did Day not print these editions?

The period when the initial translations commenced, around the year 1575, was when Day seems to have been consolidating his business and focusing on the steady sellers that would make him money. It may be that there were further distractions, either in Day's personal life or in his business life, that we do not know of, which made him hesitant about committing his resources to large-scale projects without the certainty of any return. As the Luther translations progressed into the years 1577–8, Day was certainly preoccupied in protecting his steady sellers from pirates.[119]

By the middle of the 1570s, it would appear that the interests of Foxe and Day were moving them away from their successful working relationship. It is true that Foxe had promised readers of the *Acts and Monuments* a history of:

---

[116] Martin Luther, *A right comfortable treatise containing fourteene pointes of consolation* ... (London, 1578), STC 16989.

[117] STC 16975, 16975.5, 16976 and 16977.

[118] STC 16989, 16990 and 16991; STC 16993 and 16994 respectively. In comparison, of the eight other translations of Luther from Elizabeth's reign to the Civil War, only three went through more than one edition: *A methodicall preface prefixed before the epistle to the Romanes* went through two editions, one before 1594, the other in 1632 (STC 16985 and 16986); *A treatise, touching the libertie of a Christian* went through two editions in 1579 and a third in 1636 (STC 16995, 16996 and 16997), as well as Thomas Becon's translation, *A very comfortable, and necessary sermon, concerning the comming of Christ* (STC 16997.5 and 16998).

[119] See *PPP*, chapter 7.

the yeare and reigne of the Queene that now is, where we have more conveniently to inferre not onely of these matters of the Martyrs ... but also of the whole Inquisition of Spayne and Plackard of Flaunders, with the tragicall tumults and troubles happening within the last memorie of these our latter dayes.[120]

Presumably this ambitious enterprise would have been undertaken with Day, and in fact both Foxe and Day seem to have stubbornly clung to this dream. At the conclusion of both the 1576 and the 1583 editions, Foxe promised his readers a history of all that 'within [the] sayd compass of this Queenes reigne hitherto hath hapned in Scotland, Flaunders, France, Spayne, Germany, besides this our own countrey of England and Ireland ... as it shall please the Lord to geve grace and space'.[121] In fact the Lord provided neither. There are not many indications that Foxe got seriously to work on this project, although he may have begun gathering some material for it. Instead, his energies seem to have been taken up more and more with his pastoral activities – which included the Luther translations. If events had continued on this course, Foxe and Day would probably have moved into separate spheres of activity, with the second edition of the *Acts and Monuments*, their greatest collaborative achievement, and the *Whole Workes of Tyndale, Frith and Barnes*, their last.

VI

By 1576 the careers of Foxe and Day, so long intertwined, had seemingly diverged. From its beginnings in Edward VI's reign, the great martyrological project which bound Foxe and Day together had been rather like the universe as we now understand it: it was expanding from the moment it was born. From the completion of almost every phase, a new stage was envisioned by its creators. This had changed with the printing of the 1570 edition. It now seemed that the great project had reached its conclusion and that the subsequent careers of Foxe and Day would follow separate trajectories. In April 1575 the greatest of the Luther translations that Foxe was to supervise, *A Commentarie Vpon the Epistle to the Galathians*, had just been printed by Thomas Vautrollier. Foxe had also become increasingly involved with pastoral activities in London. In the meantime, John Day had been busy producing his lucrative steady sellers – the primers and the metrical psalms. It is entirely conceivable that the informal but enduring

[120] *1570*, p. 2259.   [121] *1576*, p. 208; repeated in *1583*, p. 2154.

working partnership of Day and Foxe might never have been revived, except for two random events: a young man falling in love and an old one dying.

In 1576 John Day's eldest son, Richard, returned home to Aldersgate. Richard had been educated at Eton, and had then taken the high road that led from Eton to King's College, Cambridge, where he took his BA in 1572.[122] He had been studying theology with the intention of fulfilling his father's cherished dream of having his son become a clergyman.[123] The importance John Day placed on his son's education is reflected in the printer's generous donations of books to King's College. These donations included a copy of the first edition of the *Acts and Monuments* and an edition of *The Whole workes of W. Tyndale, John Frith and Doct. Barnes*, and this largesse continued to flow until shortly before his son's departure from the college.[124] In fact Richard himself donated manuscripts to the college, which he may have received from his father, in the year of his unexpected departure.[125] If Richard intended to leave permanently, this was not known to his tutors, as his name continues to appear in both the Mundum and Commons books for the college, listing, for example, his absence at meals for several months after his return to London. These records suggest that he was expected back in Cambridge at some point, although such expectations were ultimately unfulfilled.[126]

Richard's return was thus unexpected and unwelcome, and the reasons for it were controversial. In a Chancery suit he brought against his step-mother shortly after John Day's death, Richard claimed that his departure from Cambridge was on account of her desire to rid the family of the expense of financing Richard's education.[127] The great Cambridge biblio-grapher, A. N. L. Munby, accepted the suggestion that it was the machina-tions of the wicked stepmother that brought about the premature conclusion of Richard's scholarly career.[128] However, the story told by Richard in the case he brought against Alice Day contained a great deal of exculpatory embellishment. From the depositions made in Alice's

---

[122] See the entry on Richard Day in the *ODNB*.   [123] See TNA, C 24/181, ints. to deps. 15.

[124] John Day probably donated the *Acts and Monuments* shortly after publication, perhaps with a mind to his son studying there. (Richard matriculated in November 1571: see Venn and Venn, *Alumni Cantabrigienses*). The work is meticulously corrected, with minor printing errors corrected by hand and additional slip cancels not found in other copies. See, for example, sigs. B1r, B5r, Uu7r, XXx5v for hand corrections; sigs. Gg1v and 3G5r for additional slip cancels.

[125] *Augustini et Boethii quaedam, cent. XII–XIII, Opus imperfectum in Matthaeum, Allegoriae Abbreviatae, Gregorii Homilia XL* and *Augustinus De Vita Christiana, cent. XIV–XV*.

[126] King's College Archives, Commons and Mundum Book entries for the years 1576–77, *passim*.

[127] TNA, C 24/180, int. 4; TNA, C 24/181 int. 7.

[128] A. N. L. Munby, 'The Gifts of Elizabethan Printers to the Library of King's College, Cambridge', *The Library*, 5th series, 2 (1947), pp. 224–32, esp. p. 224.

counter-suit (to which Munby did not refer), it is clear that Richard did in fact leave university because of a woman, but that this woman was not Alice Day.[129] Instead, Richard had fallen in love with Ellen Bowles, a young woman who lived near his father's printing house in London.[130] We know nothing of Ellen's family, but it is clear that Richard's hope of marrying her continued long after his return home.[131] However, the relationship was ultimately doomed, as Richard eventually forsook her, choosing to marry another woman, the daughter of a gentleman, in a marriage that was supposed to ensure his financial security.[132]

After (presumably) feasting on the fatted calf, John put the prodigal to work in his printing house. Day had recently lost his chief corrector, William Gace, and workers in John Day's printing house later testified that it had been his intention that Richard should be trained in the post.[133] Under any circumstances Gace would have been hard to replace, but it soon became apparent that Richard was a less than satisfactory substitute.[134] This was neither initially apparent nor was it inevitable. Richard brought real assets to his father's business: few correctors of the period had the formal education that Richard had received and witnesses hostile to Richard would later concede that his abilities as a translator had proven to be of use to his father.[135] Moreover, Richard was not without inherent ability and he sometimes displayed flashes of business acumen.[136] And when he put his mind to it, he was capable of doing first-rate work; for example, when reprinting the *Prayer Book of Elizabeth*, he completely transformed and vastly improved it.[137] However, Richard's work was extremely inconsistent; he was also capable of turning out inferior productions, such as his work on editions of the psalms or his edition of Becon's *The Demaundes of holy scripture*, which appears to have been reprinted directly from volume III of the collected works of Becon.[138] The problem seems to have been that

---

[129] TNA, C 24/181.   [130] Ibid., ints. 6–8.

[131] TNA, C 24/180, deps. to ints. 10–11; TNA, C 24/181, ints. 6–8.

[132] He married Douglas Pope, the daughter of Nicholas Pope. TNA, C 24/180, deps. to ints. 10–11; TNA, C 24/181, deps. to ints. 26–7. See the entry on Richard Day in *ODNB*.

[133] TNA, C 24/180, deps. to int. 4.

[134] See P. Simpson, 'Correctors of the Press', in *Proof-reading in the Sixteenth, Seventeenth and Eighteenth Centuries* (Oxford, 1935), pp. 138–9.

[135] TNA, C 24/180, deps. to int. 6.

[136] Richard, for example, clearly saw the potential for the bookshop acquired by his father in St Paul's Churchyard. See below, p. 292.

[137] Richard may also have been responsible for introducing the modern distinctions between the letters 'i' and 'j' and 'u' and 'v' into books printed in his father's shop. John Day was the first English printer to differentiate between these letters and he began doing so while his son worked for him as corrector (Oastler, *John Day*, p. 17).

[138] STC 1718. See *PPP*, p. 182.

Richard's heart was not in his work and his ambitions soared far beyond his subordinate role in his father's shop.

In any case, Richard's employment as a corrector was something of a temporary expedient, designed to teach him the basics of his father's trade and to keep him engaged in useful employment until a more permanent niche could be arranged in John Day's business. The decision to print a new edition of the *Acts and Monuments* was probably a second step in this process. The work would be printed under John Day's patent, and undoubtedly it was his decision to print this third edition, but all the evidence points to Richard overseeing the actual production of the work, and it is doubtful that this third edition would have been printed at all if it did not provide a useful baptism of fire for John Day's son. Entrusting Richard with the job of printing the *Acts and Monuments*, a complex and challenging task that had strained John Day's resources and abilities, would give Richard a mighty task to undertake. It would not only provide Richard with comprehensive experience of all aspects of the business, from the initial planning and the acquisition of supplies, particularly paper, to organising the sale of the work, it would also supply John with an opportunity to see if his eldest son was capable of succeeding him in the family business.

That this was indeed John Day's intention is suggested by his unusual failure to take an active role in the production of the book. This work was almost entirely shaped in both its physical layout and in the revisions made to its contents by the son rather than the father, and it was unquestionably Richard Day who directly supervised the entire production of this edition.[139] Furthermore, this decision seems to have been made suddenly. For one thing, whereas with both the first and the second editions Day had been careful to advertise their appearance in works of related interest, no such announcement appeared for this work.[140] Indeed, there does not appear to have been much time for any sort of preparation. Most importantly, Foxe himself seems to have had little notification of Day's plans for a new edition, and its printing would come at a time when he was engaged on other important projects.

---

[139] John King maintains that it 'is inappropriate to assign responsibility for this edition wholly to Richard Day, who assumed a degree of oversight for the printing of this book and some others when he worked in his father's printing house after his return from Cambridge University' (King, *Print Culure*, p. 123). We feel that close examination of the 1576 edition, as well as the documents generated in later law suits involving Richard, indicate that it was Richard who was in charge of the edition (see below, pp. 268–74).

[140] See above, pp. 100 and 184–5, for these announcements.

VII

The second random event that reunited Foxe and Day was the death of the eminent Latinist Walter Haddon in 1572. For nearly a decade Haddon had been involved in a running controversy with the distinguished Portuguese scholar Jerónimo Osório da Fonseca, bishop of Silva, who had an international reputation as a Latin stylist. The controversy began in 1563 when Osório sent Queen Elizabeth an open letter, written in extremely elegant Latin, exhorting her to restore the true Catholic religion in England.[141] Manuscript copies of Osório's letter to the queen circulated freely among the English elites and, worse yet, at least from the viewpoint of the English authorities, it was printed that same year in three major continental printing centres: Louvain, Venice and Paris. In Paris in particular, where the work appeared in both Latin and the vernacular, it enjoyed great popularity, and the entire edition (500 copies) of the Latin edition sold out.[142]

William Cecil, the Maecenas of Elizabethan propaganda, wasted no time in responding to this challenge and turned to an old client, Walter Haddon, to rebut Osório in similarly elaborate and polished Latin. After Cecil put pressure on the French government, Haddon's reply was published in Paris, where Osório's work had been so popular, in 1563.[143] But instead of smothering further controversy, the publication of Haddon's reply only incited it; in 1565 an English translation of Osório's letter was printed in Antwerp.[144] There was an almost immediate rejoinder: in the same year Abraham Hartwell responded with a translation of Haddon's reply.[145] (It is worth noting that Hartwell's translation was published by William Seres, who had been orbiting around Cecil for decades.) Osório returned to the fray in 1567 with an attack on Haddon, and a year later John Fenn published an English translation of Osório's new work in Louvain.[146]

[141] *Epistola ad Elizabetham Angliae Reginam de Religione* (1563).

[142] See Lawrence V. Ryan, 'The Haddon–Osorio Controversy (1563–1583)', *Church History*, 22 (1953), pp. 142–54. Matthew Racine, '*A Pearle for a Prynce*: Jerónimo Osório and Early Elizabethan Catholics', *Catholic Historical Review*, 87 (2001), pp. 401–27, says little about Foxe or his contribution to the debate, but it is useful in exploring other dimensions of the controversy.

[143] Ryan, 'Haddon–Osorio', pp. 143 and 147–9.

[144] *An Epistle of the Reverend Father in God Hieronymus Osorius Bishop of Arcoburge in Portugale, to the most excellent Princesse Elizabeth ... Translated oute of Latten in to Englishe by Richard Shacklock* (Antwerp, 1565), STC 18887. (The running title is *A Pearle for a Prynce*.)

[145] *A sight of the Portugall Pearle, that is the Aunswere of D. Haddon Maister of the requests, against the epistle of Hieronimus Osorius, a Portugall, entitled a Pearle for a Prynce* (London, 1565?), STC 12598.

[146] *Amplissimi atque Doctissimi Viri D. Hieronymi Osorii, Episcopi Sylvensis, in Gualterum Haddonum Magistrum Libellorum Supplicum apud clarrisimam Principem Helisabetham Angliae, Franciae, & Hiberniae Reginam. Libri tres* (Lisbon, 1567); *A Learned and very Eloquent Treatise, writen in Latin by the famouse man Hieronymus Osorius ...* (Louvain, 1568), STC 18889.

Haddon began to reply to Osório's attack, but his death in 1572 left it incomplete.

Matters were not allowed to rest there. At some point during the next few years Foxe was asked to complete Haddon's unfinished response. In a letter, probably written in 1575, whose vehemence indicates the importance English Protestants attached to rebutting Osório, Laurence Humphrey, taking time from his duties as president of Magdalen College, urged his old friend 'to go on to confute Osório, to stab him, even to cutting his throat'.[147] Nevertheless it was probably Cecil who was responsible for enlisting John Foxe in the long-running campaign against the Portuguese bishop. Cecil had taken a considerable interest in this controversy from its inception and Haddon himself had been linked to Cecil by several threads of the intricate spider's web that was the patronage network of Elizabeth's chief minister.[148] To continue Haddon's work, Cecil now approached Foxe, another eloquent Latinist who had been the great man's client since the reign of Edward VI. And when Foxe's reply to Osório was finally written, it would be printed by Seres' former partner, and then in an English translation, by Cecil's past and present client, John Day.[149]

We do not know exactly when Foxe began penning his reply to Osório. It may have taken quite some time to write. For one thing, his reply was extremely verbose; the work would number over 800 pages, of which only the first 70 were written by Haddon. For another thing, there were at least two other important works in which Foxe was involved over this period: his edition of the complete works of Tyndale, Frith and Barnes and the translation of Luther's commentary on Galatians. It is very unlikely that Foxe finished his response to Osório before the second half of 1575, when the printing of the third edition of the *Acts and Monuments* began. If the

---

[147] 'Perge Osorium confutare ut confodias et iugules' (BL, Harley MS 417, fo. 118ʳ). The letter is dated 21 February but unfortunately no year is given. However, the letter goes on to discuss the progress John Foxe's son, Samuel, was making in Greek studies. Samuel Foxe entered Magdalen College in 1574, was elected demy in July of that year and matriculated on 10 January 1575 (Joseph Foster *Alumni Oxonienses*, 8 vols. (Oxford, 1888–92). Therefore, this letter must have been written after 1574 but before the publication of Foxe's reply to Osório in 1577. The most likely date is 1575 but it is possible that it was written in February 1576. By February 1577 Foxe would have finished writing the work.

[148] Stephen Alford, *Kingship and Politics in the Reign of Edward VI* (Cambridge, 2002), pp. 200–2.

[149] *Contra Hieron. Osorium, eiusque odiosas insectationes pro Evangelicae veritatis necessaria Defensione, Responsio Apologetica. Per clariss. virum, Gualt. Haddonum inchoata: Deinde suscepta & continuata per Ioann. Foxum* (London, 1577), STC 12593. Walter Haddon, *Against Jerome Osorius ... and his slavnderous invectives ... continued by John Foxe*, trans. James Bell (London, 1581) STC 12594. That Day produced the English translation of this work is particularly interesting because he did not usually print the English translations of Foxe's Latin works, and this was coming at a time when he and Foxe were busy preparing the fourth edition of the *Acts and Monuments*. This is another sign of continuing official interest in the publication of responses to Osório.

response to Osório had been finished by this point, given the interest Cecil and others had in seeing this work printed, its production would not have been delayed. As it was, we know from the title page of the 1576 edition of the *Acts and Monuments* that it was published on 27 June of that year. We also know that another work printed by John Day, John Dee's *The perfect arte of navigation*, was completed during September 1577.[150]

Once started, the *Contra Osorium*, which clearly, from its clean layout, was printed with some care, would have taken months to print. (Since we do not know the print run for the volume, it is impossible to be more precise, but it should be borne in mind that Day would not have been using all his presses for this work.)[151] It is furthermore very likely that the *Arte of navigation* would not have been printed simultaneously with the *Contra Osorium* in order that Day's best staff, who would have been involved in the *Acts and Monuments* and with Foxe's response, could then be assigned to the *Arte of navigation*. Since we know from its title page that the *Contra Osorium* was printed in 1577 it therefore must have been printed before the *Arte of navigation*, otherwise there would not have been time to complete it that year. The printing of the *Contra Osorium* must have commenced by the winter of 1576, and it probably began earlier than that.[152] Thus it is likely that Foxe finished his response to Osório by the autumn of 1576, making it certain that he was engaged with this work while the third edition of the *Acts and Monuments* was being printed.

VIII

One would expect that under these circumstances the third edition would show few signs of Foxe's editorial intervention. A close examination of the text reveals that this is in fact the case. In general the text of the third edition of the *Acts and Monuments* largely duplicates the text of the second edition.

---

[150] STC 6459. An additional clue to dating Foxe's composition of the reply to Osório comes from a letter to Foxe written in September 1575 in which Foxe's correspondent states that he has heard that Foxe will reply to Osório's work (BL, Harley MS 417, fo. 127ʳ).

[151] After the lengthy time in which all of his presses were engaged in printing the third edition of Foxe's book, Day would have had to devote some of them to producing some of the smaller works that would have provided a quick profit.

[152] For additional evidence of the *Perfect arte of navigation* being delayed in order to allow the completion of the *Acts and Monuments* and the *Contra Osorium*, see above, n. 152. Although printed in 1577, the work was not entered into the Stationers' Register until 26 March 1579. This, however, was not an unusual situation; books were often added to the register *after* they had been completed. This could have been for a number of reasons: that the work was originally considered to be covered by another, more general patent, that the work was issued without authorisation (often evidence of a corresponding fine would survive), or that the work simply missed being put into the register at the correct time, the error only being noticed after the book had been issued. We are grateful to Ian Gadd for this information.

Very few changes were made to the text in 1576, and almost all of these concerned Mary's reign. There are two exceptions to this. One, which clearly stemmed from the martyrologist himself, was a new table of 'The mysticall numbers of the Apocalips opened', the latest attempt by Foxe to correlate his exegetical interpretation of Revelation with the hard fact that the world obstinately refused to end on schedule.[153] The other change is more problematic: the *Prayer and Complaint of the Ploughman*, an anti-clerical treatise, was also dropped from this edition. The reasons for this deletion are very unclear, particularly since it is the only full *document* dropped from this edition.[154] It is hard to see that there was anything politically or ideologically embarrassing about this work, and in fact it was reinserted into the 1583 edition.[155] It is possible that it was deleted by accident but its relatively large size makes this seem unlikely.

In contrast to the Herculean archival research that had underpinned the first two editions, the third edition contained only three new documents. One of these was a denunciation of Protestant sympathisers in Ipswich that had been submitted to royal commissioners on 15 May 1556.[156] A letter from the Marian martyr William Hunter to his mother was also added to this edition; how and when this document reached Day's printing house is unknown.[157] The final document, the printing of a speech by the MP John Hales made at the accession of Elizabeth, is one of the few clear cases we have of material being added to this edition by Foxe himself.[158] This speech, in the context of 1576, was a caustic indictment of Elizabeth's ecclesiastical politics and conformed closely to Foxe's own convictions and his general treatment of the queen.[159] Neither document appears to have been uncovered as a result of Foxe's recent research; in fact the martyrologist probably possessed Hales's oration for years before it was printed.[160]

---

[153] *1576*, p. 102. Foxe's apocalyptic beliefs will be discussed in Chapter 8.

[154] *Pace* John King, who claims that 'many documents' were omitted from this edition (King, *Print Culture*, p. 124). John Davis's account of his sufferings in 1546 was also dropped, very probably by accident, from the 1576 edition. See n. 163.

[155] Cf. *1576*, pp. 402–3 with *1570*, pp. 494–501 and *1583*, pp. 398–408.

[156] This was added in *1576*, p. 1981.   [157] *1576*, p. 2008.   [158] This was added in *1576*, pp. 2005–7.

[159] Hales' oration is analysed in Freeman, 'Providence and Prescription', pp. 42–4. It is perhaps significant that this oration, with its pointed political message, was placed at the very end of the third edition.

[160] An important collection of letters, first printed in 1563, between Princess Mary and Edward VI's Privy Council, had been dropped from the 1570 edition, perhaps inadvertently. In 1563 they were printed out of sequence (see above, p. 119), but in the 1576 edition they were not only restored but were placed in their proper chronological position in the text (*1576*, pp. 1289–97).

Apart from this, new material came from oral sources and none of this seems to have resulted from Foxe's inquiries. Instead there were anecdotes that came from people interested in glorifying or excusing what they or others had done during Mary's reign. Whether the account of the near-arrest of Mrs Roberts of Hawkhurst, Kent – a Protestant sympathiser who only avoided arrest when the magistrate who came to apprehend her suffered a 'providential' attack of gout, which prevented him from climbing the steps of her house – came to Foxe or to Richard Day remains uncertain.[161] Similarly the original recipient of Thomas Rose's detailed and self-justifying account of his career, spanning three reigns and two recantations, is unknown.[162]

One of the most remarkable narratives added to the 1576 edition was that of John Kemp, a minister from the Isle of Wight, who supplied an account of his movements and activities in the years 1554–5.[163] His purpose in doing so was to demonstrate that he was not the leader, also named John Kemp, of the 'Freewillers'.[164] Although the John Kemp who contributed this narrative appears to have shared a mutual friend with Foxe, it is very unlikely that Foxe approved or even knew that Kemp's account was added to his book, as it violated one of Foxe's cardinal rules in writing about the Marian period: to avoid mentioning at all costs internal divisions between the Marian Protestants, particularly the quarrels over predestination.[165] In all likelihood Richard Day added Kemp's narrative to the edition himself; this, together with Foxe's almost automatic rejection of references to the 'Freewillers', explains why it would not be reprinted in the fourth edition.

---

[161] This was added in *1576*, pp. 1965–6. This addition was probably the cause of one of the very rare deletions of material that occurred in this volume: the narrative of John Davis describing his imprisonment and mistreatment in 1546 was dropped from this edition and replaced by the account of Mrs Roberts (cf. *1570*, p. 2277 with *1576*, p. 1966). That this omission was accidental can be inferred from the reinsertion of Davis's narrative into the 1583 edition (p. 2073).

[162] *1576*, pp. 1977–81.   [163] Ibid., pp. 1975–7.

[164] This account has created a good deal of confusion, with a number of scholars assuming that this John Kemp was the 'Freewiller' leader John Kemp who had been mentioned very cryptically in the first edition of the *Acts and Monuments* on pp. 1530 and 1605. M. T. Pearse, *Between Known Men and Visible Saints: A Study in Sixteenth Century English Dissent* (Cranberry, NJ, 1994), pp. 45–6, and C. J. Clement, *Religious Radicalism in England 1535–1565* (Carlisle, 1995), p. 348. Actually the John Kemp from the Isle of Wight seems not to have been the 'Freewill' leader but rather a former draper of the same name, who guaranteed the first fruits of Alexander Wimshurst, a friend of Foxe's. See Freeman, 'Dissenters from a Dissenting Church', p. 147, n. 99. For a general discussion of the 'Freewillers' see the same article, pp. 129–56.

[165] On Foxe's determination to avoid discussion of the 'Freewillers' and the reasons for it, see Freeman, 'Dissenters', pp. 153–5. On the mutual friendship John Foxe and John Kemp had with Alexander Wimshurst, see previous note.

Another interesting narrative added to this edition was that of the burning of Christopher Wade in Dartford in 1555, with its vivid details of vendors selling cherries to the crowd and of the martyr holding his hands above his head as he slowly burned to death.[166] In this case, the *Acts and Monuments* was most explicit in identifying the sources for this vivid eyewitness account: Richard Fletcher, the vicar of Cranbrook, and his son, also named Richard, at the time minister of Rye (the first rung on a ladder that would eventually lead to the bishopric of London).[167] The reasons for this unusually detailed and precise citation of informants was that the Fletchers had their own motives for recounting this incident. The authority of both the father and the son was challenged in their parishes by more radical Protestants and by discontented laymen. By relating this story the Fletchers were associating themselves with the venerated heroes of the Marian Church, thereby enhancing their prestige and blunting any criticism that they were less than godly.[168] The account of Christopher Wade's burning was received only while the third edition was being printed; it is therefore very likely that this tale was not the fruit of painstaking enquiry by Foxe but was instead the result of the Fletchers seizing an opportunity once they heard about the new edition.[169] Although the elder Richard Fletcher had informed Foxe of an incident in Mary's reign that had been recorded in the 1570 edition, it is improbable that the account of Christopher Wade's death was sent by the Fletchers directly to Foxe.[170] Another addition to the 1576 edition was a Latin poem by Giles Fletcher, a fellow of King's College along with Richard Day. Giles was the son of the elder Richard Fletcher and he was probably the means by which his family heard of the new edition and the intermediary from whom Richard Day received the account.

One alteration to the volume, which must have been laborious, was the systematic removal of the name of John Dee, the celebrated Elizabethan

---

[166] *1576*, p. 1600.

[167] The *Acts and Monuments* reads: 'spectatores praesentes, Richard Fletcher pater, nunc minister ecclesiae Cranbroke; Richardus Fletcher filius, minister ecclesiae Riensis'.

[168] See Collinson, 'Cranbrook and the Fletchers: Popular and Unpopular Religion in the Kentish Weald', in *Godly People*, pp. 416–23, and Freeman, 'Notes on a Source for John Foxe's Account of the Marian Persecution', pp. 203–11. Both Collinson and Freeman, however, err in declaring that the narrative of Wade's burning first appeared in the 1583 edition; the reasons for this error will become clear in the next note.

[169] The late acquisition of this narrative is demonstrated by the fact that it appears in the 1576 edition on p. 1600, nine pages after an account of Christopher Wade's martyrdom had been given (there is no cross-referencing in this edition between these two accounts). The only explanation for this anomaly is that the account reached the printing house just after the account of Wade's martyrdom had been printed. In the next edition, that of 1583, the two separate accounts of Christopher Wade's martyrdom would be merged together (*1583*, pp. 1678–80).

[170] Fletcher had witnessed the story about Edmund Allin; see *1570*, p. 2165.

mathematician and occult philosopher, wherever it occurred in the text. Dee had been arrested in May 1555 for casting a horoscope predicting the accession of Elizabeth to the throne.[171] Eventually he was released on bond and placed in the custody of Bishop Bonner, in a form of glorified house arrest.[172]

These Marian activities led to a number of unflattering references to Dee throughout Foxe's first edition. He was described as interrogating John Philpot and being rebuked by him as inexpert in divinity. Dee was also described as interrogating the Marian martyr Bartlett Green. Worse yet, Foxe himself referred to 'Doctour Dee the great conjurer', and a letter written by a friend to John Philpot which was printed in Foxe's book also referred to 'Doctour Dee the great conjurer'.[173] In February 1570, Dee expressed his displeasure at this epithet – although he did not refer to Foxe, directly or indirectly – when in his preface to an edition of Euclid's *Geometrie*, he vehemently denied being a conjurer.[174] Worse was to come. Foxe, in his second edition, reprinted all the negative references to Dee.[175] He also added a new one. In a narrative printed in the first edition of Foxe, the Marian martyr, Robert Smith, mentioned that he was examined by one of Bonner's chaplains, 'a conjurer by report'.[176] In the first edition this conjurer was never named but in the second edition a marginal note help-fully identified him: 'This was D. Dee'.[177]

Dee was furious, and his anger erupted all over the preface to his *Perfect arte of navigation*. In the draft of this preface, Dee expressed his outrage that 'diverse . . . impudent lyes (long syns) are placed among the records of those mens Acts who were accownted to have dyed, onely in the cause of verity, and to have byn constant, in the conflict of martyrdom'.[178] A little later on, Dee hoped that 'the wise and *the . . . authorised* will use due discretion to discredit . . . this horrible sklaunder, spreading and establishing all this realm over ([that] is to wete) that the foresaid jentleman, is, not only a conjurer, or caller of dyvells, but a great power therein; yea the great or arch conjurer of this whole kingdome'.[179] In fact, by the time Dee's protests appeared in print, the offending passages had already been removed from

---

[171] *Acts of the Privy Council of England*, ed. John Roche Dasent, new series, 32 vols. (London, 1890–1964), v, pp. 137, 143 and 176.

[172] Whether Dee was formally a chaplain of Bonner's is unclear, but he had been ordained as a priest on 17 February 1555 (GLL, MS 535/1, fos. 26^v–7^r). Dee was on good terms with Bonner, and in a note he made in one of his books he described the bishop as his 'singularis amicus' (Roberts, 'Bibliographical Aspects', p. 36).

[173] *1563*, pp. 1408, 1460, 1427 and 1445.   [174] Euclid, *Elements of geometrie*, sigs. A1^v–A3^r.

[175] *1570*, pp. 1978, 1988, 1999 and 2023.   [176] *1563*, p. 1253.   [177] *1570*, p. 1871.

[178] Bodleian Library, Ashmole MS 1789, fo. 51^v.   [179] Ibid., fo. 52^r; our emphasis.

the third edition of the *Acts and Monuments*.[180] Foxe did not delete these passages but, in a marginal note added in the 1576 edition, he scrupulously clarified Dee's situation: 'M. Dee was yet under band of recogniscance for the good of bearing and forthcommyng till Christmas next after.'[181]

There are two plausible explanations for this rapid resolution of Dee's complaints. Glyn Parry has claimed that Foxe 'personally' eliminated Dee's name from the third edition. Parry also argues that 'political leverage' (apparently exercised by Leicester, Walsingham and their followers) led Foxe to excise Dee's name.[182] Parry even asserts that Dee, in his preface to the *Perfect arte of navigation*, emphasised 'that Foxe had been pressured into removing the conjuring accusations from *Actes and Monuments*'.[183] This last statement is an exaggeration. Nowhere in either draft of his preface or in the printed version of it does Dee state that Foxe removed these accusations, much less that the martyrologist had been pressured into removing them. In fact, Dee, in urging that Foxe remove them, was obviously assuming that this had not been done. Moreover, there is no evidence that Foxe had anything to do with the removal of Dee's name.[184] However, even if Foxe did not make the changes himself, it is quite possible that the political circumstances, which Parry outlines, did lead to Dee being airbrushed out of Foxe's text.

But there is another, equally plausible explanation, and that is that Dee's rehabilitation owed a great deal to the relationship he had forged with John Day. A number of Dee's works were printed by Day in the 1570s and on all

---

[180] Cf. *1570*, p. 1871 with *1576*, p. 1602, *1570*, pp. 1978–9 with *1576*, pp. 1702–4, *1570*, p. 1980 with *1576*, p. 1705, *1570*, p. 1999 with *1576*, p. 1721, *1570*, p. 2023 with *1576*, p. 1744, and *1570*, p. 2049 with *1576*, p. 1745. This deletion of Dee's name was observed by Roberts, 'Bibliographical Aspects', p. 49. The fact that Dee's protests only appeared in print after the publication of the third edition of the *Acts and Monuments* had made them superfluous is another indication that Dee's work was delayed in order for both the new edition of Foxe's martyrology and the *Contra Osorium* to be produced as soon as possible.

[181] *1576*, pp. 1744–5.

[182] Glyn Parry, 'John Dee and the Elizabethan British Empire in its European Context', *Historical Journal*, 49 (2006), pp. 658–63.

[183] Ibid., p. 662.

[184] Admittedly there are extracts, made in Foxe's hand, of entries from the Privy Council Register covering the period from April 1555 to December 1557 (BL, Harley MS 419, fos. 133ʳ–4ᵛ). One entry, for 29 May 1555, directs Sir Francis Engelfield to apprehend 'one John Dye in London'. Someone – in a different hand from Foxe's – crossed out the name Dye on this document and wrote the initial D. over it (Harley MS 419, fo. 133ᵛ). His document is clearly a cast-off, since there is a large 'B.9' written next to the entry on Dee. When this entry was first printed in 1583, it began on sig. 4B4ᵛ. Therefore the evidence would seem to indicate that the decision to remove Dee's name was not made by Foxe but was made in Day's printing house. Moreover, this entry was first printed in the 1583 edition, whereas the deletion of Dee's name had already occurred in the 1576 edition.

of them the printer and the mathematician were close collaborators.[185] It may well have been the sensitivity of the Days, father and son, to the mathematician's distress that led to the careful removal of passages harmful to Dee's reputation. There are two indications of this. The first is that the passages in the preface to the *Perfect arte of navigation* that criticise Foxe were reworded when the work was finally printed, to make these complaints more general and less focused on the martyrologist himself.[186] The second is that while passages copied from the Privy Council register concerning Dee's arrest and his examination for the 'lewd and vain practices of calculing or conjuryng' were printed in the fourth edition, Dee's name was replaced by 'D'.[187] By 1583 Dee had long outlived his political usefulness, and in fact in September of that year he left England for eastern Europe.[188] If the *Acts and Monuments* had been rewritten for political purposes, why did this rewriting continue when there was no political advantage to be gained from it? It is more likely that John Day continued to be loyal to an old friend and associate. The painstaking care shown in this matter contrasts markedly with the editorial sloppiness generally displayed in this volume, and indicates the importance the Days attached to placating the offended mathematician.

Thus much of the newly added material was supplied by Richard Day's contacts and much that was newly deleted was removed at their wish. Richard Day's influence, however, is even more apparent in the additions made to the introductory material to the *Acts and Monuments*. All of the introductions to the 1570 edition were reprinted in the 1576 edition. Yet the 1576 edition also contained one additional introduction; Samuel Fleming's letter 'To the Reader'. This epistle praised historians of the Church – Eusebius, Socrates Scholasticus, Platina and the Magdeburg Centuriators – 'but for playne understanding, manifest proofe, and sufficient discourses, this work of maister John Foxe is to be preferred before any other that hath been written in time past'. Yet if Fleming was generous to Foxe, he was charitable to almost no one else. Seldom has a letter addressed to readers of a volume been more critical of those very readers. The entire letter is a lamentation on the failure of the laity of all ranks to live godly lives, and in particular to respect and obey the clergy. As far as princes, magistrates and nobles were concerned, Fleming observed that history showed that

---

[185] Roberts has also suggested that Day was responsible for the alterations, rather than Foxe, and that the printer was reacting to 'pressure' from Dee (Roberts, 'Bibliographical Aspects', p. 49).

[186] Cf. Bodleian Library, MS Ashmole 1789, fos. 51ᵛ–2ʳ with Dee, *Perfect arte of navigation*, sig. Δ3ʳ.

[187] *1583*, pp. 1578 and 1581, cf. Dasent, *Acts of the Privy Council*, v, pp. 137 and 143.

[188] Parry, 'John Dee', pp. 670–5.

'they had been most enemies to gods Church, which have receaved most honor in the common wealth and most nobility in kin[d]red'. And as for the 'common people', reading the work:

they shall finde how variable their mindes have been in old time, how in one yeare they preferred the Gospell, in another oppressed it, how they have gladly seen the bodies of their pastors violently wronged and consented to all the trouble of Gods people, much like those Iewes under the Roman Empire, that in one day would have made Christ a King and almost in the next would have them crucified.[189]

Perhaps it is unsurprising that this tactless hectoring of potential purchasers of the work would never be reprinted in any subsequent edition.

Fleming undoubtedly owed his opportunity to use the third edition as a pulpit to his status as a fellow of King's College, Richard Day's alma mater.[190] Contributions by fellows of King's streamed into introductory sections of the new edition. No fewer than five poems were added to the section of Latin poems introducing the new edition of the *Acts and Monuments*. Of these, three were by fellows of King's contemporary or nearly contemporary with Richard Day: Giles Fletcher, Sir Thomas Ridley and Thomas Barwick.[191] The other two poems were by an unidentified 'M. M. S.' and by Richard Day himself.[192] Clearly Richard Day, either in an effort to win friends or to simply gratify them, was using Foxe's martyrology as a showcase for the talents of influential fellows of his former college. This may also be another indication that Richard planned to return to Cambridge at some point. It is certainly a sign that he was making the most of the opportunities provided to the person printing the *Acts and*

[189] Sig. ¶3r. Jesse Lander describes Fleming's letter as an address to a socially diverse audience, extolling the edifying qualities of Foxe's book. Jesse M. Lander, *Inventing Polemic: Religion, Print and Literary Culture in Early Modern England* (Cambridge, 2006), pp. 64–5. While these elements are present in Fleming's letter, what to us seems more marked is the triumphant clericalism of the piece and its denigration of the laity of all social classes.

[190] Fellow of King's 1568–81. Venn and Venn, *Alumni Cantabrigienses*.

[191] Giles Fletcher was a fellow in 1568–81 before becoming chancellor of the diocese of Chester (ibid.). Sir Thomas Ridley was a fellow at King's in 1569–79, before going on to be headmaster of Eton and eventually Chancellor of Winchester (ibid. and *ODNB*). Although Thomas Barwick was at King's in 1557–59, he may have been included in this edition for other reasons. He was a member of Edward Grindal's household and for this reason might have already been known to John Foxe. Certainly a letter of his dated 1 October 1578 and written to Foxe survives (BL, Harley MS. 417, fos. 120ᵛ–21ʳ). Whether it was his connection to Foxe or his connection to Richard Day that ensured the placement of his poem in the edition is uncertain. If it was the former, however, it is surprising that the poem was not reprinted in 1583.

[192] All of these poems were reprinted in the 1583 edition except for those by Thomas Barwick and Richard Day. The reasons for the exclusion of Barwick's poem remain obscure but Richard Day's was undoubtedly dropped because at the time of the 1583 edition he was on the worst possible terms with his father.

Monuments. Above all, it is evidence of the controlling influence Richard had over the printing of this volume.

This influence is reflected in other changes that Richard made to the layout of the book. A minor change was to move (apparently on his own initiative) two pages of caveats that Foxe had written regarding certain passages in his work from the front of the book to the back.[193] Richard also created new tables at the beginning of the 1576 edition, listing 'Certaine places of the scripture expounded' and 'Common places handled at large in their place figured'.[194] The most fundamental changes were made to the index, which was completely transformed by Richard. Previously the people in the index had been listed alphabetically by their Christian names; now they were listed alphabetically by their surnames. At the same time Richard also listed subjects as well as individuals; he stated that he modelled this novel arrangement on commonplace books.[195] Richard was proud of these innovations and made sure that he received the credit for them, taking the unusual step of writing a short introduction to the index that discussed his improvements and signing his name to it. Once again it becomes clear that it was Richard Day who was in the fullest sense the editor of the work and that it is he who bore the responsibility for the end-result.

Richard's index has been the subject of some important recent analysis. Jesse Lander has attempted to locate the index, especially what Lander sees as an emphasis in it on the Primitive Church, in its religious and political contexts. He argues that the emphasis on the Primitive Church is a polemical response to both Presbyterians and Catholics.[196] If Richard was indeed using his index to participate in the religious disputes of the period, this was the only time he waded into these turbulent waters. Christine Hutchins has acutely observed that Richard Day's index and other finding aids in the 1576 edition were modelled on tools developed for biblical exegesis. Hutchins has suggested that Richard Day's critical apparatus was intended to assist both in the study of Foxe's text and in simultaneous

---

[193] See Freeman, 'Fate, Faction and Fiction in Foxe's *Book of Martyrs*', pp. 618–19.   [194] Sig. ✠1r.

[195] The introduction to the index is on the unpaginated page immediately following p. 2008. The errata list occurs at the very end of the prefatory material, directly after the Latin poems, and takes up only a quarter of the second column of the page.

[196] Lander, *Inventing Polemic*, pp. 67–8. Parenthetically, we are hesitant to accept that Richard's references in the index to 'the Popish Pagane' is, as Lander asserts, a reference to the Presbyterians. Furthermore, we do not see any direct reference to the Presbyterians in the index. Finally, while Lander sees polemical and political significance in the complete removal of Richard's critical apparatus from the 1583 edition, we would simply observe that this could be easily explained by the disastrous relations between John Day and his son when the 1583 edition was printed.

scriptural exegesis.[197] This is one of the earliest and clearest indications of the special regard in which English Protestants held Foxe's work and their tendency to place it on a nearly equal level with Scripture.

IX

Richard Day's unusual ability to shape the development of the third edition was largely the result of one negative factor: the minimal engagement that either John Foxe or John Day had with it. Foxe's lack of involvement may have been involuntary, on account of the pressures of other work at that time, but John Day's was a remarkable vote of confidence, perhaps not in Richard, but certainly in the marketability of John Foxe's book. Day's willingness to give a novice printer – even his own son – a free hand with such a costly undertaking would seem to indicate considerable confidence that despite everything the book would sell.

Whatever the truth of this may be, it is indisputable that Richard was preoccupied with reducing the biggest single expense of the volume: the cost of paper. Unfortunately, this preoccupation undermined the quality of the book. The paper used for this edition is very thin, with the result that the legibility of the text was obscured because of bleed-through. Moreover the thin paper tore easily – particularly when the pages were turned. Many surviving copies of this edition are torn – especially at the bottom of the page around the middle, where the page is weakest. Some of the sheets used were thicker than others, but these thicker sheets were rougher, resulting in the smudging of the ink and further reducing legibility. The poor quality of the paper in this edition was frequently criticised by contemporaries, and Richard defensively blamed his father, claiming that John had been responsible for the inferior paper.[198] It is plausible that John might have tried to cut costs, especially since he was entrusting such an expensive project to his inexperienced son. However, years later one of John Day's workmen would testify on oath that it was in fact Richard who purchased the paper for this edition.[199]

---

[197] Christine E. Hutchins, 'Sacred Concordances: Figuring Scripture and History in Foxe's *Acts and Monuments*', *Reformation*, 8 (2003), pp. 41–62. However, we do not necessarily agree with Hutchins's argument that Richard Day's index specifically and explicitly referred the reader to the Geneva Bible.

[198] Simon Parrett's letter, for example, criticised the quality of paper in the 1576 edition. See below on pp. 274–5. For Richard's accusation against his father see TNA C 24/180 ints. and deps. 6.

[199] See ibid., Richard Chambers, dep. 6.

Furthermore, other cost-cutting measures were clearly carried out on Richard's initiative. Once again, legibility was sacrificed on the altar of economy, as smaller type was used throughout the edition. This allowed Richard to increase the number of words per page; John King has estimated that ninety lines of type were squeezed onto a page of the 1576 edition, whereas a page of the 1570 edition contained only seventy-four lines.[200] This resulted in the consumption of less paper (the 1570 edition is 2,302 pages long; the 1576 edition, containing fewer than twenty additional pages of text, still only comes to 2,008 pages). This expedient may well have eased the financial strain on those who printed the book but increased the eyestrain on those who read it. The use of smaller type made the book harder to read. Moreover, it was aesthetically rebarbative: type of the size Richard used was normally deployed in marginal notes, and spread out across a whole page it looked distinctly odd. Furthermore, because this type was usually used in smaller quantities and in more peripheral places on the page, there was a smaller stock of it and it was replaced less frequently. Thus, in order to print entire folio pages with this size of type, Richard was compelled to rely on mixing together several different sets of type, some of whose sorts were worn out or damaged. The unfortunate reader thus not only had to struggle with a smaller size of type, but his or her eyes would also be scanning type from different sets. Added to the difficulties of bleed-through and smudging, Richard's economies resulted in serious inconveniences for the reader. However, by utilising the smaller type, Richard not only saved paper, he was able to reduce what was essentially the text of the 1570 edition (which had been printed with larger type and had taken up two separately bound volumes) into a body of text capable of being fitted into one unwieldy, bound tome.[201] In addition to the obvious savings in the cost of paper that this represented, Richard Day may also have calculated that he would be able to sell more *bound* copies of a one-volume work than of a two-volume work, further increasing his profits.[202]

---

[200] King, *Early Modern Print Culture*, p. 129.

[201] The title page of the 1570 edition, announcing that the work was in two volumes, was reprinted without change for the 1576 edition. A perusal of current booksellers' catalogues and internet websites reveals how modern booksellers who own a 1576 edition are frequently confused by this, and believe they only have one volume of a two-volume work. Their internal examinations of the book fail to spot that the 'second volume' commences on p. 772 (an unnumbered page between p. 771 and p. 773).

[202] It is worth noting that Day employed two binders and that it would have been tempting for the Days to have bound a certain number of the copies of this edition and offered them for sale at a higher price in their Aldersgate shop. See Evenden, 'The Fleeing Dutchmen?', pp. 63–77. John King has maintained that 'the condensed physical dimensions of the third edition invited binding in either one or two volumes' (King, *Print Culture*, p. 128). Unfortunately, King has supplied no evidence to

There were other flaws in this edition that were not related to scrimping but rather to negligence. It is ironic that Richard, who was hired as a corrector in the first place, produced an edition whose proofreading was markedly inferior to the 1570 edition. Part of this may well have been due to the absence of John Foxe in the printing house. But Richard bears a great deal of the responsibility for this negligence. In fact, in later law suits hostile witnesses would claim that Richard did not fulfil his duties as a corrector adequately because of his lack of commitment and inattention to detail.[203] Indications of this same slackness appear throughout the 1576 edition, where mistakes frequently occur that should have been spotted by competent proofreaders. For example, lines were skipped by compositors and words were sometimes carelessly transformed by them.[204] Far more serious was the marked deterioration in the accuracy of one of the most impressive features of the 1570 edition: the network of cross-references guiding the reader to material in different sections of the work.[205] One common mistake was that of simply reprinting the page numbers cited in cross-references in the 1570 edition, without making the necessary alterations for the different pagination of the 1576 edition.[206] Sometimes Richard got lazy and simply removed bothersome cross-references.[207] Occasionally the cross-reference was duly changed but the citation was inaccurate: an informative example occurs when a cross-reference to the standard form of articles presented to heretics in the diocese of Canterbury instead directs the reader to the different form used for heretics in the diocese of London.[208] For this mistake to have occurred, some attention – but not enough – must have been paid to updating the cross-reference. Another

support this suggestion. We have, however, found no example of a surviving copy of the 1576 edition that was bound in two separate volumes, nor is there any mention in churchwardens' accounts or other relevant documents of this work ever being bound in two separate volumes.

[203] See, for example, TNA, C 24/180 ints. and dep. 6.

[204] For an example of a line of text being omitted, cf. *1570*, p. 1763, col. 2, lines 2–4 with *1576*, p. 1505, col. 2, lines 44–5. For another example of a careless line skip, cf. *1570*, p. 1763, col. 1, lines 1–3 with *1576*, p. 1505, col. 2, first sentence. One rather striking example of ways in which words were carelessly transformed is the metamorphosis of 'Pharasitical flattery' (*1570*, p. 1864) into 'Parasiticall flattery' (*1576*, p. 1596).

[205] It should be made clear that these cross-references were invariably references back to earlier sections of the text, which had already been printed. It was virtually impossible to cross-reference forwards in the text because the type for the pages would not have been set that far in advance.

[206] For example, cf. *1570*, p. 1952, col. 1, line 11 with *1576*, p. 1679, col. 2, paragraph 3, line 17, or cf. *1570*, p. 1961, col. 1, line 5 with *1576*, p. 1688, col. 1, line 4 on the history of John Philpot.

[207] For example, cf. *1570*, p. 2032, col. 1, line 4 on the account of Joan Catmer with *1576*, p. 1752, col. 1, end of line 3 on the account of Joan Catmer, or *1570*, p. 2137, col. 1, the last line of the examinations of John Newman, with *1576*, p. 1851, col. 1, the last line of the examinations of John Newman.

[208] Cf. *1570*, p. 2165, col. 1, line 31 with *1576*, p. 1870, col. 1, paragraph 1, line 33.

worrying symptom of carelessness is that the errata list for this volume is brief to the point of being perfunctory.[209]

Apart from the improved index and finding aids, which seem to have been of special concern to Richard, and the dubious benefit of additional Latin poems and Samuel Fleming's prefatory letter, the only improvements to the 1576 edition were in the slight, although not insignificant, additions to the text and the addition of two further woodcuts, both of which, it must be said, had been used in works previously printed by John Day. One of these, a map of Saxon England showing the seven kingdoms of the Heptarchy, was first printed in William Lambarde's *Archaionomia*.[210] The second, which appeared on the final pages of each volume of the 1576 edition, was the remarkable illustration of the blindfold figure representing Justice weighing the 'Verbum Dei' in a pair of scales against communion wafers, rosaries, decretals and papal decrees, reprinted from the last page of *The whole workes of W. Tyndall, John Frith and Doct. Barnes* (see Figure 14).[211]

X

These modest improvements do not change the fact that this edition, physically and even aesthetically, was markedly inferior to its predecessor. Even the text – at least if the annotations and cross-references are considered – had deteriorated. In fact never again would the critical apparatus of the *Acts and Monuments* attain the level of accuracy and comprehensiveness achieved in the second edition. In this area, the threads that had begun to slip from Richard Day's fingers would never be completely regathered.

These flaws appear to have gone unremarked by contemporaries, but the decline in the physical standards and appearance of the work were commented on. The best evidence for this is a letter written to Foxe in 1582, while he was preparing the fourth edition of his martyrology, which would be issued the following year. It was sent to him by Simon Parrett, an old friend who had been a contemporary of Foxe's at Magdalen, and it was forwarded to Foxe by Laurence Humphrey, who urged him to follow Parrett's advice. Parrett made a number of useful suggestions but was particularly insistent that the new edition be 'printed in good paper, and a

---

[209] The errata list occurs at the very end of the prefatory material, on the bottom right-hand corner of sig. ✠5r (the verso is blank).

[210] Cf. Lambarde, *Archaionomia*, STC 15142, sig. D4ᵛ with *1576*, p. 110.

[211] Cf. Foxe, *The whole workes of W. Tyndall, John Frith and Doct. Barnes*, final page, with the final page of *1576*. See above for a discussion of this woodcut.

Figure 14 Image of Justice in John Foxe (ed.), *The whole workes of W. Tyndale, John Frith and Doct. Barnes* (1573), [no sig.]. Courtesy of Lambeth Palace Library.

fair and legible print and not in blacke, blurred, and torne paper as the last edition is ... It is pittifull to see such a notable peece of worke to bee darkned with foule paper and obscure print.'[212]

---

[212] BL, Harley MS. 416, fo. 204ʳ.

Comments by Foxe and John Day on the third edition have not survived, but the latter's feelings at least are not difficult to gauge. Soon, if not immediately, after the third edition was issued, John Day and Foxe resolved to produce yet another edition, one more worthy of their talents. By 1579 Foxe had already begun collecting oral information for his new edition.[213] John Day's reasons for wanting to restore his professional reputation were particularly acute. His renown as the most technically accomplished printer in England had secured him valuable privileges that were up for renewal again in 1577.[214] To gain the patronage that would procure those privileges for him, John Day had previously printed technically complex works with little commercial appeal. It was vitally important to him that this reputation was not tarnished at this crucial stage in his career. At the same time, as later events would make abundantly clear, Day had an enormous personal as well as financial investment in the *Acts and Monuments*. Religious zeal, personal and professional pride, as well as greed, all mixed together in a combustible fuel that would push him to risk his health, indeed his life, to achieve a worthy edition of the great martyrology.

It is worth noting that the decision to print a fourth edition of the *Acts and Monuments* does not appear to have been made on the basis of the sales of the third edition, nor was it in response to popular demand. As with the 1570 and 1576 editions, the decisions for embarking upon a new edition were made for personal reasons, which, while sometimes financially motivated (i.e., in the pursuit of continued patronage), were nevertheless not direct responses to the market. This alone undermines efforts to try to assert the popularity of Foxe's work merely by the fact that it was frequently reprinted. The sales of the book did permit its reprinting, but they did not dictate that it would be reprinted. This also calls into question the efforts of Ian Green to assess the appeal of early modern religious works solely by the number of editions that were printed within a particular time period, regardless of the size and nature of the book (or even the cost of producing it), and without any consideration of patronage.[215]

While it was not a technical success, the third edition of the *Acts and Monuments* nevertheless had significant consequences. Although the text was largely a reprint of the previous edition, some of the material added to it, such as the narratives of Thomas Rose and John Kemp, remain of considerable historical interest. On an unhappier note, the printing of the work marked the beginning of a precipitous decline in the relationship

---

[213] BL, Harley MS. 25, fo. 145^{r-v}.   [214] TNA, 19 Eliz., part 2, m. 5.
[215] See Ian Green, *Print and Protestantism in Early Modern England* (Oxford, 2000), *passim*.

between John Day and his eldest son – a relationship that in a few years would be irreparably damaged. And finally, the perceived failure of this edition, along with the collaboration on the response to Osório, renewed the fruitful partnership between Foxe and Day, and ensured that it would last for the remainder of Day's lifetime. And Day's desire to remedy his son's 'failure' would lead to a new, larger and, at least in physical terms, improved edition of the 'Book of Martyrs'.

CHAPTER 8

Fathers, sons and other adversaries: the making of the 1583 edition

I

Although both John Day and John Foxe seem to have decided soon after the printing of the 1576 edition that a new edition of the 'Book of Martyrs' was needed, it would still inevitably be a few years before this project could be initiated. In the meantime both Foxe and Day turned their attention to other matters in the years immediately after the third edition was printed. However, the events of these years, particularly a series of unexpected conflicts that engulfed both author and printer, not only gave immediacy and strength to their decision to print a fourth edition, they also shaped the contents and purposes of the new edition. By the time the new edition was being printed, it would have been clear to both printer and author that they had much more at stake in its success than they might originally have imagined.

As we have already described, Foxe continued with his general editorship of various works by Martin Luther; at the same time he burnished his credentials as an anti-Catholic polemicist. On 1 April 1577 he preached a sermon at All Hallows, Bread Street in London celebrating the conversion of a London Jew to Christianity. This sermon, translated by Foxe himself into Latin, was printed as *De oliva evangelica* that same year.[1]

This was the first of a series of Latin works that Foxe would write in the next five years that were not printed by John Day. There is no evidence that there was any falling out between author and printer; Foxe's decision probably stems, rather, from Day's reluctance to print works in Latin that showed no sign of commercial success unless he received considerable concessions for them. Despite the fact that the *De oliva evangelica* was dedicated to Sir Francis Walsingham – and according to Foxe read by the

---

[1] John Foxe, *De oliva evangelica* (London, 1578), STC 11236. This sermon was translated from Latin back into English by James Bell (*A sermon preached at the christening of a certaine Jew at London* (London, 1578), STC 11248).

author to the long-suffering Privy Councillor while the latter was convalescing – there is no sign of any official support for the book, except perhaps the fact that it was printed by Christopher Barker, the Queen's Printer.

Nevertheless, the sermon is an important work and an excellent indication of the major issues that dominated Foxe's thought during this time. *De oliva evangelica* compared the Jews to the Catholics in their blind adherence to the old Law, their rejection of the Gospel (in Foxe's eyes, Catholics had rejected the Gospel by rejecting justification by faith) and their following the leadership of blind and hypocritical castes of priests. But in the sermon Foxe also argued, based on his reading of Revelation, that the conversion of both groups was nigh, during the approaching end times of the world. In fact, Foxe sent a copy of this sermon to a Frankfurt printer, Andreas Wechels, expressing the hope that it might be translated into German and disseminated among the Jewish communities in Germany, further hastening their conversion.[2] Moreover, Foxe was not without influential supporters in his efforts: Archbishop Whitgift entrusted the martyrologist with 40 gold pieces to be used for the relief of converted Jews.[3] The growing preoccupation with the threat of Catholicism, linked with the waxing of Foxe's fascination with the final book of the Bible, would shape the martyrologist's activities in the last decade of his life.

Foxe followed *De oliva evangelica* with an overtly anti-papal work, *Papa confutatus*, printed anonymously in 1580.[4] The first part, or 'actio', of this work consists of an address by the True Church, speaking in the first person to the papal Antichrist, denouncing the Petrine succession and claims of papal primacy over both ecclesiastical and secular rulers. This is

---

[2] BL, Harley MS 417, fo. 114ᵛ. Foxe, in his commentary on Revelation, would write that before the Final Judgement there would be a period when Babylon would be overthrown and the Turks, Jews and pagans would be converted to Christianity. Foxe, *Eicasmi*, p. 388. The major points of *De oliva evangelica* provide a further example of how deeply Foxe's apocalyptic thought was indebted to John Bale. Foxe's mentor had previously declared that the Jews and the Catholics were alike in their adherence to the Law, rejecting justification by faith, and that, because of this, biblical prophecies regarding the conversion of the Jews also applied to the Catholics, and that Jews, Turks and some Catholics would be converted during the end times. John Bale, *The image of both churches* (Antwerp, 1548?), STC 1297, sigs. N2ᵛ–N5ᵛ.

[3] LPL, MS 2010, fo. 121ʳ. In the spring of 1584 Foxe apparently negotiated with Christopher Plantin for a special printing of the Gospel of John in both Hebrew and Latin (BL Harley MS 417, fo. 113ᵛ). This may well have been one of the purposes for which the money Foxe received from Whitgift was intended. It is also probable that he turned to Plantin because John Day was then incapacitated by ill health.

[4] John Foxe, *Papa confutatus* (London, 1580), STC 11240; an English translation of this work, printed the same year, is STC 11241. Both works were printed by Thomas Dawson. A year earlier, one of Foxe's first works, his translation of Urbanus Rhegius's *Necessary instruction*, was reprinted. In the same year, Richard Day printed his own translation of the *Panegyricon* from Foxe's earlier play, *Christus Triumphans*.

a counterpart to Foxe's *Solemne Contestation*, written twenty years earlier, in which the papal Antichrist addressed the reader and boasted of his power. The dialogues in both works were essentially scissors-and-paste compilations extracted from other writings by various authors. (In the case of *Papa confutatus*, one of the chief works that Foxe drew on was his 'Book of Martyrs'.) The second part, or 'actio', is a denunciation of the doctrinal 'errors' of the Catholic Church, particularly the rejection of justification by faith and the belief in transubstantiation. This work also saw Foxe repeat and elaborate his comparison of the Jews with the Catholics. Finally, an English translation of Foxe's book against Osório was printed in 1581, topping off the reservoir of Foxe's anti-papal writings in this period.[5]

The urgency of both Foxe's apocalyptic expectations and his mounting apprehension of Catholic aggression was accelerated by events on the continent – most particularly the Saint Bartholomew's Day massacre and the atrocities that had occurred in the Low Countries. To Foxe these were not random horrors, but unmistakable signs of Satan's fury in the final days before Christ's triumphant return.[6] The linkage between these themes is perfectly illustrated in an exchange of letters between Foxe and Thomas Croke, rector of Great Waddingfield, Suffolk. In the summer of 1575, Foxe was travelling in Suffolk and apparently suffered some sort of mishap. Croke lent him a horse or provided transport, and also accompanied him part of the way back to London. Foxe wrote a letter of thanks that August, and in September Croke, taking advantage of the chance to correspond with a renowned spiritual physician, replied with a letter confessing his own feelings of hypocrisy and his lack of confidence in his salvation. He also deplored what he regarded as the cruel and inhumane persecution of Protestants on the continent. Foxe responded, comforting Croke, but also declaring that the persecutions in Flanders and France – especially in France where, according to Foxe, cruelty reached unheard-of levels – were indeed the result of Satan's increasing rage in the final days of the world.[7]

---

[5] Walter Haddon and John Foxe, *Against Jerome Osorius*, trans. James Bell (London, 1581), STC 12594.

[6] In his commentary on the book of Revelation, Foxe would postulate that there were ten persecutions – paralleling the ten persecutions of the early Church – that would afflict the True Church in the final days of the world. The last three of these persecutions were, respectively, the persecution in France during the reign of Charles IX, 'under whose rule over 20,000 martyrs suffered with unheard of cruelty in the space of one month' ('sub cuius imperio occubuerunt unius mensis spacio, supra viginti martyrum milia inaudita crudelitate sublata'), the Marian persecution, and finally the persecution 'in Hispania atque Flandria' under Philip II (Foxe, *Eicasmi*, p. 55).

[7] BL, Harley MS 417, fos. 126ᵛ–7ʳ (Croke's letter); 127ᵛ–8ᵛ (Foxe's reply). Interestingly, Foxe used the same phrase, 'unheard of cruelty' ('inaudita crudelitate'), to describe the St Bartholomew's Day Massacre in both the letter to Croke and the *Eicasmi*. It is also noteworthy that about this time

While Foxe's enthusiasm for anti-Catholic polemic in this period was certainly motivated by his deeply held personal conviction that the end of the world was nigh, it should also be remembered that he was also marching in step with some of his closest friends, such as Laurence Humphrey, John Field and Robert Crowley. During this period each of these writers had rehabilitated, at least temporarily, their status with the Elizabethan authorities, tarnished with past radicalism, by devoting their considerable polemical abilities to the struggle with Rome. In large part this was a response to the Jesuit mission to England; most particularly these authors wrote in response to Edmund Campion's defiant apologetic works, the 'Challenge' and the *Rationes decem*.[8] Crowley was one of the participants in the notorious disputation with Campion in the Tower and Field was one of the notaries recording the event. One of Foxe's other close friends (and another earlier opponent to clerical vestments), Alexander Nowell, co-wrote the official account of these debates.[9]

Significantly, there is evidence that indirectly suggests that Foxe intended to write against Campion himself. Among his papers are narratives and transcripts of the debates with Campion in the Tower, while a partial list of books in the martyrologist's library indicates that he possessed copies of many key works dealing with Campion's trial and execution.[10] In any case,

Foxe made one of his few additions to the text of the 1576 edition, an unusually personal account of how the proper interpretation of Revelation 13:5 – the forty-two months of power given to the Beast – came to him while he lay awake in bed pondering the issue. Revealingly, Foxe also says that he first embarked on this train of thought while wondering why God permitted the persecution of his True Church (*1576*, p. 101).

[8] In 1582 Laurence Humphrey printed *Jesuitismi pars prima* (STC 13961), which began as a response to Campion's *Rationes decem* but developed into an argument against claims for papal jurisdiction over secular monarchs. Two years later he followed this with *Jesuitismi pars secunda* (STC 13962), a rebuttal of John Drury's *Concertatio*, itself a reposte to William Whitaker's attack on Campion (STC 25358). In 1558 Humphrey had printed his *View of the Romish hydra and monster* (STC 13966), a collection of seven sermons denouncing Catholics as traitors to the queen. John Field's 1580 translation of Phillippe de Mornay's treatise on the Church (STC 18160) provoked Robert Persons's *A brief discours containing certayne reasons why catholiques refuse to goe to church* (East Ham, 1580), STC 19394. Field shot back with his own rebuttal, *A caveat for Parsons Howlet* (London, 1581), STC 10844. Crowley made his own contribution to the literature against Campion with *An aunswer to sixe reasons* (London, 1581), STC 6075. Crowley also wrote anti-Catholic works in 1586 (STC 6091) and 1588 (STC 6084).

[9] Alexander Nowell and William Day, *A true report of the disputation ... with Ed. Campion Jesuite* (London, 1583), STC 18744.

[10] BL, MS. Harley 422, fos. 132ʳ–72ᵛ contain two copies of Campion's 'challenge' and transcripts of three disputations with Campion in the Tower in September 1581. Interestingly, some of these papers (fos. 136ʳ–47ʳ and 161ʳ–72ᵛ) are transcripts of these debates, compiled by Catholics and confiscated by Thomas Norton when he raided the house of William Carter, the Catholic printer. This would indicate that Norton, at least, was aiding Foxe in composing an anti-Campion work and it is even possible that Foxe's access to these papers was a sign of official support for his projected work against Campion. The list of books in Foxe's library is in BL, Lansdowne MS 819, fos. 95ʳ–6ᵛ. Among these books were:

Foxe's last explicitly anti-Catholic work, printed in 1583, *De Christo gratis justificante*, although ostensibly a further reply to Osório, was also directed against Campion's *Rationes decem*.[11] Strikingly, Foxe gave a copy of this last work to the noted recusant lawyer Edmund Plowden.[12] Throughout his dealings and projected dealings with Jews and Catholics, Foxe not only believed that they were ripe for conversion, he was also remarkably certain that his writings would facilitate the process.

II

While Foxe and his friends Humphrey, Crowley, Nowell and even Field were busy thrusting their pens into the dragon of the papal Antichrist, they were also fighting another enemy. During the 1570s, fissures between the first and second generations of the Elizabethan godly were widening into chasms. Nowhere was this more apparent than at Magdalen College, which under the presidency of Laurence Humphrey had become in fact – if not in name – a puritan seminary. By 1575 two factions had been formed in the college. Laurence Humphrey led one, which consisted largely of the senior fellows; many of the junior fellows, including the future puritan luminaries John Barebon and Edward Gellibrand, felt that Humphrey had become dangerously lukewarm in pursuing a godly reformation of the Church. In 1575, six junior fellows, including Barebon and Gellibrand, were expelled from the college, initiating a dispute that was only settled when Sir Francis Walsingham intervened and secured the readmission of the expelled fellows. In 1578 John Barebon and his supporters tried to block the confirmation of one John Everie as a fellow. This time the dissenting fellows had overreached themselves. Everie was the son of one of the queen's Sergeants at Arms, and Elizabeth had personally recommended his election; in the ensuing uproar Barebon and four supporters were expelled from their fellowships. In the college elections that followed, Humphrey triumphed. His brother-in-law, Roger Inkforby, was elected vice-president, another

Edmund Campion, *Rationes decem* (Henley-on-Thames, 1581) STC 4536.5; Alexander Nowell and William Day, *A true report of the disputation ... with Ed. Campion Iesuit* (London, 1583) STC 18744; William Allen's hagiography of Campion and other Jesuits executed in Elizabeth's reign, *A briefe historie of the glorious martyrdom of XII reverend priests* (Rheims, 1582), STC 369.5; and the *Concertatio Ecclesiae Catholicae in Anglia*, ed. John Fenn and John Gibbons (Rheims, 1583), a compilation of documents dealing with Campion's 'Challenge', examinations, torture and martyrdom.

[11] John Foxe, *De Christo gratis justificante* (London, 1583), STC 11234.

[12] Parry, 'John Foxe, "Father of Lyes"', pp. 295–305. Foxe may have been inspired to make this gesture because Plowden had attempted to write a report of Campion's treason trial but had been refused permission (ibid., pp. 303–4).

brother-in-law, William Inkforby, was made bursar, and other supporters of Humphrey became the deans of divinity and arts.[13]

In 1581 the remaining radicals at Magdalen, frustrated by Humphrey's dominance and completely disillusioned with his regime, engineered the expulsion of John Foxe's son, Samuel, from the college. Samuel had entered Magdalen in 1574, and from the beginning Laurence Humphrey had taken Samuel under his wing; in fact at one point the president was personally coaching him in Greek.[14] Humphrey's mentorship had its drawbacks: the close association between Samuel and Humphrey made the martyrologist's son a target for the president's opponents. A first dark cloud, no bigger than a man's hand, appeared in the spring of 1577 when John Foxe wrote to Humphrey asking that his son's tutor, no less a figure than Edward Gellibrand himself, be replaced.[15] In December 1577 Samuel Foxe suddenly left the college and departed for France without obtaining a leave of absence or informing his family. We do not know the reasons for this precipitous flight, which caused John Foxe considerable paternal anxiety, but it is impossible to avoid the conclusion that Samuel was trying to escape an increasingly ugly situation at the college.[16] Foxe somehow persuaded his son to return to the college and also persuaded the college to readmit him without imposing any disciplinary measures.[17] The next few years passed peacefully enough and in 1580, Samuel became a fellow of the college.[18] Then the next year lightning struck and Samuel was expelled.

John Foxe responded to this with frenetic lobbying, which included an appeal to Cecil. Once again, Foxe did not turn to his patron in vain; Samuel was restored to his fellowship by royal command.[19] However, John Foxe was at once deeply wounded and deeply angered. At first he had been somewhat sympathetic to the young radicals at Magdalen. He had even intervened on behalf of Henry West, a fellow at Magdalen who got into serious trouble, apparently in the wake of the Everie affair, for defamatory, perhaps even

---

[13] The best narrative of these events is C. M. Dent, *Protestant Reformers in Elizabethan Oxford* (Oxford, 1983), pp. 48–58, but this account may be overly sympathetic to Humphrey's opponents. For another view see the article on Laurence Humphrey in *ODNB*.

[14] Bodleian Library, MS Rawlinson C 936, fos. 5^r and 6^r.

[15] Ibid., fo.5^r. (This is Humphrey's reply to Foxe's request; it is dated 8 April.)

[16] For Foxe's anxiety about his son, see his agitated letter to Sir Amias Paulet, the English Ambassador in Paris (BL, Harley MS 417, fo. 116^v). Foxe asked Paulet to detain Samuel if he should arrive in Paris, and expressed his fears for his son's safety.

[17] Ibid., fo. 117^r. (This is Foxe's successful appeal to Humphrey for Samuel's readmission.)

[18] BL, Lansdowne MS 679, fo. 46^v.

[19] In a letter to his friend Daniel Rogers, thanking him for his offer to intervene on Samuel's behalf, Foxe declared that he had written to Cecil to ask for Samuel's reinstatement (BL, Harley MS 417, fo. 117^r). For Samuel Foxe's restoration by the queen's command see BL, Lansdowne MS 679, fo. 46^v.

seditious, remarks.[20] Foxe had also engaged in amicable correspondence with both Barebon and Gellibrand.[21] The expulsion of his son clearly changed his views. In a letter to an unnamed bishop, Foxe denounced those responsible for Samuel's expulsion as 'those factious puritans' ('factiosa ista Puritanorum') and as 'those thrice-pure puritans' ('ista ter puritani') claiming, not without justification, that Samuel was expelled simply because he was Humphrey's supporter.[22] John Foxe warned his correspondent that the faction that had expelled Samuel threatened all bishops, and indeed the very stability of the Church.[23]

[20] BL, Harley 416, fo. 150[r]. (This is actually the draft of a letter, without date or address.) However, the letter is fairly clear about why West was in trouble; it was because he had uttered defamatory remarks against 'superiores potestates'. What remains obscure is who these authorities were. It is quite possible that they included Humphrey and Bishop Horne, the visitor to the college, but it is also possible that West's remarks might also have been directed against secular authorities and even the queen herself. A sign of the seriousness of West's situation is the fact that Foxe states in the letter – which was apparently written to the fellows of Magdalen – that West was incarcerated. Henry West had already been expelled and readmitted in 1575. In 1578 he would finally be expelled by Bishop Horne for slanderous statements; at the time, Horne expressed surprise that West had not been expelled two years previously. *A Register of the Members of St Mary Magdalen College, Oxford*, ed. W. D. Macray, 8 vols. (London, 1894–1915), II, p. 183. This would suggest that West had made his remarks during Bishop Horne's 1576 visitation of the college and that Foxe's letter dates from this period. Certainly Foxe's intervention would explain why West was not expelled in 1576, as Bishop Horne clearly believed he should have been.

[21] On 19 February 1577 Barebon wrote a very respectful letter to Foxe, addressing him as 'reverende pater' (BL, Harley 417, fo. 117[v]). In 1576 Gellibrand wrote to Foxe asking for advice as to whether he could, in good conscience, wear the surplice and academic robes. Foxe responded by saying that the chasuble, alb, amice, stole and maniple were tainted by their association with popish idolatry and could in no circumstances be worn. However, gowns worn by laymen, not priests, and worn not only in church but in college and on the street, such as the academic gown, academic cap and surplice could be worn in suitable circumstances (Bodleian Library, MS Rawlinson C 936, fos. 7[r]–8[v]). Foxe's letter already indicates a more moderate response to these issues than that of Gellibrand and his associates. Gellibrand's inquiries seem to have stemmed from Bishop Horne's visitation to Magdalen in 1576, when the bishop enjoined the wearing of the surplice and academic gowns by the Magdalen fellows (Macray, *Register*, III, p. 23). A letter from Gellibrand to Foxe indicates Gellibrand's more extreme views on this issue, as he denounced Horne's visitation in no uncertain terms (BL, Harley MS 416, fo. 195[r]). Gellibrand's relationship with Foxe, however, was further complicated by his being Samuel Foxe's tutor. In 1577 Humphrey reported to John Foxe that Gellibrand was angered by the martyrologist's request that he step down as Samuel's tutor (Bodleian Library, Rawlinson C 936, fo. 5[r]). However, good relations between John Foxe and Gellibrand were apparently restored as Gellibrand wrote a letter, in a friendly tone, to the martyrologist on 26 August 1578 (BL, Harley MS 416, fo. 194[r]).

[22] The contents of this letter are particularly problematic. The letter survives but the bottom section of one page has been torn away. However, the letter was printed by Thomas Fuller, who stated that he had seen the original, which he printed in full. When Fuller saw the letter, there was already a small tear in it. Fuller, *A Church History of Britain*, IV, pp. 391–5. Of the phrases just quoted, 'thrice pure puritans' survives in the original but 'those factious puritans' only survive in Fuller's version (cf. Harley 416, fos. 152[r–v] with Fuller, *Church History*, IV, pp. 392–3). It is both interesting and ironic that this, one of the earliest uses of the word 'puritan' as a term of abuse, was made by a person whom modern scholars refer to as a puritan himself.

[23] Once again, these comments only survive in Fuller's version of the letter (cf. Harley 416, fo. 152[v] with Fuller, *Church History*, IV, p. 393).

Another indication of how sharply Foxe's views had altered came in a letter he wrote to Archbishop Whitgift in 1584 concerning Whitgift's policy of compelling clergymen to subscribe to articles proclaiming their conformity. Here again the element of generational conflict becomes apparent in Foxe's references to nonconformists as 'callow spirits addicted to unreasonable demands'.[24] Thirteen years earlier Foxe had fought for the revision of the Book of Common Prayer, but now, though he could not bring himself to approve fully of Whitgift's programme of mandatory subscription to the Prayer Book, he saw it as an understandable reaction to young and factious agitators.[25] It must be added, however, that Foxe's acceptance of Whitgift's programme stemmed not only from personal disenchantment with the new generation of nonconformists but from his fears that divisions among English Protestants would fatally weaken them against the omnipresent Catholic threat: 'my sole concern is that both sides join in arming themselves and watching against those Roman Philistines, the enemies of our peace and salvation'.[26]

The composition of the fourth edition of the *Acts and Monuments* brought together all Foxe's concerns during the seven years that preceded its printing. The volume would take note of recent atrocities, such as the Saint Bartholomew's Day massacre, and it would reflect Foxe's increasing preoccupation with the Apocalypse.[27] His sense of the imminence of the last days led him to magnify the Catholic threat and thus the need to unite

[24] 'juveniles animorum addictiones inconsideratae petitiones'. (LPL, MS 2010, fos. 117^r–21^v. The quotation is on fo. 118^r.) Further on in the letter Foxe placed the blame for conflict within the English Church on Whitgift's opponents: 'but would that these restless innovators and troublesome reformers had stayed within the proper boundaries from the beginning, so that the higher authorities had not been driven to these extreme solutions' ('Atque utinam irrequieti isti novatores, ac reformatores tam turbulenti initio ita intra modum sese continuissent, ut superiores potestates ad extrema haec remedia non adegissent') (ibid., fo. 118^v).

[25] In this letter Foxe conceded that the Book of Common Prayer did contain flaws but dismissed them as relatively minor. 'For what among all human writings is, except for the Scriptures alone, free from any blemish?' ('Quid enim in scriptis humanis ita numeris omnibusque praesertim est scripturas solum exceperis in quo insideat naevus?') (ibid., fos. 119$^{r–v}$). What is especially striking about this rhetorical question is that it very closely echoes remarks Foxe had made in the preface to the *Reformatio*, where he declared that 'there never is, nor ever was anything so happily produced by human ingenuity that it is completely free from flaws' ('nihil est, nec umquam fuit tam foeliciter humano elucubratum ingenio, cui non aliquid inhaesit naevi'), except of course Scripture (*Reformatio*, fos. A 4^v–B1^r). However, while the wording of the two passages is very similar, their purposes are entirely different. In the *Reformatio*, Foxe was pointing out that all human works, including the Book of Common Prayer and the canon law code, were flawed, as part of a justification for revising these works. Now Foxe was making the same observation to argue that the Book of Common Prayer should be accepted in spite of its imperfections.

[26] 'hoc ago solum optoque ut mutuis praesidiis nos invicem muniamus adversus philisteos istos Romanos pacis nostrae et salutis inimicos' (LPL, MS 2010, fo. 119^r).

[27] See below, pp. 301 and 317–18.

against it.[28] The threat from foreign enemies, backed as it was, at least in Foxe's eyes, by the full might of Satan's wrath at his forthcoming defeat, along with the consequent imperative need to rally against these foes, inevitably meant that the thrust of Foxe's work was less critical of established authority than it had been in the past. Purging the Church of all traces of 'popery' remained important, but it was less of a priority in the final days of the world when both Satan and God were making a last convulsive effort to win souls, and the struggle against the forces of darkness had become the paramount obligation of all members of the true Church.

This changing set of priorities is also readily apparent in Foxe's treatment of Elizabeth. In this edition he reproduced the second of his dedications to the queen (i.e., that of 1570), even though it was implicitly critical of her. Nor did he remove John Hale's oration to her, although this, in the context of the 1580s, compared Elizabeth to Saul, the backsliding king of Israel. However, Foxe added no further material critical of the queen to the fourth edition. And the first of the four 'considerations' that he added to this edition unabashedly praised the tranquillity and peace of Elizabeth's rule and particularly extolled her for 'defending us agaynst such as would els devoure us'.[29] Thus the fourth edition is the most conservative of the editions of the 'Book of Martyrs' printed during Foxe's lifetime – indeed arguably the most conservative complete edition of the work printed in the early modern era – and in it the calls to reform, which had sounded throughout the previous editions, were muted, although not entirely stilled.

III

In the meantime, during the few years after the printing of the third edition of the 'Book of Martyrs', Day produced very few landmark works. An

---

[28] The fear of the Catholic threat and the need for the members of the true Church to unite against it are apparent in the only completely new addition to the introductory material in the fourth edition: four 'considerations' for English Protestants to meditate upon (*1583*, sig. ¶2ᵛ). Another addition to the 1583 edition, which further illustrates Foxe's fears of the Catholics, is his printing for the first time of an oration given by Nicholas Bacon in 1567, in which Bacon demanded the punishment of those smuggling Catholic literature into England (*1583*, pp. 740–2).

[29] *1583*, sig. ¶2ᵛ. Foxe had earlier similarly, but at greater length, praised Elizabeth for the peace that she brought to the realm in a prayer that he composed for the 1578 edition of Sternhold and Hopkins's metrical psalms, printed by John and Richard Day. However, even here, there was just a soupçon of criticism for the queen's unwillingness to purge the Church of 'popish' remnants and deal firmly with English Catholics. Foxe, lavishly praising her mercy, went on to observe, perhaps a trifle sardonically, that she was 'more like a naturall mother than a Princes' to her Catholic subjects. Thomas Sternhold and John Hopkins, *The whole book of Psalmes collected into English meter* (London, 1578), STC 1828.02, sig. N2ᵛ.

exception to this was his printing of John Dee's *The perfect arte of navi-gation*. This was a work that had been privately commissioned by an unnamed patron.[30] It was an elegantly produced piece, with large, clear roman type and wide margins. The title page boasted a particularly fine woodcut illustration and the woodcut capital C, depicting an enthroned Elizabeth, which was recycled from the 'Book of Martyrs'. But the work had an extremely small print run of only 100 copies, which in effect made this a privately printed work. Another work noteworthy for the technical skill with which it was produced is John Banister's *The historie of man*, a work on anatomy and surgery, which John Day printed in 1578.[31] This book con-tained a number of detailed illustrations, clearly modelled on those in Vesalius's classic work, of the skeleton and muscles of the human body. Unusually, it also contained an illustration in the margin (depicting a human bone).[32] Unfortunately it is not known whether these illustrations were subsidised or not. Finally, it should also be mentioned that in 1578 John Day printed two works by his old friend Thomas Becon and a further collection of the sermons of Hugh Latimer. These clearly represent John Day's personal preferences and were intended neither to impress patrons nor to garner particularly large sales.[33] Moreover, in producing books of the quality of *The perfect arte of navigation* and *The historie of man*, Day seized the chance to demonstrate, after the debacle of the 1576 edition, that he had not lost his technical skills.

For the most part, however, the period between the third and fourth editions of the *Acts and Monuments* saw Day largely preoccupied with defending the printing empire that he had painstakingly built up. The greatest threat to it came not only from within the ranks of his own profession but from within his household as well. For years most members of the Stationers' Company had chafed under the system of monopolies imposed on them, which benefited Day and a small coterie of others to the

[30] Although the work is dedicated to Christopher Hatton, it is unlikely that he was the work's patron. William Sherman has pointed out that the dedication to Hatton was a last-minute interpolation to the work. William H. Sherman, *John Dee: The Politics of Reading and Writing in the English Renaissance* (Amherst, MA, 1995), pp. 152–70. Edward Dyer certainly financed the publication of other works by Dee, but none of them was printed by Day and Dyer was always credited in those works. Whoever did patronise the work is simply referred to as an 'unknown Freend' who paid for the work solely at his own expense (unsigned sheet between sigs. Δ1 and Δ2).

[31] John Banister, *The historie of man sucked from the sappe of the most approued anathomistes . . .* (London, 1578), STC 1359.

[32] The marginal illustration of an 'unnamed bone' occurs on fo. 16v (sig. F4ʳ).

[33] Thomas Becon, *The governaunce of virtue* (London, 1578), STC 1729 and Thomas Becon, *The pomaunder of prayer* (London, 1578), STC 1748; Hugh Latimer, *Frutefull sermons* (London, 1578), STC 15279.

exclusion of almost everyone else. These men had succeeded in gaining a stranglehold on all the lucrative monopolies in the book trade, and while they grazed in the tall grass they forced the remaining London printers to scrabble over the few lush areas left, or to try to make a living in more arid pastures. In August 1577 a substantial group of printers, stationers, booksellers and journeymen complained to Cecil about the monopolies held by a handful of people over the printing of certain books. Among those criticised in this complaint was John Day; it was charged that his monopoly of primers and catechisms deprived 'the porest sort' of the Stationers' Company of their 'onelie relief'.[34] This and subsequent vehement complaints brought no satisfaction to the aggrieved printers and booksellers; Day's monopolies, along with all the other monopolies over the printing and selling of books, remained in force.[35] Yet it was becoming clear that the very system of monopolies that was the foundation of Day's business was under threat, and much of his energy in subsequent years was to be spent in struggling to retain the privileges that the authorities had granted him.

In fact in the very next year Richard and John Day were forced to defend their monopolies in a series of disputes with John Day's former partner, William Seres, and his son.[36] The Stationers' Company mediated in these quarrels, which were quite bitter – the Stationers' Register records that 'by means of the which controversies and questions greate sute and debate in lawe was like to have folowed betwene the said parties' – through the autumn of 1578 and the following winter.[37] Although it is not clear what the specific grievances were, quite probably the *casus belli* was the introduction of extra prayers (including one written and signed by John Foxe) into the metrical psalms printed by the Days in 1578. Seres and his son had a licence to print psalms but they were not allowed to print them with accompanying music; this was the monopoly of the Days. Seres and his son

---

[34] BL, Lansdowne MS 48, fo. 180[r].

[35] See, for example, ibid., fo. 182[r]. For John Wolfe's merciless attack on Day's monopolies in the early 1580s, see Arber, II, pp. 759 *et seq.*, and Harry R. Hoppe, 'John Wolfe, Printer and Publisher 1579–1601' in *The Library*, 4th series, 14 (1933), p. 246.

[36] The quarrel appears to have been initiated by William Seres and his son. The account of the mediation in the Stationers' Company Register does not specify whether it was the Day family or the Seres family who were the complaining parties. However, there are two indications that suggest that it was Seres and his son who were threatening to sue the Days. The first is that the register records the Seres' names first and lists the Days as (apparently) the respondents. The second is that the settlement of the issue of the right to print prayer books lists which prayer books the Days and various other printers were allowed to produce but does not mention those that Seres and his son were allowed to produce. This would seem to indicate that it was not the works printed by the Seres family that were being called into question, and this would imply that the Days were the defendants.

[37] SCA, Liber A, fo. 36[r]. The incident is not recorded in Arber's transcript of the registers.

probably felt that the Days were increasing an already unfair advantage by inserting written prayers into the psalms. Such prayers were the one thing that Seres and his son could add to their editions of the psalms and they must have resented the Days competing with them in their own arena.

However, once started, the quarrel spilled over into other contested areas. Fundamentally, the arbitration of the Stationers' Company favoured John and Richard Day, whose wealth and connections were superior to those of William Seres and his son.[38] John and Richard Day appear to have been restricted to one book of prayers, Richard Day's edition of *A booke of Christian prayers*.[39] However, the right of John and Richard Day to 'the sole and only imprintinge' of that coveted cash cow, the metrical psalms, was confirmed and their privileges over Nowell's catechism were also upheld.[40] Thus in the years 1577 to 1579 John Day had fought off a series of complaints about his monopolies; his determination and his connections made it difficult, if not impossible, for his frustrated rivals to obtain legal redress.

However, other printers chose not to take legal action and found another means of attacking Day's stranglehold on the trade. Some were quite ready to act illegally and poach in Day's rich preserves. This problem had already arisen, most dramatically in 1566, when Day was re-elected warden of the Stationers' Company, along with Richard Jugge. At the behest of the Privy Council, Day and Jugge appointed two men to search out those printing and selling books in violation of patents. One smells a rat here; it is quite possible that the Privy Council was in its turn reacting to requests by John Day and other holders of printing monopolies to act against the producers and sellers of 'pirated' books. The whiff of rodent increases upon consideration of the two printers chosen to conduct the investigation: Hugh Singleton (Day's successor as City Printer) and Thomas Purfoot.[41] Apparently their search took them far and wide as they were paid £5 for their travels in the quest for illicit books.[42] However, this expenditure of

---

[38] The Seres' cause was probably further damaged by the death of William Seres the elder some time between 9 December 1578 and 18 January 1579 (see Seres, *ODNB*). William Seres, his son and namesake, was not a printer himself and may have been less inclined to pursue this case vigorously. It is perhaps worth noting that the last grievances to be resolved were settled rapidly after the elder Seres' death.

[39] SCA, Liber A, fo. 36[r]. Richard Day, *A booke of Christian prayers, collected out of the auncient writers, and best learned in our tyme* (London, 1578), STC 1094.04.

[40] SCA, Liber A, fo. 37[r] and 39[r] respectively. These were the issues that were finally resolved on 18 January 1579.

[41] Arber, *Transcripts*, i, p. 322.

[42] Arber notes that 'the amount evidently implies a long and continuous search'. Ibid., i, p. 347.

energy was unnecessary, as it was Purfoot himself who was chiefly responsible for printing illicit works. Moreover, as Purfoot was printing unlicensed primers, it was Day's patents he was violating and Day who was personally aggrieved. It is more than likely that Day knew that Purfoot was responsible and placed him in charge of the investigation to watch him squirm, as Purfoot finally had to admit that he was in fact the culprit he was supposed to be pursuing. However, Day's revenge went further than this, as Purfoot was severely fined, being forced to pay £6 12s 4d.[43] His public humiliation was not only a warning to other pirates, it was the precedent for another occasion when Day would once again publicly shame someone who dared to infringe his monopolies.

In the long run, Purfoot's activities had inflicted very little damage on John Day. Over a decade later circumstances were different; other printers, increasingly resentful of the printing monopolies, and frustrated by their inability to end the practice, were increasingly ready to violate the monopolies, and many of the printers who were not pirates were nevertheless increasingly ready to sympathise with those who were. Towards the end of the 1570s there are a number of indications that Day began to be pressured by rival printers who were producing works covered by his patents without bothering to pay him for the privilege. It was this pirating of books – particularly the primers and catechisms – that finally brought matters to a head between John Day and his son Richard.

IV

Although there had been tensions between father and son dating from Richard's sudden departure from Cambridge, nevertheless by 1577 they seem to have been resolved. In that year John even entrusted Richard with the delicate yet essential negotiations involved in securing the renewal of his patents. These negotiations are worth examining in some detail because they provide the first indications both of Richard's ambitions and of his unwillingness to play a subordinate role to his father. A key feature of these negotiations appears to have been the gift of a specially prepared and luxurious copy of the *Acts and Monuments* costing £10 to a 'Master Killigrew'.[44] The recipient of the gift (or bribe) was almost certainly Sir

---

[43] Ibid., I, p. 348.

[44] This was very probably a coloured copy of the book bound, tooled and edged with gold, and, if so, it provides another example of how colouring the illustrations was designed to appeal to elite readers. We know about this volume because Richard would claim in later litigation that he was not

Henry Killigrew or his younger brother, Sir William Killigrew. Sir Henry would have been a shrewd choice as an intermediary, since he was not only a close friend of Leicester, he was also Cecil's brother-in-law.[45] However, the book may have been given to William Killigrew, since Richard Day, in 1579, would dedicate to William Killigrew an English version of a portion of Foxe's drama, *Christus Triumphans*, which Richard himself had translated, thanking him for his 'great goodness and unfained favour' when Richard was a 'cold selly suitor in the Court'.[46] In any case, William was a close ally of his older brother Henry, and thus it is somewhat academic to speculate exactly which Killigrew's assistance was being sought.[47]

Yet while Richard was cultivating one or both of the Killigrew brothers in a successful bid to renew his father's patents, he also took great pains to advance his own interests. The selection of *Christus Triumphans* as a work to dedicate to William Killigrew may be revealing. This book was a translation of the 'Panegyricon' from John Foxe's earlier Latin play, *Christus Triumphans*. Apart from being a compliment to the martyrologist himself, the choice of this work, together with the gift of the 'de luxe' copy of the 'Book of Martyrs', may indicate that William or Henry or both may have had a special interest in Foxe's writings.[48] But it was presented as a highly personal gesture from Richard to William Killigrew. Although the title page of the work proclaims that it was 'Printed by John Daye, and Richard his Sonne, dwelling at Aldersgate', the dedication is signed by Richard Day alone, with no mention of his father.[49] In any case, Richard emerged from these negotiations with the patents issued to his father *and to him* as well. Clearly Richard saw himself as his father's equal partner. John Day, however, did not. The father did not expect the son to be involved in the running of the business until after his death.[50]

In 1578 Richard took an important step toward realising his ambition by being granted the livery of the Stationers' Company. The fact that this was possible, despite his not having served the required minimum of seven years as an apprentice, can only mean that his father fully supported the

---

reimbursed for the cost of it. This provides another indication that Richard took the lead in the negotiations over the renewal of the patents (TNA, C 24/181, ints 15–18, and deps. See also ibid., Thomas Duffield, dep. 9).

[45] See Killigrew, Henry, in *The House of Commons, 1558–1603*, ed. P. W. Hasler, 3 vols. (London, 1981) and *ODNB*.

[46] John Foxe, *Christ Jesus Triumphant* (London, 1579), STC 11231, sig. A2[r]. 'Selly' or 'silly' in the sixteenth century did not mean foolish; it meant innocent, vulnerable or unprotected.

[47] See Killigrew, William, in *HOC*.

[48] It is interesting that the name of John Foxe is printed on the title page, in capital letters, and in larger type than anything else except the title of the book and the place of its publication.

[49] *Jesus Christ Triumphant*, sig.A4[r].   [50] See TNA, C 24/181, deps. to int. 17.

manoeuvre.[51] In the same year John entrusted Richard with the management of his bookshop in St Paul's Churchyard.[52] Apparently the arrangement involved John selling some of his stock to Richard; therefore it can be safely inferred that Richard was supposed to keep the profits from this venture for himself. Richard would later claim, after his father's death, that John had cheated him by selling him shoddy, older or damaged books that were unsaleable.[53] As was often the case with Richard's recollections, they are not supported by the surviving evidence. This appears instead to be a distortion of what seems to have been a long-standing policy of John Day's, which was to sell the expensive and high-quality books he had printed at his Aldersgate shop, and to use his other two bookshops at St Paul's and Cheapside to sell smaller and cheaper books.[54] In fact, Day seems to have bent this policy in his son's favour, selling him copies of the *Acts and Monuments*. It is also noteworthy that the one high-quality work printed in 1578, John Banister's treatise on anatomy – in fact almost everything printed in 1578 – was sold exclusively at the St Paul's shop. Far from crippling his son's business enterprise, it appears that John was going out of his way to assist it. At the same time, during the years 1578–80 Richard spread his wings still further and printed books on his own.

It is possible that Richard's marriage, also in 1578, may have displeased his father; certainly the marriage, which involved the termination of his long-term understanding with Ellen Bowles, was sudden and unexpected.[55] However, if John Day was not satisfied with his son's conduct, he was prepared to help his newly married son by assisting him in a number of ways – not least by helping him to pay off his debts, and allowing him the use of a house backing onto the garden of his own property in Aldersgate.[56]

The turning point, however, in the relations between the father and the son came in 1580 when John Day discovered that Richard was pirating his own father's works. Apart from the insult, Richard was injuring his father in two ways: he was not only depriving him of the revenue from books

---

[51] SCA, Liber A, fo. 52ʳ. See also TNA, C 24/181 dep. 19 (to Richard's stepmother, Alice).

[52] TNA, C 24/181, ints. to deps. 13 and 14. See also Oastler, *John Day*, pp. 65–7.

[53] TNA, C 24/180, deps. 12–20 (to Richard's stepmother, Alice).

[54] This can be deduced from a study of John Day's colophons, which contain instructions as to where the book will be sold.

[55] Richard did not marry Ellen Bowles, to whom he appears to have been betrothed, but instead married a woman with the unusual name of Douglas Pope, the daughter of Nicholas Pope, a gentleman from Buxted, Sussex. See TNA, C 24/181 ints. 6–8 for the suggestion that Richard was indeed considered the suitor of Ellen Bowles and so wronged her by marrying another woman.

[56] After John Day's death, it would be hotly disputed whether or not he had given his son money to pay off his debts or only loaned him the money to do so. (TNA, C 24/181, deps. to ints. 9–12 and ibid., deps. to ints. 26–7.) For Richard's use of the house see TNA, C 24/180, dep. 5.

protected by his patents, he was also flooding the market with cheaper versions of these same works, forcing John Day to lower his own prices.[57] Richard's father may have been old but he was far from toothless. He needed to show all potential pirates that no one could infringe his monopolies with impunity, and he decided to make an example of his son. In 1580 Day had been re-elected warden of the Stationers' Company and, once again, he used his office as a whip to chastise his adversaries. That year, accompanied by the leading officers of the Stationers' Company, he broke into the bookshop in St Paul's Churchyard, not only seizing the pirated books but carting off the entire stock and all the printing equipment as well. This last action was particularly harmful to Richard because he had borrowed the money from his father to buy the equipment in the first place. He was left with the debt but without the means to repay it. But John Day had not only ensured that Richard would no longer have the resources to pirate any of his works, he had also humiliated him in the most public fashion possible. As a result Richard was driven out of the printing business permanently. By December of that year he had entered holy orders; possibly he hoped that by entering the service of his heavenly father he might assuage the wrath of his earthly one.

v

John Day, however, did not emerge unscathed from this episode. The trouble with amputations is that even when successful they still leave the body weakened. By publicly humiliating his son, John broadcast to his competitors how vulnerable he was to piracy. A number of London printers were not slow to seize the opportunity. In 1582 John Day sued the printer Roger Ward in Chancery for his piracy of Nowell's catechism. Day, with a zeal and acumen that indicates his alarm at the violation of this valuable patent, apparently traced the work back to Ward through the type that had been used. Ward, whose demeanour during the proceedings was described as 'very contemptuos' claimed that he had 'borrowed' the type required for the work from a young man named Adam Islip, one of Thomas Purfoot's servants.[58] Purfoot unsurprisingly denied that he had returned to piracy and disavowed any participation in the scheme. Ward also testified against another participant in the elaborate conspiracy: a 'Frenchman dwelling in

---

[57] TNA, C 24 /181, dep. 37.
[58] Adam Islip would later be one of the printers of the seventh edition of the *Acts and Monuments*.

Blackfriars' who apparently made a false imprint and claimed Day's printing house as the source for the counterfeit work.[59]

The biggest assault upon John Day's patents, however, came from one of his former apprentices, John Wolfe. After leaving Day's employment, Wolfe travelled in Italy doing some printing there and subsequently returned to London around 1579.[60] On his return, Wolfe challenged the authority of the Privy Council to inhibit printers from printing whatever they wished.[61] Moreover, no mere theoretician, he immediately began to put his ideals into practice. By 1583, Wolfe had flagrantly violated over half of the printing privileges then in force. In particular, he was pirating so many of Christopher Barker's books that Barker claimed to have offered Wolfe employment if he would agree to enter the Stationers' Company, where his activities could be regulated.[62] A series of protracted and ultimately unsuccessful negotiations between Barker and Wolfe took place in which Wolfe, negotiating from strength, made a series of extraordinary demands, which led to Barker complaining that Wolfe was 'a man unreasonable to deale withall'.[63]

By now Wolfe was acknowledged as the 'captaine' of a group of printers ready and willing to challenge the rights of privilege holders.[64] His enemies even charged that Wolfe compared himself to one of the great Protestant heroes – and implicitly compared his opponents to the papacy – by boasting that 'Luther was but one man, and reformed all the world for religion, and I am that one man, that must and will reforme the government in this trade'.[65] The similarity did not end there. Like the great reformer, Wolfe suffered for his cause, enduring no fewer than two spells in prison for his defiance. However, unlike Luther, Wolfe ultimately recanted. Following a raid on his shop that uncovered two printing presses in a secret vault, Wolfe 'accknowledged his error' and after this submission was 'lovingly receved into the [Stationers'] companie'.[66]

Wolfe may have become a respectable character but he was not yet a reformed one. In April 1584 Day complained to the Privy Council that Wolfe had continued his clandestine and illegal printing of Day's works.[67] Later that year Day, acting in his capacity as Warden, rose from his sickbed and led a party consisting of around twenty people, including William Fleetwood, the City Recorder, the two sheriffs of London, Gregory Seton,

---

[59] TNA, STAC 5/D13/7.　　[60] Hoppe, 'John Wolfe', pp. 243–4.　　[61] Ibid., p. 245.
[62] See entry on Wolfe in *ODNB*.　　[63] Arber, *Register*, II, p. 780.　　[64] Ibid., II, p. 773.
[65] See the entry on John Wolfe in *ODNB*.　　[66] Arber, *Register*, I, p. 248.
[67] See Hoppe, 'John Wolfe', p. 257.

who ran his Aldersgate bookshop, and his son Edward, who was to play a conspicuous part in what ensued. According to Wolfe, a considerable amount of force was used during the raid, and if Wolfe's account contains any tincture of truth, Richard Day may have got off lightly, by comparison, when his shop was raided. Wolfe claimed that the party broke into his house with swords and daggers drawn and proceeded to ransack the place and destroy the printing equipment. Edward even grabbed Wolfe's 'poore oulde father by the throate', beating and threatening him.[68] Wolfe responded with an indignant but apparently fruitless suit in Star Chamber against John Day for damages caused to his house and property during this search.[69]

Nevertheless, John Day's sound and fury signified nothing. Within a few months he was dead. Richard inherited his father's patents and he proceeded to do a deal with Wolfe, assigning the valuable privilege for the metrical psalms to Wolfe and four others.[70] Nevertheless, if John Wolfe eventually triumphed, he had to wait until the death of John Day to do so; until almost literally his last breath John Day fought with both the force of the law and the law of force against anyone who dared to infringe his cherished patents.

VI

The decision to embark on a final edition of the *Acts and Monuments* involved considerable commitment, on different levels, from Foxe and Day. For Foxe it meant the final abandonment of any hope of the projected history of Elizabeth's reign ever reaching fruition. If this was not clear by 1579, when preparation for the new edition was well underway, it would shortly become manifest as Day's health precipitously declined. Although the customary announcement that the history of Elizabeth's reign would be forthcoming was duly printed on the final page of the 1583 edition, circumstances transformed confident assertion into hollow boasting. Moreover, the production of a new edition of the 'Book of Martyrs' meant that other projects, including a work on Campion (if indeed there was supposed to be one) and a commentary on Revelation, the writing of which was, as time

---

[68] TNA, Star Chamber Proceeding, 26 Eliz., Bundle W 34, no. 23.

[69] See Hoppe, 'John Wolfe', pp. 252–8.

[70] John Day's death had a remarkable effect on both Richard Day and John Wolfe, apparently persuading them to revise their views on free markets and the iniquity of monopolies. Within weeks of John Day's death, his son Richard and John Wolfe both complained to the Star Chamber in the strongest possible terms against individuals who had dared to violate *their* patents (TNA, STAC 5/ D4/1). The Luther who would reform the printing trade had entered the Vatican.

would indicate, a deeply held ambition on Foxe's part, had to be delayed. And for a man of Foxe's advancing years – he was well into his sixth decade when preparation for the fourth edition commenced – there was always the possibility that death would intervene and transform a temporary delay into a permanent one.

However, as Day's health began to deteriorate, it was also becoming painfully clear that producing this last edition would be, literally and physically, a painful struggle for him. And finally, as always, it would be a significant financial commitment on Day's part; in fact, it would be a larger commitment than in the past, because he had learned from past mistakes and was determined that *this time* fine-quality paper in sufficient quantity would be obtained before printing.

So why did these two old men decide to invest precious energy and resources into polishing old trophies instead of winning new ones? The *Acts and Monuments* had been the greatest triumph for both Foxe and Day, and it was now a triumph of which they wished to remind the world. Day had achieved pre-eminence and Foxe had achieved celebrity, only for both men to see their reputations challenged. By reprinting Foxe's book in a new edition, more impressive than any that had come before it, Day could remind both the authorities and his competitors of his mastery of the printing trade and thereby justify the retention of his coveted and contested prized monopolies. As for Foxe, the new edition not only gave him yet another chance to address fellow Protestants from what was, metaphorically, one of the greatest pulpits in England, upon the burning issues of the turbulent and crucial end times in which they lived, it also enhanced the authority by which he spoke. The reissuing of his book served to remind people of the solid foundations on which his fame and reputation ultimately rested. Yet, as circumstances would show, there was something beyond these motivations, important as they were in the production of the fourth edition. For both men, the making of this last edition was a matter of passion. Pride certainly played a part, but beyond that it is safe to say that for Foxe and Day it was a sacred mission, and that both felt in producing what would be their last edition of their great book they were fulfilling God's will.

VII

A great advantage of knowing God's will is that it helps to clarify one's objectives and maintain the correct priorities. However, it does not obviate the need for careful planning and preparation. Noah may have received divine instruction to build the ark but it was still left to him to gather both the wood and the animals. Similarly, the production of the fourth edition of the *Acts and Monuments* required careful preparation from both Day and Foxe. Day, as we shall see, seriously set about accumulating the necessary materials for printing the book. Foxe also set about doing research for the volume, albeit in a rather more casual and desultory manner than that he employed in researching the first two editions.

One major difference between the first two editions and the fourth is that Foxe added very little new archival material. The one significant exception to this was that he did add material extracted from the Privy Council Registers to the new edition.[71] This, however, was more the fruits of opportunism than of systematic research. In 1576 Thomas Heneage and his younger brother Michael became joint keepers of the Tower Records. In later years Simeon Foxe would testify to his father's close friendship with both brothers, particularly Michael.[72] These connections would persist after John Foxe's death as Sir Thomas Heneage (as he became in 1577) was a generous patron to Samuel Foxe and would act as godfather to Samuel's oldest son, Thomas Foxe.[73] Even during Foxe's lifetime Thomas Heneage demonstrably assisted him in his researches, so it is almost certain that Foxe's foray into the Privy Council Register was simply due to his good fortune in suddenly having these records placed in the keeping of close friends.[74]

Occasionally there were also random documents gleaned for the fourth edition. For example, the second and third editions of Foxe's work included a brief account drawn from London episcopal registers of the imprisonment of Thomas Patmore, the minister of Much Hadham, Essex, for marrying his curate to a housemaid and maintaining that a priest might be married without offence to God.[75] In the 1583 edition, however, Foxe was able to build substantially on this slender foundation. He related that Patmore had

---

[71] Cf. *1583*, pp. 1409, 1417–18, 1465, 1561, 1557–8 with Dasent, *Acts of the Privy Council*, IV, pp. 317, 368–9, 384, and 389, and ibid., V, pp. 63, 110, 115, 118–20, 126, and 136–7.

[72] *1641*, II, sig. B6r.

[73] See Samuel Foxe in *ODNB*. For the complicated and extensive networking of the Foxe and Heneage families see Freeman, 'Through a Venice Glass Darkly', p. 314.

[74] For an example of Heneage supplying other records to Foxe it is worth noting that he personally examined and attested to the authenticity of medieval records from the town and castle of Quinbrough, Kent, which survive among Foxe's papers (BL, Harley MS 590, fos. 80r–126r). Moreover, there may have been an ulterior motive behind the Heneages' generosity in making these records accessible. They had only gained control of the Tower Records after a bruising fight with the Master of the Rolls, Sir William Cordell, which triggered a dispute that lasted for years. The Heneages were only finally confirmed in their position in 1581 (see the article on Michael Heneage in *ODNB*). It may well be that cooperation with Foxe's researches provided the Heneages with a justification for their continued control of these records, just as Bowyer's similar cooperation with Foxe may have helped him secure control of the Tower Records.

[75] *1570*, p. 1188 and *1576*, p. 1017.

been preferred to his living by Bishop Fitzjames and held it for sixteen years 'without any publike blame or reproach' until John Stokesley became the bishop of London. Shortly after his installation, Stokesley, out of malice or a desire to seize his benefice, 'as it is supposed and alleged by his brethren in sundry applications exhibited unto the king, as also unto Queene Anne then Marchionesse of Pembroke', had Patmore arrested. He was imprisoned 'above two years without fire or candle or any other relief but such as his friends sent him'. Foxe then provided Patmore's answers to the charges against him and concluded by adding that, upon Anne Boleyn's intercession, Henry VIII established a commission to investigate the case. Foxe added that he did not know the outcome of this.[76]

Although he did not give a source for this account, it is obvious that Foxe's information came directly from a petition sent to Anne Boleyn. For one thing, the summation of Patmore's career, the recitation of specific and detailed grievances, and the defence of Patmore's conduct would be the appropriate components of such a document. The accuracy of Foxe's declaration that Anne was marchioness of Pembroke is revealing; Anne held that title from 1 September 1532 until her recognition as queen in March 1533. This fits with Foxe's statements that Patmore had been arrested in 1530 and imprisoned for over two years, and it also agrees with a petition on Patmore's behalf that was sent to Thomas Cromwell before Michaelmas 1532.[77] This accuracy also contrasts sharply with the normal confusion regarding chronology that characterises the *Acts and Monuments*. Foxe's statement about a commission being obtained is also accurate. Presumably he had a document describing this as well.[78] Clearly Foxe, while compiling the 1583 edition, obtained a file of documents relating to Patmore's case; unfortunately there is no way to tell from whom he obtained them, but they are typical of the documents occasionally inserted into the fourth edition. Apart from his work with the Tower Records, however, Foxe did no systematic research in archives for this edition. Instead, he relied on the serendipity and personal contacts, at least for his documents.

For the most part Foxe confined his researches to gathering information from informants, which, among other things, effectively meant that almost all of the material added to this edition concerned events that had happened in the sixteenth century. Surviving among Foxe's papers is a fairly sizeable collection of anecdotes relating to the English Reformation from 1522 until

---

[76] *1583*, pp. 1044–5.
[77] J. S. Brewer, J. Gairdner and R. H. Brodie (eds.), *Letters and Papers, Foreign and Domestic, of the Reign of Henry VIII*, 21 vols. (London, 1862–1932), VII, p. 1923.
[78] Brewer *et al.*, *Letters and Papers*, VIII, p. 1063.

1559, which were sent to him in 1579 by an old friend, John Louth, the archdeacon of Nottingham.[79] Interestingly, it seems Louth sent this material to Foxe unsolicited and it is also worth noting that Foxe only printed one or two of the stories that Louth sent to him. Nevertheless, Louth's diligence in collecting this material and his zeal in sending it on to Foxe are reminders of the wealth of individual recollections and anecdotes on which Foxe was able to draw.

As was always the case, information obtained from informants could be unreliable – particularly when it related to providential episodes, where wishful thinking and sheer *Schadenfreude* coloured individual memories. A noteworthy example of this came with Foxe's account of Stephen Gardiner being stricken by the hand of God as he sat at dinner with the third duke of Norfolk at the very moment when Ridley and Latimer were burned.[80] Foxe heard this story fourth-hand and it was in fact demonstrably inaccurate. The third Duke of Norfolk died on 25 August 1554, while Latimer and Ridley were not burned until 16 October 1555. In this case, Foxe's over-enthusiastic readiness to repeat stories showing the workings of providence undermined another of his paramount concerns, that of making his martyrology impregnable to hostile criticism. Contemporaries noticed the impossibility of this chronology and pounced on it.[81]

Nevertheless, this dubious story was inserted carefully into the narrative of Stephen Gardiner's life and iniquities. Other anecdotes from informants were also carefully integrated into the text. For example, the description of the Scots reformer George Wishart, which Foxe received from Wishart's old college friend, Emery Tilney, was placed within the already existing narrative of Wishart's life.[82] Similarly, the two stories that Louth supplied that Foxe did print are also inserted seamlessly into the narrative.[83] Probably the most important of these new materials are ten letters from John Bradford to the Manchester merchant John Traves written in the years 1548–50.[84] Another striking addition to this text is the detailed narration presumably

---

[79] BL, Harley MS 425, fos. 134ʳ–45ᵛ.   [80] *1583*, pp. 1787–8.

[81] This story was repeated in the 1586 edition of Holinshed's *Chronicles*. The offending passages in the copy of this edition in York Minster Library (V/1.B.5) are crossed out and a contemporary has written comments in the margins, disparaging both the author and his intelligence in repeating the story. Raphael Holinshed, *The first and second volumes of Chronicles* . . . (London, 1587), STC 13569, p. 1130.

[82] *1583*, pp. 1267–8.   [83] Cf. *1583*, pp. 1911–12 and 2105 with BL, Harley 425, fos. 135ᵛ–6ᵛ.

[84] *1583*, pp. 1659–65. Copies of other letters, not in Foxe's hand, from Bradford to Traves, which Foxe did not print, survive as BL, Harley MS 416, fos. 33ʳ–4ʳ, 34ᵛ, 37ʳ and 37ᵛ. These copies reveal that Foxe was still relying on scribes to provide copies of the documents he used. On the identity of John Traves see Christopher Haigh, 'The Reformation in Lancashire to 1558', 2 vols. (PhD thesis, University of Manchester, 1969), II, pp. 537–8.

supplied by a well-placed informant, of the Marian martyr George Tankerfield's behaviour in the hours before his death.[85]

However, a number of other anecdotes were not inserted into the main body of the text. Many of these were added into a final section of the 1583 edition: 'The Appendix of such Notes and Matters as either have bene in this History omitted or newly inserted.' This appendix was something of a hotchpotch: a mixture of old and new ingredients thrown together. The basis of it was the material in the appendix of the 1563 edition (likewise acquired by Foxe too late to be inserted into the text of that edition), which had been deleted from the second and third editions and was now revived and presented to the reader of the fourth edition.[86] But new anecdotes, which had not been acquired by Foxe in time for ready integration into the text of the 1583 edition, were also thrown in.[87] Nevertheless, many of these stories are of very considerable interest, often demonstrating a particular desire to exonerate individuals, both living and dead, of their misdeeds or to highlight their accomplishments. One important new story eagerly taken up by Foxe was that of one of Archbishop Cranmer's servants offering the Henrician martyr John Frith a chance to escape from the primate's custody, thereby giving the martyrologist a chance to minimise Cranmer's role in Frith's martyrdom.[88] Also printed for the first time in this appendix was a story related by William Holcot of his unsuccessful attempt to assist Cranmer during the archbishop's trial. This disastrous intervention led to Holcot's own arrest and ultimate recantation; now, thirty years later, Holcot passed the story on to the martyrologist to relieve his own conscience.[89]

In addition to these anecdotes, Foxe also added some miscellaneous documents that he had apparently acquired during the printing of the 1583 edition: an account of the examination and condemnation of

---

[85] *1583*, pp. 1690–1.

[86] Cf. *1563*, pp. 1703, [recte 1730]–37 with *1583*, pp. 2128, 2130–2, 2136, 2144–5 and 2149–50.

[87] One case where this manifestly happened is in a letter that William Wood sent to John Foxe, dated 25 July 1583, relating his narrow escapes from the Marian authorities (*1583*, p. 2146). Wood had previously sent Foxe, for use in the 1570 edition, an account of his examination by Archdeacon William Chedsey and the chancellor of the diocese of Rochester (*1570*, p. 2281). It is an interesting question why Wood wrote to Foxe with a continuation of his adventures over thirteen years after he sent him his first account. It may be that Wood had personal reasons for doing so of which we know nothing; it may also be that Foxe wrote to Wood – and perhaps others – asking them for more information about their providential rescues in Mary's reign. For a discussion of Foxe's re-interrogating his sources for further information, see Freeman, 'Notes on a Source', pp. 203–11.

[88] *1583*, pp. 2127–8. See the discussion of this story in MacCulloch, *Thomas Cranmer*, p. 102.

[89] *1583*, p. 2135.

Thomas Hitton in 1529, an account of the examination of William Hastlen for heresy in Boulogne in 1547, verses denouncing Mary Tudor, a verse denunciation of the Eucharist attributed to Edward VI, a letter by John Melvin (a Protestant imprisoned in Newgate during Mary's reign), the confession of faith by the Marian martyr Patrick Patchingham, a letter from the Marian martyr William Tyms, and even letters connected, rather tenuously, with the martyrdom of Julins Palmer.[90] Foxe also reprinted a letter from John Hooper to Convocation, written in 1554, which had only previously been printed in Foxe's *Rerum*.[91] A striking addition was a treatise on the evils of worshipping images, which Foxe erroneously attributed to Nicholas Ridley.[92] Nicholas Bacon's oration, mentioned above, was also added to this section.[93] Finally, Foxe also added accounts of recent events that he considered noteworthy. One was the execution of Richard Atkins, an Englishman visiting the Eternal City in 1581 who, ignoring the old adage about what to do when in Rome, tried to snatch the Eucharist from a priest celebrating Mass in St Peter's and was painfully executed for this offence. Others were the kidnapping and equally painful execution, in 1571, of Dr John Story, one of the most important of the Marian persecutors; the massacre of Saint Bartholomew's Day; and the siege of La Rochelle in 1573.[94] The fact that Foxe chose to conclude the last edition of his great book that he would ever edit with an account of events in the French religious wars is yet another striking indication of the paramount importance that he attached to the fate of Protestants on the continent.

VIII

Despite the addition of new material, the scope of the *Acts and Monuments* remained largely unchanged. A striking feature of this edition, which will be discussed in more detail further on in this chapter, is the reprinting of material that had been dropped from the first edition due to the shortage of

---

[90] Ibid., pp. 2136–42.   [91] Cf. Foxe, *Rerum*, pp. 306–8 with *1583*, pp. 2135–6.

[92] *1583*, pp. 2128–31. In fact the treatise is probably by Edmund Grindal: see Patrick Collinson, *Grindal*, pp. 97–8, and Stephen Buick, '"Little Children Beware of Images": "An Homily against Peril of Idolatry" and the Quest for "Pure Religion" in the Early Elizabethan Church', *Reformation*, 2 (1997), pp. 301–30.

[93] *1583*, pp. 2150–1. See n. 28 of the previous chapter.

[94] *1583*, pp. 2152–4. It is worth noting that although the Saint Bartholomew's Day massacre and the siege of La Rochelle took place about a decade before the fourth edition was printed, Foxe drew his account of these events from Richard Dinoth's *De bello civili gallico*, which was first printed in 1582. Cf. *1583*, pp. 2152–4 with Richard Dinoth, *De bello civili gallico* (Basle, 1582), pp. 336–41, 346–50, 355, 359–60 and 364–6.

paper. Thus the introductory material – Latin poems, prefaces, introductions, dedication, etc. – noticeably swelled, although only one entirely new item was added to it: an introduction consisting of 'Four considerations', which Foxe addressed to English Protestants.[95] The remainder of the 'new' material was simply reprinted from the first edition of nearly twenty years before.[96] The most striking of these newly resurrected pieces was the re-erection of that lightning rod of controversy, the calendar of Protestant martyrs.[97] The calendar may have been reintroduced on Day's specific orders. However, it is more likely that the calendar was simply added to the fourth edition as part of the wholesale reintroduction of prefatory materials printed in the first edition and subsequently excluded in the others.

It would also seem that the reintroduction of the calendar was not a matter of careful calculation by John Foxe and quite possibly was not planned by anyone.[98] (This also serves as a reminder that changes in page layout should not necessarily be attributed either to Foxe or to Day. In many cases – particularly with the 1576 and 1583 editions, where the involvement of Foxe in supervising the composition of the page was not extensive – these changes were probably made by staff in Day's printing house.)

Even allowing for material dusted off and reprinted from the first edition, the fourth edition remained substantially unaltered in its scope. It covered the same basic time period, beginning with the Apostolic era, and in fact nothing significant was added to Foxe's history of the early Church. Strikingly, no new illustrations were created for this volume either. Disappointingly, very little was done to correct some of the disorganisation, caused by the insertion of material out of chronological order, that had prevailed in earlier volumes. In a few cases some efforts and such corrections were made. For example, the account of the executions of Christopher Wade and Margery Polley, which had been contributed by the Fletchers, was now moved to its proper chronological place in the 1583 edition.[99] However, such cases were exceptional. All too often material continued to

---

[95] *1583*, sig. ¶2ᵛ.
[96] In fact the only thing not reintroduced from the introductory material of the first edition was the original dedication to Elizabeth.
[97] *1583*, sigs. §2ʳ–4ᵛ.   [98] Evenden and Freeman, 'Red Letter Day'.
[99] On the Fletchers and the introduction of this material see above, p. 265. Also cf. *1576*, pp. 1591 and 1600 with *1583*, pp. 1678–80. Freeman, 'Notes on a Source', pp. 203–11, and Collinson, 'Cranbrook and the Fletchers', p. 405.

be printed out of order and, worse still, material on the same individual or event remained separated by scores or even hundreds of pages.[100]

In fact, a few efforts made in the fourth edition to integrate disparate and scattered material on the same martyr seemed to have backfired. For example, Foxe's account of the Marian martyr Edmund Allin's escape from the authorities was mysteriously removed from the 1583 edition.[101] This story was separate from the chief account of Edmund Allin, and it is possible that it was inadvertently removed in the process of trying to join the two separate accounts of this martyr together. In other words, somebody might have removed the story of the escape, planning to incorporate it into the rest of the narrative on Allin, but then forgot to reinsert it.

Another attempted reorganisation of material had the opposite effect. In the 1570 edition Foxe printed a description drawn from the register of Archbishop Warham of the proceedings against John Browne, who was executed for heresy in 1511. (Although his martyrdom took place early in Henry VIII's reign, it only appears in Foxe's conclusion of the narrative of the reign; in fact, the account of Browne's martyrdom appears to have been part of the material Foxe used to fill up space at the end of Book 8.[102])

A little further on in the second edition Foxe reported that Browne was denounced to Archbishop Warham following an incriminating conversation with a priest, and that burning coals were applied to the unfortunate man's feet in an effort to extract a recantation from him. Foxe also stated that he had heard this account from John Browne's daughter, Alice, and that she had heard it from her mother, Elizabeth Browne.[103] These two separate narratives of John Browne's ordeals were reprinted in exactly the same places in the text in both the 1576 and 1583 editions; they were never joined together and they were never moved to that portion of Foxe's text that covered the year 1511. In the 1583 edition, however, Foxe added a third

---

[100] For example, the basic account of the Marian martyr John Hullier remained separated from the eyewitness account of his execution by nearly 100 pages (*1583*, pp. 1906–9 and 2004).

[101] See Freeman, 'Notes on a Source', pp. 203–11, for a detailed discussion of this.

[102] *1570*, pp. 1480–1. For Foxe having extra pages to fill at the end of Book 8, see Elizabeth Evenden 'Closing the Books: The Problematic Printing of John Foxe's Histories of Henry VII and Henry VIII in his Book of Martyrs (1570)', in *Tudor Books and Readers*, ed. John N. King (Cambridge, 2010), pp. 68–91. It is worth noting that when Foxe printed the articles charged against Browne, he deleted the first article that read 'item, that [he believes that] the sacraments of baptism and confirmation are not necessary for the salvation of the soul' ('Item, quod sacramenta baptismi et confirmacionis non sunt necessaria ad salutem animae'). Foxe also added a qualifying clause to the fifth article: where the original stated that God had given no power to priests to minister sacraments, celebrate Mass or conduct divine services, Foxe added 'more than to laymen'. Foxe's emendation subtly changed an absolute denial of the efficacy of religious services into a denial of the sacral status of the clergy. (Cf. *1570*, pp. 1453–5 with LPL, Warham Register, fos. 169ʳ–74ʳ.)

[103] *1570*, p. 1480.

account of Browne's martyrdom. This was merely an abridged version of Alice Browne's narrative and it was correctly placed in the text of the *Acts and Monuments* among the events of 1511.[104] Apparently Foxe, in an effort to organise this material for the fourth edition, decided to shorten Alice Browne's account of her father's sufferings and shift it to the appropriate chronological place in the text. However, either through an error at the printing house or through Foxe's forgetfulness, Alice Browne's original account was never removed from the text. Furthermore, Foxe apparently forgot about the account in Warham's Register, which remained unaltered. As a result, there were three separate accounts of John Browne in the 1583 edition, separated from each other by hundreds of pages (they were on pages 805, 1276–7 and 1292–3), and this confusing arrangement was slavishly reprinted in all subsequent unabridged editions of the book.

Just as individual anecdotes or documents had been added to the text of the 1583 edition for apologetic, exculpatory or downright propagandistic reasons, so material was dropped from this new edition from similar motivations. For example, the narrative of John Kemp, which only served to remind Foxe's readers of the ancient but embarrassing disputes over predestination among Marian Protestants, was quietly discarded. Material was occasionally added to this edition for similar reasons. The narrative of Edwin Sandys's ordeals during Mary's reign provides an excellent example of this. The thrust of the story, presumably supplied by Sandys himself, is to demonstrate that his release from captivity in Mary's reign was not due to any lack of godliness or courage. The story painstakingly explains how Sandys was freed through the intervention of Sir Thomas Holcroft, who was his jailor and also a staunch Protestant sympathiser.[105] Foxe's story not only insists that Holcroft had to work hard to persuade Sandys to accept release on bond, it also declares that Sandys only agreed to flee overseas to avoid having to attend Mass. Sandys also made a point of relating that the martyrs John Bradford, Lawrence Saunders and Robert Ferrar all urged him to escape. The narrative even adds that when Sir Thomas Wyatt's men briefly occupied London they offered to release him but he refused, primly telling them that they lacked the legal authority to release him.[106]

Foxe seems to have held Sandys in high regard since at least the days of their exile and, as we have seen, the two worked closely on the Luther

---

[104] *1583*, p. 805.
[105] For Holcroft's Protestant sympathies also see BL, Harley MS 425, fo. 115[r–v]; printed in Nichols, *Narratives*, p. 210.
[106] *1583*, pp. 2086–9.

translations.[107] It was natural that Foxe would want to do his old friend a favour, and by 1583 Sandys badly needed one. Following his elevation to the see of York in 1577, he had become embroiled in a sordid scandal, which dragged on from 1581 to 1584 and involved his being blackmailed over an alleged affair with an innkeeper's wife.[108] It is worth noting that in 1585 Edwin Sandys printed a collection of his sermons, many of which denounced clerical abuses.[109] Such a collection of a living cleric's sermons was a rarity in sixteenth-century England, and this may represent another effort by Sandys to rehabilitate himself. Once again, as had been done in the third edition, by printing Thomas Rose's self-justifying autobiography, or, as had been done in the second edition, by printing John Winram's exculpatory anecdotes about the early Scottish Reformation, the *Acts and Monuments* was used to provide justification for clerics with chequered pasts.[110]

IX

There were two paramount factors that shaped the 1583 edition and made it different from all of its predecessors. The first was that this time Day, having learned from past mistakes, took steps to ensure that there was an ample supply of paper for this edition. This foresight involved paying substantial sums, all in advance. Although at this time Day was apparently as wealthy as he had ever been, he did not have the ready cash to meet these expenses. This meant that he had to borrow very substantial sums of money to finance the new edition. However, he was no longer able to use his properties as securities for his loans: after his break with Richard, in an effort to disinherit his eldest son, he had conveyed most of his property and assets to his brother-in-law, John le Hunte.[111] As a result, he had to borrow the necessary money from a narrow circle of family and friends who would be willing to invest without collateral. The amounts involved were, moreover, quite large. We know that Day borrowed at least £500 or £600 to pay for paper and wages for the workmen, and that £200 of this was borrowed directly from John le Hunte. This borrowing, moreover, continued throughout the

---

[107] In 1559 Foxe, writing about the Marian martyr John Bland, mentioned that Bland had been schoolmaster to Sandys. Foxe praised Sandys as being 'of singular gifts of mind and doctrine' ('ab singulares ingenii et doctrinae dotes lubenter') and declared that he was 'a worthy student of such a teacher' ('dignus tali paedadogo alumnus') (Foxe, *Rerum*, p. 503).

[108] See Edwin Sandys in *ODNB*.

[109] Edwin Sandys, *Sermons made by the most reverende Edwin, archbishop of York* (London, 1585), STC 21713.

[110] See above, pp. 144 and 264.   [111] This conveyance lay behind the suit TNA, C 24/180.

volume as expenses rose; as Day's health waned, his wife Alice was forced to borrow money on his behalf.[112]

Day, however, simply had no choice; he not only had to buy paper, he had to buy high-grade paper. The poor quality of paper used in the 1576 edition had met, as we have seen, with considerable criticism, and John Day, with his reputation at stake, was determined not to expose himself to such censures again. In the event, and for the first time, Day not only had enough paper, he had more than enough. Foxe and Day were able to execute an obviously agreed-upon strategy to incorporate much of the material that had been dropped from the second and third editions into the fourth. They were also able to include some items of only secondary, or even tertiary, importance, such as a letter from Hooper to Convocation, which Foxe had not bothered to include in any previous edition, and a letter from John Moyer to Thomas Parry denouncing Thomas Thackham, a peripheral participant in the martyrdom of Julins Palmer.[113]

However, throughout most of the 1583 edition, Day seems to have kept a cautious eye on his paper supply, carefully refraining from printing too much material and running out of paper prematurely. This can be seen most clearly from his treatment of Hugh Latimer's famous 'card' sermons. These had been printed in the 1563 edition and for lack of space were merely paraphrased in succeeding editions.[114] In 1583, the first sermon on the cards was reinserted at its correct place in the life of Hugh Latimer. However, the second sermon was only included about 400 pages later, in the appendix to the edition.[115] The only apparent explanation for this bizarre arrangement is that a compromise was made to reincorporate the first of these sermons and then see if there was enough paper to allow the reprinting of the second sermon. This in turn can only mean that even when around 80 per cent of the edition had been printed, Day was still cautiously husbanding his precious reserves of paper.

Another sign that Day, at least, was keeping a careful eye on the stock of paper is that some items dropped from the second edition were still not reprinted: for example, Foxe informs his readers about a prayer by the Marian martyr John Hullier – printed in the first edition – and advises them 'if any be disposed to peruse it, it is extant in the olde booke of Acts'.[116] In these cases, we can see a slight conflict between Day and Foxe. Simon Parrett had complained to Foxe that readers disliked being referred to

---

[112] TNA, C 24/181, deps. 7–16.   [113] *1583*, pp. 2135–6 and 2141.
[114] Ibid., pp. 1298–1308; *1570*, p. 1903; *1576*, pp. 1630–1.
[115] *1583*, pp. 1731–4 and 2142–4.   [116] Ibid., p. 1909.

another edition that they probably did not have at hand. Effectively there were two possible solutions to this problem. One was to reprint everything; the other was to eliminate any reference to material that had not been reprinted. The fact that the first course was not completely followed is undoubtedly on account of Day's concern about the paper supply. The fact that the second course was not followed is probably on account of Foxe's perfectionism. Finally, it is worth observing that the old promises of an appendix of documents, which had first appeared in the second edition, were finally removed. This time Day was careful not to commit himself to promises that he might not be able to fulfil.[117]

Only at the end of the volume were Day and Foxe safely able to indulge in a conspicuous display of excess – an appendix containing around thirty pages of additional material. In fact this appendix appears to have been an unplanned afterthought: an account of John Whitman – a Flemish shoe-maker, resident in England, who returned to his native land and was executed in 1572 after publicly desecrating the Host – was printed in the section dealing with the providential death of persecutors, whereas the story of his fellow iconoclast, Richard Atkins, was printed in the appendix.[118] This would suggest that when Foxe inserted the account of Whitman – in a section where it was clearly out of place – there were no certain plans for an appendix. If true, this would indicate that the decision to have an appendix was only made when Day was absolutely sure that they had enough paper on hand.

But Day's money – or more accurately the money he borrowed – had not been spent in vain. The problem of bleed-through, which was so chronic in the 1576 edition, did not affect this edition at all. This time the paper was dense enough to absorb the ink cleanly. Moreover, there was no need to resort to desperate, and ultimately counterproductive, expedients such as pasting together smaller sheets of paper. The legibility of this edition was further increased by the use of a new black letter type averaging 70–1 mm. The type was of good quality with no major signs of damage and wear. The visual layout of the pages was also impressive: the margins were wide (averaging 38 mm) and the column widths were regular.

Visually, this was the most impressive of all the editions of the *Acts and Monuments* that would ever be printed. No future edition would match its legibility and its elegant layout. It was the crowning technical achievement

---

[117] On the removal of these promises of an appendix, cf. *1570*, p. 1950 with *1583*, p. 1785.

[118] The account of John Whitman's martyrdom appears in *1583*, p. 2113. Foxe states that the account was sent to him by two sailors from Rye who were eyewitnesses.

of Day's career as a printer and his own monument to his skill. Under any circumstances, the physical aspects of this volume were an achievement that any printer in Europe would have taken pride in. For Day to have produced this at all in his fraught, indeed desperate, circumstances of 1583 was a triumph of his will.

x

John Day's rupture with Richard certainly took an emotional toll, and it may have taken a physical toll as well: staff at his printing house later testified that Day was afflicted with 'palsy' around the time that he turned on his son and heir. By 1582, the dire state of his health was manifest and his life began, like a leaf falling from a tree, to spiral in inexorably downward circles towards his death. He lost the power of speech, had difficulty moving about and was clearly in pain.[119] (However, Day led the party that ransacked John Wolfe's house *after* he was stricken. The fact that he was able to rise and watch on silently as rough justice was meted out to his adversary is testimony to his implacable determination to preserve his endangered monopolies.)

Predictably, Day's rapid decline increased exponentially the pressure to complete the volume. John le Hunte and the others who had loaned Day money were understandably anxious, perceiving that, without Day, the book could not be completed, and they would not recover their investments. At the same time Day's resolve to complete the book was at least the equal of that of his investors. Enfeebled and wracked with pain, he nevertheless still drove the last edition of Foxe's book through the press. At one point Alice Day, concerned about her husband's health – if not his life – tried to sell off the paper so that work on the edition, which was sapping so much of Day's strength, would have to be halted. However, Day persevered in his race with his own mortality, never lifting his eyes from the prize – an edition of the *Acts and Monuments* that would at the same time give glory to God and lustre to his own reputation.

The consequent rush to finish the work before his life ebbed away, however, had a detrimental effect on some aspects of the quality of the new edition. Even more than before, material was being inserted into this edition up until the last minute. One letter that Day printed was dated 25 July 1583.[120] As a result, the fundamental defect of the fourth edition is its

---

[119] For testimony about Day's 'palsy' see TNA, C 24/181 int. 16–25. For testimony about his clearly observable bad health see deps. to these ints. (especially Alice Day and Edward Day).
[120] *1583*, p. 2146.

lack of organisation; time was simply not taken to organise the last section of the work or to polish off its rough edges. The problem was exacerbated by Day's desire (and presumably Foxe's) to reintroduce material from the first edition that had been subsequently deleted. Resurrecting this old material was a job that, given the complexities of Foxe's text over four editions, demanded careful attention to detail, and yet at the same time the work was being prepared in haste.

Naturally enough, mistakes occurred. For example, two letters from the Marian martyr, Bishop Robert Ferrar, allegedly written to Thomas Goodrich, the Lord Chancellor, ended up being printed twice in the 1583 edition only a few pages apart.[121] Most of the documentation surrounding Robert Ferrar's battles with his cathedral chapter during Edward VI's reign was dropped from the 1570 edition, but these two letters were simply removed to the conclusion of the narrative on Ferrar.[122] They were reintroduced in the fourth edition at the proper chronological place in the narrative of Ferrar's life. However, some less than attentive person simply reprinted the letters as they were in the previous edition (at the conclusion of the life of Ferrar). As a result, within five pages, two sets of the same letters were printed.[123] This mistake is annoying but not particularly harmful. However, a more serious and lasting error resulted from the reinsertion of materials into Ferrar's narrative. In his first edition Foxe stated that Robert Ferrar was imprisoned for the last two years of Edward VI's reign.[124] In the 1570 edition he corrected his earlier account and stated that Ferrar was simply released on bond.[125] In the fourth edition, however, when the documentation was reintroduced, so was the erroneous statement that Ferrar had been in prison, while the correct statement of his release was disregarded in the shuffle, creating a myth accepted to the present day – that Ferrar remained in prison until Mary's reign.[126]

Similar distortion occurred with two letters written by John Alcock, who was imprisoned for heresy during Mary's reign. In the first edition, along

---

[121] At least Foxe believed that the two letters were to Thomas Goodrich. A. J. Brown, the meticulous biographer of Robert Ferrar, persuasively argues that one of these letters was actually written to Thomas Cranmer (Andrew J. Brown, *Robert Ferrar: Yorkshire Monk, Reformation Bishop, and Martyr in Wales (c. 1500–1555)* (London, 1997), p. 166).

[122] The letters occur in *1563*, pp. 1096–8 and in *1570*, pp. 1722 and 1725–6.

[123] Cf. *1583*, pp. 1552–3 with 1555–6.

[124] *1563*, p. 1098. Here Foxe was repeating what he had said in the *Rerum* (on p. 424) and there he was undoubtedly reporting garbled information he had heard during his exile.

[125] *1570*, p. 1722. This was repeated in the 1576 edition, pp. 1470–1.

[126] *1583*, p. 1553. For proof that Ferrar was not imprisoned see Brown, *Robert Ferrar*, pp. 216–18. Brown, however, does not realise that Foxe's mistake had been corrected and then lost again due to incompetent editing.

with the letters, Foxe printed two contradictory statements – on the *same* page – as to Alcock's fate, maintaining that he was burned at Smithfield and that he died in prison.[127] This mistake arose because Foxe was getting information about Alcock from two different sources and, in the haste with which the 1563 edition was compiled, he failed to notice the inconsistency. By the time the second edition was being printed Foxe had noticed the inconsistency and he removed the statement that Alcock was burned at Smithfield; he also, however, removed the two letters.[128] In the 1583 edition the letters were reinserted in the appendix but so was the erroneous statement that Alcock was burned.[129] Thus readers of the fourth edition would eventually come across two contradictory statements: one in the life of John Alcock in the main body of the text, stating correctly that he died in prison, and the other in the appendix, claiming that he was burned. Numerous further examples, all due to inadequate editing, appear throughout the text.[130]

An even more serious editorial problem was the virtually complete breakdown of the network of cross-references that had graced the 1570 edition. As we have seen, some of these had already been eliminated or were reproduced inaccurately in the 1576 edition.[131] The need for haste in the printing of the 1583 edition, however, meant that the effort to reproduce the cross-references was largely abandoned. This occurs throughout the edition. In a few cases it is particularly egregious. For example, at one place in the 1583 edition the reader is simply referred to 'pag.'.[132] Similarly, in the 1570 edition Foxe had – in an indication of how close his oversight of this edition was – referred ahead to a document that would be printed eight pages later: 'Wherof read hereafter following pag. 1959'.[133] In 1583, however, they did not bother to supply the cross-reference and the note simply reads 'Whereof

---

[127] *1563*, pp. 1663–7.   [128] *1570*, p. 2245.   [129] *1583*, pp. 2146–9.

[130] Such examples are too numerous to give here. One further typical one will have to suffice. A note was added to the appendix of the first edition relating that the Marian martyr Elizabeth Pepper was pregnant when she was burned (*1563*, p. 1734). The information about her pregnancy was not repeated in the 1570 and 1576 editions. In the 1583 edition someone – possibly Foxe – observed the story and added it to the narrative of her life (*1583*, p. 1913). However, when the realisation that there was enough paper led Foxe and Day to reprint the notes from the appendix of the 1563 edition in the 1583 edition, the note regarding Pepper's pregnancy was one of these reprinted notes and thus the material regarding the pregnancy was printed twice (*1583*, p. 2145).

[131] See above, p. 273.

[132] *1583*, p. 1804. The note, which occurred in Foxe's account of the life of John Bradford, referred back to Foxe's earlier narrative of Bradford saving bishop Gilbert Bourne from rioting Londoners. Accurate cross-references at this place in the narrative occurred in both the 1570 and 1576 editions (*1570*, p. 1780 and *1576*, p. 1339).

[133] *1570*, p. 1951. This cross-reference was reprinted with the correct page numbers in the 1576 edition (*1576*, pp. 1679 and 1687).

read hereafter following'.[134] On the rare occasions when a cross-reference was supplied in the 1583 edition, it was often incorrect. An example of this occurred with Foxe's account of Joan Warne. Joan's mother, Elizabeth, was also burned for heresy in Mary's reign, and in his account of the daughter Foxe cross-referenced back to the account of the mother.[135] In the 1576 edition the cross-reference was back to page 1608; this was a mistake, as the correct page number was actually 1600.[136] In the 1583 edition Foxe simply reprinted the – by now doubly – incorrect cross-reference to page 1608.[137] For the most part, however, the cross-references were simply removed, and since the fourth edition would be the basis for subsequent reprintings of the work, the elaborate, systematic web of cross-references painstakingly spun by Foxe was effectively whisked away, never to be restored.

The decision of the Victorian editors of the *Acts and Monuments* – the first unabridged editions of the work to be printed since 1684 and the ones which, until very recently, were the standard modern editions of the martyrology – to use the 1583 edition as the basis for their own version had serious consequences for our understanding of Foxe's book, and in particular for our understanding of his editorial supervision of it. By standardising the 1583 edition, the Victorian editors perpetuated and disseminated an edition of Foxe's work that was hastily compiled and inevitably disorganised. They also preserved the only one of the first four editions largely bereft of cross-references, thus concealing from modern scholars Foxe's meticulous concern to link up the various sections of his work.

The question arises, what was Foxe's editorial involvement in the 1583 edition? He certainly did new research for the work. It was probably at his insistence that material deleted from the 1563 edition was reprinted in the 1583 edition, and it can be additionally presumed that he encouraged Day to spend lavishly on paper. However, there is very little evidence of his being in the printing house and assuming the direct supervisory role that he had done with the 1570 edition. In fact a look at Foxe's other publications at about this time would suggest that he was much less engaged with the actual printing process than he had been for the first or second editions. In 1583 Foxe printed a theological treatise, *De Christo gratis justificante*, which also included his translation into Latin of a sermon by William Fulke.[138] This work would have required a certain amount of time to prepare, yet we know from internal evidence that the fourth edition was being printed as late as July 1583.[139] The implication is that Foxe was spending at least part of his

[134] *1583*, p. 1785. [135] *1563*, pp. 1251 and 1468; *1570*, pp. 1878 and 2030. [136] *1576*, p. 1750.
[137] *1583*, p. 1857. [138] Foxe, *De Christo gratis justificante*, STC 11234. [139] *1583*, p. 2146.

time composing and translating other works while the 1583 edition was being printed.

In almost every respect, this was Day's edition. He was the one who at the cost of undermining his health saw the work through the press. The relative involvement of the two men in the production of the last edition that they would both live to see printed is reflected in its strengths and weaknesses. Admittedly, the volume suffered because of the haste with which it had to be completed, but the ways in which it suffered are interesting. What was sacrificed was some of its scholarly apparatus and its organisation; what emerged unscathed were its visual qualities: its legibility and aesthetic appeal. Day, in printing this volume, was determined that it would showcase his mastery of his craft. In this he succeeded admirably.

XI

This success came at a price. Day was dead within a year of the completion of the fourth edition. In July 1584, against the wishes of his family who were concerned about his continuing wretched health, he set out to visit his wife's relations in Little Bradley, Suffolk, about 50 miles from the capital. En route he fell fatally ill. With a last flickering of the will power that had built a printing empire and defended it against all challengers, Day, so long bereft of speech, was able to utter these final words to Alice: 'Good wife content thyself; God doth all for the best.'[140] He finished his journey posthumously and was buried in the le Hunte family church at Little Bradley on 2 August.[141]

Day left behind a considerable estate and one that was to become the eye of a storm of legal controversy. As has been mentioned, John Day, in his implacable determination to ensure that Richard did not get any share of his wealth, conveyed his property to his brother-in-law, John le Hunte.[142] He even tried, unsuccessfully, to ensure that his letters patent did not revert to his son.[143] Richard Day, enraged by all of these manoeuvres against him, sued Alice and John, arguing that his father was of unsound mind when he

---

[140] TNA, C 24/181, dep. 77.

[141] Bury St Edmunds, Archives Office, Sudbury archdeaconery registers, cited in Oastler, *John Day*, p. 4.

[142] The deed of conveyance has not survived and therefore our knowledge of exactly what was transferred to le Hunte is unclear, as are what conditions, if any, were attached to this gift. Also unclear is what provisions Day made for his wife and his other children, although there is some evidence of his conferring cash on a son-in-law. (See the depositions of George Pen, TNA, C 24/181.) What is clear is that the bulk of Day's property – if not all of it – was conveyed to John le Hunte.

[143] TNA, C 24/180, Duffield, int. 22.

made the deed of conveyance.[144] Richard apparently won this suit (no record of it survives), as Alice and her brother countersued him.[145] Unfortunately, once again, we do not know the result of this suit. However, what we do know is that no one seems to have carried on with Day's business. There is no record of anything ever being printed at the Aldersgate printing house after Day's death or of Richard resuming his activities as a printer. Presumably the ongoing legal battles and the lack of an undisputed heir made it difficult, if not impossible, for Day's business to continue. Admittedly, Richard continued to hold the patents that had been assigned to him during his father's lifetime, and, moreover, he went to court a number of times to protect them against pirates.[146] But he assigned these rights to other printers and does not seem to have resumed printing himself. Ultimately, Richard was to sell several of these patents, including that for the *Acts and Monuments*, to the Stationers' Company.

Although the internecine squabbles within the Day family undoubtedly played their part in terminating the printing empire that John Day had built up, there were probably other, more important factors that worked to end it. Richard does not seem to have had the determination and combative zeal necessary to maintain such an extensive business against competitors and pirates. But by the end of his life even John Day was struggling desperately to preserve what he had built. Most fundamentally, the tide was simply turning against him; it was becoming harder and harder to preserve a business built on monopolies in the face of increasing hostility to them. It is telling that no printer after Day was ever granted the same extensive patents that he had held, and that gradually but inevitably, over the final decades of the sixteenth century, the government tended to cease granting monopolies to individual printers. The impetus in the book trade had shifted from the individual entrepreneur to syndicates and groups of printers and booksellers.

This guides us to the real measure of John Day's achievement. He seized the particular opportunities open to him in the mid-sixteenth century – such as the arrival of talented foreign printing staff in England, and the desire of Elizabethan statesmen (particularly Cecil) to exploit the propaganda potential of print – and forged a unique role for himself. He became England's master printer and the chosen agent for most of the difficult and complicated printing tasks that Elizabethan statesmen and officials sponsored. He was, in fact, the book trade's chief 'man of business': that is, a private individual who placed his particular expertise at the service of

[144] Ibid. [145] TNA, C 24/181. [146] See in particular TNA, STAC 5/D4/1 (1 and 2).

members of the government without holding an official position or office himself. His relationship with figures such as Cecil, Robert Dudley and Parker were close and mutually beneficial, but they were also private and personal. His counterparts were figures such as William Fleetwood and Thomas Norton; the difference between them is that the expertise of Fleetwood and Norton was in law and politics, and the chief rewards for their services lay in their access to the inner circles of power and in a limited ability to influence policy. Day's expertise was in printing and his rewards were commercial: monopolies, privileges and concessions, which allowed him to dominate his trade.

Within his trade Day's greatest long-term achievement, apart from simply elevating the quality of English printing and pioneering the extensive use of illustrations, lay in his shrewd use of cheap printing to underwrite the costs of expensive printing. In this Day was following a strategy deployed by other great European printers, most notably Christopher Plantin, who financed his master work, the Polyglot Bible, through his monopoly of liturgical works within the Spanish Habsburg territories.[147] But this was ultimately a circular process; Plantin gained his priceless monopolies by printing the Polyglot Bible and Day gained his monopolies by printing the *Acts and Monuments* and other high-quality works. To produce the high-quality books these printers needed monopolies of cheap, perennially selling works; to gain the monopolies of such works they needed to produce the high quality volumes that would win them influential patronage. If a printer had the technical skill and the connections to make such a system work the sky was the limit. Day reached as high as the skies of England allowed.

However, Day probably saw his achievement in different terms. On his tomb Day's family bragged of only one of the master printer's accomplishments: 'he sett a Foxe to wright how Martyrs runne By death to lyfe'. Day had earned the right to this boast. Less directly, but just as surely as any of the martyrs, he had sealed Foxe's work with his own blood.

XII

If, as we have speculated, Foxe was supposed to be working on a refutation of Campion (and *De Christo gratis justificante*, which responds to Campion's *Rationes decem*, may well have been part of this effort), it would not come to fruition. It may be that Foxe had already begun to turn his attention to his last great project, his commentary on the book of

---

[147] See Kingdon, 'Patronage, Piety and Printing', pp. 35–6.

Revelation. It may also be that age was finally sapping his already precarious health. In 1585 Foxe did write a preface to a commentary on the book of Nehemiah, written by his old friend James Pilkington.[148] It is unclear why an unfinished biblical commentary was suddenly printed ten years after its author had died, but Foxe's interest in the work is rather easier to ascertain. Pilkington's exegesis on Nehemiah was topical; he used the work to denounce greedy officials and courtiers who sought leases and raised rents.[149] (This is an expression of Pilkington's heroic efforts to safeguard the property and revenues of his diocese against the queen and the court.) The thrust of his commentary was to emphasise the need for magistrates to do God's will and to foster the rebuilding of the Temple (i.e., the reformation of the True Church, purged of all papal corruptions).[150] Pilkington also urged the need for all people, clerical and lay, to put aside their quarrels and to unite together in rebuilding the Temple.[151]

Unlike Pilkington, Foxe, in his preface to the book, did not interpret the rebuilding of the Temple allegorically. Instead, he interpreted it prophetically. Foxe understood Nehemiah as a divine prophecy of a historical event unfolding within Foxe's lifetime: the ravaging of the True Church and its subsequent rebuilding. Specifically Foxe felt that this prefigured the corruption of the True Church from within by the papal Antichrist and its restoration by the godly.[152] Where Foxe agreed with Pilkington was in the need for unity among all labourers gathering to rebuild the Temple. However, Foxe differed from Pilkington on the role that the magistrates and the governor played in the restoration of the Temple; where Pilkington emphasised the role of the magistrate (or monarch) strongly, Foxe offered only the mildest praise of the governor in restoring peace so that the Temple could be rebuilt.[153] (In other words, Foxe was once again praising Elizabeth for ending persecution but omitting, in silent criticism, any commendation of her for actively reforming the Church.) What is clear from all of this is that whether or not he was responsible for the reprinting of Pilkington's commentary, Foxe used it to present ideas that had already been adumbrated in the fourth edition of the *Acts and Monuments*. These formed his final word on Elizabeth and

---

[148] James Pilkington, *A godlie exposition upon certaine chapters . . . of Nehemiah* (Cambridge, 1585), STC 19929. Pilkington died before this work could be completed. It is actually a commentary on the first five chapters of Nehemiah.

[149] Ibid., fo. 4^{r-v}. Pilkington, while conceding that courtiers were not inherently evil, warned them strongly against the temptation to avarice (fos. 4^{v}–6^{r}).

[150] Ibid. See especially fos. 36^{v}–7^{r} and 47^{r-v}.   [151] Ibid., fos. 1^{r}–8^{r}.

[152] Ibid., sigs. ¶3^{r}–4^{r}.   [153] Ibid., sig. ¶4^{r}.

marked the end of his transformation from panegyricist of the queen to caustic critic, to disappointed yet mildly approving observer.

In 1585 Foxe may have had intimations of his own death. He certainly began taking steps to secure his eldest son's future. As a first step, he wrote to Samuel, who had been studying overseas for several years, urging him to return home.[154] Samuel finally arrived back in England in June 1586. Upon his arrival in England, he immediately tried to obtain the 'lawyer's place' among the Magdalen fellows. The controversy surrounding Samuel's departure from the college, as well as his prolonged absence, made him rather unsure of his standing with the fellows of the college. In a letter canvassing two fellows of the college he put the matter baldly: 'now is the time to trye whether my frends be glad or wery of my company'.[155] But Samuel – or his father – was far too cagey to rest this case merely on Samuel's charm; both William Cecil and Archbishop Whitgift were asked to write on Samuel's behalf. Cecil frankly told the college that he was writing in support of Samuel 'upon good likeinge of the man *and* for the love I bear to his old father ... to request you that the rather for my sake you will bestow that preferment upon him'.[156] In the event – and this is perhaps a further indication of how divided Magdalen College remained – the fellows did not yield to Cecil's pressure. Instead, in an obvious attempt at compromise, they granted Samuel the lesser 'physician's place', even though Samuel had no medical education.

Meanwhile, John Foxe was also attempting to provide his son with an inheritance. He had previously leased the lands attached to his prebend to Thomas Randall, his brother-in-law. Randall had died in 1585 and Foxe now manoeuvred to have the leases granted to Samuel. Unfortunately, John Piers, the bishop of Salisbury, had secured the reversionary rights to the prebend from the queen and had promised it to his domestic chaplain, who was also his son-in-law. Foxe appealed to Archbishop Whitgift and the Primate of All England was apparently very persuasive, because on 14 July 1586 Bishop Piers wrote, agreeing to renounce all interest in the prebend, out of his desire 'to pleasure that good man Master Foxe'. The leases were to remain in the hands of Foxe's descendants until 1761. In his letter notifying Samuel of Bishop Piers' acquiescence, Whitgift also promised that he would help defray the expenses of Samuel's younger brother, Simeon, at Cambridge, and that he would provide Simeon with a prebend later on.[157]

---

[154] BL, Harley MS 417, fo. 118[r].   [155] BL, Lansdowne MS 819, fo. 107[r].

[156] Ibid., our emphasis. A letter asking Whitgift to write on Samuel's behalf is also copied on the same folio.

[157] BL, Harley MS 416, fo. 208[r].

Having provided for his son's future, Foxe devoted his energies to his commentary on Revelation.[158] These energies suddenly failed. As Katherine Firth has acutely observed of Foxe's commentary, 'after about the three hundredth page the quality and clarity of his exposition declines steadily, eloquent if sad testimony to his determination to continue and to the pain he suffered in the final months of his life'.[159] Foxe's sudden and ultimately fatal collapse is also described in a postscript that he appended to a letter that his wife Agnes wrote to Samuel, stating that he had been unable to eat, sleep, write or even go upstairs to his study for a month.[160] John Foxe would never recover. He died on 18 April 1587, leaving his commentary unfinished. Nevertheless, it would be printed the following year under the title of the *Eicasmi* (a Greek word meaning speculations), even though it stopped at the seventeenth chapter of Revelation. It was edited by his son Samuel and dedicated to Archbishop Whitgift.[161]

In certain fundamental respects this book was the culmination of Foxe's work during his entire lifetime. His researches had never had the mere accumulation of historical knowledge as their goal; these inquiries were always intended to fulfil spiritual functions: for example, providing pastoral comfort, describing conduct to be emulated and providing proofs of the antiquity of Protestant doctrine. Another, and a particularly important one, of the spiritual purposes underlying Foxe's work as an historian was that he felt a correct understanding of history was a crucial step in understanding scriptural prophecies, particularly those in the last book of the Bible. As he stated of Revelation, 'which booke as it conteineth a Propheticall history of the Church, so likewise it requireth by histories to be opened.'[162]

The *Eicasmi* is a detailed exegesis of Revelation that follows the interpretative framework of John Bale, which understood the events of the Apocalypse, which preceded Christ's second coming, as prophecies of events that *had* occurred in human history. Foxe, however, was much more systematic in his equating of every detail in St John's vision with a historical event. He was also much more systematic in rejecting other Protestant readings of Revelation, most notably those of François Lambert, Heinrich Bullinger and Willliam Fulke, which interpreted the book allegorically.[163] Because Foxe's exegesis was so historically orientated,

---

[158] The work was entered in the Stationers' Register on 7 March 1586. By this point Foxe was not only clearly intending to produce this work but he had come to an understanding with a printer about it.
[159] Firth, *The Apocalyptic Tradition*, p. 106.   [160] BL, Harley MS 416, fo. 146^{r-v}.
[161] Foxe, *Eicasmi*.   [162] *1570*, sig. *4^{v}.   [163] Foxe, *Eicasmi*, pp. 42–6.

his commentary on Revelation rested on the foundations of the *Acts and Monuments*. He summarised a considerable amount of the material from his martyrology in the *Eicasmi* and he frequently darted from this material to analysis of the text of Revelation and back again. Thus Foxe's commentary on Revelation 8:7 is followed by a six-page description of the first ten persecutions of the Church, which is essentially a precis of the first book of the *Acts and Monuments*.[164]

Foxe's novel identification of Jan Hus and Jerome of Prague as the two witnesses of Revelation 11 is a particularly striking example of this process. First Foxe thoroughly discredited (at least to his own satisfaction) traditional identifications of the two witnesses and followed this with his own identification of Hus and Jerome.[165] He then supplied a detailed narrative of the careers and executions of Hus and Jerome, drawn entirely from the *Acts and Monuments*.[166] Foxe then proceeded to identify the details of these verses with specific events from history. For example, Revelation states that the bodies of the two witnesses will lie on the streets of Sodom and Egypt for three and half years (Rev. 11:8–9); Foxe interpreted this as a prophecy of the Council of Constance, which condemned Hus and Jerome and which met for about three and a half years.[167] Foxe followed this with a discussion of the Hussite wars – including the reprinting of documents from the 'Book of Martyrs' – and of subsequent historical events, notably the Council of Basle and the invention of printing, up until the advent of Luther.[168] To Foxe the *Eicasmi* was a guide to understanding not only the events in Revelation, but the *Acts and Monuments* as well. The two works, his martyrology and his commentary on Revelation, were related to each other in the way that an Ordnance Survey map is related to a globe: the former supplies the detailed contours of the land, the latter places it in its universal context. From the moment he began work on the *Commentarii* over three decades earlier, to the moment that he died, Foxe, at least in his own mind, was working on what was essentially one large project, which depicted the historical unfolding of biblical prophecy.

Foxe's 'Book of Martyrs', particularly in its later editions, was disorganised – at times, almost chaotically so – and his narrative was always marred by repetition, poor chronology and occasionally factual inconsistency. But the central messages and themes of the work never varied. From the death of

---

[164] Ibid., pp. 72–3 (interpretation) and pp. 73–9 (narrative of the ten persecutions).
[165] Ibid., pp. 142–50.   [166] Ibid., pp. 150–75.
[167] Foxe's exegesis of the prophecy is ibid., pp. 176–85; his identification of Revelation 11:8–9 as a prophecy of the Council of Constance is pp. 181–2.
[168] Ibid., pp. 186–93.

Christ until his second coming, the history of mankind – especially that of Christ's Church – was presented in the most positive and uncompromising terms; good and evil were unwaveringly identified and everything was explained and shown to be not only God's will but the fulfilment of prophecies that had been made centuries before. These messages resonated powerfully in Foxe's lifetime. Whether they would have the same impact, or whether they would be read at all after his death, remained to be seen.

Conclusion: Foxe after Foxe: the making of the Acts and Monuments *in the seventeenth and eighteenth centuries*

I

Looking back over the creation of the first four editions of the *Acts and Monuments*, one appreciates that Foxe's great martyrology was a work that was produced against enormous odds. It was largely the conception of one person, Foxe himself, but his dreams could not have become reality without the skill and determination of John Day. And even this would not have succeeded without the readiness of Cecil, Parker and others to provide the financial concessions and support necessary to produce a work of over three million words. Since without these buttresses the walls of this cathedral would have come crashing down, it is at first glance surprising to find that the work continued to be reprinted in various editions for almost a century after its first printer had died. How was it possible for new editions to appear continually when its author, its printer and the monopolies that had made its printing possible had all vanished?

In his celebrated study of the reception of early modern Protestant books, Ian Green has focused attention on the importance of 'steady sellers'. Green has defined these as works that go through five editions in England in thirty years.[1] Green has excluded the *Acts and Monuments* from the list of 'steady sellers' because, with five editions in its first thirty-three years, it narrowly misses his criteria.[2] In a large survey of Protestant books in England, this standard is useful. However, when it is applied to the printing history of the *Acts and Monuments*, this rigorous standard presents some problems. For

---

[1] Green, *Print and Protestantism*, p. 178.

[2] Green does acknowledge that although Foxe's work went through 'a surprisingly small number of editions' it was 'extremely influential' (ibid., pp. viii–ix). Later Green lists the *Acts and Monuments* as among the influential books that were not reprinted four times in thirty years (pp. 173–4).

320

one thing, it does not take into account the durability of the *Acts and Monuments*: it was reprinted with some regularity in unabridged editions for almost a century after Foxe and Day had died. Moreover, while Green acknowledges that Foxe's book was influential, his model does not sufficiently take into account that for three centuries the *Acts and Monuments* would spawn numerous other books, differing in size, quality and purpose, but all tracing a common origin back to the original editions, like so many icebergs broken off from a single massive glacier. These included, but were not limited to, the dozens of abridgements of Foxe's work. Admittedly, at best these restricted the themes and messages of Foxe's originals, and at worst they distorted them. Yet they invariably also disseminated and perpetuated some of the contents of Foxe's original editions.[3] Most fundamentally, Green's criteria inherently prioritise small works, which are inexpensive to produce, over large books, which are more costly to manufacture.[4] Inevitably, the latter will be produced less frequently than the former; that does not necessarily mean that these larger works are less influential. Inherent in Green's model is the assumption that the success and influence of an early modern book can be measured in terms of sales and numbers of editions. This maintains that early modern book production and dissemination were solely driven by market forces and, as we have seen throughout this book, such was not the case with the *Acts and Monuments* during the lifetimes of Foxe and Day. Moreover, as we shall see in this chapter, this was not to be the case in the unabridged editions that came out after Foxe's death.

Green is far from being alone in making these suppositions. Time after time scholars make assumptions about the popularity and impact of the *Acts and Monuments* based on the conviction that the printing (or non-reprinting) of the book was solely based upon its sales. For example, John King claims that 'demand for the unabridged edition of the *Book of Martyrs* levelled off after 1610, *because it took a full generation for the sixth edition to sell out*'.[5] Sheila Lambert has similarly argued that it was slow sales, rather

---

[3] See Lander, *Inventing Polemic*, pp. 76–7, Damian Nussbaum, 'Whitgift's "Book of Martyrs": Archbishop Whitgift, Timothy Bright and the Elizabethan Struggle over John Foxe's Legacy', in *John Foxe: An Historical Perspective*, pp. 135–53, and David Scott Kastan, 'Little Foxes', in *John Foxe and his World*, pp. 117–29.

[4] Green acknowledges that the cost of printing an edition of some works might prevent their having attained the status of 'steady seller' (Green, *Print and Protestantism*, p. 174).

[5] King, *Print Culture*, p. 145 (our emphasis). For example, Green claims that the *Acts and Monuments* was 'too expensive *to sell* more than one edition every seven years at the outset and then at increasingly long intervals thereafter' (Green, *Print and Protestantism*, p. 174; our emphasis).

than official censorship, that delayed the printing of the eighth edition of the *Acts and Monuments*.[6] These scholars apparently presuppose that there were no other factors – such as patronage or the cost of production – involved in the decisions to reprint the work. The evolution of the *Acts and Monuments* after Foxe and Day were dead differed considerably from its development while they were alive, but there was one element in common in both cases: in neither the sixteenth nor the seventeenth century were the decisions to print this book determined solely by sales.

II

In the sixteenth century five editions of the *Acts and Monuments* were produced in thirty-three years. In the seventeenth century four editions were produced in seventy-four years. Yet the basic reason for the diminishing number of new editions probably lay less with the demand for the work than with changes that had taken place in the book trade as a whole. By 1596, when the first posthumous edition of the *Acts and Monuments* appeared, monopolies had passed from the hands of the individual printers into the hands of the Stationers' Company. These changes apparently affected the 'Book of Martyrs'. Richard Day, now an ordained minister, tried to protect his patent by assigning the production of the 'Book of Martyrs' to various printers approved by the Stationers' Company.[7] By doing this, Richard secured allies in any attempt to preserve his privilege. They were soon needed, as that privilege was challenged as early as 1588, when Timothy Bright, utilising a sweeping patent granted to him by the crown, decided to print (over the apparent objections of Day and other parties) an abridgement of the *Acts and Monuments*.[8] Whoever Richard Day's supporters in this struggle were, their efforts and influence were not sufficient to thwart those of Bright and his patrons, particularly Archbishop Whitgift; this abridgement of Foxe duly appeared in 1589. There is a mordant irony in that the elder Day was only able to print the *Acts and Monuments* on the basis of a sweeping patent acquired by powerful patrons

[6] Sheila Lambert, 'Richard Montagu, Arminianism and Censorship', *Past and Present*, 124 (1989), pp. 62–4.
[7] The exact nature of Day's arrangements remain obscure. Our basic knowledge of them comes from an entry in records of the court of the Stationers' Company (Register B), which makes it clear that more than one party was involved by January 1589, although Richard Day still retained the privilege. See *Records of the Court of the Stationers' Company 1576–1602 – from Register B*, ed. W. W. Greg and E. Boswell (London, 1930), p. 30.
[8] Nussbaum, 'Whitgift's "Book of Martyrs"', pp. 135–53, covers the entire matter in detail.

and that his son's rights to the work were threatened by an even more expansive patent granted by a different set of powerful patrons.

About the time that this struggle was taking place, or perhaps even as a result of it, Henry Denham, a former employee and close associate of John Day's, started work on a new edition of the 'Book of Martyrs'. (In 1587 Denham had already signalled his interest in printing Foxe's work by announcing his intention to produce an abridgement of it.[9] These plans, however, were squashed by the juggernaut of influential support that Bright had enlisted for his abridgement.) At some point Denham began work on this project but his labours were brought to a close with his death in 1590. The Stationers' Company intervened to salvage the project and work on the fifth edition was completed by Peter Short, still officially operating as Day's assign in 1596.[10] Peter Short was financed by a syndicate of ten booksellers, which was formed on 7 April 1595. Under the terms of an agreement set down and closely monitored by the Stationers' Company, Short was paid 17s 6d per book; partial payment on this fee was paid weekly at the rate of 10s for every press that was involved in printing the book. Clearly the risk of significant financial loss for the printer was being alleviated by this weekly payment. At the same time, the payment ensured that the project would run smoothly. The risk was further reduced because the members of the syndicate agreed to pay the costs of the paper used on a quarterly basis. The print-run was established at 1,200 copies, with eight members of the syndicate receiving 100 copies apiece and two members receiving 200 copies apiece. Peter Short was permitted to print up to 150 additional copies at his own expense. The Stationers' Company maintained its careful oversight of this project as the agreement mandated that all of the unbound books were to be delivered to Stationers' Hall before they were sold.[11]

We do not know how well this edition sold. John King has suggested that 'Initial sales may have disappointed Short or the syndicate, because he substituted a variant title page during the following year. It conveyed the impression that he had published a new, and therefore more saleable,

[9] Arber, *Transcripts*, II, p. 473.

[10] The court entry identifying Short's role in the book's production appears on 7 April 1595 in Register B. See *Records of the Court of the Stationers' Company 1576–1602*, p. 51.

[11] Ibid., p. 51. King maintains that the 'stationers' (presumably the members of the syndicate) would have sold the books for 'at least £1.5' (King, *Print Culture*, p. 137). It is not apparent what information King is basing this conclusion upon. There is certainly nothing in the agreement that dictates the retail price of the book. There is, however, one piece of solid evidence about the price of this edition. In October 1600 the court of the Stationers' Company ordered that one Joseph Hunt pay 21s to Humphrey Lownes for a copy of the 'Book of Martyrs'. The order does not specify whether the copy was bound or unbound (*Records of the Court of the Stationers' Company 1576–1602*, p. 79).

edition.'[12] There are a number of assumptions in this statement that require examination. First of all, there is the matter of the 'title pages', which needs some explanation. There is a title page for the work as a whole, which gives the date of printing as June 1596. Some copies of the work have another title page preceding the second volume, which is for that volume only and dated 1597. This second title page, which begins 'The Seconde Volume of the Ecclesiasticall Historie . . .', was probably added when the decision was made to divide the work into two volumes. (The initial title page makes no mention of the work appearing in two volumes.) There is no evidence that this title page was added to increase sales, nor is it clear how it would have done so.[13]

The other, much more weighty, reason for arguing that book sales may have been disappointing is the delay of fourteen years between this and the next edition. However, there were other issues besides slow sales delaying another edition. For one thing, there was a complicated situation as to who would be allowed to print the book and where permission to print it would come from. Richard Day only died in 1606, and at some point the work passed into the hands of the Stationers' Company as part of their stock.[14] (Another potential complication arose upon the death of Peter Short and the subsequent marriage, in 1604, of his widow to the printer Humphrey Lownes. It is unclear what ambitions Lownes had, if any, for printing the *Acts and Monuments* at this stage, but it is certainly significant that he would be the printer of the next edition in 1610.[15]) We do not know when the Stationers' Company first acquired the book but it is certainly possible that once they obtained it the reprinting of the book proceeded smoothly.

The sixth edition, as stated, was printed by Humphrey Lownes in 1610 under the oversight of the Stationers' Company and financed by a syndicate of booksellers.[16] This arrangement – the financing of the printing by a syndicate of booksellers, who then divided the profits – would become the basic model followed in the printing of the unabridged editions of Foxe produced in the first half of the seventeenth century. What would change, as we shall see, is the number of printers who would be entrusted with the

[12] King, *Print Culture*, p. 138.

[13] In the Cambridge University Library copy of this work (shelfmark Syn.1.59.2-) there is a version of the title page for the second volume placed at the beginning of the first volume, with the word 'first' printed and pasted over the word 'second'.

[14] For a discussion of the 'English stock' see John Barnard's introduction to *The Cambridge History of the Book in Britain*, vol. V: *1557–1695*, ed. John Barnard and D. F. McKenzie (Cambridge, 2002), pp. 14–16.

[15] Leslie M. Oliver, 'The Seventh Edition of John Foxe's *Acts and Monuments*', *Papers of the Bibliographical Society of America*, 37 (1943), p. 258.

[16] W. A. Jackson, *Letter Book of the Stationers' Company* (London, 1957), pp. 434–5.

printing of the book. In printing these editions, the syndicates had one major advantage: unlike John Day, they did not face the challenge of an unstable text, in which material was constantly being added during the printing process. The main body of the 1583 edition – as opposed to preliminary material or the appendices – was essentially printed without change throughout the early modern period.[17] Additions were made to the preliminaries and appendices in subsequent editions. In the 1596 edition the only addition was a poem praising John Foxe written by John Hopkins.[18] In the 1610 edition Edward Bulkeley added material on the French wars of religion, along with a brief mention of the Gunpowder Plot.[19] The most extensive and important changes were made to the 1631–2 edition. Most notably Bulkeley's material, now reprinted, was followed by 'a treatise of afflictions and persecutions of the faithful', followed by a 106-page account of persecutions of continental Protestants, along with fairly detailed relations of the Spanish Armada and the Gunpowder Plot.[20] Also included were a subject index and a chronology.[21]

The major addition to the next edition was a memoir of John Foxe by his youngest son, Simeon.[22] This was followed by material from an appendix to the 1583 edition covering events of the reigns of Henry VIII and Edward VI.[23] No changes were made to the contents of the 1684 (ninth) edition, although some of the preliminary material was reordered into different volumes. Changes were also made to the paratext throughout these editions, which we will not list here.[24] And finally, from 1631 onwards, editions of the *Acts and Monuments* were printed in three volumes instead of two (each volume with its own title page and pagination). Despite their importance,

---

[17] Some material was added to the 1596 edition that was taken from the Tower records. For example, cf. *1596*, pp. 298–300 and 303–5 with *1583*, pp. 329–30 and 333. Perhaps this material was from notes found among Foxe's papers or, less plausibly, they were the results of someone's further research.

[18] *1596*, sig. ¶8ᵛ.

[19] *1610*, pp. 1950–2. The material on the French wars of religion consists almost exclusively of accounts of massacres and regicides, translated – as Bulkeley acknowledges – from Jacques-Auguste de Thou's magisterial *Historia sui temporis*.

[20] The treatise and the account of the continental persecutions had separate pagination from the rest of the volume: *1631–2*, III, section ii, sigs. A2ʳ–B3ʳ and pp. 1–106. The continuation and probably the treatise were written anonymously by Nathaniel Homes. (Homes's authorship was revealed in the 1641 edition.)

[21] *1631–2*, I, sigs. ( ) 1ʳ–6ᵛ and (A) 1ʳ–(I)6ᵛ.

[22] The Latin original of this memoir is *1641*, II, sigs. A1ʳ–B3ᵛ. The English translation is *1641*, II, sigs. A3ʳ–B6ᵛ. Each of the two versions of the life of Foxe have separate signatures, which both use the signatures A and B. On the provenance and contents of this memoir see Mozley, *John Foxe and his Book*, pp. 1–11, the *ODNB* life of Foxe, and Freeman, 'Through a Venice Glass Darkly', pp. 314–16.

[23] *1641*, II, pp. 1–22.

[24] The paratext has been briefly discussed by John King, *Print Culture*, p. 136.

326

the changes to the preliminaries and appendices represented only a small portion of the approximately 2,000 pages in each of these editions. The fact remains that the vast majority of Foxe's text remained remarkably stable and therefore comparatively easy to print from 1596 to 1684.

III

However, printers also faced increasing disadvantages during the seventeenth century when printing the *Acts and Monuments*. One of these was inherent in the method of production by syndicate. The fact that a large number of people were involved in the production of a book brought increasing complications regarding individual shares in the task of printing it and the profits deriving from it. This became particularly apparent with the printing of the seventh edition of the *Acts and Monuments*, which took place during the years 1631–2. On 7 September 1629 the Stationers' Company, in an obvious effort to launch a new edition, made an offer that if ten members of the Company banded together to undertake the printing of the work, they would receive the Company's permission to print in return for the modest payment of 12 pence in every pound made from sales.[25] (John King makes a good deal even better by giving the proffered figure as 'one penny per pound on the retail price'.[26])

According to John King, 'the Stationers' Company took steps to initiate production of a seventh edition' only when the previous edition had gone out of print.[27] It is true that the order confirming the reprinting of the 'Book of Martyrs' by the Stationers' Company on 5 March 1631 observes that it is 'out of print'.[28] However, it does not describe how long it has been out of print and it certainly does not state that it has recently sold out. Furthermore, the order goes on immediately to declare that 'certayne persons of quality' wished that a new edition be made 'for the generall good of the Kingdome'. These people had warned the wardens of the Company 'that if the Company would not print it for themselves that they would take a Course for the speedy doeing of it elsewhere'.[29]

The motivation behind this may well have been political. At the beginning of March 1629 Charles I suddenly dissolved parliament. Prior to its dissolution, the Commons had been preoccupied with attacking

---

[25] See *Records of the Court of the Stationers' Company 1576–1602*, p. 237.
[26] King, *Print Culture*, p. 146.   [27] Ibid.
[28] See *Records of the Court of the Stationers' Company*, p. 230.   [29] See ibid.

Catholicism and uncovering Arminianism in high places.[30] It was clear with the dissolution of parliament that these attacks would necessarily be muted and, additionally, that peace with France and Spain, the major Catholic powers, would necessarily follow. Trying to resurrect Foxe's work six months later may well have been an attempt to continue parliament (and the wars) by other means. Admittedly this is speculative, but there is evidence to support this hypothesis. The large continuation on the persecution of the Protestants that was added to this edition is not only manifestly anti-Catholic, it also places Catholic attempts to overthrow the English crown, through either conquest or subversion, within the context of persecution of Protestants within French and Spanish territories.[31] It should be remembered that although the entry in the Stationers' records describing this intervention by 'persons of quality' is dated August 1631, it clearly took place some time previous to that, quite possibly before the Company's attempt, in September 1629, to inaugurate a new edition.

An entry of 1 August 1631 in the Company's court book (Register B) states that no single printer was willing to undertake the printing of the work proposed by the Company nearly two years previously. Instead, three printers, Adam Islip, Felix Kingston and Robert Young, had agreed to print it and obtained finance from a group of sixteen members of the Stationers' Company.[32] The three printers were all well positioned to undertake a work of this size. Islip, who may have been the most prominent of the three, had been a warden of the Stationers' Company and one of its leading members for years. He had acquired the printing equipment of the late, and not necessarily lamented, John Wolfe, which gave him sufficient resources to undertake a large edition.[33] Felix Kingston was another well-established printer, having been made King's Printer for Ireland on 21 May 1618.[34] Robert Young had been an agent in Dublin for the Irish stock and King's Printer for Scotland. Because he had first been an apprentice and then later partner to Humphrey Lownes, Young had spent a significant

---

[30] Conrad Russell, *Parliaments and English Politics 1621–29* (Oxford, 1979), pp. 404–16.
[31] For a more detailed analysis of the political themes of this continuation, see Damian Nussbaum, 'Appropriating Martyrdom: Fears of Renewed Persecution and the 1632 Edition of the *Acts and Monuments*', in *John Foxe and the English Reformation*, ed. Loade, pp. 185–8. It is also interesting and probably significant that it was Nathaniel Homes who compiled this continuation. Although later a prominent Independent minister, at this time Homes was a more obscure figure, who had just been made rector of Whipsnade, Bedfordshire. The question arises, did he come forward voluntarily with this continuation, or was he encouraged to compile it by someone else? For a discussion of Homes's editorial interventions see King, *Print Culture*, pp. 148 and 286–8.
[32] See *Records of the Court of the Stationers' Company 1576–1602*, pp. 231 and 237.
[33] See John Wolfe in *ODNB*.
[34] See Robert Steele, 'The King's Printers', *The Library*, 7th series (1926), p. 321.

portion of his working life acquainted with the 'Book of Martyrs'.[35] The establishment of this triumvirate is a telling indication of the challenges printers, lacking Day's web of patents, faced in producing the *Acts and Monuments*. It required the combined efforts of three of the most important printers in the three kingdoms, financed by no fewer than sixteen people, to undertake this project. By the beginning of August 1631 the three printers had already purchased some of their paper supply and commenced work on the impression; the purpose of the August entry in the register was merely to note that the Company approved the existing agreement between the printers and the syndicate.

By 5 March 1632 serious tensions had divided Robert Young from the other members of the syndicate.[36] They complained to the Stationers' Company that Young had entered into a partnership with two other printers, Miles Fletcher and John Haviland, to reprint a new edition of Thomas Mason's abridgement of Foxe, *Christs victorie over Sathans Tyrannie*.[37] This seems an odd choice for several reasons. Mason's book had only sold in one edition back in 1615. Presumably Young was taking advantage of an arrangement he had made with Mason's widow Helen (who crucially still held the patent to produce the work) in order to print his own independent version of Mason's book in addition to the unabridged edition of the 'Book of Martyrs', of which he was only one of three printers. The syndicate had some major grounds for objection. The first was that the unabridged edition was already delayed and that Young's abridgement was impeding its completion. The second issue was that Young was expanding Mason's original text by as much as a third by adding material from the new edition of Foxe. The syndicate was worried that Mason's already substantial abridgement, enhanced with the new material pilfered by Young, would cause the new edition of Mason to do 'much hurt' to the sale of the new edition of Foxe. The court of the Stationers' Company sided with the syndicate and ruled that, since new material was being added to Mason's original book, Young's edition of *Christs victorie* was not covered by Helen Mason's patent. The Company ordered that the presses of Fletcher and others involved in the printing of the new edition of Mason be dismantled

---

[35] See Arnold Hunt, 'Book Trade Patents, 1603–1640', in *The Book Trade and its Customers 1450–1900: Historical Essays for Robin Myers*, ed. Arnold Hunt, Giles Mandelbrote and Alison Shell (Winchester, 1997), pp. 27–54.

[36] *Pace* King, this entry is 5 March 1632 (in new style) and not 1631. This is not a trivial error because, as a result of this misdating, King's narrative of events is out of sequence (see King, *Print Culture*, pp. 146–7).

[37] Thomas Mason, *Christs victorie over Sathans Tyrannie . . .* (London, 1615), STC 17622.

and that the sheets of the edition be brought to Stationers' Hall where they would be sequestered.[38]

IV

The difficulties in printing the seventh edition of the *Acts and Monuments* epitomise the increasing difficulties involved in reprinting Foxe's work during the seventeenth century. The financial and logistical problems necessitated the involvement of large numbers of people; this created the seeds for potential conflict, as these people all had their own agendas and interests. There was an additional complication in the proliferation of rights generated by the printing of Foxe in both abridged and unabridged editions; as was the case in 1632, there was the potential for these to come into conflict.[39] There was also the question of the degree to which the increasing number of abridgements of Foxe hampered the sales of the unabridged editions. This is difficult to answer definitively. The abridgements were often so different in scope and content from each other and from the unabridged editions that it would seem that there was room for all of them to coexist because of their appeal to different markets and incomes.[40]

Nevertheless, as the dispute over the reprinting of *Christs victorie* indicates, the fear certainly existed among printers that the abridgements would eat into their profits. Nor was this fear confined to the vigilant self-interest of those who had capital invested in printing an unabridged edition of Foxe. At his trial Archbishop Laud would declare that Robert Young – who had apparently not abandoned the idea of printing an abridgement of Foxe – had repeatedly sought his support for such a project and that he had refused, 'lest it should bring the large Book it self into disuse'.[41] Even if the sales of the abridged editions of Foxe did not compete with the unabridged editions, the prevalent anxiety that they did may well have hindered the production

---

[38] *Records of the Court of the Stationers' Company 1576–1602*, pp. 237–8.

[39] In addition to the problems with the seventh edition, it is instructive to look at the complications over the right to print the different editions of Clement Cotton's abridgements of the 'Book of Martyrs'. See Kastan, 'Little Foxes', pp. 123–4.

[40] The great successes among the abridgements were Clement Cotton's *The Mirror of Martyrs*, which was a collection of anecdotes and aphorisms of the martyrs, arranged by topic in a duodecimo of over 200 pages, and John Taylor's versified abridgement of Foxe's book. See Green, *Print and Protestantism*, pp. 387–8, and Kastan, 'Little Foxes', pp. 123–4 and 128. Two common elements to these abridgements, apart from their popularity, are their low cost and their radical restructuring of Foxe's text.

[41] William Laud, *The Works of William Laud*, ed. W. Scott and J. Bliss, 7 vols. (Oxford, 1847–60), IV, p. 265.

of new editions of the *Acts and Monuments*, as it would have caused people to hesitate in either producing or financing them.

In fact it could be argued that the seventh edition would not have been printed if it had not been for the consistent intervention of the Stationers' Company in its production. They allowed its reprinting in return for only token payment; without this encouragement, there might well have been no reprinting at all. They intervened decisively to defend the interests of those financing the work when they appeared to be threatened, and they even advertised the new work. As part of the English stock, the Stationers' Company held the rights to almanacs printed in London. In 1633 and 1634 the Company apparently used the leverage this gave them to insert identical advertisements for the new edition in many – but not all – of the almanacs known to have been printed in London during those two years.[42] These advertisements read: 'The Booke of Martyrs newly printed in London 1632, in 3. Volumes, with Additions of divers Martyrs that have suffred for the Gospell in forraine parts, together with the barbarous cruelties exercised upon the Professors of the Gospell in the Valtoline, and with divers other Additions.' This is a rather surprising measure, since the Stationers' Company did not have a large financial stake in the sales of the new edition. The fact that they were ready to take this unprecedented step is indicative of both the diligence with which the Company protected those who financed the edition and perhaps also the concerns of these financiers over its sales. And finally it underscores the crucial role the Company played in seeing that the seventh edition was undertaken at all.

Another consequence of the increasing number of participants necessary for the *Acts and Monuments* to be produced was an increase in the price of the book beyond the normal inflation of the period. Partly this was because the size of the book grew as the individual printers added additional material, either for ideological reasons or to make the new editions distinct from the old. (Without denying the validity of Damian Nussbaum's analysis of the ideological motivations behind the major additions to the seventh edition, it is also interesting that the advertisements that the Stationers' Company placed in almanacs focused on the additions made to the *Acts and Monuments*, presumably because this made the edition more marketable.) Even more fundamentally, there was the split of the seventh

---

[42] A cursory examination of the surviving almanacs printed in 1633 and 1634, now held at Lambeth Palace Library and the British Library, supplies the following examples: STC 407.16, 529.7, 495.9, 490.10, 529.8, and 496.

edition into three volumes. The reason for this appears to have been quite simple: each one of the three printers produced one volume apiece. (Kingston, Islip and Young produced the first, second and third volumes respectively.[43]) Whatever other effects dividing the work into three volumes had, it certainly increased the price of the book by adding to the charge for binding, if nothing else. The retail price of the *Acts and Monuments* seems to have climbed from about 25s to about 40s during the sixteenth century and up to £2–3 in the next century.

In 1570 Westminster Abbey purchased the two-volume 1570 edition for 38s, while three years later St Michael Cornhill purchased the same edition for 42s 6d, which, however, included the price of a chain, a lock and four keys.[44] In contrast, an edition of the 1610 *Acts and Monuments* in the town library at Ipswich was valued in a 1618 inventory at £2 14s.[45] The syndicate behind the seventh edition agreed that the wholesale price of the new edition would be 46s 8d.[46] Purchases of the *Acts and Monuments* by churches across England give a fairly consistent price for the 1631/2 edition as being somewhat under £3. In 1633 Waltham Holy Cross in Essex spent £2 13s on a copy (plus another shilling for having it transported from London).[47] The parish of All Saints, Derby, managed to purchase the 1631/2 edition of the *Acts and Monuments* the previous year for only £2 13s; it is unclear if this included any transportation cost, since none is listed in their accounts.[48] In 1633 Cratfield parish in Suffolk paid the higher price of £2 19s for the 'Book of Martyrs'.[49] The price may have risen further, as in 1641 the London parish of St Christopher le Stocks paid £3 for '3 bookes of Mart[yrs]'.[50] In 1708 the Kentish parish of Milton Regis paid £3 3s 'for a book of martyrs and monuments of the church in three volumes in folio'.[51]

A price of around £3 must have had a serious effect on the sales of the work. Although wages for labourers were rising through to the middle of the seventeenth century, eventually climbing from about 4s 8d in 1589 to around 6s a week seven decades later, at that point a new edition of the

[43] Oliver has determined, on the basis of printer's ornaments and initial capitals, how the task was divided between the three men. See Oliver, 'The Seventh Edition', pp. 249–51.

[44] Westminster Abbey Muniments, MS 33629, fo. 6ᵛ, and Guildhall Library, London, MS 4071/1, fo. 99ᵛ.

[45] John Blatchly, *The Town Library of Ipswich Provided for the Use of the Town Preachers in 1599* (Woodbridge, 1989), pp. 110 and 180.

[46] Jackson, *Letter Book*, p. 434. [47] ERO, MS D/P 75/5/1, fo. 39ʳ.

[48] Derbyshire Record Office, MS D3372/86/, fo. 20ᵛ. We would like to thank John Craig for this reference.

[49] SRO, MS FC 62/A6, pp. 156–7. We would like to thank John Craig for this reference.

[50] *Accomptes of the Churchwardens of the Paryshe of St. Christofer's in London 1575–1662*, ed. Edwin Freshfield (London, 1885), p. 95.

[51] Centre for Kentish Studies, Maidstone, MS P253/5/1 (unpaginated).

Acts and Monuments would still have consumed more than three months' wages.[52] Even for those further up the social and economic ladder, purchase of one of the three-volume editions was a substantial investment. Keith Wrightson has estimated that an early modern English husbandman, owning about 30 acres of land, might reasonably have expected to produce an annual surplus of £3–4 after meeting the subsistence needs of his family.[53] The considerable cost of this book must have lessened the demand for it by the reading public. In fact it is only the political and religious interests of an influential minority that ensured that the book was reprinted at intervals throughout the seventeenth century. This is not to say that sales were a negligible factor, but rather that other factors contributed to outweigh the difficulties inherent in producing a book that demanded such an expenditure of time, energy and money.

V

This can be seen readily in the printing of the eighth edition and the fortunes of the book during the 1630s. William Prynne famously charged in 1637 that Archbishop Laud had denied a licence for a new edition of the *Acts and Monuments*.[54] Prynne, who was the prosecutor at Laud's trial, had an obvious motive in wishing to vilify the archbishop and managed to work up a considerable amount of indignation, claiming that Laud, by preventing the printing of the *Acts and Monuments*, was acting 'against our own English martyres, the Professors of the Protestant religion in all ages and so by consequence against our Religion it selfe'.[55] Laud, at his trial, defended himself, stating, as we have seen, that what had actually happened was that Robert Young had 'laboured me earnestly and often' for permission to print an abridgement of the *Acts and Monuments* and that he had refused in order to protect the sales of the unabridged editions of Foxe's book.

A number of scholars have taken Laud at his word. Sheila Lambert has pointed to the difficulties in printing the 1631/2 edition, thus implying that it was these difficulties, rather than overt censorship, that prevented the *Acts and Monuments* from being produced. She also declares that the agreement

---

[52] Peter J. Bowden, 'Statistical Appendix, 1500–1640', in *Economic Change: Prices, Wages, Profits and Rents, 1500–1750*, ed. P. J. Bowden (Cambridge, 1990), p. 166; also see Ann Jennalie Cook, *The Privileged Playgoers of Shakespeare's London, 1576–1643* (Princeton, NJ, 1981), p. 279.

[53] Keith Wrightson, *English Society 1580–1680* (London, 1982), pp. 32–4.

[54] William Prynne, *Canterburies doome, or, The first part of a compleat history of the commitment, charge, tryall, condemnation, execution of William Laud . . .* (London, 1646), Wing P3917, p. 184.

[55] Ibid., p. 193.

for the seventh edition 'shows that 1,600 copies were expected to sell over three years, but this estimate must have proved optimistic for there was no new edition for nine years'.[56] Once again, a scholar is assuming that once an edition was sold out it was then automatically reprinted. There is no evidence to support this assumption, and it is possible that calls for an edition in 1637 – if they existed – came from influential people, as was the case with past editions, rather than because of the market. Lambert goes on to declare that printing of the eighth edition in 1641 must have commenced before Laud's fall in December 1640 and thereby implies that the archbishop did not oppose the printing. However, it was obvious to all, at least by April 1640, when Charles summoned parliament and ended his personal rule, that Laud's powers would certainly be curtailed and his advocacy would become irrelevant. Lambert also accepts at face value Laud's claims, declaring that 'What Laud prevented was a pirate edition which would have ruined the sale of the complete work.'[57] There is no way of knowing if, in fact, this was Laud's motivation in refusing to allow Young's abridgement (if indeed he refused to support it at all; we only have Laud's version of his dealings with Young).

King repeats Lambert's arguments and extends them by pointing out that Laud owned a copy of the *Whole workes of W. Tyndale, John Frith and Doct. Barnes* and that Charles I had a copy of the 1641 edition of the 'Book of Martyrs' in his library. King concludes that these facts render 'the view that Laud attempted to block its [i.e., the *Acts and Monuments*] publication all the more unlikely'.[58] This seems to be a bit of a stretch, however, as we all own books whose contents we either disagree with or disapprove of. In fact, Laud's attitudes and policies towards Foxe's martyrology are not easy to establish, but while the archbishop's own views may have remained unspoken, it is also true 'that Laudians made a point of denigrating and distancing themselves from the Elizabethan moderate puritan tradition of English Protestantism represented by figures such as John Foxe'.[59] Damian Nussbaum, in a discussion of the status of the *Acts and Monuments* in the 1630s, provides what is probably the most accurate assessment of the

[56] Lambert, 'Richard Montagu, Arminianism and Censorship', pp. 63–4.
[57] Ibid., p. 64.   [58] King, *Print Culture*, p. 151.
[59] Anthony Milton, *Catholic and Reformed: The Roman and Protestant Churches in English Protestant Thought, 1600–1640* (Cambridge, 1995), p. 539. For examples of Laudian writers disagreeing with aspects of Foxe's work see pp. 304–7 and 312–19. For the scattered examples, almost all of them capable of multiple interpretations, where Laud reacted to Foxe's book see Damian Nussbaum, 'Laudian Foxe-Hunting? William Laud and the Status of John Foxe in the 1630s', in *The Church Retrospective*, ed. Robert Swanson, Studies in Church History XXXIII (Woodbridge, 1997), pp. 329–42, and Evenden and Freeman, 'Print, Profit and Propaganda', pp. 1288–9.

situation: 'Laud may not have challenged Foxe directly but neither did he champion him.'[60] However, Laud's failure to take any action in support of a new edition may well have had the same consequences during the 1630s as opposing it actively, whatever the archbishop's intentions might have been. Given the complex organisation and logistical support that a new edition of Foxe's book demanded, the intervention of influential people was essential in the production of any new edition. Opposition, even unspoken opposition, by the primate of the Church of England, may well have caused such support to evaporate and, in effect, have worked to prevent its printing as effectively as overt censorship would have done.

In fact, it seems clear that the printing of the eighth edition was a consequence of the diminution of Laud's authority at the end of the 1630s, and that when the book appeared it did so with material support from the Long Parliament. If it were not for the Long Parliament, it is doubtful that a new edition of Foxe's book would have been printed only nine years after the seventh edition – the shortest period separating editions during the seventeenth century. Parliament appears to have been anxious to produce something along the lines of an 'official' history of the English Church. They toyed with the idea of printing Thomas Harding's gargantuan 5,400-folio annals of Church history. The cost of this was, however, prohibitive, and a new edition of Foxe's book appeared – for perhaps the only time in its printing history – as the economical alternative.[61]

Two additions were made to the second volume of the new edition. One of these consists of material from an appendix to the 1583 edition. This in turn consisted of material that had been in the first edition and had not been subsequently reprinted.[62] John King discerns a political purpose behind the inclusion of this appendix: with it the 1641 edition 'drove a wedge between bishop-martyrs such as Hooper and Ridley, on the one hand, and Caroline prelates, on the other'.[63] This is a tempting conclusion, since it would fit with the presumed motives of the Long Parliament in printing the new edition. However, an examination of the contents of the reprinted appendix does not support this interpretation. The first nine pages are a reprinting of letters by Stephen Gardiner to the duke of Somerset, which could conform readily to an anti-prelatical agenda. The same cannot be said of Hugh Latimer's *denial* (which occupies the next five pages) that he had preached that the Virgin Mary was a sinner, that saints were not to be honoured and that Hell and Purgatory did not exist. If the purpose here was to glorify Latimer as a contrast

[60] Nussbaum, 'Laudian Foxe-Hunting?', p. 339.   [61] Milton, *Catholic and Reformed*, pp. 320–1.
[62] *1641*, II, pp. 1–22.   [63] King, *Print Culture*, p. 132.

to Stephen Gardiner, these conservative sentiments would hardly serve that purpose in the 1640s. It is also difficult to comprehend the political motive in reprinting a 1531 proclamation against heretical books, which occupies the final nine pages of this section. In truth, this edition does not seem to have been made for any political reason; instead the reprinted appendix was probably the product of a search for material that could lend some novelty to the new edition and make it more commercially viable.

However, although the additional material in the eighth edition does not appear to have had the polemical thrust of the material added to the seventh edition, there is some evidence that this new edition had a particular appeal for the godly. For example, St Christopher le Stocks parish in London purchased the 1641 edition. Two years previously the parish had paid £7 14s in charges relating to a petition to the Lord Treasurer to have the communion table moved from the east end of the church. In 1641–2 the parish paid £14 2s 7d for the relief of ejected nonconformist ministers in England and a further £10 for the relief of ejected nonconformist ministers in Ireland. They also paid £17 2s 5d for the relief of the New England colonists.[64] In this context it is hard not to see the purchase of the 1641 edition of the *Acts and Monuments* as something of a political statement by the parish.

VI

Although the ninth edition would not be printed for over four decades, there are some indications that the Stationers' Company was interested in printing a new edition earlier than this. In 1660 they presented Charles II with an opulent copy of the *Acts and Monuments* at their own expense; moreover, this expense was substantial since the binding alone cost £7 10s and the Stationers' Company spent a further £2 2s 7d on ribbons and fringes for the volume.[65] In a Company not renowned for its generosity, and with a recipient not particularly known for his partiality to Foxe, this gift almost certainly had an ulterior purpose. Writing much later, Roger Morrice declared that sponsors of the 1684 edition had 'in a manner' received a promise from Charles II to renew the canon of 1571, which required that the book be purchased and displayed in all cathedrals and in the houses of senior clergy. Morrice further claimed that papists had prevented the promise from being fulfilled.[66] Presumably the gift of a splendid copy of

---

[64] Freshfield, *Accompts*, pp. 91 and 99.   [65] King, *Print Culture*, pp. 268–9.
[66] Mark Goldie, *The Entring Book of Roger Morrice, 1677–1691*, vol. 1: *Roger Morrice and the Puritan Whigs* (Woodbridge, 2007), p. 50.

Foxe's book was an initial attempt by the Stationers' Company to secure the revival of the canon. In the event, a new edition would not appear for nearly a quarter of a century after this and when it did appear it was almost certainly as a consequence of a decision made not by Charles II but by his brother, James, duke of York: his decision to convert to Catholicism.

The imminent prospect of a Catholic becoming king, with the renewed threat of persecution that many Protestants felt would be a direct consequence of this, made the *Acts and Monuments* frighteningly relevant. Subsequent events, such as the Ryehouse Plot and the execution of the conspirators, particularly Lord William Russell, created new martyrs for ardent Protestants.[67] However, the book may have been too relevant for its own good. Charles II was hardly going to lend any support to a book that would be a rallying point for those who were trying to exclude his brother from the throne. For the printing of every unabridged edition of the *Acts and Monuments* a means had been found, whether through patents or through the creation of syndicates, to secure finance for the printers before the venture even started. Patents were no longer viable in the later seventeenth century and the seventh edition had demonstrated how cumbersome the creation of a syndicate could be. A new means was found to finance the ninth edition, one which benefited from the fact that it was a project favoured by a particular political group.

This time the work was not financed by a syndicate but instead money was raised through subscription to finance the work through the press.[68] An advertisement printed in the 18 May 1683 issue of Henry Care's anti-Catholic newsletter, *The Weekly Pacquet of Advice from Rome*, provides a description of how this was arranged:

The Reprinting of Mr Fox's Book of Martyrs in Three Volumes, without any Addition or Alteration either in Sense or Word, on a new Roman Letter, with Figures Engraven on Copper Plates, having been Proposed to be done by Subscription, at Forty five shillings for one Copy in Quires of the Ordinary Paper, twenty shillings to be payd in hand, the rest on delivery, and for the best Paper in Quires, three Pounds; thirty shillings in hand. For a further Encouragement, those that Subscribe for Six to have a Seventh gratis. The

---

[67] Lois Schwoerer has gone so far as to suggest that the 1684 edition was printed as part of the controversy surrounding Lord Russell's execution. Lois G. Schwoerer, 'William Laud Russell: The Making of a Martyr, 1683–1983', *Journal of British Studies*, 24 (1985), p. 59, n. 92. As we have seen, plans for a new edition seem to have been afoot for quite a while, but it is certainly true that Russell's execution made a new edition of the 'Book of Martyrs' very topical.

[68] Interestingly another effort had been made to print Thomas Harding's sprawling annals in the 1650s and the plan was to finance this by subscription. The plan seems to have foundered because the estimated cost of printing the work was £2,000 (Milton, *Catholic and Reformed*, p. 321, n. 237).

Undertakers, William Rawlins and Samuel Roycroft, in Great Bartholomew's
Close, are preparing Letter, Paper and Plates for carrying on the said Work, and
intend to begin the same by the first of August and to have it finished by Lady-day
next: And therefore those who will take the benefit of there Proposals, are desired to
send in their Subscriptions before the end of July next, for that the Undertakers do
adhere to their resolution of Printing no more then are subscribed for. A Catalogue
of the Names of those Gentlemen whose subscriptions are already come to the
hands of the undertakers will in a few dayes be Printed.[69]

These terms were echoed in a notice Roger Morrice placed in his 'entring
book', which, once again, stated that the terms were 45s a book, and that
half had to be paid in advance.[70] Beyond these advertisements there also
seems to have been a conscious effort to drum up subscriptions throughout
the kingdom: for example, the pastor of the Presbyterian congregation in
Leeds seems to have met with parishioners in order to recruit subscribers for
the book.[71]

No changes were made to the contents of the 1641 edition; unlike
previous editions, it did not broadcast or signal its intentions through
textual changes. However, the ninth edition was clearly championed by
both Whigs and nonconformists. The advertisement of the work in Henry
Care's newsletter alone testifies to its being targeted at a Whig audience, as
does the fact that no less a figure than John Locke received subscriptions for
the work.[72] It was necessary that the drive to raise subscriptions be extensive
and well organised, since this was the sole means by which the hundreds of
pounds necessary to finance the production of the work was raised.

A key point mentioned by both Care and Morrice was that the work was in
new roman type (or, as Morrice has it, a 'good Roman character'). Clearly part
of the appeal of this volume was in the modernity of its appearance. Another
feature adding to this new look was the illustrations, which were done in
copperplate engravings. These illustrations replicated the basic content of the
earlier woodcuts but, in addition to the difference in quality between the
engravings and the woodcuts, the new illustrations were also modernised by
depicting distinctly seventeenth-century costumes and buildings.

The new engravings would have been a significant expense. Yet despite
inflation the price of these volumes seems to have remained constant with

[69] Henry Care, *The Weekly Pacquet of Advice from Rome*, v, no. 39 (18 May 1683), p. 312.
[70] *The Entring Book of Roger Morrice*, vol. ii: *The Reign of Charles II*, ed. John Spurr, p. 346.
[71] *The Diary of Ralph Thoresby, FRS*, ed. Joseph Hunter, 2 vols. (London, 1830), i, p. 166.
[72] In June 1683 John Locke received £1 from a friend as a subscription for this edition (Goldie, *Roger Morrice*, p. 50, n. 6). For further evidence of nonconformist involvement see Dr Williams's Library, Morrice MS P, p. 354.

the price of the seventh and eighth editions. This would suggest that subscription was a more efficient means of financing the work than the formation of syndicates had been. Nevertheless, the 1684 edition would be the last unabridged edition of Foxe for about a century and a half. This might be explained by a lack of interest in the 'Book of Martyrs'. However, this would seem to be belied by the proliferation of abridgements of Foxe – some of them very substantial works in their own right – throughout the eighteenth century. Perhaps a more fundamental reason for the 1684 edition having no imminent successors may be a limitation in the method of subscription: it depended on being able to muster a sizeable group of people (much larger than a syndicate) with enough interest in the *Acts and Monuments* to be able to pay a substantial amount of the cost of the book in a lump sum, well before its receipt. The *Acts and Monuments* was about to enter its period of greatest dissemination but this would be because a method was found in the eighteenth century of financing the book that was an improvement on paying for it entirely by subscription.

VII

Throughout the seventeenth century the Stationers' Company, exercising its rights, had fostered the periodic reprinting of the *Acts and Monuments*. During this time, the Company seems to have been motivated by political more than financial concerns, at least regarding the production of this book. When the Licensing Act lapsed in 1695 the Stationers' Company lost its monopolies, including that for the *Acts and Monuments*. Passage of the statute 8 Ann. c. 19 permitted unrestricted reprinting of Foxe's book.[73]

One might have expected that without the support of the Stationers' Company the book might have proved to be unprintable and thus faded into obscurity. In a sense this happened, as no further unabridged edition of Foxe's book would appear throughout the long eighteenth century. Eirwen Nicholson claims that 'in publication terms it [the *Acts and Monuments*] ceases to exist after 1684'.[74] However, in contrast, Linda Colley has maintained that Foxe's book wielded a considerable influence in the eighteenth century and enjoyed an unprecedentedly wide dissemination.[75] Despite their diametrically opposed positions, the problem is largely one of

[73] For discussion of this Act and its effects on the Stationers' Company, as well as authorial copyright, see Mark Rose, *Authors and Owners: The Invention of Copyright* (Cambridge, MA, 1993), pp. 31–48.
[74] Nicholson, 'Eighteenth Century Foxe', p. 149.
[75] Linda Colley, *Britons: Forging the Nation, 1707–1837* (New Haven, CT, 1992), pp. 25–8.

definition. Nicholson dismisses the post-1684 abridgements of Foxe's book as '"bastard" versions'.[76] Colley, on the other hand, counts those proliferating abridgements as legitimate versions of Foxe's work.

It is certainly true that abridged editions are not a full representation of Foxe's thought and that they did narrow the considerable range of his work to a few consistent themes. Nevertheless, to maintain that these abridgements do not represent Foxe's thought at all or that the *Acts and Monuments* suddenly ceased to be a factor in English religion and culture is a fundamental distortion. For example, David Wykes, discussing the diary of the Yorkshire antiquarian Ralph Thoresby, observes that while Thoresby drew on Samuel Clarke's *General Martyrologie*, he did not have access to a copy of Foxe. Wykes concludes that 'It is clear from the diary that it was Clarke's *General Martyrologie* and not Foxe's *Acts and Monuments* which shaped Thoresby's understanding of Catholic persecution.'[77] This is imposing a not unjustified but nevertheless misleading distinction between the two works. While it is important to note that Thoresby was not drawing on Foxe directly, it is also important to remember that Clarke's martyrology is almost entirely derived from Foxe's much larger work.[78]

In fact, in a preface he added to the third edition of his *General Martyrologie*, Samuel Clarke was somewhat defensive about his indebtedness to Foxe, claiming that 'some may think this labour of mine superfluous, because these things have been so largely, and fully, handled by that faithful, and laborious servant of Christ, Master Fox in his *Acts and Monuments*'. After admitting that he had gathered much of his work out of Foxe, Clarke reassured his readers (inaccurately) that he had 'turned over many other authors'.[79] A poem by Thomas Dugard, also added to this edition, comparing Foxe and Clarke, simply presents Clarke's *General Martyrologie* as an abridgement of Foxe:

> Our martyrs here he does present
> Epitomiz'd: what's his intent?
> To pleasure such as cannot buy
> The greater Martyrology

---

[76] Nicholson, 'Eighteenth Century Foxe', p. 149.

[77] David L. Wykes, 'Dissenters and the Writing of History: Ralph Thoresby's "Lives and Characters"', in *Fear, Exclusion and Revolution: Roger Morrice and Britain in the 1680s*, ed. Jason McElligott (Aldershot, 2006), p. 18.

[78] Eirwen Nicholson describes Clarke's *General Martyrology* as a 'Foxe-derived publication' (Nicholson, 'Eighteenth Century Foxe', p. 146), while Patrick Collinson declares that it is 'Foxe *redivivus*' (Patrick Collinson, 'Foxe and National Consciousness', in Highley and King, *John Foxe and his World*, pp. 10–36, at p. 31).

[79] Samuel Clarke, *General Martyrologie* (London, 1677), STC Wing C4515, sigs. A1ᵛ–A 2ʳ.

And such as leisure want to read
What's largely there historied.[80]

It should always be remembered that while the content of abridgements of Foxe varied considerably, most of them, especially the more substantial ones, did accurately represent portions of the text of the *Acts and Monuments*.

It should also be remembered that abridgements are not necessarily small works. In 1732 the London printers John Hart and John Lewis printed *The Book of Martyrs Containing an Account of the Sufferings and Death of the Protestants in the Reign of Queen Mary the First*. This work was an almost complete reprinting of the *contents* of Books 10–12 of the 1641 *Acts and Monuments*, as well as the material added by Bulkeley and Homes. This 'abridgement' was just under a million words. The work also formed the nucleus for a line of abridgements of Foxe that would be printed throughout the eighteenth century.

Hart and Lewis had apparently struck gold. Their massive edition was reprinted by John Lewis as well as other publishers in 1741, 1746 and 1760. In 1761 a London publisher named John Fuller tried to improve on this success. He reprinted the Lewis/Hart 'Book of Martyrs' but he added a preface by the then popular Methodist minister and hymn writer Martin Maden. With more enterprise Fuller also published a companion volume the same year, which compressed the first nine books of the *Acts and Monuments* (covering the Apostolic era through to the death of Edward VI) into around 400,000 words.[81] In a significant indication of the interests of the eighteenth-century reading public, the Fuller volume covering Mary's reign (apart from Maden's preface this was a reprinting of the Lewis/Hart volume) continued its successful run, but Fuller's innovatory volume, covering the first nine books of Foxe, was never reprinted. His volume covering Mary's reign was also reissued by another London publisher, Henry Trapp, in 1776, as the first volume of a two-volume set.[82] The *second* volume of the set was *The Lives of the Primitive Martyrs from the Birth of our Blessed Saviour to the Reign of Queen Mary I*. Despite its similarity to the title of Fuller's earlier volume, this was *not* (*pace* John King) a reprinting of Fuller's abridgement of the first nine books of the *Acts and Monuments*

---

[80] Ibid., sig. a4[r–v].

[81] John Foxe, *The Book of martyrs Containing an Account of the Sufferings and Deaths of Protestants from the Birth of our Saviour Down to Queen Mary I* (London, 1761).

[82] The title of the first volume was identical to that of the Fuller volume covering Mary's reign.

but a considerably smaller work.[83] Once again, the volume covering Mary's reign enjoyed some success; it was reprinted by Trapp in 1784, whereas the companion volume, covering the pre-Marian period, was never reprinted.

In 1782, Alexander Hogg had printed a major new abridgement of Foxe, edited by Paul Wright, an Anglican clergyman. This new abridgement was similar to the previous ones by Fuller and Trapp in its length but differed from them in a number of important ways. It was a single volume and a folio of nearly a thousand pages. The bulk of the volume, the first 725 pages, is an abridged version of Books 10–12 of Foxe's work. This was followed by an abridgement of Homes's account of later persecutions, which first appeared in the 1631/2 edition of the *Acts and Monuments*. This is followed by brief accounts of Quaker and Whig martyrs (extracted from John Tutchin's *Western Martyrology*) and an account of the 'persecution' of Lord George Gordon. Almost as an afterthought, this was followed by a section of just over 110 pages devoted to martyrs from the Maccabees through to the end of the reign of Henry VIII. The next three pages covered martyrs in Lithuania, Poland, China, Japan, Africa and the New World, before another section of seven pages devoted to pre-Marian English martyrs and a final section dealing with various massacres of Protestants in Ireland down to 1690. The heavy emphasis on the Marian period, so typical of the eighteenth-century abridgements of Foxe, thus continued.

The lack of chronological order in the volume was facilitated by the fact that the volume was printed in fascicles. (We will discuss this in more detail shortly.) Hogg reprinted this volume in 1784 but broke it into two volumes of unequal length, whilst retaining the same pagination. Hogg's two-volume edition was a conspicuous success, being reprinted in 1785, 1790, 1795, 1807 and in two editions in 1811. Readers of these 'abridgements' might not have been presented with the entirety of Foxe's history of the Church but they were certainly being presented with a significant portion of it.

With the eighteenth-century abridgements of Foxe we are entering a different system of production from that of the unabridged editions. During the seventeenth century the unabridged editions were reprinted to serve the political agendas of certain influential people. The abridged editions of the eighteenth century were printed for purely commercial reasons and their continued reprinting depended solely on the work's popularity for the first time. The continued sales of all types of abridgements of Foxe, large and small, without monopolies or syndicates of

---

[83] John King maintains incorrectly that Trapp republished the 'two part Fuller text'. John N. King, 'Eighteenth-Century Folio Publication of Foxe's *Book of Martyrs*', *Reformation*, 10 (2005), p. 102.

backers, or any support from the great and the good, indicate that, perhaps for the first time, editions of the *Acts and Monuments* were an unqualified commercial success. Since there had been no unabridged editions of Foxe's book printed since 1684, how can the success of these abridged editions be explained, particularly when some of them were many hundreds of pages in length? Clearly there were elements in Foxe's work that consumers were still anxious to read. What were the ways in which the abridged editions catered to the needs of readers that the unabridged editions did not? One was that the abridged editions almost invariably reworded Foxe, although some of them followed the substance of his text quite closely. A number of them made a point of reassuring readers that they were couched in current speech, rather than in the obsolete syntax and vocabulary of the unabridged editions.[84]

The most fundamental reason, however, for the success of the abridged editions was that they were affordable. One aspect of the reception of Foxe's work that remained constant, going back to William Turner's letter complaining about the price of the 1563 edition, was reader dissatisfaction with the expense of the volume. The seventeenth and eighteenth centuries produced a number of readers anxious to swell this chorus of complaint and printers ready to offer them an alternative. In 1657 the poet and Presbyterian minister Nicholas Billingsley described his abridgement of Foxe as 'the Book of Martyrs in a little room' and declared that it was suitable for those 'for whom the Tyrannie of thine affairs are so imperious, or the weakness of thy purse so injurious, as to impede thy perusal of the History of the Church'.[85] A collection of stories from the *Acts and Monuments*, printed almost half a century later, pointedly described itself as 'a Cheap and Useful book'.[86]

But while it is easy to see why the smaller abridgements of Foxe were inexpensive, it is not as apparent why the large abridgements could remain affordable, particularly since most of these were illustrated. Eighteenth-century printers were able to find the El Dorado, which had eluded their predecessors, of being able to print a large illustrated work that was affordable through a combination of methods. The first was to

---

[84] For example, in an abridgement of Foxe printed in 1701, the anonymous author acknowledged that there was nothing in his work that could not be found in the unabridged *Acts and Monuments*, but he boasted that his new edition had the benefit of not being 'lock'd up in obscure and obsolete Language'. John Foxe *et al.*, *The Book of Martyrs . . . From the time of our blessed Saviour to the year 1701*, 2 vols. (London, 1702), I, sig. A2ᵛ.

[85] Nicholas Billingsley, *Brachy-martyrologia* (London, 1657), STC Wing B2910, sig. A6ᵛ.

[86] John Foxe, *A Select History of the Lives and Sufferings of the Principal English Protestant Martyrs* (London, 1746), title page.

sell subscriptions to the complete book. The second way *combined* with the first was to sell the work in instalments, which could be purchased at weekly intervals and then, if the reader wished, be bound together as a book. The advantage of this method *for publishers* was that it provided them with funding to defray the cost of printing. The advantage for purchasers was that it made the book affordable to those unwilling or unable to put up the entire cost of the book in advance.[87] The preface to the 1732 abridged edition of Foxe (which was published by Hart and Lewis in thirty-one instalments and which was the model for subsequent eighteenth-century large-scale abridgements of Foxe) explained the method:

> The purchase of so voluminous a work cannot be reached by every one's purse at once; and therefore the expedient was resolv'd upon, of publishing a certain number of sheets *weekly*, by subscription, that the common people might also be enabled by degrees to procure it.[88]

Publication of the *Acts and Monuments* by subscription and in instalments continued throughout the eighteenth century, as abridgements of Foxe grew larger and larger. The Fuller (1761) abridgement was published in fifty-nine instalments and the Alexander Hogg edition (1782) in eighty instalments. The abridged editions of the eighteenth century have been unjustly neglected on at least two scores. They hardly deserve the epithet of 'bastard editions' that Nicholson has assigned to them and they certainly do not deserve the neglect of scholars. A number of them were substantial works that communicated a large portion of the material in Foxe to numerous readers. Scholars such as Linda Colley and Colin Haydon, who have emphasised both the influence and wide dissemination of these abridgements during the long eighteenth century, are almost certainly correct in their observations.[89]

---

[87] Linda Colley has pointed to the importance of printing in cheap instalments as a means of disseminating the *Acts and Monuments* (Colley, *Britons*, pp. 40–2). Eirwin Nicholson has suggested that the purpose of serialisation may not have been to reach a wider and less affluent market but rather may 'have been a tactic for the evasion of copyright' (Nicholson, 'Eighteenth Century Foxe', p. 155). However, printing a book in instalments would not have prevented it from being a violation of copyright.

[88] John Foxe, *The Book of Martyrs* (1732), preface (without signature). Contrary to King ('Eighteenth-Century Folio Publication', p. 105), it was Lewis and Hart, not Alexander Hogg, who first published the *Acts and Monuments* in fascicules.

[89] See Colin Haydon, *Anti-Catholicism in Eighteenth Century England* (Manchester, 1993), pp. 28–30; for another example see J. C. D. Clark, *The Language of Liberty 1660–1832* (Cambridge, 1994), pp. 47–8.

VIII

Study of the making of the *Acts and Monuments* provides an excellent vantage point to consider not only the history of the book and authorship in early modern England, it also allows us to question anachronistic assumptions that have been made about both. Some of these assumptions are made about John Day. Scholars commonly refer to Day as either a publisher or a printer–publisher. Day was a printer but he was *not* a publisher in the modern sense of a publisher–wholesaler.[90] Correctly understood, publishing a book involves financing it (as well as distributing it) and there is no evidence that Day was ever expected to shoulder the cost of the *Acts and Monuments*. In all of the editions Day would pay expenses out of his own pocket but it was always because he was guaranteed to recoup his money because of his monopolies. This difference separates Day from a purely capitalist printer speculating on the success of a book. Day was not laying out his money in the hope of recouping it through sales but rather in the assurance of recouping it through monopolies on printed works that were guaranteed to sell.

Similarly, Day would print technically demanding and costly works at the behest of Matthew Parker and other notables but in these cases his expenses were defrayed by cash payments, or he was clearly operating in the hope of concessions from the great and the good. A number of scholars, notably Pettegree and King, have correctly emphasised the crucial role of John Day in producing the *Acts and Monuments*. As David Kastan has succinctly put it, 'No Day, no book.'[91] However, it should be remembered that it was not merely Day's enterprise and expertise – essential as these were – that made the printing of the *Acts and Monuments* possible, but also the fact that Day was able to work within (and knew how to exploit) the system of monopolies that supplied him with the assurance of receiving the necessary capital before the type was set.

Another, almost universally held anachronistic assumption about the printing of the *Acts and Monuments* is that the different editions of the book were produced as a direct result of consumer demand. In other words, the assumption is made that every time a new edition was printed it was because the previous edition had sold out. As we have seen, the editions were produced for various reasons: for example, the personal circumstances

[90] On the division of the *modern* book trade into publisher–wholesaler, printer and retail bookseller see Gaskell, *Bibliography*, p. 297.
[91] Kastan, 'Little Foxes', p. 121.

of John Day and his son or the political agenda of the Long Parliament. This is not to say that there was no concern about sales, just that it does not appear that market forces were the most important agents in the production of the unabridged editions of Foxe. This situation would, of course, change in the eighteenth century as the last vestiges of the monopoly system disappeared.

Examination of the making of the *Acts and Monuments* through the sixteenth and seventeenth centuries provides a graphic illustration of the dangers of assuming that the sales of a book and the number of editions it went through are an accurate guide to its importance or influence. It is also worth keeping in mind that while the *Acts and Monuments* was, we would argue, a very influential and important book, this was not necessarily because it was a tremendously popular or widely read work; rather, it was influential because it was diligently read, and its dissemination was championed, by an active and zealous minority.[92] If the *Acts and Monuments* had not been of such interest to this minority it probably would not have been reprinted after 1610.

Yet there is another fundamental misconception that people have regarding the making of the *Acts and Monuments* and that concerns Foxe's 'authorship' of the work. In the past Romantic ideas about Foxe as the sole author of the work predominated, so much so that the standard biography by J. F. Mozley is entitled *John Foxe and his Book* (1940). More recently Patrick Collinson has opined that 'there are few instances in English literary history of a more complete fusion of author and text'.[93] Yet the pendulum has been increasingly swinging in the opposite direction. John King, for example, in his recent monograph, *Foxe's 'Book of Martyrs' and Early Modern Print Culture*, eschews the use of the term 'author' to describe Foxe's role, instead almost invariably referring to him as the 'compiler'. The fundamental problem with this is that this difference of interpretation hinges upon a modern conception of 'authorship': that the author is the person who creates and composes the entire text that bears his or her name.

Another problem in dubbing Foxe a compiler is that it can be easily misunderstood to mean that Foxe did not write any section of the *Acts and*

---

[92] This does not mean that everyone who read or praised Foxe shared the same views as those groups who urged its reprinting in 1631/2, 1641 and 1684. For example, both William Lamont, and more recently Judith Maltby, have pointed to readers who cited Foxe's work to defend episcopacy. William Lamont, *Godly Rule: Politics and Religion 1603–60* (London, 1969), pp. 23–4 and 78–9, and Judith Maltby, *Prayer Book and People in Elizabethan and Early Stuart England* (Cambridge, 1998), pp. 91, 116 and 161–2.

[93] Collinson, 'Foxe and National Consciousness', p. 16.

Monuments. In a review of John King's volume on the 'Book of Martyrs' one scholar went so far as to assert that 'Foxe did not, in the modern sense, produce original material. Foxe went so far as to distinguish his own contribution from others' through the use of a different typeface.'[94] There are sections of the *Acts and Monuments* – notably the prefatory materials – that are unquestionably written by Foxe. This is also true of a number of narratives in the book, including, for example, the execution of William Cowbridge in 1538 and a panic that broke out at a supposed fire in Oxford.[95] In any sense, whether it be modern or early modern, this is original material. It is also somewhat contradictory to assert that on the one hand there is no original material by Foxe and on the other that his contributions are in a separate typeface. For the record, a different typeface is often not used for Foxe's contributions and it is apparent that this reviewer has misunderstood what King has written.

Contemporaries certainly emphasised Foxe's authorship of the book – Collinson has observed that editions of the *Acts and Monuments* proclaimed on the title pages that they were 'by the Authour JOHN FOXE' – but they did not necessarily mean that Foxe was an author in the modern sense.[96] He was certainly not the sole creator of the text; some of it, but only a relatively small portion, was actually composed by him, but much of it was the hidden compilation of fellow authors such as John Bale and Henry Bull, and probably most of the work was excerpted from the books of dozens of authors. Nevertheless, it is misleading to view Foxe as merely a compiler in the sense that Holinshed and Hakluyt were. For one thing, this obfuscates the painstaking research done either by Foxe or the teams of people cooperating with him at various levels. Neither does it take into account Foxe's meticulous, almost obsessive, editorial interventions in the text – especially in the 1570 edition. And it ought to be remembered that those sections of the work that were composed by Foxe – such as the preliminary materials, the marginal notes and sections explaining the relationship between history and the Apocalypse – were disproportionately important in shaping readers' responses to the work.

The making of the *Acts and Monuments* places us at a crossroads where crucial aspects of early modern English culture converge. We can see in the *Acts and Monuments* both the methodologies of practising history that guided Foxe, Bale, Parker and others, and the different interpretations of

---

[94] Joseph Chi, 'Review of King, *Print Culture*', *Sixteenth Century Journal*, 39 (2008), p. 795.
[95] *1563*, pp. 570–1 and *1583*, p. 1131 and pp. 621–5.
[96] Collinson, 'Foxe and National Consciousness', p. 16.

history that these methodologies were meant to support. We can also see the close intellectual relationships between English and continental Protestants and gauge some of the intellectual currents that moved back and forth between the two. From this perspective we can observe and analyse the development of the English book trade as it moved through a system of monopolies to syndication to subscription in order to finance substantial works. The making of the *Acts and Monuments* also provides insight into the disputed questions regarding not only the illustrations of books in early modern England but also the role of images within a Protestant culture. The activities of both John and Richard Day demonstrate the varying roles of the sixteenth-century printer and the constraints under which they operated as part of one of the less sophisticated Protestant printing centres (and one which, especially with regards to paper supplies, faced unique inherent problems of its own).

Last, and perhaps of least importance, but nevertheless worthy of consideration, we see the genesis of a particularly influential book, one that was perhaps not as popular or widely read as is often maintained but which had a printing life of remarkable longevity. It is ludicrous to maintain, as so many scholars have done, that the *Acts and Monuments* was one of the most widely read books of the age – almanacs, primers and catechisms all had much greater, if perhaps more ephemeral, popularity. Nevertheless, there was a substantial segment of the population that for decades, if not centuries, regarded the *Acts and Monuments* as absolutely essential reading. And the *Acts and Monuments* was also a book that through myriad channels seeped into all levels of English culture in ways too numerous to be detailed here. A simple consideration of the works of authors such as Bunyan and Milton are merely the first steps on what would be a fascinating cultural odyssey. Foxe's 'Book of Martyrs' belongs to that select company of books – Charles Darwin's *Origin of Species*, Karl Marx's *Das Kapital* and Sigmund Freud's *Interpretation of Dreams* being among them – that are not only widely known but whose authors and central ideas are similarly known to multitudes who have not actually read the books themselves.

Glossary

bleed through	when text printed on one side of a sheet is visible on the opposite side
(to) cast off **(copy)**	to estimate how much printed matter a given amount of copy (i.e., text) will make, or how large the page must be in order that the copy may make a given number of pages. **Cast-offs** are pages of copy that have been marked up by the printing house staff with signs that indicate which text is to go on which signature page
catchword	a partial or complete word located at the lower-outer corner of a page, corresponding to the first word on the first line of the following page
chase	an iron frame containing one or more pages of set type from which one side of a sheet is printed
collation	a description of the sequence of pages and their gatherings (signatures) in a book
colophon	information at the close of a volume, relating details of the printing history of the volume – usually including the printer, their location details (sometimes their printer's mark or sign also), as well as the date of printing
compositor	a workman who sets lines of type by hand in a composing stick; these lines are then imposed into pages and then locked into formes
duodecimo **(12°)**	a format of book in which each sheet is folded five times in order to create twenty-four pages
em	a linear space taken by a roman capital M; twice the space of an N
en	a linear space taken by a roman capital N, one-half of an M

folio (2°)	a format of book in which each sheet is folded only once
format	the relation of the initial sheet to the total number of leaves in each gathering
forme	typeface or pages assembled within a chase and ready for printing
gathering	a sheet folded to produce a particular number of leaves according to the chosen format
gutter	the inner edge of a book where conjugate leaves come together and typically where gatherings are sewn
imposition	the arrangement of pages of set type in the chase so that, when printed and folded according to the required format, the resulting pages will appear in the correct order
imprint	information provided on the title page about the printer of the volume, and where and when the volume was printed
leaf (or folio)	a piece of paper that contains one page on each side
octavo (8°)	a format in which each sheet is folded three times to produce sixteen-page gatherings
quarto (4°)	a format in which each sheet is folded twice to produce eight-page gatherings
quire	*n.* one or more gatherings; *v.* to collect multiple gatherings into a single binding unit
quoins	wooden wedges used by printers to lock up a forme within a chase, to ensure that the type is held firmly in place
recto	the front side of a leaf
signature	letters of the roman alphabet placed at the bottom-right of a recto page in order to identify the sequence of the gathering; other symbols are often used, particularly for preliminary pages (usually printed last) or late additions to a print run
slip cancel	a small slip of paper added to a copy text to indicate a required substantial change to the text. It is positioned over the top of text no longer required (which is crossed out), and pasted in place on the left-hand side only, to allow the compositor to see underneath. This allowed him to check where the text has been deleted and to

read the replacement text on the slip cancel. Such a method avoids the new text being squeezed above the crossed-out words or placed in the margin, which might lead to mistakes.

sort   an individual piece of type

Stop press   this is where the press is stopped as an error has been
correction   found or an urgent change is required to the text
currently being printed. This can lead to the sheet (and therefore the edition) surviving in more than one 'state' – where one copy might have the sheet pre-stop press, another the sheet post-stop press. (The survival of a text in more than one state can indicate that paper was in short supply, or that the printer was reluctant to discard the original sheet. In some instances, first-state copies could be corrected by hand before they left the printing house.)

tip-in   an illustration inserted into a gathering, but which is
not part of that gathering. A single half sheet, illustrated on the recto and usually blank on the verso, is added by the binder in the required place. The tip-in will often have printed instructions at the bottom of the recto, indicating where it should be bound into the volume. Often the size of the tip-in is such that it must then be folded into the book. It can then be folded out to reveal a large illustration that accompanies the text at that point. Because of poor binding, the passage of time, or even wilful removal, these tip-ins are now often missing from early modern texts or are found rebound in the wrong place.

verso   the reverse side of a leaf

Select bibliography

MANUSCRIPTS

Bodleian Library, Additional MS 14995
Bodleian Library, Ashmole MS 1789
Bodleian Library, Bodley MS 73
Bodleian Library, Bodley MS e Museo 86
Bodleian Library, Bodley MS Tanner 165
Bodleian Library, Douce MS 128
Bodleian Library, Rawlinson MS C 936
British Library, Add. MS 19400
British Library, Add. MS 34727
British Library, Add. MS 48040
British Library, Add. MS C. 37.h.2
British Library, Cotton MS Otho, Cii
British Library, Cotton MS Titus B.ii
British Library, Cotton MS Titus D.X
British Library, Harley MS 25
British Library, Harley MS 416
British Library, Harley MS 417
British Library, Harley MS 418
British Library, Harley MS 419
British Library, Harley MS 421
British Library, Harley MS 422
British Library, Harley MS 425
British Library, Harley MS 426
British Library, Harley MS 590
British Library, Harley MS 3634
British Library, Harley MS 3838
British Library, Lansdowne MS 10
British Library, Lansdowne MS 15
British Library, Lansdowne MS 48
British Library, Lansdowne MS 202
British Library, Lansdowne MS 335
British Library, Lansdowne MS 388

British Library, Lansdowne MS 679
British Library, Lansdowne MS 819
Cambridge University Library, Add. MS 748
College of Arms, Arundel MS 4
College of Arms, Arundel MS 7
Corpus Christi College Cambridge, MS 7 (3)
Corpus Christi College Cambridge, MS 96
Corpus Christi College Cambridge, MS 128
Corpus Christi College Cambridge, MS 135
Corpus Christi College Cambridge, MS 175
Corpus Christi College Cambridge, MS 195
Corpus Christi College Cambridge, MS 281
Corpus Christi College Cambridge, MS 1152
Derbyshire Record Office, Matlock, MS D3372/86/
Devon Public Record Office, Register of George Neville
Emmanuel College Library, MS 260
Emmanuel College Library, MS 261
Emmanuel College Library, MS 262
Essex Record Office, Chelmsford, MS D/P 75/5/1
Gonville and Caius College Library MS 427
Guildhall Library London, MS 535/1
Guildhall Library London, MS 4071/1
Guildhall Library London, MS N531/9
Inner Temple Library, Petyt MS 538/47
King's College Archives, Commons and Mundum Book
Lambeth Palace Library, Arundel Register
Lambeth Palace Library, Courtenay Register
Lambeth Palace Library, MS 2010
Lambeth Palace Library, Warham Register
Magdalen College Oxford, Latin MS 36
Magdalen College Oxford, Latin MS 53
Magdalen College Oxford, Latin MS 172
Stationers' Company Archives, Liber A
Suffolk Record Office, Ipswich, MS FC 62/A6
The National Archives, 7 Ed. VI, part 3, m.23
The National Archives, 1 Eliz., part 1, m.24
The National Archives, 9 Eliz., part 9, m.19
The National Archives, 19 Eliz., part 2, m.5
The National Archives, C 24/180
The National Archives, C 24/181
The National Archives, C 24/182
The National Archives, C 85/115/10
The National Archives, PROB 11/30
The National Archives, SP 12/152
The National Archives, STAC 5/D4/1

The National Archives, STAC 5/D13/7
Trinity College, Cambridge, MS B.14.45
Trinity College, Dublin, MS 516
Trinity College, Dublin, MS 775
Westminster Abbey Muniments, MS 33629
Westminster Diocesan Archives, MS B.2
Dr Williams's Library, Morrice MS P
Zurich Zentralbibliothek, MS F 62

PRIMARY SOURCES

Aelfric, *A Testimonie of antiquities shewing the auncient faith in the Church of England* (London, 1566?), STC 159

Alesius, Alexander, *Of the auctorite of the word of god agaynst the bisshop of London* (Strasbourg, 1544?), STC 292

Allen, William, *A briefe historie of the glorious martyrdom of XII reverend priests* (Rheims, 1582), STC 369.5

Anon., *A christen sentence and true judgement of the sacrament . . .* (London, 1548?), STC 5190

  Newes from Vienna the 5 day of August 1566 (London, 1566), STC 24716

  The trueth of the most wicked murthering of J. Brewen (London, 1592), STC 15095

  A brief discourse of the troubles at Frankfort, 1554 – 1558 A.D. . . ., ed. E. Arber (London, 1908)

Askew, Anne, *The fyrst examinazion [sic] of Askew . . .* ed. John Bale (London? 1550?), STC 852.5

Asser, John, *Aelfredi Regis res gestae* (London, 1574), STC 863

Bale, John, *A brefe chronycle concerning the examinacyon and death of syr J. Oldecastell* (Antwerp, 1544), STC 1276

  The actes of Englysh votaryes . . . (Wesel, 1546), STC 1270, reprinted in London in 1551, STC 1273.5

  Rhithmi vetustissimi de corrupto ecclesiae statu (Antwerp, 1546)

  Illustrium maioris Britannie Scriptorum . . . Summarium (Wesel, 1548) STC 1295

  The laboryouse iourney and serche of Iohan Leylande (London, 1549), STC 15445

  The first two partes of the actes of the English votaryes (London, 1551), STC 1270

  The Epistle exhortatorye of an Engliyshe Chrystyane (Antwerp, 1554), STC 1291

  Scriptorum Illustrium maioris Brytanniae . . . Catalogus, 2 vols. (Basle, 1557–9)

  Acta Romanorum Pontificum (Basle, 1558)

  Select Works of John Bale, ed. Henry Christmas (Parker Society, Cambridge, 1849)

  King Johan, ed. J. H. P. Pafford (Oxford, 1931)

  The Complete Plays of John Bale, ed. Peter Happé, 2 vols. (Woodbridge, 1985–6)

  Index Britanniae Scriptorum: John Bale's Index of British and Other Writers, ed. Reginald Lane Poole and Mary Bateson, revised by Caroline Brett and James P. Carley (Woodbridge, 1990)

The vocacyon of John Bale, ed. Peter Happé and John N. King (Binghamton, NY, 1990)

Banister, John, *The historie of man sucked from the sappe of the most approued anathomistes* . . . (London, 1578), STC 1359

Bateman, Stephen, *A christall glasse of Christian reformation wherein the godly maye beholde the coloured abuses vsed in this our present tyme* (London, 1569), STC 1581

Becke, Edmund (ed.), *The Byble, that is to say, all the holy Scripture* (London, 1549), STC 2077

Becon, Thomas, *The governaunce of virtue* (London, 1578), STC 1728
The pomaunder of prayer (London, 1578), STC 1748

Bede, The Venerable, *The history of the church of England* trans. Thomas Stapleton (Antwerp 1565), STC 1778

Benet, John, 'John Benet's Chronicle for the years 1400–1462', ed. G. L. and M. A. Harriss, Camden Society, 4th series, 9 (1972)

Bertrandus, Petrus, *Libellus de iurisdictione ecclesiastica contra Petrum de Cugnieres* (Paris, 1495)

Bibliander, Theodor, *Machumetis Saracenorum principis . . . Alcoran* (Basle, 1550)

Billingsley, Nicholas, *Brachy-martyrologia* (London, 1657), STC Wing B2910

Bullinger, Heinrich, *Bullae papisticae . . . contra reginam Elizabetham . . . refutatio* (London, 1571), STC 4043
A confutation of the popes bull against Elizabeth queene of England, trans. Arthur Golding (London, 1572), STC 4044

Bunyan, John, *The Pilgrim's Progress*, ed. Roger Sharrock (Harmondsworth, 1965)
The Miscellaneous Works of John Bunyan, vol. V, ed. Graham Midgely (Oxford, 1986)
Grace Abounding with Other Spiritual Autobiographies, ed. John Stachniewski with Anita Pacheco (Oxford, 1998)

Campion, Edmund, *Rationes Decem* (Henley-on-Thames, 1581), STC 4536.5

Care, Henry, *The Weekly Pacquet of Advice from Rome*, v, no. 39 (18 May 1683)

Cartwright, William, *The Plays and Poems of William Cartwright*, ed. G. Blakemore Evans (Madison, WI, 1951)

Case, John, *Summa veterum interpretum in universam dialecticam Aristotelis* (London, 1584) STC 4762

Chalkokondyles, Laonikos, *De origine et rebus gestis Turcorum* . . . (Basle, 1556)

Cisner, Nicholas, *De Fredericus II Imp. Oratio* (Strasbourg, 1608)

Clarke, Samuel, *General Martyrologie* (London, 1677), STC Wing C4515

Cochlaeus, Johannes, *Historiae Hussitarum* (Mainz, 1549)

Coverdale, Miles [Henry Bull] (ed.), *Certain most godly, fruitful and comfortable letters* . . . (London, 1564), STC 5886

Crakanthorp, Richard, *Defensio ecclesiae Anglicanae* (London, 1625)

Cranmer, Thomas, *An answer of . . . Thomas archbyshop of Canterburye unto a crafty cavillation by S. Gardiner* (London, 1551), STC 5991
An aunsvvere by the reuerend father in god Thomas archbyshop of Canterbury . . . (London, 1580), STC 5992

Reformatio Legum Ecclesiasticarum, ed. John Foxe (London, 1571), STC 6006

Crespin, Jean, *Histoire memorable de la persecution et saccagement du peuple de Merindol et Cabrieres et autre circonvoisins, appelez Vaudois* (Geneva, 1555)

Recueil de pluisiers personnes qui ont constamment enduré la mort pour le nom de Nostre Seigneur (Geneva, 1555)

Actiones et monumenta martyrum (Geneva, 1560)

Actes des martyrs (Geneva, 1564)

Crowley, Robert, *The confutation of .xiii. articles, whereunto N. Shaxton, late byshop subscribed* (London, 1548), STC 6083

An aunswer to sixe reasons (London, 1581), STC 6075

Cunningham, William, *The cosmographical glasse conteinyng the pleasant principles of cosmographie, geographie, hydrographie, or nauigation* (London, 1559), STC 6119

Cuspinian, Johann, *De Turcorum origine* (Antwerp, 1541)

De Roover, Raymond, 'The Business Organisation of the Plantin Press in the Setting of Sixteenth Century Antwerp', in *Gedenboek der Plantin-Dagen 1555–1955* (Antwerp, 1956), pp. 230–46.

Dee, John, *General and rare memorials pertayning to the perfect arte of navigation* (London, 1577), STC 6459

Digges, Leonard, *A Boke Named Tectonicon* (London, 1556), STC 6849.5

Dinoth, Richard, *De bello civili Gallico* (Basle, 1582)

Erasmus, Desiderius, *Adagia* (Basle, 1528)

Euclid, *Elements of geometrie*, trans. Henry Billingsley (London, 1570), STC 10560

Fabian, Robert, *The newe Cronycles of Englande and of Fraunce* (London, 1516), STC 10659

The Chronicle of Fabian (London, 1559), STC 10664

Fenn, John and John Gibbons (eds.), *Concertatio Ecclesiae Catholicae in Anglia* (Rheims, 1583)

Field, John, *A caveat for Parsons Howlet* (London, 1581), STC 10844

Flacius, Matthias, *Catalogus testium veritatis* (Strasbourg, 1562)

Catalogus testium veritatis (Basle, 1556)

Foxe, John, *De non plectendis morte adulteris* (London, 1548), STC 11235

De lapsis in ecclesiam recipiendis consultatio cum pastoribus (London, 1549), STC 11235.5

De censura sive excommunicatione ecclesiastica rectoque eius usu (London, 1551), STC 11233

Commentarii in ecclesia gestarum rerum (Strasbourg, 1554)

Ad inclytos ac praepotentes Angliae proceres (Basle, 1557)

Rerum in ecclesia gestarum (Basle, 1559)

Actes and monuments of these latter and perillous dayes touching matters of the Church . . . (London, 1563), STC 11222

Syllogisticon hoc est argumenta, seu probationes & resolutiones (London, 1563), STC 11249

The first volume of the ecclesiasticall history contaynyng the actes and monumentes of thynges passed in euery kynges tyme in this realme, especially in the Church of England (London, 1570), STC 11223

A sermon of Christ crucified (London, 1570), STC 11242

De Christo crucifixo concio (London, 1571), STC 11247

The Gospels of the fower Evangelistes translated into vulgare toung of the Saxons, newly collected out of auncient Monumentes of the sayd Saxons, and now published for testimonie of the same, ed. John Foxe (London, 1571), STC 2961

Pandectae locorum communium, praecipua rerum capita & titulos, iuxta ordinem elementorum complectens . . . (London, 1572), STC 11239

The whole workes of W. Tyndall, Iohn Frith, and Doct. Barnes, three worthy martyrs, and principall teachers of this Churche of England collected and compiled in one tome togither, beyng before scattered . . . (London, 1573), STC 24436

The first volume of the ecclesiasticall history contayning the actes [and] monumentes of things passed in euery kinges time, in this realme, especially in the Churche of England (London, 1576), STC 11224

De oliva evangelica (London, 1578), STC 11236

A sermon preached at the christening of a certaine Iew at London (London, 1578), STC 11248

Papa confutatus (London, 1580), STC 11240

Actes and monuments of matters most speciall and memorable, happenyng in the Church with an vniuersall history of the same, wherein is set forth at large the whole race and course of the Church, from the primitiue age to these latter tymes of ours (London, 1583), STC 11225

De Christo gratis justificante (London, 1583), STC 11234

Eicasmi seu meditationes in sacram Apocalypsin, ed. Samuel Foxe (London, 1587), STC 11237

Christ Jesus Triumphant, trans. Richard Day (London, 1607), STC 11232

The Book of Martyrs (London, 1732)

A Select History of the Lives and Sufferings of the Principal English Protestant Martyrs (London, 1746)

The Book of Martyrs Containing an Account of the Sufferings and Deaths of Protestants from the Birth of our Saviour Down to Queen Mary I (London, 1761)

Two Latin Comedies by John Foxe the Martyrologist, ed. and trans. John Hazel Smith (Ithaca, NY and London, 1973)

Foxe, John, *et al.*, *The Book of Martyrs . . . From the time of our blessed Saviour to the year 1701*, 2 vols. (London, 1702)

Frarin, Peter, *Oratio P. Frarini . . . Quod male, reformandae religionis nomine, arma sumpserunt Sectarii nostri temporis* (Louvain, 1565)

An oration against the unlawful insurrections of the Protestants of our time, under pretence to refourme religion (Antwerp, 1566), STC 11333

Frith, John, *Vox Piscis* (London, 1627), STC 11395

Fuchs, Leonhardt, *De historia stirpium commentarii insignes* (Basle, 1542)

Fuller, Thomas, *The History of the Worthies of England*, ed. P. Austin Nuttall, 3 vols. (London, 1840)

A Church History of Britain, ed. J. S. Brewer, 6 vols. (Oxford, 1845)

Gardiner, Stephen, *The communication betweene my lord chauncelor and judge Hales* ... (Stamford, 1553), STC 11583

De vera obedientia (Wesel [i.e., Stanford], 1553), STC 11587

Gervase of Canterbury, *The Historical Works of Gervase of Canterbury*, ed. William Stubbs, 2 vols. (Rolls Series, London, 1879–80)

Gesner, Conrad, *The treasure of Euonymus conteyninge the vvonderfull hid secretes of nature ... Translated (with great diligence, et laboure) out of Latin, by Peter Morvvying felow of Magdaline Colleadge in Oxford* (London, 1559), STC 11800

Goltwurm, Kaspar, *Kirchen Calendar* (Frankfurt, 1559)

Gratius, Ortwin, *Fasciculus rerum expetendarum et fugiendarum* (Cologne, 1535)

Greg W. W. and E. Boswell (eds.), *Records of the Court of the Stationers' Company 1576–1602* (London, 1930)

Haddon, Walter, *A sight of the Portugall Pearle, that is the Aunswere of D. Haddon Maister of the requests, against the epistle of Hieronimus Osorius, a Portugall, entitled a Pearle for a Prynce* (London, 1565?), STC 12598

Contra Hieron. Osorium, eiusque odiosas insectationes pro Evangelicae veritatis necessaria Defensione, Responsio Apologetica. Per clariss. virum, Gualt. Haddonum inchoata: Deinde suscepta & continuata per Ioann. Foxum (London, 1577), STC 12593

Haddon, Walter and John Foxe, *Against Jerome Osorius*, trans. James Bell (London, 1581), STC 12594

Haemstede, Adriaan van, *De Geschiedenisse ende den doodt der vromer Martelaren* (Emden, 1559)

Hall, Edward, *The vnion of the two noble and illustre famelies of Lancastre [and] Yorke, beeyng long in continual discension for the croune of this noble realme* (London, 1548), STC 12721

The unyon of the twoo noble and illustre families of Lancastre and York (London, 1550), STC 12723a

Harding, Thomas, *A Confutation of a booke intituled an apologie of the Church of England* (Antwerp, 1565), STC 12762

A reioinder to M Jewels Replie Against the sacrifice of the Masse (Louvain, 1567), STC 12761

Harpsfield, Nicholas, *Dialogi sex contra summi pontificatus, monasticae vitae, sanctorum, sacrarum imaginum oppugnatores et pseudomartyres* (Antwerp, 1566)

Harrington, John, *A briefe view of the state of the Church of England as it stood in Q. Elizabeths and King James his reigne* (London, 1653), STC Wing H770

Henry of Croyland, *Vita processus sancti Thomae Cantuariensis martyris super libertate ecclesiastica* (Paris, 1495)

Holinshed, Raphael, *The first and second volumes of Chronicles* ... (London, 1587), STC 13569

Hooper, John, *An apologye made by the reverende father and constante Martyr of Christe John Hooper* ..., ed. Henry Bull (London, 1562), STC 13742

Hornschuch, Hieronymus, *Orthotypographia 1608*, ed. and trans. Philip Gaskell and Patricia Bradford (Cambridge, 1972)

Humphrey, Laurence, *Jesuitismi pars prima* (London, 1582), STC 13961

Jesuitismi pars secunda . . . (London, 1584), STC 13962

A view of the Romish hydra and monster . . . (London, 1588), STC 13966

Hus, Jan and Jerome of Prague, *Johannis Hus et Hieronymi Pragensis Confessorum Christi Historia et Monumenta*, 2 vols. (Nuremberg, 1558)

Hutchinson, Roger, *A faithful declaration of Christes holy supper comprehended in thre sermons, preached at Eaton Colledge* (London, 1560), STC 14018

Jewel, John, *The Works of John Jewel*, ed. J. Ayre, 4 vols. (Parker Society, Cambridge, 1845–50)

John of Worcester, *The Chronicle of John of Worcester 1118–1170*, ed. J. R. H. Weaver (Oxford, 1908)

Joye, George, *A contrarye (to a certayne manis) consultacion* (London, 1549), STC 14822

Lambarde, William, *Archaionomia, sive de priscis anglorum legibus libri, sermone Anglicae, vestustate antiquissima, aliquot abhinc sculis conscriptio* . . . (London, 1568), STC 15142

Lambert, François *In regulam Minoritarum* (Wittenberg, 1523)

Latimer, Hugh, *A notable sermon of ye reuerende father Maister Hughe Latemer* . . . (London, 1548), STC 15291

27 sermons preached by the rught Reverende father in God and constant martir . . . *Hugh Latimer* (London, 1562), STC 15276

Frutefull sermons (London, 1578), STC 15279

Laud, William, *The Works of William Laud*, ed. W. Scott, and J. Bliss, 7 vols. (Oxford, 1847–60)

Leland, John, *Commentarii de scriptoribus Britannicis: auctore Joanne Lelando Londinate* . . ., ed. Anthony Hall (Oxford, 1709)

Lindsay, David, *The tragical death of David Beaton* . . . (London, 1548?), STC 15683

Luther, Martin, *A frutfull sermon of the moost euangelicall wryter M. Luther*, trans. John Foxe (London, 1548), STC 16983

A very comfortable, and necessary sermon, concerning the comming of Christ, trans. Thomas Becon (London, 1570), STC 16997.5

A Commentarie Vpon the Epistle to the Galathians (London, 1575), STC 16965

A commentarie upon the fiftene psalmes, translated Henry Bull (London, 1577), STC 16975

A right comfortable treatise containing fourteene pointes of consolation . . . (London, 1578), STC 16989

Special and chosen sermons, trans. William Gace (London, 1578), STC 16993

A treatise, touching the libertie of a christian (London, 1579), STC 16995

A methodicall preface prefixed before the epistle to the Romanes (London, 1594), STC 16985

Machyn, Henry, *The Diary of Henry Machyn, Citizen and Merchant-Taylor of London, from A.D. 1550 to A.D. 1563*, Camden Society, original series, 42 (London, 1848)

Macray, W. D. (ed.), *A Register of the Members of St Mary Magdalen College, Oxford*, 8 vols. (London, 1894–1915)

Mason, Thomas, *Christs victorie over Sathans Tyrannie* (London, 1615), STC 17622

Montagu, Richard, *De originibus ecclesiasticis* (London, 1636), STC 18034

Montanus, Reginaldus Gonsalvius, *A discovery and playne declaration of sundry subtill practices of the holy inquisition of Spayne*, trans. V. Skinner (London, 1568), STC 11996

Mornay, Philippe de, *A notable treatise of the church in which are handled all the principall questions, that haue beene mooued in our time concerning that matter*, trans. John Field (London, 1580), STC 18160

Moxon, Joseph, *Mechanick Exercises in the Whole Art of Printing*, ed. H. Davis and H. Carter, 2nd edn (London, 1962)

Münster, Sebastian, *Cosmographia universalis* (Basle, 1559)

Mush, John, *An abstracte of the life and martirdome of Mistres M. Clitheroe*, 3 vols. (Newton Abbot, Devon, 1619), STC 18316.7

'A True Report of the Life and Martyrdom of Mrs. Margaret Clitherow', in *The Troubles of our Catholic Forefathers*, ed. John Morris (London, 1877)

Norton, Thomas, *A warning agaynst the dangerous practices of Papistes* (London, 1569?), STC 18685.3

Norton, Thomas and Thomas Sackville, *The tragedie of Gorboduc* (London, 1565), STC 18684

The tragidie of Ferrex and Porrex . . . (London, 1570), STC 18685

Nowell, Alexander and William Day, *A true report of the disputation . . . with Ed. Campion Jesuite* (London, 1583), STC 18744

Ochine, Bernardine, *Fouretene sermons of Barnardine Ochyne*, trans. Anne Cooke (London, 1551), STC 18767.

Oecolampadius, Johann, *A sarmon . . . to yong men, and maydens*, trans. John Foxe (London, 1548), STC 18787

Oliver, Thomas, *De sophismatum praestigiis cavendis admonitio* (Cambridge, 1604), STC 18809

Osório, Jerónimo, *An Epistle of the Reverend Father in God Hieronymus Osorius Bishop of Arcoburge in Portugale, to the most excellent Princesse Elizabeth . . . Translated oute of Latten in to Englishe by Richard Shacklock* (Antwerp, 1565), STC 18887

Amplissimi atque Doctissimi Viri D. Hieronymi Osorii, Episcopi Sylvensis, in Gualterum Haddonum Magistrum Libellorum Supplicum apud clarrisimam Principem Helisabetham Angliae, Franciae, & Hiberniae Reginam. Libri tres (Lisbon, 1567)

A Learned and very Eloquent treatie [sic] writen in Latin by the famouse man Hieronymus Osorius . . . (Louvain, 1568), STC 18889

Pantaleon, Heinrich, *Martyrum historia* (Basle, 1563)

Paris, Matthew, *Chronica maiora*, ed. H. R. Luard, 7 vols. (Rolls Series, London, 1872–83)

Parker, Matthew, *De antiquitate Britannicae ecclesiae & priuilegiis ecclesiae Cantuariensis cum Archiepiscopis eiusdem 70* (London, 1572), STC 19292

Pecock, Reginald, *Reginald Pecock's Book of Faith*, ed. J. L. Morison (Glasgow, 1909)

Persons, Robert, *A brief discours containing certayne reasons why catholiques refuse to goe to church* (East Ham, 1580), STC 19394

A treatise of three conversions of England, 3 vols. (St Omer, 1604), STC 19416

Peucer, Caspar, *Chronicon Carionis*, ed. Philipp Melanchthon and Caspar Peucer (Wittenberg, 1580)

Philpot, John, *Vera expositio disputationis . . . in Synodo Ecclesiastica, Londini in Comitiis regni ad 18 Octob. Anno 1553* (Rome [i.e., Cologne], 1554)

Piccolomini, Aeneas Silvius, *De Gestis Concilii Basiliensis Commentariorum*, ed. and trans. Denys Hay and W. K. Smith (Oxford, 1967)

Pilkington, James, *A godlie exposition upon certaine chapters . . . of Nehemiah*, ed. John Foxe (Cambridge, 1585), STC 19929

    The Works of James Pilkington, ed. James Scholefield (Parker Society, Cambridge, 1842)

Platina, Bartolomeo, *Vitae pontificum* (Venice, 1479)

Prynne, William, *Canterburies doome, or, The first part of a compleat history of the commitment, charge, tryall, condemnation, execution of William Laud . . .* (London, 1646), Wing P3917

Rabus, Ludwig, *Der Heyligen ausserwoehlten Gottes Zeugen, Bekennern und Martyrern . . . Historien . . .*, 8 vols. (Strasbourg, 1552–8)

Rhegius, Urbanus, *An instruccyon of Christen fayth*, trans. John Foxe (London, 1548?), STC 20847

Ridley, Nicholas, *A frendly farewel, which Master Doctor Ridley . . . did write*, ed. John Foxe (London, 1559), STC 21051

    A pituous lamentation of the miserable estate of the church of Christ in Englande, in the time of the late revolt from the gospel. Never before imprinted. Whereunto are also annexed letters of J Careless (London, 1566), STC 21052

    The Works of Nicholas Ridley, ed. Henry Christmas (Cambridge, Parker Society, 1841)

Rivery, Jean and Adam, *Recueil de pluisiers personnes qui ont constamment enduré la mort pour le nom de Nostre Seigneur* (Geneva, 1556)

Robert of Avesbury, *De Gestis Mirabilibus Regis Edwardi Tertii*, ed. E. M. Thompson (Rolls Series, London, 1889)

Roger of Howden, *Chronica magistri Rogeri de Hovedene*, ed. W. Stubbs, 4 vols. (Rolls Series 51, London, 1868–71)

Rotuli Parliamentorum vt et Petitiones et Placita in Parliamento, ed. Richard Blyke and John Strachey, 6 vols. (Basle, 1528)

Sabellico, Mark Antonio, *Opera Omnia*, 4 vols., ed. J. Ayre (Cambridge, 1845–50)

Settle, Elkanah, *The female prelate* (London, 1680), STC Wing S2684

Sleidan, Johann, *A Famouse cronicle of our time, called Sleidanes Comantaires*, trans. John Daus (London, 1560), STC 19848

Staphylus, Fredericus, *Defensio pro trimembri theologica M. Lutheri contra aedificationes Babylonicae turris* (Augsburg, 1559)

Stapleton, Thomas, *A Fortresse of the Faith* (Antwerp 1565), STC 23232

    A counterblast to M. Hornes Vayne blast against M. Fekenham (Louvain, 1567), STC 23231

Sternhold, Thomas and John Hopkins, *The whole book of Psalmes collected into English meter* (London, 1578), STC 24876

Sztrárai, Mihály, *Historia Cranmerus T. Erseknek . . .* (Debrecen, 1582)

Thoresby, Ralph, *The Diary of Ralph Thoresby, FRS*, ed. Joseph Hunter, 2 vols. (London, 1830)

Thorpe, William, *The examinacion of Master William Thorpe* (Antwerp, 1530), STC 24045

Tyndale, William, *The practyse of Prelates* (Antwerp, 1530), STC 24465
  An Answere unto Sir Thomas Mores dialoge (Antwerp, 1531), STC 24437
  The souper of the Lorde (Antwerp?, 1533), STC 24468
  An exposicion vppon the v.vi.vii. chapters of Mathew (London, 1548), STC 24441a

Vergil, Polydore, *De rerum inventoribus* (Basle, 1536)
  The Anglica Historia of Polydore Vergil A.D. 1485–1537, ed. and trans. Denys Hay, Camden Society, new series, 74 (1950)

Viret, Pierre, *A verie familiare and fruiteful exposition of the. xii. articles of the christian faieth conteined in the co[m]mune crede, called the Apostles Crede . . .* (London, 1548), STC 24784

Voragine, Jacobus de, *Legenda Aurea*, trans. W. Caxton? (London, 1483), STC 24873

Walsingham, Thomas, *Historia Anglicana*, ed. H. T. Riley, 2 vols. (Rolls Series 28, London, 1863–4)
  The St Albans Chronicle: The Chronica Maiora of Thomas Walsingham ed. and trans. John Taylor, Wendy R. Childs and Leslie Watkiss (Oxford, 2003)
  The Chronica maiora of Thomas Walsingham 1376–1422, ed. James G. Clark, trans. David Preest (Woodbridge, 2005)

Walter of Guisborough, *The Chronicle of Walter of Guisborough*, ed. Harry Rothwell, Camden Society, 3rd series, 89 (1957)

Whethamsted, Johannes, *Registrum Abbatiae Johannes Whethamsted, abbatis monasterii Sancti Albani*, ed. H. T. Riley, 2 vols. (Rolls Series, London, 1872)

Whitaker, William, *Ad Rationes decem Edmundi Campiani Iesuitae, quibus fretus certamen Anglicanae Ecclesiae ministris obtulit in causa fidei* (London, 1581), STC 25358

Wied, Herman von, *A Simple and Religious Consultation by what means a Christian Reformation May Be Begun* (London, 1547), STC 13213

SECONDARY SOURCES

Alford, Stephen, *Kingship and Politics in the Reign of Edward VI* (Cambridge, 2002)

Arber, Edward (ed.), *Transcripts of the Registers of the Company of Stationers of London . . . 1554–1640 A.D.*, 5 vols. (Birmingham, 1875–94)

Archer, Ian W., 'John Stow: Citizen and Historian', in *John Stow (1525–1605) and the Making of the English Past*, ed. Ian Gadd and Alexandra Gillespie (London, 2004), pp. 13–26

Armstrong, Elizabeth, *Robert Estienne, Royal Printer* (Cambridge, 1954)

Aston, Margaret, *The King's Bedpost: Reformation and Iconography in a Tudor Group Portrait* (Cambridge, 1993)

Aston, Margaret and Elizabeth Ingram, 'The Iconography of the *Acts and Monuments*', in *John Foxe and the English Reformation*, ed. David Loades (Aldershot, 1997), pp. 66–141

Baender, Paul, 'The Meaning of Copy-text', *Studies in Bibliography*, 22 (1969), pp. 311–18

Bauckham, Richard, *Tudor Apocalypse* (Abingdon, 1978)

Betteridge, Tom, 'From Prophetic to Apocalyptic: John Foxe and the Writing of History', in *John Foxe and the English Reformation*, ed. David Loades (Aldershot, 1997), pp. 210–32

Bibl, Victor, 'Der Briefweschsel zwischen Flacius and Nidbruck', *Jahrbuch der Gesellschaft für die Geschichte des Protestantismus in Österreich*, 18 (1896), pp. 205–7

Bidwell, John, 'French Paper in English Books', in *The Cambridge History of the Book*, vol. IV: *1557–1695*, ed. John Barnard and D. F. McKenzie (Cambridge, 2002), pp. 583–601

Binns, James, 'STC Latin Books as Evidence for Printing House Practice', *The Library*, 5th series, 32 (1977), pp. 1–27

Blatchly, John, *The Town Library of Ipswich Provided for the Use of the Town Preachers in 1599* (Woodbridge, 1989)

Blatt, Thora B., *The Plays of John Bale* (Copenhagen, 1968)

Blayney, Peter W. M., 'William Cecil and the Stationers', in *The Stationers' Company and the Book Trade 1550–1990*, ed. Robin Myers and Michael Harris (Winchester and New Castle, DE, 1997), pp. 11–34

  'John Day and the Bookshop that Never Was', in *Material London, ca. 1600*, ed. Lena Cowen Orlin (Philadelphia, 2000), pp. 321–43

  'The "Bishops' Bible"', in *Elizabeth I: Then and Now*, ed. Georgianna Ziegler (Seattle, 2003), p. 43

Bloy, C. H., *A History of Printing Ink, Balls and Rollers 1440–1850* (London, 1967)

Bowden, Peter J. (ed.), *Economic Change: Prices, Wages, Profits and Rents, 1500–1750* (Cambridge, 1990)

Bray, Gerald (ed.), *The Anglican Canons 1529–1947*, Church of England Record Society VI (Woodbridge, 1998)

Brigden, Susan, *London and the Reformation* (Oxford, 1989)

Brown, A. J., *Robert Ferrar: Yorkshire Monk, Reformation Bishop and Martyr in Wales (c. 1500–1555)* (London, 1997)

Brown, Nancy Pollard, 'Robert Southwell: The Mission of the Written Word', in *The Reckoned Expense: Edmund Campion and the Early English Jesuits*, ed. Thomas M. McCoog (Woodbridge, 1996), pp. 193–213

Bruce, John and T. T. Perowne (eds.), *Correspondence of Matthew Parker* (Parker Society, Cambridge, 1853)

Burks, Deborah, 'Polemical Potency: The Witness of Word and Woodcut', in *John Foxe and his World*, ed. Christopher Highley and John N. King (Aldershot, 2002), pp. 263–76

Buscher, Hans, *Heinrich Pantaleon und sein Heldenbuch* (Basle, 1946)

Cameron, Euan, 'Medieval Heretics as Protestant Martyrs', in *Martyrs and Martyrologies*, ed. Diana Wood, Studies in Church History xxx (Oxford, 1993), pp. 185–207

Carley, James P., 'Polydore Vergil and John Leland on King Arthur: The Battle of the Books', in *King Arthur: A Casebook*, ed. Edward Donald Kennedy (New York and London, 1996), pp. 185–204

Christianson, Paul, *Reformers and Babylon: English Apocalyptic Visions from the Reformation to the Eve of the Civil War* (Toronto, 1978)

Clark, J. C. D., *The Language of Liberty 1660–1832* (Cambridge, 1994)

Clebsch, William A., *England's Earliest Protestants, 1520–1535* (New Haven, CT, 1964)

'The Elizabethans on Luther', in *Interpreters of Luther: Essays in Honor of Wilhelm Pauck*, ed. Jaroslav Pelikan (Philadelphia, 1968), pp. 97–120

Clement, C. J., *Religious Radicalism in England 1535–1565* (Carlisle, 1995)

Clement, Richard W., 'A Survey of Antique, Medieval, and Renaissance Book Production', in *Art into Life: Collected Papers from the Kresge Art Museum Medieval Symposia*, ed. Carol Garrett Fisher and Kathleen L. Scott (East Lansing, MI, 1995), pp. 9–28

Cochrane, Eric, *Historians and Historiography in the Italian Renaissance* (Chicago and London, 1981)

Colley, Linda, *Britons: Forging the Nation, 1707–1837* (New Haven, CT, 1992)

Collinson, Patrick, *Archbishop Grindal 1519–1583: The Struggle for a Reformed Church* (Berkeley and Los Angeles, 1979)

Godly People: Essays in English Protestantism and Puritanism (London, 1983)

'England and International Calvinism, 1558–1640', in *International Calvinism, 1541–1715*, ed. Menna Prestwich (Oxford, 1985), pp. 197–223

The Birthpangs of Protestant England (Basingstoke, 1988)

'William Tyndale and the Course of the English Reformation', *Reformation*, 1 (1996), pp. 72–97

'Truth, Lies and Fiction in Sixteenth Century Protestant Historiography', in *The Historical Imagination in Early Modern Britain: History, Rhetoric and Fiction, 1500–1800*, ed. Donald R. Kelley and David Harris Sacks (Cambridge, 1997), pp. 37–68

'John Stow and Nostalgic Antiquarianism', in *Imagining Early Modern London: Perceptions and Portrayals of the City from Stow to Strype 1598–1720*, ed. J. F. Merritt (Cambridge, 2001), pp. 27–51

Cook, Ann Jennalie, *The Privileged Playgoers of Shakespeare's London, 1576–1642* (Princeton, NJ, 1981)

Cooper, W. R., 'Richard Hunne', *Reformation*, 1 (1996), pp. 221–51

Copsey, Richard, *Carmel in Britain: Studies on the Early History of the Carmelite Order*, vol. III (Faversham and Rome, 2004)

Crompton, James, '*Fasciculi Zizaniorum*', *Journal of Ecclesiastical History*, 12 (1961), pp. 35–45, 155–66

Daniell, David, 'Tyndale and Foxe', in *John Foxe: An Historical Perspective*, ed. David Loades (Aldershot, 1999), pp. 15–28

Davies, Catharine, *A Religion of the Word* (Manchester, 2002)

Davies, C. and J. Facey, 'A Reformation Dilemma: John Foxe and the Problem of Discipline', *Journal of Ecclesiastical History*, 39 (1988), pp. 37–65

Davies, J. S. (ed.), *An English Chronicle*, Camden Society, original series, 64 (1856)

Davis, John F., 'The Trials of Thomas Bilney and the English Reformation', *Historical Journal*, 24 (1981), pp. 775–90

Deneke, Bernward, 'Kaspar Goltwurm: Ein lutherischer Kompilator zwischen Überlieferung und Glaube', in *Volkserzählung und Reformation*, ed. Wolfgang Brückner (Berlin, 1974), pp. 125–77

Dent, C. M., *Protestant Reformers in Elizabethan Oxford* (Oxford, 1983)

Diener, Ronald E., 'The Magdeburg Centuries: A Bibliothecal and Historiographical Analysis' (ThD dissertation, Harvard University, 1979)

Diefendorf, Barbara B., *Beneath the Cross: Catholics and Huguenots in Sixteenth Century Paris* (New York and Oxford, 1991)

Dillon, Anne, *The Construction of Martyrdom in the English Catholic Community, 1535–1603* (Aldershot, 2002)

Dimmock, Matthew, *Newe Turks: Dramatizing Islam and the Ottomans in Early Modern England* (Aldershot, 2005)

Driver, Martha, *The Image in Print: Book Illustration in Late Medieval England and its Sources* (London, 2004)

Duff, E. Gordon, *A Century of the English Book Trade* (London, 1905)

Duggan, A., *Thomas Becket: A Textual History of his Letters* (Oxford, 1980)

Dunkin, Paul S., 'Foxe's *Acts and Monuments*, 1570 and Single-Page Imposition', *The Library*, 5th ser., 2 (1947), pp. 159–70

Eccles, M., 'Bynneman's Books', *The Library*, 5th series, 12 (1957), pp. 81–92

Eisenstein, Elizabeth, 'Defining the Initial Shift: Some Features of Print Culture', in *The Book History Reader*, ed. David Finkelstein and Alistair McCleery (London, 2002), pp. 151–73

Elton, G. R., 'Luther in England', in *Studies in Tudor and Stuart Politics and Government*, 4 vols. (Cambridge, 1974–92), IV, pp. 230–45

Evenden, Elizabeth, 'The Fleeing Dutchmen? The Influence of Dutch Immigrants upon the Print Shop of John Day', in *John Foxe: At Home and Abroad*, ed. David Loades (Aldershot, 2004), pp. 63–78

'The Michael Wood Mystery: William Cecil and the Lincolnshire Printing of John Day', *Sixteenth Century Journal*, 35 (2004), pp. 383–94

Patents, Pictures and Patronage: John Day and the Tudor Book Trade (Aldershot, 2008)

'Closing the Books: The Problematic Printing of John Foxe's Histories of Henry VII and Henry VIII in his Book of Martyrs (1570)', in *Tudor Books and Readers*, ed. John N. King (forthcoming)

Evenden, Elizabeth and Thomas S. Freeman, 'John Foxe, John Day and the Printing of the "Book of Martyrs"', in *Lives in Print: Biography and the Book Trade from the Middle Ages to the 21st Century*, ed. Robin Myers, Michael Harris and Giles Mandelbrote (New Castle, DE and London, 2002), pp. 23–54

'Print, Profit and Propaganda: The Elizabethan Privy Council and the 1570 Edition of Foxe's "Book of Martyrs"', *English Historical Review*, 119 (2004), pp. 1288–1307

'Red Letter Day: Protestant Calendars and Foxe's "Book of Martyrs"', *Archiv für Reformationsgeschichte* (forthcoming, 2012)

Facey, Jane, 'John Foxe and the Defence of the English Church', in *Protestantism and the National Church in Sixteenth Century England*, ed. Peter Lake and Maria Dowling (London, 1987), pp. 162–92

Fairfield, Leslie P., *John Bale: Mythmaker for the English Reformation* (West Lafayette, IN, 1976)

Firth, Katherine R., *The Apocalyptic Tradition in Reformation Britain, 1530–1645* (Oxford, 1979)

Foot, Mirjam M., *Eloquent Witnesses: Bookbindings and their History* (London and New Castle, DE, 2004)

Foster, J., *Alumni Oxonienses*, 8 vols. (Oxford, 1888–92)

Frauenknecht, E., *Die Verteidigung der Priesterehe in der Reformzeit* (Hanover, 1997)

Freeman, Thomas S., 'From Catiline to Richard III: The Influence of Classical Histories on Polydore Vergil's *Anglica historia*', in *Reconsidering the Renaissance*, ed. Mario Di Cesare (Binghamton, NY, 1992), pp. 191–214

'A Library in Three Volumes: Foxe's "Book of Martyrs" in the Writings of John Bunyan', *Bunyan Studies*, 5 (1994), pp. 48–57

'Notes on a Source for John Foxe's Account of the Marian Persecution in Kent and Sussex', *Historical Research*, 67 (1994), pp. 203–11

'*A Solemne Contestation of Divers Popes*: A Work by John Foxe?', *English Language Notes*, 31 (1994), pp. 35–42

'"The reik of Maister Patrik Hammylton": John Foxe, John Winram and the Martyrs of the Scottish Reformation', *Sixteenth Century Journal*, 27 (1996), pp. 43–60.

'The Importance of Dying Earnestly: The Metamorphosis of the Account of James Bainham in Foxe's "Book of Martyrs"', in *The Church Retrospective*, ed. R. N. Swanson, Studies in Church History xxxiii (Oxford, 1997), pp. 267–88

'"The Reformation of the Church in this Parliament": Thomas Norton, John Foxe and the Parliament of 1571', *Parliamentary History*, 16 (1997), pp. 131–47

'John Bale's Book of Martyrs?: The Account of King John in *Acts and Monuments*', *Reformation*, 3 (1998), pp. 175–223

'Fate, Faction and Fiction in Foxe's "Book of Martyrs"', *Historical Journal*, 43 (2000), pp. 601–23

'"The Good Ministrye of Godlye and Vertuouse Women": The Elizabethan Martyrologists and the Female Supporters of the Marian Martyrs', *Journal of British Studies*, 39 (2000), pp. 8–33

'"As True a Subiect being Prysoner": John Foxe's Notes on the Imprisonment of Princess Elizabeth, 1554–5', *English Historical Review*, 117 (2002), pp. 104–16

'Dissenters from a Dissenting Church: The Challenge of the Freewillers, 1550–1558', in *The Beginnings of English Protestantism*, ed. Peter Marshall and Alec Ryrie (Cambridge, 2002), pp. 129–56

'Providence and Prescription: The Account of Elizabeth in Foxe's "Book of Martyrs"', in *The Myth of Elizabeth*, ed. Susan Doran and Thomas S. Freeman (Basingstoke, 2003), pp. 27–55

'Through a Venice Glass Darkly: John Foxe's Most Famous Miracle', in *Signs, Wonders, Miracles: Representations of Divine Powers in the Life of the Church*, ed. Kate and Jeremy Gregory (Woodbridge, 2005), pp. 307–20

'The Power of Polemic: Catholic Responses to the Calendar in Foxe's "Book of Martyrs"', *Journal of Ecclesiastical History*, 61 (2010), pp. 475–95

Freeman, Thomas S. and Marcello J. Borges, '"A grave and heinous incident against our holy Catholic Faith": Two Accounts of William Gardiner's Desecration of the Portuguese Royal Chapel in 1552', *Historical Research*, 69 (1996), pp. 1–17

Freeman, Thomas S. and Sarah Elizabeth Wall, 'Racking the Body, Shaping the Text: The Account of Anne Askew in Foxe's "Book of Martyrs"', *Renaissance Quarterly*, 54 (2001), pp. 1165–96

Freshfield, Edwin (ed.), *Accomptes of the Churchwardens of the Paryshe of St. Christofer's in London 1575–1662* (London, 1885)

Garrett, Christina H., *The Marian Exiles: A Study in the Origins of English Puritanism* (Cambridge, 1938)

Gaskell, Philip, 'The Decline of the Common Press' (PhD thesis, Cambridge University, 1956)

New Introduction to Bibliography: The Classic Manual of Bibliography (New Castle, DE, 2002)

Gerritsen, Johan, 'Printing at Froben's: An Eyewitness Account', *Studies in Bibliography*, 44 (1991), pp. 144–63

Gilmont, Jean-François, *Bibliographie des éditions de Jean Crespin 1550–1572*, 2 vols. (Verviers, 1981)

Jean Crespin: un éditeur réformé du XVIe siècle (Geneva, 1981)

Goldie, Mark, *The Entring Book of Roger Morrice, 1677–1691, vol. 1: Roger Morrice and the Puritan Whigs* (Woodbridge, 2007)

Grafton, Anthony, *Bring Out Your Dead: The Past as Revelation* (Cambridge, MA, and London, 2001)

Graham, Timothy and Andrew G. Watson, *The Recovery of the Past in Early Elizabethan England: Documents by John Bale and John Joscelyn from the Circle of Matthew Parker*, Cambridge Bibliographical Society XIII (Cambridge, 1998)

Green, Ian, *Print and Protestantism in Early Modern England* (Oxford, 2000)

Greenberg, Devorah, 'Community of the Texts: Producing the First and Second Editions of *Acts and Monuments*', *Sixteenth Century Journal*, 36 (2005), pp. 695–715

Gregory, Brad, *Salvation at Stake: Christian Martyrdom in Early Modern Europe* (Cambridge, MA, 1999)

Highley, Christopher and John N. King (eds.), *John Foxe and his World* (Aldershot, 2002)

Gwyn, Peter, *The King's Cardinal: The Rise and Fall of Thomas Wolsey* (London, 2002)

Haigh, Christopher, 'The Reformation in Lancashire to 1568' (PhD thesis, University of Manchester, 1969)

Hall, Basil, 'The Early Rise and Gradual Decline of Lutheranism in England, 1520–1660', in *Reform and Reformation: England and the Continent c. 1500–c. 1750*, ed. Derek Baker, Studies in Church History: Subsidia II (Oxford, 1979), pp. 576–95

Hall, Catherine, 'The One-Way Trail: Some Observations on CCC MS 101 and G&CC MS 427', *Transactions of the Cambridge Bibliographical Society*, 11 (1998), pp. 272–84

Hanna, Ralph, 'An Oxford Library Interlude: The Manuscripts of John Foxe the Martyrologist', *Bodleian Library Record*, 17 (2002), pp. 314–26

Happé, Peter, *John Bale* (New York, 1996)

Harris, Jessie W., *John Bale* (Urbana, IL, 1940)

Harris, Oliver, 'Stow and the Contemporary Antiquarian Network', in *John Stow (1525–1605) and the Making of the English Past*, ed. Ian Gadd and Alexandra Gillespie (London, 2004), pp. 27–35

Hartley, T. E. (ed.), *Proceedings in the Parliaments of Elizabeth I*, 3 vols. (Leicester, 1981–95)

Hartmann, Martina, *Humanismus und Kirchenkritik: Matthias Flacius Illyricus als Erforscher des Mittelalters* (Stuttgart, 2001)

Hasler, P. W. (ed.), *The House of Commons, 1558–1603*, 3 vols. (London, 1981)

Hay, Denys, *Polydore Vergil: Renaissance Historian and Man of Letters* (Oxford, 1952)

Haydon, Colin, *Anti-Catholicism in Eighteenth Century England* (Manchester, 1993)

Hessels, J. H., *Ecclesiae Londino–Bataviae Archivum*, 3 vols. in 4 (Cambridge, 1889–97)

Hill, Christopher, *Antichrist in Seventeenth Century England* (Oxford, 1971)

Hill, Richard L., *Papermaking in Britain 1488–1988: A Short History* (London, 1988)

Hirsch, Rudolph, *Printing, Selling and Reading 1450–1550* (Wiesbaden, 1967)

Hoffman, George, 'Writing Without Leisure: Proof-reading as Work in the Renaissance', *Journal of Medieval and Renaissance Studies*, 25 (1995), pp. 17–31

Hoppe, Harry R., 'John Wolfe, Printer and Publisher 1579–1601', *The Library*, 4th series, 14, no. 3 (1933), pp. 241–87

Howlett, Richard (ed.), *Chronicles of the Reigns of Stephen, Henry II and Richard I*, 5 vols. (Rolls Series 82, London, 1884–9)

Hudson, Anne, *Lollards and their Books* (London, 1985)

The Premature Reformation (Oxford, 1988)

Hunt, Arnold, 'Book Trade Patents, 1603–1640', in *The Book Trade and its Customers 1450–1900: Historical Essays for Robin Myers*, ed. Arnold Hunt, Giles Mandelbrote and Alison Shell (Winchester and New Castle, DE, 1997), pp. 27–54

Hutchins, Christine E., 'Sacred Concordances: Figuring Scripture and History in Foxe's *Acts and Monuments*', *Reformation*, 8 (2003), pp. 41–62

Jackson, W. A. (ed.), *Letter Book of the Stationers' Company* (London, 1957)

James, M. R., *A Descriptive Catalogue of the Manuscripts in the Library of Corpus Christi College Cambridge*, 2 vols. (Cambridge, 1912)

Jenner, Mark S. R. and Paul Griffiths, *Londonopolis: Essays in the Cultural and Social History of Early Modern London* (Manchester, 2000)

Johnson, Francis R., 'Notes on English Retail Book-Prices, 1550–1640', *The Library*, 5th series, 2 (1950), pp. 83–112

Jones, Norman L., 'Matthew Parker, John Bale and the Magdeburg Centuriators', *Sixteenth Century Journal*, 12 (1981), pp. 35–49

Jotischky, Andrew, 'Gerard of Nazareth, John Bale and the Origins of the Carmelite Order', *Journal of Ecclesiastical History*, 46 (1995), pp. 214–36

Kastan, David Scott, 'Little Foxes', in *John Foxe and his World*, ed. Christopher Highley and John N. King (Aldershot and Burlington, VT, 2002), pp. 117–29

Ker, N. R. and A. J. Piper, *Medieval Manuscripts in British Libraries*, 4 vols. (Oxford, 1983–1992)

Kess, Alexandra, *Johann Sleidan and the Protestant Vision of History* (Aldershot, 2008)

Kinder, A. Gordon, 'Spanish Protestants and Foxe's Book: Sources', *Bibliothèque d'Humanisme et Renaissance*, 60 (1998), pp. 107–16

King, John N., *English Reformation Literature: The Tudor Origins of the Protestant Tradition* (Princeton, NJ, 1982)

    Tudor Royal Iconography: Literature and Art in an Age of Religious Crisis (Princeton, NJ, 1989)

    '"The Light of Printing": William Tyndale, John Foxe, John Day, and Early Modern Print Culture', *Renaissance Quarterly*, 54 (2001), pp. 52–85

    'John Day: Master Printer of the English Reformation', in *The Beginnings of English Protestantism*, ed. Peter Marshall and Alec Ryrie (Cambridge, 2002), pp. 180–208

    'Eighteenth-Century Folio Publication of Foxe's *Book of Martyrs*', *Reformation*, 10 (2005), pp. 99–105

    Foxe's 'Book of Martyrs' and Early Modern Print Culture (Cambridge, 2006)

Kingdon, Robert M., 'The Plantin Breviaries: A Case Study of the Sixteenth-Century Business Operations of a Printing House', *Bibliothèque d'Humanisme et Renaissance*, 22 (1960), pp. 133–50

    'The Business Activities of Printers Henri and François Estienne', in *Aspects de la propagande religieuse*, ed. G. Berthoud (Geneva, 1957), pp. 258–75

    'Patronage, Piety and Printing in Sixteenth-Century Europe', in *A Festschrift for Frederick B. Artz*, ed. David Henry Pinkney (Durham, NC, 1964), pp. 19–36

Kirk, R. E. G. and E. F. Kirk (eds.), *Returns of Aliens in London,* Huguenot Society of London x, 4 vols. (Aberdeen, 1900–8)

Kisby, Fiona, 'Books in London Parish Churches before 1603: Some Preliminary Observations', in *The Church and Learning in Later Medieval Society: Essays in Honour of R. B. Dobson*, ed. C. Barron and J. Stratford (Donnington, Lincs., 2002), pp. 305–26

Knapp, James A., *Illustrating the Past in Early Modern England: The Representation of History in Printed Books* (Aldershot, 2003)

Kolb, Robert, *For All the Saints: Changing Perceptions of Martyrdom and Sainthood in the Lutheran Reformation* (Macon, GA, 1987)

Kusukawa, Sachiko, 'Leonhardt Fuchs on the Importance of Pictures', *Journal of the History of Ideas*, 58 (1997), pp. 403–27

Lake, Peter, 'Anti-Popery: The Structure of a Prejudice', in *Conflict in Early Stuart England*, ed. Richard Cust and Ann Hughes (Harlow, 1989), pp. 72–106

Lambert, Sheila, 'Richard Montagu, Arminianism and Censorship', *Past and Present*, 124 (1989), pp. 36–68

Lamont, William, *Godly Rule: Politics and Religion 1603–60* (London, 1969)

Lander, Jesse M., *Inventing Polemic: Religion, Print and Literary Culture in Early Modern England* (Cambridge, 2006)

Latré, Guido, 'Was van Haemstede a Direct Source for Foxe? On le Blas's *Pijnbanck* and other Borrowings', in *John Foxe at Home and Abroad*, ed. David Loades (Aldershot, 1997), pp. 151–5

Leinbaugh, Theodore H., 'Aelfric's *Sermo de Sacrificio in Die Paschae*: Anglican Polemic in the Sixteenth and Seventeenth Centuries', in *Anglo-Saxon Scholarship: The First Three Centuries*, ed. Carl T. Berkhout and Milton McGatch (Boston, 1982), pp. 56–8

Loades, David (ed.), *John Foxe and the English Reformation* (Aldershot, 1997)
  John Foxe: An Historical Perspective (Aldershot, 1999)
  John Foxe: At Home and Abroad (Aldershot, 2004)

Lowry, Martin, *The World of Aldus Manutius: Business and Scholarship in Renaissance Venice* (Oxford, 1979)

Luard, H. R., 'A Letter from Bishop Bale to Archbishop Parker', *Cambridge Antiquarian Society Communications*, 3 (1864–79), pp. 157–73

Luborsky, Ruth Samson and Elisabeth Morley Ingram, *A Guide to English Illustrated Books, 1536–1603*, 2 vols. (Tempe, AZ, 1998)
  'The Illustrations: Their Pattern and Plan', in *John Foxe: An Historical Perspective*, ed. David Loades (Aldershot 1999), pp. 67–84

Lucas, Peter J., 'Parker, Lambarde and the Provision of Special Sorts for Printing Anglo-Saxon in the Sixteenth Century', *Journal of the Printing Historical Society*, 28 (1999), pp. 41–70

MacCulloch, Diamaird, *Suffolk and the Tudors: Politics and Religion in an English County 1500–1600* (Oxford, 1986)

McCusker, Honor C., *John Bale: Dramatist and Antiquary* (Bryn Mawr, PA, 1942)

McKerrow, Ronald B., *An Introduction to Bibliography for Literary Students* (Oxford, 1927)

McKisack, Mary, *Medieval History in the Tudor Age* (Oxford, 1971)

McKitterick, David, *Print, Manuscript and the Search for Order 1450–1830* (Cambridge, 2003)

Maltby, Judith, *Prayer Book and People in Elizabethan and Early Stuart England* (Cambridge, 1998)

Milton, Anthony, *Catholic and Reformed: The Roman and Protestant Churches in English Protestant Thought, 1600–1640* (Cambridge, 1995)

Momigliano, Arnaldo, 'Pagan and Christian Historiography in the Fourth Century A.D.', in *Essays in Ancient and Modern Historiography* (Middletown, CT, 1977), pp. 79–99

Moore, J. K., *Primary Materials Relating to Copy and Print in English Books of the Sixteenth and Seventeenth Centuries* (Oxford, 1992)

Mozley, John, *John Foxe and his Book* (London, 1940)

Munby, A. N. L., 'The Gifts of Elizabethan Printers to the Library of King's College, Cambridge', *The Library*, 5th series, 2 (1947), pp. 224–32

Murphy, Michael, 'John Foxe, Martyrologist and "Editor" of Old English', *English Studies*, 49 (1968), pp. 516–23

Nave, F. de and L. Voet, *Plantin-Moretus Museum, Antwerp* (Brussels, 1989)

Nichols, J. G. (ed.), *Chronicle of the Grey Friars of London*, Camden Society, original series, 53 (1852)

   Narrative of the Days of the Reformation, Camden Society, original series, 77 (1859)

Nicholson, Eirwen, 'Eighteenth Century Foxe: Evidence for the Impact of the *Acts and Monuments* in the "Long" Eighteenth Century', in *John Foxe and the English Reformation*, ed. David Loades (Aldershot, 1997), pp. 143–77

Nussbaum, Damian, 'Laudian Foxe-Hunting? William Laud and the Status of John Foxe in the 1630s', in *The Church Retrospective*, ed. Robert Swanson, Studies in Church History XXXIII (Woodbridge, 1997), pp. 329–42

   'Reviling the Saints or Reforming the Calendar? John Foxe and his "Kalendar" of Martyrs', in *Belief and Practice in Reformation England*, ed. Susan Wabuda and Caroline Litzenberger (Aldershot, 1998), pp. 113–36

   'Whitgift's "Book of Martyrs": Archbishop Whitgift, Timothy Bright and the Elizabethan Struggle over John Foxe's Legacy', in *John Foxe: An Historical Perspective*, ed. David Loades (Aldershot, 1999), pp. 135–53

O'Sullivan, W., 'The Irish "Remnaunt" of John Bale's Manuscripts', in *New Science out of Old Books: Studies in Manuscripts and Early Printed Books in Honour of A.I. Doyle*, ed. R. Beadle and A. J. Piper (Aldershot, 1995), pp. 374–87

Oastler, C. L., *John Day the Elizabethan Printer* (Oxford, 1975)

Ogier, D. M., *Reformation and Society in Guernsey* (Woodbridge, 1997)

Oliver, Leslie M., 'The Seventh Edition of John Foxe's *Acts and Monuments*', *Papers of the Bibliographical Society of America*, 37 (1943), pp. 243–60

   'Single-Page Imposition in Foxe's *Acts and Monuments*, 1570', *Library*, 5th series, 1 (1946), pp. 49–56

Parent, Annie, *Les métiers du livre à Paris au XVIe siècle (1535–60)* (Geneva and Paris, 1974)

Parry, Glyn, 'John Foxe, "Father of Lyes", and the Papists', in *John Foxe and the English Reformation*, ed. David Loades (Aldershot, 1997), pp. 295–305

   'John Dee and the Elizabethan British Empire in its European Context', *Historical Journal*, 49 (2006), pp. 643–75

Pearse, M. T., *Between Known Men and Visible Saints: A Study in Sixteenth Century English Dissent* (Cranbury, NJ, 1994)

Peel, Albert (ed.), *The Seconde Parte of a Register*, 2 vols. (Cambridge, 1915)

Pettegree, Andrew, 'Haemstede and Foxe', in *John Foxe and the English Reformation*, ed. David Loades (Aldershot, 1997), pp. 278–94

'Illustrating the Book: A Protestant Dilemma', in *John Foxe and his World*, ed. Christopher Highley and John N. King (Aldershot, 2002), pp. 133–44

Pettegree, Andrew and Matthew Hall, 'The Reformation and the Book: A Reconsideration', *Historical Journal* 47 (2004), pp. 785–808

Phillips, Peter, *English Sacred Music, 1549–1649* (Oxford, 1991)

Pohlig, Matthias, *Zwischen Gelehrsamkeit und konfessioneller Identitätsstiftung* (Tübingen, 2007)

Pollard, A. W., G. R. Redgrave, P. R. Rider, K. F. Panzer, W. A. Jackson, and F. S. Ferguson (eds.), *A Short-title Catalogue of Books Printed in England, Scotland, and Ireland and of English Books Printed Abroad, 1475–1640*, 3 vols. (London and Oxford, 1976–91)

Racine, Matthew, '*A Pearle for a Prynce*: Jerónimo Osório and early Elizabethan Catholics', *Catholic Historical Review*, 87 (2001), pp. 401–27

Reames, Sherry L., *The Legenda Aurea: A Re-examination of its Paradoxical History* (Madison, WI, 1985)

Richardson, Brian, *Printing, Writers and Readers in Renaissance Italy* (Cambridge, 1999)

Roberts, Julian, 'Bibliographical Aspects of John Foxe', in *John Foxe and the English Reformation*, ed. David Loades (Aldershot, 1997), pp. 36–51

Robinson, Benedict Scott, '"Darke Speech": Matthew Parker and the Reforming of History', *Sixteenth Century Journal*, 29 (1998), pp. 1061–83

Robinson, Hastings (ed.), *The Zurich Letters*, 2 vols., Parker Society (Cambridge, 1842–5)

  Original Letters Relative to the English Reformation, 2 vols. (Parker Society, Cambridge, 1846–7)

Rose, Mark, *Authors and Owners: The Invention of Copyright* (Cambridge, MA, 1993)

Russell, Conrad, *Parliaments and English Politics 1621–29* (Oxford, 1979)

Ryan, Lawrence V., 'The Haddon–Osorio Controversy (1563–1583)', *Church History*, 22 (1953), pp. 142–54

Ryrie, Alec, 'The Strange Death of Lutheran England', *Journal of Ecclesiastical History*, 53 (2002), pp. 64–92

Scholderer, V., 'Michael Wenssler and his Press', *The Library*, 3rd series, 3 (1912), pp. 283–321

Schwoerer, Lois G., 'William Laud Russell: The Making of a Martyr, 1683–1983', *Journal of British Studies*, 24 (1985), pp. 41–71

Scribner, R. W., *Popular Culture and Popular Movements in Reformation Germany* (London, 1987)

Sharpe, Kevin, 'Representations and Negotiations: Texts, Images, and Authority in Early Modern England', *Historical Journal*, 42 (1999), pp. 853–81

Sherman, William H., *John Dee: The Politics of Reading and Writing in the English Renaissance* (Amherst, MA, 1995)

Simpson, Percy, *Proof-reading in the Sixteenth, Seventeenth and Eighteenth Centuries* (Oxford, 1935)

Small, Ian and Marcus Walsh (eds.), *The Theory and Practice of Text-Editing: Essays in Honour of James T. Boulton* (Cambridge, 1992)

Southern, A. C. *Elizabethan Recusant Prose* (London, 1956)

Steele, Robert, 'The King's Printers', *The Library*, 4th series, 7 (1926), pp. 321–2

Steinmann, Martin, *Johannes Oporinus: Ein Basler Buchdrucker um die Mitte des 16 Jahrhunderts* (Basle and Stuttgart, 1967)

Strype, John, *Historical Collections of the Life and Acts of . . . John Aylmer* (Oxford, 1821)

   Memorials of Archbishop Cranmer, 4 vols. (Oxford, 1848–54)

Sypher, G. Wylie, '"Faisant ce qu'il leur vient à plaisir": The Image of Protestantism in French Catholic Polemic on the Eve of the Religious Wars', *Sixteenth Century Journal*, 11 (1980), pp. 59–84

Tanner, Norman P. (ed.), *Heresy Trials in the Diocese of Norwich, 1428–31*, Camden Society, 4th series, 20 (1977)

Tanselle, G. Thomas, 'The Meaning of Copy-Text: A Further Note', *Studies in Bibliography*, 23 (1970), pp. 191–6

Thomas, A. H. and I. D. Thornley (eds.), *The Great Chronicle of London* (London, 1938)

Trefnant, T., *Registrum Johannis Trefnant, Episcopi Herefordiensis*, AD MCCCLXXXIX–MCCCCIV, ed. William W. Capes, Canterbury and York Society xx (London, 1916)

Trueman, Carl, *Luther's Legacy: Salvation and English Reformers, 1525–1556* (Oxford, 1994)

Truman, James C. W., 'John Foxe and the Desires of Reformation Martyrology', *English Literary History*, 70 (2003), pp. 35–66

Usher, Brett, 'In a Time of Persecution: New Light on the Secret Protestant Congregation in Marian London', in *John Foxe and the English Reformation*, ed. David Loades (Aldershot, 1997), pp. 233–51

   'Backing Protestantism: The London Godly, the Exchequer and the Foxe Circle', in *John Foxe: An Historical Perspective*, ed. David Loades (Aldershot, 1999), pp. 105–34

Venn, J. and J. A. *Alumni Cantabrigienses*, 10 vols. (Cambridge, 1922–58)

Voet, Léon, *The Golden Compasses: A History and Evaluation of the Printing and Publishing Activities of the Officina Plantiniana at Antwerp*, trans. Raymond H. Kaye, 2 vols. (Amsterdam, 1969)

Wabuda, Susan, 'Henry Bull, Miles Coverdale and the Making of Foxe's *Book of Martyrs*', in *Martyrs and Martyrologies*, ed. Diana Wood, *Studies in Church History* xxx (Oxford, 1993), pp. 245–58

Walker, Greg, 'Saint or Sinner? The 1527 Heresy Trial of Thomas Bilney Reconsidered', *Journal of Ecclesiastical History*, 40 (1989), pp. 219–38

Walsham, Alexandra, *Providence in Early Modern England* (Oxford, 1999)

Watson, Andrew G., 'Christopher and William Carye, Collectors of Monastic Manuscripts, and "John Carye"', in *Medieval Manuscripts in Post-Medieval England*, ed. Andrew G. Watson (Aldershot, 2004), pp. 135–42

Watson, David, 'Jean Crespin and the first English Martyrology of the Reformation' in *John Foxe and the English Reformation* ed. David Loades (Aldershot, 1997), pp. 192–209

Watt, Tessa, *Cheap Print and Popular Piety, 1550–1640* (Cambridge, 1991)

Williamson, Magnus, 'Evangelicalism at Boston, Oxford and Windsor under Henry VIII: John Foxe's Narratives Recontextualised', in *John Foxe: At Home and Abroad*, ed. David Loades (Aldershot, 2004), pp. 31–45

Wood, Anthony à, *Athenae Oxonienses*, ed. Philip Bliss, 5 vols. (London, 1813–20)

Woolf, Daniel, *The Social Circulation of the Past: English Historical Culture 1500–1730* (Oxford, 2003)

Wrightson, Keith, *English Society 1580–1680* (London, 1982)

Wriothesley, Charles, *A Chronicle of England During the Reigns of the Tudors*, ed. William D. Hamilton, 2 vols. Camden Society new series, 11 and 20 (London, 1875–7)

Wykes, David L., 'Dissenters and the Writing of History: Ralph Thoresby's "Lives and Characters"', in *Fear, Exclusion and Revolution: Roger Morrice and Britain in the 1680s*, ed. Jason McElligott (Aldershot, 2006), pp. 174–88

Yates, Frances A., *Astraea: The Imperial Theme in the Sixteenth Century* (Harmondsworth, 1977)

ONLINE SOURCES

Aston, Margaret, 'The Illustrations: Books 10–12', in John Foxe's 'Book of Martyrs' Online Variorum Edition: www.hrionline.ac.uk/john/foxe

Economic History Services, 2004: www.eh.net/hmit/ppowerbp/

Freeman, Thomas S., '"St Peter Did Not Do Thus": Papal History in the *Acts and Monuments*': www.hrionline.ac.uk/johnfoxe/apparatus/freemanStPeterpart1.html

International Institute of Social History (Amsterdam): www.iisg.nl/hpw/

Oxford Dictionary of National Biography: www.oxforddnb.com

Index

Milton Keynes UK
Ingram Content Group UK Ltd.
UKHW021444130524
442635UK00050B/1495

9 781107 662933